SYMPOSION 2005

ÖSTERREICHISCHE AKADEMIE DER WISSENSCHAFTEN
PHILOSOPHISCH-HISTORISCHE KLASSE
KOMMISSION FÜR ANTIKE RECHTSGESCHICHTE

AKTEN DER GESELLSCHAFT FÜR GRIECHISCHE UND HELLENISTISCHE RECHTSGESCHICHTE

HERAUSGEGEBEN VON

EVA CANTARELLA
JOSEPH MÉLÈZE MODRZEJEWSKI
GERHARD THÜR

in Verbindung mit
Michael Gagarin, Alberto Maffi,
Julie Vélissaropoulos-Karakostas

Band 19

Verlag der
Österreichischen Akademie
der Wissenschaften

Wien 2007

ÖSTERREICHISCHE AKADEMIE DER WISSENSCHAFTEN
PHILOSOPHISCH-HISTORISCHE KLASSE
KOMMISSION FÜR ANTIKE RECHTSGESCHICHTE

SYMPOSION 2005

Vorträge zur griechischen und hellenistischen Rechtsgeschichte

(Salerno, 14.–18. September 2005)

Comunicazioni sul diritto greco ed ellenistico

(Salerno, 14–18 Settembre 2005)

herausgegeben von / a cura di
Eva Cantarella

Verlag der
Österreichischen Akademie
der Wissenschaften

Wien 2007

Vorgelegt von k. M. Gerhard Thür
in der Sitzung am 15. Dezember 2006

Il XV Convegno della Società Internazionale di Diritto Greco ed Ellenistico è stato organizzato con il contributo dell'Università degli Studi di Milano, della Provincia di Salerno e del CNR.
Il volume Symposion 2005, che ne contiene gli atti, è stato stampato grazie al contributo della Facoltà di Giurisprudenza dell'Università degli Studi di Milano e del Ministero dell'Università e della Ricerca.

Die verwendete Papiersorte ist aus chlorfrei gebleichtem Zellstoff hergestellt, frei von säurebildenden Bestandteilen und alterungsbeständig.

ISBN 978-3-7001-3823-5

Satz: Eva Schellnast, Institut für Römisches Recht, 8010 Graz
Druck und Bindung: Börsedruck Ges.m.b.H., 1230 Wien

http://hw.oeaw.ac.at/3823-5
http://verlag.oeaw.ac.at

ARNOLD
KRÄNZLEIN
UND
PANAYOTIS
DIMAKIS
ZUM
GEDENKEN

INDICE

I. DIRITTO GRECO ARCAICO E CLASSICO

II. DIRITTO ELLENISTICO, GRECO-ROMANO E BIZANTINO

RIFLESSIONI FINALI

PREMESSA

Nei giorni tra il 15 e il 17 settembre del 2005, si è tenuto a Salerno il XV Symposion della *Società Internazionale per la Storia del Diritto greco ed ellenistico / Internationale Gesellschaft für griechische und hellenistische Rechtsgeschichte.*

Organizzata dall'Istituto di diritto romano dell'Università di Milano, la riunione si è svolta a Salerno, per un duplice ordine di ragioni.

La prima è che Salerno è stata, un tempo, parte del mondo greco. Organizzare un convegno di diritto greco in Magna Grecia significava mettere in evidenza la carenza di ricerche sul contributo dato da questa terra a un aspetto fondamentale della cultura, qual è il diritto. Di qui, la decisione non solo di scegliere Salerno come sede del Symposion, ma anche di aprire i lavori della sessione con due contributi dedicati a rinnovare alcune prospettive di ricerca in quel settore.

La seconda ragione – meno scientifica, ma non priva di importanza – è stata quella di consentire a quelli, tra i partecipanti al Symposion, che ancora non avevano visitato questa Grecia, di constatare *de visu* (e a quelli che già vi erano stati di meglio ricordare) quali e quanto importanti siano le tracce che la cultura greca ha lasciato in questa terra.

I lavori serrati dei tre giorni di Symposion, i cui atti sono raccolti in questo volume, pubblicato grazie ai fondi generosamente concessi dalla facoltà di Giurisprudenza dell'Università di Milano, sono stati dunque intervallati da una gita a Paestum, con visita al Museo, alla Tomba del Tuffatore e ai meravigliosi templi, testimonianza di livello artistico che nulla ha da invidiare ai pure splendidi templi della madrepatria.

Al Symposion, come d'abitudine, hanno partecipato studiosi giunti da molti, diversi paesi. Dall'Austria sono giunti Kaja Harter-Uibopuu, Federico Morelli, Bernhard Palme, Gerhard Thür; dalla Francia, Barbara Anagnostou-Canas, Jean-Marie Bertrand, Bernard Legras, Joseph Mélèze Modrzejewski, Claude Mossé; dalla Danimarca, Karen R. Kristensen; dalla Germania, Martin Dreher, Andreas Jördens; dalla Gran Bretagna, Edward Harris, Lene Rubinstein, Stephen Todd; dalla Grecia, Sophie Adam, Andréas Helmis; dalla Polonia, Jakub Urbanik; dagli Stati Uniti, Edward E. Cohen, Michael Gagarin, Adriaan Lanni, Adele Scafuro, Robert W. Wallace; dall'Ungheria, Éva Jakab; dall'Italia – oltre a chi scrive – Mario Amelotti, Antonio Banfi, Felice Costabile, Michele Faraguna, Lorenzo Gagliardi, Alberto Maffi, Livia Migliardi, Laura Pepe, Mario Talamanca.

L'incontro, importante e fruttuoso, non avrebbe potuto aver luogo senza la generosità di numerose istituzioni e personalità: il Rettore dell'Università di Milano, la provincia di Salerno (che oltre a elargire un importante contributo ha consentito l'uso della splendida Villa Guariglia) e il Consiglio Nazionale delle Ricerche. A tutti va il ringraziamento più vivo degli organizzatori e della comunità di giusgrecisti, cui è stato consentito proseguire l'avventura, iniziata oltre trent'anni or sono, che tanto ha contribuito alla diffusione della ricerca sul diritto greco e all'insegnamento di questa materia nelle Università di tutto il mondo.

Un ringraziamento particolare devo ai colleghi Joseph Mélèze Modrezejewski e Gerhard Thür, che insieme a me dividono la responsabilità e l'onore di tenere in vita questa ormai storica Società, e insieme ai quali sono state prese tutte le decisioni relative all'organizzazione del convegno.

A rendere possibile la pubblicazione degli atti, oltre al contributo appositamente stanziato dalla facoltà milanese di Giurisprudenza, hanno contribuito il lavoro redazionale di Eva Schellnast e la gentilezza di Gerhard Thür, che ha costantemente e sollecitamente fatto da tramite con l'editore. La dottoressa Nunzia Donadio ha redatto l'indice delle fonti.

A tutti loro va un sentito, sincero ringraziamento, che si estende alla continua, attiva, infaticabile presenza e collaborazione del collega Lorenzo Gagliardi e del Segretario amministrativo dell'Istituto di Diritto romano, Sergio Longo. Se il Convegno ha avuto luogo e i suoi atti vengono oggi pubblicati è grazie al contributo di tutti loro.

Milano, 15 dicembre 2006 Eva Cantarella

I. DIRITTO GRECO ARCAICO E CLASSICO

MICHAEL GAGARIN (AUSTIN)

FROM ORAL LAW TO WRITTEN LAWS: DRACO'S LAW AND ITS HOMERIC ROOTS

According to tradition, Draco wrote a homicide law for Athens in 621 BCE. My question is, Why did Draco write this law when, as far as we know, no law had ever before been written in Athens (*Ath. Pol.* 41.2)? We may think that writing down laws is a natural step to take, but for people who knew nothing of written public documents, it was far from obvious. So, why did Draco decide to write this law? What could a written law do that oral customs and rules could not? One answer was offered in the fifth century by Theseus in Euripides' *Suppliants* (433-34): "When the laws are written down, the weak and the rich have equal justice."[1] Many scholars today dismiss this explanation as misguided democratic ideology. They note that most early laws were written in communities that were not democratic and argue that the poor and the weak could not read. Instead, they argue, inscribed laws were intended to make a visual impression on ordinary people, thereby strengthening the control of the ruling elite.[2]

Evidence in the inscriptions themselves, however, indicates that, on the contrary, they were intended to be read and used by members of the community beyond the small ruling elite.[3] On the question of literacy, our evidence is limited and inconclusive, but it is becoming clearer all the time that even in the seventh

[1] γεγραμμένων δὲ τῶν νόμων ὅ τ' ἀσθενὴς
ὁ πλούσιός τε τὴν δίκην ἴσην ἔχει.

[2] "Une écriture destinée à être vue plutôt que lue," as Camassa (1988: 151) says of early written texts, slightly misquoting Detienne 1981: 69. Stratton argues that the state could not control the earliest writing in Greece, and this made necessary "the development of a state system based on repressive written laws created and amended by the government" (1980:118). Eder sees the codification of law as "a reaction of the few aiming at preserving their political influence as completely as possible"; it thus served the political interests of the ruling class and preserved the control of the few over the many (1986: 264). "Wichtiger als die Lesbarkeit war offenbar die Sichtbarkeit der Satzung im konkreten Sinne, nämlich als Symbol und Garantie ihrer unabänderlichen und dauerhaften Geltung" ("Evidently the readability of a statute was less important than its visibility in the concrete sense, as a symbol and guarantee of its unchanging and lasting validity"), Hölkeskamp 2000: 88.

[3] I discuss this issue and the whole subject of writing and law at greater length in *Writing Greek Law* (forthcoming).

century, especially in Athens, a fairly broad range of people knew how to write and presumably how to read, at least in a rudimentary fashion. Striking evidence for this has been collected by an American archaeologist, Merle Langdon, who has found dozens of inscriptions, most from the sixth century but a few perhaps earlier, that were carved on flat stones in the countryside of Attica, and the authors of some of these identify themselves as shepherds![4] And even if the number of readers was relatively small, say 5-10% of the population, this would still mean that many who were not part of the ruling elite would have been able to read. This is not to deny the visual or monumental aspect of some of these texts, but as a monument like the Vietnam War Memorial in Washington DC makes clear, an inscription can make a visual impact and at the same time be important as a text.

Now if Draco wrote his law so that people could read it, we must still ask, why was it important that it be written? The most common answer is that Draco was responding to a crisis that had arisen out of the attempted coup of Cylon fifteen years earlier.[5] We have slightly different versions of the story in Herodotus, Thucydides and Plutarch, but they agree that after Cylon's coup failed, he and his followers were trapped, either on the Acropolis or in a sanctuary, and many of them were sacrilegiously killed there. The family of the Alcmeonids, led perhaps by Megacles, appear to have played a leading role, and they were later considered polluted because of the sacrilege.[6]

No ancient source mentions a continuing crisis or connects Draco with Cylon, but many scholars make the connection anyway. The most detailed case for this was presented by Sally Humphreys at the 1990 Symposion (Humphreys 1991: 21-22):

> It seems likely enough that many of the questions with which Drakon was concerned would be raised with particular insistence at some interval after the defeat and massacre, when sons of the slain had grown to manhood, when those who had sympathized with Kylon or were related to his supporters gathered confidence to voice their claims in public, perhaps when some of the killers who had initially left Attika began to explore the possibility of return.
>
> Drakon, then, is preoccupied in the first place with killers who claim to have acted defensibly. His phrase μὲ 'κ προνοίας, non-intentionally, is well chosen to cover the variety of claims that will have been made: that the killer acted in self-defense, that he had no personal animosity against his victim, that he was acting under orders.

Besides the difficulty of seeing why issues arising out of Cylon's attempted coup would be more urgent fifteen years later than at the time of the coup, there are

---

4 Personal communication; these texts are not yet published, but see the notice in *SEG* 49.2

5 636 is the generally accepted date for Cylon, though this is not certain; for details see Rhodes 1981: 79-84, and for a full account of the ancient sources, see Stroud 1968: 70-74.

6 More details in Thür 2002: 633-34.

significant problems with this thesis. First, in Athenian law μὴ ἐκ προνοίας ("unintentionally") is never used of killing in self-defense, or killing without personal animosity, or killing under orders. And even if it could apply to any of these types of killing, there is no evidence for such killings in the massacre of the Cylonians, which appears to have been carried out quite intentionally in a period of civil strife. Humphreys might have a somewhat easier time positing a link to the Cylonian episode if she accepted, as I do but she does not, that Draco's law as we have it apples to intentional as well as unintentional homicide. But even then, the connection remains purely hypothetical.

In addition, the killing of the Cylonians must have raised political and religious concerns. Cylon had been attempting to gain control of Athens by force, which amounted to establishing a tyranny, and Athens later had legislation protecting anyone who killed a would-be tyrant. But Draco's law as we have it says nothing about killing a tyrant. Nor does it address the religious crime of killing someone who was either in a sanctuary or, as a suppliant, was somehow protected by the gods. This religious concern was probably the reason why for years after this event the Alcmeonids were said by some to be under a curse. Surely a law responding to this particular crisis would address these two factors.

Forsdyke (2005: 83-84) argues that the tyranny law cited in *Ath. Pol.* 16.10 was aimed specifically at the Cylonians, but there are problems with this view. The passage reads,

> They [the Athenians during the time of Pisistratus] had the following law (*nomos*): "These are ancestral ordinances (*thesmia*): If any people set up to be tyrants in a tyranny, or if anyone joins in establishing a tyranny, both he and his family (*genos*) will be outlawed (*atimos*)."[7]

This report cites an Athenian *nomos*, usually dated to the fifth or late sixth century,[8] which officially establishes as law a long-established (*thesmia*) ancestral rule, that anyone establishing or helping to establish a tyranny will be outlawed. If this information is accurate, the *nomos* cannot be as old as Draco because he was the first to write laws in Athens (*Ath. Pol.* 41.2).[9] But the *thesmia* cited in this *nomos* may be the kind of *thesmia* that are reported in *Ath. Pol.* 3.4 to have been written

---

[7] νόμος γὰρ αὐτοῖς ἦν ὅδε. "θέσμια τάδε 'Αθηναίων καὶ πάτρια· ἐάν τινες τυραννεῖν ἐπανιστῶνται ἐπὶ τυραννίδι, ἢ συγκαθιστῇ τὴν τυραννίδα, ἄτιμον εἶναι καὶ αὐτὸν καὶ γένος." The pleonasm and abrupt shift from plural to singular have stimulated most scholars to emend, and editors have usually deleted the expression ἐπὶ τυραννίδι as redundant with τυραννεῖν (see Rhodes 1981: 223); but it is defended by Ostwald 1955: 121 n. 97, who sees similar pleonasm in Draco's law. See also Gagarin 1981b.

[8] Rhodes 1981: 222-23.

[9] The law would not, of course, have been called a *nomos* in the seventh century, but the *Ath. Pol.* is probably responsible for this term.

down by the Thesmothetai. In that case, we can imagine that the Cylonians went into exile after their failed coup and the Thesmothetai, either at that time or in some later trial, wrote the rule down as a note to themselves for future reference, that anyone who attempts a tyranny is to be outlawed (which would have forced him into exile).

If this hypothetical scenario is accurate, and the Cylonians later were agitating to return to Attica, then Draco may have needed to reaffirm this traditional rule. But this rule would not be part of his homicide law. And if, as Forsdyke further suggests (2005: 84-88), the Cylonians and their supporters returned to Attica despite this rule, seeking revenge and thus continuing the intra-elite conflict that Forsdyke sees as characteristic of this period, then, again, it is not clear why Draco needed to write down a law rather than just reaffirm (orally) the customary rules for the treatment of homicide, including the rule that only family members can prosecute for homicide, which Forsdyke sees as a significant factor in her reconstruction of events (2005: 87, following Humphreys).

Besides Humphreys and Forsdyke, many other scholars link Draco to the Cylonian conspiracy because the two events are close in time.[10] We do have evidence that a generation later Solon responded to a crisis in Athens in part by writing laws, and my suspicion is that this later event has led scholars to conclude by analogy that Draco must also have been responding to a crisis.[11] But the main steps Solon took to resolve the crisis he faced were the *seisachtheia* and the prohibition of debt-bondage, and he may have had other reasons for writing laws, many of which were on matters not related to this crisis. Moreover, by Solon's time the Athenians had already had enough experience with written law that he could more easily understand the significance and effect of writing. But whatever Solon's reasons, there is no reason why Draco must have had the same motive.

In fact, we have no evidence for any crisis in Athens at the time of Draco. The explanation that Draco was responding to some sort of crisis may seem plausible at first glance, but we need to ask exactly how writing a law would resolve a crisis. How, in other words, would the act of writing down a law resolve a conflict that could not be resolved by traditional methods of dispute settlement that did not use writing?

To understand why Draco's law needed to be written, we must ask first, how homicide was treated in Athens before Draco, and then what changed after Draco wrote his law. We have no direct evidence for Athenian law before Draco, but it is likely that procedures similar to the traditional methods of dispute settlement that are illustrated in the poems of Homer and Hesiod were also used in early Athens (and in Greece in general). In particular, in the famous trial scene on the shield of Achilles (*Iliad* 18.497-508) Homer presents a dispute arising out of a homicide, which

[10] E.g., Stroud 1968: 70-74 with references; Thür 2002.

[11] Hölkeskamp 1999 argues that almost all early laws were written as responses to crises.

evidently would be settled before a group of elders.[12] The poems also present many general rules and customs for the treatment of homicide and other matters which were preserved and transmitted orally. These rules are sometimes stated explicitly by one of the characters in the poem, but they are also illustrated by many examples of homicide and other wrongs.

Among the rules voiced explicitly by a character, two in particular apply to homicide. First, as Odysseus advises Telemachus after they have killed the suitors (*Odyssey* 23.118-20), "even when one has killed one man in a community, a man with few helpers following him, he flees into exile, leaving behind his kinsmen and country."[13] Examples in both epics confirm that this is the usual response to a killing, and also indicate that once a killer has fled into exile, the victim's relatives do not normally pursue him any further. On the other hand, in a different context Homer presents a very different rule about the treatment of homicide, namely that the killer should be reconciled with the victim's relatives. This rule is proclaimed by Ajax in an angry speech to Achilles (*Iliad* 9.632-36): "A person accepts from the killer the blood-price for his dead brother or son, and when he has paid a large compensation, the killer remains in his land, and the person's heart and manly anger are curbed, when he has received the blood-price."[14] Finally, one other relevant rule concerning homicide may be implicit in the story of Agamemnon's murder, various accounts of which are given in the *Odyssey* (see 1.35-43, 3.254-312, 11.405-34, etc.). The fact that Clytemnestra is killed by Orestes along with Aegisthus, even though (unlike in Aeschylus' *Agamemnon*) she is only an accomplice, and that everyone seems to approve of her murder, suggests that it was generally accepted that an indirect participant in a homicide should be punished together with the actual killer.

All Greeks knew Homer well and it is likely that in early Greece Athens and other communities continued to follow the same general rules and customs for responding to a homicide, either by exile or by compensation and reconciliation, or by both. The Cylonian episode shows that exile was one possible response to homicide because at least some of those who killed the Cylonians were exiled, though the sacrilegious nature of the crime may have played a role in the

[12] I have discussed this scene in Gagarin 1986: 26-33 and elsewhere. The most recent treatment is by Cantarella (2002), who reaches very different conclusions on some points.

[13] καὶ γάρ τίς θ' ἕνα φῶτα κατακτείνας ἐνὶ δήμῳ,
ᾧ μὴ πολλοὶ ἔωσιν ἀοσσητῆρες ὀπίσσω,
φεύγει πηούς τε προλιπὼν καὶ πατρίδα γαῖαν·

[14] καὶ μέν τίς τε κασιγνήτοιο φονῆος
ποινὴν ἢ οὗ παιδὸς ἐδέξατο τεθνηῶτος·
καί ῥ' ὃ μὲν ἐν δήμῳ μένει αὐτοῦ πόλλ' ἀποτίσας,
τοῦ δέ τ' ἐρητύεται κραδίη καὶ θυμὸς ἀγήνωρ
ποινὴν δεξαμένῳ.

punishment. We have no such evidence for compensation and reconciliation, but it is certainly possible that some killers were reconciled with their victims' families, perhaps after a period of exile. And still others, presumably the more powerful members of the community, probably resisted any punishment and refused to submit to traditional procedures for dispute settlement, perhaps claiming that the traditional rules did not apply to them, or perhaps that they were not directly involved in the killing.[15]

But if such people were still present in Athens fifteen years later, or if some of those who had been exiled were anxious to return and willing to pay compensation but were not being allowed to do so by their victims' relatives, and if either situation (or both) were causing serious conflict in the community, how would writing a law resolve this situation? Why would those who were unwilling to accept a peaceful settlement reached through traditional procedures agree to abide by a rule just because it had been put in writing for the first time? And if the written law contained innovations that somehow made it more attractive to those who had previously refused to abide by the rules, why could Draco not simply modify the existing procedures to make them more effective? Why would changes have to be put in writing?

Consider, for example, the scenario Thür (2002) reconstructs, that Megacles or some other leader claimed that although he had encouraged others, he did not participate in the killings (and perhaps even argued against them) and therefore was not liable to a charge of homicide, and (fifteen years later) relatives of some victims were still demanding that he be punished. In such a situation, why could Draco not simply declare that those who lead others but do not themselves kill either are or are not liable? Why did he need to put this rule in writing? Surely if Megacles had been refusing to go to court for fifteen years and if he continued to refuse even after Draco declared (orally) that those who lead are liable, he would react no differently when Draco wrote this rule down. And if Draco ruled the other way and declared (orally) that leaders are not liable, and the relatives refused to accept this, what difference would writing down the rule make? And if the main rules in Draco's law closely resembled traditional Homeric rules and practices (as I think they do), it is especially hard to see any reason why he would need to put them in writing. Many reasons have been proposed why Draco created the specific rules we find in his law, but no reason has been given for writing them down rather than declaring them orally. Nor has anyone explained why writing down these rules would have been more effective at resolving a crisis, whether or not it was related to the killing of the Cylonians.

To understand the reasons, we must turn to the one piece of solid evidence we have, the text of the law. The original inscription is lost, but a copy survives, made

[15] So Thür 2002: 634-35.

in Athens in 409, which many scholars think accurately reproduces the original text of the law, though there is considerable disagreement whether these provisions originally stood at the beginning of the law.[16] Even if significant parts of the original law are missing from this later inscription, as long as the text we have reflects Draco's actual words, my argument about Draco's motives in writing the law should still be still valid. For reference purposes I have divided my translation into numbered clauses.[17]

ΠΡΟΤΟΣ ΑΧΣΟΝ

1. καὶ ἐὰμ μὲ 'κ προνοίας κτένει τίς τινα, φεύγεν.
2. δικάζεν δὲ τὸς βασιλέας αἴτιον φόνο ε͂[ναι τὸν ἐργασάμενον] ε̄͂ βολεύσαντα· τὸς δὲ ἐφέτας διαγνο͂ναι.
3. αἰδέσασθαι δ' ἐὰμ μὲν πατὲρ ε͂ι ε̄͂ ἀδελφὸς ε̄͂ hυε͂ς hάπαντας, ε̄͂ τὸν κολύοντα κρατε͂ν.
4. ἐὰμ δὲ μὲ hοῦτοι ο͂σι, μέχρ' ἀνεφσιότετος καὶ ἀνεφσιο͂, ἐὰν hάπαντες αἰδέσασθαι ἐθέλοσι, τὸν κολύοντα κρατε͂ν.
5. ἐὰν δὲ τούτον μεδὲ hε͂ς ε͂ι, κτένει δὲ ἄκον, γνο͂σι δὲ hοι πεντέκοντα καὶ hε͂ς hοι ἐφέται ἄκοντα κτε͂ναι, ἐσέσθον δὲ hοι φράτορες ἐὰν ἐθέλοσι δέκα· τούτος δὲ hοι πεντέκοντα καὶ hε͂ς ἀριστίνδεν hαιρέσθον.
6. καὶ hοι δὲ πρότερον κτέναντες ἐν το͂ιδε το͂ι θεσμο͂ι ἐνεχέσθον.
7. προειπε͂ν δὲ το͂ι κτέναντι ἐν ἀγορᾶι μέχρ' ἀνεφσιότετος καὶ ἀνεφσιο͂.
8. συνδιόκεν δὲ κἀνεφσιὸς καὶ ἀνεφσιο͂ν παῖδας καὶ γαμβρὸς καὶ πενθερὸς καὶ φράτορας.
9. (passage into exile?)
10. ἐὰν δέ τις τὸν ἀνδροφόνον κτένει ε̄͂ αἴτιος ε͂ι φόνο, ἀπεχόμενον ἀγορᾶς ἐφορίας καὶ ἄθλον καὶ hιερο͂ν 'Αμφικτυονικο͂ν, hόσπερ τὸν 'Αθηναῖον κτέναντα ἐν τοῖς αὐτοῖς ἐνέχεσθαι· διαγιγνόσκεν δὲ τὸς ἐφέτας.
11. [ἐξ]ε͂[ναι δὲ τὸς ἀνδροφόνος ἀποκτένεν ε̄͂ ἀπάγεν ἐὰν ἐν] τε͂ι ἐμεδ[απε͂ι ...]
12. ἄρχον]τα χερο͂ν ἀ[δίκον ... χερ]ο͂ν ἀδίκον κτέ[νει ... διαγιγνόσκ]εν δὲ τὸς ἐ[φέτ]ας.
13. ...]εις ε̄͂ ἐλεύθερος ε͂ι· καὶ ἐὰν φέροντα ε̄͂ ἄγοντα βίαι ἀδίκος εὐθὺς ἀμυνόμενος κτένει, νεποινὲ τεθνάναι.

---

[16] Indications that the original text was not revised before being reinscribed include the fact that the fifty-one are to choose ten members from the phratry by (aristocratic) rank (*aristindên*) and that the text refers to itself as a *thesmos*. In the first case, a more democratic process would surely have been implemented in the fifth-century if the law had been revised, and in the second, the law would have been called a *nomos*, as it is in the prescript from 409 ("let the Anagrapheis inscribe the *nomos* of Draco concerning homicide"). In addition, the provision for retroactivity would have been without force by the time a generation or so had passed, yet it is still preserved in the reinscribed text (provision 6), as is a reference to frontier markets (provision 10), which no longer existed by 409. See further Stroud 1968: 60-64.

[17] *IG* I^3 104. I give Stroud's text, preserving the spelling of the inscription but removing most of the epigraphical details. In provision 2 (line 12) and provision 11 (lines 30-31) I include *exempli gratia* supplements that illustrate the generally agreed sense of the missing words. I omit the prescript from 409 (lines 1-9).

[Seventeen lines]
ΔΕΥΤΕΡΟΣ ΑΧΣΟΝ

The law begins after the heading FIRST AXON in line 10. Provision 1 is concise and simple and clearly reflects the traditional practice of exile for homicide.

(1) Even if someone does not kill someone intentionally, he goes into exile.

Provision 2 is also expressed concisely and it too reflects a rule implicit in Homer, that an accomplice would be treated just like an actual killer.

(2) The kings judge guilty of homicide the killer or the planner, and the *ephetai* decide.[18]

By referring to *hoi basileis* and *hoi ephetai* ("the kings and the *ephetai*"), Draco implies that both groups already existed in Athens. The kings would almost certainly have had judicial duties before Draco, as they do in Homer and Hesiod, and perhaps the *ephetai* too, though the particular division of duties between the kings and the *ephetai* specified here may be a change from their earlier division of duties, about which we know nothing.

After the first two clauses come three provisions concerning reconciliation between the killer and the victim's relatives, the practice referred to by Ajax (see above):

(3) Reconciliation, if there is a father or brother or sons, all of them; or the objector prevails.
(4) But if these are not (alive), up to the degree of first cousin once removed and first cousin, if all are willing to reconcile, the objector prevails.
(5) But if not one of these is (alive), and he killed unintentionally, and the fifty-one, the *ephetai* decide he killed unintentionally, let ten phratry members admit him if they wish; and let the fifty-one choose these by rank.

Here too, in allowing reconciliation, presumably accompanied by compensation, Draco is following traditional practices, though his rules provide considerably more detail than we find in Ajax's brief summary, which only mentions accepting

[18] Because Thür thinks that the function of the *basileis* was to determine the oaths to be sworn by the two sides, he translates this provision, "Die Könige sollen anordnen (dass der Kläger schwört, der Verklagte) sei schuldig der Tötung, entweder 'mit der Hand, die er geregt hat' oder 'durch Ratschlag'" (2002: 634). Even if we accept that *dikazein* here means "anordnen" ("order, direct") – and I and others would disagree – nothing justifies the words in parentheses except Thür's preconception about the function of the *basileus* in a homicide case. If Draco had wished to prescribe that the *basileis* should order a litigant to swear a decisive oath, surely he would have stated this explicitly. No reader could be expected to supply for himself the words Thür adds in parentheses.

compensation from the killer of a brother or son. Moreover, Ajax says nothing about disagreements among relatives, which in practice may have been a source of conflict.[19] Draco's requirement for unanimity may have been an important innovation intended to reduce the potential for confusion and conflict in such situations. And Draco goes further in 4 and 5, addressing contingencies for which there were probably no earlier rules, and he sets forth these rules in detail. In giving detailed rules for the procedure to be followed in such cases, Draco is almost certainly innovating.

Provisions 3-5 are also interesting for style. 3, which reaffirms a traditional practice, continues the same concise style as 1 and 2, but 4 has a little more detail; and in 5, which addresses a remote contingency for which almost certainly no earlier rule existed, Draco spells out the procedure in greater detail. Thus, his method seems to be to combine traditional, general rules, which are stated concisely, with new rules containing extensive details.

After these, Provision 6 provides that the law is retroactive.

> (6) And let those who killed earlier be bound by this ordinance (*thesmos*).

Here Draco returns to the concise style of provisions 1 and 2. He evidently sees no reason to clarify whether this means that all the provisions thus far are retroactive, as I think is more likely, or only that the provisions on reconciliation are retroactive. But in fact, since the latter contain the most significant innovation in the law thus far, retroactivity would be most important for these provisions, and so in the end it matters little which alternative we choose.

These first six provisions contain the essence of the homicide law. They state the basic penalty for homicide, specify who judges homicide cases and include accomplices in the process, allow for reconciliation no matter which relatives (if any) remain, and designate these rules as retroactive. In a modern legal code, this would be Section One of the law. The next five provisions (7-11) can be designated Section Two; they give rules about procedures that both accuser and accused must follow in homicide cases. First we are told quite precisely who makes the initial proclamation (7) and who shares in the prosecution (8).

> (7) There is to be a proclamation against the killer in the agora [by relatives] up to the first cousin once removed and first cousin.
> (8) Sharing the prosecution are cousins and cousins' sons and sons-in-law and fathers-in-law and phratry members.

[19] For the suggestion that the dispute on the shield of Achilles might be caused by disagreement among relatives, see Gagarin 1981: 13-16.

In the next four lines only a few letters can be read: "is responsible for a homicide," "the fifty-one" (in the accusative case), and "they convict of homicide." If these last words were part of a conditional clause, the missing provision (9) may have regulated the convicted killer's journey into exile after the trial, perhaps specifying that he not be harmed on the way and setting a time limit. Such a provision might have occupied all four lines, or there may have been another provision before it.

After these lines comes a rule protecting a killer in exile (10), followed by a provision that makes clear that a killer who returns to the territory will not be not protected (11).

> (10) But if someone kills the killer (in exile) or is responsible for his killing while he is avoiding a frontier market and athletic contests and Amphictyonic sacrifices, he is liable to the same treatment as someone who kills an Athenian; and the *ephetai* are to decide.
> (11) It is permissible to kill or summarily arrest (a killer) in our territory.

All these rules reflect the traditional practices we observe in Homer, a victim's relatives take the lead in prosecuting a killer, but after the killer goes into exile, they no longer pursue him. But Draco has added precision and has specified a number of details that almost certainly were not traditionally specified: for example, where outside of Attica the killer would or would not be protected. These details are especially important, since one of the main reasons why a killer had to go into exile was to prevent future contact between him and the victim's family and friends. Frontier markets, athletic contests and Amphictyonic sacrifices were relatively new international events on the border of Attica or outside the territory. Both sides would need to know whether the killer in exile would be protected if he attended these events, and Draco specifies that he would not. Thus the victim's family and friends would know that they could attend these events with little likelihood of encountering the killer, who would lose his protection if he attended them, just as he would if he returned to Attica.

After this section of procedural details, no clear sense can be made of the next three lines. Then provision 12 says something about beginning a fight – most likely the person who strikes the first blow will be held responsible for any death resulting from the fight. And 13 allows a person to kill someone who is attacking him and not owe compensation for the death.

> (12) ... beginning a fight ... he kills beginning a fight ... and the *ephetai* are to decide.
> (13) ... or is free; and if someone kills defending himself immediately against someone who is forcibly and unjustly plundering or seizing him, the death shall be without recompense.

After 13, no sense can be made of the next seventeen lines, but then there is another heading, SECOND AXON, corresponding to FIRST AXON at the beginning of the law.[20] This shows that additional provisions continued as far as that point and certainly farther, though only a few traces of letters can be seen after this. Thus, the reconstructable provisions of Draco's law constitute less than half of the forty-five lines of text on the first axon, and assuming that the law continued farther down the second axon, we can calculate that Draco's original law was at least three or four times as long as the text we now have, and maybe longer.

Now, what does this text reveal about Draco's reasons for writing his law? First, we do not know whether the original seventh-century inscription had some of the same physical features as other early inscriptions, such as dividing marks between words or phrases, which would make the text easier to read, but the clear organization of provisions in the law is evident even in this later copy. Section One contains the most essential elements: the crime and its punishment, procedures for judging and reconciliation, and a statement of retroactivity. Section Two then gives precise and detailed rules for litigation procedures, in the order in which a homicide case would normally proceed, beginning with the initial public proclamation accusing the killer of homicide and ending with rules protecting the convicted killer who has gone into exile, but not if he returns to Attica. After this come additional rules covering special situations that would probably arise more rarely. Not enough of this third section survives for us to know whether these rules were arranged in a particular order, but the overall organization of the law is clear enough. It is also clear that Draco must have consciously arranged the provisions in such a way that it would be easy for a reader to follow, or to find a specific provision he was looking for. Thus, one of Draco's primary goals was to make his law accessible to readers who might need to use it.

Also of help to a reader would be certain stylistic features. First, several provisions have a chiastic arrangement of subjects and verbs.[21] This marks the beginning and end either of a provision (2, 3) or of a period within a provision (5, 10). Second, Draco begins several provisions (2, 3, 7, 8, and perhaps 11) with an infinitive followed by *de*. In these provisions the infinitive acts like a heading stating the subject of that provision – *dikazein*, *proeipein*. Third, 4, 5, and 10 begin with *ean de*, indicating that these provisions add a qualification to the preceding clause. Like the numbered sections and subsections of modern legislation, these features would

---

20 Although only traces of this second heading survive, the greater size of the letters, the larger spacing between this line and the line that precedes, and the uninscribed space at the end of the preceding line all are paralleled for the first heading (line 10) and nowhere else. We can thus accept the reconstruction of this second heading as certain.

21 See, for example, provision 2, which begins δικάζειν δὲ τοὺς βασιλέας and ends with τοὺς δὲ ἐφέτας διαγνῶναι (Verb, Subject, Subject, Verb).

help readers more easily understand the organization of the law and find specific provisions they might wish to read.

It is clear, then, that Draco tried to write a law that was reader-friendly, but we must still ask, why write this law down in the first place? The historical context is important. Evidence from archaeology reveals a steady pattern all over Greece, including Attica, of population growth and economic prosperity as well as greater diversity. By the late seventh century, the unification (*synoecism*) of Attica had been completed,[22] bringing together towns and villages that may previously have had their own local traditions. Athens was now head of a large territorial unit that included all of Attica (whether or not it was called by this name at the time), and its population had been growing because of immigration as well as territorial expansion.[23]

The growing prosperity suggests that the community was generally law abiding, and that before Draco wrote his law, traditional procedures for dispute-settlement must therefore have been functioning effectively, even for major offenses such as homicide. On the other hand, the growth and greater diversity of the population would have increased the likelihood that certain areas of Attica or segments of the population had different customs and practices, and such differences would have increased the chance for uncertainty and conflict about traditional rules. The resulting increase in the number and complexity of disputes would have strained the traditional procedures for dispute settlement, which had developed to serve smaller, more coherent communities. The situation did not necessarily call for entirely new rules – it would be reasonable to keep well-known and effective rules, such as the rule that a killer should go into exile – but some traditional rules might need to be changed or supplemented. And for many aspects of the treatment of homicide existing rules (such as the rules for reconciliation) would need greater precision and specificity. And in other areas new rules would be needed to govern less common situations or to spell out new details of procedure. Finally, the relatively recent development of new institutions, such as international festivals, would also have led to the need for new rules.

In order to clarify traditional rules or to legislate for new situations, it would be especially important to give full details about these rules, to make these details as clear as possible so as to prevent misunderstanding or disagreement, and to ensure

22 See Rhodes 1988: 200 (on Thucydides 2.15.2): "If there was in fact a unification of Attica in the bronze age, it will almost certainly have been undone in the breakdown of the Mycenaean civilization, and the unity of the classical period will have been created toward the end of the dark age." The last village to be joined to Athens was Eleusis, probably in the eighth or seventh century.

23 Osborne (1996: 70-81) speaks of "slow and steady growth" (80). See Whitley 2001: 98-99 on population growth in the eighth century ("that there was a general increase in population ... seems undeniable"). Manville 1990: 55-78 has a good summary of the social organization of Attica and its development up to Draco's time.

the stability of the details so that they would not change over space or time. It is this need for precise, clear, and stable details, especially details about points of procedure, that explains why Draco did not just formulate new rules orally, as had been done in the past. Traditional pronouncements that could be preserved and transmitted orally were adequate for expressing general, easily-remembered rules, but they were not adequate for expressing rules with many details, or for ensuring that the details did not vary from case to case.

Recall Ajax's statement about compensation and reconciliation which we cited earlier: "A person accepts from the killer the blood-price for his dead brother or son, and when he has paid a large compensation, the killer remains in his land, and the person's heart and manly anger are curbed, when he has received the blood-price" (*Iliad* 9.632-36). This traditional rule (or statement of custom) says only that a brother or father accepts compensation, stops being angry, and allows the killer to remain in the land. It says nothing about whether a relative must accept compensation, which relative (if there is more than one present) can or must agree to accept the compensation, what happens if no father or brother is alive, or countless other details. As a general oral pronouncement, it has the virtue of being easily remembered and communicated to large audiences. But it will not be effective in regulating conduct in a community growing ever larger, more diverse, and more complex, where the absence of such details would increasingly result in uncertainty and disagreement.

A more detailed rule, however, would be difficult, if not impossible, to compose in a version that could be easily remembered and transmitted orally. Just imagine trying to put the text of Draco's law into hexameters! And even if one could express Draco's law in verse, it would be nearly impossible to communicate the text orally to a wide audience with all the details intact, especially over time. As many studies of oral cultures have shown, details in oral texts are unstable and often change with successive retellings. Only in exceptional circumstances could orally transmitted details perhaps remain constant over time, and the examples given are usually small religious communities transmitting a sacred text.[24] Thus, when Draco wanted to communicate precise details of homicide procedure – which family members should participate, or where a killer in exile could and could not go – he had to put this information in writing. This is the main reason why he wrote his law.

Draco may have had other reasons, but nothing suggests that in writing this law he aimed to further his own interests or those of a small ruling class by imposing his authority on the common people. On the contrary, his law would have served in several ways to strengthen the nascent sense that all inhabitants of Attica belonged

---

24 The *Vedas* are often cited as the extreme case of exact memorization of a large body of material, but scholars have recently expressed doubts whether these were in fact transmitted without writing; see Goody 1987: 110-22, Finnegan 1992: 139-53

to a single political community, a polis, that was Athens.[25] First, the mere fact of writing and displaying rules that applied, by implication at least, to all Athenians (or to all inhabitants of Attica) and only to them would have conveyed a sense of political unity. In fact, this sense of inclusion was not only implicit in the opening *tis*, "someone" – that is, some Athenian – but is especially evident in provision 10, where Draco provides that anyone who kills a killer in exile "is liable to the same treatment as someone who kills an Athenian." By making the killer of an Athenian subject to different treatment from the killer of anyone else, this law would convey to the reader that, as an Athenian he was a privileged person and was protected by this law, as others were not.

The law would also convey a sense of political unity by implying, perhaps for the first time, that Athens, or Attica, was a territory with clear, demarcated boundaries.[26] Provision 10 suggests this concept of a territory with known boundaries when it speaks of a frontier market, and provision 11 conveys the same idea when it allows a killer to be killed or arrested "in our territory." Thus, by writing a law for all the inhabitants of Attica, by making an Athenian a privileged person, and by implying that Athens (or Attica) is a single territorial unit, Draco would have fostered a growing sense of Athenian political unity. This may not have been his conscious aim, since these details are inserted almost by the way in later provisions of the law, but it may have been one of the effects of writing this law. And the desire to clarify rules for an increasingly diverse population would suggest a general awareness on Draco's part of the need to create a more closely unified community out of these diverse elements.

Finally, Draco did not write rules addressing only one issue or one specific crisis. He wrote a comprehensive and detailed homicide law concerning a wide range of issues and situations, including some rather remote contingencies.[27] He organized it, moreover, into a logical and coherent whole, not simply a collection of individual provisions that might have been enacted as ad-hoc responses to crises. Past conflicts or recent crises may have made Draco aware of the need for new, detailed rules concerning homicide, but his aim in writing this law was not to resolve these past conflicts or to address them directly, but to provide a comprehensive and detailed set of rules that could easily and effectively be used in homicide cases that would arise in the future.

---

25 On this point see Manville 1990: 79-82, Forsdyke 2005: 88-89.

26 Manville (1990: 80) notes that "probably such boundaries were not carefully surveyed demarcations but primarily natural limits and marginal lands."

27 By this I do not mean to imply that Draco wrote a "code" in the modern sense of a "complete and systematic set of rules" about homicide (see Hölkeskamp 1999, and most recently Thür 2002: 632); this issue of "codification" in the modern sense is, in my view, a red herring.

BIBLIOGRAPHY

Camassa, Giorgio. 1988. "Aux origines de la codification écrite en Grèce." In *Les savoirs de l'écriture en Grèce ancienne*, ed. Marcel Detienne. 130-55. Lille.

Cantarella, Eva. 2002. "Dispute Settlement in Homer: Once Again on the Shield of Achilles. In *Mélanges en l'honneur Panayotis Dimakis: Droits antiques et société*, 147-65. Athens.

Detienne, Marcel. 1981. *L'invention de la mythologie*. Paris: (English trans. 1986. *The Creation of Mythology*. Chicago)

Eder, Walter. 1986. "The Political Significance of the Codification of Law in Archaic Societies: An Unconventional Hypothesis." In *Social Struggles in Archaic Rome: New Perspectives on the Conflict of the Orders,* ed. Kurt A. Raaflaub, 262-300. Berkeley.

Finnegan, Ruth. 1992. *Oral Poetry: Its Nature, Significance and Social Context,* 2nd ed. Bloomington, IN. (1st ed. 1977)

Forsdyke, Sara. 2005. *Exile, Ostracism, and Democracy: The Politics of Expulsion in Ancient Greece*. Princeton.

Gagarin, Michael. 1981. *Drakon and Early Athenian Homicide Law*. New Haven.

Gagarin, Michael. 1986. *Early Greek Law*. Berkeley.

Goody, Jack. 1987. *The Interface Between the Written and the Oral*. Cambridge.

Hölkeskamp, Karl-Joachim. 1999. *Schiedsrichter, Gesetzgeber und Gesetzgebung im archaischen Griechenland. Historia Einzelschrift* 131. Stuttgart.

Hölkeskamp, Karl-Joachim. 2000. "(In-)schrift und Monument. Zum Begriff des Gesetzes im archaischen und klassischen Griechenland," *Zeitschrift für Papyrologie und Epigraphie*: 132: 73-96.

Humphreys, Sally. 1991. "A Historical Approach to Drakon's Law on Homicide." In *Symposion 1990*, ed. Michael Gagarin, 17-45. Cologne.

Manville, Brook. 1990. *The Origins of Citizenship in Ancient Athens*. Princeton.

Osborne, Robin. 1996. *Greece in the Making 1200-479 BC*. London.

Ostwald, Martin. 1955. "The Athenian Legislation against Tyranny and Subversion." Transactions of the American Philological Association 86: 103-28.

Rhodes, P.J. 1981. *A Commentary on the Aristotelian* Athenaion Politeia. Oxford.

Rhodes, P.J. ed. 1988. *Thucydides History II*. Warminster.

Stratton, Jon. 1980. "Writing and the Concept of Law in Ancient Greece." *Visible Language* 14: 99-121.

Stroud, Ronald S. 1968. *Drakon's Law on Homicide*. Berkeley and Los Angeles.

Thür, Gerhard. 2002. "Gesetzeskodizes im archaischen und klassischen Athen." In *Mélanges en l'honneur Panayotis Dimakis: Droits antiques et société*, 397-404. Athens.

Whitley, James. 2001. *The Archaeology of Ancient Greece*. Cambridge.

EVA CANTARELLA (MILANO)

RESPONSE TO MICHAEL GAGARIN

When I wrote to Michael Gagarin that I would be his respondent, he promise that he will try to make sure he won't say anything I will agree with him. I must tell him he succeeded only in part. In spite of my own efforts to totally disagree with him, I must confess that I share many of his points.

In this paper, that represents a further important step in the progress of his research dedicated to the interaction of writing and Greek Law, Gagarin faces one of the most important moments in legal history, the first appearance of written Laws.

Gagarin approaches this difficult and highly controversial topic asking a preliminary question: why, after a century or more of private writing, did the Greeks decide to write down the laws?

According to some scholars, laws were written down in order to guarantee a minimum of "equal justice". According to others, laws were not written to be read, but in order to make a visual impression on ordinary people and to strengthen the control of the ruling elite.

Gagarin endorses the opinion that they were written to be read; and rightly so, in my opinion. The "control-of-the-ruling-class" theory might deserve to be taken in account, perhaps, for other historical periods and countries. The visual impact of Hammurabi's law is really imposing and I would say frightening (not to speak of the content of the code, as well as of other Near Eastern Law Codes); but Gagarin interest is explicitly limited in Greece, and I think that he has more than sufficiently demonstrated that Greek laws were written to be read.

The further question is: why the Greeks wanted the laws to be read? To answer this question Gagarin turns to the first Athenian written law, whose original was lost, but whose copy, made in 409 B.C., reproduces, in Gagarin opinion, Draco's actual word (we will go back to this problem, later on). With strong arguments, that I don't need to repeat, he rejects the hypothesis that this law was written down in order to resolve a crisis stemmed from the failed attempt of the Cylonian, as well as the hypothesis that it was aimed to resolve a more general situation of crisis or feuding in Athens, at that time.

His analysis of the law is very accurate and original. In order to understand the reasons why it was written, Gagarin proceeds with a two steps method: the first step consists in the illustration of the non written traditions regulating homicide in the poems of Homer and Hesiod (the tradition of the oral laws period, as he calls it).

The second step consists in the comparison of these traditions and the Draconian provisions, in order to register analogies and differences, and find out if they were such to suggest or request the necessity of a written code.

Gagarin's conclusion, at the end of this comparison, is that Draco wrote a law whose aim "was not to solve specific conflicts in the past, but to provide a comprehensive set of rules for homicide cases that would arise in the future". And I fully agree with his opinion: I am not certain, instead, to share his opinion concerning the relation between the law and oral tradition.

According to Gagarin, Draco's law reaffirmed the basic oral laws (provisions 1 and 2, in his handout) adding new rules that, again, followed traditional practice, but spelled out the procedures in greater details (provision 3, concerning reconciliation), or addressing contingencies for which almost certainly no earlier rules existed (provisions 4 and 5). In other words, Gagarin thinks that the law combined general rules, which were traditional, with detailed new rules.

This poses a first question: did really the new provisions concern only detailed, non general rules? In my opinion, some of the Draconian new rules were so general that the homicide law may be considered the moment of a fundamental passage in the legal history of Athens. The reasons of my opinions are tied to these considerations: in Gagarin's interpretation, the basic oral rules reaffirmed by Draco were the followings:

1) the person who has committed an homicide flees into exile leaving his kinsmen and country (*Od.*, 23, 118-120)
2) the killer should be reconciled with the victim's relatives (*Il.*, 9, 632-636)
3) the accomplice is equated to the actual killer, as demonstrated by the story of Clytemnestra, being killed by Orestes along with Aegystus, in the various account of the Odyssey.

Furthermore, notes Gagarin, in Homer already existed a pacific dispute-settlement system (the system followed in the trial on Achille's shield), and it is very likely that in the pre-Draconian period the Athenians followed the traditional Homeric practices.

As far as this last point is concerned (the fact that in pre-Draconian period the Athenian followed the traditional Homeric practices) I share Gagarin's opinion, but I would like to add that the traditional Homeric practice did not consist only in the alternative between exile and the possibility of compensation. In Homer a person who had committed an homicide fled the country in order to avoid to be killed in revenge by the victim's relatives. This was the first, basic Homeric rule. Voluntary exile was only a *de facto* remedy to avoid to be killed.

Therefore, when Draco stated the penalty of exile for the *phonos mê ek pronoias*, he was not following the Homeric practice. By the way, the Homeric practice did not distinguish voluntary and involuntary homicide: self revenge, exile or compensation were alternatives offered (so to say) to any person who had committed an homicide, either voluntary or involuntary. When Draco stated the penalty of exile for homicide he was introducing some very important innovations: he introduced a distinction between *phonos ek pronoias* and *phonos mê ek pronoias* (we don't have here the time, nor the need, to discuss which was the penalty for homicide *ek pronoias*); he prohibited revenge, a basic Homeric rule; he stated a civic (the first civic) penalty for homicide.

A second doubt that I want to express concerns the possibility that in the oral law period the accomplice was treated just like an actual killer. I don't think that we can deduct the existence of a legal rule (an oral legal rule) from the dramatic narrative of a mythical event such as the killing of Clytemnestra, in the Odyssey. Finally, connected with the character of Clytemnestra, I think that it is necessary to discuss a problem, connected with the meaning of provision 2 of Draco's law .

According to Gagarin this provision "follows the Homeric practice in declaring that an accomplice would be treated just like an actual killer". But provision 2 does not mention an accomplice. The Greek word to be translated, in order to understand this provision is *bouleusas* (which follows, line 11 of Draco's law, a lacuna of 17 letters, which has been filled in many different ways) translated by Gagarin with "planner" ("the kings judge guilty of homicide the killer or the planner, and the *ephetai* decide").

This translation, however, raises serious questions: which is the technical meaning of the expression "to plan" a crime? Is a planner an accomplice, as Gagarin seems to suggest, if I did not misunderstand his line or reasoning? Is he rather a person whose criminal behavior is different from the behavior of an accomplice, as I believe? In the second case, provision 2 of Draco's law does not reaffirm the Homeric rule, whose existence would be proved by the case of Clytemnestra. It introduces a new criminal behavior, called *bouleusis*, a crime that in my opinion was not connected with involuntary, but only with voluntary homicide.[1] Again, a very controversial problem, that deserves to be discussed, as well as the moment when the crime of *bouleusis* was first previewed by the Athenian law.

In my opinion, the conceptualisation of a crime such as *bouleusis* is too sophisticated to be present in the first Athenian law: *bouleusis* was introduced when the *anagrapheis*, in 409-408, copied the law. It was in that moment, in my opinion, that *bouleusis* was equated to *phonos mê ek pronoias,* as far as the penalty was concerned. That is to say from a procedural point of views.

Had Draco been the author of such a rule, he would have stated it in a substantive rule, not in a procedural one; he would have said something like "*ean mê ek pronoias kteine tis tina, ê ean bouleuse, feugen*". He would not have equated *bouleusis* to *phonos mê ek pronoias* only in an indirect way, through the statement, for both, of the competence of the Ephetai. But this is a secondary point, not central

[1] As I wrote many years ago (E. Cantarella, *Studi sull' omicidio in diritto greco e romano*, Milano, 1976, p. 92-93) and as I still believe.

to the topic addressed by Gagarin. Going back to his main topic, I agree with the following points:

a) Drako's law was written to be read;
b) it was aimed to provide a comprehensive set of rules for homicide cases that would arise in the future;
c) the knowledge of the Homeric traditions is indispensable to understand Drako's Law: Draco's law is a further step in the process of dealing with the homicide cases, already present in Homeric times.

However, as I said, in my opinion Draco did not introduce only details, but many substantial innovation. The function of Homeric courts (I am speaking of course of the court in Achilles' shield), was not to decide if the accused person had or had not committed an homicide, as the Draconian courts did. The *gerontes*, in Achilles' shield, were not summoned by the relatives of the victim, as the Draconian courts: they judged on demand of the murderer pursued by the relatives of the victim and claiming that the revenge was unjust, because in contrast with the rules governing the system of the vendetta.

The Draconian trial, therefore, differed from the Homeric justice for substantial reasons. Both the Areopagus and the Ephetic Courts had to decide if the accused person had committed the homicide (voluntary or involuntary not to speak of the so called *phonos dikaios*), and they had the power to condemn him to the prescribed penalty, if proved guilty.

The Homeric trial belongs to a world where the concept of crime did not yet exist, where the same behavior was acceptable or unacceptable according to the balance between the honour of the persons involved. In other words, it belonged to a world where the necessity to react was a matter of honor, not of justice.

The Draconian law, therefore, was a turning point in the history of Athenian punishing system. This was the reason why it was necessary to write down the law. My explanation of the reason why laws were written down, then, is different from Gagarin's. For Gagarin, the reason for writing is to be found in the new details: oral tradition may be adequate for expressing general rules, not details; details need to be written down. In my opinion, instead, new rules need to be written down, in order to be read, known and observed, when they are general and revolutionary, such as the ones which in my opinion were enacted by Draco.

LAURA PEPE (MILANO)

A PROPOSITO DI UNA LEGGE SICELIOTA SULL'OMICIDIO*

Nel corso di una campagna di scavi condotta tra il 1903 e il 1905 nella località di Monte S. Mauro presso Caltagirone, Paolo Orsi rinvenne una dozzina di piccoli frammenti di lamine bronzee, sui quali, seppur con molte lacune, è leggibile un'iscrizione bustrofedica in alfabeto calcidese e dialetto ionico datata alla seconda metà del VI secolo a.C.[1]. Alcuni elementi significativi permettono di ricostruire la storia di queste lamine: innanzitutto, nove dei dodici frammenti ritrovati sono opistografi[2], e riportano sul *recto* e sul *verso* formule simili e ricorrenti; in secondo luogo, un frammento angolare rinvenuto[3] mostra il segno di un taglio netto che ha troncato a metà orizzontalmente le lettere scritte sul rigo iniziale del *verso*, rigo che invece è integro sul *recto*: indizio, questo, di un riutilizzo successivo delle lamine. La combinazione di queste due circostanze – formule ricorrenti e riutilizzo – fa pensare che sul documento siano state riportate due differenti redazioni dello stesso testo, di cui una, quella sul *recto*, più recente rispetto a quella contenuta nel *verso*[4]. Altro fattore significativo è l'assenza di scrittura su un lato di tre dei frammenti

---

* Nelle tavole riportate di seguito al presente contributo si riproducono i disegni di Rosario Carta, pubblicati da Paolo Orsi, *Di un'anonima città siculo-greca a Monte S. Mauro presso Caltagirone*, in *Monumenti Antichi dei Lincei*, 20 (1910) 831ss.

[1] P. Orsi, *Di un'anonima città* cit. 729ss. (nell'articolo, alle coll. 831-844, è contenuto anche il contributo epigrafico per la lettura e l'integrazione del testo di D. Comparetti). Le lamine – oggi esposte al Museo Archeologico Regionale Paolo Orsi di Siracusa, con il numero di inventario 30839 – sono state ripubblicate da V. Arangio Ruiz/A. Olivieri, *Inscriptiones grecae Siciliae et infimae Italiae ad ius pertinentes*, Milano 1925, 171ss., con il titolo *lex incertae civitatis de homicidio*, e si trovano poi in *SEG* IV.64. I frammenti rinvenuti dovevano appartenere ad almeno due lamine, come si ricava dalla circostanza che due di essi (il 4 e il 5) hanno conservato l'angolo superiore destro: Orsi, *Di un'anonima città* cit. 831s.; F. Cordano, *Le leggi calcidesi di Monte San Mauro di Caltagirone*, in *Decima Miscellanea greca e romana*, Roma 1986, ora in Ead., *Studi Siciliani. Miscellanea (1974-2000)*, Milano 2000, 211ss., part. 221. Per la datazione si rimanda a Orsi, *Di un'anonima città* cit. 845s.

[2] Si tratta dei frr. 1,3,5,6,7,8,9,10,11.

[3] Si tratta del fr. 5; si vedano al proposito le osservazioni di Comparetti, in Orsi, *Di un'anonima città* cit. 111-114.

[4] Orsi, *Di un'anonima città* cit. 845.

superstiti: ciò dà credito all'ipotesi che la seconda redazione sia stata dettata dalla necessità di aggiunte, ovvero di varianti più dettagliate, rispetto alla prima[5].

Le lamine dovevano essere esposte in pubblico, come confermano tanto la verosimile funzione pubblica dell'edificio in cui esse sono state ritrovate[6], quanto, soprattutto, il contenuto del documento, su cui doveva essere incisa una legge sull'omicidio. A far pensare a una legge, infatti, è la struttura scandita e articolata del testo, su cui dovremo tra breve soffermarci; che poi questa legge trattasse di omicidio si desume da alcuni vocaboli significativi che, seppur mutili, si leggono su alcuni dei frammenti. Si riconoscono in almeno cinque circostanze, infatti, vocaboli legati alla radice *phon-*: i termini sono stati ricondotti in quattro casi al sostantivo *phoneus* (frr. 1 *recto*, l. 1; 3 *recto*, l. 9; 3 *verso*, l. 5; 6 *verso*, l. 1) e una volta all'aggettivo *phonios* (fr. 6 *recto*, l. 2)[7]; ancora, su un frammento (fr. 3 *recto*, l. 7) si legge con ogni verosimiglianza il termine in caso dativo *tha]natoi*[8]; ed è infine possibile, benché in questo caso l'ipotesi sia più labile, che le lettere *nai*, sul fr. 6 *recto*, l. 1, rappresentino la terminazione di un infinito, che potrebbe essere *tethna]nai* oppure *kte]nai*[9].

Questa legge sull'omicidio, come si è prima accennato, è scritta in alfabeto calcidese, ed è stata inoltre rinvenuta in un insediamento che, come i più recenti scavi archeologici hanno dimostrato, doveva segnare l'estrema propaggine dell'estensione territoriale verso l'interno delle colonie calcidesi di Catania e di Leontini, a segnare il confine rispetto all'area di influenza dorica facente capo a

---

5 Cordano, *Le leggi calcidesi* cit. 221.

6 Orsi, *Di un'anonima città* cit. 736ss. ritenne che tale edificio, da lui denominato *anaktoron* e datato attorno all'VIII secolo, dovesse essere la dimora del capo tribù indigeno. Per i più moderni orientamenti della dottrina in merito al problema della funzione (sacrale o pubblica) del cosiddetto *anaktoron*, si rimanda per tutti a U. Spigo, *L'anonimo centro greco di Monte s. Mauro di Caltagirone nel quadro dell'arcaismo siceliota: prospettive di ricerca*, in *Decima Miscellanea greca e romana*, Roma 1986, 1ss., part. 5ss., 9s. e rell. ntt., più propenso da parte sua a ritenere che l'edificio in questione avesse carattere pubblico; nello stesso senso anche Cordano, *Le leggi calcidesi* cit. 213ss.

7 In particolare (segnalo d'ora in poi con il solo nome gli autori delle integrazioni proposte; le opere in cui queste sono riportate sono state menzionate *supra*, nt. 1): *phone[a*, fr. 1 *recto*, l. 1 (Arangio Ruiz/Olivieri); *phon[e]a[s*, fr. 3 *recto*, l. 9 (Comparetti); *phon[eas*, fr. 3 *verso*, l. 5 (Comparetti); *pr]os phone[as*, fr. 6 *verso*, l. 2 (Comparetti); *ph]oniai*, fr. 6 *recto*, l. 2 (Comparetti). Comparetti, peraltro, proponeva di leggere *pho]niai* anche al fr. 2, l. 4: ma nell'apparato di Arangio Ruiz/Olivieri si sottolinea come la seconda lettera del rigo, identificata da Comparetti come *i*, è più verosimilmente *t*, per cui l'integrazione proposta non può essere accettata.

8 L'integrazione è di Arangio Ruiz/Olivieri; Comparetti, al contrario, postulava *-s* finale in luogo di *-i*, e leggeva quindi *tha]natos*.

9 Al riguardo Arangio Ruiz/Olivieri annotano: «*tethna[nai, kte[nai vel quid simile supplendum*».

Gela[10]: esporre a Monte S. Mauro la legge di una colonia calcidese, se non addirittura una legge comune all'intera area calcidese, era dunque una chiara operazione antigeloa[11]. Ora, la natura calcidese della legge rende opportuno almeno un accenno a quel complesso di disposizioni, tradizionalmente conosciute come *nomima Chalkidikà*, che le fonti antiche attribuivano a Caronda di Catania[12]. Questo corpus di norme caratteristiche era ben noto a Tucidide, il quale, parlando della fondazione di Imera da parte di coloni calcidesi provenienti da Zancle e di esuli siracusani, ricorda che la lingua affermatasi nella colonia fu un misto tra il dorico e il calcidese, mentre soltanto calcidesi furono le istituzioni – *nomima Chalkidikà*, appunto – che ebbero il sopravvento[13]. Anche Platone, nella *Repubblica*, individua una specifica legislazione calcidese accanto a quella dorica e a quella attica, indicando inoltre i nomi dei padri delle tre: rispettivamente Caronda, Licurgo e Solone[14]. Sono peraltro diversi gli autori che nominano Caronda additandolo come l'autore di tale "codice", uno tra i primi scritti, destinato ad avere una fortuna straordinaria: le sue leggi vennero infatti adottate non solo nelle città calcidesi della Sicilia e della Magna Grecia[15], ma a quanto pare anche nella penisola calcidica[16], nell'isola di Kos[17], e nella città di Mazaka, in Cappadocia[18]; esse, inoltre, erano ben note nella stessa Atene[19]. Alla luce di ciò, risulta poco rilevante la questione relativa

[10] *Contra* Orsi, *Di un'anonima città* cit. 845, considerava Monte S. Mauro come un insediamento gelese, e giustificava quindi la presenza di leggi calcidesi in quest'area con l'ipotesi che esse fossero state «messe fuori uso e forse rubate in una scorreria». Per l'evidenza offerta dalle più recenti indagini archeologiche si rimanda a Cordano, *Le leggi calcidesi* cit. 219s. (con relativa bibliografia) ed Ead., *L'evoluzione sociale dei Calcidesi di Sicilia*, in *Tredicesima Miscellanea greca e romana*, Roma 1988, ora in *Studi Siciliani* cit. 303ss., part. 306s.

[11] Cordano, *Le leggi calcidesi* cit. 217.

[12] Tra le fonti che indicano Catania come patria di Caronda ricordiamo Arist. *Pol.* 1274 a 23; Porph. *Vit. Pyth.* 21; Iambl. *de Vit. Pythag.* 7.33; 27.130; 30.172; 36.267. Isolata l'opinione di E.A. Freeman, *The History of Sicily from the earliest Times*, Oxford 1891-94, II, 399ss., secondo il quale Caronda proveniva da Sibari: contro tale posizione si rimanda a C.F. Crispo, *Contributo alla storia della più antica civiltà della Magna Grecia*, Roma 1940, 9.

[13] Thuc. 6.5.1.

[14] Plat. *Resp.* 599 d-e.

[15] Plat. *Resp.* 599 e; Aristot. *Pol.* 1274 a 23; in particolare, per il codice di Caronda vigente a Reggio cfr. Heracl. Lemb. fr. 55 ed Ael. *V.H.* 3.17, il quale aggiunge che Caronda giunse a Reggio dopo essere stato esiliato dalla patria Catania, notizia della cui attendibilità dubita tuttavia T.J. Dunbabin, *The Western Greeks. The History of Sicily and South Italy from the Foundation of the Greek Colonies to 480 b.C.*, Oxford 1948, 74.

[16] Aristot. *Pol.* 1274 b 23.

[17] Herond. *Mim.* 2.46ss.

[18] Strab. *Geogr.* 12.2.9.

[19] Athen. *Deipn.* 14.10.40, che cita al riguardo Ermippo di Smirne: *êdonto de Athênêsi kai hoi Charôndou nomoi par'oinon*. Il passo è stato oggetto di molteplici discussioni, non solo per la proposta di A. Hecker (*Epistolae criticae ad F.G. Schneidewinum V. Cl.*, in

alla storicità di Caronda, posta da una parte della dottrina contemporanea[20]. Ciò che conta, infatti, è solamente la consapevolezza, da parte delle fonti antiche, dell'esistenza di norme caratteristiche comuni all'intera area calcidese – ben distinte da quelle di matrice attica o dorica –, che si diffusero con ogni probabilità grazie al tramite della madrepatria[21], e che si svilupparono in modo tale da non alterare il modello originario, attribuito all'antico legislatore Caronda.

Quale fosse poi il contenuto specifico di queste leggi è molto difficile dire: Aristotele, nella *Politica*, tramanda poche ma preziose notizie, che saranno oggetto di successiva analisi. Maggiori informazioni si trovano in autori più tardi, principalmente Diodoro Siculo e Stobeo, che rappresentano tuttavia fonti per più versi infide. A tacer d'altro, Diodoro, nel suo corposo resoconto delle leggi di Caronda[22], attribuisce a quest'ultimo molte disposizioni che da fonti più attendibili sono invece riferite a Zaleuco di Locri, secondo la tradizione il primo autore di un "codice" scritto[23]. Inoltre, lo storico risente fortemente della tradizione che vuole

---

Philologus 5 [1850] 421) di emendare *Athênêsi* in *Katanêsi*, ma anche per la possibilità che le leggi fossero cantate (tant'è che [Arist.] *Probl.* 919 b-920 a, ricorda che le melodie note come *nomoi* vennero così chiamate dalle leggi che, prima di essere scritte, venivano cantate per poter essere ricordate più facilmente). Per l'intera questione si rimanda a L. Piccirilli, *«Nomoi» cantati e «nomoi» scritti*, in *Civiltà Classica e Cristiana* 2 (1981) 7ss. e a J. Triantaphyllopoulos, *Cantar le leggi*, in *Atti della Accademia Mediterranea delle Scienze* 1 (1983) 27ss.

20 K.J. Beloch, *Griechische Geschichte*, I² 1, Strassburg 1912, 350 e I² 2, 1913, 257s.; A. Delatte, *Essai sur la politique pythagoricienne*, Liège-Paris 1922, 177. I dubbi sulla reale esistenza di Caronda furono sollevati dal fatto che il suo nome, derivato da Charon (il traghettatore dei morti che in origine doveva indicare il Sole), richiama quello di una divinità solare, proprio come quello di Zaleuco, legislatore di Locri (la cui storicità venne già messa in dubbio da Timeo di Tauromenio: cfr. Cic. *de Leg.* 2.6.5) e dello spartano Licurgo; a riaffermare la storicità di Caronda fu G. De Sanctis, *Storia dei Greci*, 1, Firenze 1939, 469, la cui opinione rimane oggi quella dominante. Per una diversa interpretazione dell'abbondante materiale leggendario contenuto nelle fonti relative agli antichi legislatori cfr. A. Szegedy-Maszak, *Legends of the Greek Lawgivers*, in *GRBS* 19 (1978) 199ss.

21 Arist. 1274 b 23-24, a proposito di Androdama di Reggio mandato come legislatore per i calcidesi di Tracia; sul punto cfr. Dunbabin, *The Western Greeks* cit. 75; F. Cordano, *Leggi e legislatori calcidesi*, in *Sesta Miscellanea greca e romana*, Roma 1978, 89ss., part. 90s.: G. Camassa, *La codificazione delle leggi e le istituzioni politiche delle città greche della Calabria in età arcaica e classica*, in AA.VV., *Storia della Calabria antica*, Roma 1987, 619.

22 Diod. 12.11-19.

23 Eph. *FGrHist.* 70 F 139 *apd* Strab. 6.1.8; Eus. *Chron.* p. 86 Schöne. Lo stretto rapporto tra Zaleuco e Caronda è peraltro sottolineato da molti autori: Ael. *V.H.* 3.17; Porphyr. *Vit. Pyth.* 21; Iambl. *De vit. Pythag.* 7.33; 30.172; Sen. *Ep.* 90.6; Aristotele riporta, senza darle eccessivo credito, la notizia secondo cui il legislatore di Locri sarebbe stato maestro del catanese (Arist. *Pol.* 1274 a 25ss.); ma esiste in effetti anche un'opposta tradizione che fa di Zaleuco il discepolo di Caronda (Theodoret. *de Cura Graec. aff.* 9.8.221). Circa la possibilità di distinguere, tra le leggi riportate da Diodoro, quelle di Caronda e di

Caronda discepolo di Pitagora[24], con il risultato che molte tra le leggi che egli gli attribuisce appaiono più delle massime morali che non delle norme giuridiche[25]. La stessa considerazione vale per Stobeo: un chiaro influsso del pensiero pitagorico, e forse anche stoico[26], si avverte nel proemio[27] che, a suo dire, Caronda avrebbe utilizzato come introduzione per le sue leggi, e la cui genuinità è peraltro messa in dubbio dal fatto che esso è per il resto sconosciuto alle fonti[28]. Risulta dunque evidente che è necessaria molta cautela nel riconoscere come calcidesi le norme

---

Zaleuco, cfr. E. Ciaceri, *Storia della Magna Grecia,* II, Milano 1940, 32ss.; G. Vallet, *Rhègion et Zancle. Histoire, commerce et civilisation des cités chalcidiennes du détroit de Messine*, Paris 1958, 317.

[24] Nello stesso senso cfr. Diog. Laert. 8.16; Porphyr. *Vit. Pyth.* 21; Iambl. *De vit. Pythag.* 7.33; 27.130; 30.172; Sen. *Ep.* 90.6; al riguardo si rimanda a F.E. Adcock, *Literary Tradition and Early Greek Code-Makers*, in *Cambridge Historical Journal* 2 (1927) 95ss., part. 102ss.; Crispo, *Contributo* cit. 130; B. Pace, *Arte e civiltà della Sicilia antica*, III, Genova 1945, 248s.; Dunbabin, *The Western Greeks* cit. 73s.; Vallet, *Rhègion et Zancle* cit. 314s.; Szegedy-Maszak, *Legends* cit. 203s.

[25] Alle osservazioni svolte nel testo va poi aggiunto il fatto che Diodoro, prima di citare le norme di Caronda, rammenta che egli venne scelto per dare leggi a Turi, la colonia panellenica fondata da Atene per volontà di Pericle sulle ceneri dell'antica Sibari, nel 444/443 a.C. Mentre la notizia di Diodoro è confermata da Val. Max. 6.5 *ext.* 4 e da Schol. ad Plat. *Resp.* 599 e, altri autori riferiscono ora che Turi adottò il "codice" di Zaleuco (Eph. *FGrHist.* 70 F 139 *apd* Strab. 6.1.8; Athen. *Deipn.* 11.117, 508 a), ora che la costituzione della città fu opera di Protagora, il filosofo amico di Pericle (Diog. Laert. 9.50); per l'analisi delle fonti e della questione nel suo complesso si rimanda ad Adcock, *Literary Tradition* cit. 104s.; Ciaceri, *Storia della Magna Grecia* cit. 33; Crispo, *Contributo* cit. 10ss. In ogni caso, l'informazione di Diodoro si presenta dubbia anche per il fatto che egli assegna Caronda a una città diversa rispetto a quella tradizionalmente indicata come sua patria, Catania (per cui cfr. *supra*, nt. 12), e inoltre colloca il legislatore in un'epoca ben più recente rispetto al VI secolo, a cui egli va piuttosto attribuito sulla base di più attendibili fonti: un *terminus ante quem* è al riguardo fornito dalla notizia di Heracl. Lemb. *Exc. Pol.* 55, secondo il quale Reggio avrebbe fatto uso delle leggi di Caronda prima della tirannide di Anassila, la cui presa di potere risale al 494 a.C. (sul punto si veda, per tutti, Cordano, *Leggi e legislatori calcidesi* cit. 90ss. ed Ead. *L'evoluzione sociale* cit. 307s.). Tali deformazioni giustificano poi il fatto che Diodoro finisce anche per sminuire l'originalità di Caronda quando afferma che, nello svolgere il suo compito di dare leggi alla città, egli «esaminò le legislazioni di tutti i popoli, scelse i principi migliori e li registrò nelle sue leggi» (Diod. 12.11.4; va tuttavia sottolineato che il tema della scelta delle leggi migliori in uso presso altre popolazioni è ricorrente nelle biografie dei legislatori greci più illustri, come ha dimostrato Szegedy-Maszak, *Legends* cit. 204s.).

[26] Sul punto si rimanda a M. Mühl, *Die Gesetze des Zaleukos und Charondas*, in *Klio* 22 (1929) 105ss. e 432ss., part. 118ss. e 347; Dunbabin, *The Western Greeks* cit. 71.

[27] Stob. *Anth.* 44.2.24; menzione di tale proemio si trova anche in Cic. *de Leg.* 2.6.

[28] Platone (*Leg.* 722 e) rivendica a se stesso il primato nell'uso di un proemio introduttivo a leggi; sul valore del proemio di Stobeo si rimanda a Delatte, *Essai* cit. 177ss.; Crispo, *Contributo* cit. 131; Dunbabin, *The Western Greeks* cit. 68 ss; Vallet, *Rhègion et Zancle* cit. 314 nt. 7.

ricordate da Diodoro e Stobeo; tanto più che il tentativo di riportare con certezza al nome di Caronda alcune leggi presenti in queste fonti, condotto negli anni passati da diversi studiosi, non ha prodotto alcun risultato definitivo[29].

Alla scarsità e incertezza delle notizie si aggiunge poi il fatto che la tradizione letteraria non ricorda alcuna legge di Caronda sull'omicidio. Vero è, tuttavia, che Aristotele in un passo della *Politica* attribuisce una normativa in materia ad Androdama[30]: questi, chiamato come legislatore dai Calcidesi di Tracia, probabilmente portò qui le leggi della sua città, Reggio, dove vigeva il codice di Caronda; nulla tuttavia lo Stagirita aggiunge circa il contenuto di tali disposizioni sull'omicidio. Più puntuale è l'informazione contenuta in un altro passo della *Politica*, ove si dice che a Cuma – verosimilmente la colonia calcidese della Magna Grecia e non Cuma eolica[31] – vigeva la regola per cui l'imputato di un processo per omicidio era ritenuto colpevole se l'accusatore produceva un numero bastevole di testimoni presi tra i suoi parenti più stretti[32]: dato che, forse, potrà essere di qualche utilità nel contesto di quanto risulta leggibile sulle nostre lamine.

Della struttura e del contenuto di queste dovremo ora occuparci: il confronto tra i dati riferiti dalla tradizione letteraria e gli elementi più certi che possono essere complessivamente individuati nell'iscrizione potrà servire a formulare delle ipotesi circa il tenore generale del nostro documento[33].

Innanzitutto, si può affermare con sicurezza che la legge era articolata in modo tale da comprendere e da descrivere diverse fattispecie: lo conferma infatti la frequente ricorrenza di *ian* (attico *ean*), accompagnato una volta dalla particella *de*[34];

---

29 Per una sintesi dello *status quaestionis* si rimanda ad Arangio Ruiz/Olivieri, *Inscriptiones* cit. 189ss. (le pp. 195-227 raccolgono tutte le testimonianze letterarie che riportano presunte leggi di Zaleuco e Caronda); M. Mühl, *Die Gesetze* cit. part. 432ss.; Crispo, *Contributo* cit. 116ss.; Ciaceri, *Storia della Magna Grecia* cit. 32ss. e 143s. Una recente panoramica sulla legislazione di Caronda si trova in S. Link, *Zur archaischen Gesetzgebung in Katane und im epizephyrischen Lokroi*, in *Rechtskodifizierung und soziale Normen im interkulturellen Vergleich*, hrsg. von H.-J. Gehrke, Tübingen 1994 (*ScriptOralia* 66), 165ss.

30 Arist. *Pol.* 1274 b 23.

31 In questo senso cfr. G. Smith, *Early Greek Codes*, in *CPh* 17 (1922) 187ss., part. 189; R.J. Bonner/G. Smith, *The Administration of Justice from Homer to Aristotle*, I, Chicago 1930, 79 nt. 2.

32 Arist. *Pol.* 1269 a 1. Per un'interpretazione di questa legge come «customary practice which was seized upon by the legislator and introduced into the code» cfr. Smith, *Early Greek Codes* cit. 193.

33 Un esame complessivo della legge è stato svolto, in un breve articolo, da Cordano, *Le leggi calcidesi* cit. e *L'evoluzione sociale* cit. 307s. Qualche accenno si trova anche in Pace, *Arte e civiltà* cit. 255s.; Dunbabin, *The Western Greeks* cit. 128s.; Vallet, *Rhègion et Zancle* cit. 318; E. Cantarella, *Studi sull'omicidio in diritto greco e romano*, Milano 1976, 83 e nt. 16; G. Maddoli, *Il VI e il V secolo a.C.*, in *Storia della Sicilia, II*, Napoli 1979, 23, 94 nt. 55; Camassa, *La codificazione delle leggi* cit. 619.

34 L'espressione *ian de* è leggibile per intero sul fr. 1 *recto*, l. 5; *ian* soltanto si legge chiaramente sul fr. 3 *recto*, l. 3 (che Arangio Ruiz/Olivieri hanno proposto di integrare

gli editori hanno spesso integrato il *de* dopo la congiunzione ipotetica, e questa integrazione, oltre a essere confortata dal raffronto con la celebre legge di Draconte in cui pure le singole previsioni sono introdotte da *ean de*[35], risulta abbastanza attendibile quando *ian* è preceduto sull'epigrafe da un segno simile ai nostri due punti: questo infatti, nella maggior parte delle sue occorrenze, sembra avere la funzione di dividere i diversi commi in cui la legge è strutturata. Analoga funzione di scansione tra i diversi articoli della legge doveva assolvere anche il pronome relativo indefinito *hostis*, che, tra attestazioni sicure e integrazioni attendibili, si legge in sette circostanze[36]. L'impressione generale, dunque, è che si tratti di una legge estremamente minuziosa, dettagliata e puntuale, caratteristiche che ben si accordano con la *akribeia* che Aristotele affermava essere la più apprezzabile qualità di Caronda[37], e che si segnalò come uno dei tratti distintivi delle leggi calcidesi: la medesima precisione si riscontra infatti nella legge di Kos attribuita a Caronda di cui è menzione nel secondo *Mimiambo* del poeta alessandrino Eronda, e nella quale erano previste pene pecuniarie differenziate per diversi reati, dettagliatamente elencati[38].

Sebbene la frammentarietà del testo non permetta di stabilire il contenuto delle diverse fattispecie, nondimeno qualche ipotesi può essere formulata anche a partire dai termini isolati, soprattutto quando questi offrono occasione per un confronto con le informazioni che le fonti letterarie ci hanno lasciato. Ci soffermeremo quindi ad analizzare i vocaboli la cui lettura si può ricostruire con un buon livello di certezza.

Alcuni termini significativi, che ricorrono con ogni verosimiglianza su diversi frammenti, sembrano mostrare la partecipazione della famiglia alla persecuzione dell'omicida: si tratta di *ui*[*os* o *ui*[*eon* (Comparetti, fr. 2, l. 2), di *pai*]*das* (Arangio Ruiz/Olivieri, fr. 3 *recto*, l. 6), di *gamb*]*ron* o *penthe*]*ron* (Arangio Ruiz/Olivieri, fr. 7 *recto*, l. 4), e di un sostantivo a tema *anephsio-* (Arangio Ruiz/Olivieri, fr. 8 *verso*, l. 4). Sono gli stessi vocaboli che compaiono nella legge di Draconte[39], la quale è

---

con *prono*|*ian*: ma a mio avviso è più plausibile leggere nella parola la consueta congiunzione ipotetica: vedi *infra*, nel testo), con qualche dubbio sul fr. 5 *verso*, l. 4 e sul fr. 9 *recto*, l. 1. Ancora, si segnalano le integrazioni *ia*[*n de* al fr. 7 *recto*, l. 2 (Comparetti); *i*[*an de* al fr. 7 *verso*, l. 7 (Arangio Ruiz/Olivieri; gli autori per questo frammento invertono la disposizione stabilita da Orsi, ritenendo questo, pertanto, il *recto*; in questo contributo verrà mantenuta la disposizione assegnata da Orsi: le motivazioni sono quelle addotte da Cordano, *Le leggi calcidesi* cit. 221, 227); *ia*[*n de*, al fr. 8 *verso*, l. 2 (Arangio Ruiz/Olivieri).

35 La notazione è di Arangio Ruiz/Olivieri, *Inscriptiones* cit. app. cr. ad l. 6.

36 *Hostis* si legge per intero al fr. 5 *recto*, l. 4, e in modo assolutamente riconoscibile al fr. 3 *recto*, l. 5 (*host*[*is*) e al fr. 12, l. 2 (*hos*[*tis*); il pronome va con ogni probabilità integrato anche al fr. 1 *recto*, l. 6 (*ho*[*stis*: Arangio Ruiz/Olivieri), al fr. 5 *verso*, l. 2 (*ho*[*stis*: Arangio Ruiz/Olivieri), al fr. 9 *verso*, l. 1 (*ho*[*stis*: Comparetti), e al fr. 10 *recto*, l. 2 (*h*[*ostis*: Arangio Ruiz/Olivieri).

37 Arist. *Pol.* 1274 b 5.

38 Herond. *Mim.* 2.46 ss; sul passo si veda anche più diffusamente *infra*, nel testo.

39 IG I^3.104, ll. 14,15,21-22.

peraltro servita come imprescindibile punto di riferimento per le ipotesi di integrazione avanzate; e il confronto con essa può far pensare che anche nel codice calcidese la famiglia della vittima intentasse l'azione contro l'omicida. Ma io ritengo che si possa andare oltre: si è parlato, infatti, del comune denominatore alla base dei *nomima Chalkidikà*; e si è inoltre visto che nella legge cumana riportata da Aristotele nella *Politica* i parenti dell'ucciso prestavano una testimonianza che da sola serviva a far condannare il reo[40]. Non è forse impossibile, allora, pensare che lo stesso principio valesse anche nel nostro testo, tanto più se si considera il rilievo che Caronda nelle sue leggi volle attribuire alla testimonianza: egli, come Aristotele stesso ancora afferma, sarebbe stato infatti il primo a istituire una particolare procedura, la *episkepsis*, a carico di chi fosse sospettato di aver testimoniato il falso[41].

Accanto alla compagine genetica, compare nelle nostre lamine anche quella politica: essa è indicata dal numerale *tetraq(o)*, ricorrente su ben tre frammenti[42], che deve con ogni probabilità riferirsi a un collegio magistratuale[43]. Due le integrazioni proposte per il termine. La prima è *tetraqo*[*nta*, "quaranta", postulata nell'edizione del *SEG*[44] e a quanto mi risulta ignorata dai commentatori dell'iscrizione: si tratterebbe, in effetti, di un *hapax*, ricostruito sulla forma dorica *tetrôkonta* (alternativa a *tetarakonta*) attestata in diverse iscrizioni[45]. Proprio l'unicità della forma *tetraqo*[*nta* deve tuttavia indurre a preferire l'integrazione di Comparetti unanimemente accettata, ossia *tetraqo*[*si*-, "quattrocento". Nell'accogliere questa lettura, Arangio Ruiz/Olivieri hanno stabilito un parallelo con la legge di Draconte in cui vengono menzionati i 51 efeti[46]: e l'ipotesi del collegio giudicante è oggi pacificamente accolta[47]. Ora, come credo, va messo in luce che, se davvero i

---

40 Arist. *Pol.* 1269 a 1.

41 Arist. *Pol.* 1274 b 5.

42 In particolare: *tetraqo*[, fr. 1 *recto*, l. 4; *tetraq*[, fr. 2, l. 5; *tetraqo*[, fr. 7 *recto*, l. 1 (corrispondente al *verso* dell'edizione di Arangio Ruiz/Olivieri: cfr. *supra*, nt. 34).

43 Comparetti, in Orsi, *Di un'anonima città* cit. 843s., sollevò inizialmente il dubbio che la cifra (da lui integrata, come tra breve si vedrà, con *tetraqo*[*si*-) si riferisse a una pena pecuniaria, ma concluse che essa, di gran lunga superiore rispetto alle altre che, come vedremo, figurano nell'iscrizione, sia molto più adatta a designare i giudici, o i membri di una *boulê*; nello stesso senso cfr. anche Arangio Ruiz/Olivieri, *Inscriptiones* cit. app. cr. ad fr. 1.

44 *SEG* IV.64, app. cr. ad A4: «*magistratus ad quem ius capitale pertinebat*».

45 Cfr. H.G. Liddel/R. Scott/H.S. Jones, *A Greek-English Lexicon*, Oxford 1966[9], s.v. *tessarakonta*.

46 Cfr. in part. IG I[3].104, ll. 17,19,24-25, a loro volta restituite grazie a Dem. *C. Macart.* 1069.

47 Dunbabin, *The Western Greeks* cit. 128; Cordano, *Le leggi calcidesi* cit. 227. Nel corso del dibattito, il prof. M. Gagarin ha espresso i propri dubbi in merito al fatto che una cifra tanto alta possa riferirsi ai cittadini di pieno diritto, in grado di far parte di un tribunale: verosimilmente, ha sottolineato, essa doveva equivalere alla totalità della cittadinanza. Non mi sento tuttavia di condividere tale dubbio: posto infatti che la legge in questione

quattrocento fossero il corrispettivo degli efeti (o anche degli areopagiti, competenti nei casi di omicidio più grave), dovremmo postulare una partecipazione su scala molto più vasta della cittadinanza calcidese, rispetto a quella ateniese, all'attività dei tribunali per i delitti di sangue. Una prova in tal senso potrebbe essere fornita da un importante passo della *Politica* aristotelica, in cui lo Stagirita ricorda il provvedimento di Caronda teso a imporre a coloro che non prendevano parte alle attività del tribunale un'ammenda cospicua se ricchi, e irrisoria se poveri[48]. Il passo, per la sua menzione di pene pecuniarie differenziate, è in genere usato in dottrina per supportare l'ipotesi che la costituzione di Caronda poggiasse su basi censitarie[49], ipotesi confortata anche dal parallelo posto da Platone tra il legislatore catanese e Solone[50]; esso, inoltre, serve anche a dimostrare che nelle colonie calcidesi tutti i cittadini erano tenuti a partecipare come giudici ai tribunali. Proprio l'informazione

---

era la legge di una colonia calcidese (e non deve essere riferita al piccolo insediamento di Monte S. Mauro, dove essa era soltanto esposta), la possibilità di identificare nei quattrocento i componenti di un collegio giudicante non mi sembra irragionevole: benché non sia noto il numero medio dei cittadini di una colonia calcidese, dobbiamo tuttavia supporre che esso, nella seconda metà del VI secolo, superasse ampiamente le quattrocento unità. Una conferma indiretta potrebbe trovarsi, per esempio, nella notizia di Diod. 11.49, in cui si legge che Gerone, impadronitosi di Catania e di Nasso nel 476 a.C. (e dunque poco più tardi rispetto all'epoca in cui il nostro documento va collocato), trasferì gli abitanti delle due città a Leontini, e immise nel territorio conquistato 10.000 individui, presi per metà da Siracusa e per metà dal Peloponneso; sul punto si rimanda a G. Manganaro, *Per una storia della Chora Katanaia*, in *Catania antica, Atti del convegno della S.I.S.A.C.* (Catania, 23-24 maggio 1992), a cura di B. Gentili, Pisa-Roma 1996, 19ss.

48 Arist. *Pol.* 1297 a 23; l'attendibilità del passo aristotelico è stata messa in dubbio, ma senza grande successo, da Mühl, *Die Gesetze* cit. 115s.

49 A. Holm, *Catania antica*, Catania 1925, 9; Ciaceri, *Storia della Magna Grecia* cit. 44s.; Cordano, *Leggi e legislatori calcidesi* cit. 94; *contra* si veda tuttavia Pace, *Arte e civiltà* cit. 252, che intende il passo aristotelico nel senso che la legge di Caronda impediva ai ricchi di rifiutare la funzione di giudice, possibilità che era invece offerta ai poveri.

50 Plat. *Resp.* 599 d. In aggiunta alle testimonianze di Platone e Aristotele ricordate nel testo, e a conferma delle basi censitarie della costituzione di Caronda, si deve ricordare innanzitutto la notizia di Heracl. Lemb. *Exc. Pol.* 55, che, pur definendo aristocratica la costituzione di Reggio, città retta dalle leggi di Caronda, ricorda tuttavia che i Mille, titolari del potere, erano scelti proprio su base censitaria (*apò timêmatôn*); in secondo luogo va menzionato il passo di Theophr. *Peri symbol.* fr. 97.5 *apd* Stob. *Anth.* 4.2.20, ove a Caronda è attribuita la legge sulla compravendita in base alla quale il venditore doveva esigere immediatamente il pagamento della merce, pena la perdita di ogni successivo diritto sull'acquirente: disposizione che, probabilmente, era intesa a mantenere la originaria suddivisione del censo (in questo senso cfr. Cordano, *Leggi e legislatori calcidesi* cit. 95, in cui è contenuta anche una breve discussione sulle diverse interpretazioni del passo). Sulla possibilità che la costituzione censitaria delle città calcidesi si fosse formata dopo la tirannide di Panezio, impadronitosi del potere a Leontini intorno al 600 a.C. (Aristot. *Pol.* 1310 b e 1316 a; Polyaen. 5.47), cfr. Cordano, *L'evoluzione sociale* cit. 306ss.

aristotelica, combinata con l'evidenza offerta dalle lamine, potrebbe dunque fornire una prova dell'esistenza, nelle città calcidesi, di un bacino di reclutamento dei giudici chiamati a pronunciarsi su fatti di sangue ben più ampio rispetto a quello ateniese del VI secolo: ad Atene, come è ben noto, gli efeti erano solo 51, ed erano scelti su basi aristocratiche[51]; il medesimo criterio serviva anche per la selezione degli areopagiti, ex magistrati chiamati a decidere sugli omicidi più gravi, il cui numero doveva essere sicuramente inferiore, e di molto, alle 400 unità[52].

Quanto all'attività che il tribunale dei quattrocento era chiamato a svolgere, è evidente che essa dovesse contemplare l'irrogazione della pena. E proprio l'entità della pena, di cui nel nostro testo sono rimasti alcuni notevoli indizi, potrebbe rappresentare una delle più significative novità della legge di Caronda. I termini chiave si leggono su due distinti frammenti: su uno di questi, che rappresenta l'angolo superiore destro di una tavoletta (fr. 5 *recto*), le due righe iniziali (continue visto il carattere bustrofedico della scrittura) hanno conservato le parole *duo talan[ta* (Comparetti)[53]; sul secondo (fr. 6 *recto*, l. 3) ricorre un altro numerale, questa volta *t]ria*, seguito dall'indicazione *ta*, integrato in *ta[lanta* (Comparetti). L'ammontare della somme previste – due e tre talenti – è considerevole[54], e per questo la dottrina è concorde nel riconoscere che si trattasse di pene pecuniarie a carico del reo[55]; invero,

---

51 Poll. 8.125.

52 D.M. MacDowell, *Athenian Homicide Law in the Age of Orators*, Manchester 1963, 39ss. part. 41s., ritiene che il numero degli areopagiti, ovviamente variabile a seconda dell'età di elezione ad arconte e della longevità dei singoli, dovesse ammontare al massimo a 200 unità, risultando quindi molto più basso rispetto ai 500 o più componenti delle giurie popolari eliastiche. R.W. Wallace, *The Areopagos Council, to 307 b.C.*, Baltimore-London 1989, 11ss., pensa invece che dopo Draconte gli areopagiti altro non fossero se non gli efeti che sedevano nell'Areopago, e dunque in numero di 51.

53 Il numerale è scritto in effetti con il digamma intervocalico, e Comparetti annotava: «non trovo esempio del *duo* con digamma; ma non è strano» (cfr. infatti ind. *duva*, umbr. *tuva*).

54 Si è pensato che il talento a cui i frammenti si riferiscono sia quello euboico, e non quello siceliota, più leggero, il cui uso è però attestato soltanto a partire dal primo quarto del V secolo, e dunque da un'epoca più recente, anche se di poco, rispetto a quella in cui le nostre lamine vano collocate: cfr. Comparetti, in Orsi, *Di un'anonima città* cit. 843; N. Parise, *Il sistema della litra nella Sicilia antica tra V e IV secolo*, in *AIIN* 25 (1979), *Atti del IV Convegno del Centro Internazionale di Studi numismatici* (Napoli, 17-22 aprile 1977), 293ss., part. 301. Proprio la considerazione dell'alto valore di questa somma fa escludere la possibilità di un confronto con i due talenti menzionati nel processo raffigurato sullo scudo di Achille in *Il.* 18.507, che dovevano al contrario rappresentare una cifra alquanto irrisoria; sul punto si rimanda a G. Glotz, *La solidaritè de la famille dans le droit criminel en Grèce*, Paris 1904, 127s.

55 Comparetti, in Orsi, *Di un'anonima città* cit. 843; Dunbabin, *The Western Greek* cit. 128; Vallet, *Rhègion et Zancle* cit. 318; Cordano, *Le leggi calcidesi* cit. 225; Ead., *L'evoluzione sociale* cit. 308; S. von Reden, *Money, Law and Exchange: Coinage in the Greek Polis*, in *JHS* 117 (1997) 154ss., part. 162 (in quest'ultimo contributo si accenna

altri elementi presenti nel testo contribuiscono a confermare questa ipotesi. Così, è stata ravvisata un'ulteriore indicazione di somma pecuniaria al rigo successivo del frammento su cui si legge *duo talanta* (fr. 5 *recto*, l. 3): qui si possono distinguere le lettere *era ena*, che Comparetti volle integrare con *stat*]*era hena*. Ma questa integrazione non fu accolta da Arangio Ruiz/Olivieri, e appare in effetti dubbia tanto per la strana collocazione del numerale, che segue anziché precedere l'indicazione della moneta, quanto anche per il suo ammontare, di gran lunga inferiore rispetto ai due e ai tre talenti altrove indicati. Nessuno ha poi segnalato, a quanto mi risulta, due ulteriori difficoltà formali che l'integrazione *statera hena* solleva: la lettura del numerale *hena* appare incerta per il fatto che nel testo manca il segno grafico *het*, altrove sempre utilizzato per segnalare l'aspirazione iniziale; certo, si può pensare a un errore dello *sculptor*, ma la circostanza si presenta anomala proprio per la correttezza ortografica che questi dimostra nelle altre parti leggibili delle lamine. Per di più, il rigo successivo (che continua *ena*, dato il *boustrophedon*) inizia con un segno grafico verticale in tutto simile a quello che altrove, e in modo incontrovertibile, indica *iota*. Comparetti, per giustificare la lettura *stat*]*era* (*h*)*ena*, intese questo segno come barra di divisione tra due differenti articoli della legge: ma sarebbe, questa, un'ulteriore stranezza, visto che altrove lo *sculptor* fa sempre uso, a questo scopo, dei due punti. Per queste ragioni io ritengo sia possibile e opportuno leggere non già *hena* ma *enai*, infinito presente di *eimì*: così facendo sarebbero superate le due difficoltà create dall'assenza dell'aspirazione *het* e dall'interpretazione del segno grafico verticale. *Enai* invece di *einai* non rappresenta un problema, e non deve indurre a pensare a un errore di scrittura: l'assenza del dittongo si può intendere come normale alternanza grafica *e*/*ei*, comune nei documenti epigrafici del tempo (si pensi, nella legge di Dracone, a *ktenai*, in luogo di *kteinai*[56]). Nel quadro così delineato, con la lettura *stat*]*era enai*, troverebbe una sua più opportuna collocazione l'ipotesi formulata da F. Cordano, secondo la quale la parola *statera* poteva essere menzionata in aggiunta a un valore posto prima, e di cui non è rimasta traccia, come variante di pena[57].

Al di là di questo passaggio controverso, comunque, vi sono nelle lamine altri spunti che, oltre alle indicazioni numeriche individuate, possono confermare l'ipotesi delle somme pecuniarie come pene a carico del reo. Un primo indizio può forse trovarsi in un frammento su cui sono leggibili le lettere *emoi* (fr. 2, l. 6): Comparetti propose l'integrazione *d*]*e moi*[*ran*, a indicare la "parte della somma" che l'omicida era tenuto a versare alla famiglia dell'ucciso[58]. Un dato più attendibile ricorre su un altro frammento (fr. 8 *recto*, l. 4), dove si legge *apoi*, integrato da

---

anche alla possibilità che il talento possa essere inteso, al pari di stateri, dracme e oboli, come unità di peso).

56 IG I^3.104, *e.g.* (per limitarci solo alle attestazioni sicure) ll. 16-17, 18, 20.

57 Cordano, *Le leggi calcidesi* cit. 225; la lettura *era enai*, priva però di integrazione, si trova nell'edizione del *SEG*.

58 Nel *SEG* si propone invece la lettura *d*]*emoi*.

Comparetti con *apoina* e da Arangio Ruiz/Olivieri con *apoinan*: in entrambi i casi, comunque, con un termine atto a indicare la composizione tra le parti[59]. Il medesimo termine poteva forse comparire anche in un ulteriore frammento (fr. 3 *recto*, l. 8), dove, tuttavia, sono riconoscibili soltanto le prime tre lettere, *apo*, suscettibili di integrazioni differenti rispetto ad *apoina* o *apoinan*: il confronto con la l. 30 della legge di Draconte (*tos de androphonos echseinai apoktenen*) ha indotto Arangio Ruiz/Olivieri a considerare anche l'ipotesi di leggere sul frammento in questione un termine legato al tema *apokten-*. Comunque sia, la verosimile presenza del termine *apoina* o *apoinan* in almeno una circostanza può portare a pensare che la legge parlasse di un "riscatto": in questo senso, come tariffa fissa di composizione stabilita dalla *polis*, potrebbero essere allora intese le somme *tria talanta*, *duo talanta*, ? *statera*[60].

---

[59] La possibilità di una composizione tra le parti potrebbe essere confermata anche dalle parole contenute nel rigo successivo (fr. 8 *recto*, l. 5), se si potesse provare la correttezza dell'integrazione di Comparetti *the*]*lei di*[*donai*.

[60] Così già Comparetti, in Orsi, *Di un'anonima città* cit. 830ss. Se davvero la legge parlava di un riscatto (*apoina*), si dovrebbe mettere in discussione la supposizione avanzata da Vallet, *Rhègion et Zancle* cit. 318, secondo cui le somme previste avrebbero potuto corrispondere contemporaneamente a una composizione per la famiglia e a una ammenda dovuta alla città. Tale conclusione, di cui l'autore non fornisce ulteriori delucidazioni, è probabilmente giustificata dal confronto con la già ricordata legge che nella *Politica* (1297 a 23) Aristotele attribuisce a Caronda, e che prevedeva una multa dovuta – evidentemente alla *polis* – dai cittadini che non partecipavano alle attività dei tribunali: multa considerevole per i ricchi e minima per i poveri. Tale dato non può tuttavia portare alla conclusione che nel sistema normativo calcidese la *polis* debba essere sempre, in tutto o in parte, destinataria delle pene pecuniarie stabilite dalla legge, tanto meno se tale legge riguarda, come nel nostro caso, l'omicidio, reato che nel diritto greco fu sempre sentito come questione essenzialmente privata anche quando venne sottoposto al controllo della *polis*. L'ipotesi di Vallet è peraltro smentita dal significato etimologico del sostantivo *apoina* e del verbo derivato *apoinao*, derivati per aplologia da *apo-poinê* (sull'etimologia e la storia del termine si rimanda a Glotz, *La solidaritè* cit. part. 109s. nt. 3), nonché dal valore dei termini nel contesto in cui sono di regola inseriti. Sin dai poemi omerici, infatti, tanto *poinê* quanto *apoina* sono sempre usati a indicare il complesso dei beni offerti da un privato a un altro privato a titolo di riscatto o di compensazione: se ci limitiamo agli esempi più significativi, è così per gli *apoina* infiniti che Crise offre ad Agamennone per la liberazione della propria figlia (*Il.* 1.13; 20; 23; 95; 111; 372; 377); è così per gli *apoina* che l'Atride è pronto a versare ad Achille perché questi desista dalla propria ira (*Il.* 9.120; 19.138); è così per la *poinê* che, nella celeberrima descrizione del processo raffigurato sullo scudo di Achille, l'omicida offre di pagare o ha pagato (l'interpretazione, come è noto, è controversa) a uno dei familiari dell'ucciso (*Il.* 18.498 e in questo senso cfr. anche 9.633; 636). Tale valore i termini conservano anche in una fase più matura, più "giuridica" rispetto a quella dei poemi omerici. Vero è, in effetti, che negli autori del V e del IV secolo *poinê* e *apoina*/*apoinan* possono indicare la somma di denaro versata allo stato a titolo di riscatto di un prigioniero (cfr. *e.g.* Hdt. 6.79; 7.134.13 e 136.9.); ma è altrettanto vero che il significato originario si mantiene con riferimento a quegli ambiti – come quello dell'uccisione di un uomo – sentiti di competenza esclusiva

Si tratta, come è evidente, di una soluzione ben più mite rispetto al taglione che Zaleuco aveva previsto nel "codice" locrese[61]; e ben più mite anche dalle sanzioni fissate per l'omicidio da Draconte, il quale aveva stabilito la condanna a morte per chi avesse ucciso con premeditazione (*ek pronoias*), e l'esilio per chi fosse risultato colpevole di un omicidio commesso senza premeditazione (*mê ek pronoias, akousios*)[62]; vero è che in quest'ultimo caso i parenti potevano accordarsi per la concessione del perdono (*aidesis*) e dunque per una composizione pecuniaria, ma questa non era poi quantificata, bensì solamente regolamentata come possibilità[63].

A questo proposito, peraltro, va posto in luce un altro importante fattore: qui tanto il termine *apoina* quanto l'indicazione delle somme di denaro si trovano o sulla parte più recente, il *recto*, o su frammenti non opistografi, che come abbiamo detto dovevano rappresentare delle aggiunte rispetto al testo originario della legge. Sebbene questo fatto possa essere ascritto a una mera casualità, tuttavia non si può neppure escludere che le somme rappresentino una delle novità introdotte nella seconda redazione della legge: forse le disposizioni più antiche autorizzavano i parenti dell'ucciso a uccidere a loro volta l'omicida, e dunque mantenevano la

---

della famiglia, e dunque dei privati, in cui la *polis* può al limite intervenire con una funzione di controllo o per stabilire la pena, che la famiglia deve poi far scontare. Una conferma della funzione "privata" del termine si trova nella legge di Draconte: questa, alla l. 31, integrata sulla scorta di un passo della *Contro Aristocrate* demostenica (28), stabilisce la possibilità di uccidere, o in alternativa di condurre con *apagogê* davanti agli Undici, gli assassini che, dopo essere stati condannati all'esilio in quanto giudicati colpevoli di omicidio non premeditato (*phonos mê ek pronoias*), fossero ritornati in patria senza aver ottenuto il perdono (*aidesis*) dai parenti dell'ucciso; non era lecito però torturarli né patteggiare un riscatto (*apoinan*) per risparmiare loro la vita, pena il pagamento del doppio del danno. È significativo che, nel commento che segue la citazione della legge (33), Demostene glossi *to mêd'apoinan* con *mê chrêmata prattesthai*, in cui *prattesthai*, alla diatesi media, indica proprio il fatto di esigere il pagamento a proprio esclusivo vantaggio, e senza dunque che la *polis* tragga profitto alcuno da tale transazione.

[61] Per il taglione in vigore a Locri cfr. Dem. *C. Tim.* 140.

[62] La distanza tra le soluzioni adottate da Caronda, Zaleuco e Draconte è in effetti più apparente che reale, se si pensa che le tre realtà giuridiche possono essere considerate come tre modalità diverse, ma comunque afferenti a un comune bacino, di superamento del sistema della vendetta privata. Zaleuco, con la sua legge del taglione, trasforma la vendetta privata in una pena prevista e controllata dalla *polis*. Caronda e Draconte proseguono invece le strade che già in epoca precittadina, come i poemi omerici attestano, erano state percorse per porre fine alle faide tra *genê*: il primo sostituisce la precedente composizione volontaria tra le parti con una composizione obbligatoria e legale; l'altro fa assurgere l'esilio, che in età omerica era soltanto un rimedio di fatto, a una vera e propria pena.

[63] Sulle regole della *aidesis* nella legge di Draconte si vedano, per tutti, Glotz, *La solidarité* cit. 309ss.; MacDowell, *Athenian Homicide Law* cit. 110ss., part. 123ss.; sulle finalità della regolamentazione dettagliata della *aidesis* si veda poi il contributo di M. Gagarin in questo volume.

vendetta privata limitandosi a controllarla e a regolamentarla; la legge più recente, al contrario, poteva essere volta a mitigare questo regime, in modo tale che il reo avesse la possibilità di riscattarsi pagando la pena pecuniaria preventivamente stabilita dalla *polis*[64].

La previsione di una simile pena nelle nostre lamine trova una sua armonica collocazione all'interno del sistema normativo calcidese descritto dalle fonti. La particolare mitezza di Caronda è ricordata da Diodoro a proposito della sanzione da lui prevista per chi avesse abbandonato lo schieramento in battaglia o avesse rifiutato di prendere le armi: non già la morte, come stabilito dagli altri legislatori, bensì – provvedimento che lo stesso Diodoro definisce *philanthrôpoteros* – l'esposizione per tre giorni nella pubblica piazza in vesti femminili[65]. Anche la pecuniarietà della condanna è un motivo ricorrente nelle leggi calcidesi[66]: abbiamo già ricordato della pena *megalê* per i ricchi e *mikrà* per i poveri in caso di mancata partecipazione all'attività del tribunale, che Aristotele attribuisce a Caronda[67]. E di pene in denaro stabilite dal legislatore catanese in funzione risarcitoria parla anche il poeta alessandrino Eronda nel secondo dei suoi *Mimiambi*, quando ricorda che, in base alle leggi di Caronda vigenti a Kos, esisteva uno specifico tariffario per diversi casi di danneggiamento: chi rompe la porta della casa altrui deve pagare una mina; alla stessa multa è condannato chi prende a pugni un uomo; chi incendia o viola il domicilio altrui deve pagare mille dracme; chi causa un danno è punito con una sanzione al doppio[68]. Sussiste, è vero, il dubbio sulla genuinità dell'attribuzione a Caronda del codice in vigore a Kos: nondimeno, la notizia è stata giudicata fondata

---

[64] Cordano, *Le leggi calcidesi* cit. 225.

[65] Diod. 12.11.16. Abbiamo in precedenza accennato alla scarsa attendibilità di Diodoro: ma in tale circostanza non vi sono fondati motivi per dubitare della genuinità della legge, la cui paternità è unanimemente ricondotta dalla dottrina al legislatore catanese: cfr. Ciaceri, *Storia della Magna Grecia* cit. 32; Crispo, *Contributo* cit. 118 (entrambi gli autori ritengono comunque che tale disposizione non sia originale di Caronda, in quanto già Zaleuco doveva averla prevista nella sua opera legislativa).

[66] Per la pertinenza tra il sistema delle condanne pecuniarie e la costituzione delle città calcidesi cfr. Vallet, *Rhègion et Zancle* cit. 319s.; l'autore, oltre alle disposizioni ricordate nel testo, annovera tra le leggi ispirate al principio risarcitorio anche quella relativa alle epiclere, citata da Diod. 12.18.3: il parente più prossimo poteva decidere di non sposare l'ereditiera, ma nel caso doveva sborsare a titolo di compensazione 500 dracme. Non vi sono dubbi che nella legislazione calcidese trovasse posto una normativa sulle epiclere, come conferma un passo della *Politica* aristotelica riferito ad Androdama (Arist. *Pol.* 1274 b 23): il passo di Diodoro, tuttavia, non parla della disposizione originaria, bensì di un successivo emendamento a essa, che dunque potrebbe appartenere alla legislazione di Turi. Sul punto cfr. Cordano, *Leggi e legislatori calcidesi* cit. 97 e nt. 2.

[67] Arist. *Pol.* 1297 a 23.

[68] Herond. *Mim.* 2.46ss.

da Carlo Castello, nel suo intervento al *Symposion* del 1988[69], ed è inoltre confermata dai minuziosi dettagli nella descrizione delle offese e delle relative pene, in perfetto accordo con la già ricordata *akribeia* attribuita a Caronda da Aristotele[70].

La *akribeia* analitica e la mitezza come criterio ispiratore delle pene pecuniarie della legge di Monte S. Mauro ben si combinano, dunque, con le informazioni delle fonte letterarie, confermandole. Più arduo è invece stabilire quali fossero le ragioni della diversificazione (due, tre talenti, ? statere) delle pene, ovvero il contenuto sostanziale delle singole previsioni.

Un'ipotesi al riguardo venne avanzata da Orsi e sostenuta poi da Arangio Ruiz/Olivieri: questi postularono che al fr. 4 (non opistografo) fosse prevista l'eventualità di un omicidio commesso in un tempio, ovvero la possibilità che l'omicida avesse trovato rifugio in un tempio. Nel frammento, infatti, le lettere del primo rigo, *ephonana*, potrebbero essere integrate con *Pers]ephona na[os*, e di conseguenza quelle dei due righi successivi, *kaitesathen*, con *kai tes Athen[as*, da riferire al tempio di Atena. Sussiste tuttavia il dubbio, già segnalato da Comparetti, della forma dorica *Persephona*, in un testo ionico in cui i dorismi sono del tutto assenti: e infatti lo stesso Comparetti proponeva di integrare alla l. 1 *epistr]ephon* piuttosto che *Pers]ephona*[71].

Al di là di questa ipotesi, è possibile pensare che le pene pecuniarie presenti sulle lamine fossero «calibrate su differenti circostanze nella colpa»[72], e dunque diversificate sulla base del grado di volontarietà dell'agente: il paragone proposto, e in verità più spontaneo al riguardo, è ancora quello con la legge di Draconte, che allo stesso modo aveva indicato pene diverse a seconda del diverso atteggiamento mentale di chi uccideva. Ma è davvero possibile che la medesima classificazione fosse contemplata anche nelle tavolette calcidesi? L'ipotesi è timidamente avanzata da Arangio Ruiz/Olivieri nell'apparato critico al fr. 3 *recto*, l. 3, che conserva le lettere *iant*; le prime tre potrebbero in effetti rappresentare la terminazione di *pronoian*, congettura formulata proprio sulla base del confronto con la linea 11 della legge di Draconte: *kai eam me ek pronoias ktenei tis tina*. Ma si tratta a mio avviso di ipotesi dubbia: infatti mi pare che si potrebbe con uguale verosimiglianza intendere *ian* come la consueta particella condizionale introduttiva dei diversi

---

69 C. Castello, *Sulla legislazione attribuita a Caronda nel secondo Mimiamo di Eroda*, in *Symposion 1988*, Köln-Wien 1990, 361ss., part. 366ss.

70 Sulla legge contenuta nel mimiambo di Eroda cfr. inoltre Arangio Ruiz/Olivieri, *Inscriptiones* cit. 224 (in cui viene formulata l'ipotesi che le leggi di Caronda siano state portate a Kos per il tramite del siciliano Cadmo, di cui è notizia in Hdt. 6.22 e 7.164).

71 Alle ll. 2-3 lo stesso Comparetti, in luogo di *kai tes Athen[as*, leggeva *naites* (= *naetes*) *Athen[aiou*, "abitante o rifugiato nel tempio di Atena": lettura ben poco plausibile visto che la prima lettera del rigo 2 non è N (<u>*n*</u>*aites*) ma piuttosto K (dunque <u>*k*</u>*ai tes*). A proposito di questo frammento, va ancora segnalato che Comparetti, proponendo di intendere il segno di incerta lettura dopo *Athe* come M piuttosto che come N, annotava: «ed allora si potrebbe pensare ad *athemistos*, o ad altro di simile a base di *themis*».

72 Così Cordano, *Le leggi calcidesi* cit. 225.

commi della legge, e integrare poi la successiva *t* con *te*, in modo da leggere *ian te*, “e se”.

Nella nostra legge non vi sono dunque indizi sicuri per affermare che la valutazione dell’elemento soggettivo del reato era alla base della diversificazione della pena. Del resto non è per nulla scontato che essa, al pari di quella di Draconte, prendesse in considerazione l’atteggiamento mentale dell’omicida: elemento notoriamente irrilevante nel regime di vendetta privata che la legge mirava gradualmente a superare. Credo pertanto che per spiegare la presenza di differenti pene pecuniarie nelle nostre lamine si possa formulare una differente ipotesi, ancora una volta grazie al confronto con le fonti letterarie. L’informazione che interessa è di nuovo quella fornita dal passo già menzionato della *Politica* aristotelica relativa alle pene maggiori o minori imposte rispettivamente ai ricchi e ai poveri per la loro assenza dai tribunali[73]. Abbiamo visto che tale previsione di pene differenziate in base al reddito trova la sua collocazione e giustificazione più opportuna in un sistema censitario. È lecito dunque domandarsi se proprio questo criterio, e non già quello della valutazione dell’elemento soggettivo, non possa servire a dare ragione anche delle pene pecuniarie presenti nella legge di Monte S. Mauro[74]. Se così fosse, allora, la legge non si limiterebbe a presentare carattere mitigativo rispetto alla precedente vendetta, ma si arricchirebbe anche di contenuti “democratici”: la composizione pecuniaria non era più stabilita dai parenti della vittima, secondo quanto attesta per l’età più antica l’*epos* omerico, ma era fissata per legge in modo proporzionale alla ricchezza del reo, in modo tale da essere accessibile a tutti[75]. Sarebbe allettante, al riguardo, mettere a confronto il nostro documento con il “codice” di Gortina, in cui pure era previsto un tariffario – non in caso di omicidio ma di violenza sessuale e di *moicheia*[76] – differenziato sulla base dell’appartenenza di offeso e offensore alle diverse classi in cui la popolazione era suddivisa[77]. Ma a

[73] Arist. *Pol.* 1297 a 23.

[74] Alla medesima possibilità accenna anche, in quello che sembra un ripensamento rispetto a quanto affermato nell’articolo del 1986 (*Le leggi calcidesi* cit.), Cordano, *L’evoluzione sociale* cit. 303ss., part. 308s.

[75] Ci si potrebbe domandare che cosa accadeva nel caso in cui l’omicida non fosse stato in grado di pagare la pena prevista dalla *polis*. Nel quadro delineato, in cui si è supposto che la seconda redazione della legge fosse tesa a mitigare un precedente regime che autorizzava sangue in cambio di sangue, è lecito pensare che la sanzione alternativa rimanesse la morte: tanto più se intendiamo in questo senso il dativo strumentale *tha*]*natoi* alla l. 7 del fr. 3 *recto*.

[76] IC IV 72 col. II 2-45, sulla cui interpretazione si veda, per tutti, A. Maffi, *Il diritto di famiglia nel Codice di Gortina*, Milano 1997, 21ss.

[77] L’opportunità di un simile confronto parrebbe peraltro suggerita dallo stesso Aristotele (*Pol.* 1274 a 23), che, pur senza accoglierla, riferisce della tradizione che in qualche modo legava Caronda a Creta, facendo del legislatore catanese un discepolo di Zaleuco, a sua volta istruito nella *nomothesia* da Taleta di Gortina. La convinzione che Creta sia stata patria delle prime leggi scritte (cfr. G. Camassa, *Aux origines de la codification ècrite des lois en Grèce*, in M. Detienne [cur.], *Les savoirs de l’ècriture en Grèce*

ben vedere, nell'ipotesi che ho formulato per le lamine di diversificazione delle pene in base al reddito, la somiglianza tra la legge calcidese e quella cretese è più apparente che reale: la suddivisione in classi presupposta dal "codice" di Gortina, infatti, nulla ha a che fare con il reddito, perché si basa piuttosto sullo *status libertatis* (liberi – schiavi) e probabilmente *civitatis* (liberi/cittadini – *apetairoi*[78]).

Con la sua previsione di pene proporzionali al censo, dunque, la nostra legge sull'omicidio confermerebbe da sola la distanza, implicitamente sottolineata da Platone[79], della normativa calcidese rispetto a quella attica-draconiana, e si rivelerebbe inoltre unica nel suo genere. Si potrebbe obiettare che tale aspetto, tanto importante e innovativo, sarebbe stato messo in luce da Aristotele, che invece si limita a sottolineare come l'unica novità introdotta da Caronda sia la *episkepsis* per la falsa testimonianza[80]: ma tale silenzio non è necessariamente significativo, se si pensa che anche a proposito di Draconte lo Stagirita annotava come nella sua *politeia* non vi fosse alcun elemento particolare, fatta eccezione per la gravità delle pene[81]. Si potrebbe inoltre supporre che della legge non rimase più evidenza quando la costituzione censitaria delle città calcidesi venne cancellata con le conquiste dei tiranni di Gela, Ippocrate prima e Gelone poi, all'inizio del V secolo[82]: data che coincide con quella della distruzione del centro di Monte S. Mauro[83]. Fortunatamente, il bronzo su cui la nostra legge venne incisa sopravvisse, anche se in modo molto malconcio, all'incendio dell'edificio in cui era stata esposta.

---

ancienne, Lille 1992, 130ss., part. 139ss., anche in Id., *La codificazione* cit. 619ss. con bibliografia ivi citata) potrebbe senza dubbio deporre a favore di questa ipotesi, per la quale in effetti alcuni autori sembrano propendere: cfr. Pace, *Arte e civiltà* cit. 250s.; Smith, *Early Greek Codes* cit. 196; Bonner-Smith, *The Administration of Justice* cit. 80s., questi ultimi a proposito della somiglianza tra il codice gortinio (cfr. IC IV 72 col. II 7-9) e quello di Caronda (cfr. Herond. *Mim.* 2.46ss.) riguardo la violenza a una schiava, punito rispettivamente con una pena di 5 dracme e con la condanna a pagare il doppio del danno.

78 Al riguardo cfr. Maffi, *Il diritto di famiglia* cit. 12.

79 Plat. *Resp.* 599 d-e (il passo, già in precedenza menzionato, distingue nettamente le leggi calcidesi da quelle attiche e da quelle doriche).

80 Arist. *Pol.* 1274 b 5.

81 Arist. *Pol.* 1274 b 15. Va aggiunto che altrettanto irrilevante è il silenzio di Diodoro, non solo per la generale inattendibilità delle leggi che egli attribuisce a Caronda, ma anche perché, a tacer d'altro, non vi è in lui alcuna traccia del provvedimento contro i rei di falsa testimonianza, che era invece tanto significativo per Aristotele.

82 Hdt. 7.153-156. cfr. Dunbabin, *The Western Greeks* cit. 378s.; Spigo, *L'anonimo centro greco* cit. 31ss.; Cordano, *L'evoluzione sociale* cit. 309ss.

83 Orsi, *Di un'anonima città* cit. 845s. ipotizzava invece che la fine dell'insediamento greco fosse stata opera di Ducezio, che nella prima metà del V secolo guidò i Siculi a una rivolta nazionale contro tutto ciò che era greco.

Frgm. 1 (mm. 73 × 66)

a) *recto*

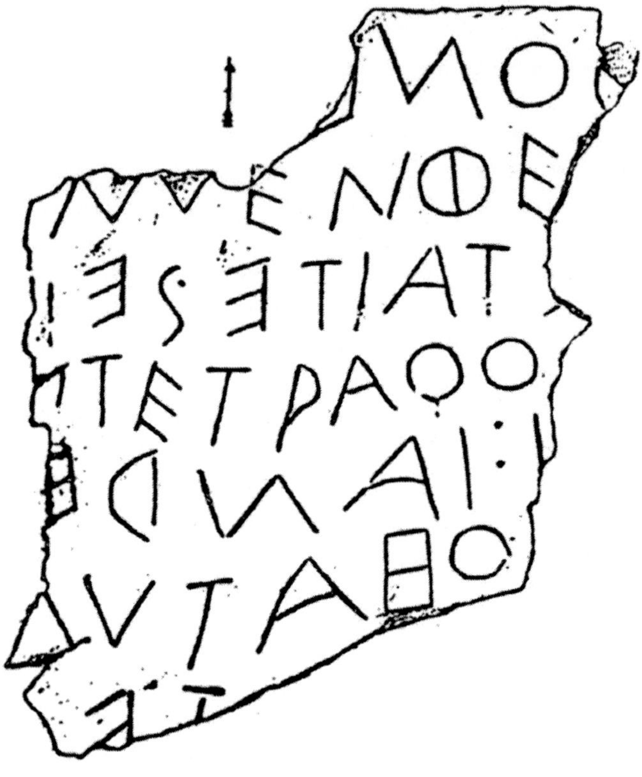

. . . . φ̣ονε̣[α . . . .
. . . . μένφε[ται
. . . . ται τες ει . . . . . .
. . . . τετραϙο[σι . . . . . .
. . . . ν̣ : ἰὰν δὲ . . . . . .
. . . . α̣υτα *ho* . . . . . .
. . . . τ̣ε̣ . . . . . .

Frgm. 1

b) *verso*

. . . . ρρ (?)
ο απ . . . .
. . . . γ' .

L. 1 ρα
L. 3 ς

Frgm. 2 (ex multis reliquiis restitutum)
(mm. 75 × 65, non opisthographum)

. . . . μον . . . .
. . . .: ταδε υι . . . .
. . . . ϙαναι: . . . .
. . . . νṭαι: . . . .
. . . . τετραϙ[οσι . . . .
. . . . ε μοι . . . .

Frgm. 3 (mm. 90 × 50)

Fr. 3 « accartocciato nei lembi inferiori, che non si possono aprire, svolgere e leggere, senza sottoporli ad un'altissima temperatura, che danneggerebbe la lamina » Orsi.

a) *recto*

. . . . σιι . . . .
. . . . εF . . . .
. . . . ιαν τ . . . .
. . . . τ̣αμ . . . .
. . . . : *h*οστ[ις . . . . .
. . . . δας . κ . . . . .
. . . . νατοι : ε̣ . . . . .
. . . . απο . . . .
. . . . φ̣ον̣[έ]α̣[ς . . . . .

Frgm. 3

b) *verso*

. . . .

. . . .

. . . . δαι : χ̣α . . . . .

. . . . τοὺ]ς : φον[έας . .

. . . . α̣φεγε. . . . . . .

. . . . ανο . . . .

. . . . ενοις . . . .

. . . . μεδ . . . .

. . . . τα̣. . . . .

Frgm. 4 (mm. 68 × 49)

Angulus superior laminae, non opisthographus

ẹφονα: να . . . . . .
. . . . . νος : καὶ τε-
ς̣ αϑ̣εν . . . .
. . . . δαυ
. . ις . . . .

Frgm. 5

(mm. 64 × 55)

Pars superior dextera laminae rectis angulis. « Poiché anche il frammento precedente costituisce l'angolo superiore d. di una lamina non opistografa, se ne conclude che le tabellette erano per lo meno due » Orsi.

a) *recto*

. . . . . ο]ῦτις : δύ-
Ϝο τάλαν[τα . . . .
. . . . ερα ενα
I *h*όστις α . . . .
. . . . κλειδα .
. . σοι . . . .

L. 3 στατ]έρα
L. 6 σον

Frgm. 5

b) *verso*

. . . . ει

*h*ό[στις . . . .

. . . . μ . . υτε

ἰὰν . . . .

Frgm. 6

« Risulta da due pezzetti opistografi congiunti, che uniti misurano mm. 44 × 44 » Orsi.

recto

verso

. . . . ναι ε . . . . .

. . . . . φ]όνιαι . . . .

. . . ṭρία τά[λαντα . . . . .

. . . . . αυ τε . . . .

. . . . . . hεπεριο̣ν . . . . .

. . . . . πρ]ὸς φονέ[ας

Frgm. 7

mm. 65 × 40 « molto contorto a caldo » Orsi.

recto	*verso*
. . . . . τ̣ετραϙο̣[σι	. . . . ε . . . .
. . . . . ας : ἰὰ[ν δὲ	. . . . οιοι . . . . . .
. . . . . ον αφ	. . . . χο . . . .
. . . . . ρον̣	. . . . . . ο̣πετ̣ . . . .
	. . . . . . αν συ . . . . . .
	. . . . . . ον : τ . . . . . .
	. . . . . . οχοι : ἰ[ὰν δὲ . .

L. 1 τετραϙό[σιοι

Frgm. 8 (mm. 59 × 38)

recto

. . . . α : . . . .
. . . . ειπ̣ . . . .
. . . . σ̣ιαρ̣ . . . . . .
. . . . . . απoι . . . .
. . . . . λ̣ει δι . . . .
. . . . θ̣ . . . .

verso

. . . . ιδ . . . .
. . . . : ἰὰ̣[ν δὲ . . . . .
. . . . ον̣ . . . .
. . . . φ̣σι . . . .
. . . . νε . . . .
. . . . . . τρ̣ . . . .

Frgm. 9 (mm. 54 × 28)

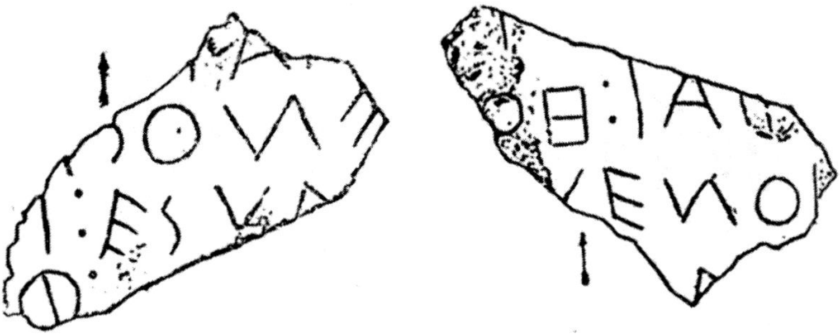

recto	*verso*
. . . . ι̣ὰ̣ν [δὲ	. . . . αι : *h*ό[στις δὲ . . .
. . . . ενος ν̣	. . . . . ενοι . . . .
. . . . ι : ἔ συν̣	. . . . . δ̣ . . . .
. . . . φ̣	

Frgm. 10 (mm. 30 × 47)

(« di lettura disperata » Orsi)

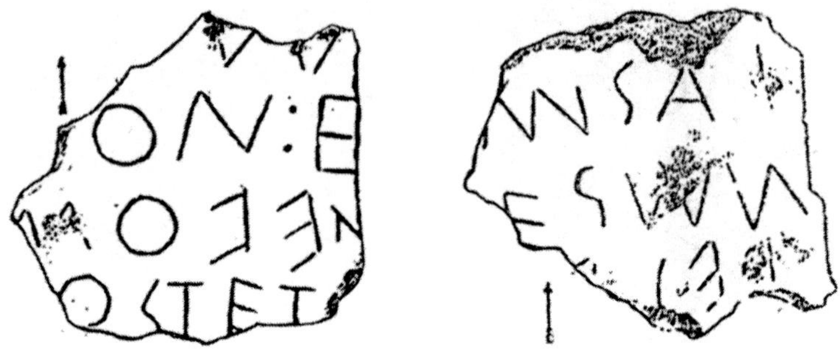

recto

. . . .
. . . . ον : *h*[όστις δὲ . . .
. . . . ϵFο . . . .
. . . . οστετ . . . .

verso

. . . . . . ασμ . . . .
. . . . . . εσυνδ . . . . . .
. . . . ει . . . .

Frgm. 11 (mm. 29 × 28)

recto

verso

. . . . . ι χο . . . . καὶ . . . .
. . . . χεσθ . . . . ?
. . . . . π . . . . . .

1 « Il prof. Comparetti ritiene impossibile il segno χ, per quanto evidente nell'originale e quindi nel facsimile » Orsi 2 ... χεσθ[αι Comparetti, fortasse ἐνέ]χεσθ[αι.

Frgm. 12 (mm. 30 × 22, non opisthographum)

. . . . ι . . . .
. . . . *h*όσ[τις δὲ . . . . . .
. . . . προτ . . . .

FELICE COSTABILE (REGGIO CALABRIA)

RISPOSTA A LAURA PEPE

La relatrice ha affrontato nelle lamine bronzee di Monte S. Mauro quello che è senza dubbio uno dei più importanti documenti epigrafici di contenuto giuridico ritrovati nell'area siceliota nell'ultimo secolo. Infatti, il testo che esse contengono – una legge sull'omicidio – se non può colmare il vuoto derivante dal silenzio delle fonti letterarie circa la regolamentazione dell'omicidio, tuttavia ci fornisce importanti dati che l'acribia filologica ed epigrafica può tentare di recuperare alla ricostruzione del quadro legislativo nelle città calcidesi d'Occidente, dove vigevano quei *nomima* da ricondurre all'attività del più celebre legislatore della zona, Caronda.

Benché unico e prezioso, tuttavia, questo testo è stato finora ben poco studiato nei suoi dettagli, visto lo stato estremamente lacunoso e frammentario in cui ci è giunto. Su questo documento, dunque, il contributo della Dr.ssa Laura Pepe riporta un interesse sopito e lo illumina di nuova luce: si tratta indubbiamente di un'analisi iniziale, che in futuro dovrà e potrà giovarsi – cosa finora impedita da difficoltà burocratiche – di uno studio autoptico, mediante il quale potranno essere verificate le affermazioni di chi per primo si incaricò di ordinare, catalogare e pubblicare le lamine, nonché di nuove immagini fotografiche, acquisite ed elaborate con tecniche ben più avanzate rispetto a quelle del secolo scorso.

Ma già ora l'analisi dettagliata e complessiva del testo che è stata proposta presenta numerosi e importanti elementi di originalità: essa si avvale di un metodo efficace che consiste nel confronto puntuale con le più fededegne testimonianze letterarie, *in primis* quella della *Politica* aristotelica, e giunge ad alcune conclusioni che appaiono senza dubbio condivisibili.

Interessante, innanzitutto, è il confronto istituito dalla relatrice tra la legge di Monte S. Mauro e il testo della *Politica* aristotelica (1274 b 5), in cui lo Stagirita afferma che caratteristica principale di Caronda è la *akribeia*; una *akribeia* che è sicuramente dato riscontrare nel nostro documento e che si riconosce, nonostante la lacunosità del testo, come sua caratteristica evidente.

Si possono poi indubbiamente condividere le soluzioni proposte dalla relatrice per alcune letture del testo alternative a quelle finora offerte da Comparetti, ovvero da Arangio-Ruiz e Olivieri: è legittima (e in questo caso l'autopsia delle lamine potrà confermarla) la lettura *statera enai* (verbo *eimi*) rispetto alla tradizionale *statera ena*, che darebbe luogo alle diverse difficoltà evidenziate dalla Pepe nel corso della sua relazione. Ed è altrettanto verosimile intendere *ian* non già come la parte conclusiva di *pronoian*, come ipotizzava Arangio-Ruiz, ma piuttosto come la consueta particella condizionale che tanto di frequente appare sulle nostre lamine; come pure è infine verosimile che il *tau* che segue sia da integrare con *epsilon*, e sia dunque da intendere quale *te* enclitico.

È parimenti corretto rigettare, sulla scorta di quanto già segnalato da Comparetti, la lettura di Orsi *Persephona naós*: essa infatti indurrebbe a postulare dorismi, che sono attesati – sia pure ben più tardi – nel dialetto di una *polis* calcidese-messenica come *Rhegion*, ma che non si giustificherebbero altrettanto in ambiente puramente calcidese, e che comunque nel nostro testo sembrano del tutto assenti.

Soltanto un dubbio vorrei invece sollevare a proposito dell'interpretazione che è stata fornita del testo aristotelico di *Pol.* 1269 a 1-3 in cui, secondo la traduzione che ci è stata proposta, "l'imputato era ritenuto colpevole di omicidio se l'accusatore produceva un numero bastevole di testimoni presi tra i suoi parenti più stretti". Credo infatti che potrebbe essere possibile anche una differente e più attendibile lettura di questo passo, a cui si giunge intendendo il genitivo *ton autou suggenon* come dipendente da *ton phonon*: dunque, "colpevole di omicidio dei propri parenti".

In conclusione, l'avere avuto il coraggio di riprendere un testo così frammentario e difficile, ed affrontato in passato da patriarchi delle scienze giuridica ed epigrafica, conseguendo ciò nonostante progressi di lettura come di esegesi, fa sperare che lo studio possa ulteriormente progredire grazie all'autopsia del documento ed alle moderne tecniche di riproduzione fotografica ed ingrandimento elettronico dei particolari, che l'autrice si ripromette fin d'ora di compiere.

MARTIN DREHER (MAGDEBURG)

DAS BÜRGERRECHT IM GRIECHISCHEN SIZILIEN ZWISCHEN RECHT UND POLITIK

„Denn die Poleis dort (sc. in Sizilien) sind übervölkert mit zusammengewürfeltem Gesindel, und es kommt leicht zu Umwälzungen (μεταβολαί) und Vergrößerungen der Bürgerschaft“ (Thuk. 6,17,2). Diese Worte sind Teil einer Rede, die Thukydides in seinem sechsten Buch Alkibiades in den Mund legt. Alkibiades will damit seine Landsleute dazu bringen, der Expedition nach Sizilien zuzustimmen. Daher steht seine These im Verdacht, die Lage in Sizilien schlechtzureden, um den Athenern eine schnelle und leichte Eroberung der Insel in Aussicht zu stellen.

Dennoch hat die Aussage eine historische Grundlage, denn die Insel Sizilien hatte schon vor der Zeit des Thukydides viele Bevölkerungsbewegungen und daher viele Änderungen in der Zusammensetzung ihrer Bürgerschaft erlebt. Solche Bewegungen setzten sich nach dem 5. Jahrhundert fort und hörten selbst unter der römischen Herrschaft nicht völlig auf; aber die folgende Betrachtung wird sich zeitlich auf die archaische und klassische Zeit und geographisch auf Sizilien beschränken.

Unter dem Terminus ‚Bevölkerungsbewegung‘ sind hier mehrere Phänomene zusammengefaßt, die in der Forschungsliteratur bisher zu wenig differenziert worden sind[1]. Ich will das an anderer Stelle näher ausführen und hier nur kurz andeuten. Erstens gehört dazu die *Ansiedlung* von Menschen an einem bestimmten Ort. Zweitens haben wir den umgekehrten Vorgang einer *Aussiedlung* vor uns, wenn Menschen ihren Wohnort verlassen. Eine Aussiedlung mit einer gezielten Ansiedlung derselben Bevölkerung an einem anderen Ort ist als *Umsiedlung* zu bezeichnen. Davon läßt sich wiederum die *Umbesiedlung* unterscheiden als eine Entfernung von Bevölkerung von einem Ort und dessen Wiederbesiedlung mit anderen Menschen. Diese Bevölkerungsbewegungen erfolgen teils freiwillig, teils unter Zwang.

Es ist evident, daß solche grundlegenden Veränderungen in der Zusammensetzung eines Gemeinwesens zahlreiche soziale, wirtschaftliche, kulturelle, rechtliche und politische Probleme mit sich brachten, die hier selbstverständlich nicht umfassend behandelt werden können. Vielmehr sollen im folgenden nur wenige exempla-

---

[1] Vattuone 1994 z.B. spricht ohne weitere Unterscheidung manchmal von espianto/impianto, manchmal von trapianto (z.B. S. 113).

rische Fälle von Bevölkerungsbewegung angeführt werden[2], um zu untersuchen, *in welcher Form* die Migranten in eine politische Gemeinschaft ein- oder aus ihr ausgegliedert wurden. Seit wann gab es eine formalisierte, also rechtlich festgelegte Mitgliedschaft in der Polis, seit wann also das Institut des Bürgerrechts? Und welchen Wert haben die Bewohner einer Polis diesem Rechtsinstitut beigemessen? Die Ergebnisse sollen auch dazu beitragen, die umfassendere Fragestellung zu beantworten, ob bzw. in welchem Umfang die westgriechischen Poleis sich von denen des Mutterlandes und des östlichen Mittelmeerraumes unterschieden[3].

Ich möchte drei Phasen der Entwicklung unterscheiden, die im Kern chronologisch eingeteilt sind, aber bestimmte Phänomene, besonders die Formen politischer Herrschaft, auch zeitübergreifend verbinden.

1. Die Zeit der Kolonisation und der aristokratischen Herrschaft.
Es kann wohl keinem Zweifel unterliegen, daß die griechischen Kolonisten, die sich seit der zweiten Hälfte des 8. Jahrhunderts an den Küsten Siziliens ansiedelten, sozusagen selbstverständlich, vollwertige Mitglieder ihres jeweiligen Gemeinwesens, ihrer Polis, gewesen sind. In der historischen Forschung ist umstritten, ob die frühen Koloniegründungen noch vorstaatliche oder bereits staatliche Unternehmungen waren[4]. Mit dem Zeitpunkt, an dem eine politische Herrschaft innerhalb der Polis etabliert wurde, den wir aber meist nicht genau festlegen können, können wir jedoch von den Poleis als Staaten und von ihren Mitgliedern als Staatsbürgern sprechen. Daß alle Kolonisten „politisch gleichberechtigte Bürger" gewesen seien[5], gilt aber nur in dem Sinn, daß sie die gleiche Rechtsstellung hatten, daß sie also gleichermaßen die passive Staatsbürgerschaft innehatten; gleiche politische Rechte hatten sie damit nicht. Der aktive Anteil an der Regierung der Polis war vielmehr abgestuft, sonst würden wir nicht überall in der Frühzeit auf oligarchisch bzw. aristokratisch regierte Poleis treffen, in denen mithin nur eine eingeschränkte Zahl von Bürgern die Regierung ausübte. Die Forschung hat vielfach nachgewiesen, daß auch Nachzügler

---

[2] Ich beabsichtige, an anderer Stelle eine systematische und vollständige Auflistung der Bevölkerungsbewegungen zu geben und sie auch unter mentalitätsgeschichtlicher Fragestellung zu untersuchen.

[3] Zum Terminus Westgriechen vgl. Dreher, Westgriechen (im Druck); dieser Aufsatz versteht sich ebenfalls als Beitrag zu der umfassenderen Fragestellung. Ein weiteres Problem ist das Asylwesen, das bei den Westgriechen eine erstaunlich geringe Rolle gespielt hat, vgl. vorläufig Dreher 2003, 7.

[4] Vgl. zum status quaestionis etwa Lomas 2000, 171f.

[5] Seibert 1979, 221.

und später ankommende Gruppen von Kolonisten in den Polisverband integriert wurden[6].

Aus der Frühzeit der Kolonien werden vor allem Fälle von internen Machtkämpfen zwischen adligen Gefolgschaften überliefert, wie z.B. die Vertreibung der Myletiden aus Syrakus um die Mitte des 6. Jahrhunderts oder die Auswanderung einer unterlegenen Gruppierung aus Gela, die ganz in der Nähe den Ort Maktorion gründete, bald aber von der siegreichen Partei zur Rückkehr bewogen wurde[7]. Ethnische Gegensätze scheinen dabei, wenn überhaupt, eine geringe Rolle zu spielen. In mehreren sizilischen Kolonien lebte eine ethnisch gemischte Bevölkerung über lange Zeit zusammen[8]. In den zwischenstaatlichen Bereich führt uns der Krieg von Syrakus gegen die eigene Kolonie Kamarina, wobei die wenige Jahrzehnte alte Stadt zerstört und ihre Einwohner vertrieben wurden[9]. Zum Ende der hier betrachteten Phase hin stoßen wir schließlich auf eine Stasis mit sozialen Motiven, nämlich die Vertreibung der bis dahin herrschenden Schicht der Gamoren aus Syrakus in den Jahren nach 492, die vom gesamten Demos unter Einschluß der unfreien Kyllyrier ins Werk gesetzt wurde. Die Gamoren siedelten sich in Kasmenai an, einer weiteren Apoikie von Syrakus selbst[10].

Diese und weitere Bevölkerungsbewegungen, vor allem die Aufnahme und Ansiedlung von Vertriebenen in anderen Orten, mußten bereits in früher Zeit die Frage aufwerfen, wer zu einer Polis gehörte und wer nicht. Eine Abgrenzung zu Nichtmitgliedern der Gemeinschaft bzw. dann zu Nichtbürgern des Staates war zweifellos von Anfang an selbstverständlich und blieb es auch in der Folgezeit, und zwar in zwei Richtungen: Zum einen gegenüber anderen Polisgemeinschaften; ein Kamarinäer war kein Syrakusaner, auch wenn er sich zeitweise in der Mutterstadt seiner Polis aufhielt, und umgekehrt. Olympiasieger aus allen Poleis, auch aus Kolonialstädten, wurden als Mitglieder ihrer Heimatpolis ausgerufen[11], und Stifter von Wei-

---

6 Zum Phänomen der *epoikoi* vgl. grundlegend Asheri 1971; besonderen Wert legt Lombardo 2004, 359ff., auf diesen Sachverhalt.

7 Thuk. 6,5,1 zu Syrakus; Hdt. 7,153 zu Gela.

8 Vgl. besonders die Frühgeschichte von Himera, Thuk. 6,5,1; vgl. Seibert 1979, 221. Allgemein Lomas 2000, 173.

9 Thuk. 6,5,3. Seibert 1979, 222 vermutet, daß bereits die Aussiedlung der Kamarinäer nicht freiwillig erfolgt sein könnte.

10 Hdt. 7,155,2; Aristot. Pol. 1302b25-33; Dion. Hal. 6,62,1. Vgl. Dunbabin 1948, 100; Seibert 1979, 226. In der älteren Forschung, z.B. Hüttl 1929, 54, wurde auch ein Datum um 520 v.Chr. vertreten; Syrakus hätte dann bereits vor der Machtergreifung Gelons eine längere Phase der Demokratie durchlaufen, was aus verschiedenen Gründen sehr unwahrscheinlich ist.

11 Bereits im 7. Jahrhundert, nämlich für die Olympiade von 648 v.Chr., ist ein Olympiasieger aus Syrakus verzeichnet, zwei weitere kamen aus den griechischen Städten Süditaliens. Im 6. Jahrhundert hat sich die Zahl der westgriechischen Sieger signifikant erhöht. Zu den Olympiasiegern aus Westgriechenland vgl. Philipp 1994, 78ff.; Dreher, Westgriechen (im Druck). Zu „victors in panhellenic games as evidence for polis identity“ vgl. Hansen/Nielsen 2004, 107ff.

hegeschenken in überregionalen Heiligtümern gaben ihre Herkunft an, wobei die ersten inschriftlichen Zeugnisse ins 7. Jahrhundert zurückgehen[12]. Jede Polis, aus der wir entsprechende Nachrichten aus der archaischen Zeit haben, unterschied zwischen ihren *politai* (bzw. *astoi* und weitere Bezeichnungen)[13] und zum einen den Fremden (*xenoi*), die persönlich frei waren, und zum anderen den Unfreien, Sklaven. Schon die homerische Gesellschaft kennt Sklaven (*douloi*), die nach Sizilien kommenden Kolonisten mögen schon Sklaven mitgebracht haben. Wenn sie bei oder nach ihrer Ankunft Teile der einheimischen Bevölkerung versklavten, wie man es im allgemeinen, nach dem Vorbild der spartanischen Heloten, für die Kyllyrier in Syrakus annimmt, dann lebte auch in den sizilischen Poleis von Anfang an eine Schicht von Nichtbürgern. In anderen Poleis mögen erst später Kriegsgefangene oder Kaufsklaven zur Bevölkerung dazugekommen sein. Aristoteles stellt also grundsätzlich zu Recht fest, daß bloße Ortsansässigkeit für die Mitgliedschaft in einer Polis nicht genüge[14].

Für die Sklaven war – von der Aufhebung des Sklavenstatus durch Freilassungen sehen wir hier ab – ein Eintritt in die Polisgemeinschaft grundsätzlich unmöglich: Die persönliche Freiheit war überall Voraussetzung für die Poliszugehörigkeit. Von Seiten der freien Nichtbürger her gab es im wesentlichen zwei Fälle. Der erste Fall betrifft die Nachkommen der Politen. Die Kinder aus einer rechtmäßigen Ehe zwischen einem Syrakusaner und einer Syrakusanerin wurden sicher problemlos ihrerseits Syrakusaner. Wenn ein Elternteil aber Nichtbürger war, verfuhr man im agnatischen Erbschaftssystem höchstwahrscheinlich so, wie es, wiederum höchstwahrscheinlich, in Athen bis zur Mitte des 5. Jahrhunderts v.Chr. praktiziert wurde, daß die Poliszugehörigkeit des Vaters zählte[15]. Auf diese Weise konnten (bis zum Bürgerrechtsgesetz des Perikles von 451) auch mit Ausländerinnen gezeugte legitime Kinder Athener werden. Der zweite Fall, der uns hier besonders interessiert, betrifft Ausländer, die sich in einer Polis niederlassen wollten oder sich, weil sie

[12] Vgl. die Nikandre von Delos, ca. 650 v.Chr. (CEG 403) und die Weihinschrift DGE 757 ebenfalls aus Delos. Vgl. Walter 1993, 87f., der diese Phänomene in die Staatswerdung der Polis einordnet. Vgl. auch das Tötungsgesetz Drakons, das, aufgezeichnet am Ende des 5. Jahrhunderts, ins 7. Jahrhundert zurückgeht und in Z. 28 von dem Athener (*Athenaios*) spricht. Allerdings hat Greg Anderson in einem Vortrag „The Invention of Citizenship in Ancient Athens“ am 17.4.2005 an der North Western University, Evanston, gezeigt, daß das Ethnikon bis zum Ende des 6. Jahrhunderts noch selten und erst in der Phase ab 520 v.Chr. sprunghaft häufiger verwendet wird. Hansen/Nielsen 2004, 58ff., behandeln „ethnics as evidence for polis identity“, befassen sich aber nicht mit der vorklassischen Zeit.

[13] Die verschiedenen Termini für ‚Bürger' sind zusammengestellt von Davies 2004, 27f. Mit der Terminologie befaßt sich jetzt ausführlich Blok 2005.

[14] Aristot. Pol. 1287a7-8. Finley 1979, 63, wiederholt diese Aussage, läßt aber keine positiven Kriterien folgen. Vgl. auch Whitehead 1991, 137.

[15] Vgl. Busolt 1920, 222; Patterson 1981, 8ff. Blok 2005, 39f., stellt die These auf, daß in Athen vor 451 auch die Bürgerschaft der Mutter ein hinreichendes Kriterium gewesen sei, aber die angeführte Stelle aus Euripides' Ion liefert dafür keinen eindeutigen Beweis.

Flüchtlinge waren, mehr oder weniger niederlassen mußten. Nach allem Anschein galten in den griechischen Poleis folgende Voraussetzungen für eine Aufnahme in die Bürgerschaft. Erstens mußte die Person, wie gesagt, persönlich frei sein. Zweitens mußte sie in den allermeisten Fällen als Grieche gelten. Zwar scheinen in mehreren süditalischen Poleis auch Italiker Bürger geworden zu sein, aber die Hinweise auf entsprechende Namen beginnen erst ab dem Ende des 5. Jahrhunderts[16] und setzen dann individuelle Bürgerrechtsverleihungen voraus. Für die sizilischen Poleis liegen solche Hinweise nicht vor, und die Aufnahme von sikulischen Männern ist trotz vielfältiger Beziehungen der ethnischen Gruppen auch nicht wahrscheinlich. Noch in klassischer Zeit hat man sich gegen die Aufnahme von Söldnern, die oft Fremde waren, vehement gewehrt (s.u.). Hingegen wird man annehmen müssen, daß die sizilischen Kolonisten und ihre Nachfahren nicht selten sikulische Frauen geheiratet haben und daß diese Frauen in die Polisgemeinschaft integriert wurden[17]. Drittens aber war, das ist allerdings keine rechtliche Bedingung mehr, für hinzukommende Bürger eine ökonomische Existenzgrundlage nötig. Zuwanderer konnten entweder ein ausreichendes Vermögen mitbringen, oder sie bekamen das Nötige von der aufnehmenden Polis; im allgemeinen erhielten sie, wie die ursprünglichen Kolonisten selbst, Landstücke. Landverteilungen an Neubürger sind literarisch vielfach bezeugt, inschriftliche Zeugnisse treten hinzu, auf die wir zum Teil zurückkommen werden[18].

Rechtshistorisch ist nun, was das Bürgerrecht betrifft, die Frage wichtig, ob es für die Aufnahme in die Polisgemeinschaft eines förmlichen Beschlusses von seiten der aufnehmenden Polis bedurfte, oder sogar, ob die frühe Polis ein formales Bürgerrecht und damit die Bürgerrechtsverleihung gekannt hat. Unsere literarischen Quellen, die frühestens aus der klassischen Zeit stammen, sind in dieser Hinsicht, selbst wenn sie präzise Informationen verarbeiten würden, wenig hilfreich, da sie nur sehr zusammenfassend und allgemein formulieren und dabei immer unter dem Verdacht des Anachronismus stehende Termini verwenden wie z.B. συμπολιτεύω für die in Leontinoi aufgenommenen Megarer[19].

[16] Vgl. Lomas 2000, 175.177ff.; die Autorin weist ausdrücklich auf die Unterschiede zwischen Süditalien und Sizilien hin.

[17] Vgl. etwa Lomas 2000, 176.

[18] Z.B. Hdt. 5,45f.; Diod. 11,70,5; 11,76,3; 14,78,3.5; Allgemein vgl. Asheri 1966, 24ff.; Walter 1993, 80: „Die Gemeinde war Siedlungsgemeinschaft; wer ein Stück Land besaß, gehörte dazu. ... Die ‚Einbürgerung' von Fremden bestand daher in diesem Stadium vor allem in der Zuweisung von Land".

[19] Thuk. 6,4,1. Allerdings haben wir für diese Phase recht wenig Material, v.a. weil die entsprechenden Bücher Diodors nicht erhalten sind.

Ich glaube, daß es eine formale Bürgerrechtsverleihung nicht gegeben hat. Dafür ist zunächst eine grundsätzliche Gegebenheit anzuführen, die hier nicht *in extenso* begründet werden kann[20]: Die frühe Polis war, selbst wenn sie schon staatliche Grundzüge ausgebildet hatte, im allgemeinen noch so wenig institutionalisiert, und die politischen Beschlüsse waren noch so wenig formalisiert, daß man besser noch gar nicht von Bürger*recht* sprechen sollte[21]. Dennoch muß es eine Art von Aufnahme in die Polis gegeben haben. Zwar konnten sich einzelne Ausländer, die vermögend genug waren, wahrscheinlich form- und problemlos in einer anderen Polis niederlassen. Aber die Ansiedlung größerer Gruppen, von anderswo Vertriebenen etwa, wie die syrakusanischen Gamoren in Kasmenai (s.o. Anm.10) oder die nach Maktorion Ausgesiedelten in Gela (Hdt. 7,153) bedurfte sicherlich eines politischen Beschlusses, zumal wenn aus dieser Ansiedlung politische Komplikationen für die aufnehmende Polis erwachsen konnten. Der juristisch wichtige, aber sachlich weniger bedeutsame Unterschied bestand darin, daß den Aufgenommenen nicht das Bürgerrecht verliehen, sondern ein Aufenthaltsrecht eingeräumt wurde: „sie dürfen hierbleiben". Indem die Neuankömmlinge dann Land bebauten oder in Einzelfällen auch von Handwerk oder Handel lebten, Abgaben leisteten, sonstige Rechte und Pflichten erfüllten, gab es zwischen ihnen und den Alteinwohnern keine wirklichen Unterschiede mehr, sie waren Kasmenäer oder Geloer wie die anderen. Waren sie das? Zwei Bedingungen müssen wohl noch erfüllt gewesen sein. Die erste war in der ökonomischen Lebensgrundlage impliziert und gewissermaßen selbstverständlich: Die Neuankömmlinge mußten einen dauerhaften Wohnsitz in ihrer neuen Polis haben, in einem eigenen Haus oder im Haus von anderen wohnen. Das zweite brachte gegebenenfalls doch noch eine gewisse Förmlichkeit in die Neuansiedlung hinein, wenn auch nicht auf der Ebene der Gesamtpolis. Wenn diese Polis aber gegliedert war in Personenverbände, die im allgemeinen auch kultische Funktionen hatten, dann mußten, wie das auch im nachkleisthenischen Athen noch mit den Phratrien der Fall war[22], die Neuankömmlinge in diese Verbände eingegliedert werden. Andernfalls konnten auch zusätzliche, für die Neuankömmlinge reservierte Einheiten eingerichtet werden. Allerdings darf man sich hier keine formalisierten Vorgänge vorstellen, wie wir sie gleich in der klassischen Zeit kennenlernen werden – mündliche, kultisch sanktionierte Handlungen haben der archaischen Zeit durchaus genügt[23].

---

[20] Zu Athen und Sparta vgl. Dreher 2001, 16f. 43; genauer zu Sparta dens. 2006.

[21] Vgl. die Formulierung „Zugehörigkeit zur Polisgemeinschaft" von Walter 1993, Titel und 21f.

[22] P.Oxy. 2538 col. II (Lysias); Aristoph. Av. 1661-70; Demosth. 57, 54.

[23] Michael Gagarin weist in seinem Beitrag zu diesem Symposion darauf hin, daß die schriftliche Fixierung öffentlicher Angelegenheiten, die ab der Mitte des 7. Jahrhunderts einsetzte, sich für etwa ein Jahrhundert lang fast ausschließlich auf das Aufschreiben von Gesetzen beschränkte. Vgl. dazu auch Hölkeskamp 1999, 274.

Wir kommen also zu dem Schluß, daß die Mitgliedschaft in einer Polis-Gemeinschaft dadurch erworben wurde, daß sich persönlich freie Griechen, die sich dauerhaft niederlassen wollten, in einer Polis angesiedelt haben bzw. ansiedeln durften, sich dort ihren Lebensunterhalt erwarben und ggfs. in die Personenverbände der Polis eingliederten. Eine Bürgerrechtsverleihung fand in der archaischen Zeit bei Ansiedlungen ebensowenig statt wie es bei Aussiedlungen eine Aberkennung des Bürgerrechts gegeben hat. Aussiedler haben ihre Mitgliedschaft in einer Polis dadurch verloren, daß sie *de facto* ihren Wohnsitz und ihren immobilen Besitz aufgegeben haben bzw. aufgeben mußten. Denn auch diesem Vorgang konnte durchaus ein politischer Beschluß zugrundeliegen, indem eine bestimmte Gruppe von Politen, etwa die syrakusanischen Gamoren, vertrieben wurde. Faktische Vertreibung oder Aussiedlung bedeutete automatisch auch Ausbürgerung. Für diejenigen, die von einem Gericht zu Verbannung (*phyge*) verurteilt wurden, trat dieselbe faktische Folge ein: sie mußten ihre Polis verlassen und hoffen, sich in einer anderen ein neues Leben aufbauen zu können. Der Kreis schließt sich dadurch, daß erst damit, daß jemand faktisch seine bisherige Poliszugehörigkeit aufgegeben hatte, die Voraussetzung für ihn entstand, sich eine neue Poliszugehörigkeit zu erwerben[24]. Das moderne Problem einer doppelten Staatsangehörigkeit stellte sich daher für die frühe Polis nicht[25].

2. Tyrannen und Politen.

Bevölkerungsbewegungen im eingangs definierten Sinn kamen in der aristokratischen Phase der sizilischen Poleis nicht allzuoft vor, da diese Gemeinwesen sich ganz überwiegend als soziale Einheiten verstanden, in denen die grundsätzliche Einteilung der Bürgerschaft in eine kleinere, besitzende Oberschicht, der auch die Führung der Polis zustand, und in die größere Schicht derer, die weniger besaßen und die sich nur durch den Besuch der Volksversammlung an der Verwaltung des Gemeinwesens beteiligten, weitgehend selbstverständlich akzeptiert war.

Aber ab dem 6. Jahrhundert, mit besonderem Erfolg ab dem Ende des Jahrhunderts, gelang es einzelnen Adligen bzw. Adelsgeschlechtern, sich eine beherrschende Stellung innerhalb ihrer Polis zu sichern und eine Tyrannis zu errichten[26]. In bezug auf die Bevölkerung wirkte sich der Machtanspruch dieser Tyrannen zunächst, in der Phase, in der sie sich in den Kämpfen gegen Rivalen durchsetzen

[24] Das solonische Gesetz (Plut. Solon 24), es dürfe nur eingebürgert werden, wer aus seiner Heimat verbannt sei oder wer mit seiner ganzen Familie nach Athen ziehe, um dort ein Gewerbe zu treiben, sanktionierte wahrscheinlich nur die entsprechende Tradition.

[25] Das schließt selbstverständlich nicht aus, daß jemand, der faktisch die Poliszugehörigkeit wechselte, sich weiterhin seiner früheren Heimat verbunden oder sogar zugehörig *fühlen* konnte; aber Zeugnisse für eine solche Mentalität haben wir erst aus der nachfolgenden, tyrannischen Periode (s.u.).

[26] Vgl. zur westgriechischen Tyrannis grundlegend Luraghi 1994.

mußten, verschiedentlich so aus, daß die Gegenpartei vertrieben wurde[27]. Nachdem aber der Einzelwille des Tyrannen sich in der Polis allgemeine Geltung verschafft hatte und nun über allen Fraktionen und Gegensätzen stand, vermochte der Herrscher seine Interessen so nachdrücklich durchzusetzen, daß in der Phase der sizilischen Tyrannen besonders viele Aus-, An- und vor allem Umsiedlungen zu verzeichnen sind. Zur Veranschaulichung nenne ich nur die jeweilige Anzahl der Maßnahmen aus den einzelnen Rubriken, und nur ausnahmsweise die Ereignisse selbst, wobei die frühe Tyrannis mit der späteren ab Dionysios I. zusammengefaßt wird[28]. An *Ansiedlungen* haben wir also sieben Fälle, darunter die Ansiedlung von zehntausend Söldnern durch Gelon in Syrakus nach 485 v.Chr. und von derselben Anzahl an Söldnern durch Dionysios I. in Leontinoi 396 v.Chr. Diesen stehen ebenfalls sieben *Aussiedlungen* gegenüber. An *Umsiedlungen* sind elf Fälle bekannt, womit diese Gruppe die größte unter den Bevölkerungsbewegungen darstellt. Als *Umbesiedlungen* schließlich lassen sich vier Fälle bezeichnen.

Alle diese Bevölkerungsbewegungen beruhten auf der Initiative der Tyrannen. Während die reinen Ansiedlungen durchgehend Angebote an ansiedlungswillige Menschen waren, also keinen Zwangscharakter trugen, gilt für die Aussiedlungen das Gegenteil. Umsiedlungen konnten den Wünschen der Betroffenen entsprechen oder ihnen Gewalt antun, oft ist für uns aber nicht mehr feststellbar, wie diese sich dazu stellten. Umbesiedlungen schließlich lassen sich normalerweise in die zwei Phasen einer Aussiedlung mit Zwangscharakter und einer freiwilligen Ansiedlung aufteilen.

Die Gründe und Ziele dieser tyrannischen Maßnahmen waren mehrschichtig und können schwerlich auf einen einzigen Gesichtspunkt reduziert werden. Am ehesten lassen sich die Maßnahmen unter die Stichworte Machtgewinnung, Machterhaltung, Machterweiterung subsumieren. Die Beseitigung von Opposition, der Ausbau von Syrakus zu einer Art Hauptstadt des beherrschten Territoriums, die Förderung der Wirtschaftskraft und die militärische Stärkung strategischer Bastionen bilden die wichtigsten Motive.

Spezifisch für die Tyrannis ist der Einsatz von Söldnern. Während die freien Stadtstaaten nur in außerordentlichen Notlagen auf dieses militärische Instrument zurückgriffen[29], waren Söldner geradezu konstitutiv für die Machtgewinnung und Machterhaltung von Tyrannen[30]. Diese Funktion brachte es mit sich, daß die Söldner den Tyrannen längerfristig dienten und nicht nur für einen bestimmten Kriegszug angeworben wurden. Der Tyrann war auch gut beraten, wenn er Söldner, die nicht mehr benötigt wurden oder ihren Dienst beendeten, nicht einfach entließ und somit

[27] Vgl. Seibert 1979, 223ff.

[28] Die meisten dieser Episoden finden sich bei Seibert 1979 und Vattuone 1994 verzeichnet. Auf diese Bevölkerungsbewegungen, ihre Systematik und ihre Konsequenzen will ich an anderer Stelle genauer zurückkommen.

[29] Vgl. z.B. Griffith 1935, 194.

[30] Vgl. z.B. Tagliamonte 1994, 99ff.

zu einer Gefahr für die Ordnung und Sicherheit seines Territoriums werden ließ, sondern ihnen eine neue ökonomische Existenz ermöglichte. Zu diesem Zweck mußte er ihnen, wie später die römischen Feldherren ihren Soldaten, Land verschaffen, was zu Problemen mit den bisherigen Eigentümern dieses Landes führen konnte. Die Anzahl der jeweils angesiedelten Söldner wird wahrscheinlich meist nicht so hoch gewesen sein wie von unseren Quellen angegeben, und auch die runden Zahlen von meist zehntausend Mann sind ebenso verdächtig wie sie es bei anderen Siedlerzahlen sind[31]; aber daß es sich jeweils nicht nur um mehrere hundert, sondern eher um mehrere tausend Männer handelte, dürfen wir schon annehmen.

Gerade bei den Söldnern, die meist aus ganz verschiedenen griechischen und nichtgriechischen Gebieten kamen[32], aber auch bei den anderen Neusiedlern, die der Polis, in der sie sich ansiedeln durften bzw. mußten, nicht angehörten, stellt sich die Frage nach ihrer Integration. Die Forschung scheint diesbezüglich keinen Zweifel zu kennen: Die Neusiedler erhielten jeweils das Bürgerrecht; z.B.: Die Tyrannen „... siedelten die Bevölkerung um und verliehen Söldnern und Einwanderern in großer Zahl das Bürgerrecht“ (so Finley und viele andere)[33]. Solche Formulierungen setzen voraus, daß von Seiten der Tyrannen ein bewußter politischer Akt der Einbürgerung vorgenommen wurde, daß ein vom Tyrannen in Auftrag gegebener Volksbeschluß oder eine konkrete Entscheidung des Tyrannen selbst verkündet wurde. Es wird ein irgendwie formalisierter Vorgang angenommen, den man sich wohl ebenso wie in späterer Zeit am ehesten als Einschreibung in Bürgerlisten vorstellt: „Die von Gelon Inskribierten“, heißt es etwa bei Seibert[34].

Für all diese Vorstellungen gibt es weder zuverlässige Quellenhinweise noch hinreichende Gründe, die in der historischen Situation liegen würden. Viel näher liegt hingegen die Annahme, daß sich die informelle Einbürgerung, wie sie oben für die Frühzeit angenommen wurde, auch unter den Tyrannen nicht wesentlich geändert hat. Der allgemeine Grund dafür bleibt der gleiche: Auch in der Tyrannenzeit war die Polis noch nicht wesentlich weiter institutionalisiert und formalisiert, war die Schriftlichkeit der politischen Vorgänge nicht viel weiter vorangeschritten. Diese Ausgangslage wurde durch die spezifische politische Herrschaftsform der Tyrannis noch verstärkt. Denn die eigentlichen Entscheidungen fielen nicht mehr in den Institutionen der Polis, in einem Adelsrat und/oder der Volksversammlung, sondern sie wurden, vielleicht nach Beratungen in einer persönlich ausgewählten Gruppe, im

[31] Erstaunlicherweise werden sie im Unterschied zu sonst in den Quellen gegebenen Heereszahlen in der Literatur normalerweise nicht in Zweifel gezogen.

[32] Vgl. Tagliamonte 1994, 99ff.

[33] Finley 1979, 69. Vgl. etwa Seibert 1979, 226: „wo sie das Bürgerrecht erhielten“; „Durch die Verleihung des Bürgerrechts waren die Umgesiedelten keine Phygades.“ 246: „und erhielten dort das Bürgerrecht“; „Verleihung des Bürgerrechts“; Stroheker 1958, 59: „ wo sie das Bürgerrecht erhielten“; Moggi Nr.17, S.106ff: „ottennero la cittadinanza“, „concessione della cittadinanza“ u. ä.

[34] Seibert 1979, 228.

Kopf eines einzelnen getroffen und den entsprechenden Institutionen bestenfalls mitgeteilt. Die Vorstellung der früheren Forschung, der Tyrann habe *neben* der Polis gestanden, habe ich immer für begrifflich unzutreffend gehalten; vielmehr stand der Tyrann *innerhalb* der Polis, war aber allem und allen informell übergeordnet und lenkte die Polis nach seinem Willen. Wo aber nach der persönlichen Macht des Tyrannen lange nichts kam, außer allenfalls der ebenso informellen Macht seiner Familie und seiner Adjutanten, wo also niemand Rechte besaß, da gab es auch keine ungleichen Rechte, da gab es also auch keine Unterschiede zwischen Altbürgern und Neubürgern[35]. Wen der Tyrann als freien, griechischen Einwohner in seiner Polis duldete, wen er gar selbst aufnahm und ansiedelte, indem er dafür sorgte, daß er durch ein Stück Land sich und seine Familie ernähren konnte, der war selbstverständlich Bürger dieser Polis. Das dürfte denn auch gemeint sein, wenn Herodot formuliert: πολιήτας ἐποίησε (vgl. καὶ πολιτείαν δούς, Diod. 14,106,3 über Dionysios I.). Politen, Bürger wurden die Angesiedelten[36]. Wer aber sollte ihnen das noch, und gegebenenfalls wie, extra und förmlich bestätigen?

Die spätere Terminologie insbesondere Diodors τοῦ γὰρ Γέλωνος ... πολιτογραφήσαντος ξένους μισθοφόρους (11,72,3) setzt zwar eine schriftliche Eintragung in Bürgerlisten o.ä. voraus; der von Diodor noch an anderer Stelle[37] gebrauchte Terminus *politographein* dürfte aber erst hellenistischen Ursprungs[38] und durch die spätere, ab der klassischen Zeit geübte Praxis geprägt sein und kann daher nicht als *terminus technicus* gelten, der für die archaische Zeit wörtlich zutreffend wäre[39]. Das gilt übrigens analog auch für ähnliche Vorgänge, die später in Schriftform erfolgten und die man sich daher auch für die frühere Zeit als verschriftlicht vorgestellt hat, wie z.B. die Anwerbung der Söldner[40]: (sc. Hieron) στρατιώτας πολλοὺς κατέγραψεν εἰς τὴν στρατίαν (Diod. 11,48,2). Es verwundert daher nicht, daß man bei Diodor selbst durchaus auch neutrale Termini für die Ansiedlung von Neubürgern findet, die keine bestimmte Form implizieren, meist die Verben μετοικίζειν oder κατοικίζειν, so auch für die Ansiedlung der oben genannten Söldner durch Gelon: κατοικισθέντας ὑφ' Ἱέρωνος (Diod. 11,76,3).

In derselben Weise müssen wir auch die Ansiedlungen von Einzelpersonen interpretieren, die nun, in der Zeit der Tyrannis, erstmals dokumentiert sind. Einschlägig sind in unserem Zusammenhang fünf Fälle.

---

35 Vgl. auch Busolt 1920, 223.

36 Hdt. 7,156,2, wo die Formulierung, die Gelon als Subjekt voraussetzt, zweimal verwendet ist.

37 11,49,3 sagt Diodor ἐπολιτογράφησεν von Theron, der in Himera nach Tötung vieler Gegner Dorier und andere Kolonisten ansiedelte.

38 Bezeugt ist er in kleinasiatischen Inschriften des 3. Jh. v.Chr. (Liddell/Scott s.v.). Vgl. Brulé 1990.

39 Das scheint aber Asheri 1966, 26 vorauszusetzen.

40 Für die hellenistische Zeit nimmt Chaniotis Listen an, die den Namen, das Ethnikon und den Rang des Angeworbenen enthielten, vgl. Chaniotis 2004, 487.

a) Glaukos aus Karystos auf Euböa hatte um 500 v.Chr. mehrere Siege in panhellenischen Boxwettbewerben errungen; er scheint geradezu eine antike „Boxlegende" geworden zu sein. Glaukos kam aus Gründen, die sich nicht mehr ermitteln lassen, nach Sizilien, wo Gelon ihn zu seinem Stellvertreter in Kamarina machte[41]. Wir dürfen vielleicht annehmen, daß Glaukos sich im Dienste Gelons militärisch bewährt hatte; zur Sicherung der Deinomeniden-Herrschaft über Kamarina waren sicherlich Qualitäten als Söldnerführer gefragt[42]. Vom Bürgerrecht ist in den Quellen und (deswegen?) in der Literatur nicht die Rede.

b) Pausanias (6,13,1) beschreibt die in Olympia aufgestellte Statue des Astylos aus Kroton: „Dieser hat bei drei aufeinanderfolgenden Spielen den Stadionlauf und den Doppellauf gewonnen. Weil er sich aber bei den beiden letzten Olympiaden als Syrakusaner ausrufen ließ, um Hieron, dem Sohn des Deinomenes, zu Gefallen zu sein, beschlossen die Krotoniaten, sein Haus in ein Gefängnis umzuwandeln, und sie stürzten die Statue um, die im Heiligtum der Hera gestanden hatte". Es läßt sich rekonstruieren[43], daß Astylos 488 als Krotoniate, 484 und 480 als Syrakusaner gewonnen hat, so daß er eher von Gelon (gestorben 478) als von dessen Bruder Hieron nach Syrakus geholt wurde; eine Verwechslung durch Pausanias ist durchaus vorstellbar. Zweifellos hat ihn der syrakusanische Tyrann an seinen Hof gezogen, um den Glanz des Olympiasiegers auch auf sich selbst und seine Residenzstadt fallen zu lassen. Es ist durchaus möglich, daß Astylos bei der Neugründung von Syrakus durch Gelon im Jahr 485 unter den Neubürgern war. Aber wenn Mann recht darin hat, daß der Sprinter seine Heimatpolis aufgrund von Auseinandersetzungen mit demokratischen Gegnern verließ[44], so wäre es doch ein Zufall, wenn die entsprechenden innenpolitischen Anlässe in Kroton genau mit der Neugründung von Syrakus durch Gelon zusammengefallen wären. Außerdem erwähnen unsere Quellen nur drei Kategorien von Neusiedlern in Syrakus: die zurückgeführten Gamoren, die Söldner Gelons und die umgesiedelten Kamarinäer. Es ist daher genauso gut denkbar, daß Astylos zunächst, vor 485, zu Gelon nach Gela kam und von dort aus mit dem gesamten Tyrannenhof nach Syrakus übersiedelte[45]. Christian Mann nimmt sicherlich zu Recht an, daß Astylos dauerhaft nach Syrakus übersiedelte, nicht zu-

---

41 Schol. Aisch. 3,189; Anecd. Bekker I p.232 s.v. Γλαῦκος Καρύστιος. Vgl. Dunbabin 1948, 416.

42 Luraghi 1994, 150f. 275f.und Mann 2001, 246 stellen den agonistischen Ruhm und die politischen Fähigkeiten in den Vordergrund. Die Gründe mögen sich durchaus überschnitten haben.

43 Vgl. noch Dion. Hal. 8,1,1; 8,77,1 und Mann 2001, 246ff. mit früherer Literatur, auch zum folgenden.

44 Mann 2001, 188f.

45 Mann spricht einmal zu Recht von dem ganzen Zeitraum 488-484 (S.247) für den Poliswechsel und engt diesen dann mit Luraghi auf das Ereignis der Neugründung von Syrakus 485 ein (ebd.), gibt aber an anderer Stelle ohne Begründung das Jahr 484 an (S.189).

letzt weil er sich in Kroton den Volkszorn zugezogen hatte, wie Pausanias schreibt[46]. Mann fügt dann allerdings noch hinzu, „er erhielt das Bürgerrecht von Syrakus", was offenbar, da sonst kein Anhaltspunkt vorliegt, nur aus dem dauerhaften Aufenthalt des Astylos dortselbst geschlossen ist[47].

c) Ergoteles wurde, so berichtet Pausanias, im Verlauf einer Stasis aus seiner Heimatstadt Knossos vertrieben, ging nach Himera und erhielt dort das Bürgerrecht sowie viele andere Ehren: πολιτείας τετύχηκεν [ὅς] καὶ πολλὰ εὕρετο ἄλλα ἐς τιμήν (Paus. 6,4,11)[47a]. Im allgemeinen wird angenommen[48], daß er 476/5 oder kurz danach nach Himera kam, als der Tyrann Theron von Akragas die zuvor dezimierte Bürgerschaft der Stadt wieder auffrischte[49]. Bezeichnend ist, daß der Zeitgenosse Pindar in seiner zwölften olympischen Ode, die einen wohl 472 errungenen Sieg des Ergoteles besingt und auf frühere Siege bei den Pythischen und Isthmischen Spielen verweist, zwar auch die Vertreibung des Kreters wegen einer Stasis, aber nichts über das Bürgerrecht in Himera erwähnt, das dann für Pausanias eine selbstverständliche Ehrung war. Daß die Formulierung des Pausanias nicht wörtlich zu nehmen ist, ergibt sich auch daraus, daß sie den Erhalt des Bürgerrechts in eine Reihe mit weiteren Ehrungen stellt, also eine Gleichzeitigkeit nahelegt, während die Forschung mit guten Gründen annimmt, daß Ergoteles erst nach seiner Umsiedlung Siege in den

46 Strenggenommen könnte Pausanias auch so interpretiert werden, daß Astylos sich rein als Reverenz an Gelon als Syrakusaner ausrufen ließ und erst, nachdem ihn seine Mitbürger in Reaktion auf diesen „Verrat der Heimat" bestraft hatten, nach Syrakus auswanderte. Allerdings ist eine solche, abstrakte „Bekenntnis-Staatsbürgerschaft" zumindest in dieser Zeit nirgendwo bezeugt (die von Hornblower 2004, 140. 283 angeführte Proklamation des Spartaners Lichas als (Pseudo-) Boioter setzt spätere Verhältnisse voraus und unterstützt keineswegs die These Hornblowers, ebd., Dorieus sei kein Bürger von Thurii gewesen). Weiterhin handelt es sich bei den krotoniatischen Maßnahmen gegen Astylos nicht einfach um eine spontane Entladung des Volkszorns, sondern offenbar um gerichtsförmig beschlossene Strafen, wobei der Tatbestand im unklaren bleibt, denn der Wechsel der Polis-Zugehörigkeit galt den Griechen eigentlich nicht als Delikt; gegebenenfalls wurde Astylos wegen Hochverrats angeklagt, und dieses Delikt wird in Kroton genauso dehnbar gewesen sein, wie wir es aus Athen wissen. Schließlich war es das Bestreben Gelons und seiner Nachfolger, sich die tatsächliche und nicht nur virtuelle Präsenz berühmter Männer an ihrem Hof zu sichern; Astylos steht daher in einer Reihe von mehreren solcher Personen.

47 Mann 2001, 247. Auch die Fortführung des Satzes „... und kehrte nicht mehr in seine Heimat zurück" ist nicht beweisbar. Die Statue in Olympia ist auch von Plin. nat. 34,59 erwähnt, sportliche Siege des Astylos werden auch in einem Gedicht des Simonides gepriesen, Simon. Frg. 1.

47a In einer neuen Siegerinschrift aus Olympia werden die Siege des Ergoteles ausdrücklich auf Himera bezogen: H. Taeuber/R. Pausz (Hgg.), Neue Inschriften von Olympia (im Druck), Nr. 23 (ich danke H. Taeuber für die Erlaubnis, auf diesen noch unveröffentlichten Text hinweisen zu dürfen).

48 Mann 2001, 245 Anm.811 mit Literaturverweisen.

49 Diod. 11,48,6ff; 49,3.

Laufdisziplinen der großen Spiele errungen habe – und nur diese Siege kommen als Anlaß für Ehrungen in Frage.

d) Ausführlich beschreibt Pausanias die in Olympia aufgestellten Weihegeschenke des Phormis, der Mainalier, dann aber (auch?) Syrakusaner gewesen sei und für Gelon und Hieron Kriegsdienste geleistet habe (Paus. 5,27,1-7). Offenbar verdingte sich Phormis wie viele seiner arkadischen Landsleute als Söldner, muß aber in Syrakus eine Führungsposition eingenommen haben, die er entweder von Beginn an innehatte oder in die er schnell aufstieg, denn nur als besonderer Günstling der Deinomeniden und mit deren Billigung konnte er das kostbare Pferdegespann aus Bronze in Olympia aufstellen lassen. Das Schicksal des Phormis weist also Ähnlichkeiten mit dem des Glaukos auf. Pausanias beschreibt aber noch ein zweites Weihegeschenk, das ebenfalls als Weihung des Phormis gegolten habe, der Inschrift nach aber von einem Syrakusaner namens Lykortas für den Mainalier Phormis gestiftet worden sei. Interessanterweise wird in dieser Inschrift die Zugehörigkeit des Phormis zu Syrakus nicht erwähnt, vielleicht sollten wir sogar sagen: verschwiegen. Denkbar ist, daß das Denkmal nach dem Sturz der Deinomeniden-Tyrannis, etwa aus persönlicher Dankbarkeit, in Auftrag gegeben wurde und daß die Syrakusaner die unter Gelon und Hieron selbstverständlich gegebene Poliszugehörigkeit des Phormis dann nicht mehr akzeptierten. Lykortas, der sich offenbar persönlich eng mit Phormis verbunden fühlte, wie auch Pausanias schließt, – sie mögen auch Waffengefährten gewesen sein – mag es deswegen für nicht opportun gehalten haben, seinen Freund noch als Syrakusaner zu bezeichnen, obwohl er selbst als solcher auftritt[50]. Vielleicht war Phormis sogar wieder in seine arkadische Heimat zurückgekehrt und die Zugehörigkeit zu Syrakus damit obsolet geworden.

e) Ohne literarische Vermittlung, sondern direkt aus einer Inschrift in Olympia erfahren wir, daß Praxiteles, der Stifter eines weiteren Weihegeschenks, Syrakusaner und Kamarinäer war, aber ursprünglich aus Mantineia in Arkadien stammte. Er könnte wie Phormis als Söldner(führer) oder aber als Siedler nach Sizilien gekommen sein[51]. Für den historischen Moment der Ansiedlung oder auch Umsiedlung des Praxiteles sind mehrere Vorschläge gemacht worden. Wir sollten jedoch in diesem wie auch in den anderen Fällen nicht unbedingt nach konkreten, uns bekannten Anlässen für Ansiedlungen suchen, die vielmehr jederzeit möglich und nicht immer an wichtige Ereignisse gebunden waren. Die Zugehörigkeit zu zwei Poleis, die der

[50] Hornblower 2004, 186 weist darauf hin, daß Lykortas ein typisch arkadischer Name war und reiht deshalb auch ihn selbst unter die arkadischen Einwanderer ein. Zwingend ist dieser Schluß jedoch nicht. Die Pausanias-Stelle ist jetzt ausführlich kommentiert von Zizza 2006, 247ff.

[51] Nomima I 20. Vgl. Dunbabin 1948, 416: „a mercenary leader in the service of the tyrants"; Morgan 1999, 392: „perhaps a mercenary or a colonist involved in the refoundation of Kamarina". Vgl. zur möglichen Söldneranwerbung in Olympia den Beitrag von B.Forsén, in: N. Birgalias (Hg.), War, peace and the panhellenic sanctuaries, Kongreßakten 2005 (im Druck).

Stifter in seiner Inschrift ausdrückt, scheint jedenfalls am ehesten eine gleichzeitige Zugehörigkeit zu sein[52], nicht eine nacheinander erfolgte Ansiedlung, wie man meistens vermutet hat[53]. Dies deutet auf die Zeit ab 485 v.Chr., in der Kamarina, sofern es überhaupt noch besiedelt war, von den syrakusanischen Tyrannen beherrscht wurde; insofern erinnert Praxiteles an Glaukos, unseren oben zuerst besprochenen Fall. Mit der Doppelnennung wird Praxiteles nicht nur seine eigene Verbundenheit mit beiden Städten, sondern sicher auch die Zusammengehörigkeit, sprich die Abhängigkeit Kamarinas von Syrakus, zum Ausdruck gebracht und damit den Herrschern von Syrakus gehuldigt haben. Eine formalisierte Verleihung des Bürgerrechts für zwei verschiedene Städte durch einen Tyrannen wäre jedenfalls weder als gleichzeitiger noch als ungleichzeitiger Akt leicht vorstellbar.

Auch aus dieser Gruppe von individuellen Ansiedlungen[54] ergeben sich also keine überzeugenden Hinweise auf formalisierte oder gar institutionelle Bürger-

---

[52] Dafür spricht die Verbindung mit *kai*, während die zeitlich vorausgehende Herkunft aus Mantineia deutlich zum Ausdruck gebracht ist. Van Effenterre und Ruzé sprechen von einer „double citoyenneté".

[53] Mehrere Vermutungen sind im Kommentar von van Effenterre/Ruzé wiedergegeben. Wenn doch eine Reihenfolge angenommen werden müßte, dann die in der Inschrift gegebene, die schwerlich die Annahme zuläßt, Praxiteles sei zuerst nach Kamarina und dann, etwa 484 wegen der Zerstörung der Stadt durch Gelon, nach Syrakus gezogen.

[54] Wenn zu dieser Gruppe von Umsiedlern auch Mikythos gerechnet wird, so liegt dem die wahrscheinlich falsche Annahme zugrunde, dieser Gefolgsmann des Tyrannen Anaxilas stamme aus Tegea (so z.B. Philipp 1994, 88). Die Annahme dürfte aus dem Umstand abgeleitet sein, daß Mikythos nach dem Tod des Anaxilas nach Tegea auswanderte, wie Herodot (7,170) und Pausanias (5,26,4) übereinstimmend berichten. Daß sich Mikythos gerade nach Tegea begab, setzt zweifellos voraus, daß er schon vorher Beziehungen dorthin gehabt hatte. Aber welcher Art diese waren, läßt sich nicht mehr eruieren. Es mögen durchaus Freundschaften zu anderen Arkadern gewesen sein, die als Militärs in die Magna Graecia gekommen waren wie Phormis (oben d) oder Praxiteles (oben e). Wäre aber Mikythos selbst arkadischer Herkunft, so hätte der zeitweilige Tyrann (vgl. auch Diod. 11,48,2), der offenbar seinen ganzen Reichtum nach Tegea mitnehmen und von dort aus zahlreiche kostspielige Weihegeschenke in Olympia aufstellen konnte, also dort gut lebte, das sicherlich in seinen Inschriften gesagt und Pausanias hätte es so wiedergegeben. Pausanias referiert aber aus den olympischen Inschriften ganz im Gegenteil, daß Mikythos aus Rhegion und Messene stamme. Der Bevölkerungstransfer zwischen Arkadien und Westgriechenland ging also nicht ausschließlich von Osten nach Westen, sondern, wenngleich wohl nur in Einzelfällen, auch einmal in die Gegenrichtung.
Die Angabe des Pausanias, Mikythos habe die griechischen Poleis Rhegion und Messene als Vaterstadt (πατρίδα, also Singular) gehabt, ist wohl kaum so zu verstehen, daß auf den einen Inschriften Rhegion, auf den anderen Messene angegeben gewesen wäre. Das wäre nämlich nur denkbar, wenn die Weihgeschenke in zeitlichem Abstand aufgestellt worden wären und Mikythos zwischenzeitlich seine Poliszugehörigkeit gewechselt hätte, also ursprünglich aus Rhegion stammte und nach der Eroberung Zankles durch Anaxilas dorthin gezogen wäre und sich dann als Bürger der in Messene umbenannten Stadt präsentiert hätte. Demgegenüber legt Pausanias (5,26,5) nahe, daß alle Weihgeschenke – obwohl sie wahrlich zahlreich waren! – in Erfüllung eines Gelübdes aufgestellt wurden,

rechtsverleihungen. Hingegen stoßen wir auf Unregelmäßigkeiten. Vom Bürgerrecht sprechen nur späte Quellen, aber auch sie nicht in allen Fällen. Die moderne Literatur übernimmt, wohl ohne darüber zu reflektieren, diese Formulierungen, spricht aber auch in einem Fall, in dem die Quellen das nicht tun, vom Erwerb des Bürgerrechts. Angesichts dessen können wir uns in der Position gestärkt fühlen, daß in der archaischen Zeit, auch unter tyrannischer Herrschaft, die Eingliederung von neuen Bürgern in die Polis ohne formalisiertes Beschlußverfahren und ohne schriftliche Eintragungen vorgenommen wurde.

Auf dieser Grundlage bietet es sich umso mehr an, unseren Texten auch dort zu folgen, wo sie die gleichzeitige Zugehörigkeit einer Person zu zwei Poleis nahelegen. Nur wenn wir ein förmliches Bürgerrecht voraussetzen würden, müßten wir in Erwägung ziehen, daß ein Polisbürger jeweils nur einer Polis angehören könnte, und müßten die Nennung von zwei Poleis gegebenenfalls auf eine unterschiedliche Zeitphase zurückführen. Das aber ist nach dem bisher Gesagten weder nötig noch sinnvoll[55]. Wenn sich Praxiteles (oben e) als Syrakusaner und Kamarinäer bezeichnet, so ist das ebenso ein Bekenntnis zur Politik des herrschenden Tyrannen wie die Angabe des Mikythos, Rhegion und Messene seien seine „Vaterstadt“ (s. Anm.54)[56]. Phormis bezeichnet sich als Mainalier und als Syrakusaner, und auch wenn wir für gesichert halten, er sei aus Arkadien nach Syrakus gezogen, so gibt es doch keinen Grund anzunehmen, er habe sich nach seinem Transfer nur noch als Syrakusaner und nicht mehr als Arkader gefühlt[57]. Eine solche Unterscheidung hätte ihn wahrscheinlich sehr verwundert[58].

---

als Mikythos bereits in Tegea wohnte. Die Angabe von zwei Heimatstädten gleichzeitig dürfte aber auch politisch besser zu dem passen, was wir über Mikythos wissen: Indem Mikythos durch seine fiktive Doppelherkunft die enge Verbindung der beiden Städte betonte, wollte er, als treuer Diener, sogar Schatzmeister, des Anaxilas (Pausanias macht aus dem *oikeios* Herodots einen *dulos*, könnte allerdings mit diesem Terminus nicht die Rechtsstellung des Mikythos, sondern seine Stellung im politischen Sinn als „Tyrannenknecht“ bezeichnen wollen), die Annexion von Zankle und auch die Wahl des Namens Messene für diese Stadt (Thuk. 6,4,6) nachträglich sanktionieren. Außerdem mögen noch folgende Assoziationen im Hintergrund gestanden haben: Bei der Gründung von Rhegion von Zankle aus sollen bereits messenische Siedler beteiligt gewesen sein; nach 490 wurden von Anaxilas Messenier ins Land geholt und Anaxilas selbst soll messenische Wurzeln gehabt haben.

55 Vgl. auch Busolt 1920, 229, nach dem die Annahme des Bürgerrechts eines anderen Staates nicht den Verlust des indigenen Bürgerrechts nach sich zog. Allerdings ist der Unterschied, den Busolt zu den Koloniegründungen macht, m.E. nicht aufrechtzuerhalten. Außerdem differenziert er zu wenig zwischen den verschiedenen Perioden der griechischen Geschichte.

56 Als Parallele eines solchen politischen Anspruchs auf Herrschaft über eine andere Stadt könnte die Formulierung Xen. hell. 1,5,19 gelten: φυγάδα ἐξ Ἀθηνῶν καὶ Ῥόδου; vgl. Hornblower 2004, 136f. und Anm.30 mit der weiteren Parallele Teos – Abdera.

57 Hornblower 2004, 140 wirft diese Alternative in seiner Übersetzung auf: „an Arkadian from Mainalos but (or ‚and'?) now a Syracusan“; der Verweis auf S. 186 führt dort zu derselben Übersetzung mit Rückverweis auf S. 140. Erklärt wird diese Stelle also nicht,

3. Die Zeit der „freien Poleis“[59].

Zwar sind die meisten der uns bekannten Bevölkerungsbewegungen in Sizilien von Tyrannen veranlaßt worden, das Phänomen war aber, wie wir bereits im ersten Abschnitt gesehen haben, nicht auf diese Phase beschränkt, sondern auch in der Zeit nach dem Sturz des Thrasybulos in Syrakus 466 zu beobachten. Allerdings müssen die recht intensiven Aus-, An- und Umsiedlungen am Anfang dieser Phase insofern noch als indirekte Nachwirkungen der tyrannischen Politik gelten, als es sich teilweise um die Revision von Maßnahmen der Deinomeniden handelte.

Das gilt besonders für die von Diodor (11,72ff.) unter den Jahren 462 und 461 berichteten Ereignisse, die in Wirklichkeit einen längeren Zeitraum umfaßt haben werden. In Syrakus kam es zu Auseinandersetzungen zwischen den ehemaligen Söldnern Gelons und der übrigen Bürgerschaft. Die Umsiedlungen Hierons in Katane wurden rückgängig gemacht. Kamarina wurde wieder von den früheren Siedlern in Besitz genommen. Neben diesen konkreten Beispielen berichtet Diodor (11,76,5) ganz grundsätzlich, daß alle Poleis gemeinsam beschlossen (κοινὸν δόγμα), die Verbannten wieder aufzunehmen, die Poleis den ursprünglichen Bürgern (τοῖς ἀρχαίοις πολίταις, vgl. 11,72,3) zurückzugeben und die ehemaligen Söldner der Tyrannen in Messene anzusiedeln. Dann hätten sie ihr jeweiliges Land unter alle ihre Bürger aufgeteilt. Auch wenn wir die von Diodor sehr euphorisch vorgestellte und von der Forschung meist ähnlich ausgemalte „Rückwanderungswelle“ etwas redimensionieren, so kann doch kein Zweifel bestehen, daß die Bevölkerungsstruktur in vielen sizilischen Poleis neu geordnet und die Zusammensetzung der Bürgerschaft neu organisiert wurde[60].

Diese Situation ist also der gegebene Anlaß, der es erstmals in der sizilischen Geschichte erforderte, daß „standardisierte“ Kriterien für die Zugehörigkeit von

---

aber die Übersetzung ‚but' ist umso unverständlicher, als Hornblower in seinem ausführlichen Kommentar zu dem im Peloponnesischen Krieg prominenten Rhodier Dorieus zu dem Schluß kommt: „that *déraciné* elite figures like Dorieus moved freely between *poleis* and in some sense they retained their original identity, just as Phormis ...“ (140). Ich glaube nicht, daß Dorieus in Thurii einen nichtbürgerlichen Status als Metöke o.ä. hatte, wie Hornblower (ebd.) annimmt, und ich glaube auch nicht wie er, daß das Bürgerrecht in den freien Poleis des 5. und 4. Jahrhunderts noch immer so wenig formalisiert war, daß man von ständig und unkompliziert die Poleis wechselnden Personen sprechen könnte (s.u. 3.) Für die archaische Zeit und die Zeit der Tyrannenherrschaft trifft dies aber eher zu. Das Problem einer Wiederaufnahme des Bürgerrechts, das von Hornblower auch angesprochen wird und das zeitweilige „Ruhen“ dieses Status impliziert, wäre noch separat zu diskutieren.

58 Dem könnte die Situation junger Deutscher ausländischer Herkunft entsprechen, denen penetrante Journalisten partout entlocken wollen, ob sie sich mehr als Deutsche oder mehr als Türken fühlten.

59 Diese Bezeichnung verwendet Seibert, 1979, 229 für die Zeit ab 466 v.Chr. Sofern in manchen Poleis, wie z.B. Himera, zeitweise keine Tyrannis bestand, wird sie hier sinngemäß auch für diese Phasen in der ersten Hälfte des 5. Jahrhunderts gebraucht.

60 Vgl. dazu Dreher, Kongreßakten 2006 (im Druck).

Polisbewohnern zur Bürgerschaft eingeführt und in rechtsförmigen Verfahren überprüft wurden. Wer gehörte zu den Söldnern der Tyrannen, wer nicht? Wer lebte erst seit kurzem in der Polis und hatte Land inne, das von früheren Polismitgliedern beansprucht wurde? Wer durfte also das Land der Polis bebauen? Zwar mußte nicht jeder Bürger Landbesitz haben, aber die Zahl derer, die in den sizilischen Städten teilweise oder sogar ganz von Handwerk oder Handel lebten, wird noch im 5. Jahrhundert nicht groß gewesen sein. Umgekehrt aber war sehr wahrscheinlich jeder Landbesitzer auch Bürger, wenn das Bürgerrecht wie in Athen und anderen Städten die Voraussetzung für immobiles Eigentum gewesen ist[61]. und die sizilischen Städte waren ausgesprochen landwirtschaftlich geprägt.

Von einer Landverteilung zu Anfang des 5. Jahrhunderts haben wir ein noch nicht lange bekanntes inschriftliches Zeugnis aus dem sizilischen Himera. Eine Landverteilung an neue Siedler aus Zankle, die 493 v.Chr. ihre Heimatstadt verlassen mußten, liegt auch dann vor, wenn die Erwähnung eines *ges anadasmos* in Z. 14 nicht, wie die Erstherausgeberin Brugnone meint, die Neuverteilung des gesamten Territoriums vorsieht, sondern, wie Manganaro argumentiert, für die Verletzung des vorliegenden Dekrets dieselbe Strafe vorsieht wie für denjenigen, der eine Neuaufteilung des Landes vorschlagen sollte; denn die Verteilung eines halben *schoinos* an jeden der neuen Siedler ist durch Z. 1 gesichert[62]. Parallelen für solche gesetzlichen Landzuweisungen an Neusiedler haben wir aus anderen griechisch besiedelten Gebieten: Vermutlich um 500 v.Chr. regelte in Naupaktos ein Gesetz, die sogenannte Bronze Pappadakis, die Aufteilung eines bestimmten Landstückes zwischen Alt- und Neusiedlern je zur Hälfte[63]; in Kerkyra Melaina im sogenannten Psephisma von Lumbardo (6.-3. Jahrhundert) sollten den Neusiedlern Landstücke zugelost werden; das Ergebnis der Erlosung mußte schriftlich fixiert werden[64].

Die Frage, wer zur Bürgerschaft gehörte, hatte aber nicht nur ökonomische und soziale, sondern auch eminent politische Bedeutung. Denn erst in der freien Polis war nicht mehr der über allen stehende Wille eines Tyrannen für die Geschicke der Polis maßgeblich. Jetzt waren es die bürgerlichen Institutionen der Polis, also Rat und Volksversammlung, die wirklich etwas zu entscheiden hatten, und zwar Angelegenheiten, von denen sowohl die individuellen Verhältnisse der Bürger, etwa bei Eigentumsregelungen, als auch das Schicksal der Gesamtpolis, etwa bei Bündnisfragen, abhing. Auch insofern wurde nun wichtig, wer in diesen Institutionen mitzuent-

---

61 Davon ist auszugehen, zumindest ist keine Polis bekannt, in der Landbesitz nicht auf die Bürgerschaft beschränkt gewesen wäre, vgl. Asheri 1966, 26 A.5; Whitehead 1991, 146; Chaniotis 2005, 84.

62 Brugnone 1997; Manganaro 2000; vgl. Lombardo 2004, 359. Unklar bzw. unbegründet bleibt, warum Manganaro 2000, 750 die Inschrift ins 6. Jahrhundert setzt.

63 Meiggs/Lewis Nr.13; Körner 1993, Nr.47. Auch die Deukalion-Inschrift aus Elis ließe sich hier anführen (Nomima I 21), in ihr wird allerdings einer Einzelperson Land zugewiesen.

64 Syll.^{3} 141; vgl. Lombardo 1992; dens. 2001, 78ff.

scheiden hatte, wer mithin zur Bürgerschaft gehörte. In Syrakus wollte man die von Gelon angesiedelten Söldner nach dem Sturz der Tyrannis zunächst als Bürger minderen Rechts einstufen, denen der Zugang zu den Ämtern verwehrt bleiben sollte. Dieser Status wurde von den Betroffenen nicht akzeptiert, so daß es zum Bürgerkrieg und schließlich zur Vertreibung der ehemaligen Söldner kam[65]. Die Episode zeigt, wie wichtig den Betroffenen der Bürgerstatus, und zwar der ungeschmälerte, volle Bürgerstatus gewesen ist.

Wir wissen, daß in Athen nach der kleisthenischen Phylenreform die Bürger in den Demen registriert wurden, das Bürgerrecht aber auch an eine Mitgliedschaft in den Phratrien gebunden war[66]. Es waren also die Untereinheiten der Polis, die die Aufgabe wahrnahmen, Verzeichnisse ihrer Mitglieder und damit der Polisbürger zu führen. Wenn wir nun auch aus Sizilien Hinweise auf ähnliche Vorgänge haben, so liegt die Annahme nahe, daß auch hier der Bürgerstatus an solche Untereinheiten der Polis geknüpft war, für die jüngst der englische Terminus sub-ethnics als Oberbegriff vorgeschlagen wurde[67]. Dementsprechend erhalten in unserer Inschrift aus Himera die Neuankömmlinge nicht nur Land, sie werden vielmehr auch in neu eingerichteten, sogenannten zankleischen Phylen zusammengefaßt (Z. 2-3: φῦ]ỉλα Δαγκλαῖα ποέσαι) und bilden als solche einen Teil der Bürgerschaft[68]. Die Phratrien sollen die schon registrierten Festlegungen (i.e. die Verteilung der Landlose wie in Kerkyra Melaina?) veröffentlichen. Einen Beleg für eine schon veröffentlichte Registrierung nicht unbedingt von Landstücken, aber auf jeden Fall von der Zugehörigkeit der Bürger zu einer Phratrie, eventuell innerhalb von drei dorischen Phylen, liefern die 1992 von Cordano veröffentlichten Täfelchen des Athenatempels von Kamarina, die mit der Neuordnung der Polis nach der Tyrannenzeit in Verbindung gebracht werden müssen und daher von Cordano auf das Jahr 461 v.Chr. datiert werden[69]. Da die Phratrien keine Eigennamen, sondern Nummern tragen, handelt es sich ganz eindeutig um eigens geschaffene, bewußt vorgenommene Untergliederungen der Bürgerschaft[70]. Nach Murray könnten die Täfelchen „original title to citizenship or (which may be effectively the same thing) original participation in the

---

65 Diod. 11,72,3. 76,1f.

66 S.o. Anm.22.

67 Hansen/Nielsen 2004, 160.

68 Ich lese mit Brugnone (und Lombardo 2004, 359) φῦ]ỉλα im Plural, weil das Wort Objekt zum aktiven Infinitiv ποέσαι sein muß. Manganaro hingegen sieht in φῦ]ỉλὰ Δαγκλαι̣̂α die dorische Form des Singulars φυλή, was inhaltlich attraktiver wäre, aber grammatisch nicht konstruierbar erscheint.

69 Nach Diod. 11,76,5 Cordano 1992, 86.94.

70 Cordano 1992, 91.93. Die Termini hικάς und τριακάς dürften weitere bürgerschaftliche Untergruppen bezeichnen, ebd. 83.92; zustimmend Murray 1997, 496f.

distribution of land" anzeigen, sie sind jedenfalls „primarily symbols of citizenship"[71].

Die Formalisierung und Verschriftlichung des Bürgerrechts in der ersten Hälfte des 5. Jahrhunderts ist natürlich kein isolierter Vorgang, sondern fügt sich in eine allgemeinere Entwicklung ein. In den Poleis, die von Tyrannen frei oder befreit waren, wurden zunehmend häufiger Gesetze und Beschlüsse inschriftlich veröffentlicht, gerade in den Städten Siziliens entwickelte sich die Rhetorik, und etwa auch der Petalismos in Syrakus, bei dem die Namen der für die Verbannung vorgeschlagenen Männer auf Olivenblätter geschrieben wurden, zeigt die allgemeine Verbreitung der Schriftlichkeit.

Erst durch eine solche formale, rechtsförmige Feststellung des Bürgerstatus kann man im eigentlichen Sinn vom Bürger*recht* sprechen. In der Terminologie unserer Quellen spiegelt sich die hier angenommene Veränderung in der nachtyrannischen Zeit erwartungsgemäß nicht wider, weil die in der klassischen Zeit üblichen Formulierungen auch für die früheren historischen Phasen verwendet werden[72]. Es findet sich aber bei den Autoren der klassischen Zeit umgekehrt auch kein eindeutiger Beleg dafür, daß in der Zeit der freien Polis das Bürgerrecht nunmehr, wie hier angenommen wird, in einem rechtsförmigen Akt verliehen wurde. Am nächsten kommen dieser Annahme die Formulierungen des Thukydides, daß die Leontiner nach 424 viele neue Bürger eingeschrieben hätten (5,4,2: πολίτας τε ἐπεγράψαντο πολλούς), und daß sich die Oberschicht Leontinois nach ihrer Vertreibung in den syrakusanischen Bürgerverband eingegliedert habe: ἐπὶ πολιτείᾳ ᾤκησαν. Inschriftliche Quellen existieren für Sizilien leider nicht.

Wie mit dem Verweis auf die Ereignisse in Leontinoi nach dem Frieden von Gela 424[73] angedeutet wurde, haben die Bevölkerungsbewegungen in Sizilien mit den Revisionen nach dem Tyrannensturz noch kein Ende gefunden, wenngleich sie nicht mehr so zahlreich wie unter den Deinomeniden erfolgten. Nicht zufällig hören wir von ähnlichen Maßnahmen und Problemen, wie der Einbürgerung von Söldnern, gehäuft wieder in der Zeit der jüngeren syrakusanischen Tyrannis, besonders unter Dionysios I., und die Zeit Timoleons erinnert in vieler Hinsicht an die Neustrukturierung der Poleis in den 460er Jahren. Die seit damals anzunehmende Formalisierung und Schriftlichkeit des Bürgerrechts dürfen wir dann auch bei diesen weiteren Bevölkerungsbewegungen des 5. und 4. Jahrhunderts voraussetzen, vielleicht sogar bei denen der jüngeren Tyrannis, die insofern Errungenschaften der freien Polis übernommen haben könnte.

---

[71] Murray 1997, 498. 501. Landverteilung scheint auch Brugnone 1997, 276 anzunehmen. Zu weiteren Beispielen außerhalb Siziliens vgl. etwa Lombardo 2004, 359ff. Cordano 1992, 94 denkt eher an die Aufteilung des städtischen Wohngebiets.

[72] Vattuone 1994 folgt dieser unkritischen Praxis, indem er für alle Phasen den späten Terminus *politographein* verwendet.

[73] Zu diesen Vorgängen vgl. ausführlich Dreher 1986.

Die Entwicklung des Bürgerstatus von einer quasi selbstverständlichen Gegebenheit hin zu einem formellen Recht folgte in den sizilischen Poleis grundsätzlich denselben Entwicklungslinien wie in den Poleis des griechischen Mutterlandes. Die relativ späte und lange Phase der Tyrannis bedeutete jedoch auch für die Herausbildung des formellen Bürgerrechts eine gewisse Verzögerung. Die ungewöhnlich intensiven Bevölkerungsbewegungen in Sizilien trugen dazu bei, daß der Bürgerstatus leichter als in anderen griechischen Regionen erworben bzw. gewechselt werden konnte. Voraussetzung dafür war die überdurchschnittliche Verfügbarkeit von bebaubarem Land, auf dem Neubürger angesiedelt werden konnten[74]. Diese Voraussetzung dürfte spezifisch für Sizilien bzw. die Magna Graecia sein und wird in den Darstellungen der gesamtgriechischen Verhältnisse im allgemeinen vernachlässigt[75]. Auf sie dürfte aber auch zurückgehen, daß in Sizilien weniger und weniger intensive Staseis zu verzeichnen sind als anderswo. Aus der für Sizilien erkennbaren größeren Mobilität und Flexibilität der Bürgerschaften sollten wir aber keineswegs schließen, daß der Bürgerstatus bzw. dann das Bürgerrecht in Sizilien als weniger attraktiv oder weniger bedeutsam als andernorts angesehen worden wären.

BIBLIOGRAPHIE

Asheri, D., Distribuzioni di terre nell'antica Grecia, Torino 1966.

Bergemann, J., Der Bochumer Gela-Survey. Vorbericht über die Kampagnen von 2002 bis 2004. Mit einem Beitrag von Ulrich-Walter Gans, MDAI(R) 111, 2004, 437-476.

Ders., Supplementi coloniari e condizione giuridica della terra, RSA 1, 1971, 77-91.

Blok, J.H., Becoming Citizens. Some Notes on the Semantics of „Citizen" in Archaic Greece and Classical Athens, Klio 87, 2005, 7-40.

Brugnone, A., Legge di Himera sulla ridistribuzione della terra, PP 53, 1997, 262-305.

Brulé, P., Enquête démographique sur la famille grecque antique. Étude de listes de politographie d'Asie mineure d'époque hellénistique (Milet et Ilion), REA 92, 1990, 238-242.

Busolt, G., Griechische Staatskunde I, München 1920 (HdAW).

Cataldi, S. (Hg.), Poleis e Politeiai. Esperienze politiche, tradizioni letterarie, progetti costituzionali, Atti del Convegno Internazionale di Storia Greca, Alessandria 2004.

Chaniotis, A., Mobility of Persons During the Hellenistic Wars, in: C. Moatti (Hg.), La mobilité des personnes en Méditerranée de l'antiquité à l'époque moderne. Procédures de contrôle et documents d'identification, Rom/Paris 2004, 481-500.

Ders., War in the Hellenistic World. A Social and Cultural History, Malden/Oxford 2005.

---

[74] Die jüngsten archäologischen Untersuchungen auf dem Territorium von Gela haben gezeigt, daß den Siedlern zumindest in archaischer Zeit viel Land zur Verfügung stand; man nutzte nur die besten und leicht zu bebauenden Flächen. Vgl. den Bericht von M. Siebler in der Frankfurter Allgemeinen Zeitung vom 8.6.2005; vgl. auch Bergemann 2004.

[75] Vgl. etwa Walter 1993, 80: „Da in kaum einer Gemeinde sehr viel überschüssiges Land zur Verfügung gestanden haben kann, das die Eingesessenen großzügig zu vergeben bereit waren, ...".

Consolo Langher, S.N., Siracusa e la Sicilia greca tra età arcaica ed alto ellenismo, Messina 1996.

Cordano, F., Le tessere pubbliche dal tempio di Atena a Camarina, Rom 1992.

Davies, J.K., The concept of the ‚citizen', in: S. Cataldi (Hg.) 2004, 19-30.

Deininger, J., „Krise" der Polis? Betrachtungen zur Kontinuität der gesellschaftlichen Gruppen und der inneren Konflikte im Syrakus des 5. und 4. Jahrhunderts v.Chr., in: Klassisches Altertum, Spätantike und frühes Christentum, Festschrift A. Lippold, hg. v. K. Dietz u.a., Würzburg 1993, 55-76.

Dreher, M., Sophistik und Polisentwicklung, Frankfurt a.M. u.a. 1983.

Ders., La dissoluzione della polis di Leontini dopo la pace di Gela (424 a.C.), ASNP ser. 3, vol. 16, 1986, 637-660.

Ders., Athen und Sparta, München 2001.

Ders. (Hg.), Das antike Asyl. Kultische Grundlagen, rechtliche Ausgestaltung und politische Funktion, Köln u.a. 2003.

Ders., Die Primitivität der frühen spartanischen Verfassung, in: A. Luther u.a. (Hgg.), Das frühe Sparta, Stuttgart 2006, 43-62.

Ders., Die Westgriechen und die panhellenischen Heiligtümer des Mutterlandes, in: N. Birgalias (Hg.), War, peace and the panhellenic sanctuaries, Kongreßakten 2005 (im Druck).

Ders., Frieden und Eintracht nach dem Sturz der Tyrannen? Die Neuordnung Siziliens 466 v.Chr., in: S. Cataldi (Hg.), Salvare le poleis. Costruire la concordia. Progettare la pace, Kongreßakten 2006 (im Druck).

Dunbabin, T.J., The Western Greeks. The history of Sicily and South Italy from the foundation of the Greek colonies to 480 B.C., Oxford 1948.

Finley, M.I., Das antike Sizilien, München 1979.

Griffith, G.T., The Mercenaries of the Hellenistic World, London 1935 (ND Groningen 1968).

Hansen, M.H.H./Nielsen, T.H. (Hgg.), An Inventory of Archaic and Classical Poleis, Oxford 2004.

Hölkeskamp, K.-J., Schiedsrichter, Gesetzgeber und Gesetzgebung im archaischen Griechenland, Stuttgart 1999.

Hornblower, S., Thucydides and Pindar. Historical Narrative and the World of Epinikian Poetry, Oxford 2004.

Hüttl, W., Verfassungsgeschichte von Syrakus, Prag 1929.

Lomas, K., The Polis in Italy. Ethnicity, Colonisation, and Citizenship in the Western Mediterranean, in: R. Brock/S. Hodkinson (Hgg.), Alternatives to Athens. Varieties of Political Organization and Community in Ancient Greece, Oxford 2000, 167-185.

Lombardo, M., Lo *psephisma* di Lumbarda: note critiche e questioni esegetiche, in: Hesperìa, hg. v. L. Braccesi, III, Rom 1992, 161-188.

Ders., La documentazione epigrafica, in: Problemi della chora coloniale dall'Occidente al Mar Nero. Atti del XL Convegno Internazionale di Studi sulla Magna Grecia (Taranto 2000), Taranto 2001, 73-152.

Ders., Poleis e politeiai nel mondo „coloniale", in: S. Cataldi (Hg.), 2004, 351-367.

Körner, R., Inschriftliche Gesetzestexte der frühen griechischen Polis, hg. v. K. Hallof, Köln u.a. 1993.

Luraghi, N., Tirannidi arcaiche in Sicilia e Magna Grecia. Da Panezio di Leontini alla caduta dei Dinomenidi, Florenz 1994.

Manganaro, G., Revisione di un'iscrizione di Segesta e di un decreto frammentario di Himera, in: Terze Giornate Internazionali di Studi sull'Area Elima (Gibellina-Erice-Contessa Entellina 23-26 ottobre 1997) Atti II, Pisa-Gibellina 2000, 747-753.

Mann, C., Athlet und Polis im archaischen und frühklassischen Griechenland, Göttingen 2001.

Manville, P.B., The Origins of Citizenship in Ancient Athens, Princeton 1990.

Moggi, M. (Hg.) I sinecismi interstatali Greci I. Dalle origini al 338 a.C., Pisa 1976.

Morgan, C., Cultural Subzones in Early Iron Age and Archaic Arkadia?, in: T.H. Nielsen/ J. Roy (Hgg.), Defining Ancient Arkadia (CPCActs 6), Kopenhagen 1999, 382-456.

Murray, O., Rationality and the Greek City: the Evidence from Kamarina, in: M.H. Hansen (Hg.), The Polis as an Urban Centre and as Political Community (CPCActs 4), Kopenhagen 1997, 493-504.

Parke, H.W., Greek Mercenary Soldiers. From the Earliest Times to the Battle of Ipsus, Oxford 1933.

Patterson, C., Pericles' Citizenship Law of 451-50, Philadelphia 1981 (ND Salem 1988).

Philipp, H., Olympia, die Peloponnes und die Westgriechen, JDAI 109, 1994, 77-92.

Raaflaub, K.A., Homer to Solon: The Rise of the Polis. The Written Sources, in: M.H. Hansen (Hg.), The Ancient Greek City State (CPCActs 1), Kopenhagen 1993, 41-105.

Seibert, J., Die politischen Flüchtlinge und Verbannten in der griechischen Geschichte, 2 Bde., Darmstadt 1979.

Ders., Die Bevölkerungsfluktuation in den Griechenstädten Siziliens, AS 13-14, 1982-83, 33-65.

Sordi, M., La Grecità assediata e le premesse di una colonizzazione panellenica, in: M. Sordi (a cura di), Emigrazione e immigrazione nel mondo antico (CISA 20), Milano 1994, 133-140.

Stroheker, K.F., Dionysios I. Gestalt und Geschichte des Tyrannen von Syrakus, Wiesbaden 1958.

Tagliamonte, G., I figli di Marte. Mobilità, mercenari e mercenariato italici in Magna Grecia e Sicilia, Rom 1994.

Van Effenterre, H./Ruzé, F., Nomima. Recueil d'inscriptions politiques et juridiques de l'archaisme grec I, Rom 1994.

Vattuone, R., ‚Metoikesis'. Trapianti di popolazione nella Sicilia greca fra VI e IV sec. A. C., in: M. Sordi (a cura di), Emigrazione e immigrazione nel mondo antico (CISA 20), Milano 1994, 81-113.

Walter, U., An der Polis teilhaben. Bürgerstaat und Zugehörigkeit im archaischen Griechenland, Stuttgart 1993.

Whitehead, D., Norms of Citizenship in Ancient Greece, in: A. Molho/K. Raaflaub/J. Emlen (Hgg.), City States in Classical Antiquity and Medieval Italy, Stuttgart 1991, 135-154.

Zizza, C., Le iscrizioni nella *periegesi* di Pausania. Commento ai testi epigrafici, Pisa 2006.

ANTONIO BANFI (MILANO)

RISPOSTA A MARTIN DREHER

Nel rispondere a Martin Dreher, vorrei tentare di ampliare il discorso ad alcune questioni generali e di metodo concernenti il problema della cittadinanza presso i Greci d'Occidente.

E' ben nota la frase che Tucidide attribuisce ad Alcibiade, secondo la quale le città di Sicilia erano caratterizzate da una popolazione disomogenea e mutevole, sicché più facile sarebbe stata la conquista, visto lo scarso patriottismo di cittadini privi di saldi legami con la loro terra[1]. Con questa osservazione di carattere quasi etnografico, l'ambizioso leader ateniese postula uno strettissimo rapporto fra comunità di stirpe, coesione sociale e impegno bellico. Uno degli effetti dell'eterogeneità dei componenti il corpo civico, infatti, è costituito dal frazionamento della città in piccoli gruppi in lotta fra loro, sicché un abile comandante saprebbe, dice Alcibiade, indurne molti alla defezione[2]. Si può certo convenire sul fatto che una simile rappresentazione è espressione di un'esagerazione retorica e polemica, tutta interna al dibattito con Nicia sull'apertura di un nuovo fronte in Sicilia. Non vi è dubbio, però, che essa esprima anche un certo senso di estraneità rispetto al mondo coloniale d'Occidente, nel quale sarebbe venuta a mancare quella comunanza di origini che specialmente nell'Atene del V secolo costituisce un elemento fondamentale per definire l'appartenenza di un soggetto alla propria comunità[3]. In tal senso, le parole riportate da Tucidide (o da lui stesso composte secondo verosimiglianza) non fanno altro che confermare quanto è stato scritto intorno alla "diversità" dei greci d'occidente, i quali sarebbero stati caratterizzati da una peculiare mobilità, flessibilità e tendenza ad integrarsi, non solo con gruppi greci estranei alla fondazione della colonia, ma anche con elementi indigeni[4]. Si tratterebbe, dunque, di una concezione del diritto di cittadinanza (da

---

1 Thuc., VI.17.

2 *Ibid.* Cfr. K. Lomas, *The Polis in Italy: Ehtnicity, Colonization and Citizenship in the Western Mediterranean*, in R. Brock – S. Hodkinson (eds.), *Alternatives to Athens, Varieties of Political Organization and Community in Ancient Greece*, Oxford 2001, p. 180-181.

3 Lomas, *Polis in Italy*, *cit.*, p. 181; P. Gauthier, *La citoyenneté en Grèce et à Rome: participation et intégration*, "*Ktema*" 6 (1981), p. 167 e sgg.

4 *Ibid.*, p. 169 e sgg.; E. Lepore, *Problemi dell'organizzazione della chora coloniale*, in M. Finley (ed.), *Problèmes de la terre en Grèce ancienne*, Paris 1973, p.16 e sgg.

intendersi come *legal form of acceptance and integration*[5]) differente da quella che siamo abituati a conoscere, attraverso le fonti, per le grandi città del continente in età classica. Una concezione che sottintende un modo diverso, più "aperto" di intendere la *polis* e l'appartenenza ad essa.

Premesso che la pretesa di Wilamowitz di "leggere il mondo greco con gli occhi dei greci"[6], non è più oggi scientificamente accettabile, mi pare sia comunque necessaria una certa cautela nell'utilizzare i concetti che caratterizzano alcuni lavori intorno al problema della cittadinanza nel mondo greco. Concetti di una evidentissima attualità, e dai contenuti piuttosto indefiniti, quali integrazione, mobilità e flessibilità. E' possibile, certo, che categorie del tutto estranee all'oggetto osservato ne consentano comunque un migliore intendimento, e si tratta, del resto, di un fenomeno tipico della storia del mondo antico, poiché, come osservava Finley, è naturale che "i concetti e le presupposizioni su cui essa si fonda derivano in ampia proporzione dall'esperienza più o meno recente"[7]. Tuttavia, resta la necessità di un'attenta messa alla prova delle categorie concettuali che si applicano al mondo antico, evitando ogni generalizzazione.

Per quanto riguarda il rapporto fra cittadinanza, mobilità, e integrazione di diversi gruppi, rapporto al quale sono naturalmente connesse le cosiddette "questioni di etnicità", mi pare che sia utile rimarcare, in primo luogo, la differenza fra il periodo della *Pentecontaetia* e della Guerra del Peloponneso, e le altre fasi della storia greca, poiché la polarizzazione del mondo greco intorno a due differenti modelli politici e costituzionali ebbe ricadute significative anche su questo piano. Penso alla famosa legge di Pericle del 451-450 ,[8] che, restringendo la cittadinanza ai soli figli di genitori entrambi ἀστοί intese tra l'altro colpire le grandi famiglie aristocratiche che, per tradizione, stringevano legami transnazionali con un'accorta politica matrimoniale (si pensi, ad esempio, a Cimone, figlio di una Tracia di stirpe regale[9]). Mi pare lecito supporre che la forte ideologizzazione del periodo della Guerra Peloponnesiaca abbia prodotto qualche conseguenza anche sul modo in cui la composizione e l'organizzazione del corpo civico era concepita dai Greci d'Occidente, tanto più che la propaganda ateniese cercò attivamente di fomentare il conflitto fra le città siceliote opponendo Dori a Calcidesi[10]. Insomma, è probabile che la diversità dell'occidente greco, con la sua minor rigidezza nel concepire il diritto di cittadinanza rispetto a un modello di *polis* "basato su di un rigoroso

---

5 Lomas, *Polis in Italy*, *cit.*, p. 168.

6 Nella premessa a *Der Glaube der Hellenen*.

7 M. Finley, *Le generalizzazioni nella storia antica*, in *Uso e abuso della storia*, Torino 1981, p. 99.

8 E. Cantarella, *Filiazione legittima e cittadinanza*, in *Symposion 1995, Vorträge zur griechischen und hellenisticschen Rechtsgeschichte*, Wien 1997, p. 97 e sgg.

9 Plut., *Cim*. 4.1

10 M. Gras, *L'Occidente e i suoi conflitti*, in *I Greci*, vol. 2 t. 2, *Definizione*, Torino 1997, p. 89 e sgg.

esclusivismo"[11], si debba spiegare con il continuo emergere di *staseis*, anche assai violente, e con la connessa persistenza, specialmente, ma non solo, in Sicilia, di forme di governo di origine arcaica (tirannidi e comunque poteri personali), che si segnalano per una minor carica ideologica, che sono sostanzialmente prive di quegli ideali partecipativi che caratterizzano la democrazia ateniese e per le quali spostamenti e mutamenti di popolazione sono attuati in funzione di una politica di potenza[12]. Non è dunque un caso, che si assista ad una più chiara formalizzazione del diritto di cittadinanza proprio nel momento in cui ai regimi tirannici si sostituiscono costituzioni democratico-moderate: infatti, non è interesse né delle aristocrazie né dei tiranni una troppo stringente definizione dell'appartenenza al corpo civico, mentre lo è dei regimi democratici o, se si vuole, "repubblicani"[13], che prevedono un certo grado di partecipazione del cittadino al governo della cosa pubblica, sicché cresce la differenziazione verso l'esterno, mentre si riduce quella all'interno della cittadinanza. Si potrebbe comunque sostenere che in Sicilia ed in Magna Grecia, anche nel periodo post-tirannico, l'ampia disponibilità di terre rese comunque più facili i numerosi spostamenti di popolazione e rese possibile una maggiore disponibilità all'integrazione fra soggetti di diversa provenienza, facendo sì, allo stesso tempo, che fossero meno cruenti e meno numerosi i conflitti per la redistribuzione delle terre[14].

Questa tesi, che in linea generale può sembrare corretta, non mi pare sia sempre confermata, nei singoli casi storicamente determinati: occorre ricordare la forte presenza indigena, con la quale vi fu una lunga storia di scambi ma anche di conflitti sanguinosi[15] ed anche la forte conflittualità interna allo stesso mondo coloniale greco. Tutto ciò faceva sì che una potenziale ampia disponibilità di terre si traducesse, in concreto, in una relativa scarsità[16], tant'è che i terreni di una colonia erano tanto più appetibili quanto più si trovavano vicini al centro urbano che poteva assicurare rifugio e difesa, mentre diverso era lo *status* delle terre più lontane (*eschatià*)[17]. Infatti, sia Platone che Aristotele ritenevano che si dovesse organizzare la *chora* coloniale con l'assegnazione ai cittadini di due lotti, uno vicino al centro cittadino e l'altro lontano, proprio per assicurare un'equa distribuzione dei rischi fra

---

[11] U.E. Paoli, *Lo stato di cittadinanza in Atene*, in *Studi di diritto attico*, Firenze 1930, p. 201.

[12] Lomas, *Polis in Italy*, *cit.*, p. 182 e sgg.

[13] D. Musti, *Storia greca*, Bari 1990, p. 368 e sgg.

[14] E' quanto sostenuto, in riferimento al caso siciliano, da M. Dreher, in *Old and New Citizens in Ancient Sicily*, conference held at the Northwestern University (*Troubles Over Citizenship in the Greco-Roman World*, April 17, 2005). Ringrazio vivamente l'Autore per avermi fornito il testo.

[15] E. Lepore, *I Greci in Italia*, in M. Finley – E. Lepore, *Le colonie degli antichi e dei moderni*, Roma 2000, p. 66 e sgg.

[16] Lepore, *Problemi dell'organizzazione*, *cit.*, p. 19 e sgg.; *Id.*, *I Greci in Italia*, cit., p. 73 e sgg.

[17] *Ibid.*, p. 27 e sgg.

tutti i proprietari[18]. Inoltre, Aristotele loda le leggi di quegli Stati che privano i proprietari di terre lontane dal centro politico del diritto di voto in assemblea, proprio perché i rischi ai quali costoro sono esposti non garantiscono una chiara percezione dell'interesse collettivo[19].

Per tutti questi motivi, credo che, se si vuole effettivamente discutere della "diversità" dei Greci occidentali, non ci si possa limitare all'esame del mero diritto di cittadinanza, che di per sé può assumere i *contenuti* più vari, ma occorra, per l'appunto, ampliare il discorso ai due temi, fra loro strettamente connessi, della partecipazione dei cittadini al governo della città e della proprietà fondiaria;[20] in ciò, mi pare perfettamente condivisibile l'invito di Ettore Lepore ad analizzare nel suo complesso "il tipo particolare di *demos* che viene a formarsi nelle *apoikiai* di Occidente" e la composizione del corpo civico e politico[21].

Spostando lo sguardo dalla Sicilia all'area magno-greca, mi pare di notevole interesse il caso della città di Thurii e le vicende che ne segnarono la storia politica e costituzionale in piena età classica, fra V e IV secolo.

Si tratta di un caso unico nella storia della colonizzazione greca, poiché era stato deciso di fondare una colonia panellenica e perché la deduzione della colonia fu predisposta e pianificata in modo – per così dire – scientifico. Ciò nonostante, il tentativo non si può dire riuscito, dato che presto si produsse una situazione assai simile a quella descritta da Alcibiade in Tucidide, con il rischio reale del fallimento dell'impresa coloniale.

Come cercherò di mostrare, la capacità di integrazione, che avrebbe dovuto assicurare la coesione della cittadinanza, fu gravemente messa in discussione non appena emerse la questione della distribuzione delle terre e dell'assegnazione delle principali magistrature, poiché parte dei coloni non accettarono quei principi isonomici ai quali si sarebbe dovuta ispirare la colonia. Infatti, è fenomeno proprio delle colonie il fatto che, una volta raggiunto il sito designato per la fondazione, si diano in contemporanea l'acquisizione dello *status* di cittadino da parte dei partecipanti alla spedizione, che di norma si accompagna alla perdita della cittadinanza della città di provenienza[22], e la ripartizione e assegnazione delle terre ai nuovi cittadini. Sicché la cittadinanza è interamente costituita di proprietari. Per questo molti decreti di fondazione contengono precise istruzioni sulla distribuzione delle terre[23], talora accompagnate dalla designazione di appositi funzionari

---

18 Plat., *Leg.* 5, 745c-d; Arist., *Pol.*, VII.9.7-8 (1330 a).

19 *Ibid.*

20 M. Moggi, *Organizzazione della chora, proprietà fondiaria e homonoia: il caso di Turi*, "ASNP" 27 (1987), p. 77 e sgg.; D. Lotze, *Il cittadino e la partecipazione al governo della polis*, in *I Greci*, vol. 2 t. 2, Definizione, Torino 1997, p. 369 e sgg.

21 Lepore, *I Greci in Italia*, *cit.*, p. 79.

22 E. Szanto, *Das griechische Burgerrecht*, New York 1979, p. 61 e sgg. Vi sono però casi nei quali i coloni mantengono anche la cittadinanza della metropoli. E' il caso, ad esempio, di Locri (Polyb. XII.10.a).

23 A.J. Graham, *Colony and Mother City in Ancient Greece*, Manchester 1964, p. 44 e sgg.

(geonomi), incaricati, appunto, di provvedere alla ripartizione dei lotti[24]. Non è certo un caso, quindi, che si siano ben presto affermate formule tipiche della propaganda coloniaria quali *epi tê isêi kai omoiai*[25] che mostrano la forte presenza di principi isonomici e, si potrebbe forse dire, egualitari – anche se non sempre è detto che tali principi si siano effettivamente realizzati[26].

Venendo ora ai fatti, è ben noto come sul finire del VI secolo, la ricca e potente città di Sibari, già travagliata da alcuni rivolgimenti costituzionali che avevano portato all'affermazione di una tirannide con la fuga o l'espulsione di buona parte degli aristrocratici, fu sconfitta dai rivali crotoniati, appoggiati dagli esuli sibariti, e rimase disabitata per lungo tempo[27]. Seguì un tentativo (fallito) di rifondare la città con un nuovo insediamento nel 453, ed un ulteriore tentativo nel 446, quando gruppi di sibariti si rivolsero contemporaneamente a Sparta e ad Atene sollecitando le due città a partecipare alla nuova fondazione, con l'invio di coloni[28]. Al rifiuto di Sparta si contrappose invece la disponibilità dell'Atene di Pericle, che vide nell'impresa un buon modo per consolidare le proprie ambizioni imperiali[29]. Si decise così di inviare messi nel Peloponneso per invitare non più le singole *poleis*, ma chiunque, semplice cittadino, lo avesse voluto, a partecipare alla colonia panellenica[30]. Per certo, sappiamo che alla spedizione, guidata dall'esegeta Lampone, uomo molto vicino a Pericle[31], e da Senocrito, parteciparono fra gli altri Erodoto, Protagora, Ippodamo di Mileto ed anche lo stratego spartano Cleandrida, in esilio perché accusato di essersi fatto corrompere da Pericle[32]. Significativamente la colonia ebbe come ecista proprio Lampone e non, com'era uso, l'oracolo delfico[33], ed assunse il nome di Thurii: la scomparsa dell'antico nome di Sibari è indice della volontà di marcare la

---

24 E' il caso, ad esempio, di Brea (Tod, ep. 44). Cfr. Graham, *op. cit.*, p. 35 e sgg.

25 Cfr. Thuc. I.27.1.

26 E. Lepore, *Problemi dell'organizzazione*, *cit.*, p. 23 e sgg. Sia detto per inciso, il legame linguistico fra *nomos* e *nemein* non è mai andato perso alla coscienza dei greci; *isonomia*, quindi (al pari di *eunomia*) era concetto che evocava immediatamente l'idea della divisione dei beni (e in particolare delle terre) fra i componenti il corpo civico. Lo mostra bene il titolo di un'opera di Tirteo, detta appunto *Eunomia*, nella quale si trattava della *stasis* verificatasi a Sparta al tempo della guerra messenica, quando una parte degli spartiati reclamò una nuova divisione delle terre (Arist., *Pol.* 1306 b). Cfr. L. Piccirilli, *Dall' "anomia" all' "eunomia"*, in *Scritti in onore di G. Guarino*, vol. III, Padova 1998, p. 10333.

27 G. Pugliese Carratelli, *Le vicende di Sibari e Thurii*, "*Atti e memorie della Società Magna Grecia*" XIII-XIV (1972-73), p. 21 e sgg. V. Ehrenberg, *The Foundation of Thurii*, "AJPH" 69 (1948), p. 149 e sgg.

28 Diod., XII. 9-11. Pugliese Carratelli, *Le vicende*, cit., p. 24 e sgg.

29 Moggi, *Senocrito, Tucidide di Melesia e la fondazione di Turi*, "ASNP" 9 (1979), p. 499 e sgg.; Ehrenberg, *Foundation of Thurii*, *cit.*, p. 155 e sgg.

30 Ehrenberg, *Foundation of Thurii*, cit., p. 154.

31 Cfr. Aristoph., *Nub.* 332; *Schol. ad loc. cit.*;

32 Diod. XIII.106.10.; Plut., *Per.* 22. Pugliese Carratelli, *Le vicende*, cit., p.27.

33 Graham, *Colony*, cit., p. 26 e sgg.

discontinuità della nuova fondazione rispetto al passato, mentre la scelta degli ecisti, entrambi ateniesi, mostra chiaramente il ruolo egemonico di Atene verso la colonia panellenica[34]. E' di particolare interesse l'organizzazione che fu data al corpo civico della colonia: esso fu diviso in dieci tribù costituite *iure sanguinis*, che rispecchiavano le diverse provenienze dei coloni: tre tribù ai peloponnesiaci (con i nomi di Arcade, Acaide ed Elea), tre alla Grecia centrale (Beotica, Amfictionide e Doride) e quattro ai coloni di origini ioniche (Iade, Atenaide, Euboide, Nesiote)[35]. Stando alle fonti, le leggi della città furono scritte da Protagora di Abdera, che non a torto buona parte della moderna dottrina considera come uno dei maggiori teorici del pensiero democratico del V secolo[36]. E' comunque verosimile che egli si sia almeno in parte ispirato, nella sua attività di legislatore, alle antiche leggi attribuite dalla tradizione a Caronda[37], ma mi pare significativo che – stando ad Eforo[38] – i Turini abbiano superato i Locresi per la precisione ed i dettagli della loro legislazione, il che, come ha ben dimostrato Domenico Musti, è indice di "un tipico atteggiamento mentale, che è tanto più democratico, quanto più soddisfa l'esigenza della precisione, determinazione, specificazione"[39]. L'impostazione della costituzione della nuova *polis* fu dunque di stampo democratico, anche se la lettura dei pochissimi frammenti rimastici della legislazione della città non sembra lasciare intendere che si sia trattato di una democrazia "radicale"[40]. Il fatto che Thurii sia sorta come democrazia, è sia pure indirettamente provato dalla stessa struttura urbanistica della città. Come si è da tempo riconosciuto, infatti, l'urbanistica ippodamea (della quale tracce, ancorché scarse, sono emerse negli scavi[41]) è espressione essa stessa di una sorta di "razionalismo democratico" con connotazioni egualitarie, poiché essa mirava ad assicurare agli edifici residenziali privati una disposizione uniformemente felice, senza privilegiarne alcuno[42]. Poste queste

[34] Segnalo che, secondo Ehrenberg (*Foundation of Thurii*, cit., p. 152 e sgg.), vi sarebbe stata, prima della fondazione di Thurii, la fondazione di una terza Sibari, nella quale si sarebbe consumato lo scontro fra i nuovi venuti e i sibariti.

[35] Diod. XII.11.

[36] Cfr. J.S. Morrison, *The Place of Protagoras in Athenian Public Life*, "CQ" 35 (1941), pp. 1-16; Ehrenberg, *Foundation of Thurii*, *cit.*, p. 168 e sgg.

[37] Her. Pont., fr. 150; Strab., *Geogr.* VI.1.8.

[38] *ap.* Strab., *Geogr.* VI.1.8.

[39] D. Musti, Demokratia, *Origini di un'idea*, Bari 1995, p. 65.

[40] V. Arangio-Ruiz, A. Olivieri, *Inscriptiones Grecae Siciliae et infimae Italiae ad ius pertinentes*, Milano 1925, p. 227-229; cfr. N.K. Rutter, *Diodorus and the Foundation of Thurii*, "*Historia*" 22 (1973), p. 167 e sgg.; Ehrenberg, *Foundation of Thurii*, cit., p. 166 e sgg.

[41] P.G. Guzzo, *I risultati degli scavi*, "*Atti e memorie della Società Magna Grecia*" XIII-XIV (1972-73), p. 38 e sgg.; F. Castagnoli, *Ancora sull'urbanistica di Thurii*, "*Parola del Passato*" 28 (1973), p. 220 e sgg.

[42] Castagnoli, *Topografia ed urbanistica*, "*Atti e memorie della Società Magna Grecia*" XIII-XIV (1972-73), p. 51 e sgg.; *Id.*, *Sull'urbanistica di Thurii*, "*Parola del Passato*" 26 (1971), p. 301 e sgg.

premesse, è lecito supporre che anche la distribuzione dei lotti di terra ebbe luogo secondo criteri isonomici: del resto, sappiamo da Aristotele che furono approvate leggi allo scopo di evitare, nel tempo, l'accentramento della proprietà in poche mani[43].

Sta di fatto che, nonostante quanto si è detto sin ora, né la *isomoiria* né in generale i principi isonomici che erano stati programmaticamente posti alla base della nuova fondazione[44] bastarono ad evitare che si producesse una grave *stasis*, che vide contrapposti i cittadini di origine sibarita a quelli provenienti dalla Grecia. Infatti, secondo quanto riferisce Diodoro[45], in breve tempo si giunse alla *stasis*, poiché i sibariti di origine pretesero di godere di speciali privilegi, quasi che vi fosse una differenza di *status* giuridico fra gli autoctoni e coloro che essi consideravano come "successivamente naturalizzati" (*tois ysteron prosgegrammenois politais*). Sembra quasi che i sibariti abbiano rifiutato di accedere alla logica di una fondazione coloniale, che crea *ex novo* una nuova *polis*[46], e considerassero essi stessi come cittadini di pieno diritto di una *polis* preesistente ed i nuovi venuti alla stregua di cittadini ascitizi (o forse *epoikoi*), con una ridotta capacità giuridica di diritto pubblico e, parimenti, con una meno piena personalità sacrale[47]; inoltre, essi rivendicavano i propri antichi diritti di proprietà sui fondi circostanti la città, pretendendo di escluderli dalla lottizzazione[48]. Pertanto, scrive Diodoro[49], pretesero per loro stessi le magistrature principali, tentarono di affermare la posizione privilegiata delle donne di stirpe sibarita nei culti cittadini loro riservati, lasciando alle nuove venute posizioni affatto secondarie ed infine si assegnarono le terre più vicine alla città, lasciando agli altri le più lontane. Per quanto riguarda quest'ultimo punto, è chiaro che le terre più vicine alla *polis* sono le migliori in quanto più facilmente difendibili (si consideri la costante situazione di conflittualità con i Crotoniati); inoltre, ed è questo un punto di non secondaria importanza, è evidente che gli assegnatari delle terre più vicine al centro politico avranno anche molto maggiore agio nel partecipare attivamente alla vita politica cittadina[50].

Sta di fatto che il comportamento dei sibariti provocò la violenta reazione degli altri coloni, i quali ne massacrarono buona parte ed espulsero quindi i sopravvissuti dalla città: essi finirono poi per fondare – recuperando l'antico nome della loro patria – una nuova Sibari sul Traente[51].

---

43 Arist., *Pol.* V. 7 (1307 a).

44 Lepore, *Problemi dell'organizzazione*, cit., p. 26.

45 Diod. XII. 11.1-2.

46 Moggi, *Organizzazione della chora, cit.*, p. 68.

47 S. Berger, *Revolution and Constitution in Thurii: Arist. Pol. 1307 a,b*, "*Eranos*" 88 (1990), p. 10.

48 Arist., *Pol.* V.3 (1303 a).

49 Diod., XII. 11.

50 Moggi, *Organizzazione della chora, cit.*, p. 72 e sgg.

51 Diod., XII.22.

L'espulsione dei Sibariti non bastò, comunque, ad assicurare la concordia nella colonia. Anche se le fonti presentano qualche problema interpretativo e non consentono una facile ricostruzione cronologica degli eventi, sappiamo che vi furono significativi mutamenti costituzionali accompagnati da tensioni all'interno della cittadinanza[52]. Tensioni che videro scontrarsi le diverse etnie presenti fra i coloni e che, ancora una volta, furono causate da problemi di redistribuzione delle terre e di assegnazione delle principali magistrature. Sappiamo infatti da Aristotele che l'ordine costituzionale della città mutò a causa del progressivo accentramento della proprietà fondiaria nelle mani di pochi[53]. Ciò avveniva, scrive Aristotele, "contro la legge" ed in certo modo in contrasto con l'estensione dell'elettorato passivo alle cariche cittadine anche ai meno abbienti. Sta di fatto che i meno abbienti presero le armi, cacciarono coloro che avevano esteso le loro proprietà oltre il consentito e procedettero ad una redistribuzione delle terre. Un nuovo scontro si produsse a causa della legge che stabiliva un intervallo minimo di cinque anni per la rielezione alla strategia: alcuni ex strateghi, valendosi della fama guadagnata sul campo si adoperarono per far abrogare la legge, e vi riuscirono nonostante l'opposizione dei magistrati (*simbuli*) che avevano il compito di controllare la legittimità costituzionale delle deliberazioni degli organi legislativi. Questa modifica, per quanto di portata apparentemente limitata, aprì la via – secondo quanto scrive Aristotele – al completo sovvertimento della costituzione cittadina[54].

Con ogni verosimiglianza, gli eventi riferiti da Aristotele devono essere collegati a nuove lacerazioni del corpo civico della colonia, ed in particolare a scontri fra la componente ionica ed ateniese e quella peloponnesiaca[55]. Si trattò di una contesa fra quelle parti della cittadinanza che ambivano ad affermare il proprio ruolo guida nella colonia, nel momento in cui si preparava lo scoppio della Guerra del Peloponneso. Non a caso, venne in questione anche l'identità stessa dell'ecista; i contrasti vennero sedati, ma quale fondatore della colonia fu indicato Apollo, in vece di Lampone[56]. Ebbe la meglio la componente peloponnesiaca e infatti la città assunse negli anni seguenti un orientamento moderatamente filospartano[57]. Lo stesso Alcibiade, nel 415, diretto a Sparta dopo la convocazione in patria per la vicenda della mutilazione delle erme, fece scalo a Thurii[58]. Ma la serie dei rivolgimenti non ebbe fine: poco tempo dopo, una nuova *stasis* portò dapprima all'espulsione di

[52] Berger, *Revolution*, *cit.*, p. 11 e sgg.
[53] Arist., *Pol.* V.7 (1307 a).
[54] Arist. *Pol.* V.7 (1307 b).
[55] Pugliese Carratelli, *Le vicende*, cit., p. 28.
[56] Diod., XII. 35. Ehrenberg, *Foundation of Thurii*, *cit.*, p. 164 e sgg.
[57] Pugliese Carratelli, *Le vicende*, cit., p. 29 e sgg.
[58] Thuc., VI.61.

cittadini anti-ateniesi[59] e successivamente, con un nuovo rovesciamente, all'epulsione di 300 filo-ateniesi, fra i quali spicca il nome di Lisia[60].

Non è certo questa la sede ove approfondire ulteriormente le complesse vicende politiche e costituzionali della polis di Thurii. Piuttosto, mi pare particolarmente significativa l'attenzione dedicata alla città da Aristotele nel libro quinto della Politica, quello dedicato alle cause dei rivolgimenti costituzionali ed ai mezzi con i quali preservare ciascuna costituzione[61]. Nei capitoli dedicati all'esame delle cause di trasformazione delle costituzioni in generale, il filosofo cita il caso di Thurii quale esempio di sovvertimento dovuto alla origine non omogenea della cittadinanza: "causa di *stasis*" scrive Aristotele "può essere la diversità di stirpe (*stasiôtikon de kai to mê omophylon*), finché non si riesce a raggiungere una situazione di concordia. Infatti, la città non nasce da una qualsiasi mescolanza di popolo e parimenti essa non nasce in un qualsiasi volgere di tempo. E' questo il motivo per cui coloro che si associarono altri popoli nella fondazione di una città o li coinvolsero successivamente, dopo averla fondata, per lo più furono afflitti da *staseis* (*diestasiasan*)"[62].

In conclusione, è forse eccessivo parlare *tout court* di crisi e disintegrazione della *polis* nelle colonie occidentali, come sosteneva una certa dottrina[63]. Tuttavia, la tesi più recente, che postula una diversa mentalità dei greci d'Occidente rispetto alla identificazione del cittadino ed alla individuazione, *per differentiam*, dell'altro (sia esso lo straniero oppure il barbaro), sicchè diverso sarebbe stato il modo di concepire il diritto di cittadinanza, maggiori la flessibilità, la mobilità e – in somma – la capacità di integrazione, anche tale tesi – si diceva – dev'essere considerata con attenzione e sottoposta a verifica in relazione ai singoli casi.

Non v'è dubbio alcuno che non solo in ambito coloniale e non solo in occidente diverse popolazioni si siano incontrate, conosciute e mescolate; tuttavia, il comportamento della componente sibarita di Thurii e le successive vicende della città, con la contesa emersa fra le due grandi componenti "etniche" della cittadinanza, ciascuna portatrice di diversi modelli politici e costituzionali e – oserei dire – di due diverse ideologie, provano a mio avviso che delineare una troppo forte contrapposizione fra Grecia continentale e colonie occidentali, limitandosi a considerare unicamente la pura e semplice concessione del diritto di cittadinanza, a prescindere dalla più generale articolazione della costituzione delle singole città e dai problemi della proprietà fondiaria, rischia di restituire un'immagine che non sempre corrisponde alla reale complessità dei fatti.

---

59 Thuc., VII.33; 57. Pugliese Carratelli, *Storia civile*, in *Megale Hellas*, Milano 1983, p. 68 e sgg.

60 Dion. Hal., *Lys.* 1; Plut., *Vit. Orat.*, 835 e. Cfr. Berger, *Revolution*, *cit.* p. 11.

61 Arist., *Pol.* V.1.1 (1301 a)

62 *Ibid.*, V. 2.10 (1303 a)

63 Cfr. ad es. Lepore, *I Greci in Italia*, cit. p. 72.

KAREN RØRBY KRISTENSEN (ODENSE)

INHERITANCE, PROPERTY, AND MANAGEMENT: GORTYNIAN FAMILY LAW REVISITED[1]

The role played by women in relation to the acquisition and management of property is endlessly emphasised in modern scholarship. Their precise role, however, is much debated. The question I am addressing is more or less what we may find embraced by the concept of *kyrieia* within fifth century Gortynian society. *Kyrieia* in Gortyn covers the capacity to control and dispose of property (ones own), to manage property on behalf of other members of the *oikos* (female members' property, and minor children's property) and to provide legal representation for women and children in the household. Strictly speaking the dependent labourers, whether termed *woikees* or *doloi*, were not included in the *kyrieia*. Economically *kyrieia* was expressed by the phrase '*karteron emen*' (that is the equivalent to the Athenian expression '*kyrion einai*'). The master of a dependent labourer was called *pastas*, and the term *pastas* only applied in this capacity. I shall return to the question of *kyrieia* in relation to the dependent population at the end of my paper.

I have argued elsewhere that all Gortynian women in fact had a *kyrios*. He would be the woman's father, brother, husband or son.[2] The alleged freedom of Gortynian women whether in respect to non-economic matters or mattes of economics is to be observed only in marginal situations. In other words, women acting in their own right are to be found when no *kyrios* existed or when their *kyrios* violated the confidence entrusted to him. The most clear-cut example of the former concerns the divorcee during divorce proceedings. The famous oath of denial in III.5-12 of the Law Code[3] serves as a substitute for a process of litigation between her *kyrios* and her previous husband. The text is as follows:

But as regards things, which she denies (the judge) shall decree that the woman take an oath of denial by Artemis, before the statue of the Archeress in the Amyklaian temple.

---

1 Whilst the available space does not allow for a thorough comment on Alberto Maffi's response, I shall confine myself to clarify one point only. This concerns no. 2b in Maffi's response, see below in n.7. The remainder, I shall return to in future papers.

2 Kristensen 1994.

3 All references are columns of the Law Code = IC IV 72, unless otherwise indicated. All translations are from the edition of the Law Code by R.F. Willetts, besides slight modifications of XII.13-17. The translation of II.16-20 is my own, though.

The circumstance for this oath is further elaborated in the supplementary section of the Code in XI.46-55.

Some women apparently had a relative as *kyrios*. We learn in II. 16-20 that

If someone assaults a free woman under the guardianship of a relative with the intent of forceful intercourse, he shall pay 10 staters if a witness testifies.

Many interpretations exist with respect to this law. Amongst these, we find the suggestion that the law dealt with the attempted rape of an heiress.[4] However, besides the problem relating to whatever issue the witness was to testify (the status of the relative as *kyrios* for the woman, or the attempted rape)[5] I believe that this law was not intended for heiresses. It encompassed, however, other cases of free women under the *kyrieia* of a relative. II.16-20 could be applied to all women who had no 'natural' *kyrios*, that is to say no father, no brother, no husband and no son. If we do not distinguish between, on the one hand, a biological father, brother or son, and, on the other hand, these relatives in a legal-social capacity we would, nonetheless, end up with only heiresses. Yet if we were to interpret the free woman as an heiress we would have more problems to answer than we would solve. A very evident problem is to explain why rape or seduction of an heiress only amounts to a tenth of the value of the fine for the same offence if the woman were not an heiress. One could argue that the offence was even more serious in case of an heiress; that is to say for her relatives. If an heiress became pregnant and gave birth to a child, she would have an heir to her property. There would no longer be any need for a groom-elect. The Law Code does, however, provide a hint to the meaning of the law of II.16-20. Within the Code, we find a number of free women who only had maternal relatives in a legal sense. These could be the offspring of a mixed marriage – the father would then be a dependent labourer who could not represent his daughter. Assuming the *dolos*-father, although he had married a free woman, still had a *pastas* like all dependent labourers in Gortyn we cannot expect this *pastas* in his capacity as *pastas* representing a free women in a case of rape. By analogy to the conditions of debt-bondage, it becomes clear that the *pastas* was the term for the master of a dependent labourer (or for the women and children of his household). In connection with debt

[4] See Gernet (1955) 51-59 (arguing that this was a case of rape of an heiress, whilst we should pay attention to the preposition *epi* of *epiperetai*), and Willetts (1967) 58-59 (who holds this was a case of attempted seduction of an heiress, since *kartei* is omitted in this law). Cautadella (1973) holds that the offence is committed under the supervision of the relative acting as guardian. The witness was then to give evidence of the role played by the guardian in the case. Finally, Maffi (1984) and (1997) 24-29, holds that the law deals (interpreting *epiperetai* as *epipheretai* in the sense of 'respond to an accusation') with a mitigation of sentence, which is caused by the complicity of the guardian of the woman. Along these lines, see most recently also Link (2004). I find, nonetheless, the suggestion as 'make an attempt upon with force' as the sense of *epiperetai* the most favourable.

[5] See Headlam (1892-93) 48-69, especially p. 59 (witnesses were only testifying to procedural or contractual matters). This is refuted in Gagarin (1984) who holds that II.16-20 is an example of a witness testifying to the facts of a case.

bondage, we learn that a free *katakeimenos* did not acquire a *pastas* but a *katathemenos*, whilst the *dolos* who became a *katakeimenos* would retain his *pastas* along with an additional master, the *katathemenos*.[6] Even if a free woman with a free mother and a dependent father had a brother, it is far from certain he would be able to represent her in court. He would certainly not be a citizen, but an *apetairos* somebody who was not admitted to an *etaireia* for the lack of paternal relatives.[7] In addition, it is striking that rape or seduction of a member of an *apetairos'* household amounts to the same as the fine in II.16-20: 10 staters.

Other women to whom this law could apply were women who were rejected by their fathers at birth when born after divorce. We learn in III.44-49:

If a wife who is separated (by divorce) should bear a child, (they) are to bring it to the husband at his house in the presence of three witnesses; and if he should not receive it, the child shall be in the mother's power either to rear or expose;

Whether this really was an option for a woman to raise a child on her own need not concern us here. The legal implication does, however. If a family for whatever reason chooses to let a daughter keep her rejected child that girl or boy would not automatically have a *kyrios*. The relative of II.16-20 could, nonetheless, be the child's maternal grandfather or uncle. In reality the Gortynians made use of three kinds of *kyrioi*: a 'natural' *kyrios* (father, brother, son or husband – the latter two obviously applied to women only), an 'appointed' *kyrios* that is a relative as in II.16-20, and a 'nominated' *kyrios*, namely the evasive *orpanodikastas* of XII. 6-19.

Did an heiress have a *kyrios*? To answer this question we need to consider on the one hand the heiress ripe for marriage, on the other the minor heiress. Much of the legislation on the heiress deals with the minor heiress. She was by definition deprived of a *kyrios* (no father, no brother) and as minor obviously also without a husband or son. It is not clear whether she was to be raised by her paternal family, if a groom-elect existed. We are told that the paternal relatives should be in charge of the administration of the heiress' property, whilst she would receive half the income (VIII.42-46). She was, nonetheless to be raised by her mother or her maternal relatives, if no groom-elect existed, being in control of her own property (VIII.47-53). We find, however, this to be modified in the supplementary legislation in case no groom-elect existed, or she did not enjoy the protection offered by the *orpanodikastai* (whom we may suspect to be a rather novel institution in Gortynian society). She was to be raised by her mother, whilst

---

6 See Kristensen (2004).

7 It is true that an *apetairos* could offer legal representation to female members of his household (see Maffi'a response no. 2b). Maffi's objection is, however, only valid on the presumption that this son of a mixed marriage automatically would become head of his mother's *oikos* and, thus, *kyrios* for his mother and sister(s). At least before the son became of age, these women would need other legal representation. In addition, one may wonder if the son of a mixed marriage could replace his father as head of the family, although his father could not represent his family legally.

The prescribed paternal and maternal relatives shall administer the property and the income to the best of their ability until she is married. (XII.13-17).

It seems, however, far from certain that the minor heiress had one specific person appointed as her *kyrios*. She had, nonetheless, clearly a range of relatives to conduct the management of her property. It seems likely that one or several of these would act as her *kyrioi* if needed. We may consider the fact that the relatives of the heiress assisted in arranging her marriage, in at least two respects: if the groom-elect resisted marrying the heiress (VII.40-45) and no one from the *pula* was willing to marry her, or if there were no groom-elects (VIII.13-17). Her relatives would assist her if needed. An heiress' admission to refuse to marry a groom-elect also supports the *ad hoc*-based nature of *kyrieia*. In other words, before she became heiress her father or brother would be her *kyrios* (as is evident from VIII.20-30),[8] and at the time of her marriage, her husband. In between, she could rely on the help from her relatives as '*ad hoc kyrioi*' or possibly from the otherwise evasive *orpanodikastai*. A minor heiress did not have a specific *kyrios* until the time of her marriage.[9]

The father of an heiress could leave an indebted estate to her (that is the law of IX.1-24).

We learn in IX.1-7 that

If someone owing money should leave behind an heiress, she either personally or through her paternal and maternal relatives shall mortgage or sell to the value of the debt, and the purchase and mortgage shall be legal. (IX.1-7).

The last statement underlines the unusual nature of the act. Obviously, heiresses did not commonly sell or mortgage their property. They may not legally have been able to, unless out-standing debts were to be paid. We may compare to the case of the divorcee who was accused by her husband for stealing. Her oath settled the matter before she legally returned to her father. The heiress could act on her own (or choose the assistance of her relatives) to settle debts, before the property was legally hers and she was to marry in due course. There is, thus, the possibility that the heiress only could engage in one particular economic transaction – that of covering the debt of her father. The law also stipulates the consequences if either her relatives or her husband (we may assume the law was intended for both situations: the minor as well as the married heiress) violated the economic responsibility entrusted to them. If they did, she would be *kyria* of her own property. The law is parallel to VI.2-46 to which I shall return shortly.

Like the heiress, other women acquired property as inheritance. The year when Kyllos and his colleagues from the Aithaleus-*startos* held the office as *kosmoi*,

[8] See Maffi (1987) for an interpretation of VIII.20-30.

[9] We may wonder if that mattered. Most likely the property of the minor heiress could not be subject to sale, nor to any kind of transaction of mortgage. Despite her freedom of choice of husband, she would have to give a rejected groom-elect half her property. Additionally, although her property in a sense belonged to her, she also had an obligation towards her future sons.

statutory female inheritance rights were introduced in Gortyn. It has been argued that this meant a deterioration of the rights for women, as has the opposite case – that women's rights were improved.[10] Without resorting to the arguments beyond what is found in the Code itself, it is clear that dowry existed in the pre-Kyllonian Gortynian society. That is in fact what we learn in V.1-9, which is the law introducing statutory female inheritance rights:

Whatever woman has no property either by gift from father or brother or by pledge or by inheritance as (enacted) when the Aithalian startos, Kyllos and his colleagues, formed the kosmos, such women are to obtain their portion; but there shall be no ground for actions against previous female beneficiaries.

It is evident that some women gained from inheritance becoming statutory. Since an upper limit was imposed on the female share of the inheritance, it is equally evident that others lost compared to what they might have received prior to the law. In addition, an upper limit was also imposed on gifts to women otherwise not entitled to inherit (wives and mothers) at 100 staters. However, the consequences for the redistribution of wealth within Gortynian society would not have been affected significantly. The law regulated the sizes of female property, which had an impact on the size of male property. Every *oikos* would absorb female contributions, which in some cases were returned; in others, they were part of the new redistribution of inheritance amongst children of both sexes. This property would then form part of the sons' *oikoi* and become daughters' contributions to their husbands' *oikoi* as well. Eventually the property ended up as inheritance divided amongst children of both sexes.

The Gortynian man was *kyrios* for the women in his household: his wife, his widowed mother, divorced, widowed or immature sisters or daughters, and finally his immature sons. It meant clearly that he would represent them in legal matters as long as they were members of his household. Their individual properties were also to some extent within his *kyrieia.*

The law in IV.23-V.1 commences stipulating the status of the properties in the *oikos*:

The father shall be in control of the children and the division of the property and the mother of her own property. So long as they are living, there is no necessity to make a division; but if anyone should be fined, the one fined shall have his share apportioned to him as is written. (IV.23-31).

This is further elaborated in the law of VI.2-46: In VI. 2-12 we learn that:

As long as the father lives, no one shall offer to purchase any of the paternal property from a son nor take out a mortgage on it; but whatever (the son) himself

[10] In respect to a weakening of women's rights (and strengthen of the power of the *kyrios*) see for example Gagarin (1994), whilst for example Schaps (1979) 58-60 and Link (1994) 53-58, 62-66, argue that *kyrieia* was abolished in the Law Code. Maffi (2003) 187-201 in discussing the point of view presented by Link dismisses this interpretation of the condition of Gortynian *kyrieia*. Mostly I agree with Maffi (2003).

may have acquired or inherited, let him sell, if he wishes. Nor shall the father sell or mortgage the possessions of his children, whatever they have themselves acquired or inherited. Nor shall the husband sell or pledge those of his wife, nor the son those of his mother.

In VI.31-36, we learn that:

If a mother dies leaving children, the father is to be in the control of the mother's property, but he shall not sell or mortgage unless the children consent and are of age (i.e. dromees).

There is a small adjustment to this law: the mother's debt was to be covered from the maternal inheritance, whilst the father's debt was to be levied from the paternal inheritance as we learn in the supplementary section of the Code: XI.31-45.

Except for one single case, children had no claim on their parents' property before it became their inheritance: if someone[11] was fined that child was entitled to the prescribed share of the inheritance. The unpleasant alternative would be to enter the state of debt bondage, for example. On the other hand, the head of the household (whether in the capacity as father, husband or son) had no rights to sell or mortgage property, apart from what was legally his own. Several times, it is emphasised that the management of property is to be transferred to the rightful owner (wife, mother, or children) if the *kyrios* exceeds the powers entrusted to him. A father could not legally dispose of his children's maternal inheritance before they consented and were *dromees*! Does this mean that a man was not legally mature before he became a *dromeus*, or was the state as *ebion* sufficient for a young man to become a *kyrios* in his own right? We are facing some inconsistencies relating to the terms *ebion* on the one hand and *dromeus* on the other.[12] The term *dromeus* is otherwise found in the Law Code as qualifying witnesses along with *eleutheros*.[13] There are, however,

---

[11] Although the participle *toi atamenoi* is in the masculine, we may assume that daughters were included as well. Women could also be fined, see for example IV.8-14: if a divorced woman exposes her baby before it is presented according to what is written, she is to pay 50 staters in case of a freeborn child, in case of a slave-born child 25 staters, if she is convicted.

[12] Tzifopoulos (1998), argues that *dromees* constituted yet another age group: 'By becoming a *dromeus* the Cretan was perhaps only entering adulthood that entailed certain privileges mainly inheritance rights, but not yet full citizenship.' (p.155). He holds that '*dromees*' in a sense served as a negative qualification. The cases where *dromees* could appear as witnesses were limited to those involving matters of inheritance, whilst non-qualified witnesses meant 'adult citizens with full rights.' (p.154). I do not find his argument at all conclusive, although I must admit to his critique (p. 154n50) of my assumption that all witnesses were *dromees* (1994) 11: I do, however, believe they were, as it has become clear above. *Dromees* served as a condition of the requirement for witnesses. See further Maffi (2003) 163-166.

[13] Witnesses are required to be *dromees eleutheroi* in I.41-42, III.21-22, and V.52-54, whilst in XI.53-55, the witness was required to have been *dromeus* for at least fifteen years. It is not mentioned that he should be an *eleutheros*, but it is implicit in the requirement of being a *dromeus*.

far more examples when witnesses are not qualified at all. Some of these refer to the very existence of one or more witnesses and, therefore these would not need any qualification.[14] In several cases, we would, nonetheless, expect witnesses to be qualified. The number of these cases exceeds the amount of cases where qualification of witnesses exists.[15] The explanation for this is rather that need arose for specifying who could serve as witnesses. It hardly constituted a difference in specific requirement for the witnesses in relation to the subject matter of a particular case.[16] There is one puzzling example where the witnesses were to be *ebiontes* (in IX.46-47) instead of *dromees*. In the law on agreement of commerce we learn that in cases exceeding 100 staters three adult witnesses were to testify, two in cases exceeding 10 staters and in lesser cases only one witness was required to testify.

As part of the law on adoption, it is stated that neither a woman nor an *anebos* can adopt or can be adopted. There are two problems: why is the minor termed *anebos* instead of *apodromos*, and what is the sense of *ampaineththo*? Are we to take it as active or passive?[17] If we take it as passive, I do not need to reflect further, why an *anebos* cannot be adopted. The adoption law in Gortyn did not include posthumously adoptions. Contrary, it clearly had other purposes than provide the heir to the *oikos*.[18] An adoption could be annulled including a small compensation paid to the rejected adoptee. Adoption could also be upheld even though legitimate children of either sex were born. In respect to inheritance, it meant for the adoptee that the effect of his status as heir was diminished. He would then become a 'female' heir receiving the same portion, which was allotted to women and had no further obligations towards family and cult and so on. The explanation for this peculiarity is the dual purpose of adoption. Adoption also served the purpose of admitting non-citizens to the citizenry. Such persons were embraced by the evasive expression *opo ka til lei* 'from whatever source one wishes' – *anpansin emen* 'one may adopt'.[19]

---

14 This is at issue in I.13-14, I.20-21, II.19-20, XI.26-28, and finally in X.31-32, as it is in IC IV 41 V.10-11 and IC IV 46B.4-5.

15 This concerns the proclamation of the capture of a seducer (whether free or servile) in II. 28-33 as well as it is the case in relation to the presentation of a child born after its parents divorce (III.44-IV.7). In addition, no qualification is attached to witnesses in IC IV 41 II.9-10, IC IV 47.22, IC 75A.1-3, 6-8 (= IC IV 81.4-5, 9-11). In IX.24-40 the witnesses are indirectly qualified, namely as the heirs of the deceased.

16 There is one exception: the case of XI.46-55 where the witness is required to be *pentekaidekadromeus*. This law is part of the supplementary section of the Code and deals with the divorcee's oath of denial. The sensitivity of the matter (a woman's oath of denial settling a legal issue) is stressed in two respects. On the one hand, a specific requirement is attached to the witness, on the other hand, the fact that a further piece of legislation was needed, namely this particular law.

17 See Maffi (2003) 202-204.

18 Contra Maffi (1997) who disregards the *inter vivos* aspect of the adoption law.

19 Some scholars interpret this clause as embracing only citizens (for example Maffi (1997) 75-76, and (2003) 201, or only members of the same phyle, see Koerner (1993) 549), whereas others believe members of the dependent population (Nomima II (1995) no. 40

Whilst women probably were *eleutherai* regardless of their father's legal status (that is whether he was a citizen or an *apetairos*), men could not become citizens without a paternal relative admitting them to an *etaireia*. A man could, for example, choose to adopt his sister's non-citizen offspring.[20]

If we are to take *ampaineththo* in the active sense, that is 'can adopt' we need to seek an explanation why the minor is an *anebos* instead of an *apodromos*. Whilst the Gortynians in the Law Code applied two sets of age distinctions (one biological, another political), it seems, nonetheless, most logical that the non-reproductive aspect of the minor is emphasised. Since the *etaireia* is involved, the political aspect is stressed in the first place.

Beside this evidence, we find age terminology only in relation to the marriage of an heiress. The crucial piece of legislation is VII.29-40:

As long as the groom-elect or the heiress is too young to marry, the heiress is to have the house, if there is one, and the groom-elect is to obtain half the revenue from everything; but if the groom elect should not wish to marry the heiress, though they both are of an age to marry, on the ground that he is still an minor, all the property and the produce shall be at the disposal of the heiress until he marries her.

The law continues in stipulating the legal action on part of the relatives, if the groom-elect was a *dromeus* refusing to marry the heiress. It is evident that an *ebion* could marry, although he still was an *apodromos*. It is equally evident that the intention behind the law encouraged him not to postpone the marriage to the time where he became a *dromeus*. The law favoured only the delay of the minor groom-elect. We cannot, however, argue that an *ebion* became *kyrios* in his own right while still an *apodromos*, or that young men commonly married before they were *dromees*. The case of an heiress was in many respects out of the ordinary. Although an heiress could denounce her groom-elect, her property was generally subject to great interest, particularly who would become the father of her children.

We are left with one case where a legal action is conducted by persons who were not *dromees* or *ebiontes* qualified as *poliateuontes*.[21] The context provided this criterion of *poliateuontes* in IX.46-47. I maintain then that a man was not legally mature before he reached the age where he became a *dromeus*. The precise age remains obscure.

---

p. 146), or even strangers (Link (1994) 55-59) were included as well). Most logically, however, the adoptee would have to be free as well as Gortynian. A rejected adoptee was to receive his compensation from the *mnamon* of the *ksenios kosmos*. This fact further supports that a potential adoptee could be a non-citizen. At least it is clear that an annulled adoption meant dismissal of the adoptee from the citizenry. He might of course, if initially a citizen, become member of the citizenry again through admission to his original family.

[20] Ogden (1996) 264-266 has suggested this previously.

[21] In IC IV 51 (which is a fragment stipulating conditions relating to the swearing of oaths) we find *êbiontes* qualified as *poliateuontes*.

There are several examples where persons within the *kyrieia* of another suddenly were granted the power as *kyrios* over their own property: the wife, the mother, the minor children, and the heiress. Children would become *kyrioi* over their own property, if the father illegally disposed of their maternal inheritance or he remarried (VI.37-39, and VI. 44-46). A wife and a mother became *kyria* if a husband or a son respectively exceeded the rights of management attempting either to sell or to mortgage property (VI. 9-24). The course of this action making non-legally mature persons *kyrioi* of their own property did not come about automatically, but involved court-proceedings. As it is the case a number of times, we lack information concerning the procedural measures. Whilst the women or minor children were not compensated beyond the simple restoration of their property, the purchaser or recipient of the mortgage was compensated with twice the amount of the goods in question, and an additional compensation for potential damages worth the simple value. Non-retroactive force of the law is stated in IV.24-25. We find the parallel situation in the law of IX.1-24 concerning the heiress. Both laws were most likely enacted making previous custom indisputable as the consequence of the introduction of female inheritance rights. This seems also to be the case with IV.23-31 stipulating the status of the properties within the *oikos*. Obviously, we can imagine a situation where the *kyrios* had extensive rights over the properties entrusted to him, but there is no certain indication that this was the case in the period immediately prior to the enactment during Kyllos' and his colleagues' time of office. Rather we should see the shaping and adjustment of *kyrieia* as a gradual process developing over time. We can for example observe how the segregation of the property of husband and wife is further emphasised, as it is articulated in XI.31-45: claimants could not levy execution on the maternal property to cover the debt of the husband or vice versa, nor could a husband use the property of his deceased wife to cover debt of his own.

Property could then be transferred into the *kyrieia* of a wife, a mother, minor children or an heiress. Whatever implication this had for the practical management of the property remains obscure. We may guess that new *kyrioi* were appointed (for a wife or a mother this could be their previous *kyrios*). There is also the possibility that the property in question became indisposed for sale or mortgage until the owner or the *kyrios* had been replaced. In other words, a wife's property as well as a mother's property was indisposed until it became the inheritance of the children. Children's property became transferable when, in case of girls, they got married; in case of boys when they became of age. There is, however, another possibility. In several cases, we learn that relatives were acting on behalf of women: for example, when a divorcee had given birth to a child, or an heiress had trouble getting married. This does not necessarily mean that a relative was appointed *kyrios* for a woman (as the case of II.16-20) but it would serve the immediate purpose of de facto property management. We cannot decide whether or not the *kyrios* was deprived of more than his capacity to manage property – would he for example also loose his right to represent the woman legally? That was probably not the case. The consequence of this would be that a father could not arrange the marriage for his own daughter, or apprehend his wife's seducer. We may, then, suggest a fourth category of *kyrioi*: those appointed on a strictly *ad hoc* basis amongst a woman's or a child's maternal uncles or cousins for the sole purpose of economic transactions.

So far I have addressed *kyrieia* within the citizenry. Gortynian family law did also embrace a dependent population whether termed *woikees* or *doloi*. It is quite evident that all legal representation required the *pastas* of a dependent man or woman. Apprehension of a seducer involved the *pastas* (II.42-43). Presentation of a child born after the dissolution of a *woikees*-marriage required apparently the *pastas* (although we cannot decide unequivocally that he was to be one of those presenting the child, see III.52-IV.3). A servile *katakeimenos* retained his *pastas* during debt-bondage and so on. Yet the organisation of the families in the dependent population is similar to the citizenry's family-structure. The *pastas* of the children's father would also become their *pastas*.[22] Dissolution of marriage implied the same procedures: the *woikea* went back along with whatever she had brought with her into the marriage (although no surplus were evidently the case, IV.40-44). We cannot know if she shared the *pastas* of her husband during marriage or she retained the *pastas* of her father. We may argue equally well for both cases. One example exists where the servile person acted in her own rights. This is the case of II.11-16. If the *dola endothidia* was raped, she enjoyed preference in oath. Whilst the compensation was extremely low if she was no longer a virgin, her preference in oath provided probably far more protection.[23] She could point her finger at the rapist, and did not need her *pastas* to settle the matter of guilt, though she would most certainly need him with respect to the compensation. There is, nonetheless, one question of *kyrieia* in respect to the dependent population. Who managed the property of a *woikeus*?[24] Like free women, *woikees* could be fined for offences committed in their own rights, whilst illegal actions committed on their master's order were an offence on part of the master. Cattle owned by *woikees* were excluded from sons' inheritance. In respect to *kyrieia*, we may benefit from the comparison to free women. The property of a *woikeus* was legally his, consisting of moveable property (cattle and contents of his house). However, if he for example were to sell his cattle, he would most likely need his *pastas*' legal representation.

In conclusion, we may observe many analogous cases within the Gortynian *kyrieia*-structure. We can identify several kind of *kyrioi*: natural, appointed, nominated and those serving on *ad hoc* basis. It is evident that compared to Athens we are facing a limited *kyrieia* in Gortyn where women, children, heiresses and

[22] We may infer this from IV.3-6, and IV.18-23.

[23] The right of preference in oath swearing was only given in special circumstances. Either one of the parties did not enjoy full legal rights or the matter has to be solved urgently. See further III.49-52, IV.6-8, IC IV 41 II.12-16, IC IV 42B and IC IV 45.

[24] For example Link (1994) 39-41claims that no real property rights were at issue here. He regards the property of a *woikeus* as a *peculium* with clear reference to the Roman world.

dependent labourers in some cases were able to act in their own rights.[25] The law presented a few alternatives to proper litigation: oath of denial or preference in oaths. The most striking feature of Gortynian law is a paradox. On the one hand, we find very sharp definitions for categories of property and legal status; on the other hand, a remarkable flexibility was embedded in the system.

BIBLIOGRAPHY

Cautadella, M.R. (1973) 'L'interpretazione della parole ἀκεύοντος κηδεστᾶ e il ruolo del tutore nel codice di Gortina. Col.II.17-20' *RIL* 107: 799-809.

Gagarin, M. (1984) 'Witnesses in the Gortyn Laws' *GRBS* 25: 345-349.

Gagarin, M. (1994) 'The Economic Status of Women in the Gortyn Code: Retroactivity and Change' in G. Thür, *Symposion 1993* Köln: 61-72.

Gernet, L. (1955) *Droit et société dans la Grèce ancienne* Paris.

Guarducci, M. (1950) *Inscriptiones Creticae IV* Rome.

Headlam, J.W. (1892-93) 'The Procedure of the Gortynian Inscriptions', *JHS* 13: 48-69.

Koerner, R. (1993) *Inschriftliche Gesetzestexte der frühen griechischen Polis* Köln.

Kristensen, K.R. (1994) 'Men, Women and Property in Gortyn: the *karteros* of the Law Code' *C & M* 45: 5-26.

Kristensen, K.R. (2004) 'Gortynian Debt Bondage. Some New Considerations on IC IV 41 IV-VII, 47, and 72 I.56-II.2, X.25-32' *ZPE* 149: 73-79.

Link, S. (1994) *Das griechische Kreta. Untersuchungen zu seiner staatlichen und gesellschaftlichen Entwicklung vom 6. bis zum 4. Jahrhundert v. Chr.* Stuttgart.

Link, S. (2004) 'Die Nötigung des Mündels in Gortyn (IC IV 72, col. 2, 16-20)' *DIKE* 7: 169-178.

Maffi, A. (1984) 'Le "Leggi sulle donne" IC.4.72. 16-20, Plut., Sol. 23.1-2' *Sodalitas*: 1553-1567.

Maffi, A. (1987) 'Le mariage de la patrôoque "donnée" dans le Code de Gortyne (col. VIII.20-30)' *RD* 65 (4): 507-525.

Maffi, A.(1997) *Il diritto di famiglia nel Codice di Gortyna.* Milano.

Maffi, A. (2003) 'Studie recenti sul Codice di Gortyna' *Dike* 6: 161-226.

Ogden, D. (1996) *Greek Bastardy* Oxford.

[25] Edward Cohen made a comment on my application of 'limited *kyrieia*' and referred to a recent paper by D.M. Schaps (1998). Schaps has many interesting observations in respect to the freedom of Athenian women. His paper does not, however, alter the understanding of the general legal condition (including *kyrieia*) of Athenian women. I maintain then that legally Gortynian *kyrieia* was limited in comparison to Athenian. This is not to say that women were freer in Gortyn than they were in Athens. Limited *kyrieia* refers to the fact that in Gortyn some women could legally act in their own rights, namely women who were in a marginal position one way or the other.

Schaps, D. (1979) *Economic Rights of Women in ancient Greece* Edinburgh.

Schaps, D.M. (1998) 'What was Free about Free Athenian Women?' *TAPhA* 128: 161-188.

Tzifopoulos, Y.Z. (1998) ''Hemerodromoi' and Cretan 'Dromeis': Athletes or Military Personnel? The Case of the Cretan Philonides' *Nikophoros* 11: 137-170.

Van Effenterre, H. & Ruzé, F. (1995) *Nomima II* Rome.

Willetts, R.F. (1967) *The Law Code of Gortyn* Berlin.

ALBERTO MAFFI (MILANO)

RISPOSTA A KAREN R. KRISTENSEN

1. Al centro della relazione di Karen Kristensen sta ancora una volta un tema che è stato oggetto negli ultimi dieci anni di un animato dibattito (a cui hanno contribuito in particolare, oltre alla relatrice e a me stesso, Michael Gagarin e Stefan Link): cioè se nella Gortina dell'età del CdG le donne siano sottoposte a tutela. Kristensen ed io siamo convinti che in linea di principio anche le donne gortinie, così come quelle ateniesi, siano sottoposte a una forma di *kyrieia*; Link lo nega. Il problema nasce naturalmente dal fatto che il testo delle iscrizioni non menziona mai in maniera esplicita il *kyrios* delle donne. Nella sua relazione Kristensen fa un passo ulteriore e ritiene che si possano identificare diversi tipi di *kyrios*: "naturale", da identificare con padre, fratello, figlio o marito; "designato", da identificare con un parente in linea materna nei casi in cui non esista un *kyrios* "naturale"; "istituzionale" (nominated) da identificare nei fantomatici *orpanodikastai*; infine "specifico", incaricato di compiere determinati atti giuridici relativi al patrimonio della donna senza però sottrarre il potere sulla persona della donna al *kyrios* "naturale". Infine Kristensen fa una concessione alla tesi contraria, ammettendo che in alcuni casi le donne siano sottratte alla tutela muliebre, precisamente quando il *kyrios* non è identificabile o comunque il suo intervento non è previsto, oppure quando il *kyrios* ha violato i suoi doveri.

2. Io non credo che nel diritto gortinio si possa identificare una pluralità di figure istituzionalizzate di tutore, come suppone la relatrice. Credo piuttosto che ci siano delle situazioni in cui la tutela di particolari interessi induce il legislatore a introdurre discipline speciali, che in qualche modo derogano alla struttura della *kyrieia*.

Riprendiamo rapidamente alcuni dei casi esaminati nella relazione.

a) Col. III 5-12 e col. XI 46-55. K. ritiene che il giuramento della donna, che afferma di non aver sottratto beni del marito in occasione del divorzio, non sia da considerare "as a substitute for a process of litigation between her *kyrios* and her previous husband". Il giuramento svolge qui il ruolo di prova legale che il CdG prevede nel caso in cui prescriva al giudice di *dikazein*. Quindi possiamo tranquillamente supporre che la donna stia in giudizio assistita dal suo *kyrios*, ma presti personalmente il giuramento richiesto dalla legge. La stessa cosa si ha nel caso della

schiava *endothidia* (col. II 15-16): qui è evidente che il giuramento della schiava funge da prova decisoria, ma il processo sarà stato intentato dal suo padrone.
b) Col. II 16-20. Questo passo resta uno dei più difficili da interpretare. Secondo K. si tratta di una donna che non ha un *kyrios* "naturale"; il *kadestas* di cui parla la norma sarà dunque un collaterale dalla parte di madre. L'ipotesi di K. è che si possa trattare della figlia di uno schiavo che si sia unito ad una donna libera recandosi nella casa di lei. Dunque anche se avesse un fratello, questi non sarà un cittadino di pieno diritto, ma soltanto un *apetairos*, il quale, in quanto *apetairos*, non potrebbe rappresentarla in giudizio. Per questo il *kadestas* deve essere un parente da parte di madre. Questa motivazione non mi sembra giustificata: un *apetairos* può benissimo rappresentare in giudizio una donna della sua famiglia (tanto è vero che in col. II si parla della donna di un *apetairos*). Tuttavia sembra anche a me probabile che sia il nonno o lo zio materno ad esercitare la *kyrieia* (sempre che abbiano approvato il comportamento della rispettiva figlia o sorella senza costringerla a esporre il o la neonata).

c) Il caso successivo esaminato da K. è quello dell'ereditiera: chi è il *kyrios* dell'ereditiera? Se ci sono dei parenti paterni, l'amministrazione dei beni ereditari spetterà a costoro (col. VIII 43-44 *karterons ēmēn tas ergasias*); altrimenti, se viene allevata presso la madre (che nel frattempo sarà ritornata presso la famiglia d'origine), allora saranno i parenti paterni e materni ad amministrare i beni ereditari. Questa singolare disciplina induce K. a identificare una specifica categoria di "ad hoc *kyrioi*". In realtà queste norme hanno di mira non la tutela della ereditiera, bensì del patrimonio ereditario: si parla di *ergasia* e si usa il verbo *artuen* (col. XII 16). In particolare dalla norma di col. IX 1-7, che sembra autorizzare l'ereditiera a disporre da sola dei beni ereditari, K. trae la conseguenza che in questo caso la donna possa veramente agire senza l'autorizzazione o l'assistenza di alcuno, purché gli atti di disposizione siano finalizzati al pagamento dei debiti ereditari. A parte il fatto che K. ritiene che la norma si applichi anche all'ereditiera sposata e alla minorenne, cosa che tenderei ad escludere, io credo che l'alternativa posta dalla norma si riferisca nel primo caso all'ereditiera maggiorenne (*ēbionsa*) e nel secondo caso alla minorenne. Il che può essere considerato un indizio del fatto che la donna, quando si tratta di disporre dei propri beni a favore di persone estranee alla famiglia, interviene personalmente al compimento del negozio insieme al *kyrios* (nel caso dell'ereditiera insieme agli amministratori del patrimonio ereditario). La mia conclusione è dunque che l'ereditiera costituisce un caso particolare, nel senso che non ha un *kyrios* in senso proprio perché non ha nemmeno un patrimonio proprio.

d) Lascio da parte il caso dell'adozione e passo ad esaminare il caso in cui il marito o il figlio dispongano in modo arbitrario del patrimonio della moglie o della madre (col. VI 9-31). In questo caso la norma stabilisce che i beni *epi tai matri ēmēn k'epi tai gynaiki* (ll. 17-18). Come interpretare questa terminologia? A me pare che nel testo di K. vi sia una certa ambiguità: a volte parla di "restoration of their property", ma altrove di trasferimento del "management of property to the rightful owner" (cioè la moglie o la madre) o di casi "where persons within the *kyrieia* of another suddenly were granted the power as *kyrios* over their own property". In ogni caso K. si chiede quali conseguenze aveva questo atto arbitrario e riprovato del marito o del figlio. O veniva nominato un nuovo *kyrios* (che poteva essere il precedente, ad es. il padre o il fratello della donna sposata); oppure il bene in questione veniva sottratto ad ogni ulteriore atto di disposizione, in pratica fino alla morte della donna e all'apertura della sua successione; oppure, infine, subentravano dei parenti della donna con funzioni limitate alla semplice amministrazione dei beni di lei, senza però privare il marito, ad es. del potere di arrestare il seduttore della moglie o il padre del potere di dare in moglie la figlia. Nessuna di queste soluzioni mi sembra plausibile: non la prima, perché la legge tace su un trasferimento della *kyrieia* come sanzione dell'atto di disposizione illecito; non la seconda, perché, almeno nel caso di debiti contratti dalla donna, non si vede perché i creditori dovrebbero vedersi sottrarre dei beni magari necessari per il soddisfacimento del loro credito; non la terza perché la coesistenza di poteri diversi sulla donna in capo a persone diverse non sembra probabile (oltre tutto la promessa di matrimonio comportava anche di norma risvolti economici attraverso il dono nuziale). Ma questo non significa che allora il management passa alla donna, perché, oltre tutto, non si vede perché non lo avesse anche prima. In realtà io penso che non succeda assolutamente nulla: la donna riacquista la piena titolarità del bene. Piuttosto si può immaginare che qualche parente della donna si sia fatto parte diligente e abbia intentato l'azione contro il marito o contro il figlio, un'azione che potrebbe avere avuto caratteristiche simili a quelle della *graphē kakōseōs* attica.

e) Un ultimo punto mi sembra interessante richiamare. La norma che tutela la moglie e la madre contro atti di disposizione arbitrari del marito o del figlio è dichiarata espressamente non retroattiva (col. VI 24-25). Secondo K. questa precisazione si giustifica con il fatto che il CdG ha introdotto il diritto delle donne (cioè di figlie e sorelle) ad ereditare. Ma io non credo che sia così. Anche prima del CdG il matrimonio comportava con tutta probabilità la consegna allo sposo di un dono nuziale da parte del padre della sposa, dono che doveva essere restituito in caso di scioglimento del matrimonio per morte del marito o per divorzio. Dunque escluderei che il marito abbia mai avuto la piena disponibilità dei beni della moglie. E la stessa cosa vale, *mutatis mutandis*, per il figlio, che non avrebbe certo potuto disporre a suo piacimento dei beni della madre danneggiando così le aspettative ereditarie dei propri fratelli e sorelle. Dunque per me la motivazione della nuova tutela introdotta in col. VI resta quella che ho già espresso più volte: norme come questa si giustificano nei confronti di una rapida e pericolosa crescita di un'economia monetaria. Il legislatore temeva cioè che il marito o il figlio non fossero più in grado di reintegrare il patrimonio della moglie o della madre, una volta che fosse stato trasformato in moneta.

In definitiva io ho trovato molto stimolante la discussione dei vari passi esaminati da K., che ci hanno mostrato quanto sia vasto, e ancora per molti aspetti da chiarire, il continente dei presupposti impliciti e delle conseguenze inespresse delle norme contenute nel CdG, in particolare per quanto riguarda la condizione giuridica delle donne, che è ben lungi dal risultare chiara sotto tutti gli aspetti. Io continuo a pensare che la donna non sia libera di compiere autonomamente atti di disposizione sul proprio patrimonio, a meno che non si tratti di trasferimenti interni al gruppo familiare, in particolare la divisione del proprio patrimonio tra i figli.

Dal punto di vista del metodo mi sembra interessante la conclusione che K. ricava dalla sua indagine sulla *kyrieia*, secondo cui il legislatore è capace di introdurre elementi di elasticità in un sistema di norme e di concetti che aspira invece alla sistematicità e alla coerenza.

BIBLIOGRAFIA

Maffi, A., *Studi recenti sul Codice di Gortina*, "Dike" 6, 2003, p. 161-226.

ÉVA JAKAB (SZEGED)

SEG XLVIII 96: STEUERGESETZ ODER FRACHTVERTRAG?

I. Text und Fragestellung. Bei den Ausgrabungen auf der Athener Agora wurde am 21. Juli 1986 eine Marmorstele in der Größe von 1.105 m x 0.45 m gefunden, die eine gut erhaltene Stoichedon-Inschrift überliefert. Den Text hat R.S. Stroud mit umfassendem Kommentar 1998 musterhaft ediert[1]. Es handelt sich um einen *nomos* „über die *dôdekatê* des Getreides von den Inseln“[2] (Z. 3/4) aus dem Jahre 374/3 v.Chr. Agyrrhios, der bekannte Politiker des 4. Jh. v.Chr.[3], stellte den Antrag, daß „die *dôdekatê* (8 1/3%) in Lemnos, Imbros und Skyros verkauft werden soll und die *pentêkostê* (2%) des Getreides“ (Z. 5-8). Da Überschrift und Präambel diese beiden bekannten Steuersätze erwähnen, ist der Text im Schrifttum als „Grain Tax Law“ oder „Getreidesteuer-Gesetz“ definiert worden. Nach Stroud regele es die Ausschreibung der Versteigerung des Rechts der Eintreibung der genannten beiden Steuern (*dôdekatê* und *pentêkostê*) an den Getreideerträgen der drei Kleruchen-inseln, die ab jetzt als Naturalabgabe erhoben und nach Athen geliefert werden sollen. Der *nomos* beschreibe zunächst die Pflichten der Steuerpächter und anschließend den öffentlichen Verkauf des zugestellten Getreides auf der Agora von Athen.

Die *editio princeps* ist ziemlich jung, aber die reizende neue Quelle hat bereits viele Autoren zu Ergänzungen motiviert. In den wesentlichen Punkten wird überwiegend Strouds Auslegung gefolgt und erweitert (Migeotte[4], Engels[5], Gauthier[6]); vereinzelt werden auch kritische Bemerkungen gemeldet (so besonders Harris[7] und Faraguna[8]).

---

1 R.S. Stroud, The Athenian Grain Tax Law of 374/3 B.C., Hesperia Suppl. 29, Princeton 1998.

2 M. Faraguna, Intorno alla nuova legge ateniese sulla tassazione del grano, Dike 2 (1999) 67f. bezieht sich auf die parallele Formulierung in SEG XVIII 13, Z. 11-12, wofür bereits L. Robert, Sur la loi d'Athènes relative aux Petites Panathéneés, Hellenica 11-12 (1960) 193 die Wiedergabe „dans la Néa“ überzeugend vorgeschlagen hat.

3 S. dazu den umfassenden Kommentar von Stroud, Grain Tax Law (o. Anm. 1) 16-25.

4 L. Migeotte, Taxation directe en Grèce ancienne, in: Symposion 1999, hg. von G. Thür/T.J. Fernandez Nieto, Köln 2003, 302.

5 S.J. Engels, Das Athenische Getreidesteuer-Gesetz des Agyrrhios, ZPE 132 (2000) 97-124.

6 Ph. Gauthier in BE 1999 Nr. 186.

7 E.M. Harris, ZPE 128 (1999) 269-72.

8 Faraguna, Intorno (o. Anm. 2) 63-97.

Harris beschäftigt sich mit zwei Fragen: Einerseits widerspricht er Stroud in der Deutung der *dôdekatê* (zwei Zehntel) in den Zeilen 58 und 60; andererseits bestreitet er seine These der „Ertragsteuer“[9]. Die zwei Zehntel seien nach Harris die ersten zwei *katabolai* (Teilzahlungen), welche die Steuerpächter sogleich nach dem Ersteigern bar zu entrichten hätten[10]. Die Zeilen 58 und 60 enthielten eine einmalige Übergangsregelung, wie die bereits bar geleisteten Teilzahlungen durch die Umwandlung von Geld- auf Naturalsteuer zu verwalten seien. Der zweite Punkt seiner Kritik betrifft einen tragenden Punkt in Strouds Thesen, ob die *dôdekatê* eine Naturalabgabe der Inselbewohner für das dort gewachsene Getreide, quasi eine Art Pachtzins für das gebrauchte Kleruchenland, gewesen sei[11]. Harris argumentiert gegen die herrschende Auffassung und betont, daß eine ähnliche Abgabepflicht für athenische Bürger außerhalb Athens nirgends in den Quellen belegt sei[12]. Die *dôdekatê* und *pentêkostê* definiert er eher als Durchgangszölle (transit taxes), die wegen der guten strategischen Lage der drei Inseln besonders lukrativ gewesen sein dürften[13].

Faraguna vertieft die Interpretation in zwei Themenkreisen; einerseits überlegt er den öffentlichrechtlichen Status der drei Klerucheninseln und ihrer Bevölkerung, andererseits die Bedeutung von *meris*. Nach der Schilderung des wechselhaften politischen Schicksals der Inseln führt er weitere Quellen zum Bürgerrecht der Inselbewohner an und kommt zum Schluß, daß die *dôdekatê* nur für die Urbevölkerung, nicht aber für die Kleruchen gegolten haben dürfte[14]. Mit Stroud argumentiert er dafür, daß SEG XLVIII 96 nur ein altes Gesetz über die *dôdekatê*, das seit 387/6 existiert habe, reformieren wolle. Anschließend analysiert er die Prozedur der Vergabe der Steuereintreibung, vor allem das Bedeutungsfeld des terminus technicus *meris*[15]. Mit Stroud stellt er darauf ab, daß *meris* hier eine gewisse Menge Getreide und damit auch eine „Portion“ vom Ackerland, einen geographischen Bezirk, bedeute[16], bei dessen Vergabe die von ihm für die Bergwerke ausgearbeiteten spezialen Methoden des Lizitationsverfahrens gegolten hätten; darauf ist unten noch zurückzukommen.

Liest man den relativ langen und komplizierten Text noch einmal aufmerksam durch, fällt es auf, daß darin außer den beiden technischen Worten *dôdekatê* und *pentêkostê* keine Angaben zu den Steuern oder deren Eintreibung zu finden sind.

---

9 Harris, Notes (o. Anm. 7) 269.

10 Die Zahlungspflicht der Steuerpächter wurde in Raten aufgeteilt; in jeder Prytanie war eine Teilzahlung fällig, vgl. Harris, Notes (o. Anm. 7) 270.

11 So Stroud, Grain Tax Law (o. Anm. 1) 31.

12 Harris, Notes (o. Anm. 7) 272.

13 Harris, Notes (o. Anm. 7) 272. Zu seinem Vorschlag zu Z. 55-61 s. unten bei Anm. 104ff.

14 Faraguna, Intorno (o. Anm. 2) 77f.

15 Faraguna, Intorno (o. Anm. 2) 90-96.

16 Faraguna, Intorno (o. Anm. 2) 90.

Dies führt zur Fragestellung meines Beitrags: Haben wir wirklich ein Getreidesteuer-Gesetz vor uns?

II. Widersprüche und Deutungsprobleme. Es empfiehlt sich zunächst, Strouds Modell der Steuerpacht kritisch zu überlegen; nachzugehen ist den Fragen, ob die öffentliche Ausschreibung einer Steuerpacht (des Rechts der Eintreibung der Steuer) zum Inhalt unserer Inschrift wirklich gut paßt und ob das rekonstruierte Verfahren nach dem in der Inschrift vorgegebenen Schema funktionieren konnte. Anschließend möchte ich aus Strouds Kommentar einige Bemerkungen hervorheben, die meines Erachtens gegen seine Hauptthese sprechen.

1. Zum Modell der Steuerpacht. Das Gesetz sieht vor, die *dôdekatê* und die *pentêkostê* nach *merides* zu vergeben; eine *meris* besteht aus 500 Medimnoi Getreide (Z. 8/9). Der Editor sieht darin die Steuerabgabe nach dem Ertrag eines konkreten geographischen Bezirks[17], dessen Grenzen ein früheres Gesetz gezogen haben soll. Die technischen Worte *pôlein* (Z. 6/7), *epônia* und *kêrykeia* (Z. 28) bestätigen jedenfalls die Ausschreibung einer öffentlichen Auktion. Die Auktion war die übliche Form des Kontrahierens unter Staat und Privaten, wie es auch Aristoteles bestätigt[18]. Es fragt sich jedoch, ob die Versteigerung nach *merides*, wenn jede *meris* aus 500 Medimnoi (100 Weizen und 400 Gerste) bestehe, funktionsfähig sei.

Zum Ablauf der öffentlichen Versteigerungen, insbesondere der Steuerpacht, möchte ich hier nur zwei Quellen zitieren. Plutarch (Alkibiades 5) berichtet von einem Metöken, der in Alkibiades so verliebt war, daß er all sein Habe veräußert und ihm den Erlös angeboten habe. Alkibiades war gerührt, gab ihm das Geld zurück, verlangte jedoch von ihm „am folgenden Tag die Pächter der staatlichen Zölle zu überbieten.“ Der etwas besorgte Metöke ging getreulich auf den Markt und „überbot die gebotene Pachtsumme um ein Talent ...“ Lassen wir den glücklichen Ausgang bei Seite; uns interessiert bloß die Tatsache, daß jeder Geschäftsmann (ob Athenischer Bürger oder nicht) zur öffentlichen Versteigerung Zugang hatte und seine Konkurrenten durch Überbieten ausschlagen konnte. Das Recht der Eintreibung der Steuer, der Zuschlag, wurde dem Meistbietenden erteilt[19].

Andokides schildert in seiner Verteidigungsrede[20] eine ähnliche Szene (Über die Mysterien 133): Agyrrhios[21] leitete eine Gruppe von Steuerpächtern, die im Jahre

[17] Stroud, Grain Tax Law (o. Anm. 1) 40ff. überlegt lange, wie viele *merides* nach dem geschätzten Ertrag der drei Inseln denkbar wären.

[18] Ath. Pol. 47, 2. Die *pôlêtai* definiert P.J. Rhodes, A Commentary on the Aristotelian Athenaion Politeia^2, Oxford 1993, 552 als „‚sellers‘, makers of state contracts of all kind“.

[19] Auch Harris, Notes (o. Anm. 7) 270 spricht von „competitive bidding“.

[20] Zum politischen Kontext vgl. immer noch F. Blaß, Die attische Beredsamkeit 1/3^2, Leipzig 1887/98 (N. Hildesheim 1962) 280ff.; neulich auch A. Missiou, The Subversive Oratory of Andocide, Cambridge 1992, 49-54.

[21] Zur politischen Karriere des Agyrrhios s. D. MacDowell, Andocide: On the Mysteries, Oxford 1962, 157 und Stroud, Grain Tax Law (o. Anm. 1) 16-25.

402/1 v.Chr. die *pentêkostê* in Athen[22] für 30 Talente gepachtet und dadurch 6 Talente Gewinn erwirtschaftet habe. Im folgenden Jahr wollten sie das lukrative Geschäft wiederholen. Andokides fand jedoch die angebotene Summe (erneut 30 Talente) zu gering und den Gewinn der Pächter zu üppig, deshalb stieg auch er selbst in die Lizitation vor der Boule ein[23]. Nach mehrmaligem Bieten und Überbieten wurde der Zuschlag für 36 Talente an Andokides erteilt[24].

Ich verzichte auf weitere Quellenbeispiele und fasse das hier Relevante zusammen: Die Boule oder die Poletai schreiben das Recht zur Eintreibung einer gewissen Steuer auf einem bestimmten Gebiet jährlich zur Versteigerung aus; das Angebot der öffentlichen Hand ist in diesen zwei Punkten (Steuertyp und lokale Bestimmung) genau festgelegt. Ungewiß bleibt hingegen, wie hoch die Steuereinnahmen im konkreten Jahr ausfallen werden. Die Interessenten schätzen, wohl nach den Erfahrungen der vergangenen Jahre, den erhofften Ertrag und bieten der Polis – einen gesunden Gewinn einkalkulierend – je einen (pauschalen) Betrag an. Die Höhe des Entgelts wird immer erst im Laufe der Versteigerung festgelegt, weil ein höheres Anbot die früheren selbstverständlich ausschlägt[25]; es herrscht eine Wettbewerb-Situation. Die Leistungspflicht des Steuerpächters wird also niemals im voraus, ja gar nicht gesetzlich, geregelt.

Entspricht unser *nomos* diesem Modell? In der Inschrift schreibt die Polis zweifelsohne eine *dôdekatê* und eine *pentêkostê* zur Versteigerung aus, setzt aber die Leistungspflicht der „Käufer“ (*priamenoi)* mit 500 Medimnoi Getreide fest (Z. 8-10). Wie soll es zu einem Wettbewerb kommen, wenn die Leistung bereits gesetzlich festgehalten wurde? Dies ist ein unlösbarer Widerspruch in Strouds Modell, den er übersehen hat. Bereits Faraguna hat in seinem frühen Aufsatz auf dieses Problem hingewiesen, er versucht jedoch die Definition als „Steuergesetz“ durch eine hypothetische Konstruktion der Zahlungsmodalitäten zu retten, auf die unten noch zurückzukommen ist[26]. Ich finde den Widerspruch im Ablauf des unterstellten Verfahrens unüberwindbar; deshalb möchte ich im folgenden nach einer neuen inhaltlichen Deutung suchen.

2. *Zu Strouds Beobachtungen.* Liest man Strouds Kommentar, der den Text gewissenhaft und unvoreingenommen durchleutet, stößt man auf weitere Argumente,

[22] Die *pentêkostê* ist hier ein Hafenzoll von 2% für Import und Export, vgl. MacDowell, Andocide (o. Anm. 21) 158.

[23] Es ist pikant, daß Andokides seine Steuerpacht als Wohltat für das Volk Athens hervorhebt.

[24] Zu dieser Auffassung des Imperfektes *hypeballon* (§ 133) s. MacDowell, Andokide (o. Anm. 21) 159.

[25] Neben der Höhe der Summe wird natürlich auch die Zahlungsfähigkeit des Ersteigerers berücksichtigt. Hier können sozialer Stand, Vermögen oder allgemeine Zuverlässigkeit auch eine Rolle gespielt haben. Trotzdem darf die Rolle der Lizitation nicht unterschätzt werden, wozu K. Hallof, Der Verkauf konfiszierten Vermögens vor den Poleten in Athen, Klio 72 (1990) 407ff. zu neigen scheint.

[26] Faraguna, Intorno (o. Anm. 2) 93; vgl. dazu noch unten bei Anm. 88ff.

die gegen seine Hauptthese, also gegen die Deutung als Steuergesetz, sprechen. Es sind vor allem keine anderen Belege für die Existenz einer Steuer in Höhe der *dôdekatê* aus Attica überliefert[27]; allein aus Iasos ist eine Verkaufssteuer für Wein nach diesem Steuersatz bekannt[28]. Dazu kommt, daß die Steuern in Athen zu dieser Zeit fast aunahmslos in Bargeld eingetrieben wurden; nur ganz wenige Belege sind für Naturalsteuer bekannt[29]. Außer der in unserer Inschrift genannten gibt es nur noch zwei weiteren Steuern in Athen, die lokal bestimmt sind (eine *dekatê* im Hellespontos und eine *pentêkostê* in Nea), diese beiden sind aber Hafenzölle und keine Ertragsteuern[30]. Vergleicht man unseren Text mit weiteren überlieferten Steuergesetzen, fällt es sogleich auf, daß die übrigen Gesetze die für die Versteigerung zuständigen Behörden (Poletai oder Boule) präzise bestimmen, während in unserer Inschrift jeder Hinweis darauf fehlt[31]. Hier bleiben sogar der Kreis der Steuerpflichtigen und die Methode der Eintreibung völlig ungeregelt[32]. Andere Steuergesetze schreiben genau die Zahlungsmodalitäten der Pächter vor, wie und wann die Ratenzahlungen, *katabolai*, zu leisten sind, während hier diese Frage fast völlig ausgeklammert bleibt[33]; hier scheint die Leistung als Ganzes bestimmt zu sein[34].

Ein fundamentales Problem bedeutet weiterhin, daß die Vergabe (Verpachtung) nach *merides* in Steuergesetzen sonst nie (nur in unserem Text) vorkommt[35]. Faßt man die *merides* mit Stroud als eine nach Prozentsatz bestimmte Abgabenpflicht der Steuerpächter von einem geographischen Gebiet auf, kommt man zum Ergebnis, daß die Anzahl der zu versteigernden *merides* vom Ertrag abhängig sei und eigentlich erst nach der Ernte beziffert werden könne. Nach diesem Modell wäre also die Anzahl der *merides* zur Zeit der Versteigerung noch unbekannt, aber die Poletai hätten sie nach Erfahrung schätzen sollen[36]. Doch macht m. E. das unbestimmte Objekt die Versteigerung obsolet. Würde es sich um eine Ertragsteuer handeln, wäre die gesetzlich festgelegte Zusammensetzung der *meris*, eins zu vier von Weizen und Gerste (Z. 9/10 der Inschrift), kaum zu erklären[37].

---

27 Vgl. dazu jedoch Faraguna, Intorno (o. Anm. 2) 65.

28 Diese störende Tatsache stellt bereits Stroud, Grain Tax Law (o. Anm. 1) 27 fest.

29 Stroud, Grain Tax Law (o. Anm. 1) 27.

30 Nea, SEG XVIII 13; vgl. Stroud, Grain Tax Law (o. Anm. 1) 31; Faraguna, Intorno (o. Anm. 2) 67f.

31 Bereits Stroud, Grain Tax Law (o. Anm. 1) 28 bemerkt dieses Phänomen.

32 Bemerkt bereits von Stroud, Grain Tax Law (o. Anm. 1) 32.

33 Vgl. dazu Harris, Notes (o. Anm. 7) 270, wenn seine Thesen über die Deutung der Zeilen 58 und 60 stichhaltig sind; s. dazu oben bei Anm. 10f.

34 Bemängelt bereits bei Stroud, Grain Tax Law (o. Anm. 1) 38.

35 Festgestellt bereits von Stroud, Grain Tax Law (o. Anm. 1) 40.

36 So Stroud, Grain Tax Law (o. Anm. 1) 41.

37 Stroud, Grain Tax Law (o. Anm. 1) 42 versucht durch komplizierte statistische Spekulationen eine Erklärung zu liefern, die aber die präzis bestimmten Quoten letztlich nicht nachweisen kann.

Bemerkenswert ist noch die ungewöhnliche Syntax des Textes: Der erste Teil (Z. 10-35) ist stilistisch der Gesetzessprache völlig fremd, nur der zweite Teil zeigt den üblichen Gesetzesstil[38]. Warum wäre der Verkauf des zugestellten Getreides auf der Agora (im zweiten Teil) dem traditionellen Gesetzesstil treu formuliert, aber gerade die Versteigerung des Rechts der Steuereintreibung (im ersten Teil) stilistisch abweichend gestaltet? Geht es in beiden Teilen um ein Steuergesetz, zeigt der Text einen unerklärlichen Widerspruch.

Inhaltlich hängt damit zusammen, daß der Käufer bei jeder Steuerpacht sonst angehalten wird, sogleich nach dem Ersteigern eine *prokatabolê* (Anzahlung, Vorauszahlung) zu zahlen[39], während es hier ausdrücklich abgelehnt wird (Z. 27). Dazu kommt, daß die typischen Versteigerungsgebühren, *epônia* (Verkaufssteuer) und *kêrykeia* (Heroldsgebühr), bei Steuerpacht sonst nie vorkommen, während sie hier ausdrücklich geregelt sind[40].

Zusammenfassend ist festzuhalten, daß der neu edierte *nomos* Athens aus dem Jahre 374/3 v.Chr. zahlreiche inhaltlichen Probleme zeigt, die noch nicht restlos gelöst sind. Stroud publizierte die Inschrift mit guter Lesung und musterhafter Detailanalyse der einzelnen technischen Wendungen; seiner Deutung nach handele es sich um ein Steuergesetz über Getreide von den drei Klerucheninseln. Der vorliegende Text basiere auf einem früheren Gesetz, das bereits gewisse Einzelheiten der Steuereinhebung geregelt haben soll; hier ginge es um die Verpachtung der Steuer des nächsten Jahres, die jedoch nicht mehr in Geld, sondern in Naturalien einzutreiben und nach Athen zu bringen wäre, um dort zu subventionierten Preisen von den Behörden der Polis an das Volk verkauft zu werden. Oben versuchte ich zu zeigen, daß jene vom Schrifttum überwiegend akzeptierte Interpretation zum Teil problematisch und widersprüchlich ist. Diese Unstimmigkeiten der Auslegung motivieren dazu, nach einer denkbaren neuen Deutung zu suchen.

III. Auf dem Weg zu einer neuen Deutung. Im folgenden versuche ich die Zeilen 5-36 abweichend zu erläutern; mit dem Schlußteil der Inschrift werde ich mich hier nicht beschäftigen. Mustert man den Text noch einmal durch, fallen folgende typische Worte auf: *pôlein* (Z. 6), *meris* (Z. 8), *komiei* (Z. 10/11), κινδύνωι τῶι ἑαυτõ (Z. 11), *apostêsei* (Z. 16), *xêras ... katharas* (Z. 24/25), *epônia kai kêrykeia* (Z. 28). Die Interpretation knüpft an diese an.

---

[38] Bemerkt bereits von Stroud, Grain Tax Law (o. Anm. 1) 44.

[39] Die *katabolê* wird nach Aristot. 47, 3 in jeder Prytanie als Ratenzahlung entrichtet, die *prokatabolê* besteht meistens aus zwei Zehntel der Pachtsumme, die als Anzahlung geleistet wird; s. Rhodes, Commentary (o. Anm. 18) 556 mit Quellen; Harris, Notes (o. Anm. 7) 270.

[40] Stroud, Grain Tax Law (o. Anm. 1) 62f.

1. Pôlein. Das Verbum deutet eindeutig auf eine Versteigerung hin[41]. Diese Bedeutung wird auch von den technischen Worten *epônia* und *kêrykeia* (Z. 28) bestätigt; Verkaufssteuer und Heroldsgebühr hatten Ersteigerer bei öffentlichen Auktionen vor den Poleten zu entrichten[42]. Stroud definiert das Verbum *pôlein* als „to sell the right to collect the taxes“[43]; damit beschränkt er die inhaltliche Interpretation der Inschrift strikt auf die Steuerpacht. Zweifelsohne ist dies eine mehrfach belegte Bedeutung, die aber nicht unbedingt zwingend ist. Nach Aristoteles (Ath. Pol. 47, 2) waren die Poleten für den Abschluß öffentlicher Verträge zuständig; er hebt ausdrücklich die Verpachtung der Minen und Steuern sowie den Verkauf konfiszierter Grundstücke hervor. Bereits diese Aufzählung zeigt, daß außer dem Verkauf des Rechts der Eintreibung der Steuern auch der Abschluß anderer öffentlichen Verträge mit demselben terminus technicus bezeichnet wird. Dazu kommt, daß der Katalog des Aristoteles bekannterweise unvollständig blieb: Der Kreis der denkbaren Kontrakte zwischen Staat und Privaten ist viel breiter und das Kontrahieren erfolgte immer in Form einer Auktion[44]. Die Bedeutung des Verbum *pôlein* ist also keineswegs auf einen einzigen Vertragstyp zu beschränken; es knüpft vielmehr an die Art des Vertragsabschlusses durch Versteigerung an. Der Vertragstyp ist erst nach sorgfältiger Prüfung des spezifischen Vertragsinhalts zu definieren. Bereits die oben angesprochenen Quellen zeigen, daß Kauf, Miet- oder Werkvertrag problemlos nach demselben Verfahren der Versteigerung abgeschlossen und mit dem technischen Wort *pôlein* ausgedrückt werden konnten. Dementsprechend würde ich *pôlein* neutral mit „versteigern“ und *priamenos* mit „Ersteigerer“ übersetzen.

2. *Komizein.* Der Text ab Z. 6 nennt als Objekt der Leistungspflichten den *sitos* (Z. 5/6, 8, 11, 13, 14, 17). Das Getreide wird nach Hohlmaß (*medimnoi*, Z. 9, 24 und *sêkomata,* Z. 25) gemessen bzw. bei der Erfüllung auch ins Gewicht umgerechnet (*talanton*, Z. 23, 24). Die Leistungspflicht des Ersteigerers wird mit den Verben *komiei* (Z. 10/11), *anakomiei* (Z. 12/13), *katanêsei* (Z. 14), *apostêsei* (Z. 16, 21/22, 24/25) und *anakomisêi* (Z. 18) beschrieben. Auf den ersten Blick fällt auf, daß die Hauptpflicht des Ersteigerers vor allem im *komizein* besteht. Das Verbum kommt in der Inschrift vier Mal vor[45] und seine Bedeutung ist unbestritten „liefern, zustellen, transportieren“[46]; es ist sogar das typische Wort für den Transport von Getreide[47].

---

41 In diesem Sinne bereits Stroud, Grain Tax Law (o. Anm. 1) 28; zustimmend auch Harris, Notes (o. Anm. 7) 269 und Faraguna, Intorno (o. Anm. 2) 93.

42 S. Hallof, Verkauf (o. Anm. 25) 407ff. mit weiteren inschriftlichen Belegen.

43 Stroud, Grain Tax Law (o. Anm. 1) 9. Faraguna, Intorno (o. Anm. 2) spricht von „l'appalto della riscossione di una dodicesima“; Engels, Getreidesteuer-Gesetz (o. Anm. 5) 104 formuliert: „... soll die Dodekate und die Pentekoste in Form von Getreide verpachtet werden (wörtlich: das Recht, die Steuer einzusammeln, soll verkauft werden).“

44 Vgl. Rhodes, Commentary (o. Anm. 18) 552 mit weiterer Literatur.

45 Z. 10/11, 12/13, 18, 19/20.

46 Vgl. Stroud, Grain Tax Law (o. Anm. 1) 48 mit weiteren inschriftlichen Belegen; s. auch Liddell-Scott und Preisigke für das weitere Bedeutungsfeld.

Die zwei weiteren Verben (*katanêsei, apostêsei)* bezeichnen den speziellen Modus der Erfüllung: Das Getreide wird angehäuft und durch Zumessen übergeben; darauf ist unten noch zurückzukommen.

Unvoreingenommen betrachtet besteht also die Leistungspflicht des Ersteigerers darin, Getreide von den Inseln Lemnos, Imbros und Skyros zunächst auf dem Seeweg nach Piräus, anschließend auf dem Land in die obere Stadt zu transportieren[48]. Der Abschnitt in den Zeilen 5-36 regelt also nicht die Erhebung einer Natural- oder Umsatzsteuer, sondern den Transport von Getreide von den Inseln nach Athen. Demzufolge bietet sich als Gegenmodell zur Steuerpacht die Ausschreibung von Seefrachtverträgen.

3. Kindynos. Die Wendung κινδύνωι τῶι ἑαυτõ (Z. 11) ist eine typische Klausel der Frachtverträge[49]. *Kindynos* (ungefähr dem Lateinischen *periculum* entsprechend) hat ein breites Bedeutungsfeld, das vom Risiko allgemein zur Gefahr im juristischen Sinne als „unverschuldeter Untergang des Vertragsobjekts" reicht[50]. Im Vertragsrecht bezeichnet man damit die höhere Gewalt oder das vertragstypische Risiko; das letztere wird meistens durch vertragliche Abreden geregelt[51]. In unserem Kontext, also im Zusammenhang mit dem Seetransport, hat das Wort die enge technische Bedeutung von „Seegefahr". Stroud bezieht sich auf drei parallele Quellen dazu: Dem. 52, 20, Lys. 32, 25 und Syll.^{3} 976, Z. 50-52; er will mit denen den Gebrauch und den juristischen Inhalt der Klausel demonstrieren[52]. Besprechen wirklich Demosthenes, Lysias und das Getreidegesetz aus Samos die Gefahr (Seegefahr) im juristischen Sinne? Deckt das Bedeutungsfeld von *kindynos* in den drei angesprochenen Quellen den Sinn der Klausel κινδύνωι τῶι ἑαυτõ in Z. 11 unserer Inschrift?

Demosthenes (52, 20) will in seiner Rede gegen Kallippos beweisen, daß der verstorbene Lykon ihn (Kallippos) weder in seine Geschäfte mit einbezogen noch in sein Vertrauen aufgenommen habe. Unter anderem berichtet er davon, daß Lykon 40 Minen an zwei Brüder als Darlehen für eine Seefahrt gewährt habe. Die Empfänger scheuten jedoch die Gefahren des Meeres und segelten nicht ab. Lykon fühlte sich betrogen und versuchte Kapital und Zinsen auf dem Prozeßweg zurückzuverlangen; er hat sich aber nicht einmal vor Gericht die Hilfe des Kallippos gewünscht. *Kindynos* bezeichnet hier allgemein die Risiken der geplanten Seereise, mit der

---

47 Aristot. Ath. Pol. 51.4, IG II^2 1672 (Eleusis, 329/8 v.Chr.) Z. 288-289, Agora XXVIII, S. 158 Nr. 85, vgl. Stroud, Grain Tax Law (o. Anm. 1) 48.

48 Der Erfüllungsort ist das Heiligtum des Aiakos, dessen Lage auf der Agora Stroud, Grain Tax Law (o. Anm. 1) 85ff. überzeugend nachgewiesen hat.

49 Zum griechischen Frachtvertrag s. den Überblick bei J. Vélissaropoulos, Les naucleres Grécs, Paris 1980, 282ff.

50 Vgl. bei Liddel-Scott „danger, hazard, venture, whether abstract or concrete", aber auch „trial, venture".

51 Vgl. É. Jakab, Periculum und Praxis. Vertragliche Abreden beim Verkauf von Wein, SZ 121 (2004) 189ff.

52 Stroud, Grain Tax Law (o. Anm. 1) 49.

Seegefahr als Risikozuweisung im konkreten Vertragsverhältnis hat aber die Stelle nichts zu tun[53].

Lysias (32, 25) Rede gegen Diogeiton handelt von Vormundshaft: Der Beklagte habe das Vermögen zweier Mündel, die seine Enkel waren, unterschlagen[54]. Er habe unter anderem ein Handelsschiff mit einer Ladung im Wert von zwei Talenten an die Adria geschickt; der zum Segeln ungünstige Zeitpunkt und die berüchtigte Piratenzone machten das Geschäft besonders riskant[55]. Nach der Abfahrt sagte Diogeiton der Mutter der Kinder, daß das Schiff auf deren Gefahr führe. Nach der glücklichen Heimkehr mit verdoppeltem Gewinn bestand er jedoch darauf, daß die Reise auf seine eigene Gefahr unternommen worden sei. *Kindynos* hat hier tatsächlich mit der Seegefahr zu tun, aber ebenfalls nicht im Sinne unseres Gesetzes[56]. Die knappe, im „Innenverhältnis“ zwischen Vormund und Mündel gefallene Bemerkung, auf wessen Gefahr das Schiff segele, hat mit Gefahrenzuweisung durch Parteiabreden in Fracht- oder Darlehensverträgen nichts zu tun. Nach der Textumgebung geht es hier vielmehr um die betrügerische Buchhaltung des Vormunds: Diogeiton hat offenbar die Ausgabe von zwei Talenten für die Schiffsladung bis zur Rückkehr des Schiffes nicht verbucht. Wäre das Schiff untergegangen, hätte er die zwei Talente in die Buchführung der Mündel eingetragen und sogleich als Verlust abgeschrieben; das Schiff wäre also „auf ihre Gefahr“ gesegelt, nach dem Prinzip des *casum sentit dominus*. Das Schiff ist aber heil zurückgekehrt, deshalb entscheidet er sich dafür, die zwei Talente des Startkapitals in seiner eigenen Buchführung als Ausgabe einzutragen, um auch den hohen Gewinn dort kassieren zu können.

Unsere Wendung „auf ihre eigene Gefahr“ kommt wörtlich im „Getreidegesetz“ aus Samos vor[57] (Z. 52): „Die für die Getreideverwaltung gewählten Männer sollen die Verpfändung auf ihre eigene Gefahr vornehmen“[58]. Der Kontext ist wie folgt: Der *demos* von Samos hat einen Getreidefonds mit eigener Verwaltung eingerichtet, um günstig Getreide anzuschaffen und an die Bürger in monatlichen Portionen unentgeltlich zu verteilen. In Z. 48-52 wird bestimmt, daß die Beschaffung des Getreides (nach einem *ad hoc*-Volksbeschluß) auch an Unternehmer versteigert werden

---

[53] Falsch zugeordnet bei Stroud, Grain Tax Law (o. Anm. 1) 49.

[54] Zum sozialen Hintergrund vgl. S.C. Todd, The Shape of Athenian Law, Oxford 1995, 202 ff.; zur Übersicht der Rede s. auch Blaß, Attische Beredsamkeit (o. Anm. 20) 609.

[55] Vgl. dazu S. Isager/M.H. Hansen, Aspects of Athenian Society in the Fourth Century B.C., Odense 1975, 27, 56f.

[56] Isager/Hansen, Aspects (o. Anm. 55) 27 wollen hier ein Seedarlehen feststellen: „there is a brief reference to a return loan made for sea trade ...“ Blaß, Attische Beredsamkeit (o. Anm. 20) 613 formuliert neutral und legt sich auf keine juristische Definition fest: Der Text läßt m.E. keinen Schluß auf ein Seedarlehen zu.

[57] Syll.^{3} 976; nunmehr IG XII 4/1 172.

[58] Kommentar G. Thür/Chr. Koch, Prozeßrechtlicher Kommentar zum „Getreidegesetz“ aus Samos, Anzeiger der phil.-hist. Klasse der ÖAW 118 (1981) So. 5, 66, 74f.

kann[59]; die Ersteigerer sollen Bürgen stellen und Hypotheken geben. Die zwei Getreideverwalter müssen jedoch das spezifisch juristische Risiko des Geschäfts auf sich nehmen: Sie haften also mit ihrem Privatvermögen, wenn etwa die Pfandsache untergeht, das Pfandrecht erlischt und die Forderung weder vom Verpflichteten noch von dessen Bürgen einzutreiben wäre[60]. Wie wir sehen, trifft die Wendung κινδύνωι τῶι ἑαυτῶν wieder nicht die Seegefahr. Insofern haben wir jedoch einen ähnlichen Kontext, da es auch hier um die vertragliche Zuweisung des juristisch erfaßten, vertragsspezifischen Risikos geht.

Den gesuchten juristischen Sinn von Seegefahr finden wir erst in späteren Quellen, die ich aufgrund des ähnlichen Kontextes rechtsvergleichend heranziehen möchte. Ein kleiner Exkurs in den westlichen Mittelmeerraum zeigt, daß der antike Staat meistens bemüht war, die Gefahrtragung auf seine privaten Vertragspartner abzuwälzen. Die folgenden Texte lehren uns, warum die öffentliche Hand auf dieser Klausel beharrte.

Livius 23, 49, 1 berichtet davon[61], daß das römische Heer in Hispanien im Jahre 215 v.Chr. (im zweiten punischen Krieg) große Versorgungsschwierigkeiten erlebt habe. Dazu war die Staatskasse ziemlich leer, deshalb wandte sich der Prätor an bekannte Staatspächter, die früher aus öffentlichen Aufträgen reichlich profitiert hatten, den Transport nach Hispanien ausnahmsweise auf Kredit (mit aufgeschobener Bezahlung) zu übernehmen. Die *societates publicanorum* zeigten sich bereit, verlangten jedoch Privilegien dafür, vor allem die Übernahme der Seegefahr durch den Staat: *quae in naves imposuissent ... vi publico periculo essent.* Wenn also das Frachtgut infolge von Sturm oder Angriff der Feinde verloren ginge, soll der Staat den Schaden tragen[62]. Wenn der Staat hier die Seegefahr als besonderes Privileg übernommen hat, wurde sie im Normalfall auf die Pächter abgewälzt. Den guten Grund dafür liefert die Fortführung der Geschichte, weil manche der *publicani* die günstigen Vertragsbedingungen schamlos ausgenützt haben: Bei hoch deklariertem Ladungswert haben sie Schiffbrüche vorgespiegelt oder inszeniert[63].

Aus griechischem Seefracht-Milieu stammt ein netter Witz im Philogelos, der auf die Möglichkeiten der geschickten Gefahrenzuweisung aufmerksam macht

[59] Für die Interpretation der Inschrift in diesem Sinne s. Thür/Koch, Getreidegesetz (o. Anm. 58) 75.

[60] Zum griechischen Pfandrecht s. D. MacDowell, The Law in Classical Athens, Plymouth 1978, 143.

[61] Liv. 23, 49, 1: *ubi ea dies venit, ad conducendam tres societates aderant hominum undeviginti, quorum duo postulata fuere: unum, ut militia vacarent, dum in eo publico essent, alterum, ut quae in naves imposuissent, ab hostium tempestatisque vi publico periculo essent. utroque impetrato conduxerunt ...*

[62] Vgl. dazu A. Bürge, Der Witz im antiken Seefrachtvertrag. Beobachtungen zur Vertragspraxis im antiken Mittelmeerraum, Index 22 (1994) 392f.

[63] Liv. 25, 3, 10; vgl. Bürge, Witz (o. Anm. 62) 393f.

(§ 81)[64]: „Ein Scholastikos fuhr auf einem Schiff, das in Sturm geriet. Als die Mitreisenden jammerten, sagte er: „Warum seid ihr auch so geizig? Ich zahle 10 Drachmen mehr und reise auf die Gefahr des Kapitäns.“ Der antike Witz lehrt uns, daß die vertragliche Gefahrenzuweisung immer auch eine Preisfrage war. Die Übernahme eines hohen Risikos mußte vom Vertragspartner bezahlt werden. Die Pikanterie liegt hier darin, daß der Kapitän für die „Versicherungsprämie“ gerade das Überleben nicht garantieren konnte.

Ein griechisches Vertragsformular mußte auch dem siegreichen Feldherrn Mummius vor Augen geschwebt haben[65], als er im Jahre 146 v.Chr., nach der Eroberung von Korinth, bei der öffentlichen Ausschreibung des Seetransportes der an Kunstschätzen reichen Beute unbedingt eine dem römischen Recht fremde Klausel im Formular haben wollte: *si eas perdidissent, novas eos reddituros*[66]. Gebildete Römer amüsierten sich gewaltig über den juristischen Fehlgriff: Die Klausel eignet sich nämlich zur Risikoabwälzung bei vertretbaren Sachen (etwa Getreide, Wein), aber nicht bei Kunstgegenständen, die wertvolle Einzelstücke, juristisch unvertretbare Sachen sind, die also mit irgendwelchen neuen Produkten keineswegs ersetzt werden können. Die hübsche Anekdote bestätigt erneut, daß die öffentliche Hand bemüht war, durch *lex contractus* die Seegefahr beim Transport auf den Verfrächter abzuwälzen.

Die Klausel τῶι ἑαυτοῦ κινδύνωι ist auch in staatlichen Verträgen über Getreidetransport aus dem griechischen Ägypten in reicher Fülle überliefert, allerdings erst aus römischer Zeit[67]. Sie regelt die Gefahrtragung zwischen Staat und Schiffer und wälzt den Schaden aus „Seegefahr“ (Verlust der Ladung wegen Schiffbruchs oder Sturm) auf den Privaten ab. Bei totalem Verlust hat der Pächter also sein Schiff und auch den Wert der Ladung eingebüßt.

4. Apostêsei. Die Leistungspflicht des Kontrahenten wird (neben dem Transportieren, *komizein*) mit dem Verbum *apostêsei* (*aphistêmi*) bezeichnet. Außer den eng umrissenen Fällen der Seegefahr kann das Frachtgut auch durch Veruntreuung, Diebstahl usw. vermindert werden. Die Zuwägen-Klausel sichert die objektive Haftung des Verfrächters für die Quantität der Ladung. In Z. 40 liest man: „Nachdem die Zehnmänner das Getreide gemäß dem Vorgeschriebenen zuwägen ließen ...“ Die Erfüllung erfolgt durch das Zuwägen des Transportguts, worin beide Parteien mit-

---

64 Eine griechische Sammlung von 265 Witzen aus dem 4. Jh. n.Chr.; Text und Übersetzung nach A. Thierfelder, Tusculum, München 1968.

65 Vell. Pat. 1, 13, 4: *Mummius tam rudis fuit ut capta Corintho, cum maximorum artificium pefectas manibus tabulas ac statuas in Italiam portandas locaret, iuberet praedici conducentibus, si eas perdidissent, novas eos reddituros. non tamen puto dubites, Vinici, quin magis pro re publica fuerit manere adhuc rudem Corinthiorum intellectum quam in tantum ea intellegi, et quin hac prudentia illa imprudentia decori publico fuerit convenientior.*

66 Vell. Pat. 1, 15, 4; vgl. Bürge, Witz (o. Anm. 62) 394f.

67 So etwa P.Lond. II 301, p. 256 (=M.Chr. 140), 138-161 n.Chr.; P.Hamb. I 74, 173/4 n.Chr., P.Oxy. XVII 2125, 220-1 n.Chr.

wirken und einander kontrollieren. Der Ersteigerer stellt das im Lagerhaus (Aiakeion) abgelieferte und angehäufte Getreide bereit und führt vor den gewählten Zehnmännern die Prozedur durch (Z. 21-27). Eine etwas abweichend formulierte, aber inhaltlich ähnliche Klausel findet man in behördlichen Quittungen vom staatlichen Korntransport in den Papyri[68].

Der *nomos* bringt ausführliche Vorschriften, wie das Zuwägen durchgeführt werden soll (Z. 21-27): „Der *priamenos* soll den Weizen zu einem Gewicht von einem Talent[69] fünf Hekteis[70] (je 1/6 Medimnos) und die Gerste zu einem Gewicht von einem Talent pro Medimnos[71] zuwägen ... indem man den Getreidemaßtisch bis zum Rand auffüllt, wie es die übrigen Kaufleute tun.“ Auf den ersten Blick verblüfft die Kombination von Hohlmaß und Gewicht. Einen denkbaren Zusammenhang versucht bereits Stroud plausibel herzustellen[72]. Einleuchtend ist Rathbone, der die überlieferten metrologischen Tabellen[73] analysiert und die offenbar übliche Umrechnung mit den lokal stark abweichenden Hohlmaßen begründet[74]. Dementsprechend dürfte das Talent auch in unserer Inschrift zur „Beglaubigung“ des Medimnos gedient haben. Dasselbe Problem haben die Naukleroi im ptolemäischen Ägypten so gelöst, daß das beim Einladen verwendete Maß eventuell mitgeführt haben[75]. Von einem „beglaubigten“ Maß berichtet P.Lille 23[76], es bleibt jedoch ungewiß, ob *chalkous* in Z. 25 Hohlmaß oder Gewicht ist.

Faßt man die bisherigen Beobachtungen zwischendurch zusammen, deutet vieles darauf hin, daß die Inschrift nicht die Verpachtung der in Naturalien abzuliefernden Getreidesteuern regelt, sondern die Vergabe des Transports des eingenommenen Getreides an Naukleroi. Der gewöhnliche Ablauf eines Frachtgeschäfts läßt sich nach dem reichen Papyrusfund rekonstruieren. Nachdem das Getreide in das Schiff eingeladen wurde, stellt der Schiffer (*nauklêros* oder *kybernêtês*) eine Quittung über die in Empfang genommene Menge aus[77]. Damit verpflichtet er sich, im Zielhafen dieselbe Quantität abzuliefern. Es handelt sich um eine objektive Haftung, der Schif-

---

68 Vgl. etwa P.Hamb. 19, Z. 22; P.Tebt. 370, Z. 16 oder P.Amst. 107,13.

69 In Athen hat ein Talent 26,2 kg, vgl. DNP 1, 230-31.

70 Der Hekteus ist ein gebräuchliches griechisches Trockenmaß, das vor allem für Getreide Verwendung fand; es umfaßt ein Sechstel eines Medimnos und beträgt in Attika 8,75 Liter; vgl. DNP 5,275.

71 1 Medimnos = 52,53 Liter in Athen. Die Hohlmaße hatten in den antiken Poleis sehr unterschiedliche Fassungsvermögen, weil sie von verschiedenen Gewichtssystemen abgeleitet worden sind.

72 Stroud, Grain Tax Law (o. Anm. 1) 55f.

73 P.Oxy. 3455; P.Lond. 1718, aber auch Plin. nat. 18, 66.

74 D. Rathbone, The Weight and Measurement of Egyptian Grains, ZPE 53 (1983) 265-275.

75 So war es auch in dem bereits oben zitierten P. Hibeh. 98 (=WChr. 441), 251 v.Chr.

76 Ptolemais Hormu, 222 v.Chr.

77 In P.Hibeh 98 (=WChr. 441), 251 v.Chr., bestätigt der Schiffer, 4.800 Artaben Gerste eingeladen zu haben.

fer muß also auch für unverschuldete Verluste (etwa Diebstahl, Wegschütten, Ausrinnen des Getreides) einstehen[78]. Das Zumessen des Getreides erfolgt also zweimal; für die Leistungspflicht des Verfrächters ist eher die Übergabe am Zielort von Interesse.

Diese Art der Erfüllung war bei Austauschverträgen über vertretbare Sachen[79] in der Antike allgemein üblich[80]. Meistens war auch das Entgelt (Kaufpreis, Werklohn, Frachtlohn) nach den Maßeinheiten bestimmt[81]. Das Zumessen als Erfüllungsbestimmung hat immer einen immanenten Haftungsinhalt[82], der auch für unsere Inschrift unterstellt werden kann.

5. *Xêras ... katharas*. Der *nomos* legt ausdrücklich fest, daß der Korn im Aiakeion *xêras ... katharas* (Z. 25) abzuliefern sei; es handelt sich um die Qualität der Ladung. *Xêros* bedeutet „trocken, ohne Wasserschäden" und *katharos* „rein, ohne jede Verunreinigung". Der Verfrächter garantiert durch ausdrückliche Zusage, daß die Ladung in gutem Zustand, unbeschädigt übergeben werde. In der Handelspraxis dieser Zeit wurden allgemein diese zwei typischen Mängel hervorgehoben. Die Garantie für Wasserschäden kommt auch in den Frachtverträgen der graecoägyptischen Papyri vor, obwohl dafür ein anderes Wort gebraucht wird: *aparabrochos*[83]. Inhaltlich geht es zweifelsohne um den selben Mangel, daß das Getreide beim Ein- und Ausladen bzw. während des Transports naß geworden ist. *Katharos* kommt in Garantiezusagen der Schiffer im griechischen Ägypten regelmäßig vor; einen ganz frühen Beleg dafür liefert wieder P.Hibeh. 98. Es handelt sich um die Quittung eines *naukleros*, der Gerste in die königliche Speicher nach Alexandria transportiert; das Korn ist „rein und unverfälscht" (Z. 19), durch Zumessen abzuliefern.

---

78 Durch weitere Parteiabreden kann jedoch seine Haftung eingeschränkt werden, vgl. A.J.M. Meyer-Termeer, Die Haftung der Schiffer im Griechischen und Römischen Recht, Zutphen 1978, 117ff.

79 In der lateinischen Terminologie *res, quae pondere numero mensura constant*; zum Begriff vgl. Th. Rüfner, Vertretbare Sachen? Die Geschichte der res, quae pondere numero mensura constant, Berlin 2000, 27ff. Zur juristischen Bedeutung des Zumessens s. É. Jakab, Aversione venire – Verkauf in ‚Bausch und Bogen'?, in: Usus Antiquus Juris Romani, Antikes Recht in lebenspraktischer Anwendung. hg. W. Ernst/É. Jakab, Berlin 2005, 87-110.

80 Offenbar war diese Handelspraxis auch in Attica verbreitet, weil das Verbum *aphistêmi* meistens für das Zumessen von vertretbaren Sachen gebraucht wird, vgl. IG I^3 52A, Z. 20/21 aus dem 5. Jh. oder IG XII 5.1.647, Z. 15 aus dem 5. Jh.

81 Vgl. Jakab, Periculum (o. Anm. 51) 225ff.

82 Jakab, Periculum (o. Anm. 51) 216ff., 229ff.

83 So etwa P.Ross.Georg. II 18 VI, XXIX, XXXII, XL, XLI, XLII (140 n.Chr.), P.Laur. I 6 (97/8-116/7 n.Chr.), P.Warren 5 (154 n.Chr.).

Das athenische Getreidegesetz scheint die Bedeutung mit der Wendung *katharos airôn,* „frei vom Schwindelhafer", etwas einzuschränken[84]. Nach den Papyri ist das Bedeutungsfeld des Wortes *katharos* breiter aufzufassen: In P.Oxy. IV 708 (= WChr. 432) von 188 n.Chr. lesen wir von einer verunreinigten Kornladung, die mit Gerste und Erde vermischt war und deshalb dem Absender, einem Sitologen, zurückgeschickt wurde. Anderswo[85] bestätigt ein Schiffer in seiner Quittung den Empfang von Korn, das „frei von Erde und Gerste" ist. Die Papyri verstehen also unter *katharos* alle denkbare Verunreinigung des Frachtgutes (Erde, Unkraut, falscher Korn)[86].

6. Meris. Stroud übersetzt das Wort mit „portion" und versteht darunter einen Steuerbezirk. Er gibt jedoch zu, daß er keinen Beleg für die Verwendung des Wortes in einer Steuerpacht oder in einem Steuergesetz gefunden habe[87]. Faraguna überprüft erneut die Bedeutung des Wortes und entscheidet sich ebenfalls für „genau umrissenes geographisches Gebiet"[88]. Er sieht den Widerspruch zwischen dem Lizitationsverfahren und den gesetzlich festgelegten 500 Medimnoi, glaubt aber ihn mit der Übertragung seiner These über die Vergabe der *metalla* auf die Steuerpacht lösen zu können. Demzufolge sei die Zahlungspflicht des Pächters aus zwei Summen zusammengesetzt: einerseits ein fester Betrag, andererseits eine variable „Ersteigerungsprämie" oder „Registrationsgebühr"[89]; lizitiert wäre bloß über das Letzte[90]. Problematisch finde ich dabei, daß dieses Modell aus unserem Gesetz keineswegs nachzuweisen ist.

Zweifelsohne hat *meris* auch eine gut belegte geographische Bedeutung, die aber insbesonders in den Papyri der römischen Zeit typisch ist. In früheren Quellen überwiegt der Gebrauch des Wortes im Sinne von „part, portion, share in a mine, contribution, quote"[91]. Der Kläger in Dem. 42, 3 (Vermögenstausch) bezieht sich etwa darauf, daß er in der Pacht der Bergwerke involviert ist und dem Staat für jede *meris* noch ein Talent (insgesamt drei Talente) zahlen mußte. *Meris* bedeutet hier etwa „einen vertraglich festgelegten Pachtanteil an den staatlichen Silbergruben".

Bei öffentlichen Werkverträgen war die Ausschreibung nach „Anteilen, Portionen" allgemein üblich. In den Bauverträgen wurde das gesamte zu entrichtende

---

84 Bei Stroud, Grain Tax Law (o. Anm. 1) 56 ist es „darnel sieve"; Engels, Das Getreidesteuer-Gesetz (o. Anm. 5) 104 übersetzt mit „Schwindelhafer"; Preisigke bringt für *aira* „Lolchsamenkörner (zwischen Weizenkörnern)".

85 P.Oxy. X 1259 (211/12 n.Chr.).

86 In diesem Sinne bereits Meyer-Termeer, Haftung (o. Anm. 78) 113.

87 Stroud, Grain Tax Law (o. Anm. 1) 40.

88 Faraguna, Intorno (o. Anm. 2) 94-96.

89 Faraguna, Intorno (o. Anm. 2) 95f.

90 Vgl. dazu die Kritik von G. Thür, Symposion 2003, hg. von H.-A. Rupprecht, Wien 2006, 161ff.

91 S. beim Liddel-Scott mit weiteren Belegen.

Werk in „Baulose" aufgeteilt. Die Abschnitte wurden etwa in Tegea *erga* genannt[92]; jedes *ergon* wurde einzeln vergeben, wobei der jeweilige Vertragsinhalt (Leistungspflichten, Verzugs- und Strafbestimmungen) in einer Syngraphos für den Ersteigerer zusammengefaßt wurden[93]. IG II^2 463 überliefert den Baubeschluß, die Bauanweisungen und den Bauvertrag über die öffentliche Bauvergabe einer langen Stadtmauer aus dem Jahre 307/6 v.Chr. aus Athen. Der Abschnitt in den Zeilen 117-122 bezeichnet das Baulos mit dem terminus technicus *meris*[94]. Denselben Wortgebrauch zeigt SEG XLII 145, wo das Baulos bei einem Straßenbau *meros* genannt wird[95].

Die Brücke zum Frachtvertrag schlägt etwa eine Petition der *naukleroi*, die im 3. Jh. v.Chr. in Ägypten im staatlichen Getreidetransport beschäftigt waren[96]. Der Bittsteller stellt sich vor als der *dioiketes* der *naukleroi* aus dem Hafen, die „königliches Getreide *eis ta metrêmata* (Z. 5) transportieren." Das Wort *metrêma* kommt in vielen ptolemäischen Urkunden im Sinne von „Portion, Anteil" vor[97]; nach Preisigke kann das Wort als Synonym zu *meris* verstanden werden.

All das spricht dafür, *meris* nicht als ein genau umrissenes geographisches Gebiet, sondern als vertraglich festgelegtes Auktionslos aufzufassen. Jede *meris* besteht in unserem Gesetz aus 500 Medimnoi[98] – das ist die Menge, die von einem Privaten nach den festgelegten Bedingungen ersteigert werden konnte.

7. Dôdekatê, pentêkostê. Das Verbum *pôlein* (Z. 6) hat die *dôdekatê* (Z. 6) und die *pentêkostê* des Getreides (Z. 8) zum Objekt; Stroud sieht dadurch die Deutung „to sell the right to collect these taxes" automatisch belegt[99]. Zweifelsohne liegt diese Bedeutung nahe, ich finde sie aber in unserem Zusammenhang nicht zwingend. Das Wort *pentêkostê* kann eine gewisse einzutreibende Steuer, den bereits eingetriebenen Ertrag aus dieser Steuer oder dessen Geldwert bzw. Erlös bezeichnen. Für den übertragenen Sinn bietet IG I^3 78 ein gutes Beispiel: „ ... jeweils ein ausgewachsenes Opfertier ... jeder der beiden Göttinnen darbringen von (dem Erlös aus) der Gerste und dem Weizen ..." (Z. 37/38). Gerste und Weizen werden als

---

92 G. Thür, Bemerkungen zum altgriechischen Werkvertrag (die Bauvergabeordnung aus Tegea, IG V/2, 6A), in: Studi Biscardi V, Milano 1984, 475ff.

93 Thür, Werkvertrag (o. Anm. 92) 477f.

94 Die Quelle bringt bereits Stroud, Grain Tax Law (o. Anm. 1) 40 Anm. 80, trotzdem bleibt er bei der geographischen Definition. Zur Inschrift s. F.G. Maier, Griechische Bauinschriften I, Heidelberg 1959, 66.

95 G.V. Lalonde, Greek Inscriptions from the Athenian Agora, Hesperia 61 (1992) 375-379; Faraguna, Intorno (o. Anm. 2) 91 Anm. 87.

96 P.Vindob. G 56636 (im Druck), das Manuskript wurde mir von dem Editor, Dr. Cs. Láda, freundlicherweise überlassen.

97 S. etwa P.Hels. I 6; SB VI 9367 Nr. 9; P.Tebt. III 1029.

98 Vergleicht man diese Menge mit dem typischen Fassungsvermögen der Schiffe, fällt die Geringfügigkeit der Ladung auf. Isager/Hansen, Aspects (o. Anm. 55) 58 betonen, daß die kleineren Getreideschiffe 3.000 Talente, die größeren 5.000 Talente transportieren konnten.

99 Stroud, Grain Tax Law (o. Anm. 1) 28.

aparche, Naturalabgabe, nach Eleusis geliefert. *Krithos* und *pyros* bedeuten hier nicht bloß Gerste und Weizen, sondern die spezielle Art der Abgabe. Die Inschrift formuliert etwas komprimiert und bestimmt die Opfertiere mit der Wendung *apo ton krithon kai ton pyron*. Die Opfertiere werden aus dem Erlös des Getreides angeschafft.

Als weiteres Beispiel ist das Getreidegesetz aus Samos anzuführen[100]; hier liest man καὶ μίσθωσις τοῦ ἀργυρίου τοῦ ἐκ τοῦ τόκου, „Vergabe des an Zinsen eingehenden Geldes“[101]. Die Autoren haben nachgewiesen, daß darunter die öffentliche Vergabe der „Beschaffung möglichst günstigen Getreides“ zu verstehen ist[102]. Eine ähnliche sprachliche Verkürzung ist auch in unserem Gesetz denkbar: Die *dôdekatê* und die *pentêkostê* des Getreides dürften jene Kornmenge bedeutet haben, die *in natura* eingetrieben oder aus dem Ertrag einer Geldsteuer angeschafft wurde und nach Athen zu transportieren war. Nicht das Einheben der Steuer wurde in unserer Inschrift verpachtet, sondern der Transport des Erlöses.

8. Epônia, kêrykeia. Verkaufssteuer und Heroldsgebühr sind bei öffentlichen Versteigerungen regelmäßig zu entrichten[103]. Unser Gesetz schreibt einen pauschalen Betrag von 20 Drachmen je *meris* vor (Z. 23/24). Es bleibt allein unsicher, ob die sechs Mitglieder einer Symmoria 6x20 oder insgesamt nur 20 Drachmen zahlen mußten.

Seine abweichende Deutung des Lizitationsverfahrens knüpft Faraguna an das technische Wort *epônia*[104]. Die Ersteigerer unterlägen nach ihm einer doppelten Zahlungspflicht: Einerseits seien sie verpflichtet, die fixe Menge von 500 Medimnoi zu liefern; andererseits hätten die Poleten die Lizitation über die Höhe der *epônia* (die er als „Vertragsregistrationsgebühr“ versteht) eröffnet. Dieses Modell der doppelten Zahlungspflicht hat Faraguna für die Pacht der staatlichen Bergwerke ausgearbeitet[105]. Das Thema der Bergwerke will ich hier ausklammern. Bezweifeln möchte ich jedenfalls die Übertragbarkeit des Modells auf die Steuerpacht, wo die Quellen (s. oben nur Plutarch und Andokides) eindeutig von einem einheitlichen Betrag und vom Überbieten berichten. Verzichtet man auf die Deutung unserer Inschrift als Steuerpacht, löst sich dieses Problem von selbst.

IV. Zusammenfassend ist festzustellen, daß der wirtschaftliche und juristische Inhalt der Inschrift dafür spricht, in den Zeilen 6-36 nicht die Verpachtung des Rechts der Steuereintreibung, sondern die Vergabe des Transports von Getreide (Steuererlös?) zu sehen. Die Hauptpflicht des Ersteigerers besteht zweifelsohne im *komizein* (lie-

---

100 IG XII 4/1 172, Z. 47/48.

101 So Thür/Koch, Getreidegesetz (o. Anm. 58) 66.

102 Thür/Koch, Getreidegesetz (o. Anm. 58) 75.

103 Hallof, Verkauf (o. Anm. 25) 407ff.

104 Faraguna, Intorno (o. Anm. 2) 91ff.

105 S. seinen Beitrag im Symposion 2003, (o. Anm. 95) 141ff.; mit der Kritik von G. Thür 161ff.

fern, transportieren); die anschließenden Bestimmungen sind typische Klauseln der antiken Frachtverträge. Dementsprechend würde ich die Definition als „Grain Tax Law" oder „Getreidesteuer-Gesetz" ablehnen. Korrekter scheint die Bestimmung als „Getreidegesetz", weil SEG XLVIII 96 bloß den Transport und den öffentlichen Verkauf des Getreides regelt. Agyrrhios hat den staatlichen Transport von Getreide von den drei Klerucheninseln nach Athen vorgeschlagen, um dem Demos im kommenden Frühling bzw. Frühsommer mit dem Verkauf zu fixierten Preisen entgegenzukommen[106]. Dafür hat er – wohl nach dem Muster der privaten Frachtverträge – ein Formular für den staatlichen Gebrauch entworfen. Für einen Neuentwurf spricht das Erlassen der *prokatabole* in Z. 27: Die sonst bei öffentlichen Verträgen prinzipiell verlangte Vorleistung mußte aufgehoben werden. Der Naukleros, der seine *meris* durch Unterbieten der Konkurrenten ersteigerte, mußte nämlich dem Staat keinen „Kaufpreis" zahlen, sondern bekam Entgelt für seine Transportleistung. Für die Deutung als Vertragsformular spricht auch die merkwürdige Syntax, worauf bereits Stroud aufmerksam machte[107]: Der erste Teil des Textes zeigt den typischen Stil der Syngraphai dieser Zeit. Das zum Transport ausgeschriebene Getreide stammt zweifelsohne aus Steuerquellen, aber SEG XLVIII 96 enthält überhaupt keine Normen darüber, wie oder von wem die *dôdekatê* und die *pentêkostê* auf den Inseln eingetrieben wurde. Deshalb ist die Definition als Steuergesetz abzulehnen.

[106] Der politische und wirtschaftliche Kontext ist mit Samos vergleichbar, vgl. Thür/Koch, Getreidegesetz (o. Anm. 58) 70ff.; s. auch P. Garnsey, Famine and Food Supply in the Graeco-Roman World, Cambridge 1988, 70ff. und Isager/Hansen, Aspects (o. Anm. 55) 19ff.

[107] Stroud, Grain Tax Law (o. Anm. 1) 44.

MICHELE FARAGUNA (TRIESTE)

RISPOSTA A ÉVA JAKAB

La *grain-tax law*[1] può essere chiamata a simboleggiare le difficoltà e i limiti entro cui si muove lo storico dell'antichità, impegnato col suo lavoro nel tentativo di ricostruire l'ampio e complesso mosaico della società antica sulla base di un ridottissimo numero di tessere, spesso, tra l'altro, troppo distanti l'una dall'altra nella trama del disegno originario. La stele è infatti perfettamente conservata e il testo dell'iscrizione, fatta eccezione per alcune lettere, pienamente leggibile. Eppure, l'interpretazione della legge rimane almeno in parte ancora sfuggente e controversa[2].

Il *nomos* proposto da Agirrio consta di due sezioni principali: la prima (ll. 5-36) riguarda due imposte, la *dôdekatê*, finora ignota, gravante sul grano (*sitos*) delle isole di Lemno, Imbro e Sciro, e la *pentêkostê* verisimilmente esatta sullo stesso nei porti delle tre isole, salvo poi occuparsi quasi esclusivamente della *dôdekatê*; la seconda (ll. 36-55) contiene invece provvedimenti sulla vendita a prezzo politico del *sitos* ricavato da tali imposte, che – è bene precisare – dovevano d'ora in poi pervenire alla città in natura. Oggetto delle ultime sette righe (ll. 55-61) sono infine alcune disposizioni transitorie di carattere tecnico volte a regolare la destinazione di certe entrate, nell'ambito del sistema finanziario della città, nella fase precedente all'entrata in vigore della legge. Se la seconda sezione evidenzia, sul piano storico, come Atene avesse, nel IV sec. a.C., iniziato a prendere misure per far fronte al problema degli approvvigionamenti granari già alcuni decenni prima di quanto finora si pensasse[3], la prima arricchisce considerevolmente, sul piano istituzionale,

---

1 R.S. Stroud, *The Athenian Grain-Tax Law of 374/3 B.C.*, "Hesperia" Suppl. 29, Princeton 1998 (*SEG* 48,96); cfr. anche P.J. Rhodes-R. Osborne, *Greek Historical Inscriptions, 404-323 B.C.*, Oxford 2003, nr. 26.

2 Almeno in parte questo potrebbe essere legato alle vicende "editoriali" del testo trascritto sulla stele: rispetto agli altri *nomoi* ateniesi conservati la legge non contiene la formula di sanzione (ἔδοξε τοῖς νομοθέταις) né istruzioni circa la pubblicazione del testo e si può presumere che anche le disposizioni che ne costituivano il contenuto centrale siano state riportate in forma abbreviata, o in estratto, rispetto al testo conservato, verisimilmente su papiro, nel *Mêtrôon*; sul rapporto testo epigrafico/testo d'archivio v. da ultimo P.J. Rhodes, *Public Documents in the Greek States: Archives and Inscriptions*, "G&R" 48 (2001), pp. 37-41.

3 Cfr. V.J. Rosivach, *Some Economic Aspects of the Fourth-Century Athenian Market in Grain*, "Chiron" 30 (2000), pp. 31-64, e, soprattutto, J. Engels, *Das athenische Getreidesteuer-Gesetz des Agyrrhios und angebliche 'sozialistische' Ziele in den Maßnahmen zur*

le nostre conoscenze sul sistema degli appalti pubblici e della tassazione nella *polis* attica, rivelando però nello stesso tempo quanto lacunose esse siano.

L'elemento che, da un punto di vista formale, dà unità al contenuto della stele è il titolo di νόμος περὶ τῆς δωδεκάτης τοῦ σίτου τῶν νήσων che compare sulla pietra subito dopo l'indicazione dell'arconte (ll. 3-4)[4]. A partire dall'*editio princeps* dello Stroud l'iscrizione è stata pressoché unanimemente interpretata alla luce di tale titolo, ritenendosi quindi che la legge di Agirrio mirasse a regolare, in successione temporale e logica, tutto il percorso della *dôdekatê* dalla sua esazione in natura alla destinazione ultima dei proventi della vendita del *sitos* al fondo per le spese militari, gli στρατιωτικά (ll. 54-55). La prima sezione riguarderebbe in particolare l'appalto pubblico della riscossione del grano delle isole e il successivo trasporto dello stesso da Lemno, Imbro e Sciro fino all'agorà di Atene. E' qui peraltro che sorgono le maggiori difficoltà perché, stabilendo il *nomos* già *a priori* la quantità di *sitos* (500 medimni) che gli appaltatori si impegnavano a versare alla città per ciascuna μερίς, non si comprende in che cosa potesse consistere l'elemento della "gara" tipico dei meccanismi dell'asta pubblica. Se Stroud lasciava la soluzione di tale questione tutto sommato nell'indeterminato (p. 112-114), R. Osborne ha individuato la "variabile" oggetto della competizione nel numero delle μερίδες per le quali i partecipanti all'asta si offrivano, concludendo poi che vi sarebbe stato di fatto un solo appaltatore per isola[5], mentre io stesso avevo a suo tempo suggerito che ciascuna μερίς dovesse corrispondere ad una suddivisione geografica e fiscale delle isole e che, consistendo il guadagno dell'appaltatore nel differenziale tra l'entità, necessariamente oscillante, della *dôdekatê* e la quota fissa di 500 medimni, la variabile risiedesse nell'entità della tassa di registrazione (gli ἐπώνια καὶ κηρύκεια) delle ll. 27-29, per la quale le 20 dracme della stele sarebbero da considerarsi soltanto un minimo[6]. In ogni caso gli studiosi hanno concordemente assunto che i

---

Getreideversorgung spätklassischer und hellenistischer Poleis, "ZPE" 132 (2000), pp. 97-124.

4 E' verisimile che tale intestazione, pur quasi senza confronti, rifletta di fatto le modalità di archiviazione e di classificazione dei testi nel *Mêtrôon*; cfr. a questo proposito J.P. Sickinger, *Public Records and Archives in Classical Athens*, Chapel Hill-London 1999, pp. 84-91 e 147-157, e, da ultimo, L. Boffo, *Per una storia dell'archiviazione pubblica nel mondo greco*, "Dike" 6 (2003), pp. 19-22.

5 R. Osborne, recens. a Stroud, *The Athenian Grain-Tax Law* cit., "CR" 50 (2000), p. 173: "The person bidding to deliver the highest number of portions wins. In the absence of any evidence for subdivisions of the islands into regions…we should believe that there is only one successful bidder per tax per island"; cfr. anche Rhodes-Osborne, *Greek Historical Inscriptions* cit., p. 125.

6 *Intorno alla nuova legge ateniese sulla tassazione del grano*, "Dike" 2 (1999), pp. 63-97, in part. 90-97. In maniera sostanzialmente analoga A. Moreno, *Athenian Bread-Baskets: The Grain-Tax Law of 374/3 Re-interpreted*, "ZPE" 145 (2003), pp. 97-106, ricollegando la legge alla classificazione censitaria soloniana, ritiene che soltanto i πεντακοσιομέδιμνοι fossero gravati dalla *dôdekatê* e che il guadagno dell'unico appaltatore che si aggiudicava il contratto per le *tre* isole avesse origine nella differenza

meccanismi dell'appalto non erano specificati nella legge, che si rifaceva per essi alle disposizioni generali dei νόμοι τελωνικοί citati da Dem. 24,96-101 e 122, facendo quindi appello a norme che, seppure ipotizzabili con una certa probabilità, sono in qualche modo *esterne* rispetto alla legge di Agirrio[7].

Éva Jakab ha con grande lucidità individuato il punto debole presente in tale modello interpretativo e, forte, tra le altre cose, della sua competenza nell'ambito della documentazione dei papiri, oppone ad esso un modello alternativo secondo cui l'oggetto della prima sezione non sarebbe la vendita all'asta del diritto di esigere i τέλη della *dôdekatê* e della *pentêkostê*, bensì l'appalto pubblico del trasporto del *sitos* dalle tre isole ad Atene. Non avremmo quindi una *grain-tax law* ma un "Frachtvertrag", un contratto di nolo marittimo – un *unicum* di enorme interesse nel panorama della documentazione delle città greche – che il proponente del *nomos*, Agirrio, avrebbe ideato sulla falsariga dei contratti di trasporto privati di cui doveva avere una personale esperienza. Il metodo seguito è quello di un'analisi puntuale e approfondita dei termini-chiave delle ll. 5-36. Mediante tale analisi Éva Jakab mette in luce come il verbo più frequentemente ricorrente ad indicare la prestazione richiesta all'appaltatore sia κομίζειν (con i suoi composti)[8] e come il verbo πωλεῖν indicasse genericamente la vendita all'asta di ogni tipo di contratto pubblico (e non soltanto l'appalto delle miniere e dei *telê* di Arist. *Ath. Pol.* 47,2), offrendo nello stesso tempo un'esegesi ampia e illuminante del significato giuridico di κίνδυνος in tale contesto nonché di alcuni importanti aspetti concreti della pratica commerciale previsti dalla legge, quali le modalità di controllo del volume del carico da consegnare e il lasso di tempo, apparentemente piuttosto largo, concesso a beneficio dell'appaltatore per la pesatura del grano. Viene inoltre sottolineata, a sostegno dell'ipotesi proposta, l'anomalia stilistica del testo che in questa sezione predilige l'enunciazione degli obblighi degli appaltatori mediante l'indicativo futuro, come avviene di norma nelle συγγραφαί, diversamente dall'uso tipico dei *nomoi*, dove prevalgono in genere l'imperativo e l'infinito.

Poiché la nuova interpretazione della legge nasce quasi esclusivamente da una rilettura dell'iscrizione, la sua attendibilità può essere messa alla prova soltanto attraverso una verifica della sua coerenza interna. In particolare, mi è sembrato di grande interesse il meccanismo di assegnazione del contratto postulato da Éva Jakab, e cioè quello dell'asta al ribasso. Il *nauklêros* cui veniva assegnato l'appalto non era infatti, nella sua interpretazione, il miglior offerente, colui cioè che era

---

tra l'imposizione di 1/12 sul prodotto delle terre dei ricchi cleruchi e i 500 medimni che essi dovevano versare alla città.

[7] Su questo punto cfr. L. Migeotte, *Quelques aspects légaux et juridiques de l'affermage des taxes en Grèce ancienne*, in *Symposion 1997* (edd. E. Cantarella-G. Thür), Köln-Weimar-Wien 2001, pp. 165-169.

[8] Per l'uso di questo verbo in relazione al trasporto di grano, oltre a Arist. *Ath. Pol.* 51,4, v. *IG II² 207, c*, l. 17 (su quest'iscrizione cfr. D.H. Kelly, *Charidemos' Citizenship: the Problem of* IG *II² 207*, "ZPE" 83 [1990], pp. 96-109) e 1672, ll. 297-298.

disposto a versare di più alla *polis* per aggiudicarsi il contratto (τῷ τὸ πλεῖστον διδόντι: *IG* II² 2492, l. 36; *SEG* 28,103, ll. 23-24; cfr. anche *SEG* 18,13 [= *Agora* XIX, L 7], ll. 9-10, dove l'espressione è peraltro quasi totalmente integrata)[9], bensì chi, chiedendo di meno, offriva il prezzo più basso. Il modello tenuto presente è, esplicitamente, quello del contratto d'opera, del "Werkvertrag", ed è a questo che intendo ora dedicare alcune brevi riflessioni. Sempre con riferimento ad Atene, prenderò in particolare in esame i casi, meglio documentati, dell'appalto delle stele da iscrivere con il testo di decreti e leggi e quello dell'appalto dei lavori pubblici. Tengo a precisare che nessuno dei due casi viene considerato da F. Pringsheim nel suo classico saggio su *Der griechische Versteigerungskauf*[10].

Quanto all'appalto delle stele, la legge di Nicofonte sul saggio della moneta approvata nel 375/4 a.C., un anno prima di quella di Agirrio (*SEG* 26,72; Rhodes-Osborne, *Greek Historical Inscriptions* cit., nr. 25), rivela come, nonostante il silenzio quasi totale delle fonti, i poleti continuassero anche nel IV sec. ad avere tale responsabilità (ll. 47-49: ὁ δὲ γραμματε[ὺ]ς [ὁ] τῆς βολῆς παραγγειλάτω μίσθωμα τοῖς πωλ[ηταῖς], οἱ δὲ πωληταὶ ἐσενεγκόντων εἰς τὴμ βολήν)[11]. Una recente sistematica raccolta dei dati relativi al costo dell'iscrizione di decreti e leggi tra il 408/7 e il 270 a.C. ha messo in luce come questi variassero ad intervalli fissi di 10 tra le 20 e le 50 dracme secondo la lunghezza del testo e altri non sempre ben precisabili fattori[12]. Il verbo δοῦναι con cui nei decreti viene espresso l'ordine dato al ταμίας τοῦ δήμου (o allo ὁ ἐπὶ τῇ διοικήσει) di "erogare" una certa somma indica peraltro in modo chiaro che tale somma veniva stabilita, probabilmente sulla base delle normali tariffe, già *a priori*, e non era perciò oggetto di un'asta pubblica. In relazione ad un lavoro così specializzato, ci si può anzi domandare se l'offerta potesse essere così ampia da giustificare il ricorso alla procedura dell'asta al ribasso.

La stessa cosa vale, a mio giudizio, anche per l'appalto dei lavori pubblici, che, come è noto, ad Atene venivano parcellizzati in un numero molto elevato di lotti e gestiti *direttamente* dai magistrati cittadini[13]. Gli studiosi per lo più assumono, a dire

---

9 Sul sistema della vendita pubblica all'asta cfr. M.K. Langdon, *Public Auctions in Athens*, in *Ritual, Finance, Politics. Athenian Democratic Accounts Presented to David Lewis* (edd. R. Osborne-S. Hornblower), Oxford 1994, pp. 253-265, con discussione della precedente bibliografia; utili osservazioni anche in S.D. Lambert, Rationes Centesimarum. *Sales of Public Land in Lykourgan Athens*, Amsterdam 1997, pp. 265-268.

10 F. Pringsheim, *Der griechische Versteigerungskauf*, in *Gesammelte Abhandlungen*, II, Heidelberg 1961, pp. 262-329.

11 Si veda in proposito Langdon, *Poletai Records*, in *The Athenian Agora*, XIX, Princeton 1991, pp. 62-63.

12 W.T. Loomis, *Wages, Welfare Costs and Inflation in Classical Athens*, Ann Arbor 1998, pp. 121-165.

13 G. Bodei Giglioni, *Lavori pubblici e occupazione nell'antichità classica*, Bologna 1974, pp. 51-54; R. Martini, *Lavori pubblici e appalti nella Grecia antica*, in *I rapporti*

il vero, che il sistema dell'asta al ribasso fosse in questo contesto quello dominante[14] ma, benché la documentazione sia ampia e io possa quindi sbagliarmi, nel caso specifico di Atene in età classica non mi sembra vi siano solidi elementi in questo senso. Se infatti a Tegea (*IG* V, 2, 6A; G. Thür-H. Taeuber, *Prozessrechtliche Inschriften der griechischen Poleis: Arkadien (IPArk)*, Wien 1994, nr. 3) e a Lebadea (*IG* VII 3073) nei regolamenti si fa riferimento all'"imprenditore" con il termine ἐργώνης, ad Atene e a Delo al tempo della dominazione ateniese l'appaltatore viene regolarmente definito μισθωτής o ὁ μισθωσάμενος (nel caso dei lavoratori a giornata ricorre invece ὁ μισθωτός)[15]. Ciò che più importa, al di là di questa non dirimente differenza terminologica, è tuttavia che nei documenti relativi ai lavori di costruzione (o ricostruzione) dell'Eretteo (*IG* I^3 474-479), delle mura del Pireo e delle Lunghe Mura (*IG* II^2 1656-1664 [= Maier, *Griechische Mauerbauinschriften* cit., nrr. 1-9] [395/4-392/1 a.C.]; *IG* II^2 244 [= Maier, *Griechische Mauerbauinschriften* cit., nr. 10] [337/6 a.C.]), e del Prostoon del *Telesterion* e del muro di cinta del santuario ad Eleusi (rispettivamente, *IG* II^2 1673 + *SEG* 34,122; e 1672, in part. ll. 1-78 [= Maier, *Griechische Mauerbauinschriften* cit., nr. 20)[16] i pagamenti vengono erogati nella forma di una paga fissa giornaliera o di compensi standard per ciascun pezzo finito o per misura di muro commissionata, senza che, laddove il confronto tra i dati sia possible, sia lecito riscontrare alcuna oscillazione o variazione imputabile ai meccanismi dell'appalto mediante asta pubblica[17]. Nel caso dei grandi lavori edilizi, il problema della città, come evidenziato da A. Wittenburg, era del resto soprattutto quello di assicurarsi manodopera affidabile e in numero sufficiente[18]. Numerose clausole dei contratti non a caso miravano ad agevolare gli appaltatori con esenzioni fiscali e anticipi dei pagamenti (cfr. ad es. *IG* II^2 1678 [= *IDélos* 104-4], ll. 1-24) e questo porta

---

contrattuali con la pubblica amministrazione nell'esperienza storico-giuridica, Napoli 1997, pp. 37-53.

14 F.G. Maier, *Griechische Mauerbauinschriften*, II, Heidelberg 1961, pp. 17-18; G. Thür, *Bemerkungen zum altgriechischen Werkvertrag (die bauvergabeordnung aus Tegea, IG V/2, 6A)*, in *Studi in onore di Arnaldo Biscardi*, V, Milano, 1984, pp. 476-477 e 505-506 n. 98; M.-C. Hellmann, *Choix d'inscriptions architecturales grecques*, Lyon-Paris 1999, p. 55 (con rif. a *IG* VII 3073) e *passim*; più cauta A. Burford, *The Greek Temple Builders at Epidauros*, Liverpool 1969, p. 161.

15 Martini, *Lavori pubblici* cit., pp. 38-44.

16 Sui lavori edilizi nel santuario di Eleusi in età licurghea cfr. B. Hintzen-Bohlen, *Die Kulturpolitik des Eubulos und des Lykurg. Die Denkmäler- und Bauprojekte in Athen zwischen 355 und 322 v. Chr.*, Berlin 1997, pp. 18-21 e 53-54.

17 R.H. Randall, *The Erechtheum Workmen*, "AJA" 57 (1953), pp. 199-210; Loomis, *Wages* cit., pp. 104-120.

18 A. Wittenburg, *Texte und Bemerkungen zum Werkvertrag bei den Griechen*, in *Studien zur alten Geschichte Siegfried Lauffer zum 70. Geburtstag am 4. August 1981 dargebracht von Freunden, Kollegen und Schülern* (edd. H. Kalcyk-B. Gullath-A. Graeber), III, Roma 1986, pp. 1079-1088; cfr. anche, dello stesso, *Griechische Baukommissionen des 5. und 4. Jahrhunderts*, München 1978.

nuovamente a pensare che l'assegnazione dei lotti, più che mediante una vera e propria asta al ribasso, avvenisse in seguito ad una contrattazione tra i magistrati preposti ai lavori e i singoli artigiani o imprenditori.

Se dunque il sistema dell'asta al ribasso non sembra documentato in rapporto alla città di Atene, va poi osservato che, per quanto alcune iscrizioni di Delo della fine del IV e del III sec. a.C. – e quindi nel periodo dell'indipendenza – mostrino in modo chiarissimo che l'appalto dei lavori veniva di norma pubblicizzato nell'agorà mediante l'araldo pubblico (cfr. ad es. *IG* XI, 2, 145, ll. 10-11: τοῦ Διοσκουρίου τὸν τοῖχον ἐξέδομεν...ὑπὸ κήρυκος ἐν τῆι ἀγορᾶι κατὰ τὴν συγγραφὴν οἰκοδομῆσαι; ll. 17-18; 146, A, ll. 44 (integrato) e 72-73; 162, A, ll. 42-43; 199, D, ll. 41-46), mai compare nella documentazione in questo contesto l'obbligo di versare alla città una somma a titolo di ἐπώνια καὶ κηρύκεια, che troviamo invece attestati nel caso della vendita di beni confiscati e nell'appalto dei *telê* (Harpocr. s.v. κηρύκεια; *Lexeis Rhetorikai*, s.v. ἐπώνια καὶ κηρύκεια, p. 255 Bekker)[19]. Sarebbe stato anzi paradossale se gli artigiani, che lavoravano per un compenso fisso e preventivamente stabilito, fossero stati anche tenuti a versare dei *telê* per aggiudicarsi il lavoro e il contratto. In maniera del tutto analoga, se ora ritorniamo alla legge di Agirrio, sulla base del nuovo modello interpretativo dovremmo pensare che i *nauklêroi* (o *emporoi* [ll. 26-27]) che si aggiudicavano le *merides* offrendo il prezzo più basso e accollandosi tutti i costi e i rischi della navigazione erano anche soggetti agli ἐπώνια καὶ κηρύκεια, ciò che appare eccessivamente penalizzante e tutto sommato poco plausibile. Data l'importanza del grano delle isole, tale in ogni caso da determinare l'approvazione di un nuovo *nomos* della città, era infatti nell'interesse di Atene di invogliare i potenziali appaltatori, e non di scoraggiarli o disincentivarli.

Una seconda questione riguarda inoltre la προκαταβολή, il versamento anticipato richiesto all'appaltatore, che viene menzionata nella legge alla l. 27 e nelle disposizioni di carattere tecnico-finanziario che concludono l'iscrizione (ll. 55-61). Nella prima viene esplicitamente stabilita l'esenzione per ὁ πριάμενος dal versamento della "rata iniziale" (cfr. Soud. s.v. προκαταβολὴ καὶ προσκαταβόλημα). Nelle seconde, secondo la convincente interpretazione di E.M. Harris, viene invece previsto che, nel tempo che rimaneva fino all'effettiva entrata in vigore della legge, la *prokatabolê*, pari a due versamenti mensili (da qui "i due decimi"), dovesse essere sempre destinata al fondo generale dell'amministrazione (διοίκησις), mentre in futuro tutti i proventi della vendita del *sitos* sarebbero stati versati nella cassa militare[20]. Ciò viene per lo più interpretato a significare che la legge di Agirrio in realtà *non* introduceva una nuova imposta, la *dôdekatê*, ma ne disponeva l'esazione in natura e non più in moneta. Se questa

---

[19] Documentazione in K. Hallof, *Der Verkauf konfiszierten Vermögens vor den Poleten in Athen*, "Klio" 72 (1990), pp. 407-410.

[20] E.M. Harris, *Notes on the New Grain-Tax Law*, "ZPE" 128 (1999), pp. 269-270.

lettura è corretta, ciò dimostra indirettamente che erano gli appaltatori e non la città ad effettuare i pagamenti e che il sistema dell'appalto regolato dal *nomos* era quello della vendita all'asta al miglior offerente tipico dell'appalto delle imposte e non quello dell'asta al ribasso di un "servizio", in questo caso quello del trasporto del grano dalle isole ad Atene.

E' lecito in definitiva concludere che, conformemente all'interpretazione più naturale dell'espressione τὴν δωδεκάτην πωλεῖν...καὶ τὴν πεντηκοστήν, e cioè "dare in appalto (la riscossione del)la *dôdekatê* e (del)la *pentêkostê*", piuttosto che "vendere all'asta (il trasporto del ricavato del)la *dôdekatê* e (del)la *pentêkostê*", la legge di Agirrio può a buon diritto essere ancora definita una *grain-tax law*. Più che a due modelli interpretativi antitetici e contrapposti, mi sembra di conseguenza più utile pensare ad un unico modello integrato in cui le lucide osservazioni di Éva Jakab hanno il merito di farci meglio comprendere, nei loro aspetti giuridici e pratici, le disposizioni concernenti il trasporto del *sitos* delle isole a cura di coloro che prendevano in appalto l'esazione delle due imposte.

Rimane naturalmente ancora aperta la questione delle *merides* e di come gli appaltatori ricavassero in concreto un profitto dal contratto che stipulavano con la città. Il problema sorge a causa dell'apparente anomalia di una tassa riscossa in *sitos* e non, come avveniva quasi regolarmente nel V e IV sec., in moneta (Plut. *Alc.* 5, 1-5; And. 1,133) e la soluzione deve essere cercata nei meccanismi attraverso cui economia monetaria ed economia naturale si integravano e interagivano. Nonostante un certo scetticismo dei commentatori[21], l'idea che le *merides* corrispondessero a suddivisioni territoriali e fiscali delle isole, su cui l'appaltatore acquisiva il diritto di riscuotere la *dôdekatê*, rimane sempre, a mio giudizio, quella più convincente[22]. Se la recente ipotesi di A. Moreno secondo cui le simmorie che riunivano sei *merides* sarebbero state in realtà, conformemente al significato usuale del termine, *gruppi di contribuenti*, per quanto allettante, mi sembra non facilmente giustificabile all'interno del quadro complessivo della legge[23], è utile richiamare l'attenzione su *IG* I^3 420, un frammento di iscrizione recentemente reinterpretato come una lista di beni immobili, di cui viene specificata anche l'estensione, relativa a qualche cleruchia[24]. Essa rivela una volta di più come le città greche fossero interessate a

---

21 Cfr. ad es. *BE* 2001, nr. 165.

22 Che l'unità di riferimento fosse di carattere territoriale è in ultima analisi assunto anche da R. Osborne e A. Moreno (citati alle nn. 5 e 6).

23 Essa si giustifica infatti quasi esclusivamente all'interno dell'assunto che i cleruchi soggetti alla *dôdekatê* fossero soltanto i pentacosiomedimni; sulla scarsa attendibilità (o breve vita) del sistema descritto da Pollux 8,130, che sta alla base di tale costruzione, si veda ora peraltro G.E.M. de Ste. Croix, *Athenian Democratic Origins and Other Essays*, Oxford 2004, pp. 56-60.

24 W.S. Morison, *Property Records for Athenian Cleruchs or Colonists? Notes on* IG *II^2 420*, "ZPE" 145 (2003), pp. 109-113.

tenere registrazioni scritte sull'assetto della proprietà fondiaria[25] e dimostra che una qualche semplice forma di controllo e ripartizione fiscale del territorio delle isole di Lemno, Imbro e Sciro non sarebbe stata, dal punto di vista della fattibilità pratica, del tutto impossibile[26].

[25] Cfr. a questo proposito M. Faraguna, *A proposito degli archivi nel mondo greco: terra e registrazioni fondiarie*, "Chiron" 30 (2000), pp. 65-115; Id., *Vendite di immobili e registrazione pubblica nelle città greche*, in *Symposion 1999* (edd. G. Thür-F.J. Fernández Nieto), Köln-Weimar-Wien 2003, pp. 97-122.

[26] [Non mi è stato possible tenere conto del contributo di U. Fantasia, *Appaltatori, grano pubblico, finanze cittadine: ancora sul* nomos *di Agirrio*, "MedAnt" 7 (2004), pp. 513-540, che ho potuto vedere soltanto quando questa "risposta" era ormai ultimata.]

GERHARD THÜR (GRAZ)

DAS PRINZIP DER FAIRNESS IM ATTISCHEN PROZESS: GEDANKEN ZU ECHINOS UND ENKLEMA

Tragen zwei Bürger einer staatlichen Gemeinschaft ihren Streit vor einer objektiven Stelle aus, erwartet jeder, nicht von vornherein benachteiligt zu sein. Eine allgemein akzeptierte Prozessordnung muss einerseits organisatorische Vorkehrungen dafür treffen, dass das Gericht ohne äußeren Druck oder Bestechung entscheiden kann, andererseits aber auch das Verhalten der Prozessparteien und ihrer Vertreter an gewisse Spielregeln binden. Eine dieser Spielregeln ist das sogenannte ‚Neuerungsverbot'. In modernen Prozessordnungen darf das Berufungsgericht nur diejenigen Beweismittel zur Kenntnis nehmen, welche die Parteien bereits der ersten Instanz vorgelegt haben. In jüngster Zeit wird auch ein Neuerungsverbot innerhalb der ersten Instanz diskutiert, um Prozessverschleppung zu verhindern. Der attische Prozess kannte ein ähnliches Neuerungsverbot – unbestrittenermaßen für Prozesse, welche die amtliche, obligatorische Diaita durchliefen.[1] In Athen ging es allerdings nicht um Prozessverschleppung, sondern um den Schutz der Prozessparteien vor Überraschungsangriffen des Gegners in der zeitlich limitierten Hauptverhandlung. Beide Regelungen wollen das Prinzip der Fairness in der Prozessführung fördern.

Gerichtsorganisation und Ablauf des Verfahrens sind in hohem Grad abhängig von ihrem sozialen Umfeld. Als gerecht akzeptierte Entscheidungen können auf vielerlei Wegen gefunden werden, Objektivität des Gerichts und Fairness der Parteien sind jedoch zeitlose Probleme. Für den Rechtshistoriker ist es reizvoll zu untersuchen, wie unterschiedlich und zeitgebunden diesen Prinzipien ausgeformt wurden.

Seit Generationen wird das gut dokumentierte Prozessrecht des klassischen Athen nach diesen Gesichtspunkten erforscht. Der attische Prozess wird dabei entweder als Paradigma einer demokratischen Rechtsprechung gelobt oder als Willkürjustiz einer leicht verführbaren Masse von Spießbürgern verteufelt.[2] In meinem Beitrag möchte ich jede – mir ohnedies suspekte – ideologisierende Wertung vermeiden. Spannend genug wird es sein, das Prozessrecht Athens in seiner historischen Bedingtheit zu betrachten. Dabei müssen wir allerdings von einigen modernen Vorstellungen der gerichtlichen Wahrheitsfindung Abschied nehmen. Im attischen Prozess ist das Beweisrecht geprägt von der demokratischen Gerichtsorganisation, den großen Dikasterien; und aus den Besonderheiten des Beweisrechts ergeben sich

---

[1] Harrison (1971) 97, 102.

[2] S. Todd (1973) 91 mit weiterer Literatur.

zwanglos einige Regeln der Fairness für den Umgang der Prozessparteien untereinander.

In die Augen springend und bestens erforscht ist das Bemühen der Athener, die Chancengleichheit für beide Prozessparteien am Gerichtstag selbst herzustellen. Zu den demokratischen Spielregeln des Gerichtstages zählen die gleichmäßige Auslosung der Geschworenen aus allen zehn Phylen der Bürgerschaft unmittelbar am Tag der Hauptverhandlung, die Auslosung der Sitzplätze in den bereits durch Los zusammengestellten Dikasterien und die Zulosung der Dikasterien an die an diesem Tag als Vorsitzende parallel amtierenden Gerichtsmagistrate. Bis zum letzten Augenblick weiß also niemand, welche Richter welchen Prozess zu entscheiden haben, Bestechung ist unmöglich. Ebenso unmöglich ist es auch, dass Claqueure (ähnlich wie heute im Theaterbetrieb) in Gruppen Sitzplätze einnehmen und durch Beifalls- oder Missfallenskundgebungen die Stimmung ihrer Richterkollegen für oder gegen eine Partei anheizen. Vom gefährlichen „Lärmen“ der Richter, dem *thorybos*, und seiner gruppendynamischen Funktion im Prozess wird später noch die Rede sein. Durch diese Maßnahmen und die perfekt organisierte geheime Abstimmung ist – von den äußeren Bedingungen her gesehen – eine objektive Entscheidung durch die demokratischen Massengerichte optimal gewährleistet. Der Chancengleichheit zwischen den Parteien dient auch ein weiterer, sehr einfacher Mechanismus: Durch eine Wasseruhr (*klepsydra*) wird dem Kläger und dem Beklagten exakt die gleiche Redezeit zugemessen. All das ist in den Kapiteln 63-69 der *Athenaion Politeia* mit großer Liebe zum Detail beschrieben und durch archäologische Funde aus der Agora dokumentiert.[3]

Mit ‚Fairness' haben die soeben genannten strikten Regeln des Ablaufs eines Prozesses in Athen allerdings wenig zu tun. Ich möchte sie „äußere“ Rahmenbedingungen der Chancengleicheit vor Gericht nennen. Gibt es auch „innere“, den Inhalt der Gerichtsreden bestimmende Rahmenbedingungen? Hier könnte man von Regeln der Fairness sprechen. Jeder, der die attischen Gerichtsreden etwas genauer kennt, wird sofort bezweifeln, dass die Sprecher von irgendeinem Prinzip der Fairness gleitet wurden. Die Hauptverhandlung vor den Geschworenen ist ein *agôn*, eine Redeschlacht. Die Parteien und ihre Mitstreiter, *synêgoroi*, scheinen ihre Auseinandersetzungen wie Freistilringer auszutragen; jeder üble Trick, jeder Überraschungsangriff scheinen erlaubt. Doch besteht der Prozess in Athen bekanntlich nicht nur aus den Plädoyers und der Abstimmung im Dikasterion. Um die leitenden Prinzipien zu erkennen, muss man das gesamte Verfahren zumindest von der Klageerhebung an betrachten – richtigerweise auch noch die völlig privaten Auseinandersetzungen davor. Als erstes Gebot der Fairness ist zu erkennen, dass Prozesse von den Dikasterien überhaupt zu vermeiden seien. Ein anständiger Mensch regelt seine privaten Streitigkeiten im Kreise von Freunden und Bekannten. Es ist geradezu ein Topos, dem Gegner im Prozess vorzuwerfen, die privaten Vergleichsverhandlungen zum

[3] Boegehold (1995), Thür (2000).

Scheitern gebracht zu haben.[4] Außer dem Argument vor Gericht zieht ein Verstoß gegen dieses Gebot der Fairness jedoch keine rechtlichen Konsequenzen nach sich. Der ‚Gütegedanke' darf freilich in der weiteren Erklärung des staatlichen Verfahrens nicht vernachlässigt werden.

Nach rechtlichen Rahmenbedingungen für faires Verhalten der Parteien wird man sinnvollerweise erst ab dem Erheben der Klage oder Anklage suchen. Außer Betracht kann dabei die Vorschrift bleiben, der Kläger habe den Beklagten vor Zeugen, *klêtêres*, zu laden.[5] Sie schützt den Beklagten gegen ein zu Unrecht ergehendes Säumnisurteil, gehört aber nicht zu den Vorschriften, welche sich auf den Inhalt der Plädoyers auswirken.

Ohne das Prinzip der Fairness beim Namen zu nennen, hat sich Franz Lämmli 1938 dem Thema mit einer philologisch exakten Fragestellung genähert. Anhand der 1. Rede des Andokides und Pseudo-Lysias 6 untersucht er die Fragen, wie ein Sprecher vor Gericht auf *unvorhergesehene Beweismittel* und *Argumente* seines Gegners reagiert hat und wie weit die schriftlich in den Verkehr gebrachte Fassung einer Gerichtsrede die erst vor dem Dikasterion gehörten Argumente des Gegners berücksichtigt. Die zweite, im engsten Sinn philologische Frage möchte ich hier auf sich beruhen lassen. Sie scheint mir nur aktuell für Plädoyers, an deren Publikation der Rhetor selbst ein persönliches politisches Interesse hatte, wie etwa die drei Reden des Andokides oder Demosthenes 18 und Aischines 3. Die Mehrzahl der Privatreden stammt aus der Logographenwerkstatt. Man kann davon ausgehen, dass sie Wort für Wort so publiziert wurden, wie sie die Sprecher auswendig gelernt und vor Gericht vorgetragen haben. Nicht überliefert wurden in den meisten Fällen die vor Gericht zur Verlesung gebrachten Urkunden. Ich nehme an, dass ihr Text ursprünglich – der Gerichtspraxis entsprechend – als von den Holztäfelchen abgeschriebene Dossiers am Schluss der publizierten Reden angefügt war. Der spätere rhetorische Unterricht verlor leider das Interesse an diesen für den Rechtshistoriker so wichtigen, in den Kategorien der Schule aber nur „kunstlosen" Produkten der Prozessführung, so dass überwiegend nur noch die Lemmata *martyria*, *proklêsis* oder *nomos* im Text erhalten sind, bestenfalls mit aus dem anhängenden Dossier frühzeitig eingefügten Texten der Urkunden – oder, schlechtestenfalls, mit gefälschten, aus dem Text der Rede rekonstruierten Dokumenten. Diese ‚Logographenreden' geben Aufschluss über die Regeln der Fairness.

Bereits Lämmli hat sich klar die Frage gestellt, woher die Logographen, welche die Plädoyers für ihre Kunden im vorhinein Wort für Wort konzipierten, den Standpunkt des Gegners, den dieser erst vor dem Dikasterion vortragen wird, erfahren konnten. Welche Einrichtungen garantierten dafür, dass die Parteien 1.) vor Gericht nicht hoffnungslos aneinander vorbeiredeten und 2.) nicht plötzlich im Prozess völ-

[4] Scafuro (1997) 69-75, Lanni (2005) 115f., (2006) 48f.

[5] Harrison (1971) 85.

lig unvorbereitet mit noch nie geäußerten Vorwürfen konfrontiert wurden. Beide Probleme sind im attischen Prozess einigermaßen befriedigend gelöst.

Die erste Frage löst sich bereits durch das eigene Interesse der Parteien, die materiellen Erfordernisse der erhobenen Klage zu beweisen oder zu bestreiten. Es ist eine bekannte Tatsache, dass die gegensätzlichen Standpunkte der Parteien nicht erst in der Hauptverhandlung vor dem Dikasterion aufeinanderprallten, sondern bereits in einem Vorverfahren abgeklärt wurden, welches der Gerichtsvorstand oder eine staatlich beauftragte Privatperson, der erloste Diaitet, durchführten. Diese Funktion erfüllten die *prodikasiai* in Blutprozessen, die amtliche *diaita* in den meisten Privatprozessen und die *anakrisis* in den übrigen Verfahren. Bereits Lämmli[6] hat festgestellt, dass in der Anakrisis nicht der Gerichtsvorstand den Parteien Fragen nach den Prozessvoraussetzungen stellt,[7] sondern die Parteien einander nach den für ihre Argumentation relevanten Tatsachen befragen, einander zu Stellungnahmen und Zugeständnissen provozieren und so ihre Plädoyers vor dem Dikasterion vorbereiten. Als rechtliche Maßnahmen standen zwei Gesetze zur Verfügung: Eines verpflichtet die Parteien, dem Gegner auf seine Fragen zu antworten (Dem. 46, 10): „Beide Gegner müssen einander auf Fragen antworten, bezeugen aber nicht."[8] Ein zweites hält die Parteien an einer zustimmenden Antwort fest, so dass der Zustimmende den Wortlaut vor dem Dikasterion nicht mehr abstreiten kann (Dem. 49, 12): „..., dass gegenseitige *homologiai* (Zugeständnisse) maßgeblich sind, welche die Parteien vor Zeugen machen".[9] Die prozessuale Funktion dieses ‚Homologiegesetzes' habe ich schon vor Jahren wahrscheinlich gemacht.[10]

Man kann diese Vorverfahren unter zwei Gesichtspunkten sehen: Einerseits wird der Prozessstoff so strukturiert, dass das Dikasterion eine Grundlage hat, objektiv zu entscheiden. Andererseits können die Parteien einander durch geschicktes Fragen die tragenden Argumente ihrer künftigen Plädoyers entlocken. Das Spiel von Frage und Antwort in den Vorverfahren steht, von der Technik und Methode der Verhandlungsführung betrachtet, im Gegensatz zum zusammenhängenden Plädieren vor den Dikasterien, die bekanntlich mit mehreren hundert Geschworenen besetzt waren. Man kann, zugespritzt, von einem ‚rhetorischen' Verfahrensabschnitt, der Hauptverhandlung, und einem ‚dialektischen', dem Vorverfahren, sprechen.[11] Die Ergänzung des rhetorischen, entscheidenden Abschnitts durch den vorbereitenden

---

[6] Lämmli (1938) 83, s. auch Thür (1977) 76, (2005) 156.

[7] So noch Wolff (1961) 61, (1965) 2519f.

[8] Dem. 46, 10: ΝΟΜΟΣ. Τοῖν ἀντιδίκοιν ἐπάναγκες εἶναι ἀποκρίνασθαι ἀλλήλοις τὸ ἐρωτώμενον, μαρτυρεῖν δὲ μή. S. auch Isai. 6, 12.

[9] Dem. 42, 12: ... ἀλλ' ἀνθ' ἑνὸς δύο νόμους ἥκει πρὸς ὑμᾶς παραβεβηκώς, ἕνα μὲν τὸν κελεύοντα τριῶν ἡμερῶν ἀφ' ἧς ἂν ὀμόσῃ τὴν οὐσίαν ἀποφαίνειν, ἕτερον δὲ τὸν κελεύοντα κυρίας εἶναι τὰς πρὸς ἀλλήλους ὁμολογίας, ἃς ἂν ἐναντίον ποιήσωνται μαρτύρων.

[10] Thür (1977) 155.

[11] Thür (1977) 156, 313; (2005) 152.

dialektischen war zweifellos eine Maßnahme, welche die Fairness der Prozessführung förderte.

So weit herrscht Einigkeit in der wissenschaftlichen Literatur. Höchst kontrovers werden jedoch meine folgenden Ausführungen sein. Ich werde entgegen der allgemeinen Meinung nachzuweisen versuchen, dass die Fairness im attischen Prozess so weit ging, dass die Parteien einander in *allen* Prozessen sämtliche Beweisurkunden vorlegen und diese in versiegelten Tonbehältern, *echinoi*, deponieren mussten, gleichgültig, ob das Verfahren eine obligatorische Diaita durchlaufen hatte oder eine Anakrisis. Schließlich möchte ich auch das neuerdings aufgeworfene Thema der ‚Relevanz' von Prozessbehauptungen mit dem Prinzip der Fairness in Verbindung bringen. Irrelevant – *exô tou pragmatos* – war nicht, was *rechtlich* nicht zur Sache gehört, sondern was der Kläger nicht ausdrücklich in seine *Klageschrift*, in sein *enklêma* oder seine *graphê*, aufgenommen hat.

In der Literatur hat sich zur ersten Frage, zur Verwendung von *echinoi*, die Meinung durchgesetzt, dass das ‚Neuerungsverbot' nur für jene Privatprozesse gegolten habe, die vor den Vierzigmännern, von denen je vier für eine Phyle zuständig waren, anhängig zu machen waren.[12] Die einzeln amtierenden Mitglieder der Vierzig führten im Gegensatz zur Jurisdiktion der Archonten keine Anakrisis durch, sondern losten den Parteien aus der Liste der Bürger, die das 59. Lebensjahr vollendet hatten, einen Diaiteten zu. Dieser „amtliche" oder besser „erloste" Diaitet hatte, von der Prozessordnung her, zunächst die gleiche Funktion wie der Gerichtsmagistrat im Rahmen der Anakrisis. Die Diaita hatte jedoch die Besonderheit, dass sie mit einem Urteilsvorschlag des Diaiteten endete, einer *apophasis*. Da wir nie vom Inhalt eines ‚Diaitetenurteils' hören, dürfte dieses – entsprechend den Gerichtsurteilen – nur aus einem zustimmenden oder ablehnenden Vermerk zur Klageschrift bestanden haben. Die Parteien konnten sich mit dem Vorschlag des Diaiteten beruhigen (*emmenein*, AP 53, 2) oder wie nach einer Anakrisis in den rhetorischen Verfahrensabschnitt eintreten (*ephienai*) und – nach Rede und Gegenrede – das Dikasterion über ihren Fall abstimmen lassen. In diesem Fall hatte der Diaitet sämtliches Urkundenmaterial an das zuständige Mitglied der Vierzigmänner zu übergeben, welches dann als Gerichtsmagistrat den Vorsitz im Dikasterion führte. In ihrem Katalog der Ämter beschreibt die *Athenaion Politeia* im Abschnitt über die Vierzigmänner auch das Verfahren der obligatorischen Diaita. Hier erfahren wir von der Vorschrift, dass die Parteien vor dem Dikasterion nur die beim Diaiteten vorgelegten Urkunden benutzen durften (AP 53, 3).[13] Galt dieses Neuerungsverbot nur für Diaitetenprozesse oder auch für alle übrigen Gerichtsverfahren?

---

[12] Harrison (1971) 97.

[13] Ath. Pol. 53, 2-3: ... οἱ δὲ παραλαβόντες, [ἐ]ὰν μὴ δύνωνται διαλῦσαι, γιγνώσκουσι, κἂν μὲν ἀμφοτέροις ἀρέσκῃ τὰ γνωσθέντα καὶ ἐμμένωσιν, ἔχει τέλος ἡ δίκη. ἂν δ' ὁ ἕτερος ἐφῇ τῶν ἀντιδίκων εἰς τὸ δικαστήριον, ἐμβαλόντες τὰς μαρτυρίας καὶ τὰς προκλήσεις καὶ τοὺς νόμους εἰς ἐχίνους, χωρὶς μὲν τὰς τοῦ διώκοντος, χωρὶς δὲ τὰς τοῦ φεύγοντος, καὶ τούτους κατασημηνάμενοι, καὶ τὴν γνῶσιν τοῦ διαιτητοῦ

Vor dem Fund der *Athenaion Politeia* war die Antwort anscheinend klar. Nach Meier-Schömann waren alle vor dem Dikasterion zu verlesenden Dokumente bereits in der Anakrisis vorzulegen.[14] Auf Bonner geht die Meinung zurück, die in der *Athenaion Politeia* erwähnten *echinoi* seien nur in der Vorverhandlung vor dem Diaiteten verwendet worden, in der Anakrisis hingegen nicht.[15] Es habe also in diesen Prozessen kein Neuerungsverbot gegeben. Diese Meinung hat sich bis heute gehalten, obwohl 1982 endlich ein archäologisches Zeugnis für einen solchen Dokumentenbehälter aus dem 4./3. Jh. v.Chr. publiziert wurde. Es handelt sich um den Deckel eines Tontopfes mit der Aufschrift: „... *ex anakriseôs* ...“[16] Dieser Fund hat jedoch noch niemanden zu einem Umdenken veranlasst.[17] In Symposion 1997 schreibt zum Beispiel Wallace: „... use of the *echinos* in *anakriseis* was intended only a way of preserving documents vital to the case.“[18] Es ist also an der Zeit, die Meinung Bonners aus dem Jahre 1905 kritisch zu überprüfen. Sedes materiae ist jedoch nicht Bonner, sondern Lämmli, der in dem erwähnten Werk 1938 in einem Kapitel „Die Bedeutung der Anakrisis im attischen Rechtsverfahren“ sorgsam alle Quellen behandelt, welche die These Bonners angeblich bestätigten.[19] Trotz großer Skepsis und gewichtiger Gegenargumente kommt auch Lämmli zu dem Schluss, in den Anakrisis-Prozessen habe es kein Neuerungsverbot gegeben. Das ist falsch.

Bevor ich auf die Quellen eingehe, ist noch ein Wort über die Vorstellungen zu verlieren, mit welchen die genannten Autoren an das attische Prozessrecht herangingen. Der Jurist nennt dieses Grundverständnis „Dogmatik“. Dogmatik bedeutet in der Jurisprudenz nicht ein System von Glaubenssätzen, sondern induktiv gefundene Grundsätze zum besseren Verständnis einer Rechtsordnung. Die obligatorische Diaita ist ein gutes Beispiel dafür. Bis heute wird die Meinung vertreten, der erloste Diaitet entscheide den Prozess in erster Instanz, und das Dikasterion fungiere nach dem *ephienai* der unterlegenen Partei als ‚Berufungsgericht‘.[20] Steinwenter hat bereits 1925 nachgewiesen, dass man nicht von „Berufung“ sprechen dürfe, sondern vom Anrufen des zuständigen Gerichts nach einem bloßen Versuch zur gütlichen Einigung durch den Diaiteten.[21] Der Streit um die moderne Bezeichnung der *ephesis* und ihre dogmatische Einordnung mag spitzfindig anmuten, zieht jedoch Konsequenzen nach sich, derer sich philologische Bearbeiter der Quellen nicht immer

---

γεγραμμένην ἐν γραμματείῳ προσαρτήσαντες, παραδιδόασι το[ῖ]ς δ’ τοῖς τὴν φυλὴν τοῦ φεύγοντος δικάζουσιν. (3) οἱ δὲ παραλαβόντες εἰσάγουσιν εἰς τὸ δικαστήριον, ... <u>οὐκ ἔξεστι δ’ οὔτε νόμοις οὔτε προκλήσεσι οὔτε μαρτυρίαις ἀλλ’ ἢ ταῖς παρὰ τοῦ διαιτητοῦ χρῆσθαι ταῖς εἰς τοὺς ἐχίνους ἐμβεβλημέναις</u>.

[14] Meier / Schömann (1883-87) 867.

[15] Bonner (1905) 48, s. auch (1930) 284.

[16] Boegehold (1982); s. dazu u. bei Anm. 77-87.

[17] Skeptisch immerhin Todd (1973) 129.

[18] Wallace (2001) 98.

[19] Lämmli (1938) 74-128.

[20] Z.B. MacDowell (1978) 209.

[21] Steinwenter (1925) 68-74.

bewusst sind. Vom modernen Gesichtspunkt aus erscheint es voll verständlich, dass für ein Berufungsverfahren, also angeblich für Diatetenprozesse, ein Neuerungsverbot gelten musste, für Prozesse, die nach einer bloß vorbereitenden Anakrisis stattfanden, jedoch nicht, da sie ja nur von einer einzigen Instanz entschieden würden.[22] Lämmli äußert angesichts der Erkenntnisse Steinwenters Unbehagen an diesem Ergebnis.[23] Das Bedürfnis, die Parteien vor überraschend eingesetzten neuen Beweismitteln zu schützen – in meiner Diktion, nach Fairness –, habe zwar in beiden Arten von Prozessen in gleicher Weise bestanden, doch lassen seiner Meinung nach die Quellen keinen anderen Schluss zu.[24] Lämmli hilft sich mit einer höchst gezwungenen dogmatischen Einordnung der Anakrisis,[25] auf die ich aber nicht näher eingehen möchte. Überblicken wir zunächst die Quellen.

Der negative Befund der Überlieferung, dass *echinoi* nur im Zusammenhang mit der Diaita, aber nie gemeinsam mit der Anakrisis genannt werden, ist durch die Aufschrift auf dem Tondeckel widerlegt. Dass einige Lexika[26] keine Einschränkung auf die Diaita machen, kann unter diesen Umständen immerhin als Hilfsargument gelten. Wichtiger sind die angeblich positiven Belege dafür, dass eine Prozesspartei nach einer Anakrisis dem Dikasterion neue Beweismittel vorgelegt hätte. Wieder muss man mit einem dogmatischen Missverständnis aufräumen. Ein durch *echinoi* kontrolliertes Neuerungsverbot kann natürlich nur für *Schriftstücke* gelten, die vom Schreiber vor Gericht verlesen werden. Aus diesem Grund ist das leibhaftige Vorzeigen der angeblich getöteten Sklavin im Blutprozess (Isokr. 18, 52) – von Bonner als „real evidence“ eingeordnet – für unser Thema irrelevant, genauso wie das Angebot, Sklaven vor den Augen der Richter auf der Folter zu befragen (Aisch. 2, 126). Das Neuerungsverbot galt in Athen nicht für das, was wir heute alles unter ‚Beweismittel’ einordnen würden, sondern nur für *Dokumente.* Die soeben besprochenen faktischen Inszenierungen und rhetorischen Tricks konnten durch die *echinoi* nicht verhindert werden.

In den Bereich der rhetorischen Tricks hat bereits Lämmli die Fälle der angeblich erst vor Gericht geleisteten Exomosie verwiesen (Isai 9, 18; Dem. 19, 176; 58, 7; 59, 28. 84; Aisch. 1, 45. 68; Isai. 2, 33; 8, 42; Dem. 47, 14).[27] Er geht richtiger Weise davon aus, dass die entsprechenden Schriftstücke bereits in der Anakrisis vorlagen.[28] In gleicher Weise lassen sich eine Reihe weiterer rhetorischer Tricks zwanglos auf Zeugnisse beziehen, die entweder schon vorlagen oder hätten vorgelegt werden sollen: die gespielte Unkenntnis vom gegnerischen Zeugnis (Isai. 9, 9;

---

22 Bonner (s. o. Anm. 15).

23 Lämmli (1938) 92f.

24 Lämmli (1938) 94.

25 Lämmli (1938) 88f.

26 Harpokration, Lex. Seguer. s. v. *echinos*; weitere Testimonia s. Boegehold (1995) S. 222-226.

27 Lämmli (1938) 100.

28 Ebenso Thür (2005) 167-169.

Isokr. 17, 38); die Aufforderung an den Gegner, bestimmte Zeugen zu stellen (dass in Diaitetenprozessen die Richter aufgefordert werden, bestimmte Zeugnisse zu verlangen,[29] ist eine unerhebliche Variante); das Anbieten an die Richter, weitere Zeugen zu führen oder – eine aus der Synegorie stammende Figur – für die eigene Behauptung als Zeuge zu haften (Dem. 19, 176). Lämmli ist nicht zuzustimmen, dass diese Tricks nur funktionierten, wenn in der Hauptverhandlung neue Zeugnisse zulässig gewesen wären.[30] Stets lässt sich als Basis mitdenken, dass der Weg eines Zeugnisses nur über die Anakrisis vor das Dikasterion führte.

Die erwähnten rhetorischen Tricks sind also kein starkes Argument, weder für die eine noch für die andere Seite. Nicht einschlägig sind auch die beiden Texte, die nach Lämmli außerhalb der Gerichtsreden für neues Beweismaterial in der Hauptverhandlung sprächen: Plutarch berichtet über einen politischen Prozess gegen Kallias, in dem dieser ex tempore seinen unbemittelten Vetter Aristeides bestätigen ließ, er habe freiwillig auf Unterstützung verzichtet (Plut. Aristeides 25).[31] Aus der späten Quelle sind die erheblichen prozessualen Details nicht zu entnehmen: Handelte es sich technisch um eine Zeugenaussage, eine Synegorie[32] oder einen Zwischenruf, der in den Bereich der faktischen Inszenierungen fällt? In diesen faktischen Bereich gehört jedenfalls das „Stehlen eines Zeugnisses“, zu dem Anaximenes rät (Rhet. Alex. 15, 7f., 1432a): „Bezeuge es mir, Kallikles“ – „Bei den Göttern, nicht ich: Ich suchte ihn zu hindern, als er die Tat vollbrachte.“[33] Dass Kallikles mit diesem Ausruf vor einer *dikê pseudomartyriôn* sicher sei, ist nicht dem sophistischen Inhalt der angeblichen Zeugenaussage zuzuschreiben, sondern – wie der Schlusssatz zeigt – dem Umstand, dass es sich um ein inszeniertes Störmanöver und nicht um eine ordnungsgemäß abgelegte schriftlich (im Vorverfahren) eingereichte *martyria* handelte.

Etwas ausführlicherer Erörterung bedürfen jene sechs Reden aus dem demosthenischen Corpus, die nach Lämmli das Verwenden neuen Beweismaterials in

---

[29] Lämmli (1938) 103.

[30] Lämmli (1938) 103.

[31] Plut. Aristeid. 25: Ὁ δὲ Καλλίας ὁρῶν ἐπὶ τούτῳ μάλιστα θορυβοῦντας τοὺς δικαστὰς καὶ χαλεπῶς πρὸς αὐτὸν ἔχοντας, ἐκάλει τὸν Ἀριστείδην, ἀξιῶν μαρτυρῆσαι πρὸς τοὺς δικαστάς, ὅτι πολλάκις αὐτοῦ πολλὰ καὶ διδόντος καὶ δεομένου λαβεῖν οὐκ ἠθέλησεν, ἀποκρινάμενος ὡς μᾶλλον αὐτῷ διὰ πενίαν μέγα φρονεῖν ἢ Καλλίᾳ διὰ πλοῦτον προσήκει· ... ταῦτα τοῦ Ἀριστείδου τῷ Καλλίᾳ προσμαρτυρήσαντος, οὐδεὶς ἦν τῶν ἀκουσάντων ὃς οὐκ ἀπῄει πένης μᾶλλον ὡς Ἀριστείδης εἶναι βουλόμενος ἢ πλουτεῖν ὡς Καλλίας.

[32] Aus den dem Gericht vorgetragen moralisierenden Ausführungen über Armut und Reichtum ist trotz der Wörter (*pros)martyrein* eine Synegorie am wahrscheinlichsten, s. Thür (2005) 152-155; für eine Zeugenaussage tritt Lämmli (1938) 107 ein.

[33] Rhet. Ad Alex. 15, 7-8: ... ἔστι δὲ καὶ κλέπτειν τὴν μαρτυρίαν τρόπῳ τοιῷδε· μαρτύρησόν μοι, ὦ Καλλίκλεις· μὰ τοὺς θεοὺς οὔκουν ἔγωγε· κωλύοντος γὰρ ἐμοῦ ταῦτα ἔπραξεν οὗτος. καὶ διὰ τούτου ἐν ἀποφάσει ψευδομαρτυρήσας ψευδομαρτυρίου δίκην οὐχ ὑφέξει. (8) τοιγαροῦν ὅταν μὲν ἡμῖν συμφέρῃ κλέπτειν τὴν μαρτυρίαν, οὕτως αὐτῇ χρησόμεθα· ἐὰν δὲ οἱ ἐναντίοι τοιοῦτόν τι ποιήσωσιν, ἐμφανιοῦμεν τὴν κακοποιίαν αὐτῶν καὶ συγγραψαμένους μαρτυρεῖν κελεύσομεν.

Anakrisis-Prozessen direkt belegten: Dem. 53, 17; 34, 46; 29, 28; 43, 47; 59, 5 und 37, 45.[34] Meiner Meinung nach sind sie entweder unschlüssig oder besagen genau das Gegenteil.

Zwei Reden handeln von *graphai*.

1.) In der Rede gegen Nikostratos (Dem. 53) berichtet Apollodor von einer früher gegen Arethousios erhobenen *graphê pseudoklêteias*. Während und nach der Anakrisis habe Arethousios Apollodor Schäden zugefügt, die jedoch nicht verhindern konnten, dass Apollodor den Prozess schließlich siegreich beendete (Dem. 53, 15-18). Für unsere Frage wichtig ist die unterschiedliche Erzählung zweier Vorfälle[35]: In § 16 rief Apollodor für einen während der Anakrisis verübten Anschlag auf seine Rosenbeete Zeugen herbei; als er jedoch nach der Anakrisis, kurz vor der Hauptverhandlung, beinahe in einen Steinbruch hinuntergestürzt worden wäre (§ 17), bezeichnet er seine Retter nicht als *martyres*. Aus dem auf den Hauptvorwurf, die *dikê pseudoklêteias*, zu beziehenden Wort *exelenxas* (§ 17) darf man nicht auf nachträglich zu einem Nebenpunkt beigebrachte Zeugnisse schließen.

2.) Im ersten Teil der Rede gegen Neaira (Dem. 59) berichtet Theomnestos von einer *graphê paranomôn*, die Stephanos gegen einen von Apollodor beantragten Volksbeschluss eingebracht und gewonnen hat (§ 5). Dass Theomnestos als Parteigänger Apollodors nun den Sieg der Gegner pauschal mit Verleumdung, falschen Zeugen und Anschuldigungen außerhalb des Klagegegenstandes begründet, lässt keinen Schluss auf nachträglich vorgelegte Zeugnisse zu.[36]

Die restlichen vier Texte stammen aus Privatprozessen, die eine Anakrisis durchlaufen haben.

3.) Nicht näher aufrollen kann ich hier die komplizierte Argumentation in der Rede gegen Phormion (Dem. 34).[37] Fest steht, dass der Kapitän Lampis, eine Schlüsselfigur des Prozesses, derzeit als Zeuge nicht zur Verfügung steht. In § 11 lässt sich der Sprecher die Antwort des Lampis auf eine förmlich vor Zeugen gestellte Frage bestätigen, in § 46 berichtet er von einer gegenteiligen Aussage des

---

[34] Lämmli (1938) 99, 117, 121.

[35] Dem. 53, 16-17: ... ὡς δὲ τούτου διήμαρτον, καὶ ἐγὼ μάρτυρας μὲν ὧν ἔπασχον ἐποιούμην, αὐτὸς δὲ οὐδὲν ἐξημάρτανον εἰς αὐτούς, ἐνταῦθα ἤδη μοι ἐπιβουλεύουσι τὴν μεγίστην ἐπιβουλήν· (17) ἀνακεκριμένου γὰρ ἤδη μου κατ' αὐτοῦ τὴν τῆς ψευδοκλητείας γραφὴν καὶ μέλλοντος εἰσιέναι εἰς τὸ δικαστήριον, τηρήσας με ἀνιόντα ἐκ Πειραιῶς ὀψὲ περὶ τὰς λιθοτομίας παίει τε πὺξ καὶ ἁρπάζει μέσον καὶ ἐώθει με εἰς τὰς λιθοτομίας, εἰ μή τινες προσιόντες, βοῶντός μου ἀκούσαντες, παρεγένοντο καὶ ἐβοήθησαν. ἡμέραις δὲ οὐ πολλαῖς ὕστερον εἰσελθὼν εἰς τὸ δικαστήριον πρὸς ἡμέραν διαμεμετρημένην, καὶ ἐξελέγξας αὐτὸν τὰ ψευδῆ κεκλητευκότα καὶ τὰ ἄλλα ὅσα εἴρηκα ἠδικηκότα, εἷλον.

[36] Dem. 59, 5: ... γραψάμενος γὰρ παρανόμων τὸ ψήφισμα Στέφανος οὑτοσὶ καὶ εἰσελθὼν εἰς τὸ δικαστήριον, ἐπὶ διαβολῇ ψευδεῖς μάρτυρας παρασχόμενος ὡς ὦφλε τῷ δημοσίῳ ἐκ πέντε καὶ εἴκοσιν ἐτῶν, καὶ ἔξω τῆς γραφῆς πολλὰ κατηγορῶν, εἷλε τὸ ψήφισμα. Unrichtig dazu Lämmli (1938) 121.

[37] S. dazu Wolff (1966) 63-74, bes. 69.

Lampis, welche sich Phormion von Dritten hat bestätigen lassen.[38] Der Sprecher beschwert sich darüber, dass er aus diesem Grund das Zeugnis des Lampis nicht mit *dikê pseudomartyriôn* angreifen könne – da es sich um eine *ekmartyria* handelt, geht die Beschwerde freilich ins Leere (s. Dem. 46, 7). In diesem Zusammenhang fallen die Worte (§ 46): „Wenn das Zeugnis des Lampis hier (vor Gericht) vorgelegt würde, ...“ Der Sprecher bringt damit zum Ausdruck, dass Phormion anstatt einer *ekmartyria* des abwesenden Lampis eine *martyria* des anwesenden hätte einreichen und vorlegen sollen. Davon, dass ein Zeugnis des Lampis in der Hauptverhandlung erstmals einführbar gewesen wäre,[39] ist nicht die Rede.

Die nächsten drei Stellen haben gemeinsam, dass die Sprecher – in Anwendung eines rhetorischen Topos – behaupten, vom Gegner überrumpelt worden zu sein. Der Aussagewert dieser Texte ist deshalb nicht viel höher einzustufen als jener der eingangs aufgezählten Tricks.

4.) Demosthenes verteidigt in der Rede 29 seinen im Vormundschaftsprozess geführten Zeugen Phanos gegen eine *dikê pseudomartyriôn* des Aphobos. Angeblich hatte Demosthenes nicht vorhergesehen, dass Aphobos in seiner Klägerrede Zeugnisse zur bereits entschiedenen Vormundschaftssache bringen würde, weshalb er nun seinerseits keine Zeugen zur Hand habe (§ 27).[40] Lämmli räumt zwar ein, dass Demosthenes' Überraschung gespielt sei, da in jedem Zeugnisprozess zur Hauptsache plädiert würde, doch hätte sich Demosthenes diesen Trick nicht erlauben dürfen, wenn vor der gegenwärtigen Verhandlung sämtliches Beweismaterial bekanntzugeben gewesen wäre.[41] In Wahrheit wird den Geschworenen noch viel mehr zugemutet. In § 39 führt nämlich Demosthenes genau jene Zeugen, die er angeblich nicht

---

[38] Dem. 34, 11: Αὐτὸς μὲν τοίνυν ὁ Λάμπις, ᾧ φησιν ἀποδεδωκέναι τὸ χρυσίον (τούτῳ γὰρ προσέχετε τὸν νοῦν), προσελθόντος αὐτῷ ἐμοῦ, ἐπειδὴ τάχιστα κατέπλευσεν ἐκ τῆς ναυαγίας 'Αθήναζε, καὶ ἐρωτῶντος ὑπὲρ τούτων, ἔλεγεν ὅτι οὔτε τὰ χρήματα ἔνθοιτο εἰς τὴν ναῦν οὗτος κατὰ τὴν συγγραφήν, οὔτε τὸ χρυσίον εἰληφὼς εἴη παρ' αὐτοῦ ἐν Βοσπόρῳ τότε. καί μοι ἀνάγνωθι τὴν μαρτυρίαν τῶν παραγενομένων. ΜΑΡΤΥΡΙΑ.

§ 46: ... ἐγὼ δ' οὐκ ἔχω τί χρήσωμαι τοῖς τούτου μάρτυσιν, οἵ φασιν εἰδέναι τὸν Λάμπιν μαρτυροῦντα ἀπειληφέναι τὸ χρυσίον. εἰ μὲν γὰρ ἡ μαρτυρία ἡ τοῦ Λάμπιδος κατεβάλλετο ἐνταῦθα, ἴσως ἂν ἔφασαν οὗτοι δίκαιον εἶναι ἐπισκήπτεσθαί μ' ἐκείνῳ· νῦν δ' οὔτε τὴν μαρτυρίαν ταύτην ἔχω, οὑτοσί τε οἴεται δεῖν ἀθῷος εἶναι οὐδὲν βέβαιον ἐνέχυρον καταλιπὼν ὧν πείθει ὑμᾶς ψηφίζεσθαι.

[39] So Lämmli (1938) 77, 117.

[40] Dem. 29, 28: ... αὐτὸς μὲν γὰρ μάρτυρας ψευδεῖς παρεσκεύασται περὶ τούτων, συγχορηγὸν ἔχων 'Ονήτορα τὸν κηδεστὴν καὶ Τιμοκράτην· ἡμεῖς δ' οὐχὶ προειδότες, ἀλλ' ὑπὲρ αὐτῆς τῆς μαρτυρίας ἡγούμενοι τὸν ἀγῶν' ἔσεσθαι, τοὺς περὶ τῶν ἐκ τῆς ἐπιτροπῆς χρημάτων μάρτυρας οὐ παρεσκευάσμεθα νῦν. ὅμως δέ, καίπερ οὕτως τούτου σεσοφισμένου, τὰ πράγματ' αὐτὰ διεξιὼν οἶμαι ῥᾳδίως ὑμῖν ἐπιδείξειν δικαιότατ' ἀνθρώπων τοῦτον ὠφληκότα τὴν δίκην, ...

[41] Lämmli (1938) 121.

vorbereitet hatte.[42] Auch die beiden übrigen Stellen werden zeigen, dass der rhetorische Trick der gespielten oder angeblichen Überraschung keine juristischen Schlüsse gestattet.

5.) Mit einer ungewöhnlich großen Zahl von Zeugnissen sucht Sositheos in der Rede gegen Makartatos (Dem. 43) den Anspruch des Euboulides auf die Erbschaft des Hagnias zu belegen (Dem. 43, 31-46). Am Schluss dieses Abschnitts entschuldigt sich Sositheos bei den Richtern für die unübliche Vielzahl der Zeugnisse damit, dass seine Partei einen früheren Prozess um die Erbschaft „unvorbereitet" (*aparaskeuoi*) verloren habe (§ 47).[43] Auch aus der rhetorischen Figur, eine erlittene Niederlage aus der Überraschung zu erklären, kann man keine Schlüsse auf die Zulässigkeit oder Unzulässigkeit neuer Beweismittel ziehen.[44] Selbst wenn alle Zeugnisse auf dem Tisch liegen, kann eine gut konzipierte Rede unvorhergesehene Effekte erzielen.

6.) Das beste Beispiel dafür ist der von Lämmli isoliert betrachtete Abschnitt §§ 45-47 in der Rede gegen Pantainetos (Dem. 37).[45] Der Sprecher, Nikoboulos, berichtet, Pantainetos habe in der selben Sache mit einer *dikê metallikê* bereits gegen Euergos gewonnen, weil er ihn mit unvorhergesehenen Vorwürfen (§ 47) wie der Beleidigung von Erbtöchtern überrascht und unvermutet die entsprechenden Gesetze vorgelegt habe.[46] Die Überraschung konnte indes nicht so groß gewesen sein. Nikoboulos zitiert nämlich bereits in den §§ 22-33 ausführlich die von Pantainetos gegen ihn eingereichte Klageschrift, die der gegen Euergos entsprochen habe (§ 45). Hierin

---

42 Dem. 29, 39: ... περὶ τοίνυν πάντων τούτων, πρῶτον μὲν περὶ τῆς προικός, εἶθ' ὑπὲρ ὧν καθυφεῖκεν, εἶθ' ὑπὲρ τῶν ἄλλων, ἀναγνώσεται τούς τε νόμους καὶ τὰς μαρτυρίας, ἵν' εἰδῆτε. ΝΟΜΟΙ. ΜΑΡΤΥΡΙΑΙ.

43 Dem. 43, 47: Ἀναγνῶναι μὲν τὰς μαρτυρίας ταύτας ἐξ ἀνάγκης ἦν, ὦ ἄνδρες δικασταί, ἵνα μὴ τὸ αὐτὸ πάθοιμεν ὅπερ τὸ πρότερον, <u>ἀπαράσκευοι ληφθέντες</u> ὑπὸ τούτων.

44 So aber Lämmli (1938) 121.

45 Lämmli (1938) 121f.

46 Dem. 37, 45-47: Βούλομαι δ' ὑμῖν καὶ δι' ὧν τοὺς πρότερον δικαστὰς ἐξαπατήσας εἷλε τὸν Εὔεργον εἰπεῖν, ἵν' εἰδῆθ' ὅτι καὶ νῦν οὐδὲν οὔτ' ἀναιδείας οὔτε τοῦ ψεύδεσθαι παραλείψει. πρὸς δὲ τούτοις καὶ περὶ ὧν ἐμοὶ δικάζεται νυνί, τὰς αὐτὰς οὔσας ἀπολογίας εὑρήσετε· ὅσπερ ἔλεγχος ἀκριβέστατός ἐστιν ὑπὲρ τοῦ τότ' ἐκεῖνον σεσυκοφαντῆσθαι. οὗτος γὰρ ᾐτιάσατ' ἐκεῖνον πρὸς ἅπασι τοῖς ἄλλοις ἐλθόντ' εἰς ἀγρὸν ὡς αὑτὸν ἐπὶ τὰς ἐπικλήρους εἰσελθεῖν καὶ τὴν μητέρα τὴν αὑτοῦ, καὶ τοὺς νόμους ἧκεν ἔχων τοὺς τῶν ἐπικλήρων πρὸς τὸ δικαστήριον. (46) καὶ πρὸς μὲν τὸν ἄρχοντα, ὃν τῶν τοιούτων οἱ νόμοι κελεύουσιν ἐπιμελεῖσθαι, καὶ παρ' ᾧ τῷ μὲν ἠδικηκότι κίνδυνος περὶ τοῦ τί χρὴ παθεῖν ἢ ἀποτεῖσαι, τῷ δ' ἐπεξιόντι μετ' οὐδεμιᾶς ζημίας ἡ βοήθεια, οὐδέπω καὶ τήμερον ἐξήτασται, οὐδ' εἰσήγγειλεν οὔτ' ἔμ' οὔτε τὸν Εὔεργον ὡς ἀδικοῦντας, ἐν δὲ τῷ δικαστηρίῳ ταῦτα κατηγόρει καὶ <u>δυοῖν ταλάντοιν</u> εἷλε δίκην. (47) ἦν γὰρ οἶμαι κατὰ μὲν τοὺς νόμους <u>προειδότα τὴν αἰτίαν</u>, ἐφ' ᾗ κρίνεται, ῥᾴδιον τἀληθῆ καὶ τὰ δίκαι' ἐπιδείξαντ' ἀποφεύγειν, ἐν δὲ μεταλλικῇ δίκῃ, περὶ ὧν οὐδ' ἂν ἤλπισεν αὑτοῦ κατηγορηθήσεσθαι, χαλεπὸν παραχρῆμ' ἔχειν ἀπολύσασθαι τὴν διαβολήν· ἡ δ' ὀργὴ ⟨ἡ⟩ παρὰ τῶν ἐξηπατημένων ὑπὸ τούτου δικαστῶν, ἐφ' ᾧ τὴν ψῆφον εἶχον πράγματι, τούτου κατεψηφίσατο.

ist auch der Vorwurf der Erbtochterbeleidigung enthalten (§ 33).[47] Also dürfte Pantainetos auch die Gesetze über die Erbtöchter bereits in der Anakrisis eingereicht haben. Es ist durchaus denkbar, aber durch Nikoboulos' bloße Behauptung (§ 47) keineswegs erwiesen, dass es Pantainetos damals gelungen war, die Richter durch sachfremde Argumente gegen Euergos aufzubringen, auch wenn dieser sie aus dem *enklêma* und den vorgelegten Gesetzen hätte vorhersehen können. Nikoboulos nützt nun seine Position als erster Sprecher im Paragraphe-Prozess aus, um diese Argumente im vorhinein zu entkräften.

Der Überblick über die von Lämmli zusammengetragenen konkreten Beispiele für die angebliche Vorlage neuer Beweismittel in Anakrisis-Prozessen ist damit abgeschlossen. In keinem einzigen Fall hat er nachgewiesen, dass eine Prozesspartei in der Hauptverhandlung ein Dokument benützte, das nicht schon in der Anakrisis vorgelegen wäre. Auch wenn das Neuerungsverbot zufällig nur für Diatetenprozesse überliefert ist, besteht aufgrund der neuerdings publizierten *echinos*-Inschrift und der strukturellen Gleichartigkeit von Anakrisis und obligatorischer Diaita kein Zweifel daran, dass das Verbot neuer Zeugnisse im Interesse der Fairness für beide Verfahren in gleicher Weise gegolten hat.

Damit sind wir wieder bei der Dogmatik des attischen Prozessrechts angelangt. Aus diesem Gesichtspunkt ist noch eine allgemein verbreitete Fehleinschätzung zu zerstreuen, die auch das Bild des Neuerungsverbots trübt. Ich kann mich hier sehr kurz fassen. Für Lämmli war es klar, dass ein Neuerungsverbot in Athen nur für die Vorlage von *Dokumenten* gegolten haben konnte, also nur ab dem Zeitpunkt des schriftlich vorzulegenden Zeugnisses. Eine mündliche Zeugenaussage könne man nicht einschränken.[48] Für ihn hängen die Einführung der obligatorischen Diaita,[49] des schriftlichen Zeugnisses[50] und der *echinoi* unmittelbar mit dem Neuerungsverbot zusammen. Das ist jedoch nicht denknotwendig so. Ich habe anderswo gezeigt,[51] dass sowohl das ältere mündliche als auch das jüngere schriftliche Zeugnis das selbe Formular verwenden. Beide Male bestätigt der Zeuge lediglich einen von der Prozesspartei vorformulierten Satz, so als ob er einen Eid leisten würde. Und im Blutprozess hatte der Zeuge tatsächlich seit altersher während der *prodikasiai* diesen Satz mit dem feierlichen Eid auf die Schuld oder Unschuld des Angeklagten zu verbinden. Hier war also in der Hauptverhandlung eine Überrumpelung durch neue Zeugnisse ausgeschlossen.[52] Ganz parallel zu den *prodikasiai*, nur ohne den feierli-

---

[47] Dem. 37, 33: ΕΓΚΛΗΜΑ. Ἐνταυθὶ πόλλ' ἄττα καὶ δεινά μοι ἅμ' ἐγκαλεῖ· καὶ γὰρ αἴκειαν καὶ ὕβριν καὶ βιαίων καὶ πρὸς ἐπικλήρους ἀδικήματα. τούτων δ' εἰσὶν ἑκάστου χωρὶς αἱ δίκαι καὶ οὔτε πρὸς ἀρχὴν τὴν αὐτὴν οὔθ' ὑπὲρ τιμημάτων τῶν αὐτῶν, ἀλλ' ἡ μὲν αἴκεια καὶ τὰ τῶν βιαίων πρὸς τοὺς τετταράκοντα, αἱ δὲ τῆς ὕβρεως πρὸς τοὺς θεσμοθέτας, ὅσα δ' εἰς ἐπικλήρους, πρὸς τὸν ἄρχοντα.

[48] Lämmli (1938) 111.

[49] 403-401 v.Chr., Lämmli (1938) 111; eher 399/98 v.Chr., Scafuro (1997) 126, 392.

[50] Frühestens 389 v.Chr., Lämmli (1938) 119; vgl. Rubinstein (2000) 72.

[51] Thür (2005) 154f.

[52] So schon Lämmli (1938) 106.

chen Eid, hat man sich das Auftreten der mündlichen Zeugen in der Anakrisis vorzustellen: Die Parteien müssen einander die Person des oder der Zeugen und das mündlich zu sprechende Formular des oder der Zeugnisse bekanntgeben. Mit der Schriftlichkeit hat sich nicht der förmliche Charakter des Zeugnisses gewandelt, sondern nur das Medium der Übertragung: von der Anakrisis in das Hauptverfahren und vom Hauptverfahren eventuell in den Prozess wegen falschen Zeugnisses. Schriftliche Zeugnisdokumente schließen lediglich den Streit um den genauen Wortlaut des Zeugnisformulars aus. Hält man sich den identischen Formalismus des mündlichen und des schriftlichen Zeugnisses vor Augen, kommt man zu dem Ergebnis, dass der attische Prozess das Prinzip der Fairness bereits seit altersher gekannt hat.

Worin liegt nun die Besonderheit der Diaitetenprozesse? Im Grunde genommen wurden im Jahr 399/98 lediglich die Vorverfahren der seit dem Jahr 404 aufgestauten Privatprozesse den 60jährigen Bürgern übertragen. Die Masse der Prozesse sollte gütlich entschieden werden, ohne Einsatz der teueren Dikasterien. Deshalb nannte man die quasi-amtlichen Funktionäre „Schiedsrichter“ (*diaitetai*) und führte einen Urteilsvorschlag ein, die *apophasis*, die allerdings keiner Partei den Weg vor das Dikasterion abschnitt. Möglicherweise nahm die Schriftlichkeit des Zeugnisses von der obligatorischen Diaita ihren Ausgang. Denn erstmals führte nicht der im Dikasterion präsidierende Magistrat, einer der Vierzig, das Vorverfahren durch, sondern ein erloster Privatmann. In diesen Fällen konnte der Gerichtsmagistrat die Identität der im Vor- und Hauptverfahren gesprochenen Zeugnisformulare nicht mehr kontrollieren. Schriftliche Dokumente, in versiegelten *echinoi* verwahrt – wie das für private Dokumente schon im 5. Jahrhundert üblich war[53] –, waren die technische Lösung des Problems. Doch beschränkten sich das schriftliche Zeugnis und die *echinoi* alsbald nicht nur auf die Diaitetenprozesse. Die neue Technik der Dokumentation entsprach der minutiösen Regelung des Prozesses durch die athenische Demokratie des 4. Jahrhunderts. Weder das Zeugnisformular noch das Neuerungsverbot wurden von der Einführung der Schriftlichkeit berührt.

Ich habe bis jetzt zwei prozesstechnische Maßnahmen behandelt, welche – dem Gebot der Fairness entsprechend – die Prozessparteien in der Hauptverhandlung vor unvorhersehbaren Angriffen des Gegners schützten: 1.) Das Befragen des Gegners unter Antwortpflicht, wobei der Gegner ein vor Zeugen abgegebenes Zugeständnis, eine *homologia*, nicht mehr abstreiten konnte, und 2.) das seit altersher bestehende Neuerungsverbot, das, ausgehend von den Diaitetenprozessen, durch Schriftlichkeit und *echinoi* technisch gesichert wurde. Eine letzte, von Lämmli bereits erkannte,[54] aber zur Seite geschobene Maßnahme steht noch aus. Selbstverständlich lernt der Beklagte den Standpunkt des Klägers aus der Klageschrift, der *graphê* oder dem *enklêma*, kennen und der Kläger umgekehrt den des Beklagten aus der *antigraphê*.

[53] Boegehold (1995) 79f.

[54] Lämmli (1938) 11.

Tragen diese Schriftstücke auch zur Fairness bei, sichern auch sie vor unvorhergesehenen Angriffen?

Es sind nur ganz wenige Klageschriften wörtlich überliefert. Harrison nennt fünf Beispiele,[55] zwei möchte ich noch hinzufügen. Am ausführlichsten zitiert Nikoboulos das von Pantainetos eingereichte *enklêma* einer *dikê blabês* (Dem. 37, 22-33). Auf den ersten Blick mutet der bunte Strauß der erhobenen Vorwürfe juristisch ebenso undiszipliniert an wie der Inhalt vieler Reden. Lanni erklärt den Befund der Reden sehr gut aus der speziellen Konzeption der athenischen Laiengerichtsbarkeit; die gerichtliche Wahrheitsfindung schließe in Athen die Erkenntnis des gesamten Charakters einer Prozesspartei mit ein.[56] Entgangen ist Lanni allerdings ein Mittel, welches die unsachlichen persönlichen Vorwürfe des Klägers in Grenzen hält, eine Vorschrift, die der Fairness im Prozess dient. Diese Vorschrift bezieht sich meiner Meinung nach unmittelbar auf die Klageschrift. Eine Klausel im Richtereid lautet (Dem 24, 151): „... ich werde abstimmen, worüber die Klage ist ..."[57] Dem entsprechend schwören die Prozessparteien nach Aufruf der Sache vor den Augen der Richter „zur Sache selbst zu sprechen" (AP 67, 1).[58]

Wie lassen sich diese Eide mit dem krausen Befund der Gerichtsreden vereinbaren? Rhodes[59] und Lanni[60] suchen nach sachlichen Kriterien, welche Äußerungen der Sprecher relevant seien und welche nicht. Ich meine, die Athener hatten eine andere Vorstellung von ‚Relevanz' als ein heutiger, vom modernen Prozessrecht geprägter Beobachter. Sie gingen vom Gebot der Fairness aus: „zur Sache selbst" gehörte das, was in der Klageschrift stand. Alle Vorwürfe, die der Kläger in das *enklêma* schreibt und auf diese Weise dem Gegner bekannt gibt, darf er vor dem Dikasterion erheben, ohne gegen seinen Eid zu verstoßen. Damit erklärt sich der ganze Katalog von Vorwürfen in dem schon mehrmals erwähnten *enklêma* des Pantainetos (Dem. 37, 22-33).[61] Ich habe im letzten Symposion nachgewiesen,[62] dass der

---

[55] Harrison (1971) 91f.

[56] Lanni (2005) 121-123, (2006) 59-64.

[57] Dem. 24, 149-151: ΟΡΚΟΣ ΗΛΙΑΣΤΩΝ. Ψηφιοῦμαι κατὰ τοὺς νόμους καὶ τὰ ψηφίσματα τοῦ δήμου τοῦ Ἀθηναίων καὶ τῆς βουλῆς τῶν πεντακοσίων. ... (151) καὶ ἀκροάσομαι τοῦ τε κατηγόρου καὶ τοῦ ἀπολογουμένου ὁμοίως ἀμφοῖν, καὶ διαψηφιοῦμαι περὶ αὐτοῦ οὗ ἂν ἡ δίωξις ᾖ.

[58] AP 61, 1: ... ταῦτα δὲ ποιήσ[αντες εἰ]σκαλοῦσι τοὺς ἀγῶνας, ὅταν μὲν τὰ ἴδια [δι]κάζωσι τοὺς ἰδίους, τῷ ἀριθμῷ δ', [ἕνα ἐ]ξ [ἑκά]στων [ṭ]ῶν δικῶν τ[ῶ]ν ἐκ τοῦ νόμο[υ], κ[α]ὶ δ[ιο]μνύ[ουσι]ν οἱ ἀντίδικοι εἰς αὐτὸ τὸ πρᾶγμ[α] ἐρεῖν· Lanni (2005) 113, (2006) 100 misst diesem Eid keinerlei praktische Bedeutung zu.

[59] Rhodes (2004).

[60] Lanni (2005) 114 findet, unbestreitbar richtig, doch zu wenig auf den Einzelfall bedacht, drei Typen von ‚unsachlichen' Argumenten: sozialer Kontext, Mitleid, Charakter; ausführlich (2006) 46-64.

[61] Dem. 37, 23-33: λέγε δ' αὐτὸ τὸ ἔγκλημα, ὅ μοι δικάζεται. ΕΓΚΛΗΜΑ. Ἔβλαψέ με Νικόβουλος ἐπιβουλεύσας ἐμοὶ καὶ τῇ οὐσίᾳ τῇ ἐμῇ, ἀφελέσθαι κελεύσας Ἀντιγένην τὸν ἑαυτοῦ οἰκέτην τὸ ἀργύριον τοῦ ἐμοῦ οἰκέτου, ὃ ἔφερεν καταβολὴν τῇ πόλει τοῦ μετάλλου, ὃ ἐγὼ ἐπριάμην ἐνενήκοντα μνῶν, καὶ αἴτιος ἐμοὶ γενόμενος ἐγγραφῆναι

von Pantainetos verlangte Geldbetrag, das *timema* von zwei Talenten (§ 46),[63] bereits aus dem ersten Satz hervorgeht, nämlich aus der zweifachen Verdoppelung jener 30 Minen (einem halben Talent), welche Nikoboulos' Sklave Antigenes dem Sklaven des Pantainetos weggenommen hatte. Alle weiteren Vorwürfe bis hin zur Erbtochterbeleidigung (§ 33) sind nur rhetorische Stütze des materiellen Klagebegehrens und wären nach heutiger Auffassung ‚irrelevant'. Nur um sie unangefochten vorbringen zu können, nahm Pantainetos jene weiteren Vorwürfe in sein *enklêma* mit auf.

Von den übrigen wörtlich überlieferten Klage- oder Anklageschriften wissen wir nicht, ob sie vollständig wiedergegeben sind. Dem. 45, 46 bringt vermutlich das vollständige *enklêma* (samt Klagebeantwortung) aus einer *dikê pseudomartyriôn.*[64] Dionysios von Halikarnass, Deinarchos 3 berichtet vom *enklêma* einer *dikê blabês*, die ähnlich beginnt wie die des Pantainetos.[65] Von den öffentlichen Klagen ist die Eisangelie gegen Alkibiades (Plut. Alk. 22, 4) in mehrere für den Mysterienfrevel erhebliche Vorwürfe gegliedert.[66] Die *graphê asebeias* gegen Sokrates (Diogenes Laertios 2, 40) enthält nur zwei Vorwürfe, wobei jedoch der zweite, die Jugend zu verführen, rechtlich irrelevant, rhetorisch aber vielleicht gefährlicher war als jener

---

τὸ διπλοῦν τῷ δημοσίῳ. ... (§ 25) ... Καὶ ἐπειδὴ ὦφλον ἐγὼ τῷ δημοσίῳ, καταστήσας Ἀντιγένην τὸν ἑαυτοῦ οἰκέτην εἰς τὸ ἐργαστήριον τὸ ἐμὸν τὸ ἐπὶ Θρασύλλῳ κύριον τῶν ἐμῶν, ἀπαγορεύοντος ἐμοῦ. ... (§ 26) ... Κἄπειτα πείσας τοὺς οἰκέτας τοὺς ἐμοὺς καθέζεσθαι εἰς τὸν κεγχρεῶνα ἐπὶ βλάβῃ τῇ ἐμῇ. ... (§ 28) ... Καὶ κατεργασάμενος τὴν ἀργυρῖτιν, ἣν οἱ ἐμοὶ οἰκέται ἠργάσαντο, καὶ ἔχων τὸ ἀργύριον τὸ ἐκ ταύτης τῆς ἀργυρίτιδος. ... (§ 29) ... Καὶ ἀποδόμενος τὸ ἐργαστήριον τὸ ἐμὸν καὶ τοὺς οἰκέτας παρὰ τὰς συνθήκας, ἃς ἔθετο πρός με. (§ 33 s. o. Anm. 47).

62 Thür (2006) 163f.

63 S. o. Anm. 46.

64 Dem. 45, 46: ΑΝΤΙΓΡΑΦΗ. Ἀπολλόδωρος Πασίωνος Ἀχαρνεὺς Στεφάνῳ Μενεκλέους Ἀχαρνεῖ ψευδομαρτυρίων, τίμημα τάλαντον. τὰ ψευδῆ μου κατεμαρτύρησε Στέφανος μαρτυρήσας τὰ ἐν τῷ γραμματείῳ γεγραμμένα. – ⟨Στέφανος Μενεκλέους Ἀχαρνεὺς⟩ τἀληθῆ ἐμαρτύρησα ματυρήσας τὰ ἐν τῷ γραμματείῳ γεγραμμένα.

65 Dion. Hal. Dein. 3: ... προσκειμένην δὲ ἔχει τὴν γραφὴν ταύτην· 'Δείναρχος Σωστράτου Κορίνθιος Προξένῳ, ᾧ σύνειμι, βλάβης ταλάντων δύο. Ἔβλαψέ με Πρόξενος, ὑποδεξάμενος εἰς τὴν οἰκίαν τὴν ἑαυτοῦ τὴν ἐν ἀγρῷ, ὅτε πεφευγὼς Ἀθήνηθεν κατῄειν ἐκ Χαλκίδος, χρυσίου μὲν στατῆρας ὀγδοήκοντα καὶ διακοσίους καὶ πέντε, οὓς ἐκόμισα ἐκ Χαλκίδος εἰδότος Προξένου καὶ εἰσῆλθον ἔχων εἰς τὴν οἰκίαν αὐτοῦ, ἀργυρώματα δὲ οὐκ ἔλαττον εἴκοσι μνῶν ἄξια, ἐπιβουλεύσας τούτοις.'

66 Plut. Alk. 22, 4: ... τὴν μὲν οὖν εἰσαγγελίαν οὕτως ἔχουσαν ἀναγράφουσι· 'Θεσσαλὸς Κίμωνος Λακιάδης Ἀλκιβιάδην Κλεινίου Σκαμβωνίδην εἰσήγγειλεν ἀδικεῖν περὶ τὼ θεώ, [τὴν Δήμητραν καὶ τὴν Κόρην,] ἀπομιμούμενον τὰ μυστήρια καὶ δεικνύοντα τοῖς αὐτοῦ ἑταίροις ἐν τῇ οἰκίᾳ τῇ ἑαυτοῦ, ἔχοντα στολὴν οἵανπερ ὁ ἱεροφάντης ἔχων δεικνύει τὰ ἱερά, καὶ ὀνομάζοντα αὑτὸν μὲν ἱεροφάντην, Πουλυτίωνα δὲ δᾳδοῦχον, κήρυκα δὲ Θεόδωρον Φηγαιᾶ, τοὺς δ' ἄλλους ἑταίρους μύστας προσαγορεύοντα καὶ ἐπόπτας παρὰ τὰ νόμιμα καὶ τὰ καθεστηκότα ὑπό τ' Εὐμολπιδῶν καὶ Κηρύκων καὶ τῶν ἱερέων τῶν ἐξ Ἐλευσῖνος.'

der *asebeia*.[67] Einen dreigliedrigen Vorwurf enthält der von Harrison nicht berücksichtigte *antidosis*-Antrag (*graphê*) gegen den greisen Isokrates (Isokr. 15, 5. 30): 1.) die Liturgie zu übernehmen, 2.) Bezug von unlauterem Einkommen als Logograph und 3.) wieder Jugendverführung.[68] Das letzte hat in einer Diadikasie um eine Liturgie von der Sache her nichts zu suchen. Mag man auch über die Historizität der Antidosis-Rede, Isokr. 15, streiten,[69] scheint mir jedenfalls die technische Formulierung der ‚*graphê*' der Realität zu entsprechen. Eine weitere von Harrison nicht berücksichtigte Stelle weist ebenfalls in die von mir vertretene Richtung: Zenothemis war gegen Protos in einer *dikê emporikê* mit einem Bündel von Vorwürfen vorgegangen, wovon die Trunkenheit während eines Seesturmes (Dem. 32, 27[70]) für keine der in Frage stehenden Varianten, *dikê exoulês* oder *blabês*, rechtlich relevant sein konnte.[71] Gegen Lanni[72] sehe ich deshalb im Standard der Relevanz keinen wesentlichen Unterschied zwischen ordentlichen Prozessen und Seehandelssachen. In beiden Fällen verankerten die Kläger ihre unsachlichen Angriffe im *enklêma*. Davon nicht berührt ist freilich Lannis Beobachtung, dass in Seehandelsprozessen persönliche Invektiven seltener vorkamen.[73] Beschimpfungen mussten die Parteien und Zeugen vor Gericht dulden, konkrete Vorwürfe nahm man sicherheitshalber in das *enklêma* mit auf.

Vom *enklêma* her bestätigt wird jedoch Lannis Ergebnis, dass in Blutprozessen die Pflicht, zur Sache zu sprechen, streng beachtet wurde.[74] Die feierlichen von den Parteien zu schwörenden Prozesseide, die *diômosiai*, ersetzten dort das *enklêma*. Ihr Wortlaut richtete sich immer noch nach dem Blutgesetz Drakons[75] und ließ keine

---

[67] Diog. Laert. 2, 40: Ἡ δ᾽ ἀντωμοσία τῆς δίκης τοῦτον εἶχε τὸν τρόπον· ἀνακεῖται γὰρ ἔτι καὶ νῦν, φησὶ Φαβωρῖνος, ἐν τῷ Μητρῴῳ· ‛τάδε ἐγράψατο καὶ ἀντωμόσατο Μέλητος Μελήτου Πιτθεὺς Σωκράτει Σωφρονίσκου Ἀλωπεκῆθεν· ἀδικεῖ Σωκράτης, οὓς μὲν ἡ πόλις νομίζει θεοὺς οὐ νομίζων, ἕτερα δὲ καινὰ δαιμόνια εἰσηγούμενος· ἀδικεῖ δὲ καὶ τοὺς νέους διαφθείρων. τίμημα θάνατος.'

[68] Isokr. 15, 5: Ἐδήλωσαν δ᾽ οὕτω διακείμενοι· τοῦ γὰρ ἀντιδίκου περὶ μὲν ὧν ἡ κρίσις ἦν οὐδὲν λέγοντος δίκαιον, διαβάλλοντος δὲ τὴν τῶν λόγων τῶν ἐμῶν δύναμιν καὶ καταλαζονευομένου περί τε τοῦ πλούτου καὶ τοῦ πλήθους τῶν μαθητῶν, ἔγνωσαν ἐμὴν εἶναι τὴν λειτουργίαν. ... (§ 30) Ἐκ μὲν τοίνυν τῆς γραφῆς πειρᾶταί με διαβάλλειν ὁ κατήγορος, ὡς διαφθείρω τοὺς νεωτέρους λέγειν διδάσκων καὶ παρὰ τὸ δίκαιον ἐν τοῖς ἀγῶσι πλεονεκτεῖν, ...

[69] Mirhady / Too (2000) 201f.

[70] Dem. 32, 27: ... εἰ μὲν γὰρ ἃ γέγραφεν οὗτος εἰς τὸ ἔγκλημ᾽ ἐποίει, οὐκ ὀφλεῖν ἂν δίκην δικαίως, ἀλλ᾽ ἀποθανεῖν Πρῶτος ἔμοιγε δοκεῖ. εἰ γὰρ ἐν κακοῖς καὶ χειμῶνι τοσοῦτον οἶνον ἔπινεν ὥσθ᾽ ὅμοιον εἶναι μανίᾳ, τί οὐκ ἄξιός ἐστι παθεῖν; ἢ εἰ γράμματ᾽ ἔκλεπτεν; εἰ ὑπανέῳγεν;

[71] Thür (2003) 71f.

[72] Lanni (2005) 126-128. Das Erfordernis einer Vertragsurkunde, Lanni (2006) 161-166, kann hier nicht diskutiert werden.

[73] Lanni (2005) 127, (2006) 169f.

[74] Lanni (2005) 124-126, (2006) 96-105.

[75] Thür (2004) 36f.

Geschwätzigkeit zu.[76] Aus diesem Grund scheinen uns heute die Blutprozesse ‚fairer' geführt als die übrigen.

Nach den Ausführungen zu den *echinoi*, den Tontöpfen, die meiner Meinung nach in Athen ab dem frühen 4. Jahrhundert in allen Prozessen die vor den Dikasterien zu verlesenden Dokumente enthielten, und zur ‚Relevanz', die sich meiner Meinung nach streng am Wortlaut der Klageschrift orientierte, ist nochmals auf den eingangs erwähnten Deckel eines solchen Tontopfes zurückzukommen.

Nach einhelliger Meinung weist die fragmentarisch erhaltene, mit Tinte aufgebrachte Inschrift den Topf als *echinos* aus. Eindeutig zu lesen sind in der 2. Zeile die Wörter *d]iamartyria* und *ex anakriseôs*.[77] Zwanglos lässt sich der zu Grunde liegende Prozess als *dikê pseudomartyriôn* gegen eine in einem Erbschaftsstreit vor dem Archon geleistete *diamartyria* erklären: Ein Seitenverwandter hat vor dem Archon die Zuweisung, die *epidikasia*, einer Erbschaft beantragt; dagegen ist ein Zeuge aufgetreten mit der Behauptung „der *klêros* sei nicht zuweisbar, *mê epidikos*, weil legitime Söhne vorhanden seien".[78] Dieses Zeugnis, die *diamartyria*, hat der Seitenverwandte als falsch angefochten. Der Archon musste hierauf die *epidikasia* innehalten und die Anakrisis über *die dikê pseudomartyriôn* vornehmen. Erst wenn der Seitenverwandte diesen Prozess gewinnt, also nach Verurteilung des Zeugen, darf der Archon die *epidikasia* erteilen, andernfalls hat der legitime Sohn (oder haben die Söhne) das Recht, sich der Erbschaft ohne amtliche Zuweisung zu bemächtigen, *embateuein*.

Aus der Anakrisis des Zeugnisprozesses dürfte der vorliegende Deckel stammen; es muss sich um die vier (Z. 1) Dokumente handeln, die der Kläger (Z. 4) verlesen zu lassen plante. In diesem Sinne hat Soritz-Hadler die im Text nicht erhaltenen Wörter zu ergänzen versucht.[79] Als erstes Dokument ist das angegriffene Zeugnis, die *diamartyria*, zu verlesen (Z. 2). Dieses stammt natürlich nicht aus der Anakrisis, sondern aus dem Termin der in Z. 1/2 zu ergänzenden *epidikasia*. Erst die drei weiteren Dokumente stammen aus der Anakrisis. Sie wurden, wie in griechischen Dossiers häufig, in umgekehrter chronologischer Reihenfolge abgelegt, also das älteste zu unterst.[80] Nach Verlesung der angegriffenen *diamartyria* wurden, in einer Urkunde zusammengefasst,[81] die Klageschrift und deren Beantwortung durch den Beklagten verlesen (Z. 4, großteils ergänzt). Als nächstes Dokument hatte der Kläger vermutlich eine *martyria* (am Ende der Z. 3 ergänzt) eingereicht, hierauf höchstwahrscheinlich einen am Beginn der Z. 3 zu ergänzenden *nomos*, der Misshandlung (*kakôsis*, Z. 3), regelt. Wer misshandelt wurde, ist fraglich. Aus der Rede gegen Pantainetos geht hervor, dass „Erbtöchtermisshandlung" ein mögliches Thema persönlicher Invektive war.[82]

---

[76] Vgl. Ant. 6, 16.

[77] Ich bringe den Text mit den, wie ich meine, immer noch sehr wahrscheinlichen Ergänzungen von Soritz-Hadler (1986) 106: [ἔνεστι : τά]δε : τέτταρ[α : τῶ]ν : ἐκ [: τῆς : |[2] ἐπιδικασίας : δ]ιαμαρτυρία : ἐξ ἀνακρίσεως [: |[3] νόμος : ἐπικλήρω]ν κακώσεω[ς : μαρτυρία : |[4] γραφαὶ : ἀντ]ιδί[κων : Name]ρ : ἐπέθ̣[ηκεν :|[5] Name |[6] Name. Die Fassung Boegehold (1982) 4 ist von ihm auch (1995) 81 wiedergegeben; Wallace (2001) 92f. stellt übersichtlich alle Versionen des Textes einander gegenüber.

[78] S. etwa Dem. 44, 46; dazu ausführlich Wolff (1966) 121-131.

[79] Soritz-Hadler (1986).

[80] Soritz-Hadler (1986) 106; Belege s. IPArk S. 93, Anm. 38.

[81] Vgl. die *antigraphê* in Dem. 45, 46 (o. Anm. 64).

[82] Dem. 37, 45 (s. o. Anm. 46). Hierauf hat bereits Soritz-Hadler (1986) 106 mit Anm. 25 deutlich hingewiesen.

Diese hypothetische, aber aus der athenischen Gerichtspraxis durchaus wahrscheinliche Rekonstruktion des Prozesses und der vorgelegten Dokumente hat Wallace vehement angegriffen. Sein Hauptargument ist – falsch verstandene – ‚Relevanz': „... we have no idea what documents were relevant to this particular case."[83] Gegen die von Soritz-Hadler als Grundlage einer Invektive[84] vorgeschlagene Ergänzung eines [*nomos epiklêrô*]*n kakôseôs* wendet er ein: „... would this justify sealing up in the *echinos* the text of an extraneous law?"[85] Wir haben gesehen, dass gemäß dem ‚Prinzip der Fairness' auch die im Epilog zu verlesenden, *nicht* zu Hauptsache gehörenden Dokumente dem Gegner in der Anakrisis bekannt zu geben und in den *echinos* zu legen waren. Ein Gesetz über *kakôsis* – sei es von Erbtöchtern [*epiklêrô*]*n*[86] oder, wie Wallace vorschlägt, von Waisen [*orphanô*]*n* oder Eltern [*goneô*]*n* – passt deshalb bestens in eine Zeugnisklage gegen eine *diamartyria* in Erbschaftssachen. Es scheint mir deshalb müßig, allein aus dem Wort *kakôseôs* (Z. 3) den *echinos*-Deckel für eine zweifelhafte *diamartyria* gegen eine *graphê*, *phasis* oder *eisangelia* in Anspruch zu nehmen.[87] Wallace hat nicht nur die ‚Relevanz' falsch verstanden, sondern auch das mit den *echinoi* verbundene Neuerungsverbot nicht erkannt.

Die Pflicht, zu der in der Klageschrift als ‚relevant' definierten Sache zu sprechen und darüber hinaus keine substanziellen Vorwürfe zu erheben, kann man den Regeln der Fairness zurechnen. Doch welche Sanktionen riskiert ein Sprecher, wenn er gegen diese Pflicht verstößt? Lanni beantwortet die Frage nicht.[88] Weder der Gerichtsmagistrat noch die Geschworenen hatten die Befugnis, einen Sprecher zu ermahnen und ihm schließlich das Wort zu entziehen. Es gab meiner Meinung nach nur ein einziges, archaisches Mittel, womit die Geschworenen als Kollektiv die Parteien kontrollierten: den spontanen Aufschrei, den *thorybos*.[89] Die Geschworenen hatten zwar ihrerseits die Pflicht, beide Parteien unvoreingenommen anzuhören,[90] doch konnte sich die kollektiv aufgeheizte Stimmung jederzeit entladen. Eine gut beratene Partei musste deshalb die Masse der Geschworenen umsichtig behandeln, um – eventuell durch Zwischenrufe – Missfallen gegen den Gegner und – durch packenden Vortrag – Applaus für sich selbst zu provozieren.

Um die ‚Relevanz' einer Äußerung zu kontrollieren, brauchten die Geschworenen also keine juristischen Kenntnisse. Sie mussten sich lediglich den Wortlaut des

[83] Wallace (2001) 93.

[84] S. o. Anm. 82.

[85] Wallace (2001) 95.

[86] Zu Unrecht nimmt Wallace (2001) 95 Anstoß am Genetiv Plural; vgl. τοὺς νόμους ... τῶν ἐπικλήρων in Dem. 37, 45 (o. Anm. 46).

[87] Wallace (2001) 97.

[88] Lanni (2005) 124, (2006) 98f. bleibt unschlüssig.

[89] Bers (1985). Die Geschworenen wachten aufmerksam darüber, dass die Parteien sich „an die Sache" hielten. Die Sprecher kleideten einerseits ihre eigenen Digressionen in Appelle an die Geduld der Richter zuzuhören „solange ihr hören wollt" (z.B. Dem. 21, 129f.) und forderten diese andererseits auf, Digressionen der Gegner „nicht zuzulassen" (z.B. Dem. 45, 50); weitere Beispiele von *thorybos* wegen des Inhalts und Aufbaus der Rede s. Bers (1985) 11.

[90] Dem. 24, 151 (s. o. Anm. 57).

enklêma merken und konnten bei Abweichungen protestieren. Um die Spontaneität dieser Kontrolle zu gewährleisten und Störungen durch Claqueure zu verhindern, wurden den Geschworenen sogar die Sitzplätze im *dikastêrion* zugelost.[91] So gehen die Regeln zur Wahrung der äußeren Chancengleichheit und der im Plädoyer einzuhaltenden Fairness Hand in Hand.

BIBLIOGRAPHIE

Bers, Victor (1985): Dikastic *Thorubos*, in: Essays Presented to G.E.M. de Ste. Croix on his 75th Birthday (History of Political Thought VI), hg. v. P. A. Cartledge / F.D. Harvey. London 1985, 1-15.

Boegehold, Alan L. (1982): A lid with dipinto, in: Hesperia Suppl. 19. Studies Vanderpool (1982) 1-6.

Boegehold, Alan L. (1995): The Law-Courts at Athens. Sites, Buildings, Equipment, Procedure, and Testimonia (The Athenian Agora XXVIII). Princeton 1995.

Bonner, Robert J. (1905): Evidence in Athenian Courts. Chicago 1905.

Bonner, Robert J. / Smith, Gertrude (1930): The Administration of Justice from Homer to Aristotle I. Chicago 1930.

Harrison, Alick R.W. (1971): The Law of Athens II. Procedure. Oxford 1971, [2]1998.

IPArk: Thür, Gerhard / Taeuber, Hans, Prozessrechtliche Inschriften der griechischen Poleis: Arkadien. Wien 1994.

Lämmli, Franz (1938): Das attische Prozessverfahren in seiner Wirkung auf die Gerichtsrede. Paderborn 1938.

Lanni, Adriaan M. (2005): Relevance in Athenian Courts, in: The Cambridge Companion to Ancient Greek Law, hg. v. M. Gagarin / D. Cohen. Cambridge 2005, 112-129.

Lanni, Adriaan M. (2006): Law and Justice in the Courts of Classical Athens. Cambridge 2006.

MacDowell, Douglas M. (1978): The Law in Classical Athens. London 1978.

Meier, Moritz H.E. / Schömann, Georg F. (1883-87): Der Attische Process I/II, neu bearbeitet von J.H. Lipsius. Berlin 1883-87.

Mirhady, David / Too, Yun Lee (2000): Isocrates I. Austin TX 2000.

Rhodes, Peter J. (2004): Keeping to the Point, in: The Law and the Courts in Ancient Greece, hg. v. E.M. Harris / L. Rubinstein. London 2004, 137-58.

Rubinstein, Lene (2000): Litigation and Cooperation. Supporting Speakers in the Courts of Classical Athens. Stuttgart 2000.

Scafuro, Adele C. (1997): The Forensic Stage. Settling Disputes in Graeco-Roman New Comedy. Cambridge 1997.

---

[91] Boegehold (1995) 38, 67-76.

Soritz-Hadler, Gabriele (1986): Ein Echinos aus einer Anakrisis, in: Festschrift Kränzlein. Graz 1986, 103-108.

Steinwenter, Artur (1925): Die Streitbeendigung durch Urteil, Schiedsspruch und Vergleich nach griechischem Rechte. München 1925, [2]1971.

Thür, Gerhard (1977): Beweisführung vor den Schwurgerichtshöfen Athens. Die Proklesis zur Basanos. Wien 1977.

Thür, Gerhard (2000): Das Gerichtswesen Athens im 4. Jahrhundert v.Chr., in: Große Prozesse im antiken Athen, hg. v. L. Burckhardt / J. v. Ungern-Sternberg. München 2000, 30-49.

Thür, Gerhard (2003): Sachverfolgung und Diebstahl in den griechischen Poleis, in: Symposion 1999, hg. v. G. Thür / F.J. Fernández Nieto. Köln 2003, 57-96.

Thür, Gerhard (2004): Law of Procedure in Attic Inscriptions, in: Law, rhetoric, and comedy in classical Athens: essays in honour of Douglas M. MacDowell, hg. v. D.L. Cairns / R.A. Knox. Swansea 2004, 33-49.

Thür, Gerhard (2005): The Role of the Witness in Athenian Law, in: The Cambridge Companion to Ancient Greek Law, hg. v. M. Gagarin / D. Cohen. Cambridge 2005, 146-169.

Thür Gerhard (2006): Antwort auf Michele Faraguna, in: Symposion 2003, hg. v. H.-A. Rupprecht. Wien 2006, 161-165.

Todd Stephen C. (1973): The Shape of Athenian Law. Oxford 1973.

Wallace, Robert W. (2001): Diamarturia in late forth-century Athens, in: Symposion 1997, hg. v. E. Cantarella / G. Thür. Köln 2001, 89-101.

Wolff, Hans J. (1961): Beiträge zur Rechtsgeschichte Altgriechenlands und des hellenistisch-römischen Ägypten. Weimar 1961.

Wolff, Hans J. (1965): Recht I (griechisches), in: Lexikon der Alten Welt. Artemis, Zürich 1965, 2516-2530.

Wolff, Hans J. (1966): Die attische Paragraphe. Weimar 1966.

MARIO TALAMANCA (ROMA)

RISPOSTA A GERHARD THÜR

Debbo confessare di essere sempre un po' imbarazzato nei miei interventi al *Symposion*, perché la formazione giusromanistica – soprattutto a causa del particolare orientamento dei miei interessi, prevalentemente rivolti allo sviluppo del pensiero dei giuristi come detentori di un sapere tecnico e non come generici uomini di cultura – temo mi porti ad accentuare troppo l'aspetto tecnico-giuridico del discorso, profilo che legittimamente appare particolarmente distante dalle caratteristiche del materiale verso cui, nel nostro contesto, si dirige il discorso, e che, come tutti ormai sappiamo (o dovremmo sapere), si è formato indipendentemente da qualsiasi influsso di una scienza del diritto positivo. Se ciò evidenzia una delle componenti del mio imbarazzo, quella oggettiva, dal punto di vista soggettivo, l'accentuazione dell'impostazione cui accennavo parrebbe sconsigliabile di fronte ad un pubblico, il quale – proprio perché si occupa di fonti attinenti al fenomeno giuridico, ma che restano lontane da quel tecnicismo – proviene prevalentemente dagli studi filologici (ed io apprezzo molto la filologia e cerco, nei limiti delle mie possibilità, di praticarla, anche se dal mio punto di vista "giuridicizzante") o da una storia tendenzialmente sociologizzante, ma entrambe un po' troppo spesso connotate da soverchia ingenuità allorché tentano un approccio tecnico-giuridico.

Per quanto riguarda il contributo del collega ed amico Thür, che considero, fra i giusgrecisti, una delle persone più vicine al mio modo d'essere come storico del diritto, farò una netta differenza fra la ricostruzione filologica, la valutazione tecnico-giuridica, ed il complessivo giudizio sul piano storico.

Sul piano della ricostruzione filologica, il punto che maggiormente apprezzo è la parte relativa a quello che il Thür chiama il "Neuerungsverbot", che egli ritiene in vigore anche in quei processi in cui non è prevista una *diaita* dinanzi all'arbitro pubblico, al κληρωτὸς διαιτητής. Forse il termine usato potrebbe apparire, ad un giurista *emunctae naris*, un po' fuori luogo, dato che si tratta di una terminologia e di una categoria strettamente connessa con il giudizio d'appello: quale, ed esattamente lo riconosce lo stesso relatore, non è neppure il processo che si apre dinanzi ai tribunali popolari, in seguito all'*ephesis* della parte soccombente nella *diaita*, allorché questa fase transitoria del giudizio sia prevista. Anch'io penso che il sistema dell'*echinos* si praticasse tendenzialmente in tutti i processi: ed in quella ricerca sul processo attico, di cui troppo spesso ricordo l'esagerato numero di pagine accumulatosi per finire nel mio "Nachlaß" (se, per evitare guai *post mortem*, non le manderò al macero prima), mi ricordo perfettamente di aver seguito tale tesi, pur non sovvenendomi tuttavia se ne avessi tentato una dimostrazione ovvero mi fossi riservato di farlo.

A parte il rilievo dell'iscrizione ripresa dal Thür, sulla διαμαρτυρίᾳ ἐξ ἀνακρίσεως (di cui – il libro in cui è stata pubblicata non esiste all'Istituto di diritto romano della Sapienza – non ho però visto la grafia originale, ma che, dalla trascrizione con l'omega fattane da Stephen Todd, penso sia scritta in alfabeto ionico), mi sembra che sia pienamente da condividere soprattutto la *pars destruens* rispetto all'opinione dominante e non v'insisto. Indubbiamente, anche su questo tema, si potrebbe instaurare un δισσὸς λόγος, fondato, ad es., sulla differenza funzionale tra i due tipi di processo, prodotta dall'esistenza nell'uno e dalla mancanza nell'altro di una pronuncia. Ma questa strada non mi sembra molto praticabile. Sul piano di una ragionevolezza che penso non possa totalmente negarsi al legislatore attico, v'è però un aspetto che è – a mio modesto avviso – decisivo: a che servirebbe l'*anakrisis* senza il "Neuerungsverbot"?

Venendo, invece, agli argomenti in cui sull'accertamento filologico del dato prevale il lato ricostruttivo, vorrei cominciare con un rapido accenno al carattere un po' vago, se non indefinito, dell'espressione "Fairneß der Parteien" (forse accentuata per l'ascoltatore che non rilevi dal contesto della cultura germanofona). Nella derivazione dall'inglese, fra l'altro, v'è una significativa "Verschiebung" tra il "fair process", che si colloca sul piano oggettivo, e il "Fairneß der Parteien" che va a porsi, invece, su quello soggettivo.

Se per "Fairneß der Parteien" si intende – e, in definitiva, mi sembra che ciò faccia anche il relatore – la correttezza delle parti, si tratta di una diatesi individuale: se essa manca, il diritto può cercare di ovviarvi, costringendo le parti ad esser corrette. Gli aspetti in cui, nell'esperienza attica, il legislatore interveniva a tal fine, sono – per il relatore – tre. Sul primo, rappresentato dal "Neuerungsverbot", si può esser senz'altro d'accordo, anche, come ho già detto, sull'estensione del divieto stesso a tutti i giudizi, ivi compresi quelli in cui non era prevista una *diaita* dinanzi all'arbitro pubblico. In tal modo, le parti potevano esser protette contro l'esibizione, sentita come "unfair", di nuovi mezzi di prova durante il processo dinanzi al *dikastêrion*. Altro profilo è quello dell'effettiva portata di tutto ciò nella prassi, ma indubbiamente alle parti non era consentito di far leggere documenti o testimonianze che non fossero stati previamente versati nell'*echinos*, ancorché potessero farvi riferimento nelle loro arringhe, al di là della puntuale lettura.

Sotto due diversi profili, sono, invece, molto meno sicuro sulla possibilità di costringere l'avversario a rispondere alle domande postegli. Dal punto di vista della documentazione testuale, continuo a dubitare del riferimento a questa procedura di [Dem.] 42. 12, un'interpretazione già a suo tempo avanzata dal Thür e qui ripresa, il che mi sembra escluso, oltre che dall'insufficienza a tal fine della fonte in sé considerata, dal complessivo contesto offerto dalla nostra documentazione su questo aspetto. Oltre all'assenza di una sicura base filologica, mi sembra, sul piano concettuale, molto dubbio il ricondurre questo aspetto alle norme che assicurano il

"Fairneß der Parteien". Per evidenziare il mio pensiero con un paragone col diritto attuale: a parte le diversità nella disciplina, sarebbe difficile riportare l'interrogatorio formale delle parti, nell'ambito del processo civile, agli istituti che ne regolano il corretto comportamento processuale.

Il punto, però, su cui la relazione del Thür suscita maggiori perplessità è rappresentato dal terzo aspetto, la rilevanza della dialettica fra *egklêma* ed *antigrafê* sul "Fairneß der Parteien". Tale rilevanza consisterebbe, nel pensiero del Thür, nel fatto che – per stabilire i limiti in cui le parti si riferissero o meno, nella discussione della causa dinanzi al *dikastêrion* popolare, al tema del processo, ossia parlassero εἰς αὐτὸ τὸ πρᾶγμα o ἔξω τοῦ πράγματος – si sarebbe fatto ricorso al contenuto degli atti introduttivi del giudizio. In definitiva, il problema consiste nel determinare se in effetti ἔξω τοῦ πράγματος debba esser inteso come ἔξω τοῦ ἐγκλήματος (o τῆς ἀντιγραφῆς), per andare poi a vedere se e come avrebbe potuto funzionare una tale regolamentazione.

Non mi sembra di aver trovato, nella lettura del "paper" dell'amico Thür (né nell'ascoltare l'esposizione orale dello stesso), un qualche nelle fonti aggancio della sua – in sé seducente – ipotesi. In effetti, l'unica prova della stessa, nel senso retorico del termine (come πίστις ἔντεχνος), resta il carattere molto suggestivo, e direi razionale (almeno a prima vista), dell'ipotesi stessa: il che, ai miei occhi avvezzi a cercare anzitutto il fondamento testuale di un'interpretazione storica, è spesso più un inconveniente che un pregio. Non mi sembra, infatti, e vi ritornerò brevemente, che Dem. 37. 22-38 le forniscano qualche sostegno: è, invero, ben diverso che una certa fonte possa esser letta al lume di una determinata congettura o che venga presentata per costituirne una prova. I §§ 22-38 dianzi ricordati, potrebbero, al massimo, rientrare nella prima alternativa.

Prima di proseguire, vorrei fare una precisazione. Seguendo la terminologia del relatore, io ho parlato, e parlerò, di *egklêma* e di *antigrafê*, con il che, a prender il primo termine in senso stretto, la discussione si restringerebbe alle azioni private, alle *dikai*. Il problema degli svolgimenti ἔξω τοῦ πράγματος è però più generale, ché, anzi, nei processi pubblici gli argomenti di contorno hanno un peso ancora maggiore; e, del resto, nella sua rassegna di testi relativa al "Neuerungsverbot", il relatore ha preso in considerazione anche questi processi. Io continuerò a parlare di *egklêma* e di *antigrafê*, ma non per questo limito il mio discorso ai soli processi privati, anche se per l'estensione a quelli pubblici sarebbe forse necessario, di volta in volta, saggiarne i presupposti.

Viene, anzitutto, spontanea l'osservazione che, se ἔξω τοῦ πράγματος avesse avuto, in effetti, il significato di ἔξω τοῦ ἐγκλήματος o τῆς ἀντιγραφῆς, perché mai, a mio ricordo, nelle fonti, ove vi si faccia menzione, si parla sempre di ἔξω τοῦ πράγματος senza usare le altre espressioni? Ho voluto, per soddisfare la mia curiosità, consultare TLG 32: il database non è strutturato ed implementato in modo tale da assicurare l'assoluta certezza, ma per lo scopo e per le fonti che possono aver qui rilevanza direi sia abbastanza affidante. Orbene, ἔξω τοῦ ἐγκλήματος compare solo in Dion. Hal. *ant. Rom.* 7. 61. 2, naturalmente, in contesto romano; e, com'era del resto lecito aspettarsi, non s'incontra mai ἔξω τοῦ ἀντιγραφῆς. Ma, per quest'ultima assenza v'è una spiegazione a monte, data l'irrilevanza, di cui si dirà fra un momento, per la determinazione del *thema decidendum* dell'*antigrafê* del convenuto (a meno che non avesse assunto la forma della *paragrafê*: ma anche per quest'ultima non si trova mai un accenno rilevante a favore dell'ipotesi del Thür, e ovviamente neppure il sintagma ἔξω τῆς παραγραφῆς): onde, nel prosieguo, mi riferirò soltanto all'*egklêma*.

Va, poi, osservato come l'uso di ἔξω τοῦ ἐγκλήματος sarebbe stato molto più corretto, perché meno soggetto ad equivoci di quanto non sarebbe accaduto con l'espressione ἔξω τοῦ πράγματος, l'unica corrente, dato il carattere evidentemente generico e quindi ambiguo di *pragma*. Al momento, non mi sembra ancora provato l'assunto del relatore, per cui il *pragma* di Aristot. *const.* 67. 1 (dove si parla del giuramento di εἰς αὐτὸ τὸ πρᾶγμα ἐρεῖν prestato dalle parti) e la *diôxis* del giuramento eliastico contenuto in Dem. 24. 151 (testo da trattarsi comunque con estrema cautela), si riferiscano per l'appunto all'*egklêma*, per chiamarlo così, allargato agli argomenti di contorno.

D'altro lato, sorge qui un problema di qualificazione giuridica, che, direi, solo l'interprete moderno è in grado di vedere nei suoi precisi lineamenti concettuali, ma che non è escluso potesse avere rilevanza pratica e desse quindi luogo ad una discussione su un piano pragmatico. Che cosa significava versare certi fatti nell'*egklêma*? In astratto si potrebbe pensare ad un'alternativa: i fatti venivano inclusi nell'atto introduttivo del giudizio come parte della *causa petendi*, nel senso che il *timêma* richiesto si basava anche su di essi, oppure se ne dichiarava esplicitamente il carattere di argomenti di contorno.

In concreto, mi sembra che il relatore opti nettamente per la seconda opinione, rifacendosi ad una valutazione dell'*egklêma* di Panteneto (discusso – ed in parte testualmente riportato – da Nicobulo in Dem. 37. 22-38), presentata al precedente *Symposion* del 2003, nella risposta a Michele Faraguna. Gli atti del convegno non sono ancora apparsi e, per vari motivi, non sono riuscito a sentire l'esposizione orale fatta dal collega Thür a Rauischholzhausen, onde non sono in grado valutarla.

A me sembra che proprio il caso di questo specifico *egklêma* crei all'ipotesi del Thür molte difficoltà. Mi riferisco a Dem. 37. 33-34: Nicobulo si lamenta che Panteneto abbia inserito nell'*egklêma* una serie di illeciti, nonostante che i tesmoteti non fossero competenti per le azioni che li sanzionavano. Può essere stato, senza dubbio, un "trick" retorico (ma ciò non può esser dato per scontato), nel senso che, avendo l'attore indicato quei fatti come argomento di contorno, il cliente di Demostene li presentasse invece come rientranti nella *causa petendi*.

V'è, al proposito, da valutare un aspetto che può avere una valenza contraddittoria. In ordine agli illeciti per cui i tesmoteti erano incompetenti, Nicobulo aveva inserito nella sua *paragrafê*, oltre a quello relativo all'ἄφεσις καὶ ἀπαλλαγή, un ulteriore capo, col quale faceva per l'appunto valere la detta incompetenza, ma questo capo non era stato ricevuto dai tesmoteti stessi, che lo avevano eliminato. Ad un primo approccio, ciò parrebbe andare a favore dell'impostazione del relatore: i magistrati hanno cassato questa parte della *paragrafê*, perché si trattava di argomenti di contorno, per cui non poteva rilevare un'eccezione d'incompetenza.

Ma vi sono, a ben vedere, due aspetti che incrinano decisivamente la rilevanza di questo ragionamento. Sotto un primo profilo, si può constatare che, quantunque avvertitone in tempo dall'*egklêma* dell'attore, il *paragrapsamenos* non spende una parola sul merito delle "legittime" argomentazioni di contorno, limitandosi a constatare l'incompetenza dei tesmoteti, sulla quale, del resto, non aveva bisogno di spendere troppe parole.

Sul secondo punto, bisogna partire un po' più da lontano. La possibilità d'inserire fatti di contorno nell'*egklêma* per renderne legittima l'utilizzazione avrebbe necessariamente comportato che nell'atto introduttivo si distinguessero, anche formalmente, tali fatti da quelli che costituivano il fondamento dell'azione. Disgraziatamente, in Dem. *or.* 37. 33 non viene riportata, qualsiasi ne sia stato il motivo, questa parte dell'*egklêma* di Panteneto, ma – ad accettare questa impostazione – tali fatti non potevano essere stati coordinati, come proposizioni causali, alla frase iniziale ἔβλαψέ με Νικόβουλος, al pari degli altri dedotti nell'*egklêma* stesso (§ 22: ἐπιβουλεύσας ἐμοὶ καὶ τῇ οὐσίᾳ τῇ ἐμῇ ἀφελέσθαι κελεύσας ...).

A parte il rilievo che di una tale costruzione dell'*egklêma* variamente articolata non compaiono tracce nella nostra documentazione, su questo punto, delle due l'una: o si ritiene che ciò non sia avvenuto, nel caso di Dem. 37, ed allora non ci si può più servire di questa fonte a sostegno dell'ipotesi qui discussa. O ciò era avvenuto, ma allora Nicobulo sarebbe stato veramente sprovveduto ad inserire nella sua *paragrafê* un capo sull'incompetenza dei tesmoteti, ottenendo solo il risultato di farlo cassare da questi ultimi e – dato molto importante in un'impostazione retorica della difesa giudiziaria – offrendo un argomento all'avversario, il che sarebbe stato aggravato dalla circostanza che, sul punto dell'eliminazione di tale capo, egli avrebbe addirittura richiamato l'attenzione dei giudici.

I motivi di dubbio, d'altronde, si accumulano. Nell'*egklêma* di Panteneto sarebbero stati introdotti fatti di contorno di carattere un po' particolare rispetto a quelli che normalmente conosciamo e come quelli che, del resto, vediamo discussi da Nicobulo anche nella perorazione del suo discorso (Dem. 37. 52-56). In Dem. 37. 33-34 non si tratta di notazioni di carattere personale o generale, bensì di comportamenti che, come mette in luce Nicobulo, sarebbero astrattamente stati un possibile oggetto di specifiche azioni. Il che contribuisce a comporre un quadro generale che induce a ritenere tale *egklêma* un dato più contrario che favorevole all'ipotesi avanzata dal relatore.

Con ciò non voglio formulare un definitivo rifiuto dell'ipotesi avanzata dal Thür, ma esprimere le prime – e, a mio avviso, non irrilevanti – perplessità che esso suscita. Prima prendere una posizione più decisa al riguardo, si dovrebbe approfondire la questione, anzitutto con l'esame dei passi in cui si trova l'impiego dell'espressione ἔξω τοῦ πράγματος (che non mi sembra siano moltissimi, in base ad un controllo su TLG 32, che ha confermato quanto più o meno vagamente ricordavo), accompagnato all'analisi dei contesti, nei quali – a stare al nostro modo di vedere ed alle notizie lacunose che abbiamo dalle fonti – s'incontrerebbero di siffatti svolgimenti.

Io ho l'impressione che non se ne ricaverebbe troppo nell'un senso o nell'altro, anche perché dai miei pallidi ricordi della documentazione attica (che un tempo conoscevo bene) ma anche da quelli ancor più pallidi delle fonti tecnografiche (che, sempre tanti anni fa, mi sono almeno letto), mi sembra che non vi si trovi mai una visibile traccia nel senso che si possa legittimamente parlare di circostanze che non attengono al *thema decidendum*, perché sono state introdotte nell'*egklêma*.

Se, come ritengo più probabile (ma attendo sempre di essere smentito), da un rinnovato esame delle fonti null'altro si ricavasse a favore dell'ipotesi presentata dal relatore, l'attuale impianto probatorio non parrebbe, debbo dire, sufficiente per accettare la ricostruzione così proposta. Al proposito, vorrei corroborare questa presa di posizione di qualche osservazione di carattere generale.

Se fosse stato così facile di evitare l'accusa di parlare ἔξω τοῦ πράγματος, perché di questa possibilità non si fa mai uso né menzione? Perché soltanto Panteneto sarebbe stato così accorto? o, forse, egli sarebbe stato, al contrario, soltanto un po' ingenuo nel suo eccesso di cautela, perché gli ateniesi sarebbero stati avvezzi ad inserire nelle loro arringhe tutti gli argomenti che ritenevano opportuni, senza curarsi di sfruttare l'opportunità che veniva loro data di inserirli nell'*egklêma*, per poterne legittimamente parlare, in quanto, sul piano del diritto, nessuno era in grado di impedir loro di farlo? Ma, se così stavano le cose, si trattava di una regola o di una prassi inutile.

Vi sono anche altri motivi di perplessità. Ad ammettere l'importanza di questa regola e ad inserirla in quanto altro conosciamo sul processo attico sorge una difficoltà in ordine alla parità di posizione dei contendenti, il che ha un qualche rilievo trattandosi di un argomento collegato col "Fairneß der Parteien". Sulla base delle scarse lacinie che ci sono state conservate degli atti introduttivi del giudizio, come le ha raccolte il relatore (e, al momento, non me ne sovviene d'altre), v'è una profonda differenza tra *egklêma* ed *antigrafê*. Non mi sembra di ricordare – al di fuori dei giudizi paragrafici nella mia ricostruzione[1] – esempi in cui la contrapposizione fra gli atti introduttivi del giudizio si attuasse, a parte in alcuni casi per la δίκη φόνου, in modo diverso che nello schema dello *status coniecturalis*,

[1] Che ho rapidamente esposta in una relazione al primo *Symposion* organizzato dall'indimenticabile Hans Julius Wolff, a Rheda, nel 1971, e della quale ho pubblicato, negli atti, solo una breve traccia: M. Talamanca, *Giudizio paragrafico ed ammissibilità dell'azione nel sistema processuale attico*, in *Symposion 1971*, Köln-Wien, 1975, 125ss.

della στάσις στοχασμοῦ: *feci, non feci*. Nella sua *antigrafê*, il convenuto si limitava a negare i fatti dedotti nell'*egklêma* dell'attore.

Non è facile immaginare l'inserzione – nell'*antigrafê* così strutturata – di argomenti di contorno. Non si trattava, certamente, di una cosa impossibile, ma vorrei dire che è proprio la logica che regge la contrapposizione fra *egklêma* ed *antigrafê* a render inverisimile una tale possibilità, già dal punto di vista della struttura grammaticale degli scritti difensivi. Ma è evidente che non sarebbe ammissibile che la possibilità di far rientrare nell'αὐτὸ τὸ πρᾶγμα circostanze al di fuori dello specifico *agôn* giudiziario fosse limitata all'attore.

D'altro lato, su che cosa si sarebbe basata codesta possibilità? Si trattava di una regola di diritto o di qualcosa rilevante solo al livello della prassi giudiziaria? Quest'ultima non era, di certo, in grado di trasformarsi in una consuetudine cogente (per quello che potesse valere quest'ultima qualificazione ad Atene), perché, come fonte di diritto, la consuetudine è estranea ai modi di pensare correnti nel mondo greco, anche al livello della retorica giudiziaria.

Si dovrebbe pensare ad un *nomos* che introducesse tale regola (si ricordi come manchi, in Atene, una scienza del diritto che, come la *iuris prudentia* romana, possa introdurre un principio del genere). Ma di esso manca qualsiasi traccia e, fra l'altro, basta formulare una tale ipotesi per vedere immediatamente quanto ciò sia inverisimile. Anche se è comprensibile, sul piano della retorica giudiziaria, la tecnica del convincimento globale, secondo la quale si giudica più della persona che dei fatti di causa, non sembra di certo essere stata codesta tecnica il sistema favorito dal legislatore, al quale non può imputarsi di aver creato una disciplina in cui si legalizzasse, con un espediente di carattere esclusivamente formale, la legittima possibilità di parlare al di fuori dello specifico oggetto del processo.

Vi sono, poi, non lievi perplessità sul piano della regolamentazione giuridica. Lo stesso Thür riconosce come non vi fosse alcuna sanzione per il divieto di parlare ἔξω τοῦ πράγματος (inteso nel senso di ἔξω τοῦ ἐγκλήματος), al di fuori del *thorubein* da parte dei giudici, che avrebbero così sanzionato chi andasse al di fuori dei limiti posti dagli atti introduttivi del giudizio.

Il problema si allarga in tal modo alla valutazione del *thorubein*, se esso possa effettivamente considerarsi come una sanzione al livello del diritto e non di una prassi giudiziaria collocata sul piano dell'arbitrio dei giudici eliastici, mossi – nel migliore dei casi (perché si può senz'altro pensare alle decisioni precostituite in virtù delle amicizie personali o delle simpatie politiche) – dalle emozioni suscitate dalle argomentazioni retoriche. Anche codesto punto avrebbe richiesto un'ulteriore indagine sui passi, questa volta un po' più numerosi, che si riferiscono a tale prassi nel processo attico, per vedere in quale connessione essa sia attestata o vi si faccia allusione. Su un piano astratto, mi sia permessa solo un'osservazione: mi sembrerebbe un po' fuori della realtà immaginarsi un gremio di giurati attici i quali fossero attenti solo al punto di diritto se l'oratore parlasse su punti coperti o meno dall'*egklêma*, e non si lasciassero invece trascinare dai sentimenti nutriti verso le parti e dalle sensazioni provocate da quanto ascoltavano.

Si è che il processo attico è dominato dalla retorica e non dal diritto, se non come argomento, *pistis*, da far valere in una dimensione, per l'appunto, retorica. Al Thür, profondo conoscitore dell'esperienza attica e delle relative fonti, ciò non poteva sfuggire, onde arriva alla contrapposizione, fondata o meno che sia, tra la fase "dialettica" dell'*anakrisis* (ma come si dovrebbe giudicare al proposito della *diaita*?) e quella "retorica" del dibattimento. Tale contrapposizione risulterebbe però di assai scarsa portata, quando si riconosca, col relatore, che "entscheidend" è la fase dibattimentale, dominata per l'appunto dalla retorica.

Le vere *rationes decidendi* del giudice eliastico sono senz'altro paradossalmente accentuate nel dialogo tra Filocleonte e Bdelicleonte, ma tale dialogo non potrebbe essere stato scritto né a Roma né, con tutte le critiche rivolte ai nostri giudici, neanche all'epoca presente: trovava il suo luogo naturale in Atene, in una cultura caratterizzata da quel particolare modo d'essere dei *dikastêria*.

Io posso comprendere le esigenze che stanno a base dell'impostazione che non è soltanto dell'amico Thür, ma di molti, se non di quasi tutti i giusgrecisti: quella di razionalizzare l'esperienza giuridica attica, di rappresentarla in modo non troppo difforme dalla nostra attuale, di creare una sorta di contiguità, se non di continuità che storicamente non esiste e, soprattutto, di spiegare come potesse praticamente funzionare quel sistema, di cui noi cogliamo le tracce nei discorsi giudiziari del *Corpus oratorum Atticorum* ed anche altrove.

Anch'io mi sono sempre meravigliato – e l'ho detto apertamente in un contributo alla *Mnêmê G.A. Petropoulou* – di come riucisse a sopravvivere la società attica, nei suoi bisogni essenziali, di come potesse sopportare quel tipo di giustizia: ma non è questa la sede per occuparsi ancora di questo tema.

EDWARD HARRIS (DURHAM)

WHO ENFORCED THE LAW IN CLASSICAL ATHENS?

In her book *Policing Athens*, V. Hunter claims that the enforcement of law in Classical Athens lay mainly in the hands of private citizens. She asserts that "very often arguments were settled, violence quelled, and miscreants apprehended without the intervention of the authorities at all."[1] In particular, "the apprehension of criminals and other offenders (...) generally speaking (...) was left to the private initiative of individuals who caught or had knowledge of lawbreakers. An arrest is then a classic instance of self-help since it required the use of force."[2] She concludes that "most of the major functions of policing Athens from investigations to prosecutions fell to citizens themselves."[3] In a recent article, M. Behrent has argued that the *polis* of Ancient Greece was a stateless society, and one of his main arguments in support of his view is that there was no agency in Athenian society that attempted to monopolize the use of legitimate force.[4] Behrent endorses Hunter's position and claims that the "absence of public coercive apparatuses meant that the ability to apply physical threat was evenly distributed among armed or potentially armed members of the community, that is, the citizen body." According to Behrent, officials had little or no role in enforcing the law since "policing was done by self-help and self-defence (that is, with the help of friends, neighbours, family)."[5] Behrent's general position has been endorsed by P. Cartledge.[6]

This paper will show that role played by magistrates in enforcing the law in Athens was much greater than assumed by Hunter and Behrent and that the Athenians placed strong restrictions on the use of self-help. I have four main points to make:

1) The evidence adduced by Hunter as examples of citizens employing self-help to enforce the law are not relevant to her argument.

---

[1] Hunter (1994) 120.

[2] Hunter (1994) 134.

[3] Hunter (1994) 149.

[4] Behrent (2000) 260-61.

[5] Behrent (2000) 261. Behrent (1996) contains many of the same arguments. Similar views can be found in Osborne (1985) 7: "there was no equivalent to the authority of the state, no attempt to monopolize the use of force. Such a monopoly of legitimate use of force has been seen as one defining feature of the state ..." A similar view is found in Lintott (1982) 26.

[6] Cartledge (1999).

2) In laws and decrees passed by the Athenian Assembly the main responsibility for enforcing regulations is placed in the hands of public officials.

3) Athenian citizens did not have a right to use force against other citizens engaged in criminal activity except in a few exceptional circumstances.

4) The Areopagus, which is not discussed by Hunter and Behrent, played a significant role in investigating crime and arresting offenders.

First point. None of the passages discussed by Hunter show that "very often arguments were settled, violence quelled, and miscreants apprehended without the intervention of the authorities at all."[7] The first passage is the narrative from Lysias' speech *Against Simon*, where two incidents involving violence are described. The defendant has been charged with intentional wounding (*trauma ek pronoias*). In his narrative of events, the defendant tells the court how he desired Theodotus, a boy from Plataea, and brought him to his house (Lysias 3.5). Simon too was in love with the boy and broke into the defendant's house and entered the women's quarters in an attempt to find him (6). Simon next asked the defendant to step outside the room where he was dining and, once outside, began to strike him (7). After the defendant pushed him away, Simon started to throw stones at him. He missed the defendant but hit one of his own comrades named Aristocritus (8). Instead of seizing Simon or bringing an action against him, the defendant decided to live abroad (9-10). It is difficult to see any attempt to enforce the law in this incident. Despite Simon's alleged violation of his rights, the defendant does not seize him or denounce him to a magistrate. Aside from pushing him away, the defendant does not use force against Simon.

In the second incident, Simon and some friends attacked the defendant and Theodotus in the Piraeus as they were leaving the house of Lysimachus (12). With the help of some friends, they tried to seize Theodotus, who succeeded in running away (12). Once again the defendant did not use force against Simon. In fact, he avoided him by turning down another street (13). Next Simon and his comrades dragged Theodotus out of the fuller's shop where he was hiding and started to beat him (15-16). When the defendant pulled Theodotus away, they began to strike him too (17). This developed into a brawl with both sides hitting each other, and everyone ended up with their heads battered (18). Once more one could not describe this melee as "law enforcement": no one is arrested, and no official is summoned. There is no "violence quelled" or "miscreant apprehended": the incident ends when the two sides stop throwing punches.

For her second example of self-help, Hunter cites Nicomedes' arrest of Pancleon in Lysias' speech *Against Pancleon* (23.9-11), but this passage is not relevant to her point. Pancleon is thought to be a slave (ἰδὼν ἀγόμενον τουτονὶ Παγκλέωνα ὑπὸ Νικομήδους, ὃς ἐμαρτύρησεν αὑτοῦ δεσπότης εἶναι), and Nicomedes is simply enforcing his rights of ownership in seizing him. This is not a

[7] Hunter (1994) 120ff.

case of a citizen using force against another citizen or foreigner who is breaking the law. In similar fashion Hunter claims that Phrynion's abduction of Neaira is another example of a private citizen enforcing the law ([Dem.] 59.37-40), but Phrynion too claims that Neaira is his slave (παραλαβὼν νεανίσκους μεθ' ἑαυτοῦ καὶ ἐλθὼν ἐπὶ τὴν οἰκίαν τὴν το Στεφάνου ἦγεν αὐτήν. ἀφαιρουμένου δὲ τοῦ Στεφάνου κατὰ τὸν νόμον εἰς ἐλευθερίαν, ...). In Classical Athens, as in all slave societies, masters had the power to recover slaves who ran away. In this regard they were acting no differently from a farmer who led back an animal who had wandered off his property.

For her final example, Hunter claims that the trierarch who tried to recover naval equipment from Theophemus resorted to self-help ([Dem.] 47.18-38).[8] This incident hardly qualifies as a case of self-help or enforcement of the law by a private citizen. A trierarch was a magistrate and required to render accounts after his term of office (Aeschin. 3.13-15). He was also a Supervisor of his Symmory, an official post ([Dem.] 47.21: ἔτυχον δὴ ἐγὼ μὲν τριηραρχῶν καὶ ἐπιμελητὴς τῆς συμμορίας). Finally, he was not acting on his own initiative but on the orders of a decree passed in the Council by Chaeredemus and by the terms of Periander's law about symmories ([Dem.] 47.20-21). This example actually contradicts Hunter's thesis for here we encounter an official who is enforcing the law on the instructions of the Council.

In short, none of the evidence provided by Hunter proves her point about the role played by ordinary citizens in policing Athens.

Second point. In decrees and law passed by the Athenian Assembly, the main power to implement and enforce regulations is placed in the hands of magistrates.[9] Let us begin with the law of Nicophon on silver coinage, which was passed in 375/74.[10] The main official responsible for implementing the law is a public slave called the Dokimastes, who was to sit near the tables, that is, where the bankers conducted their business in the agora, or in the Council when payments were made to the *polis* (lines 4-8). The Dokimastes was ordered to evaluate any coins given to him for examination. After testing them, he was to return the genuine ones, but to keep the counterfeit coins, cut them in two, and turn them over to the Mother of the Gods (lines 8-13). If the Dokimastes does not perform his duties, the Syllogeis of the People are to give him fifty lashes (lines 13-16). In the event that someone refuses to accept silver coins approved by the tester, all his goods on display that day are to be confiscated, presumably by officials (lines 16-18). All charges (*phaseis*) about matters in the grain market are to be made to the Sitophylakes, all those about matters in the Agora and the rest of the city to the Syllogeis of the People, and all those about matters in the port (*emporion*) to the Overseers of the Port (lines 18-23).

---

[8] Hunter (1994) 123-24.

[9] I owe the distinction between implementing and enforcing to Professor P.J. Rhodes.

[10] For the text see Rhodes and Osborne (2003) #25.

The Archons have the power to decide cases for amounts of less than ten drachmas. For larger sums, they must bring the case before the court (lines 18-26). If the offender is a slave, the officials only are instructed to give him fifty lashes (lines 30-32). If the various officials assigned to carry out the law do not perform their duties, a private citizen can report them to the Council, which has the power to impose a fine up to 500 drachmas and to remove the offender from office (lines 32-36). There will also be a Dokimastes in the Piraeus, but he too will be supervised by the Overseers of the Port (lines 36-44). In the final clause of the law, the Secretary of the Council is instructed to destroy any decree that is contrary to Nicophon's law (lines 55-56).[11]

The primary responsibility for implementing and enforcing the law lies in the hands of a public slave, the Tester, the Syllogeis who supervise him, the Sitophylakes, the Secretary of the Council and the Council, which supervises all these officials. Private individuals can provide information to these officials and receive rewards, but it is the officials who enforce the law by confiscating counterfeit coins and the goods of merchants who do not accept good coins. The officials alone have the power to impose fines and have slaves whipped. Private initiative plays a role only in reporting offences to officials or to the Council, but they may not use physical force to punish those who break the law. It is public officials who do most of the work of detecting counterfeit coins and carrying out the sanctions contained in the law.

One could also cite the duties of the ten Astynomoi, who maintained order and enforced regulations for the entire city of Athens (*Ath. Pol.* 50.2).[12] One of their duties was to supervise the hiring of women who played the flute, harp or lyre and keep their fees to no more than two drachmas. They kept watch on those who collected excrement or garbage to see that they did not dump anything too close to the city. They also enforced building regulations to stop construction that encroached on public roads or created drainage problems. Finally, they had a force of public slaves to pick up corpses found on the roads and remove them for burial. The Agoranomoi exercised an extensive jurisdiction over buying and selling in the marketplace (*Ath. Pol.* 51.1: τούτοις δὲ ὑπὸ τῶν νόμων προστέτακται τῶν ὠνίων ἐπιμελεῖσθαι πάντων, ὅπως καθαρὰ καὶ ἀκίβδηλα πωλῆται). There were ten Agoranomoi, five stationed in the city and five in the Piraeus.[13] Their duties may have extended to regulating the price of commodities.[14]

---

[11] Note that this task is usually assigned to officials, not to *ho boulomenos* (the average citizen). See *IG* ii^2 43, lines 31-35 (Council); 116, line 39 (Treasurers). For a similar clause in *IG* ii^2 98, lines 9-12 where the name of a board of officials should probably be restored.

[12] For discussion and references to other evidence about their activities see Rhodes (1981) 573-74.

[13] For their duties see Rhodes (1981) 575-76.

[14] See Bresson (2000) 151-208.

Although the *Constitution of the Athenians* lists the duties of the Agoranomoi and the Astynomoi, it does not indicate how they carried them out. More detailed information is found in an inscription containing a decree of the Assembly passed in the year 320 (*IG* ii^2 380). The decree transfers some of the duties of the Astynomoi to the Agoranomoi and instructs them how to carry out their duties. It thus gives some indication about how both boards of magistrates went about their business. The Assembly orders the Agoranomoi to keep the wide streets where the procession for Zeus the Savior and Dionysus takes place clean and in good shape (lines 19-23). They have the power to force those who dump pots into the street to clean up their mess in any way they order (lines 25-8). The next clause deals with financial matters, then prohibits any dumping into the streets and singles out excrement in particular. The penalties are fifty lashes for slaves and most likely a fine for free persons (this part of the inscription is fragmentary). There is no provision at all for private initiative in this decree; the only ones with the power to enforce these regulations are magistrates. These magistrates may have acted on information provided by private citizens in the same way that the police in modern societies rely on tips or statements made by average citizens.[15] But the task of implementing the decree's provisions is entrusted to officials and the power to impose fines on free men and physical punishment on slaves lies with them alone.

To supervise the use of weights and measures the Athenians had five Metronomoi in the city and five in the Piraeus (*Ath Pol.* 51.2).[16] The *Constitution of the Athenians* does not describe how they carried out their duties, but an inscription from the end of the second century B.C.E. gives detailed regulations about the enforcement of standard weights and measures (*IG* ii^2 1013). It is unlikely that these regulations changed very much over time so that many of its provisions are probably tralatician with minor changes to take account of modifications in standards. The magistrates responsible for implementing this law are to make sample measures for wet and dry goods and weights and to compel all those who buy and sell to use them (lines 7-9). The law is comprehensive: it applies to sellers in the agora, in workshops, in retail shops, in wine shops and storehouses (line 9). Magistrates cannot make weights larger or smaller than these prescribed weights (lines 10-1). If

---

15 For the interaction between information provided by individuals and investigation by the Council Professor Rhodes draws my attention to Antiphon 6: "the *choregos* as a private individual made an *eisangelia* against various embezzlers (§35); in the new year he became a member of the Council, and during his time as a member of the prytany he in his official capacity uncovered further malpractices and induced the council to institute an enquiry (49). That I think sets out the possibilities nicely: it is the job of the officials to 'enforce' the law against offenders; sometimes they discover offences directly in the course of their duties, but at other times a private individual has to set the machinery in motion, whether by formally acting as a prosecutor or by alerting officials in some other way."

16 They may have been helped by an official called the Prometretes. See Rhodes (1981) 577.

the magistrates do not comply, they are to owe 1,000 drachmas to Demeter and Kore (lines 10-13). Private citizens have the right to report the property of those officials who incur the fine (lines 13-14), but do not otherwise appear to play a role in enforcing the use of official weights and measures. The task of checking to see that everyone uses is placed in the hands of officials (lines 14-15) and the Council of 600 has the job of making sure no one is using counterfeit weights and measures (lines 16-18). There follow detailed regulations about how to measure various items such as nuts and beans for sale (lines 18-27). If merchants do employ containers smaller than the required size, the magistrate should sell the contents at public auction, deposit the price at the public bank, and destroy the container (lines 27-29). To keep the official weights and measures in permanent use, the law instructs a certain Diodorus, the son of Theophilus from the deme of Halieus to hand them over to three public slaves stationed in various places. These slaves are to make them available to any magistrates who request them (lines 37-42). The final clause in the law makes those who commit offenses in regard to these weights and measures subject to the law about *kakourgoi* (line 58). It is not possible to tell whether this is the same law mentioned in the orators about thieves, enslavers and clothes-snatchers, which gave private citizens the right to arrest these offenders. What is significant is that the law instructs the Areopagus to mete out punishment to those who violate its provisions (lines 56-60). The significant point for the issue of enforcement is that the law issues almost all its commands to magistrates. Private initiative comes into play only when magistrates fail to carry out their duties and fail to collect fines.

The Sitophylakes also played a major role in regulating activities in the marketplace (*Ath. Pol.* 51.3). Originally there were ten men selected by lot for this office, but the importance of their duties led the Athenians to increase their number to twenty in the city and fifteen in the Piraeus.[17] They had responsibility for overseeing the price of grain and bread (*Ath. Pol.* 51.3). Their duty was to make sure that grain was sold at just price (ὅπως ὁ ἐν ἀγορᾷ σῖτος ἀργὸς ὤνιος ἔσται δικαίως), that millers did not raise the price of flour too much over the price of grain (ὅπως οἵ τε μυλωθροὶ πρὸς τὰς τιμὰς τῶν κριθῶν τὰ ἄλφιτα πωλήσουσιν), and that bread-sellers did not raise the price of bread far over the price of flour (οἱ ἀρτοπῶλαι πρὸς τὰς τιμὰς τῶν πυρῶν τοὺς ἄρτους). In the description of their duties the *Constitution of the Athenians* says nothing about private initiative playing a role in this area.

One might object that all the evidence that presented so far pertains to the marketplace, where the *polis* had a special interest in promoting order for the sake of trade. But the enforcement of regulations by officials is also found in the sphere of the family. For example, the Eponymous Archon was responsible for looking after orphans, heiresses, and pregnant widows (*Ath. Pol.* 56.7). He directly supervised the leasing of the estates of orphans and heiresses and made sure that the lessees provide

[17] For the date of the increase see Rhodes (1981) 577.

adequate security. Finally he had the power to fine those who wronged them and could collect food from guardians who did not give it to their wards. In this case the protection of vulnerable women and children is not left in the hands of private citizens, but assigned to a public official. The Archon may have acted on information given by private citizens, but he was the one with the sole power to enforce the regulations.

One could also point to the regulations applying to schools listed by Aeschines (1.9-10). These rules are quite detailed and specify the times when boys can enter school, when they must leave, the number that can attend a school, the prescribed ages of students, and the qualifications for attendance. These rules extended to the supervision of slave-attendants given to the students (*paidogogoi*), the conduct of two festivals, the *Mouseia* in the schools and the *Hermaia* in the gymnasia, the kind of people whom the students could associate with, and the training of cyclical choruses. The task of enforcing these rules is not left to private initiative but assigned to a magistracy (ἀρχήν, ἥτις ἔσται ἡ τούτων ἐπιμελησομένη).[18]

The task of maintaining discipline in the army on campaign was the responsibility of the generals (*Ath. Pol.* 61.2). They had the power to imprison (δῆσαι),[19] "to banish by proclamation" (ἐκκηρῦξαι), which probably meant to dismiss them from the army, and to impose fines (ἐπιβολὴν ἐπιβάλλειν) on disorderly soldiers (τὸν ἀτακτοῦντα).[20] Lysias (13.67) alludes to an incident when the general Lamachus executed a soldier caught sending messages to the enemy during the siege of Syracuse (Lysias 13.67). In Demosthenes' speech *Against Conon* (54.4-5) Ariston recounts how the sons of Conon started to harass their slaves, then turned on him and his messmates. Instead of resorting to self-help, Ariston reported them to the general, who criticized their conduct. His warning did not put an end to their rowdiness: as soon as night fell, Conon's sons started another brawl. This time the general, the taxiarchs, and several soldiers intervened to quell the violence. Once again, the task of keeping order was in the hands of officials.

So far I have looked at the evidence for the fourth century where there are more literary sources for every day life. But the evidence from the fifth century does not alter this picture (see the Appendix). When decrees of this period indicate who is to enforce a law, we rarely find the possibility of prosecution by private individuals; in general the enforcement of laws and decrees is assigned to officials. Especially noteworthy is the protection afforded to *proxenoi*; in decrees awarding this title, the responsibility for ensuring that those who are honored do not come to harm lies with the Council and other officials such as the generals (e.g., *IG* i^3 156, lines 1-9; 167, lines 12-7; 181, lines 7-9). A decree about Neapolis dated to 410/9 instructs the

---

18 Athens was not unusual in this regard. For the role of officials in enforcing regulations in the gymnasium see Gauthier and Hatzopoulos (1993).

19 Cf. [Demosthenes] 50.51.

20 The *Ath. Pol.* states that the generals did not normally impose fines, but see Lysias 9.6-12; Lysias 15.5.

generals to protect the people of this community against injustice at the hands of private individuals and public officials (*IG* i^3 101, lines 44-45). If the private citizens of Neapolis were normally expected to provide for their own safety, this decree would not have been necessary.

Some scholars have observed that the Athenians never had an organization that resembled the police found in modern states.[21] From this they have concluded that the officials of the community lacked the coercive force to compel citizens and foreigners to obey their orders. This is misleading. First, as we have seen, Athenian officials had the power to levy fines. Those who did not pay fines became public debtors and incurred *atimia*, the loss of civic rights. The penalty for violating the terms of this *atimia* was harsh: Demosthenes (21.182) informs us that when Pyrrhus, one of the Eteobutadae, attempted to serve as a judge when owing money to the treasury, he was denounced to a magistrate (ἐνδειχθέντα), put on trial, and executed.[22] Second, officials were often accompanied by public slaves, who could be called upon to enforce their orders if someone refused to comply. Three passages in Aristophanes' comedies show that officials exercised a policing function as part of their duties and used Scythian archers to arrest citizens disobeying the law.[23] In *Acharnians* (54-8) the Herald of the Assembly commands archers to arrest Amphitheus, who is disrupting public business. In *Lysistrata* (433-62) the Proboulos tells archers to seize Lysistrata and other women. In *Women at the Thesmophoria* (930-34) the Prytanis instructs the Scythian archer to tie the relative of Euripides to a plank and to guard him. If anyone comes near, he is to strike him with his whip. This is not just comic fantasy; Demosthenes (21.179) reveals that the assistant (*paredros*) of an Archon had a force of attendants (*hyperetai*) who could enforce his orders. The Astynomoi had a force of public slaves who accompanied them and carried out their orders (*Ath. Pol.* 50.2). The trierarch who attempted to recover naval equipment from Theophemus took along a slave "from the magistrates" ([Dem.] 47.35: παρὰ τῆς ἀρχῆς ὑπηρέτην).[24] Androtion was helped by the Eleven in his efforts to collect arrears from the *eisphora* (Dem. 22.49-55. Cf. Dem. 24.162, 197).[25] Finally, an official might himself intervene to protect a private individual threatened with harm.

---

[21] E.g. Badian (1970) 851; Finley (1983) 18-20; Behrent (2000) 260-61.

[22] For the procedure of *endeixis* of *atimoi* such as public debtors [Demosthenes] 58.48-9; Andocides 1.73 with Harrison (1971) 172-75. Here private initiative played a role, but the denunciation was made to an official, who carried out the arrest.

[23] Hunter (1994) 145-49 discusses these public slaves, but downplays their importance. Hall (1989) claims that the average Athenian resented being manhandled by slaves, but see MacDowell (1995) 272-73.

[24] Cf. the public slave Opsigonos who accompanied the general Dicaeogenes in the dockyards. See *IG* ii^2 1631, lines 196-7, 381-2. On public slaves in Athens see Jacob (1979).

[25] Demosthenes paints a rather lurid picture of Androtion's activities, but cannot suppress the fact that the Assembly voted to have the Eleven help him to use force against defaulting debtors.

Demosthenes (21.36) refers to a Thesmothetes who was struck while rescuing a female *aulos*-player from a drunken assailant.[26] In *Acharnians* (723-24, 824-25) Aristophanes alludes to the use of whips by the *agoranomoi* to exclude banned individuals from entering the marketplace. It would thus be misleading to state that the ancient *polis* "never developed a proper police system."[27] It would be more accurate to say that in Classical Athens the functions of public administration and policing were not kept separate and assigned to different bodies but carried out by the same officials accompanied by public slaves. The officials who were responsible for conducting public business therefore had at their disposal the coercive power to compel compliance with their orders and might themselves use physical force against offenders. We should not think of Athenian officials as modern bureaucrats who sit behind desks and shuffle paper all day long. These officials did not issue orders to a police force, which arrested offenders, but did the policing themselves.

Third. There were strict limits placed on the use of force by private citizens. The citizen could arrest only three types of offenders: enslavers (*andrapodistai*), thieves (*kleptai*), and a curious category called "clothes-snatchers" (*lopodutai*).[28] The distinction between the last two categories, thieves and clothes-snatchers, is probably between those who taken another person's property stealthily and those who seize it openly.[29] Even in this case one could not arrest the offender in any circumstances. The guilt of the offender had to be obvious (*ep'autophoro*), that is, the person who arrested him had to have strong evidence for his charge.[30] In the case of the enslaver, he had to catch the offender in possession of someone who was clearly free. One could not seize someone who had made a free person into a slave at some time or another: one had to find the offender keeping the free person as a slave on his property. Dinarchus (1.23) alludes to two cases where Athenians were executed for this crime, but also makes clear that in each case the offender was caught using the free victims as slaves:

You put Menon the miller to death because he held a free boy from Pellene in his mill (...) You punished Euthymachus because he put a young girl from Olynthus in a brothel.

Neither defendant could deny his guilt since there was no question that the victim was a free person and that he was using this person as a slave, in the first case in a mill, which was considered onerous even for a slave, in the second case, in a brothel, where no respectable, free woman would work unless compelled.

---

[26] The scholion to the passage (121 Dilts) says that the Thesmothetai were required to patrol at night to stop abductions but MacDowell (1990) 255 may be right to consider this "a false inference from this passage."

[27] Badian (1970).

[28] See *Ath. Pol.* 52.1 with Harris (1990) 376-77. This may have been extended to murderers – see Lysias 13. and Antiphon 5.8-10 with Harris (2000).

[29] For analysis of these terms see Harris (1994) .

[30] On the meaning of this term see Harris (1994).

To arrest a thief or a "clothes-snatcher" one had to catch the thief in highly incriminating circumstances, that is, either in the act or with the stolen object in his possession soon after the crime was committed. The clothes-snatcher presumably had to be seized during the actual assault or just after he took the clothes. One source ([Demosthenes] 45.81) indicates that the person who arrested a thief tied the stolen object to his back and brought him before the magistrate. We cannot tell whether this was a legal requirement or only a means of proving that the offender's guilt was obvious. In any event, arrest by private individuals was highly restricted; the sources indicate that it was permitted in just these cases and not in dozens of others. It was the exception rather than the norm.

On the other hand, if one did not catch the thief with the stolen object, but suspected that someone had the stolen object in his house, one could not go ahead and enter the house simply because he thought he would discover the object. He had to conduct his search in accordance with the law. Aristophanes (*Nub.* 498-99; *Ran.* 1362-63) and Isaeus (6.42) allude to the legally prescribed form of search (*phorazo*), which required that the person who claimed his property was in the house had to enter naked. According to a scholion on Aristophanes, the purpose was to prevent people from taking something from the house without being detected or to stop them from maliciously (ὑπὸ ἔχθρας) planting the object they were looking for in the house out so as to make the owner guilty of theft.[31] In his *Laws* (954a), Plato sets forth the requirements for the search in some detail, and his rules are probably based on the Athenian procedure with some minor additions:

If someone wishes to search for something in anyone's house, he must conduct his search in the following way: naked or with a small *chiton* without a belt after first swearing an oath by the legally prescribed gods that he expects to find (the stolen object). Let him (the suspect) provide his house to be searched, both the sealed and unsealed items. If anyone does not give his house to be searched to someone which wishes to investigate, let the person who is prevented estimate the value of the object he is looking for and bring a private suit, and if he (the defendant) owes, let him pay damages double to the amount estimated.

Here we find strict regulation of a procedure carried out by a private individual to prevent its abuse as a means of personal vendetta.

Different rules applied to *moichoi*, those who seduced free women.[32] The man who caught the seducer could lock him up until he either paid compensation or made arrangements for payment.[33] But here too the Athenians placed careful restrictions on the use of force. In his speech *Against Neaera*, Apollodorus ([Dem.] 59.64-74) describes how his opponent Stephanus attempted to use this procedure against

[31] For the similarity between this procedure and *quaestio cum lance et licio* in Roman Law see Wyse (1904) 528-30.

[32] Some scholars translate the term *moichos* as adulterer, but the word also applies to those who seduce unmarried women. See Kapparis (1999) 297 for a summary of the debate.

[33] On this law see Kapparis (1999) 308-9.

Epaenetus only to find that it backfired and almost landed him in serious trouble. At the time of her trial Neaera was living with an Athenian politician named Stephanus. Apollodorus tells how Stephanus caught Epaenetus with Neaera's daughter and by threats induced him to make apromise to pay thirty *mnai*. Stephanus released him after Epaenetus named two respectable Athenians as his sureties for this sum ([Dem.] 59.65). Apollodorus claims that the entire incident was the result of a plot hatched by Stephanus and Neaera, but he provides no evidence for his allegation, which we are entitled to view with some skepticism. As soon as Epainetus was released, he brought a charge against Stephanus for wrongful imprisonment ([Dem.] 59.66). Here Apollodorus reminds the court that if someone claimed that he had been wrongfully held as a seducer, he could bring a charge against the man who detained him and, if he proved there was a plot against him, his sureties would win release from payment. If he did not convince the court, however, the defendant could do anything he wished to him provided he did not use a knife. This statute once again reveals an awareness that self-help could easily be abused and that it was necessary to protect the victims of such abuse by providing them with legal remedies.

When Epaenetus made his charge before the Thesmothetai, he admitted that he had had relations with the girl, but claimed that he was not a seducer ([Dem.] 59.67). He presented two arguments to support his point. His first argument was that the girl was not the daughter of Stephanus, but of Neaera, who was aware that he was having relations with the girl. He also pointed out that he had spent money on both mother and daughter and that they were under his care while he was in Athens. His probable reason for making this statement was to undercut Stephanus' claim to be the girl's *kyrios* or protector. His second argument was that the law states that once cannot commit *moicheia* (seduction) with women who reside in a brothel or sell themselves openly in the marketplace, that is, work as prostitutes on the street ([Dem.] 59.67).[34] At this point Stephanus grew frightened because he was worried that he would be exposed as a brothel-keeper and an extortionist. He therefore agreed to submit the dispute to arbitration provided that Epaenetus withdrew his charge and the sureties were released from their obligation ([Dem.] 59.68).[35] Epaenetus agreed, and a settlement was worked out that required Epaenetus to contribute 1,000 drachmas for the dowry of Neaera's daughter ([Dem.] 59.69-70). The entire incident reveals that the person who used self-help did so at some risk. He had to be certain that he had strong grounds for using physical force against his opponent and might be vulnerable to the charge that he had abused his power. In this case, Stephanus was forced to relinquish his claim to the payment of forty *mnai* and accept a settlement for much less. He had also exposed himself to a charge for

[34] On this law see Kapparis (1999) 311-13.

[35] There was nothing illegal about withdrawing a public charge at this stage. See Harris (1999).

wrongful imprisonment, which could have brought serious penalties if he had been convicted.

Fourth point. The Areopagus exercised a general supervision over all residents of Attica and had the power to conduct investigations and to make reports of crimes (*apophaseis*).[36] The Assembly might order the Areopagus to investigate or it might do so on its own initiative (Dinarchus 1.50). These reports were presented to the Assembly, which then decided how to proceed. The Areopagus played a major role in detecting cases of treason. Dinarchus (1.63) reports that Charinus was sent into exile for treason as a result of reports made by the Areopagus. In another case (Din. 1.58-60) the Assembly ordered the Council to investigate Polyeuctus of Cydantidae. After the Areopagus found that he was consorting with exiles, the Assembly elected prosecutors, and Polyeuctus was tried in court.[37]

The most famous case involving the Areopagus was the Harpalus affair. Harpalus was the treasurer of Alexander the Great. After Alexander's return from India, Harpalus was afraid that he would be punished and fled from Babylon in early 324 with 5,000 talents of silver and six thousand mercenaries (Diodorus 17.108.6). With thirty warships, he crossed the Aegean and came to Attica (Curtius 10.2.1). When he asked for permission to enter Athens, Demosthenes persuaded the Assembly to deny his request (Plutarch *Moralia* 846a). After leaving his mercenaries at Taenarum in Laconia, he returned with some of his money and became a suppliant for Athenian help (Diodorus 17.108.7).[38] This time his request was granted.[39]

Soon afterwards envoys sent by Philoxenus, a Macedonian naval commander, arrived in Athens to demand the surrender of Harpalus. Demosthenes persuaded the Assembly not to hand over Harpalus, but also wished to avoid causing offence to Alexander. He therefore proposed that Harpalus be taken into custody and that his money be placed on the Acropolis for safekeeping (Hyperides *Demosthenes* 8-9, 12;

[36] Wallace (1989) 115-19 argues on the basis of Dinarchus 1.62-3 that "the *apophasis* procedure was introduced by a decree of Demosthenes probably in the early part of 343." But see de Bruyn (1995) 117-18, who rightly notes that the passage has nothing to do with the introduction of the procedure, but concerns several decrees of Demosthenes aimed at applying the procedure. She attributes the procedure to Ephialtes, but her view is based on a dubious restoration in the text of *IG* i^3 102, 38-47. See Harris (1997). Wallace's view is also rejected by Rhodes (1995) 312-13.

[37] On these cases see Harris (2004).

[38] For the procedure of supplication in the Assembly see with Naiden (2004).

[39] I see no reason to follow Worthington (1992) 43-44, 315 in believing that Harpalus entered Athens by bribing Philocles in violation of the previous decree denying him entry. Worthington relies on Dinarchus 3.2, but this passage probably refers to the earlier occasion when Harpalus came with his ships and mercenaries.

Dinarchus 1.89).[40] Harpalus reported that the entire sum was 700 talents, but the amount was later discovered to be only 350 talents (Hyperides *Demosthenes* 9-10; [Plutarch] *Moralia* 846B).[41] Harpalus was allowed to escape (Hyperides *Demosthenes* 12), collected the troops left at Taenarum, and fled to Crete where he was murdered (Diodorus 17.108.7-8). Suspicion of bribery fell on Demosthenes, who declared his innocence and proposed that Areopagus investigate the matter (Hyperides *Demosthenes* 2; Din. 1.61). The Areopagus turned in its report six months later (Din. 1.45). This report listed the names of those who had taken money and the amounts they had received (Hyp. 5.5-6). Demosthenes and Aristogeiton were among those named (Din. 1.53). Ten prosecutors were appointed by the Assembly (Din. 2.6), and the accused tried in court. What is significant here is that private initiative played no role at all in the detection and the prosecution of the crime. The investigation was undertaken at the suggestion of a politician Demosthenes, but was carried out by the Areopagus on its own. The prosecutions of those reported by the Areopagus were brought by elected accusers, not by private individuals acting on their own initiative.

But the Areopagus was not only involved in detecting major crimes against the community. More routine matters also fell within its competence. Dinarchus (1.56) alludes to two incidents were the Areopagus reported minor infractions. In one case, the Areopagus fined one of its own members who had cheated a ferryman of his payment and reported him to the Assembly. In another case, it caught Conon fraudulently claiming a state payment worth five drachmas, hardly a large sum of money.

The Areopagus also pried into the private lives of Athenians. When Phano, the wife of Theogenes, the Basileus, participated in the Anthesteria, the Areopagus discovered that she was neither a virgin when she married her husband, nor even a citizen ([Dem.] 59.79-81). Theogenes persuaded the Council that he was not aware of her true status and forgiven, but it is clear that he could have been fined ([Dem.] 59.81-83).[42] The power of the Areopagus to examine the private lives of citizens is also attested in an anecdote of Athenaeus (IV 168 a-b). When the philosophers Menedemus and Asclepiades were young, the Areopagus asked them how they could be in such good shape although they owned nothing and passed their time with other philosophers. The two youths produced a miller, who told the Council that every night they worked in his mill and received two drachmas. The Areopagus was so impressed that it gave them two hundred drachmas. This incident must date to the period 330-320.[43] This amusing story may have been invented, but its details ought

---

40 Ambassadors also came from Antipater and Olympias to demand his surrender (Diodorus 17.108.7). Worthington argues against the existence of these embassies, but see Blackwell (1999) 17-27.

41 On the figures see Whitehead (2000) 385.

42 On this incident see Kapparis (1999) 344-48.

43 For the date see de Bruyn (1995) 135.

to be authentic. Contemporary evidence reveals that there was a law against idleness (Dem. 57.32), and the wage paid to the two is comparable to the rate attested for unskilled labor in this period.[44] If the Areopagus could look into Theogenes' marriage, there is no reason to doubt that it also had the power to inquire into other aspects of the personal lives of metics and citizens.

Perhaps the best illustration of the limits of self-help and the role of the Areopagus is found in the case of Antiphon (Dem. 18.132-33). Antiphon lost his citizenship through the *diapsephisis* procedure in 346. Several years later, between 343 and 340, Demosthenes seized him while "hiding" and brought him before the Assembly, charging that he was a spy for Philip, the king of Macedon.[45] During the debate in the Assembly, Aeschines objected to the arrest on the grounds that Demosthenes had entered a private dwelling without a decree.[46] The Assembly sided with Aeschines and ordered Antiphon to be released. The decision in favor of Aeschines show that it was illegal for an Athenian to enter a private house without a decree of the Council or Assembly, a significant restriction on the power to make arrests even in the case of traitors.

Antiphon's case did not end there. Demosthenes' charge aroused the suspicions of the Areopagus, which launched an investigation and arrested Antiphon shortly afterwards. This time Antiphon was tortured and evidently confessed since he was put to death. There is no need to believe that Antiphon's confession vindicated Demosthenes; confessions obtained under torture are notoriously unreliable as evidence (despite the views of some in the Bush administration). What this incident does show is the limits of private initiative in law enforcement and the key role of public bodies like the Areopagus.

The final piece of evidence to be examined comes from the decree about the Sacred *Orgas*, which is dated to 352/1.[47] The decree concerns the placing of boundary-markers around the Sacred *Orgas* (lines 7-10, 69-73) and the issue of whether or not the *Orgas* should be cultivated (lines 23-53). The decree notes that the law entrusts the administration of the *Orgas* and other sacred matters to a series of public bodies and officials: those whom the law orders to look after the *Orgas* (lines 18), the Areopagus (lines 18-19), the general elected to protect the countryside (lines 19-20), the peripolarchs (lines 20-21), the demarchs (line 21) and the Council of 500 (lines 21-22). At the very end of this list, we find almost as an afterthought "and any other Athenian who wishes" (line 22). In this case it is clear that the primary responsibility for looking after sacred business was in the hands of over eight hundred public officials.[48] The passage leaves us with the distinct impression

[44] For wages in this period see Loomis (1998), esp. 104-120.

[45] For the date see Harris (1995) 169-70.

[46] For the legal grounds for Aeschines' objection see Harris (1995) 172.

[47] For the text and discussion see Rhodes and Osborne (2003) #58.

[48] The Areopagus gained nine new members every year. If these men lived an average of twenty years after induction, that would give about 200 members. There were 133 demes

that private initiative was merely a supplement to the main work carried out by magistrates, a kind of default mechanism, which would be necessary only in exceptional circumstances when they were not able to perform their duties.

To sum up. The evidence presented here reveals that *pace* Hunter and Behrent the enforcement of law in Classical Athens was not primarily in the hands of private citizens. A study of the actual laws and decrees of the Athenians shows that officials and bodies like the Council of 500 and the Areopagus played the primary role in policing Athens. Far from entrusting private citizens with wide powers to employ self-help, the laws of Athens carefully circumscribed their right to use force. That is not to say that the Athenians had no concerns about official misconduct. But they clearly believed that it was better to place the administration of justice in the control of magistrates sworn to uphold impartially the laws and decrees of the Athenian people.[49] This was because the Athenians clearly understood the risks of leaving enforcement to the whim of private citizens who might abuse legal procedures to pursue personal feuds to the detriment of the public good.[50]

in the fourth century, each with one demarch. For the figure see Rhodes (1981) 252. The peripolarchs appear to have been officials in charge of the *peripoloi*. On these see Aeschines 2.167 with Rhodes (1981) 508.

49 For the requirement that officials perform their duties and enforce the law impartially see Rhodes and Osborne (2003) #58, lines 9-10; Dem. 57.64; 23.96-7.

50 For Athenian hostility to use of the courts to pursue private feuds see Harris (2005).

In the discussion after I presented an earlier version of this essay at *Symposion 2005* Gerhard Thür and Lene Rubinstein pointed out that I did not discuss execution of judgment by citizens and foreigners in private cases. For instance, plaintiffs were allowed to seize defaulting debtors (see Demosthenes 21.11 with MacDowell [1990] 234). But officials may have played a role here too: see Aristophanes *Clouds* 37 (cf. Harpocration *s.v. demarchos*) where Strepsiades implies that the demarch will collect the debts he owes to private lenders.

A revised version of this essay was presented to the Institute of Classical Studies at the University of London in January of 2006. I would like to thank the audience there for encouragement and helpful discussion. On that occasion several pointed out that I did not discuss the limits placed on the use of force by Athenian officials. I plan to address this topic in the future. I would also like to thank Professor P.J. Rhodes for reading over a draft of the first two sections and offering several constructive suggestions, which I have tried to incorporate into the final version.

This essay does not discuss the restricted use of deadly force by private citizens – this topic is well treated in the response of Sophie Adam.

APPENDIX

Magistrates Enforcing Laws and Decrees in the Fifth Century B.C.E.

IG i^3 1 (510-500), lines 7-8 (fine on those who lease their land in Salamis levied by Archon)

IG i^3 4 (before 485/4), lines B6-16 (Treasurers have power to impose fines for lighting fires, throwing dung, dwelling, baking, etc. on the Acropolis)

IG i^3 45 (c. 445), lines 3-6 (regulation concerning runaway slaves and thieves (*lopodytai*); three archers from the tribe holding the prytany are to act as guards)

IG i^3 58B (c. 430), lines 16-19 (Archons or architects instructed to place guards to prevent illegal access at Eleusis)

IG i^3 65 (c. 427/6), lines 11-17 (generals, Council and Prytaneis are to keep precinct of Zeus safe)

IG i^3 78 (422?), lines 8-10, 57-9 (Demarchs are to collect first-fruits and give to the Hieropoioi; provisions to be enforced by the Basileus who brings matter before Council)

IG i^3 82 (421/0), lines 24-28 (Hieropoioi responsible for keeping order at Hephaestaea and have power to impose fines. If fine is higher than fifty *dr.*, they must take case to court)

IG i^3 98 (411), lines 19-26 (Pythophanes is granted protection against harm and *asylia*; the generals and Council are responsible for his safety)

IG i^3 101 (410/09), lines 51-55 (generals to protect people of Neapolis against harm from public officials and private individuals)

IG i^3 102 (410/09), lines 32-34, 39-47 (Thrasybulus of Calydon is given *enktesis*; the Council and the Prytaneis are responsible for protecting him; Council instructed to conduct investigation about those bribed to pass a decree and to punish them and/or bring them to court as well as to report its findings.)

IG i^3 107 (c. 409), lines 3-5 (the Prytaneis, Council, and generals are ordered to see that no harm is done to an unknown honorand)

IG i^3 110 (408/7), lines 15-20 (Council, generals, and official in Sciathus responsible for protecting Oeniades of Palaeosciathus).

IG i^3 138 (before 434), lines 15-18 (two treasurers and priest are to oversee shrine of Apollo)

IG i^3 153 (440-25), lines 16-19 (fine of 1,000 dr. on captains and trierarchs. Dock-Supervisors enforce)

IG i^3 156 (440-425), lines 1-9 (Prytaneis and Council to protect the *proxenos* Leonidas ofHalicarnassus in Athens, officials in other cities when he is abroad)

IG i^3 159 (c. 430), lines 17-20 (the generals and the Council [?] are ordered to see that no harm is done to an unknown honorand, probably a *proxenos*)

IG i^3 167 (430-415), lines 12-7 (Council and Prytaneis responsible for protecting an unknown *proxenos*)

IG i^3 170 (430-405) (generals [?] and Council are ordered to see that no harm is done to an unknown honorand)

IG i^3 178 (420-405), lines 4-6 (Council is ordered to see that no harm is done Dorcis, his wife, and probably his descendants)

IG i^3 181 (c. 410), lines 7-9 (Council is ordered to see that no harm is done to an unknown *proxenos* and possibly his children)

A similar phrase is plausibly restored in *IG* i^3 183 (after 445), lines 4-6.

The identity of the archers in *IG* i^3 45 is discussed by Wernicke (1891) 60-75. He believes that they are citizens and compares the archers mentioned in *IG* i^2 60, line 17. He argues that their functions as police were later taken over by the Scythians mentioned at [Andoc.] 3.7.

One could perhaps add *IG* i^3 61 (426/5), lines 36-38, where it is clear that the Hellespontine guards have the power to control traffic through the Hellespont.

A *lex sacra* from Paeania grants Hieropoioi the right to carry a rod or staff (*rhabdos*) (*IG* i^3 250 (450-430), lines 9-11: ῥαβδοχε̂ν τὸς hιεροποιὸς καὶ hὸς ἂν κελεύοσιν). This clause may give them the power to keep order at festivals. For officials using a rod to enforce rules see Herodotus 8.59; Thucydides 5.50. For metaphorical usage see Aristophanes *Peace* 734-35; Plato *Protagoras* 338a.

By contrast, the phrase *ho boulomenos* (voluntary prosecutor) is found in fifth-century Attic inscriptions only at *IG* i^3 34, line 34 and is plausibly restored at *IG* i^3 68, line 46. The phrase is also found at *IG* i^3 14, line 8; 34, line 34; 41, line 61, but all these inscriptions are fragmentary, and not enough remains of the stone to determine whether these decrees allow for voluntary prosecution.

BIBLIOGRAPHY

Badian, E. (1970). "Police," in N.G.L. Hammond and H.H. Scullard, eds. *The Oxford Classical Dictionary*. Oxford, 1970: 851.

Behrent, M. (1996). "Hobbes and the 'Greek Tongues'," *History of Political Thought* 17: 36-59.

Behrent, M. (2000). "Anthropology and the Classics: War, Violence, and the Stateless Polis," *Classical Quarterly* 50: 257-89.

Blackwell, C.W. (1999). *In the Absence of Alexander*. New York.

Bresson, A. (2000). *La cité marchande*. Paris and Bordeaux.

De Bruyn, O. (1995). *La compétence de l'Aréopage en matière de procès publics*. Stuttgart.

Cartledge, P. (1999). Review of Nielsen (1997), Hansen (1997), and Hansen (1998). *Classical Review* 49: 465-71.

Eder, W., ed. (1995). *Die Demokratie im 4. Jahrhundert v. Chr.: Vollendung oder Verfall einer Verfassungsform?* Stuttgart.

Finley, M.I. (1983). *Politics in the Ancient World*. Cambridge.

Fisher, N.R.E. (2001). *Aeschines: Against Timarchos*. Oxford.

Gauthier, P. and Hatzopoulos, M.B. (1993). *La loi gymnasiarque de Beroia*. Athens.

Hall, E.M. (1989). "The Archer Scene in Aristophanes' *Thesmophoriazusae*," *Philologus* 133: 38-54.

Hansen, M.H., ed. (1997). *The Polis as an Urban Centre and as a Political Community* (= *Acts of the Copenhagen Polis Centre*). Copenhagen.

Hansen, M.H. (1998). *Polis and City-State. An Ancient Concept and its Modern Equivalent*. (*Acts of the Copenhagen Polis Centre* vol. 5). Copenhagen.

Harris, E.M. (1990). "Did the Athenians Regard Seduction as a Worse Crime than Rape?" *Classical Quarterly* 40: 370-77.

Harris, E.M. (1994). "In the Act or Red-Handed? *Furtum Manifestum* and *Apagoge* to the Eleven," in *Symposion 1993: Vorträge zur griechischen und hellenistischen Rechtsgeschichte* ed. G. Thür (Cologne, Weimar, and Vienna, 1994) 129-46

Harris, E.M. (1995). *Aeschines and Athenian Politics.* New York.
Harris, E.M. (1997). Review of de Bruyn (1995). *Classical Review* 47.2: 351-53.
Harris, E.M. (1999). "The Penalties for Frivolous Prosecution in Athenian Law," *DIKE*: 123-42.
Harris, E.M. (2000). "Open Texture in Athenian Law," *DIKE* 3: 27-79.
Harris, E.M. (2004). "Le rôle de l'*epieikeia* dans les tribunaux athéniens," *Revue historique de droit français et étranger* 82 (2004) 1-14.
Harris, E.M. (2005). "Feuding or the Rule of Law? The Nature of Litigation in Classical Athens: An Essay in Legal Sociology," in *Symposion 2001: Vorträge zur griechischen und hellenistischen Rechtsgeschichte* ed. by M. Gagarin and R. W. Wallace (Cologne and Vienna, 2005) 125-42.
Harris, E.M. (2006). *Democracy and the Rule of Law in Classical Athens.* Cambridge.
Harris, E.M. and L. Rubinstein (2004). *The Law and the Courts in Ancient Greece.* London.
Harrison, A.R.W. (1971). *The Law of Athens: Procedure.* Oxford.
Hunter, V. (1994). *Policing Athens. Social Control in the Attic Lawsuits, 420-320 B.C.* Princeton.
Jacob, O. (1979). *Les esclaves publics à Athènes.* New York.
Kapparis, K.A. (1999). *Apollodorus Against Neaira.* Berlin and New York.
Lintott, A. (1982). *Violence, Civil Strife and Revolution in the Classical City: 750-330 B.C.* London and Canberra.
Loomis, W.T. (1998). *Wages, Welfare Costs, and Inflation in Classical Athens.* Ann Arbor.
MacDowell, D.M. (1990). *Demosthenes: Against Meidias.* Oxford.
MacDowell, D.M. (1995). *Aristophanes and Athens.* Oxford.
Naiden, F. (2004). "Supplication as a Legal Procedure" in Harris and Rubinstein (2004).
Nielsen, T. Heine, ed. (1997). *Yet More Studies in the Ancient Greek* Polis. (*Papers of the Copenhagen Polis Centre* 4 = *Historia* Einzelschriften 117). Stuttgart.
Osborne, R. (1985). *The Discovery of Classical Attika.* Cambridge.
Rhodes, P.J. (1981). *A Commentary on the Aristotelian Athenaion Politeia.* Oxford.
Rhodes, P.J. (1995). "Judicial Procedures in Fourth-Century Athens: Improvement or Simply Change?" in Eder (1995) 303-20.
Rhodes, P.J. and Osborne, R. (2003). *Greek Historical Inscriptions 404-323 B.C.* Oxford.
Wallace, R.W. (1989). *The Areopagus Council, to 307 B.C.* Baltimore and London.
Wernicke, K. (1891). "Die Polizeiwache auf der Burg von Athens," *Hermes* 26: 51-75.
Worthington, I. (1992). *A Historical Commentary on Dinarchus.* Ann Arbor.
Wyse, W. (1904). *The Speeches of Isaeus.* Cambridge.

SOPHIA ADAM (ATHÈNES)

RÉPONSE À EDWARD HARRIS

La très intéressante communication du Professeur Edward Harris a comme point de départ certaines thèses que Virginia Hunter développe dans son livre intitulé *Policing Athens*[1]. Comme on le sait, la tâche principale du répondeur est de présenter une critique de la communication précitée. En l'occurrence, cette tâche est un peu plus compliquée, car, pour présenter la critique en question, il nous fallait mieux connaître l'ouvrage de V. Hunter, notamment les chapitres comportant les points litigieux[2].

C'est un livre bien écrit, à propos duquel David Cohen mentionne qu'il s'agit d'une «extremely important contribution to Athenian social and political history ... V. Hunter advances our knowledge on ... social practices related to litigation and prosecution, and maintenance of public order». Et Josiah Ober ajoute, de son côté, que le tableau que Hunter présente d'Athènes comme d'une «self-policed state» est singulièrement original. Il précise que V. Hunter «describes Athenian 'policing' as a form of social control that took place across a range of private and public levels».

Les thèses de ce livre se prêtent certainement à une critique, tant positive que négative. Dans plusieurs parties de l'ouvrage, l'argumentation de l'auteur est convaincante. Elle appréhende son sujet d'un point de vue à la fois historique, anthropologique et sociologique. Pour ma part, toutefois, d'un point de vue strictement juridique, il m'est impossible d'accepter toutes ses conclusions. Quant aux points précis qui viennent d'être analysés par Edward Harris, je considère, comme lui, que l'imposition du respect de la loi à Athènes n'était pas à proprement parler aux mains des particuliers, mais que les autorités de l'État y jouaient un rôle important.

En ce qui concerne le premier point développé par mon prédécesseur, ses remarques à propos des exemples de «self-help» cités par V. Hunter me semblent tout à fait justifiés (esclaves-magistrats).

En ce qui concerne son deuxième point, je tiens à remarquer qu'à mon avis, il va de soi que l'imposition du respect des lois et des décrets était confiée aux magistrats. Il me semble que la question de l'initiative privée (*private initiative* ou *self-help* ou *self-regulation*) donne lieu à une vive confusion. Les particuliers continuent, même

---

1 V. Hunter, *Policing Athens. Social Control in the Attic Lawsuits, 420-320 B.C.*, Princeton, New Jersey 1994.

2 V. Hunter, *op. cit.*, p. 120-151.

de nos jours, à prendre certaines initiatives et à assumer des obligations autres que celles du ministère public, mais assumer l'autorité des lois est une affaire de l'État.

Étant donné le temps limité dont je dispose, je m'en tiendrai surtout au troisième point développé par Edward Harris, à savoir l'existence de limites à l'usage de la violence par les particuliers. L'usage de l'initiative privée était autorisée à l'égard d'une certaine catégorie de délinquants, déterminée à la fois par le genre du délit et par la flagrance: voleurs (*kleptai*), voleurs d'hommes (*andrapodistai*), voleurs d'effets (*lôpodutai*), auquels il est permis d'ajouter les perceurs de murailles (*toichôruchoi*) et les coupeurs de bourses (*balantiotomoi*)[3]. Tous ces individus, s'ils sont pris en flagrant délit, peuvent être, sans citation (*prosklêsis*), traînés devant l'autorité compétente, le collège des Onze. S'ils avouent le délit, ils sont immédiatement exécutés. Il s'agit de la procédure de l'*apagôgê*, une procédure importante, que l'on pourrait qualifier de sommaire. Mais sur la question si on est en présence d'une vengeance privée nulle explication ne me paraît plus appropriée que celle développée par Louis Gernet dans un article de 1924[4]: «L'*apagôgê*», dit-il, «nous apparaîtra comme une procédure privée, qui ne fonctionne et ne peut fonctionner qu'entre les mains d'une victime et au service d'une vengeance. L'emploi spécifique du verbe *agein*, *apagein* ne laisse place à aucune doute; il se rapporte à une saisie privée de la personne: le volé saisit son voleur en vue d'une exécution sommaire. Mais sommes-nous pour cela dans le domaine de la pure vengeance privé? Non pas, mais dans un domaine mixte, en tout cas différente. D'abord, l'emploi de l'*apagôgê* est distingué de ce que nous appellerions la 'légitime défense': on peut tuer le voleur de nuit, on peut tuer le voleur de jour qui se défend – on peut aussi procéder contre eux à l'*apagôgê* (Démosthène, *Contre Timocrate 24*, 113) qui apparaît ainsi comme institution sociale ... Elle est privée quant à son auteur, elle est publique quant à son effet ...»

Plus précisément, non seulement il existait des limites à l'usage de la violence par les particuliers, mais en ce qui concernait la *violence mortelle*, les Athéniens ne pouvaient en faire usage que dans des cas très précis, ceux d'homicide légitime (*dikaios phonos).* Etaient qualifiés de légitime certains cas d'homicide pour lesquels la législation attique reconnaissait la suppression du caractère injuste de l'acte.

---

3 Aristote (*Constitution d'Athènes* 52, 1). Cette liste est confirmée aussi par: Isocrate, XV (*Sur Antidosis*), 90; Antiphon, V (*Sur le meurtre d'Herôdes*), 9; Lysias, X (*Pour Theomnêste*), 10; Démosthène, 35 (*C. Lacrite*), 47; Xénophon, *Mém.* I, 2, 62; Voir aussi Platon, *République*, IX, 575 b.

4 L. Gernet, «Sur l'exécution capitale: à propos d'un ouvrage récent», *R.E.G.* 37 (1924), p. 261-293, repris dans L. Gernet, *Antropologie de la Grèce Antique*, éd. Maspero, Paris 1968, p. 302-329 et dans *Droit et Institutions en Grèce antique*, éd. Flammarion, Paris 1982, p. 175-211, notamment p. 197 et suiv. Cet article, dans sa version anglaise, a été publié dans la traduction anglaise de «L'Anthropologie de la Grèce antique» (*The Anthropology of Ancient Greece*, Baltimore, John Hopkins University Press, 1981, p. 252-276) et republié dans «*Athenian Democracy*» (ed. P.J. Rhodes, Edinburgh University Press, 2004, p. 132-158).

Contrairement au meurtre et à l'homicide involontaire, l'homicide légitime était considéré comme excusable et l'auteur d'un tel acte demeurait impuni.

Des traces de ces cas d'homicide légitime sont préservées dans l'inscription de la loi de Dracon sur l'homicide (*IG* I^3 104)[5], promulguée à la fin du VIIe siècle av. J.-C. et restée en vigueur après les réformes de Solon. À ce texte se réfèrent plusieurs orateurs et philosophes[6]. Leurs citations nous amènent à conclure que la loi laisse impuni (*nêponei tethnanai*) celui qui tue en légitime défense l'auteur de prises violentes de biens ou de personne, pris en flagrant délit et agissant sans droit[7].

Était également considéré comme légitime, l'homicide du voleur saisi en train de voler durant la nuit[8]; l'homicide de toute personne convaincue de tentative de renversement de la Constitution ou d'établissement de la tyrannie[9]; et l'homicide du meurtrier exilé, de retour illégalement à Athènes[10].

Par ailleurs demeurait impuni (*mê pheugein*)[11] celui qui tuait un camarade de jeu, involontairement au cours d'une épreuve sportive (*en athlois akôn*); le brigand qui lui aurait tendu une embuscade sur la route (*en odô kathelôn*); un compagnon d'armes à la guerre par erreur (*en polemô agnoêssas*); le *moichos*[12] pris en flagrant délit d'adultère avec son épouse ou sa mère ou sa sœur ou sa fille ou encore sa

---

[5] Une stèle de marbre trouvée en 1843 porte le texte de cette loi tel qu'il a été transcrit par les *anagrapheis* en 409/8 av. J.-C. Cf. R.S. Stroud, *Dracon's Law on Homicide*, Berkeley et Los Angeles 1968 et G. Thür, *Z.S.S.*, 102 (1985), p. 774-776. Voir aussi J. Mélèze-Modrzejewski, «La sanction de l'homicide en droit grec et hellénistique», *Symposion 1990*, (Cologne et Vienne 1991), p. 3-16.

[6] Démosthène, Andocide, Antiphon, Aristote. Platon dans le chap. IX de ses *Lois* mentionne plusieurs cas d'homicide légitime (871 e, 874 b 6-d 1, 865 a 2-b 4). Voir T.J. Saunders, «Penal law and Family Law in Plato's Magnesia», *Symposion 1990*, (Cologne et Vienne 1991), p. 115-131.

[7] Démosthène, *Contre Aristocrate (23)*, 60; *IG* I^3 104, 37-8. Voir J. Vélissaropoulos-Karakostas, «Nêponei tethnanai», ainsi que la *Response* d'E.M. Carawan, *Symposion 1990*, (Cologne et Vienne 1991), p. 93-105, notamment p. 101 et p. 107-114; E.M. Carawan, *Rhetoric and the Law of Draco*, Oxford 1998.

[8] Démosthène, *Contre Timocrate (24)*, 113.

[9] Andocide, *Mystères (1)*, 96-98; *SEG* XII 87, 7-11.

[10] Démosthène, *Contre Aristocrate (23)*, 28.

[11] Démosthène, *Contre Aristocrate (23)*, 53.

[12] Voir aussi Lysias I, *Sur le meurtre d'Eratosthéne*, 30-31. Démosthène n'utilise pas le terme *moicheia*. On pense qu'à l'époque de Dracon et de Solon, la *moicheia* n'était pas réduite à l'adultère. (Voir Sally Humphreys, «A Historical Appoach to Dracon's Law on Homicide», *Symposion 1990*, Cologne et Vienne 1991, p. 17-45, note 5). Cf. *infra* note 14. La question de la définition de l'adultère a donné lieu à de nombreux débats entre Eva Cantarella («Moicheia. Reconsidering a Problem», *Symposion 1990*, Cologne et Vienne 1991, p. 289-296), David Cohen («The Athenian Law of Adultery», *RIDA* 31, 1984, p. 147-165, notamment p. 148 ainsi que son ouvrage *Law, Society and Sexuality: the enforcement of Morals in Classical Athens*, Cambridge 1991).

concubine qu'il avait prise pour avoir avec elle des enfants libres. De toute sanction était également déchargé le médecin si son patient mourait dans ses mains[13].

Même dans ces cas d'homicide légitime autorisant une justice privée, le droit attique prévoyait le renvoi de l'auteur de l'acte pour un procès par-devant le tribunal compétent, celui de *Delphinion*[14], dans le cas où la famille de la victime contestait le caractère légitime de la mise à mort. La suppression du caractère punissable de l'acte devait faire l'objet d'un jugement[15], afin que les juges puissent avoir la pleine conviction de l'existence ou non d'un concours des conditions légales de la justice privée. S'ils jugeaient que l'homicide était légitime, l'auteur était déchargé de toute sanction[16].

Ajoutons que la reconnaissance de la justice privée en cas d'homicide commis en flagrant délit se rencontre fréquemment dans tous les droits anciens, étant donné que, dans ces cas, il est difficile d'exiger de la part de la personne lésée le respect absolu de formalités procédurales souvent complexes.

Au-delà des exemples des différents procès mentionnés par Virginia Hunter et commentés par Edward Harris, j'aimerais présenter certaines réflexions plus générales sur la question.

Tous soulignent le fait qu'à Athènes, en comparaison avec les législations contemporaines, il n'existait pas de procureur général, la mise en œuvre de la procédure étant aux mains de chaque citoyen et, par conséquent, l'application des lois dépendant largement des plaignants volontaires[17].

Il convient cependant de constater qu'il y avait des affaires dans lesquelles les plaignants étaient des individus agissant en vertu d'une qualité officielle. Si un magistrat apprenait qu'un délit avait été commis et qu'il relevait de son champ de compétence, il devait engager une poursuite, comme, par exemple, dans le cas d'un stratège en cas de désertion de l'armée ou d'un agoranomos (inspecteur des marchés) en cas de pratiques illégales sur le marché. Il devait en être de même de tous les magistrats d'Athènes (la *Constitution d'Athènes* en énumère 700), dotés chacun d'attributions précises. Si le délit commis entraînait une peine plus lourde que celle que le magistrat pouvait imposer dans le cadre de son pouvoir coercitif, il

---

13 Antiphon IV, *Tetralogie*, III c 5.

14 Démosthène, *Contre Aristocrate (23)*, 74; Aristote, *Constitution d'Athènes* 57.3: si l'accusé avoue l'homicide, mais soutient qu'il a agi légitimement, par exemple s'il a surpris sa victime en flagrant délit d'adultère ou s'il a tué à la guerre par erreur ou dans le jeu en luttant, l'affaire est jugée dans le *Delphinion*. (L'autodéfense n'est pas mentionnée par Aristote parmi les cas de *dikaios phonos*).

15 A Athènes, entre autres principes procéduraux, était également en vigueur le suivant: *nulla poena sine processu*, nulle peine sans procès. Voir aussi Démosthène, *Contre Aristocrate (23)*, 36: entre l'accusation et la condamnation interfère un jugement.

16 D.M. MacDowell, *Athenian Homicide Law in the Age of the Orators*, Manchester 1963, p. 177.

17 Plutarque, *Solon* 18: *exesti tô boulomenô kai dunamenô tôn Athênaiôn.*

devait alors porter l'affaire par-devant un tribunal, afin qu'elle soit jugée par les juges et lui-même agissait alors en tant que plaignant.

Il est certain que, durant la période classique, les attributions judiciaires des magistrats furent largement réduites, leur principale tâche se limitant, en général, à la phase préparatoire. Cependant, l'archonte éponyme, par exemple, avait toujours le droit d'imposer des peines pécuniaires, à concurrence d'un certain montant en cas d'atteinte de l'*oikos* orphelin et les Onze pouvaient décréter la peine de mort contre des personnes prises en flagrant délit.

Par ailleurs, certains magistrats avaient pour unique tâche de prononcer une accusation, tels que les dix synêgores lors de la procédure de reddition des comptes (*euthyna)*, dans le cas où un magistrat était poursuivi pour malversations[18].

Il y avait, en outre, le *synêgoros* ou *katêgoros*, nommé par l'Ecclesia ou la Boulé, pour soutenir l'accusation dans une affaire donnée, lorsque le renvoi d'une personne à un procès avait été ordonné en vertu d'un décret de l'Ecclésia ou d'une *eisangelia* («impeachment») ou d'une *apophasis* de l'Aréopage. Edward Harris a déjà mentionné l'exemple de la nomination de dix accusateurs (*katêgoroi*) dans le procès de Démosthène et d'autres en 324/3 av. J.-C. (la fameuse affaire d'Harpale). En principe, était nommé *katêgoros* celui qui avait soulevé la question en premier, mais d'autres personnes pouvaient parfaitement prendre sa place.

Par conséquent, nul ne saurait prétendre qu'il n'y avait pas de «procureurs publics» à Athènes, même si la plupart des affaires publiques étaient introduites par des volontaires.

Mais, est-il finalement si important de prouver, comme Virginia Hunter et d'autres encore s'efforcent de le faire, que «private initiative and self-help or self-regulation were the rule»?

La reconnaissance à chacun des citoyens, au *boulomenos*, du droit de mettre en œuvre la poursuite pénale – grande conquête démocratique des Athéniens – ne signifiait-elle d'ailleurs pas que cette initiative privée, en ce qui concerne les affaires publiques, n'avait pas lieu pour un intérêt propre, mais s'exerçait au nom et au profit de la Cité? Parce que, comme le souligne Platon dans ses *Lois*, si la Cité est lésée par un acte illégal quelconque, tous les citoyens sont également lésés (*adikoumenoi pantes eisin, opotan tis tên polin adikê*) [19].

Qu'il y ait eu ou non abus de ce droit du *boulomenos* (*sycophantes* etc.), l'idée initiale était que la répression de l'injustice, de l'illégalité et, en général, le bon fonctionnement de la Cité constituait un bien commun et une affaire commune de tous. L'imposition du respect de la loi, suite à une initiative privée ou non, était l'affaire de la Cité elle-même, puisque, en cas d'injustice, c'est la Cité toute entière

---

[18] Aristote, *Constitution d'Athènes*, 54, 2.

[19] Platon, *Lois*, 768 a 2.

qui en était atteinte et non seulement la victime, comme le répète Démosthène dans son discours contre Midias[20].

De nos jours, un étudiant de la Faculté de Droit apprend, dans le cours de procédure pénale, qu'on distingue trois systèmes d'administration de la justice pénale: le système *accusatoire*, en vigueur en Grèce antique et en Europe jusqu'au Moyen Age; le système *examinateur*, en vigueur surtout au Moyen Age et jusqu'à la Révolution Française et le système *mixte*, une combinaison des deux systèmes précédents, en vigueur de nos jours sous une version améliorée. Dans le cadre de ce dernier, les trois fonctions, c'est-à-dire l'accusation, la défense et le jugement, sont exercées par des personnes distinctes, à cette différence près que la fonction de procureur n'est pas exercée par la partie lésée ou tout autre citoyen, mais par un agent public, membre d'un corps appelé le «ministère public». Cette autorité publique spécifique, chargée de la poursuite pénale, n'a été crée en France qu'en 1808.

Dans le Code de Procédure Pénale hellénique l'article afférent à cette fonction dispose que «le procureur exerce la poursuite pénale au nom de l'État». Cette phrase résume la juste conception, selon laquelle, pour satisfaire la revendication pénale, la poursuite pénale relève des devoirs de l'État. En effet, l'imposition de la loi pénale ne représente non seulement une exigence d'un particulier éventuellement lésé, mais aussi l'accomplissement de la mission de l'État dans l'administration de la justice.

Il me semble que, après tant de siècles de civilisation juridique, on revient à l'esprit de l'Athènes démocratique, à savoir que l'imposition de la loi et l'administration de la justice sont l'affaire de la Cité à travers les magistrats, les tribunaux ou les *boulomenoi*, citoyens agissant pour le compte de la collectivité.

---

20 Démosthène, *Contre Midias*, 45: *tên polin adikeisthai, ouchi ton pathonta monon.*

ROBERT W. WALLACE (EVANSTON)

LAW'S ENEMIES IN ANCIENT ATHENS

The Greeks invented written laws and, until 458, virtually all Greeks praised laws without qualification. Although our often fragmentary pre-Classical mentions of "nomos" are subject to the difficulty that nomos can mean other things besides statute law,[1] from the middle of the seventh century the importance of the *nomothetês,* whose legal statutes "equal for noble and commoner alike" (Solon fr. 36.18-19 West) helped end *stasis*, is one proof among many that laws were supremely valued. In 594/3 Solon wrote some hundreds of new laws which the Areopagos was to guard (*nomophylakein*)[2] and the Athenians were not to change for ten years (Hdt. 1.29; a hundred years according to Plut. *Sol.* 25). Aristotle calls Pittakos, the early sixth-century *aisymnêtês* ("elected tyrant") of Mytilene, a "craftsman of laws" (*Pol.* 1274b). According to Diogenes Laertius (1.77), "When Croesus asked him what was the greatest *archê*, he said the *archê* of the *poikilon xylon* [the shifting wood], by which he meant the law." A legend perhaps, but at any rate an archaic one: Classical Greeks did not paint laws on rotating wooden boards (*axones*). Pittakos was famous for such pithy remarks, called *pittakeia*. Respect for nomoi was characteristic of all "non-abusive" *politeiai*. In Herodotos 7.103-4, Xerxes asks the exiled Spartan king Demaratos how free men could oppose so large an army as his. Echoing Pindar's *nomos pantôn basileus* (see n. 1), Demaratos responded by stressing that the Spartans were free but feared the law as their master, *despotês*.[3] Gomme calls Thucydides' *oligarchia isonomos* (3.62.3) a "constitutional, law abiding government, in which all citizens have equal civil rights, though not equal political power" (*Hist. Comm. Thuc.* ad loc.). Even some tyrants obeyed the

---

1 See M. Ostwald, *Nomos and the Beginnings of Athenian Democracy* (Oxford 1969) 20-56 and *passim*. On Herakleitos fr. 44, "the people must fight for the nomos as for their walls," see Ostwald ibid. p. 33. On Pindar fr. 169 + *POxy* 2450 fr. 1, "nomos the king of all," see W.K.C. Guthrie, *A History of Greek Philosophy* III. *The Fifth-Century Enlightenment* (Cambridge 1969) 131-34.

2 On Solon's *nomophylakein*, see my *Areopagos Council* (Baltimore 1989) 55-64.

3 E. Millender ("*Nomos despotês*: Spartan obedience and Athenian lawfulness in fifth-century thought," in V. Gorman and E.W. Robinson [eds.], *Oikistes. Studies in Constitutions, Colonies, and Military Power in the Ancient World. Offered in Honor of A.J. Graham* [Leiden 2002] 33-59) argues that Demaratos's words are ironic, but their ambivalence must nonetheless reflect a historical truth. Furthermore, Perikles' alternative picture of Athens is also ironic (see below).

law, especially after ca. 600 when the first period of tyranny was discredited.[4] Most famously, according to the Aristotelian *Ath. Pol.* 16.8 Peisistratos, *dêmotikôtatos* and "willing to administer everything according to the laws," showed up in court when charged with murder, although his accuser lost his nerve and did not. At Sikyon the Orthagorids – the longest tyranny known to Aristotle (*Pol.* 1315b12) – ruled for a century until the mid-550s, and were only driven out by the Spartans. Aristotle remarks (ibid.), "They treated their subjects with moderation and generally obeyed the laws."

As a social value, obeying the nomoi is especially well attested for Athens' democracy, even if competing pressures from contrasting ideologies and mentalities also carried weight. The ephebes swore "to listen well to those governing at any time, and to the *thesmoi*. If anyone seeks to destroy the nomoi I will oppose him as far as I am able myself, and with the help of all" (see, e.g., Lykourg. 1.77). The dikasts swore, "I shall vote according to the nomoi and the decrees of the Athenian demos."[5] Dikasts are often called "guardians of the laws," they are often asked to apply the full strength of the law (e.g., Dem. 21.34, 57, 177, 224), and the laws are often called *kyrioi*.[6] The demos legislated that officials could not use unwritten laws (And. 1.87), they instituted the *graphê paranomôn* to eliminate confusion between laws and between laws and decrees, they appointed 500 citizen *nomothetai* annually to draft and pass new laws, and they codified their laws. Reflecting their belief in law, democratic Athenians also loved to litigate, and as Gabriel Herman has shown, in contrast to many other Mediterranean societies, they frequently proclaimed their commitment to law and legal procedure rather than private vendetta.[7]

By way of contrasting mentalities and ideologies, the Athenians also feared to be judged "professional litigants" (sykophants) and therefore in court often sought to establish that they were not litigious, *philodikoi* (Carey [n. 7] 41) or legal experts. A character in Menander remarks, "the laws are a splendid thing, but a man who looks too closely to the laws is clearly a sykophant" (fr. 545 K-T). Also contrarily, in attempting to reconcile laws with Athens' long-standing values of personal freedom and *praotês*, "gentleness," Demosthenes states that laws were to be enforced with greater vigilance against public persons than private citizens (25.85-87, 24.193).

---

4 See my essay "Charismatic leaders," in K.A. Raaflaub and H. van Wees (eds.), *Blackwell Companion to Archaic Greece*, forthcoming.

5 See, e.g., Dem. 24.150, and E.M. Harris, "Law and oratory," in I. Worthington (ed.), *Persuasion. Greek Rhetoric in Action* (London 1994) 149 nn. 6-7.

6 See M.H. Hansen, "The political powers of the people's court in fourth-century Athens," in O. Murray and S. Price (eds.), *The Greek City from Homer to Alexander* (Oxford 1990) 240 n. 117.

7 G. Herman, "Honour, revenge and the state in fourth-century Athens," in W. Eder (ed.), *Die athenische Democratie im 4. Jh. v.Chr.* (Stuttgart 1995) 43-66. C. Carey, "Nomos in Attic rhetoric and oratory," *JHS* 116 (1996) 33-46, discusses the respect for nomos in Athenian courts. For discussion and references, see also R.K. Sinclair, *Democracy and Participation in Athens* (Cambridge 1988) 220-21 with n. 112.

Anticipating J.S. Mill, the democratic intellectual Demokritos remarked, "the laws should not prevent each person from living according to his own possibilities, provided one person does not hurt another" (DK 68 B 245).[8] Perhaps most important, sometimes dikasts voted as they judged best, notwithstanding legal statutes.[9]

In ideology also, Athens' democrats and virtually all public texts praise the city's nomoi. Thucydides' Perikles says "the Athenians do not transgress the law (*paranomein*) but listen to (*akouein*) the *archai* and the nomoi" (2.37). In Euripides' *Suppliants*, Theseus's wise and noble mother Aithra observes that "all civilized order rests on this, the safekeeping of laws" (312-13). According to the Lysianic Funeral Oration (2.18-19), the early Athenians "conducted the city's affairs in the spirit of free men, by laws; humans should make law the touchstone of what is right, ... law was their king." In the early fourth century [Andokides] 4 proclaimed, "Obeying the public authorities and the laws is *sôtêria* for all. Whoever ignores these has destroyed the greatest protection of the city" (s. 19). [Demosthenes] 26 calls the laws "the rulers [*archontes*] of the city" (26.5). Aeschines' third speech excoriates contemporary *rhêtores* for defying the nomoi. "If the laws are faithfully upheld for the polis, the democracy also is saved" (3.6).

Many democratic intellectuals defended nomoi. In the single surviving ancient justification of democracy, Plato's Protagoras (*Prt.* 322a-d) argues that nomoi made civilized life possible: laws are like the lines ruled in children's copy books as they learn to write. It is also reported that Protagoras produced a lawcode for Thurioi (Herakl. Pont. ap. Diog. L. 9.50). The Anonymous Iamblichi, "this democratic sympathizer" as Guthrie calls him ([n. 1] 73), defends law as "benefiting the whole people" (3.6, 6.1, 5, etc.).

Only rarely did any Athenian publicly denigrate the laws.[10] As Rosalind Thomas has shown, three ways only were used to criticize the laws in public democratic venues such as the courts.[11] One line of attack was to proclaim that the laws were too many and contradictory. In 20.91 Demosthenes makes this point, and Anaximenes (? *Rhet. ad Alex.* 1443a) considers it helpful when litigants' cases conflict with the

---

[8] Cf. B 251: "Poverty under a democracy is as much to be preferred to so-called prosperity under an autocracy as freedom is to slavery." Abdera, Demokritos's city, was probably a democracy: D.M. Lewis, "The political background of Democritus," in E. Craik (ed.), *Owls to Athens*, Festschr. K.J. Dover (Oxford 1990) 151-54.

[9] See my essay, "Law and rhetoric: community justice in Athenian courts," in K. Kinzl (ed.), *Blackwell Companion to the Classical Greek World*, forthcoming 2006.

[10] See K.J. Dover, *Greek Popular Morality in the Time of Plato and Aristotle* (Oxford: Blackwell 1974) 306-9 ("criticism of the law"). "To judge from surviving oratory, there appears to have been a fundamental inhibition against frontal assaults on the authority of law" (Carey [n. 7] 36).

[11] R. Thomas, "Law and the lawgiver in the Athenian democracy," in R.G. Osborne and S. Hornblower (eds.), *Ritual, Finance, Politics: Athenian Democratic Accounts Presented to David Lewis* (Oxford 1994) 119-33.

law. A second way to criticize laws was to link them with self-serving politicians. In 24.142 Demosthenes remarks, "In this city, *dikastai*, our *rhêtores* rarely let a month go by without legislating to suit their private ends." In *Acharnians* 532-33 Aristophanes says that Perikles "composed laws worded like *skolia*" (drinking songs), embroiling Athens in a war with Sparta. Finally, as we shall see, especially the dramatic poets might criticize Athens' "new laws," as opposed to its tried and true ones. Similarly, litigants and others sometimes appeal to Athens' first lawgivers Drakon and Solon (e.g., Dem. 24.211, against those who propose laws not in the spirit of Drakon and Solon), just as US conservatives sometimes appeal to the "Founding Fathers."

Thus down through the Classical period, Athens' democracy generally supported the nomoi. One main reason for its support is that both in their nature and in their origin – to control "gift-devouring" aristocrats, laws were intended to be egalitarian, intolerant of elite special privilege, and protectors of the demos, "equal for *esthloi* and *kakoi* alike" as Solon said and Euripides and others (e.g., Dem. 21.45, 106, 142, 150) echo. "There is nothing worse for a polis than a tyrant, where first of all there are no common nomoi, but one man rules, taking himself for law, and equality is no more. When laws are written down, the weak and the wealthy have equal justice" (Eur. *Suppl.* 429-34). As both Aeschines and Demosthenes are pleased to say although not completely accurately, democracy is the rule of law, monarchy and oligarchy are the rule of persons (Aeschin. 1.4-6, Dem. 24.75-76). Anaximenes (? *Rhet. ad Alex.* 1420a20-22) states, "among those whose political constitution is democracy, the final appeal on all matters is to law." In contexts even broader than democracy, Greeks generally were unhappy to obey individuals,[12] but the law was impersonal and equal for everyone.

Following Ephialtes' reform of the Areopagos Council in 462/1, the democratic quality of laws at Athens came to be enhanced, as the democracy attained its full strength. With the ostracisms of Kimon and Thucydides son of Melesias, the demos more and more felt its power, at home and abroad. Aristophanes' *Knights* openly parodied the demos's conscience of its political importance, as Perikles and the "demagogues" competed for the Assembly's support, and as public awareness of democratic ideology – "the ruling hand of the demos" (Aesch. *Suppl.* 604) – strengthened. Abroad, the Athenians now openly called their allies "subjects," *hypêkooi*.

In the Assembly, *dikastêria,* and (after 403/2) as *nomothetai*, the empowered demos charged itself with drafting, enacting, and enforcing nomoi. Quite possibly and perhaps inevitably, it sometimes did so in its own interest. Although few of Athens' laws can be dated and most are known from fourth-century texts, Perikles' citizenship law of 451/0 among other things prevented aristocrats from marrying

[12] See my "Listening to the *archai* in democratic Athens," in R.W. Wallace and M. Gagarin (eds.), *Symposion* 2001 (Vienna 2005) 147-58.

foreigners (cf. Kimon's mother Hegesipyle, daughter of the Thracian king Oloros). The Coinage Decree[13] of the 440s or 420s required Athens' subjects to use Athenian weights, measures, and coins. The unwelcome Athenian "decree seller" in Aristophanes' *Birds* says he's come to sell *neous nomous*, "new laws" (1037); the three measures he mentions (against harming an Athenian; on using Athenian weights, measures, and "decrees" – *psêphismata*, a joke for *nomismata*; and against expelling or not admitting imperial officials) echo provisions of the imperial democracy.

Furthermore, however often Athens' post-462/1 democracy in fact passed laws in its own interest, conservatives hostile to the democracy repeatedly made that charge. Ca. 424 the Old Oligarch stated that at Athens "the law is *en tôi dêmôi*, in the hands of the demos" (1.18), and that people always establish laws in their own interest (1.9). Plato remarks, "each form of government enacts the laws with a view to its own advantage" (*Republ.* 338d-e, see also *Gorg.* 482e-84c, *Laws* 714b-d). In a debate at Xen. *Mem.* 1.2.41-46, Perikles tell Alkibiades that the law is simply the decision of the Assembly majority, even when it acts with force against the rich.

After 462/1 the growing power of Athens' democracy, and – at a minimum – the conservatives' view that Athens' laws served the democracy's interest, provoked democracy's critics into the extraordinary position of opposing the law. For the first time, disapproval of the city's laws is now expressed, although generally not in public fora. Most bluntly, in a pamphlet written outside Athens the Old Oligarch calls Athens a state of *kakonomia* – a *hapax*[14] – in the interests of the demos, as "the demos derives its strength and its freedom from not having good nomoi" (1.8-9). In a typically devilish manoeuvre, Thucydides puts criticism of Athens' laws into the mouth of Kleon, Athens' arch "demagogue." Kleon expresses concern that the demos "does not recognize that a city with inferior but unmovable laws is stronger than a city which has good laws that lack authority" (3.37.3). I am pretty sure that Kleon himself never called Athens' laws "inferior." Thucydides' misrepresentation at once served to criticize Athens' laws and parody the democrats' support for them. Similarly, when addressing the demos in 6.18.7, Alkibiades tells the demos that they are safest if they govern themselves by existing *êthê* and nomoi, "even if these are not the best." I ever more constantly admire Thucydides for his ability to *deinôs graphein* and make the better cause seem the worse: note in particular his verisimilitudinous euphemisms "inferior," "not the best," rather than the Old Oligarch's "bad." When Alkibiades carried his wife Hipparete back home by force (she had gone to the archon to divorce him), an enemy [Andokides] (4.14, see also Plut. *Alc.* 8.5) remarked that he thus showed scorn for the *archai*, the nomoi, and all citizens.

---

13 The Athenians did not yet distinguish laws and decrees: see, e.g., M.H. Hansen, *The Athenian Democracy in the Age of Demosthenes* (Blackwell 1991) 161-62.

14 Cf. however the Spartans *kakonomôtatoi* before Lykourgos's reforms (Hdt. 1.65.8).

Contesting something as patently, traditionally good as law required something of a *tour de force*. So, over the course of a century after Ephialtes' reforms, men unfriendly to democracy proposed no less than eight arguments against, or alternatives to, the polis's laws. Their arguments started gently, for reasons we shall see, and then turned bolder.

The first criticism of Athens' laws was directed against new laws, and was apparently first expressed against Ephialtes' reforms. In Aeschylus's *Eumenides* of 458, Athena states in her foundation speech for the Areopagos court, "here the reverence of citizens (*astoi*), their fear and kindred do-no-wrong shall hold by day and in the blessing of night alike, with the citizens (*politai*) not innovating (*epikainein*) the nomoi with evil infusions. If you stain bright water with mud, you will never find a drink" (690-95). Here is not the place to discuss the politics of Aeschylus's *Oresteia* – in this case, how far Athena's views represented the poet's. It is in any case significant that Athena's criticism of new laws is linked with the foundation of a conservative symbol against Athens' now more potent democracy. Similarly, *Prometheus Bound*, probably written not by Aeschylus but in the 440s or 430s,[15] disparages the "new laws" of tyrant Zeus's new government (150-51, 404). Although I also will not comment on the politics of *Prometheus Bound*, Griffith's remark (n. 15 [1983] 9) that Prometheus's "crime against established authority may be compared to that of Sophocles' Antigone," in my opinion points to the anti-establishment nature of *PV*'s complaint, as we shall see. Such comments against "new laws" recur. In 414, we have noted, the unwelcome Athenian decree seller in Aristophanes' *Birds* says he's come to sell *neous nomous* (1037). By contrast, supporting parents is an "old law," *palaios nomos*, written on the *kyrbeis* of the storks (*Birds* 1353-54: cf. Solon's *kyrbeis*).

Sophokles' *Antigone*, of 442, includes the earliest appearance of a second criticism of polis law: the higher claim of unwritten (*agraphoi*) nomoi, presumably an oxymoron. Thebes' ruler Kreon stresses the importance of obeying the city's nomoi (177, 191); he says that his proclamation against Polyneikes was in accordance with the nomoi (192, 449); he says, "whoever transgresses or violates the nomoi, this man shall get no praise from me" (663-65), and the chorus agree with him (213). But Antigone objects, "I did not think your proclamation strong enough to have the power to overrule, mortal as it was, the unwritten and unfailing ordinances (*nomima*) of the gods. For these have life forever" (453-57). With typical Sophoklean ambiguity, Antigone argues that she relies on a higher order against what she calls not the nomoi but Kreon's "proclamation," *kêrygma*. Also ambiguously – if less so – Ismene fears "lest with violence against nomos we override the vote and power of tyrants" (59), the chorus says Antigone "broke the

[15] Cf. M. Griffith, *Aeschylus Prometheus Bound* (Cambridge 1983) 33 and reff. (Griffith himself is cautious). Against Aeschylean authorship, see M. Griffith, *The Authenticity of Prometheus Bound* (Cambridge 1977) and M.L. West, *Studies in Aeschylus* (Stuttgart 1990) ch. 3.

king's laws, *basileioi* nomoi" (381-82), and Antigone laments the nomoi that have brought on her doom (847). Furthermore, both Ismene (79) and Antigone herself (907) say she acted "with violence against the citizens." Thus, Sophokles does not directly state but implies that the unwritten laws of the gods may come before the city's nomoi, or at any rate what a man in power (cf. 663-72) presents as its nomoi. Echoing the earliest criticism of nomoi after 462/1, Kreon himself come to say that it would have been better to follow "the established laws" (1113-14). As I shall argue elsewhere, Sophokles' *Antigone* questions or rejects virtually every Athenian democratic development since 508. It champions women, the prudent young, the family, the family gods, and elite individuals, over the polis, civil authorities, men and what I call the "gung-ho" Kleisthenic generation of men equal together and superior to all others. It also rejects a powerful *stratêgos* who degenerates into tyranny, something contemporary sources make clear the demos feared of Perikles (Plut. *Per.* 16). *Antigone*'s opposition to the city's laws, here caricatured as a ruler's laws, and its support for *agraphoi nomoi*, joins this list.[16]

In later years, Plato (*Laws* 793a), Xenophon (*Mem.* 4.4.21), Aristotle (*Rhet.* 1.13.2, 15), and Isokrates (12.169) – all conservatives – attest the ongoing importance of unwritten laws in explicit or implicit contrast with the city's laws. By contrast, we have seen, in 403 the restored democracy expressly forbade officials to enforce unwritten laws. In public speeches democrats accept both divine laws and city laws which they do not present as opposed (Carey [n. 7] 40]. For historically contingent reasons – Sophokles' opposition to the burgeoning power of the democracy and its leaders – in 442 *Antigone* struck a different stance.

Before the death of Perikles in 429, we hear no further criticisms of nomoi. This respect for legal statutes is consistent with the generally positive intellectual climate of pre-war Athens. Positive attitudes toward law are reflected in Protagoras's lawcode for Thurioi (Herakl. Pont. ap. Diog. L. 9.50), Hippodamos's ideal legal system (Arist. *Pol.* 2.8), Damon's advice to Perikles to institute dikastic pay (*Ath. Pol.* 27.4), and the *dikastêrion* designed by the architect Metiochos, another of Perikles' friends (Poll. 8.121, Bekker *Anecd.* 309.17, Phot. s.v. *Metiocheion*). These activities conformed to a prevailing mood of progressive optimism. In addition, the upper classes who patronized intellectuals continued to dominate politics.

Perikles' death marked a turning point for Athens both in politics and in intellectual history. After 429 the upper classes retained their intellectual interests as the scenes in Plato show, but with the signal exception of Alkibiades, they withdrew

[16] Sophokles briefly returned to these themes in *OT* 863-72, probably in the early 420s. Although "Perikles'" endorsement of both written and unwritten laws in Thucydides' Funeral Oration (2.37) is also complex, I note that Thucydides was anti-democratic and the Funeral Oration is both deeply ironic and undercut by the supposed moral degeneration caused by the plague which followed it. As always devilishly clever, Thucydides has his ostensibly democratic hero Perikles echo the concept of unwritten law which had recently emerged in anti-democratic circles.

from politics. Numerous texts parallel Xen. *Mem.* 3.7.1-2, where Sokrates says that Charmides is quite capable of serving in politics but is unwilling to do so. What explains this phenomenon? Contemporaries suggest two reasons: the demos no longer needed aristocratic leaders, and the aristocracy refused to play democratic politics with "inferiors," including the so-called "demagogues." No competitive honor could accrue from defeating such unworthy persons. In 428 Euripides' Hippolytos observes (*Hipp.* 986-989, see also *Ion* 595-601):

I am unpolished in speaking to the mob,
although among my age-group and among the few I am rather *sophos.*
That is as it should be. Those who are base
among the *sophoi* are rather *mousikoi* in speaking before the mob.

Like their elite patrons, intellectuals were now less involved with the democracy and in many ways became a darker, more negative force, not least in regard to nomoi. None of these later intellectuals is known to have written laws for cities. As we have seen, Thucydides' demagogue Kleon argues in favor of even inferior laws, against elite, anti-democratic and anti-nomos intellectuals. In the Mytilenean debate, Kleon says that intelligent people "always want to show that they are wiser than the laws, and to dominate public discussion. They thus cause cities disaster. Simpler people mistrust their own intelligence, and are content to be more ignorant than the laws" (3.37). Aristophanes' *Clouds* (1st ed. 423) also associates opposing law with Athens' new intellectuals. The arch sophist *Adikos Logos*, "Unjust Argument," says it was he "who first conceived the notion of arguing against the nomoi and the *dikai*" (1039-40). Having studied with the sophist Sokrates, Pheidippides rejoices in "new and clever" things and "to be able to look down on the established laws" (1399-1400). Simultaneously, various theoretical positions now evolved into more extreme and even offensive forms, as intellectuals sought fame or notoriety by bolder conceptual innovations (compare modern painting and photography). Their anti-democratic critiques of nomoi, now no longer in public like Sophokles', became bolder, and harsher.

Whatever his earlier convictions, during the war years Antiphon was a passionate conservative and anti-democrat, according to Thucydides (8.68.1). He was executed in 411 for treason against the democracy. Extant fragments of his defense speech "suggest an intellectual arrogance and reluctance to descend to the level of the jurors that we later find in Socrates' similarly unsuccessful *Apology.*"[17] Antiphon may first attest the distinction between nomos ("law," "custom," "convention") and *physis* ("nature"), a third and now much bolder attack on nomoi as mere conventions in conflict with nature. Nomos for Antiphon was entirely

[17] M. Gagarin, *Antiphon The Speeches* (Cambridge 1997) 6-7. I follow Gagarin and others in identifying Antiphon the intellectual and Antiphon the logographer; contrast G. Pendrick, *Antiphon the Sophist. The Fragments* (Cambridge 2002) 1-26.

implicated in the polis's legal system, with all the apparatus of litigation and judicial process and the dangers of imprisonment, encouragement of enmity, and fending off aggression by aggression. "Justice, then, is not to transgress the laws of whatever city one lives in," but only in the sense of not being seen to transgress them. "A person would make most advantage of justice for himself if he treated the nomoi as important in the presence of witnesses, and treated the decrees of *physis* as important when alone and with no witnesses present ... The laws are imposed, whereas nature is necessary" (fr. 44a, trans. Pendrick). Although the relativity of nomoi between different societies is a major motif in Herodotos (for example, Egyptian *êthê* and nomoi were mostly opposite to Greek: 2.35ff.), in the preceding generation he had concluded that nonetheless "nomos is king" and laws must be obeyed (3.38). Antiphon reached the opposite conclusion. Fr. 44b, if properly restored ("[the laws of those near by] we know and observe, the [laws] of those who live far off we neither know nor observe"), implies that "the chauvinistic partiality each group shows towards its own nomoi is responsible for unnatural (and therefore false) distinctions such as that between Greeks and foreigners" (Pendrick [n. 17] 354).

Similarly, in *Clouds* (423 BC), Pheidippides argues at length that it is perfectly fine to beat one's father and even one's mother. "Scorning the established nomoi" (1400), he justifies beating his father by appealing to the natural world: "Consider chickens and those other animals, how they retaliate against their fathers; and after all, what difference is there between them and us, except that they don't propose decrees?" (1427-29). Similarly, in *Birds* 755-59 (414 BC), the chorus leader says that at Athens whatever is disgraceful in terms of human nomos, like beating one's father, is *kalon* among the birds.[18]

The nomos/*physis* distinction is pervasive in Thucydides (who began to compose his *History* in 431), especially in the "Melian dialogue," set in 416 and implying a downward spiral in Athenian political morality that is historically false (Guthrie [n. 1] 85-86; see also 1.76.2 [justice never deters the stronger from advantages], and 4.60.1). In the Mytilenean debate, set in 427, in response to Kleon's point that the demos should follow even inferior laws, Diodotos counters that nomoi cannot inhibit men's natural inclination to do wrong. By nature all men err and no law will prevent them: expediency is the only valid criterion for political action (3.44.4-45).[19] It is uncertain how far Thucydides himself composed these speeches. It is significant that – no democrat – he wants his readers to agree with Diodotos, not with the democratic Kleon who supports nomoi.

In Plato's *Republic*, the Chalchedonian intellectual Thrasymachos presents a bolder version of the nomos/*physis* thesis. For him, "justice is the interest of the stronger," because all governments, whether tyranny, aristocracy, or democracy,

---

[18] See also *Birds* 1347-68 and N. Dunbar, *Aristophanes Birds* (Oxford 1995) 468-70.

[19] On nomos/*physis* in these speeches, see M. Ostwald, *From Popular Sovereignty to the Sovereignty of Law* (Berkeley and Los Angeles 1986) 308, and Guthrie (n. 1) 87. S. Hornblower, *A Commentary on Thucydides* I (Oxford 1991) 423, is more cautious.

make laws in their own interest: the government "is the thing that is strong" and laws proclaim what is just (*Republ.* 338c-339a). Like Thucydides and Antiphon, the historical Thrasymachos also seems to have been no democrat. One of his speeches mentions the *patrios politeia*, an anti-democratic motif, and the need sometimes to disobey city officials (DK 85 B1). Confirming that advocating *physis* over nomos implies hostility to democracy, Plato states that those who claimed the superiority of *physis* were attracted to "a life of domination over one's fellows and a refusal to serve others as nomos demands" (*Laws* 890a).

The most extreme version of the nomos/*physis* distinction occurs in Plato's *Gorgias*, where Kallikles says that laws and justice are not fixed by governments but by the weak, like the many in a democracy, to protect themselves from the strong. However, equality is not justice, nature is justice, and nature is self interest (482e-484c), laws are chains or bonds on nature. We know little about the historical Kallikles except that he was friendly with Andron (Pl. *Gorg.* 487c), who was a student of sophists (Pl. *Prt.* 315c) and like Antiphon one of the 400 oligarchs who misruled Athens in 411.

The fourth argument against nomoi is that they are weak. The anti-democratic Antiphon (fr. 44a) complains that laws are not very helpful in aiding sufferers or stopping perpetrators. According to Thucydides (we have noted), during the plague people stopped obeying the laws (2.53.4: but I question his description of the scale of Athens' moral collapse), and in opposing the "demagogue" Kleon, his Diodotos says that no law can prevent men from doing what they want. In Plutarch (*Sol.* 5), the sage Anacharsis remarks that laws were like spider webs, "holding the weak and delicate who might be caught in their meshes, but torn in pieces by the rich and powerful." The comment is perversely clever, as laws were intended to regulate the rich and powerful. It is therefore significant that the context is anti-democratic. Plutarch continues, "It was Anacharsis, too, who said, after attending an assembly, that he was amazed to find that here the wise men pleaded causes, but the fools decided them."

The ineffectiveness of laws is for once a theme that could be mentioned in public, where however it is given a democratic spin. In a well known passage (21.24-25), Demosthenes proclaims that without the demos, the laws themselves can do little:

> And what is the strength of the laws? If one of you is wronged and cries aloud will the laws run up and stand at his side to assist him? No. They are only letters, and incapable of such action. Wherein resides their power? In yourselves, if only you support them and make them all-powerful to help him who needs them. So the laws are strong through you and you through the laws.

In Kritias's *Perithous* (fr. 22), one speaker observes, "The upright character no orator can pervert, but the law he often turns upside down and dishonors with his talk," thus blaming politicians for corruption. In Eur. *Ion* 1045-47 the old servant proclaims, "when one seeks vengeance on one's enemies, no laws lie in the path" (cf. Hekabe in *Hecuba* 864-67).

The fifth argument against polis laws I shall cite in the "sophist" Hippias's version, at least according to the anti-democratic Xenophon (*Mem.* 4.4.14). According to Hippias in Xenophon, "laws cannot be thought of much account, since the very men who pass them often reject them or amend them."[20] Hippias of course is also associated with the nomos/*physis* distinction (Pl. *Prt.* 337c-d). By contrast, Athens' public ideal is reflected in Demosthenes' story (24.139-41) that the Lokrians changed only one law in 200 years, because would-be legislators had to propose any new measure with a noose around their neck. The promise Solon extracted from the Athenians not to change the nomoi for 10 (or 100) years implies the same notion.

Criticism of the demos's habit of changing laws also appears in public contexts, in particular on the comic stage. In *Clouds* 1420-29 when his son Pheidippides proposes to beat him, Strepsiades objects, "but nowhere is it nomos that a father should be so treated." Pheidippides retorts,

> Well, wasn't it a man who made that law in the first place, a man like you or me, and didn't he persuade the men of old by argument to accept it? Is it then any less open to me in my turn to make a new law for sons in the future, that they should beat their fathers in return?

Furthermore, as Carey writes, in Aristophanes' *Ekklesiazousai* 813-17 "the skeptical observers of the new dispensation in Athens note that Athenian *psêphismata* never last," and "the play culminates in an extensive depiction of new sex laws in action, with a grotesque pantomime in which two old hags repeatedly insist on their right under the new laws to the sexual attentions of a luckless young man"; in *Thesmophoriazousai* 361-62 the chorus pronounce an imprecation on those who replace nomoi and decrees.[21] Although we cannot determine the context, a character in Plato comicus (fr. 220) also complains about frequent changes of law. "Go away for three months, and it's no longer the same city." In the interpolated ending of Aeschylus's *Septem* (possibly from the late fifth century), the chorus states, "what the city approves as *dikaia* is sometimes this, sometimes that" (1071-72).

A sixth argument against obeying the city's nomoi was based on the demos's alleged hypocrisy in themselves not obeying these laws. This argument may make an early appearance in Thucydides, as we have seen. In the plague, he claims, the demos lost its fear of gods and nomoi, and in the Mytilenean episode the demos changed its mind and emended a decree sentencing the islanders to death, which Thucydides outrageously condemns them for although they were merciful. The most famous appearance of this argument comes in 405, when according to the anti-

---

[20] See Guthrie (n. 1) 119, 138.

[21] C. Carey, "Comic law," *Ann. Univ. Ferrara*, ns 1 (2000) 65-86.

democratic Xenophon (*Hell.* 1.7.12), the demos was told it was illegal to try the Arginousai generals as a group. At this "the masses called out that it was terrible if someone did not allow the demos to do what it wanted" – *prattein ho an bouletai.* Ostwald ([n. 19] 444) accepts this remark as historical: "for the first time in Athenian history the principle of popular sovereignty was asserted to its logical conclusion." He contends that toward the end of the fifth century, the sovereignty of laws was giving way to the power of the demos. Xenophon's phrasing, however, shows that this passage is not history but anti-democratic slander. His "masses" parody the democratic ideal of personal freedom, of "living as you like," by repeating the conservative perversion of it, "doing what you want," something even democrats condemned.[22] Xenophon's statement is not history but anti-democratic propaganda: the democracy won't obey its own laws, but wants to do whatever it wants.

This sixth argument also recurs elsewhere. For example, in *Republic* 563d, after discussing how in democracies the citizens chafe at any *douleia*, Plato says, "finally they pay no attention to the laws written or unwritten, so that they may have no *despotês* over them." In democracies, he complains, "even if some law forbids you to serve as a public official or a dikast, you nonetheless serve as a public official and a dikast if it occurs to you to do so" (557e, see also *Laws* 701b). This argument also colored anti-democratic historical reporting. The Aristotelian *Ath. Pol.* claims that after Ephialtes the demos paid no attention to the laws as it had done before (26.2), and that after 403 the demos was *kyrios* and did everything by decrees and the courts (41.2). In *Pol.* 1291b14 Aristotle admits that in a democracy the law may prevail at least in theory, but in a large state that is practically impossible. Aristotle regards as typical of extreme democracies that decrees prevail over laws and democrats do not adhere to the laws (*Pol.* 1292a4-37, cf. 1293a9-10, 30-34, 1298a28-33).

This sixth argument has a subsection: the demos did not obey the laws because they were unclear. The dikasts were therefore constrained to do as they saw best. *Ath. Pol.* 9.2 remarks,

> the fact that the laws have not been drafted simply or clearly … inevitably leads to disputes; hence, the courts have to decide everything, public and private. Some think that Solon made his laws obscure deliberately to give the people the power of decision. This is not likely; the obscurity arises rather from including the best solution for every instance in a general provision. It is not right to judge his intentions from what happens now but by analogy with the rest of his provisions.[23]

---

[22] See, e.g., Soph. *Ajax* 1073-88, Plato *Laches* 179a, Xen. *Hell.* 1.7.12, and the introduction of my book still in progress on personal freedom.

[23] In *Pol.* 1274a 5-21 Aristotle again argues that Solon was not to be blamed for the current democracy. According to *Ath. Pol.* 35.2, one of the Thirty's earliest actions was to abolish any unclear laws of Solon. See also Plut *Sol.* 18.4, 25.6 on the obscurity of Solon's laws.

In this same context and perversely, some anti-democrats now claimed that unlike the demos they *did* obey the law. In what Peter Rhodes calls a very anti-democratic chapter, *Ath. Pol.* 28 asserts that Theramenes was prepared to work for any government provided it did not transgress the laws, but he would not yield to lawlessness.[24]

Seventh and penultimately, as we have seen, Thucydides has Perikles say (2.39.4) that courage produced by character was better than courage induced by nomoi. Kritias's *Perithous* (quoted earlier) perhaps echoes this theme: "The upright character no orator can pervert, but the law he often turns upside down and dishonors with his talk." This argument from character was normally also anti-democratic (as were Thucydides and Kritias). Thus for example Isokrates writes (*Areop.* 7.39-41),

> our forefathers charged the Areopagos Council with supervising *eutaxia*, a Council which considered that those who believed that the best men are produced where laws are prescribed with the greatest exactness were blind to the truth; for in that case there would be no reason why all the Greeks should not be on the same level, in so far as it is easy to borrow written codes from each other. But they thought, virtue is not advanced by written laws but by the habits of everyday life ... Where there is a multitude of specific laws, it is a sign that a polis is badly governed ... It is not by decrees but by morals that *poleis* are well directed.

The eighth and final argument against nomoi was that a wise governing elite needed no laws. This argument is of course a central premise of Plato's *Republic*. In *Republic* 339a-340b, for example, Sokrates shows that sometimes even rulers make mistakes in the laws, which therefore do not serve their interests. The guardians should decide each case on its merits. I need not rehearse Plato's anti-democratic credentials. As Antisthenes also said, "the wise man in his activity as a citizen will be guided not by the established laws but by the law of *aretê*" (see further Thomas [n. 11]).[25] According to Plutarch (*Lyc.* 13.3), in Sparta Lykourgos prohibited written laws so that regulations could be changed as circumstances changed.

These eight arguments against the nomoi and democracy mostly had a checkered run. In the end, none prevailed against law. As we have seen, democrats mostly co-opted the notion of unwritten laws but as a supplement to written laws, not to replace them. In discussing forensic strategies, Aristotle (*Rhet.* 1368b5ff., 1373b, cf. 1375a25) and Anaximenes (? *Rhet. ad Alex.* 1421b37-22a2) mention

---

[24] P.J. Rhodes, *A Commentary on the Aristotelian* Athenaion Politeia (Oxford 1981) 285.

[25] Although anti-democratic in ancient Greece, this concept is also responsible for the principle of jury nullification in the United States. As in legal cases involving Greenpeace or other civil dissenters, an American jury has the right to ignore the law in favor of what it thinks just. However, attitudes toward law are historically contingent. In the US, people often say you can't get far by obeying the law. As in Protestantism and anti-state liberalism, each person should decide for himself what is reasonable.

appealing to unwritten law, but such appeals are rarely attested. Against divine law Euripides (*Ion* 1312-13) retorts that the gods' laws of sanctuary for criminals are unjust and unwise; lines 440-43 comment on the gods' lawlessness; in *Suppliants*, Theseus's stress on "the written laws," *gegrammenôn de tôn nomôn* (433), surely implies criticism of the unwritten kind.

We also hear little about the relativity of law after "the sophists" disappear, nor does the wartime nomos/*physis* distinction last long: it was too shocking even for Plato. In his posthumous *Bacchae*, Euripides explains at length that nomoi are based on *physis* and are linked with the divine (890-96). Complaints that the laws were bad, or could be amended, or were not necessarily obeyed by the demos, the demos took seriously at the end of the fifth century, and instituted a series of constitutional reforms to remedy these problems. Even still, Aristophon's seventy-five acquittals for proposing illegal measures suggest that the courts were reluctant to overturn Assembly decisions, whatever the law. As for the argument from character, Isokrates repudiated the point he made in *Areopagitikos* two years later in *On Peace* and then in *Antidosis,* making clear that he had been accused of being anti-democratic (see, e.g., 8.95, 15.285, cf. 7.56-70). Finally, against Plato's wise elite, his own student Aristotle objected that "to establish the rule of a human being is to bring in a wild beast ... The rule of law, on the other hand, is the rule of intelligence without appetite" (*Pol.* 1287a15-31). If it is better that certain persons rather than others should rule, let them be established as guardians and servants, *hyperêtai*, of the laws. Even Plato came to abandon this notion. His *Laws* established rule by law and by *nomophylakes*, but he now observes that no mortal soul can bear supreme and irresponsible power without losing wisdom and integrity (691c). "One of the finest of your laws," Plato's Athenian says to his Spartan, "is the one absolutely prohibiting any of the young men from inquiring whether any of the laws is good or not" (634d). In *Politicus* 302c-303, Plato states that correct constitutions rule by law. Henceforth, Aristotle's and Plato's alternative strategies were to coopt the democratic concept of the rule of law and transform it either according to a "censorial" model or else by collapsing the democracy's separation of public and private.[26]

[26] D. Cohen, *Law, Violence and Community in Classical Athens* (Cambridge 1995) ch. 3, "Theorizing Athenian society: the rule of law."

ALBERTO MAFFI (MILANO)

RISPOSTA A ROBERT W. WALLACE

Il tema affrontato nella relazione è talmente vasto che su ognuno degli otto argomenti individuati come elementi di una polemica contro la concezione democratica delle leggi, o dell'ordinamento giuridico, si potrebbe aprire una specifica discussione.

Ma la mia perplessità nasce soprattutto dal fatto che questi otto argomenti sono difficilmente riconducibili a una corrente di pensiero unitaria, sia pure definibile di matrice oligarchica, o a un solo periodo storico. Alcuni elementi emergono già nel V sec., altri caratterizzano piuttosto il IV. Quanto alle fonti da cui si possono desumere questi argomenti, esse sono molto diverse fra loro, dato che si va dalla tragedia e dalla commedia del V secolo fino all'oratoria e al pensiero filosofico del IV. La critica alle leggi "democratiche", che Wallace ha acutamente enucleato da queste fonti, a me pare dunque difficilmente isolabile dal contesto e dalle finalità specifiche di quel genere letterario e, all'interno di esso, di quella singola opera.

Per questo vorrei provare a scegliere uno di questi generi, la riflessione filosofica, e uno dei due maggiori filosofi del IV sec.: Aristotele.

Scelgo Aristotele perché, fra tutte le fonti esaminate da Wallace, mi sembra quella che, pur essendo ovviamente ideologicamente orientata, si sforza maggiormente di osservare i criteri di un discorso scientifico.

E' quindi interessante vedere come Aristotele valuta il ruolo delle leggi nella struttura giuridica della polis. Naturalmente anche questo è un tema immenso, che è quasi temerario affrontare in questo ambito.

E' ben noto quale importanza fondamentale abbia il *nomos* per la realizzazione della giustizia nella città secondo Platone: tuttavia in nessuno dei dialoghi platonici, nemmeno nelle Leggi, c'è un riferimento diretto alla realtà storica degli ordinamenti giuridici greci. E' invece in Aristotele che la riflessione sul ruolo della legge appare agganciata alla realtà storica della polis: purtroppo la perdita delle 158 Costituzioni ci impedisce di conoscere in dettaglio gli ordinamenti giuridici delle singole poleis. Nelle opere che possediamo, la realtà storica è calata nelle griglie delle classificazioni teoriche, in una prospettiva etica appunto nell'EN, in una prospettiva politica appunto nella Politica e direi in entrambe le prospettive nelle Retorica

Ma in Aristotele la legge non è trattata solo, in quanto funzione legislativa, come uno degli elementi che contribuiscono a descrivere e a classificare una costituzione. Troviamo anche delle considerazioni che affrontano il tema della funzione normativa sotto un profilo filosofico generale. Mi riferisco prima di tutto al problema, che Aristotele riprende da Platone, a cui si trova di fronte chi voglia applicare la formulazione, necessariamente generale e astratta, del *nomos* a una fattispecie concreta. E' un tema che viene ripreso da angolazioni diverse sia nella Politica, sia nell'Etica nicomachea sia nella Retorica. Non possiamo naturalmente commentare qui nemmeno tutti i passi più importanti (piuttosto deludente la sintesi che si può leggere in Piepenbrink). Possiamo però forse osservare che il problema riguarda sia le norme che delineano le strutture pubbliche sia le leggi che regolano i rapporti fra i cittadini. Per quanto riguarda le strutture pubbliche mi pare illuminante un passo come *EN* 1141 b 23-29. La *phronēsis nomothetikē*, la sapienza legislativa, è definita *architektonikē*, in quanto assicura quello che potremmo chiamare oggi il quadro istituzionale; ma è la *phronēsis politikē* che presiede al compimento degli atti di governo, e questi comportano un momento deliberativo e un momento attuativo: (in particolare la frase alle ll. 27-28 ha dato filo da torcere agli interpreti; io tradurrei: "è in qualche modo la più elevata delle cose che si possono fare", ed è noto come Platone, *Phdr*. 257-258, consideri il testo dei decreti come la trascrizione dei discorsi in assemblea dei grandi uomini politici). Dunque il rapporto fra *nomoi* (equivalenti in un certo senso a *politeia*) e *psēphismata* è considerato qui in maniera positiva, nel quadro di una dialettica necessaria a far sì che attraverso le deliberazioni concrete la costituzione trovi attuazione. Naturalmente è implicito quello che nel diritto attico di IV sec. è assicurato almeno in teoria dalla *graphē paranomōn*; e cioè che gli *psēphismata* non devono essere in contrasto con il tenore delle leggi. La polis in cui alle leggi si sostuiscono gli *psēphismata* dà luogo, come è descritto in maniera pittoresca in un noto passo della Politica (*Polit*. 1298 a), alla forma più degenerata di democrazia, dove la massa, guidata e dominata dai demagoghi, diviene l'equivalente del tiranno. Non è chiaro se qui Aristotele alluda a certi periodi della storia ateniese, dunque a una realtà storica (Hansen, *Democrazia* p. 261, lo nega perché osserva che ad Atene la distinzione fra leggi e decreti si è sempre mantenuta, anche se il passo della Politica sembra trovare un'eco in *AP* 41.2, dove si dice che dopo la caduta dei 30 tutto è nelle mani del popolo tramite decreti e sentenze). Ma se guardiamo alla critica dei demagoghi che troviamo in 1320 a, un passo che all'interno della Politica sembra riprendere la violenta critica alla democrazia degenerata, vediamo che di decreti che sostituiscono le leggi non si parla. Dunque probabilmente neanche in *Polit*. 1298 a Aristotele pensa a uno stato formalmente senza leggi. E d'altronde nell'Atene del IV sec. la *gr. paranomōn* non tutela gli interessi dei ricchi di tendenza naturalmente oligarchica contro lo strapotere del *dēmos*; appare invece come uno strumento della lotta politica all'interno del sistema democratico: basta considerare un passo come Dem. XX 91-92.

Sul terreno di quello che potremmo definire diritto privato è invece rimesso al giudice il compito di applicare la previsione di legge, generale e astratta, al caso concreto. Incontriamo qui la ben nota teoria delle lacune della legge, distinte in volontarie e involontarie, che richiede a chi deve applicare la legge, il ricorso alla *gnōmē dikaiotatē.* Quest'ultima, comunque la si voglia definire, non appare ideologicamente caratterizzata: al pari di altre formule stereotipate, come *patrios politeia*, è utilizzabile tanto in un quadro ideologico oligarchico che in uno democratico. Aristotele auspica che la previsione di legge sia in grado di ricomprendere la maggior quantità possibile di dati riscontrabili nella vita reale (*Rhet.* 1354 a 30ss.), ma sa bene che ciò non è possibile: di qui il ruolo preminente da lui attribuito alla *epieikeia* (*Rhet.* 1374 b) quale criterio che deve guidare le decisioni del giudice.

Un altro punto che è oggetto in altri tipi di fonti di una critica ideologizzata (mi riferisco al punto n. 5 dell'esposizione di Wallace: ad es. Xen. *Mem.* 4.4.14) riguarda l'instabilità delle leggi. Ma anche su questo punto si può osservare come la trattazione di Aristotele sia molto equilibrata. In *Polit.* 1269 a osserva infatti che non è bene che le leggi siano immutabili, e tuttavia che occorre innovare con molta cautela perché la forza della legge è data soprattutto dall'abitudine a osservarla; un elemento che si considera per lo più fondamento di validità della consuetudine, e che invece Aristotele applica anche alla legge scritta (in *Polit.* 1320 a affida al legislatore il compito di creare tanto leggi scritte quanto leggi non scritte).

BIBLIOGRAFIA

Hansen, M.H., *The Athenian Democracy in the Age of Demosthenes*, Oxford 1991 (= *La democrazia ateniese nel IV secolo a.C.*, tr. it. di M. Tondelli, Milano 2003, da cui cito)

Piepenbrink, K., *Politische Ordnungskonzeptionen in der attischen Demokratie des vierten Jahrhunderts v.Chr. Eine vergleichende Untersuchung zum philosophischen und rhetorischen Diskurs*, Stuttgart 2001

EDWARD E. COHEN (PHILADELPHIA)

LAWS AFFECTING PROSTITUTION AT ATHENS

Modern legal theory generally attributes considerable importance to the clarity and certainty of legal rules, and to the predictability of the consequences of their violation.[1] But at Athens an absence of specialized technical vocabulary and an aversion to statutory definition of proscribed behavior meant that the substantive content of laws was often ambiguous and open to extraordinarily varied interpretation.[2] Frequent dependence on private prosecution by volunteers (*hoi boulomenoi*) often left uncertain the consequences of transgression. This paper explores Athenian laws affecting the practice of prostitution, especially the prohibitions of "pandering" (*proagôgeia*) and "outrage" (*hybris*), and assays the social and legal consequences of uncertainty of definition and unpredictability of consequences.

The Legality of Prostitution

At Athens prostitution was lawful,[3] and pervasive.[4] In a state which accorded legal recognition to "whatever someone has willingly agreed upon with another" – a state which never did restrict "victimless sexual conduct"[5] – written arrangements for the sale of sex were commonplace, and complex contracts for erotic services were so widespread that the phrase "whoring under contract" had become idiomatic in local

1 See Lanni in this volume.

2 On the frequent "indeterminacy" of Athenian laws, see Carey 1998. Cf. D. Cohen 1995: 150, 152.

3 "Being a prostitute in itself was not an offense" (MacDowell 2005:86). Harrison, however, claims to infer from Aiskhinês 1 a prohibition on prostitution by male citizens supposedly evidenced by a court procedure allowing prosecution of "anyone who let out on hire a male citizen as a prostitute or anyone who hired one" (1968: 37). But this *graphê hetairêseôs* is explicitly described in Aiskhinês 1 as a ban on certain types of political and civic activity by male citizens who have been prostitutes, not as a prohibition of prostitution itself. See MacDowell 2000: 22; below, pp. 204-06.

4 Cf. Xen. *Apomn.* 2.2.4 (prostitutes available everywhere: τῶν γε ἀφροδισίων ἕνεκα ... τούτου γε τῶν ἀπολυσόντων μεσταὶ μὲν αἱ ὁδοί, μεστὰ δὲ τὰ οἰκήματα).

5 Wallace 1997: 151-52 and ff.; Lape 2006: 139-41. For occasional limitations on other personal freedoms, however, see Wallace 1993, 1994a, and 1994b (*pace* Rahe 1992: 196; Sissa 1999: 154-55).

discourse.[6] Lauded by comic poets as a democratic and ethically-desirable alternative to other forms of non-marital sex,[7] prostitution gained social legitimacy from its association with the goddess Aphroditê,[8] who was believed to foster prostitutes' prosperity (Athênaios 13.588c) and for whom prostitutes "clearly functioned as mediators, their sexual skills a sort of 'technology' that canalized her potent force" (Thornton 1997: 152). The shrine of Aphroditê Pandêmos, near the Akropolis,[9] was said to have been built from the proceeds of one of Solôn's innovations, the state's purchase and employment of female slaves as prostitutes. Despite the doubtful historicity of this tale,[10] the laudatory connection of democracy's founder with the foundation of brothels does provide startling insight into a fourth-century Athens that treated prostitution as a "'democratic' reform" (Kurke 1999: 199), "as an intrinsic element of the democracy" (Halperin 1990: 100). The city's Goddess, Athêna, titular deity of crafts, listed prostitutes among her benefactors (D. Harris 1995: 144-49), and a monument honoring a famed courtesan stood on the Athenian Akropolis next to a statue of Aphroditê (Pausanias 1.23.2). Female prostitutes appear even to have been welcome at the Thesmophoria,[11] religious rites of high exclusivity, and to have participated prominently in the sacred Adônia festival.[12]

In contrast, modern societies uniformly reject commercial sex as morally degenerate and humanly exploitative. In most countries, prostitutes are treated as criminals.[13] Many European nations, however, have "decriminalized" prostitution by

---

6 The prevalence and significance of these "consensual contracts" is the subject of E. Cohen 2000a and 2006.

7 See Euboulos Frs. 67 and 82 (K-A); Philêmôn Fr. 3 (K-A).

8 "Hetairai in ancient Athens prayed and made offerings to their patron deity Aphroditê, just as wives and pregnant women worshipped Hera and Artemis respectively" (Neils 2000: 216). At Korinth, supplicants to Aphroditê actively sought prostitutes' help: Athên. 13.573c. On the perceived power of Aphroditê in human affairs ("les puissances de l'amour en Grèce antique"), see Calame 1996: 11-20.

9 For this temple (located immediately below that of Athêna Nikê at the Propylaia), see Paus. 1.22.3; Beschi 1967-68; for Aphroditê's temple on the Sacred Way, see Travlos 1937; I.G. II^2 4570, 4574-85.

10 Athên. 13.569d-f= Philêmôn Fr. 3 (K-A), Nikandros of Kolophôn FGrH 271/2 F 9. *Pace* Herter 1960 [1985]: 73 and Pellizer and Sirugo 1995: 9, most scholars dismiss the report as unfounded: see Henry 2000: 505-506; Lape 2004: 77; Halperin 1990: 100-101.

11 Men. *Epitrep.* 749; Louk. 80.2.1.

12 Diphilos Fr. 42, 39 (K-A); 49 (K-A); Alkiphr. 4.14.8. For the important involvement of prostitutes in this festival, see Detienne 1977; Parker 1996: 194; Thornton 1997: 152. Cf. Winkler 1990: 198-200 and (for detailed consideration of the Adônia festival) Attalah 1966.

13 More than 90,000 arrests are made in the United States annually under statutes prohibiting prostitution, and an additional indeterminable number of prostitutes are apprehended under laws forbidding disorderly conduct or loitering (Weitzer 2000: 159-65).

eliminating direct prosecution of individual providers of purchased sex,[14] while maintaining prohibitions on soliciting, cohabitating, and/or operating commercial outlets for sex.[15] "Decriminalization" itself is often accompanied by onerous and extensive regulation (physical examinations, bureaucratic rules, complex licensing) that effectively negates, in large measure, the purported authorization of the sale of sex.

Athens likewise had adopted ancillary legislation affecting the practice of prostitution. Criminal penalties were imposed on fathers (and other men) who took money for the erotic services of boys and girls for whom they were responsible.[16] Prostitutes were monitored so closely that tax-agents collecting the annual impost on prostitution possessed precise information on individuals "practicing the trade" (*khrômenoi têi ergasiai*).[17] Male citizens who had taken money for sex were denied the right to hold political office (*arkhê*) or act as a political leader (*rhêtôr*).[18] The *polis* imposed the "harshest penalties" (*megista epitimia*) on anyone acting as a "procurer" (*proagôgos*) for free women or free youths (Aiskhinês 1.14). Were these laws then the Athenian equivalent of today's prevailing European policy of "decriminalizing" prostitution by eliminating direct prosecution of individual prostitutes, while imposing regulatory burdens and punishing tangential aspects of commercial sex, thereby obstructing the supposedly lawful practice of prostitution? Was Athenian prostitution formalistically lawful, but effectively truncated by indirect sanctions?

---

14 See O'Neill and Barberet 2000: 124-25; Barberet 1995. A number of nations, including Spain, however, are considering the restoration of direct criminal sanctions (N.Y. Times: January 18, 2004), a step taken by Sweden in 1999 (Pisano: 2002: 245-49).

15 In 2003, a new French Law on Internal Security (*loi sur la sécurité intérieure*) was adopted, explicitly criminalizing even the appearance of "soliciting" (*racolage* [par] *une attitude meme passive*) (Article 50) and similarly penalizing other aspects of the sale of sex. The Minister of the Interior has insisted that restrictions on commercial sex are part of "la lutte contre les réseaux mafieux" (Le Monde: November 16, 2002). Britain has adopted similar legislation and is considering further indirect restrictions.

16 Aiskhin. 1.13: Διαρρήδην γοῦν λέγει ὁ νόμος, ἐάν τινα ἐκμισθώσῃ ἑταιρεῖν πατὴρ ἢ ἀδελφὸς ἢ θεῖος ἢ ἐπίτροπος ἢ ὅλως τῶν κυρίων τις ... (ὁ νόμος) ἐᾷ γραφὴν εἶναι, κατὰ δὲ τοῦ μισθώσαντος καὶ τοῦ μισθωσαμένου ... καὶ ἴσα τὰ ἐπιτίμια ἑκατέρῳ πεποίηκε ... Plut. *Solôn* 23.1: Ἔτι δ' οὔτε θυγατέρας πωλεῖν οὔτ' ἀδελφὰς δίδωσι, πλὴν ἂν μὴ λάβῃ παρθένον ἀνδρὶ συγγεγενημένην.

17 Aiskhin. 1.119: καθ' ἕκαστον ἐνιαυτὸν ἡ βουλὴ πωλεῖ τὸ πορνικὸν τέλος· καὶ τοὺς πριαμένους τὸ τέλος οὐκ εἰκάζειν, ἀλλ' ἀκριβῶς εἰδέναι τοὺς ταύτῃ χρωμένους τῇ ἐργασίᾳ. Cf. Pollux 7.202, 9.29. Diod. Sik. suggests that such taxation was common throughout Greece: τῶν γὰρ ἄλλων ἁπάντων ἁμαρτανουσῶν γυναικῶν ἀργυρικὰς ζημίας τεταχότων (12.21.1). Cf. Polyain. 5.2.13. Similar tax at Kôs: Reinach 1892; Khatzibasileiou 1981: 8.55-56.

18 Aiskhin. 1.19-20, 27-33, 40, 46, 73, 119, 154, 195 and 3.175-76; Andok. 1.74; Dem. 15.32, 21.103, 22.29-31, 59.27; Lyk. ap. Harpokratiôn, s.v. *dokimastheis*. See MacDowell 2005; Fisher 2001: 39-40, 157-63.

To the contrary, Athenian law generally touched on commercial sex only as an aspect of broader concerns and treated prostitutes no differently than others in similar situations: some statutes even facilitated the sale of sex by protecting the rights of sex workers. Thus sanctions on male relatives who prostituted children were merely one element of the extensive legislation protecting youngsters from sexual exploitation – laws that included detailed prohibitions against abuse by caregivers (and others) and safeguards against exploitation of boys by mature males in school or other educational situations (including choral, athletic and gymnastic pursuits).[19] Taxation of Athenian prostitutes followed the procedures imposed on others, including farmers and merchants: Athens commonly gathered governmental funds not directly through *polis* officials but via third parties who sought to profit by purchasing the right to collect (extort?) tax money through information and procedures developed in conjunction with the Boulê, the *polêtai*, the *tamias* of the stratiotic fund, and the controllers of the theoric fund.[20] Athens denied political office, at least theoretically,[21] not only to male prostitutes but to various other persons perceived as excessively motivated by personal financial advantage (including men who had consumed ancestral property or who had failed to furnish sustenance and housing to their parents) (Aiskhinês 1.28-32). This sanction reflected traditional Hellenic concepts of manliness (*andreia*) that condemned all commerce as inherently servile, insisting that farming alone provided a proper economic arena for the "free man" (*anêr eleutheros*).[22] Thus, for Plato, "market people" (*agoraioi anthrôpoi*) were "defective men" (*phauloi*) who pursued monetary profit because they were incapable of more acceptable cultural and political pursuits[23]: the selling of sex or fish is no less censurable than the making of shoes.[24] Theophrastos is dismissive of innkeeping, auctioneering, catering, gambling, operating brothels (and even of tax collecting!).[25] Aristotle and Xenophôn explicitly group the "commercial

---

19 See Aiskhin. 1.9-11, 139; Lysias 1.32. Cf. MacDowell 2000: 15-19; E. Cohen 2000b: 159-67; Scanlon 2002: 212-14.

20 On "whore tax-farmers" (*pornotelônai*), see Pollux 7.202, 9.29. On procedures for "tax-farming," see Aristot. *Ath. Pol.* 47.2; Andok. 1.73, 133-36; Aristoph. *Sphêk.* 657-59. Cf. Stroud 1998: (esp.) 27-30.

21 For the nuances of partial, potential and full *atimia* for meretricious and other offenses, see Gagliardi 2005: 93-94; Fox 1994: 149-51; Wallace 1998; Paoli [1930] 1974: esp. 328-34; Hansen 1976: 55-98.

22 Xen. *Oik.* 5.1; Eur. *Or.* 917-22, *Hiket.* 881-87; Plato *Laws* 889d; Men. Fr. 338 (Körte/Thierfelder 1953); Aristoph. *Eir.* passim, *Akharn.* 32-36. See Hanson 1995: 214-19; Meikle 1996: 138.

23 *Rep.* 371c: οἱ ἀσθενέστατοι τὰ σώματα καὶ ἀχρεῖοί τι ἄλλο ἔργον πράττειν. Cf. *Protag.* 347c: τῶν φαύλων καὶ ἀγοραίων ἀνθρώπων; *Polit.* 289e: οἱ μὲν κατ᾽ ἀγοράς, οἱ δὲ ... νόμισμά τε πρὸς τὰ ἄλλα καὶ αὐτὸ πρὸς αὐτὸ διαμείβοντες ... μῶν τῆς πολιτικῆς ἀμφισβητήσουσί τι ...

24 *Kharm.* 163b: οἴει οὖν αὐτόν ... οὐδενὶ ἄν ὄνειδος φάναι εἶναι σκυτοτομοῦντι ἢ ταριχοπωλοῦντι ἢ ἐπ᾽ οἰκήματος καθημένῳ;

25 *Khar.* 6.5: (ὁ δὲ ἀπονενοημένος) δεινὸς δὲ καὶ πανδοκεῦσαι καὶ πορνοβοσκῆσαι καὶ

crowd" (*agoraios okhlos*) with slaves and servants.[26] Xenophôn finds the commercialization of sex no less disgusting than charging for education.[27] By aristocratic standards, men involved in non-agrarian, that is, "banausic" pursuits – production or trading of goods, labor for monetary compensation, even professional acting or musical performances – were unworthy of "citizenship,"[28] and many oligarchic states wisely and absolutely (according to Aristotle) prohibited male citizens (*politai*) from engaging actively in business.[29] Even at Athens, the right of laboring men, even practitioners of a skilled trade, to be citizens and to participate actively in public affairs was justified on the basis that engagement in such occupations was not a matter of choice but a pursuit necessary to provide sustenance.[30] But – it was feared – individuals choosing to sell themselves for money in personal dealings might similarly accept money to betray the city's public interests.[31] Yet this potential limitation on political activity seems to have had little actual effect. Political leaders at Athens were routinely accused of prostitution in the course of political debate, and routinely continued their public careers.[32] The only

---

τελωνῆσαι καὶ μηδεμίαν αἰσχρὰν ἐργασίαν ἀποδοκιμάσαι, ἀλλὰ κηρύττειν, μαγειρεύειν, κυβεύειν. Cf. *Khar.* 6.1-2: ὁ δὲ ἀπονενοημένος ... τῷ ἤθει ἀγοραῖός τις καὶ ἀνασεσυρμένος καὶ παντοποιός.

26 See Aristot. *Pol.* 1291b14-30. Cf. Aristot. *Pol.* 1289b26-34. Xen. *Hell.* 6.2.23 (τὸν ἀγοραῖόν τε ὄχλον καὶ τὸν τῶν θεραπόντων καὶ τὸν τῶν ἀνδραπόδων).

27 *Apomn.* 1.6.13: παρ' ἡμῖν νομίζεται τὴν ὥραν καὶ τὴν σοφίαν ὁμοίως μὲν καλόν, ὁμοίως δὲ αἰσχρὸν διατίθεσθαι εἶναι. τήν τε γὰρ ὥραν ἐὰν μέν τις ἀργυρίου πωλῇ τῷ βουλομένῳ, πόρνον αὐτὸν ἀποκαλοῦσιν, ἐὰν δέ τις, ὃν ἂν γνῷ καλόν τε κἀγαθὸν ἐραστὴν ὄντα, τοῦτον φίλον ἑαυτῷ ποιῆται, σώφρονα νομίζομεν. καὶ τὴν σοφίαν ὡσαύτως. ... For the equation of scholars and courtesans, see Athên. 567-573b.

28 On the virulent opposition to *banausia*, see, e.g., Aristot. *Pol.* 1337b18-22; 1258b25-27, 33-39; 1260a41-b2; 1277b33-1278a13; 1277a32-b7; 1277a36-37; 1341b8-18. Cf. Balot 2001: 22-43; Humphreys 1978, esp. 148-49.

29 Χρηματίζεσθαι (*Pol.* 1316b3-5). Cf. Ober 1991: 125.

30 Aiskhin. 1.27: ὁ νομοθέτης διαρρήδην ἀπέδειξεν οὓς χρὴ δημηγορεῖν καὶ οὓς οὐ δεῖ λέγειν ἐν τῷ δήμῳ. Καὶ οὐκ ἀπελαύνει ἀπὸ τοῦ βήματος, εἴ τις ... τέχνην τινὰ ἐργάζεται ἐπικουρῶν τῇ ἀναγκαίᾳ τροφῇ ... Cf. Thouk. 2.37, 40.

31 Aiskhin. 1.29: τὸν γὰρ τὸ σῶμα τὸ ἑαυτοῦ ἐφ' ὕβρει πεπρακότα καὶ τὰ κοινὰ τῆς πόλεως ῥᾳδίως ἡγήσατο ἀποδώσεσθαι. Cf. Lape 2006: 139.

32 Aiskhinês (1.165) claims that "one of the citizens" prominently involved in public affairs made idiomatic the phrase "whoring under contract" by working as a male prostitute under written covenants deposited with a third party. While scholars since antiquity (Oxyrhynchus Papyri no. 1012 C II 14) have suggested the political leader Androtiôn as the anonymous citizen-prostitute referred to by Aiskhinês, in an unrelated action Androtiôn is explicitly characterized as a prostitute by Demosthenes (22.29). Aiskhinês also identifies the influential political leader Hêgêsandros as a "whore" (*pornos*) and as Laodamas' paid "woman." (See Aiskhin. 1, passim and esp. 1.70, 111). In turn, Demosthenes (19.287) makes allegations of prostitution against Aiskhinês' brother Aphobêtos and his brother-in-law Nikias. A prominent member of the Boulê under the rule of the Thirty, Epikharês, is charged by Andokidês (1.100) with having been a promiscuously inexpensive male whore, compliantly and shamefully "taking

known invocation of this law involves Timarkhos, a prominent Athenian who had previously participated in Athenian politics notoriously and successfully for decades after his alleged acts of prostitution.[33] In any event, few Athenians ever reached the level of public activity targeted by the statute – that of *rhêtor*, synonymous at Athens with "political leader."[34] Indeed, thousands of Athenian men, literally the majority of citizens, chose not even to attend Assembly meetings[35] – a right of attendance retained by male prostitutes.

Two other laws offered protection for prostitutes at the pinnacle and at the nadir of sexual commerce. The prohibition of *proagôgeia* ("pandering") was especially important to courtesans in the highest rank of the profession (*tekhnê*), the free women popularly known as the "big earners" (*megalomisthoi*).[36] For them, a ban on pandering proffered security from the pimps who in numerous other societies have been a major source of sex workers' oppression. The prohibition of *hybris* ("outrage"), for its part, offered a measure of human-rights protection for even the most vulnerable of whores, the brothel slaves, who were shielded, along with all other residents of Athens, from "gross abuse" – a commitment in a "slave society"[37] that was startling even to many of the free residents of Attika (and has been improperly dismissed as "incomprehensible" by many modern scholars).[38]

---

small sums from any one inclined" (πραττόμενος δ' οὐ πολὺ ἀργύριον τὸν βουλόμενον ἀνθρώπων ἐπὶ τοῖς αἰσχίστοις ἔργοις ἔζης).

33 See Fisher 2001: 21; Dover [1978] 1989: 19. But other prosecutions were threatened: Dem. 22.21-24; Aiskhin. 1.64. Cf. Aristoph. *Hipp.* 876-79 (possible prosecution of Gryttos); Andok. 1.100 (objection to Epikharês participating in court because of his self-prostitution).

34 Davidson 1997: 252; Ober 1996: 95-96, 1989: 105-112; Hansen 1991: 143-45.

35 Archaeological evidence reveals that the fourth-century Pnyx, even after renovation and slight enlargement from the fifth-century gathering site, could barely contain the 6,000 *politai* needed for a quorum. See Thompson 1982: 138-39. For the possibility that the fourth-century expansion was never completed, see Camp 2001: 153-54. Cf. Forsén and Stanton (eds.), 1996: passim.

36 *Megalomisthoi*: "the wealthy, famous hetaeras of the law courts and the comic stage" (McClure 2003: 48). Cf. below n. 74.

37 Despite the ubiquitous presence of unfree individuals in virtually all human communities prior to the nineteenth century (Klees 1998: 1-18), Attika constitutes one of the world's few attested true "slave economies" – those in which the contribution of a huge number of unfree persons to the totality of wealth-production are so substantial that a society's overall production, distribution and consumption is highly dependent on slave labor. The Athenians believed that the servile population of Attika exceeded that of the free (Isager and Hansen 1975: 16-17). Canfora claims that "according to even the most conservative estimates, there were four slaves for every freeborn Athenian" (1995:124). Cf. Hyper., Fr. 33; Athên. 272c-d; Xen. *Por.* 4.4, 25, 28.

38 For astonishment, ancient and modern, over the protection of slaves by the *graphê hybreôs*, see below, nn. 78, 85.

Prohibition of Proagôgeia

In many historically-attested societies, and in virtually all contemporary communities, the sale of sex has been largely a phenomenon in which female prostitutes, working for men, service male customers – a pattern conforming to the general domination of commerce by men.[39] But at Athens unenslaved prostitutes seem to have been free of outside interference in their sale of sex, and women appear generally to have controlled meretricious businesses (*ergasiai*). Although scholars often assume that men were the prototypical *pornoboskoi* ("literally 'whore-pasturer,' driving his herds of women around Greece following the seasons and the festivals"[40]), few *pornoboskoi* are known to have been male, and the married free woman Nikaretê (whose business activity is chronicled at Demosthenes 59.18-23) is actually by far the fullest-attested and best-known Hellenic "herder of women" – originating in Elis, operating in Korinth, shepherding through Greece a band of well-known, high-priced whores whom she owned, bringing to Athens the young prostitute Neaira, among others. Isaios alludes to several women who operated brothels in Athens,[41] and describes with particularity a female entrepreneur who ran a house (*synoikia*) in the Piraeus, where she maintained a number of slave girls.[42] The fourth-century medical writer Hippokratês notes matter-of-factly the case of a danseuse owned by a woman who employed her as a prostitute.[43] The famed courtesan Aspasia, linked to the Athenian political leader Periklês, was allegedly the owner of large numbers of whores.[44] Masurios charges Sôkratês with consorting with Aspasia's sex workers at her brothels,[45] and Aristophanês asserts, humorously, that the abduction of two of Aspasia's whores was the proximate cause

39 However, in a number of post-classical societies women have controlled, and benefitted from, management of prostitutional enterprises: see, for example, Henriot 2001: 238-39 (19th century China); Corbin 1998: 174-81 (19th century France); Lentakis 1998: 3.109-110 (Byzantion –*pace* Leontsini 1989: 169). For the dominance of female entrepreneurs in prostitutional businesses in contemporary Manhattan, see N.Y. Times: October 12, 2004.

40 Davidson 1997: 92. Similarly: McClure 2003: 15.

41 Isai. 6. 21, 6.18. Roussel 1960: 113, n. 1.

42 Ἀπελευθέρα ἦν αὐτοῦ (sc. Εὐκτήμονος) ἣ ναυκλήρει συνοικίαν ἐν Πειραιεῖ αὐτοῦ καὶ παιδίσκας ἔτρεφε (Isai. 6.19).

43 *On Generating Seed and the Nature of the Child* 13 (=VII, 490 Littré= Lefkowitz and Fant 232). Cf. Hanson 1990: 322; Halperin 1990; Richlin 1998: 160.

44 Ἀσπασία δὲ ἡ Σωκρατικὴ ἐνεπορεύετο πλήθη καλῶν γυναικῶν, καὶ ἐπλήθυνεν ἀπὸ τῶν ταύτης ἑταιρίδων ἡ Ἑλλάς (Athên. 569f 7-9).

45 Athên. 220e: Σωκράτης ὁ μετὰ τῶν Ἀσπασίας αὐλητρίδων ἐπὶ τῶν ἐργαστηρίων συνδιατρίβων. The sexual availability of female musicial performers was proverbial. See Metagenês 4 (K-A); Adespota 1025.1 (K-A); Aristoph. *Akh.* 551; *Sphêk.* 1345-46; Theopompos FGrHist 115 F 290. Cf. Hamel 2003: 9-12; McClure 2003: 21-22; Rhodes 1981: 574. For ἐργαστήριον as brothel, see Dem. 59.67; Alkiphr. 3.27 and Fr. 4. Cf. Aiskin. 1.124; Kapparis 1999: 312.

of the Peloponnesian War.[46] Although not universally accepted,[47] these claims do illustrate the connection, in popular imagination, between meretricious commerce and female entrepreneurship. In fact, the idiomatic term for a *mastropos* (a person operating a commercial-sex business) was "Mother" (*Mêtêr*).[48] Alexis, a fourth-century comic poet, explains that courtesans generally, after achieving some personal success, moved on to acquire younger women, new to the profession, whom they might refashion for maximum profit (*kerdos*).[49] They became, in Athênaios' phrase, "the ladies who run the houses."[50] Not surprisingly then, when Antigona (a former *hetaira* now operating her own prostitutional business) receives a commission of 300 drachmas for facilitating the sale of a retail operation dealing in fragrances, she earmarks the money for the purchase of yet another female servant.[51] Theodotê, a woman portrayed as having become wealthy because of her penchant for sleeping with "men who are persuasive," commands a stable of comely and provocatively-attired young women.[52] And even when self-employed, free female prostitutes seem generally to have lived and worked without interference from men seeking to infringe on their compensation or to control their business activity[53]: they enjoyed the freedom to select their own clients and to establish the parameters of service; exercised control over their physical and familial surroundings; owned valuable personal property[54]; and independently negotiated their own business arrangements.

---

46 *Akh.* 524-29 (=Athên. 570a4-b1): πόρνην δὲ Σιμαίθαν ἰόντες Μεγαράδε / νεανίαι κλέπτουσι μεθυσκότταβοι·/ κᾆθ' οἱ Μεγαρῆς ὀδύναις πεφυσιγγωμένοι / ἀντεξέκλεψαν 'Ασπασίας πόρνα δύο· / κἀντεῦθεν ἀρχὴ τοῦ πολέμου κατερράγη / Ἕλλησι πᾶσιν ἐκ τριῶν λαικαστριῶν.

47 MacDowell, however, finds the Aristophanic treatment of the outbreak of the Peloponnesian War "not inconsistent with the account given by Thucydides; it is not illogical or incredible; and I see no reason why it should not be essentially true" (1995: 66; cf. 187-88). Fisher disagrees (1993: 37, 46 n. 30). Cf. Carey 1993: 252-53.

48 Phôtios, s.v. ματρυλεῖον. Μέγα 'Ετυμολογικόν 574.267 notes that Dorians also called *mastropoi* "mothers" [ματέρας in Peloponnesian dialects].

49 Πρῶτα μὲν γὰρ πρὸς τὸ κέρδος ... ῥάπτουσι δὲ / πᾶσιν ἐπιβουλάς. ἐπειδὰν δ' εὐπορήσωσίν ποτε, / ἀνέλαβον καινὰς ἑταίρας, πρωτοπείρους τῆς τέχνης· / εὐθὺς ἀναπλάττουσι ταύτας ... (Fr. 103 [K-A]).

50 Τὰς ἐπὶ τῶν οἰκημάτων (568d). Translation: Gulick's 1937: 71.

51 'Εκείνη προσπεριέκοψεν αὐτῇ ὡς δὴ εἰς παιδίσκην τριακοσίας δραχμὰς εὐνοίας ἕνεκα ... γυναικὸς ἣ δεινοτάτη μὲν τῶν ἑταιρῶν ἐφ' ἡλικίας ἐγένετο, διατετέλεκε δὲ πορνοβοσκοῦσα (Hyper. *Ath.* 2-3). Cf. §18: τῇ 'Αθηνογένους ἑταίρᾳ ... ἡ ἑ[ταίρα σ]ο[υ ... On this and similar relationships, see Cox 1998: 186-89, especially 187, n. 99.

52 *Apomn.* 3.11.4-5: ὁ Σωκράτης ὁρῶν αὐτήν τε πολυτελῶς κεκοσμημένην καὶ μητέρα παροῦσαν αὐτῇ ἐν ἐσθῆτί τε καὶ θεραπείᾳ οὐ τῇ τυχούσῃ, καὶ θεραπαίνας πολλὰς καὶ εὐειδεῖς καὶ οὐδὲ ταύτας ἠμελημένως ἐχούσας, καὶ τοῖς ἄλλοις τὴν οἰκίαν ἀφθόνως κατεσκευασμένην ... νὴ τὴν Ἥραν, ἔφη, ὦ Θεοδότη, καλόν γε τὸ κτῆμα.

53 See further E. Cohen 2003.

54 Courtesans' luxurious possessions are frequently mentioned in Athenian literature. See, for example, Louk. 80.4.1 (θαἰμάτια γὰρ καὶ τὰ χρυσία ταῦτα προείμην ἡδέως). Cf.

Although male aversion to business enterprise might have been an important factor in women's control of sexual businesses at Athens, not all Athenian men were dissuaded from commerce. Economic necessity or financial advantage did bring many male citizens into business: about half of all *politai* (perhaps 10,000 men) pursued non-agricultural work in hundreds of individual métiers (E. Harris 2002: 70), as did thousands of foreigners and slaves. But pandering could not lawfully be one of those pursuits. Athenian law imposed the "harshest penalties" (*megista epitimia*, a euphemism at Athens for the death penalty) on anyone who undertook the *proagôgeia* of customers for the sexual services of a "free youth or free woman."[55] Because *proagôgeia* was a word of protean and confusing significations – ranging from mere "persuasion" to criminal compulsion, from pimping to "matchmaking" to outright control of a sexual enterprise – this statute offered a basis for criminal prosecution of anyone who dared to involve himself or herself in *any* aspect of the commercial provision of sex by free women or free youths – other than the self-employment of offering one's own body for sale.

This linguistic uncertainty, although extreme, was not anomalous. At Athens "there was relatively little technical legal vocabulary and the language of the street was itself the language of the law."[56] Everyday words, however, often have multiple, and sometimes even inconsistent, meanings determined by context. But context is almost always absent from the texts of statutes. In the Athenian legal system where critical terms were not given definition by code or through judicial precedent, and in which inexact criminal prohibitions were not annullable as "unconstitutionally

---

the sumptious lifestyles and impressive property attributed to Khrysis in Menander's *Samia* (e.g. lines 373, 380) and to Theodotê in Xenophôn's *Memoirs of Sôkratês* (3.11). On women's rights of "ownership" at Athens, see Foxhall 1989; Sealey 1990: 45-49. Cf. Aristot. *Rhet.* 1361a.

55 Aiskhin. 1.14: καὶ τίνα ἕτερον νόμον ἔθηκε φύλακα τῶν ὑμετέρων παίδων; τὸν τῆς προαγωγείας, τὰ μέγιστα ἐπιτίμια ἐπιγράψας, ἐάν τις ἐλεύθερον παῖδα ἢ γυναῖκα προαγωγεύῃ. *Megista epitimia* is invoked by Aiskhinês as a fixed penalty but is probably only the orator's interpretation of a statute providing for a procedure (*agôn timêtos*) where the penalty, set by the *dikasts* if they found the defendant guilty, might be execution. Because ancient Greek (like English) permits a preceding adjective to refer to either the first or both of two following nouns – with exact meaning determined by context – some translators have rendered the Greek text literally as precluding the "proagôgeia" of any woman, including presumably enslaved females (for example, Martin and Budé 1927: I, 25: "un enfant libre ou une femme"). But social and economic context argues strongly that the ban could apply only to free women: slaves were the chattels of their masters. Plutarch understood the protection as applying only to free women (Solôn 1.23), as have most translators (e.g. Adams 1919: 14: "a free-born child or a free-born woman"; Fisher 2001: 74: "free woman or boy.)"

56 Millett and Todd 1990: 17. Perusal of Todd's Lexicon (appended to Cartledge, Millett and Todd 1990 and to Todd 1993) suggests that this comment is somewhat overstated: Athenian law may have lacked special vocabulary for criminal offenses, but it had developed many technical terms for procedural matters.

vague," each court case necessarily evoked a fresh determination of precisely what kind of behavior had been outlawed.[57] In this ambience, the very uncertainty of legal definition and the resultant unpredictability of judicial decision served as an "effective means of social control" (Lanni, this volume.)

The chilling effect of this statute on individual behavior is suggested by Sôkratês' allusion, in Plato's *Theaitêtos*, to midwives' fear of being charged with *proagôgeia*. Claiming to be a midwife (*maia*)[58] – in the metaphorical role of helping to give birth to an understanding of "knowledge" (*epistêmê*) – Sôkratês insists that midwives, because of their life experience, are best suited to bring together men and women who would make fine parents. "But they flee from this matchmaking (*promnêstikê*) because they're fearful of being charged with that wrongful and unprofessional bringing-together of man and woman which goes by the name of *proagôgeia*."[59]

Promnêstikê was not the only activity that might be conflated with *proagôgeia*. In Xenophôn's *Symposion*, Sôkratês equates *proagôgeia* with *mastropeia*. Here Sôkratês claims to be not a midwife but a *mastropos* (3.10) – one who fashions those under his/her control into attractive seducers of customers, teaching his/her charges the enticing sexual skills useful for pleasing clients.[60] But after detailed analysis of the traits required of a fine *mastropos* (4.56-61), Sôkratês identifies not himself but another participant in the *symposion* (Antisthenês) as surpassingly manifesting these characteristics of the good *mastropos* – which, Sôkratês claims, explains why Antisthenês is an excellent *PROAGÔGOS*![61] Sôkratês does know that the two activities are not absolutely indistinguishable, for he calls *proagôgeia* the

---

57 The entire case against Timarkhos (Aiskhinês 1), for example, depends on interpreting the term *hetairos*, i.e. defining "prostitution" – a word whose definition has generated decades of unresolved academic dispute. Although scholars have long sought to differentiate commercial sex from other erotic arrangements, emphasizing factors like payment, promiscuity and emotional attachment (or indifference), the defining line – if any – between prostitution and other forms of sexual exchange remains unclear. See, for example, McGinn 2004: 7-9, 1998: 17-18; Palmer and Humphrey 1990: 150; Bloch 1912: 7. Cf. Jaggar 1985; Shrage 1994: 99-119.

58 149a1-4: ἐγώ εἰμι ὑὸς μαίας ... καὶ ... ἐπιτηδεύω τὴν αὐτὴν τέχνην.

59 150a1-4: διὰ τὴν ἄδικόν τε καὶ ἄτεχνον συναγωγὴν ἀνδρὸς καὶ γυναικός, ᾗ δὴ προαγωγία ὄνομα, φεύγουσι καὶ τὴν προμνηστικὴν ἅτε σεμναὶ οὖσαι αἱ μαῖαι, φοβούμεναι μὴ εἰς ἐκείνην τὴν αἰτίαν διὰ ταύτην ἐμπέσωσιν· ἐπὶ ταῖς γε ὄντως μαίαις μόναις που προσήκει καὶ προμνήσασθαι ὀρθῶς. 149d6-8: προμνήστριαί εἰσι δεινόταται, ὡς πάσσοφοι οὖσαι περὶ τοῦ γνῶναι ποίαν χρὴ ποίῳ ἀνδρὶ συνοῦσαν ὡς ἀρίστους παῖδας τίκτειν.

60 4.57-59: ποῖά ἐστιν ἔργα τοῦ μαστροποῦ ... ἀγαθοῦ δοκεῖ μαστροποῦ ἔργον εἶναι ἣν ἂν ἢ ὃν ἂν μαστροπεύῃ ἀρέσκοντα τοῦτον ἀποδεικνύναι οἷς ἄν συνῇ; ... ἐκ τοῦ πρέπουσαν ἔχειν σχέσιν ... λόγοι οὐκ εἰσὶ μέν τινες ἀπεχθανόμενοι, εἰσὶ δέ τινες οἳ πρὸς φιλίαν ἄγουσι; Οὐκοῦν τούτων ὁ ἀγαθὸς μαστροπὸς τὰ συμφέροντα εἰς τὸ ἀρέσκειν διδάσκοι ἄν ...

61 4.64: ταῦτα ὁρῶν δυνάμενόν σε ποιεῖν ἀγαθὸν νομίζω προαγωγὸν εἶναι.

"complementary profession" of *mastropeia*: *proagôgeia* is a skilled calling (*tekhnê*) requiring the ability to identify and bring together clients and servicers who would share a mutual attraction and be good for one other.[62] This Antisthenês has done. He has worked successfully in introducing the sophist Prodikos to the wealthy Kallias (after identifying Kallias as yearning for "knowledge" [*philosophia]* and Prodikos as needing money).[63] Antisthenês had also successfully linked Kallias with Hippias of Elis, and had introduced Sôkratês himself to Aiskhylos the Phleiasian and to Zeuxippos of Hêraklea – arousing in Sôkratês enormous passion (and great gratitude to Antisthenês). A *proagôgos* of skill, writes Xenophôn,could make a lot of money – as could a good *mastropos*.[64] But a defendant charged with *proagôgeia* might have had a difficult time separating the two "complementary professions" by establishing that he was in fact teaching the sexual skills that would bring a client and prostitute together (that is, being a *mastropos*) and not functioning as a mere "go-between" (*proagôgos*).

Testifying further to the elasticity of the term *proagôgeia*, Aiskhinês cites the statute against *proagôgeia* in his case against Timarkhos – despite the absence of any contention that the defendant has been acting on behalf of anyone else. But the case involves prostitution – Timarkhos is charged with years of political activity after years of male prostitution – and the statute is cited in Aiskhinês' narration of various laws dealing with the sale of sex.[65] Its relevance is vaguely suggested within the pervasive thought that Timarkhos had "done it to himself"[66] – although, as Sôkratês claims, the essence of *proagôgeia* is a bringing-together (*synagôgê*) of others. But the language of the law, the language of the street, seems not to have known such fine distinctions – at least when interpreted by a skilled rhetorical wordsmith.[67]

---

62 Ἀγαθὸς προαγωγός: ὁ γὰρ οἷος τε ὢν γιγνώσκειν τε τοὺς ὠφελίμους αὑτοῖς καὶ τούτους δυνάμενος ποιεῖν ἐπιθυμεῖν ἀλλήλων, οὗτος ἄν μοι δοκεῖ ... πολλοῦ ἂν ἄξιος εἶναι ... (4.64). Complementary *tekhnê*: τὴν (τέχνην) ἀκόλουθον ταύτης (4.61).

63 4.62: Οἶδα μέν, ἔφη, σε Καλλίαν τουτονὶ προαγωγεύσαντα τῷ σοφῷ Προδίκῳ, ὅτε ἑώρας τοῦτον μὲν φιλοσοφίας ἐρῶντα, ἐκεῖνον δὲ χρημάτων δεόμενον.

64 *Mastropos*: καὶ πάνυ ἄν πολλὰ χρήματα λαμβάνοιμι, εἰ βουλοίμην χρῆσθαι τῇ τέχνῃ (3.10). *Proagôgos*: ἐὰν γὰρ (ἔφη) ταῦτα δύνωμαι, σεσαγμένος δὴ παντάπασι πλούτου τὴν ψυχὴν ἔσομαι (4.64). Cf. 4.60.

65 Aiskhinês' references to Athenian laws are often problematic. He sometimes purports to be quoting the text of laws verbatim when he is in fact selectively (and sometimes misleadingly) paraphrasing the actual content of the statute. Cf. Fisher 2001: 125; Ford 1999: 242. Furthermore, the manuscripts of Aiskhinês offer paleographical difficulties: they often contain the purported text of laws which Aiskhinês has cited, but these addenda are generally dismissed as illegitimate appendages composed in later antiquity. See MacDowell 1990: 43-47; Harris 1992: 71-77. But Aiskhines' reference to the statute against *proagôgeia* is straight-forward: he does not purport to quote the actual text of the law, nor is purported original language attached to his citation.

66 See, for example, §§ 15-17, 185-87.

67 Περιττὸς ἐν τοῖς λόγοις (Aiskhin. 1.119, applied to Demosthenes).

Proagôgeia had yet other – contradictory – meanings. For Aristotle, it was inherently coercive, akin to *moikheia*; for Plutarch, it was mere "persuasion" in the sense of seduction, as *opposed* to *moikheia*.[68] Thus Aristotle, in the *Nicomachean Ethics*, groups *proagôgeia* with other furtive wrong-doing imposed on victims involuntarily: theft, murder by treachery, false adversarial testimony, sexual violation of another man's female relatives (*moikheia*), poisoning, preying on slaves, *proagôgeia*.[69] Plutarch, in his *Life of Solôn* written long after the classical age of Athens, expresses bewilderment at the inconsistency of the law-giver's enactments relating to women,[70] noting with astonishment the seemingly haphazard differences in severity of sanctions for sexual offenses against free women.[71] But at least a portion of Plutarch's dismay arises from his assumption that a *proagôgos* is one who "gains his end by persuasion" – in contrast to the *moikhos* who "commits rape upon a free woman" (Perrin: Loeb translation). In Plutarch's report, both forms of behavior are forbidden – except when practiced against prostitutes (a bizarre interpretation since whores are the one group, of course, with whom "procurers" normally work). Yet "persuasion" *was* a prime classical Athenian meaning of *proagôgeia*. In *Clouds*, for example, Aristophanês actually humorously exploits this duality: a flirtatious youth is described as "walking around *proagôgeuôn* for himself with his eyes," that is, persuasively inviting sexual attention and at the same time "procuring for himself" in a meretricious way – "streetwalking" being a common manifestation of Athenian prostitution.[72]

The presumed deterrent effect of imprecise interdiction is a familiar feature of contemporary American law. The U.S. Securities and Exchange Commission, for example, systematically avoids clear and specific descriptions of prohibited

---

68 Ancient usage of *moikheia* likewise tends to be inexact, generating considerable dispute among modern scholars who often assume precision of usage. See Cantarella 2005: 241-45, 1991; Foxhall 1991; D. Cohen 1991: 98-132.

69 1131a2-8: τῶν γὰρ συναλλαγμάτων τὰ μὲν ἑκούσιά ἐστι τὰ δ' ἀκούσια ... τῶν δ' ἀκουσίων τὰ μὲν λαθραῖα, οἷον κλοπὴ μοιχεία φαρμακεία προαγωγεία δουλαπατία δολοφονία ψευδομαρτυρία, τὰ δὲ βίαια, οἷον αἰκία κ.τ.λ.

70 Although modern scholarship has discovered that Athenians of the fourth century tended to assign to "Solôn" all laws of indeterminate origin (Fox 1994: 150; MacDowell 2000: 21), Plutarch assumed that the legislation against *proagôgeia* was factually attributable to Solôn.

71 23.1-2: Ὅλως δὲ πλείστην ἔχειν ἀτοπίαν οἱ περὶ τῶν γυναικῶν νόμοι τῷ Σόλωνι δοκοῦσι. Μοιχὸν μὲν γὰρ ἀνελεῖν τῷ λαβόντι δέδωκεν· ἐὰν δ' ἁρπάσῃ τις ἐλευθέραν γυναῖκα καὶ βιάσηται, ζημίαν ἑκατὸν δραχμὰς ἔταξε· κἂν προαγωγεύῃ, δραχμὰς εἴκοσι, πλὴν ὅσαι πεφασμένως πωλοῦνται, λέγων δὴ τὰς ἑταίρας. Αὗται γὰρ ἐμφανῶς φοιτῶσι πρὸς τοὺς διδόντας ... τὸ δ' αὐτὸ πρᾶγμα ποτὲ μὲν πικρῶς καὶ ἀπαραιτήτως κολάζειν, ποτὲ δ' εὐκόλως καὶ παίζαντα, πρόστιμον ζημίαν τὴν τυχοῦσαν ὁρίζοντα, ἄλογόν ἐστι.

72 979-80: οὐδ' ἂν μαλακὴν φυρασάμενος τὴν φωνὴν πρὸς τὸν ἐραστὴν | αὐτὸς ἑαυτὸν προαγωγεύων τοῖν ὀφθαλμοῖν ἐβάδιζεν. Cf. Aristoph. *Sphêk.* 1028, *Batr.* 1079, *Thes.* 341. On the equation of "walking" and "whoring," see E. Cohen (forthcoming), Ch. 1.

behavior, seeking to deny "safe harbor" to persons seeking lawful access to activities proscribed by the Commission.[73] By banning *proagôgeia*, an inexact noun affixing itself chameleon-like to virtually every aspect of the commercial provision of sex other than self-employment, Athenian law provided maximum protection for free women and free youth in their practice of prostitution. Wealthy female prostitutes were invariably free persons.[74] Third-party control of a prostitute's life, and revenues, was effectively lawful only for enslaved women, enslaved youth, and mature free men. But Athenian *philanthrôpia* did not ignore even these victims of coercive exploitation – who were included in the all-encompassing provisions of the law forbidding "outrageous" victimization (the *graphê hybreôs).*

Prohibition of Outrageous Behavior (Hybris)

A fundamental Athenian law purported to protect every inhabitant of Attika – "whether a child or a woman or a man, whether free or slave" – from outrageous abuse (*hybris).* Under a statute preserved in the text of Demosthenes, Athenian law authorized a prosecution for *hybris* "whenever someone intentionally insults the honor (*hybrizei*) of another, whether a child or a woman or a man, whether free or slave, or does something improper (*paranomon*) against any such person."[75] Aiskhinês cites the legislation in language virtually identical with that of Demosthenes.[76] Hypereidês notes the law's explicit protection of slaves from bodily abuse,[77] and Demosthenes praises the "humane benevolence" (*philanthrôpia*) of the Athenians in forbidding the subjection of slaves to *hybris*.[78] This prohibition is so

---

73 Most recently, by failing to offer a technical definition of "security," the SEC has left unresolved the potential need for provision of detailed offering materials for the sale of Tenant-in-Common interests under the Tax-Deferred Exchange section (§1031) of the U.S. Federal Tax Code. Cf. the Commission's failure to provide a "safe harbor" for "insider trading."

74 "Unter der Gruppe der renommierten Hetären, die als Spitzenverdienerinnen galten (*megalomisthoi*) (Athênaios 570b; 558a-e), waren Sklavinnen kaum anzutreffen" (Klees 1998: 147, n. 16). Cf. Lentakis 1999: 146, 165.

75 21.47: Ἐάν τις ὑβρίζῃ εἴς τινα, ἢ γυναῖκα ἢ ἄνδρα, τῶν ἐλευθέρων ἢ τῶν δούλων, ἢ παράνομόν τι ποιήσῃ εἰς τούτων τινά ...

76 Aiskhin. 1.15: Ἐάν τις ὑβρίζῃ εἰς παῖδα (ὑβρίζει δὲ δή που ὁ μισθούμενος) ἢ ἄνδρα ἢ γυναῖκα, ἢ τῶν ἐλευθέρων τινὰ ἢ τῶν δούλων, ἢ ἐὰν παράνομόν τι ποιῇ εἰς τούτων τινά, γραφὰς ὕβρεως εἶναι πεποίηκεν ... The text of the "law" preserved at Aiskh. 1.16 is patently a forgery: MacDowell 1990: 263-64.

77 Frag. *Mantitheos*: ἔθεσαν οὐ μόνον ὑπὲρ τῶν ἐλευθέρων, ἀλλὰ καὶ ἐάν τις εἰς δούλου σῶμα ὑβρίσῃ, γραφὰς εἶναι κατὰ τοῦ ὑβρίσαντος.

78 21.48-49: τοῦ νόμου τῆς φιλανθρωπίας, ὃς οὐδὲ τοὺς δούλους ὑβρίζεσθαι ἀξιοῖ ... εἰσὶν Ἕλληνές τινες ἄνθρωποι οὕτως ἥμεροι καὶ φιλάνθρωποι τοὺς τρόπους ὥστε ... οὐδ' ὅσων ἂν τιμὴν καταθέντες δούλους κτήσωνται, οὐδὲ τούτους ὑβρίζειν ἀξιοῦσιν ... A frequent *topos* in Athenian sources is pride (and astonishment) at Athens' humane protection of even slaves through the law against *hybris*: see Aiskhin. 1.17; Dem. 21.47-49; Hyper. and Lykurg. cited at Athên. 266e-267a.

well-attested that there is "general agreement (that) we possess the actual text of the law as it stood in the fourth century" (Fisher 1992: 36), the "genuine law" (MacDowell 1990: 263).[79]

But the behavior actually banned by this legislation is uncertain, for the law contained no definition of *hybris*,[80] prohibiting instead everything encompassed by a common word having multiple and contradictory significations changing with everyday context. The term *hybris* could describe a broad scope of conduct ranging from mundane "human arrogance, overconfidence or unawareness of the reasons for one's own good fortune" through "behavior seriously injurious" (Fisher 1995: 45-46). However, the meaning of *hybris* in any specific legal context would depend on a decision-maker's conclusion in that particular matter. Not surprisingly, scholarly efforts to identify a core concept underlying or unifying the various notations of *hybris* have yielded only prolonged academic disputation – despite the profusion of surviving evidence. The standard work on *hybris* (Fisher 1992) runs 526 pages and considers hundreds of elusive testimonia. Ruschenbusch (1965), for example, sees *hybris* as inclusively covering all offenses against the person. MacDowell and Cairns insist on arrogance as the defining characteristic of *hybris*.[81] Fisher identifies *hybris* as "the deliberate infliction of serious insult on another human being."[82] Gagarin, in contrast, finds *hybris* distinguished by the use of inordinate force or violence (1979: 232). Others offer still other opinions.[83] *Tot homines, quot sententiae.* Prohibition of behavior so undefinable precludes reasonable anticipation of the situations to which the proscription might apply.

But because of modern perception of Athens as a society in which slaves had absolutely no rights (other than perhaps the right not to be murdered),[84] the statute's

---

79 Edward M. Harris, appropriating the arguments of Drerup (1898: 297-300), asserts that the text of the law at Dem. 21.47 is a "fake" (1992: 77) – a position that has found no support (see Fisher 2001: 139-40; Carey 1998). Harris' main contention is that the law treats ἤ παράνομόν τι ποιήσῃ εἰς τούτων τινά as "covering every imaginable crime." That clause, however, merely insures that any illegal action taken against a slave (and others) – even in the presence or absence of other relief – is actionable pursuant to the special severities of the *graphê hybreôs*. Harris overlooks the presence of the same clause at Dem. 43.75 (ἐὰν δέ τις ὑβρίζῃ ἢ ποιῇ τι παράνομον) – elaborated upon in 43.77-78 (ὑβριστής, παρανομώτεροι). Finally, Harris assumes that Athenian law aimed for exactitude and specificity in the drafting of criminal charges rather than for the deterrence and elasticity inherent in generalized prohibitions subject to (re)interpretation in each individual case.

80 Aiskhinês specifically notes that the statute "summarized all these offenses in a single (term)": τὸν (νόμον) τῆς ὕβρεως, ὃς ἑνὶ κεφαλαίῳ πάντα τὰ τοιαῦτα συλλαβὼν ἔχει (1.15).

81 MacDowell 1976, 1978: 129-32; Cairns 1996.

82 Fisher 1995: 45. Cf. Fisher 1992: 36-82, 1990: 126.

83 For a select survey of interpretations, see Cairns 1996; Fisher 1992: 2-5.

84 Antiph. 5.47, 6.4. Cf. Isok. 18.52; Dem. 59.9. See Harrison 1968: 171-72; Klees 1998: 176-217.

"plain meaning"– its extension of protection to slaves (and thus to unfree brothel prostitutes) – has tended to be disregarded, or even dismissed as "incoherent" or theoretically impossible.[85] Even those scholars who do acknowledge the law's explicit statement of protection for slaves and other dependents often assume the provision to have been meaningless in actual practice.[86] Yet Athenian legal protection for persons of inferior status or situation was far from theoretical. Demosthenes notes that harsh punishment had actually been meted out, pursuant to the law against *hybris*, in many cases involving victimization of slaves.[87] Deinarkhos reports that at the Eleusinian festival the Athenian *politês* Themistios had been put to death for *hybris* against a Rhodian lyre-girl,[88] and that a certain Euthymakhos was executed for forcing an Olynthian slave woman into a brothel.[89] Legal actions also appear to have been brought over the hybristic treatment of another enslaved Olynthian woman by Athenians at a Macedonian symposium after Philip's destruction of Olynthos,[90] although "we do not know enough about these cases to know in what circumstances they did, or might, reach the courts" (Fisher 1995: 69-70). To mitigate the lengthy legal delays endemic within the Athenian court system,[91] actions charging *hybris* had to be heard within thirty days after the day on which the charges were first brought[92] – a virtually unique acceleration of process.[93]

---

85 The enshrinement of slaves' rights, for example, leaves distinguished scholars grasping (unsuccessfully) for words: "such a law would have had to envisage a situation involving the treatment of free men as if they were slaves, or citizens as if they were foreigners, or slaves (who are specifically mentioned as within the scope of the law) as if they were – what?" (Murray 1990: 140). "Incoherent": Gernet 1917: 183-97. Cf. Fisher 1992: 59ff.

86 Todd 1993: 189: "When Demosthenes tells us that it was possible to commit *hybris* against a slave ... we should be careful to place a minimalist interpretation on his words."

87 Dem. 21.48-49: Ἀκούετ', ὦ ἄνδρες Ἀθηναῖοι, τοῦ νόμου τῆς φιλανθρωπίας, ὃς οὐδὲ τοὺς δούλους ὑβρίζεσθαι ἀξιοῖ ... καὶ πολλοὺς ἤδη παραβάντας τὸν νόμον τοῦτον ἐζημιώκασιν θανάτῳ.

88 Dein. *Dem.* 23: Θεμίστιον δὲ τὸν Ἀφιδναῖον, διότι τὴν Ῥοδίαν κιθαρίστριαν ὕβρισεν Ἐλευσινίοις, θανάτῳ ἐζημιώσατε ... Cf. Worthington 1992: 169. Demosthenes mentions by name a number of other persons executed for misdeeds at such religious gatherings (21.175-181).

89 Dein. *Dem.* 23: Εὐθύμαχον δέ <θανάτῳ ἐζημιώσατε> διότι τὴν Ὀλυνθίαν παιδίσκην ἔστησεν ἐπ' οἰκήματος.

90 Dem. 19.196-198; Aiskhin. 2.4, 153-55.

91 For the systemic prevalence and causes of protracted and postponed litigation, see E. Cohen 1973: 10-12; Charles 1938: 9-10.

92 Dem. 21.47: οἱ θεσμοθέται εἰσαγόντων εἰς τὴν ἡλιαίαν τριάκοντα ἡμερῶν ἀφ' ἧς ἂν γραφῇ, ἐὰν μή τι δημόσιον κωλύῃ, εἰ δὲ μή, ὅταν ᾖ πρῶτον οἷόν τε. In practice – as anticipated by the statute – state considerations could still sometimes delay prompt resolution of the matter: γραφὴν δ' ὕβρεως γράφομαι πρὸς θεσμοθέτας αὐτόν. χρόνου δὲ γιγνομένου, καὶ τῆς μὲν γραφῆς ἐκκρουομένης, δικῶν δ' οὐκ οὐσῶν, γίγνονται παῖδες ἐκ τούτου τῇ μητρί (Dem. 45.4).

Should the prosecutor prevail, there was to be an immediate determination of penalties.[94] Upon conviction, an offender was held in prison until payment of any fine that had been assessed[95]– an extraordinary remedy in a system where private litigants generally had to enforce court judgments without official assistance[96] and where even debts owed to the state often were allowed to languish for months before obligors – subject to no restraint – fled.[97]

To avoid the chimera of a protection not practically available to those unable personally to vindicate their rights against a more powerful abuser, prosecution for *hybris* could be pursued by any Athenian *politês*[98] – in contrast to the usual requirement in a private action (*dikê*) of suit by the victim directly or through his or her male representative (*kyrios*).[99] Although Harrison, for example, considers that

---

93 MacDowell 1990: 266-67 refutes Hansen's claim (1981: 167-70) that requirement of trial within thirty days was not uncommon: no other provision for εἰσαγωγὴ τριάκοντα ἡμερῶν is known at Athens (although we do know of "thirty-day cases" [τριακοσταῖαι δίκαι] from Naupaktos [Meiggs/Lewis 1969: 35-37, #20] and from Hêraklea [Dareste 1892-1904 (1965) I, 194ff., face II, ll. 26-27]). Cf. Gofas 1979: 180, n. 21. For the δίκαι ἔμμηνοι at Athens, see E. Cohen 1973: 23-26, Vélissaropoulos 1980: 242-45.

94 Dem. 21.47: ὅτου δ' ἄν καταγνῷ ἡ ἠλιαία, τιμάτω περὶ αὐτοῦ παραχρῆμα, ὅτου ἂν δοκῇ ἄξιος εἶναι παθεῖν ἢ ἀποτεῖσαι.

95 Dem. 21.47: ἐὰν δὲ ἀργυρίου τιμηθῇ τῆς ὕβρεως, δεδέσθω ἐὰν ἐλεύθερον ὑβρίσῃ, μέχρι ἂν ἐκτείσῃ. Imprisonment thus was not automatically available in cases of transgressions against slaves.

96 See Todd 1993: 144-45; Allen 1997: 34. But cf. now Harris (Symposion 2005). In the case of *hybris*, the fine was paid to the state, not to the victim or prosecutor, thereby giving the *polis* a direct financial interest in extracting payment. See Dem. 21.45: καὶ τῆς ὕβρεως αὐτῆς τὰς μὲν γραφὰς ἔδωκεν ἅπαντι τῷ βουλομένῳ, τὸ δὲ τίμημ' ἐποίησεν ὅλον δημόσιον·

97 For the rarity of imprisonment as a procedural or punitive process at Athens, see E. Cohen 1973: 74-83; MacDowell 1990: 268; Hunter 1997. For a variant interpretation, see Allen 1997. On the state's laxity even in situations involving public debtors, note the famous case of Demosthenes' father-in-law, Gylôn (Dem. 28.1-3, Aiskh. 3.171; Davies 1971: 121).

98 Dem. 21: 47: γραφέσθω πρὸς τοὺς θεσμοθέτας ὁ βουλόμενος 'Αθηναίων οἷς ἔξεστιν. Some potential cases, however, may have been discouraged by the absence of monetary incentive for a voluntary prosecutor (ὁ βουλόμενος) and by the requirement (see Lipsius [1905-15] 1966: 243-4; Harrison 1968: 195 n. 1) that the prosecutor be an Athenian citizen. For *graphai* open also to prosecution by non-Athenians, see Dem. 59.66 (Epainetos "certainly a foreigner" [Carey 1992: 121]), 59.16, 21.175, 24.105, possibly 59.52.

99 Although some commentators persist in referring to the *kyrios* as "the head of the household to which (an Athenian woman) was attached" (Just 1985: 173, n. 8) – itself an improvement over renderings of *kyrios* as "lord and master" (Wolff 1944: 46-47, n. 22) or even as "sovereign" ("in certain contexts": Todd 1993: 383) – recent studies have established that the senior male in an *oikos* was merely the household representative or "steward" in dealing publicly with household interests. See Foxhall 1989, 1996: 150. Cf. Schaps 1998: 163-67.

there was not even a "slender chance" that any outsider would actually prosecute an alleged act of *hybris* by a master against his slave,[100] even our sparse knowledge of actual Athenian litigation provides numerous examples of third parties instituting actions on behalf of women, children and other dependents. Athenian values encompassed a strong ideological commitment to aid unrelated persons who might be victimized. Solôn reportedly considered the ideal state to be one in which otherwise uninvolved persons came to the aid of those being wronged: a key element in the legislation attributed to him was authorization for volunteers to act on behalf of unrelated victims.[101] Periklês' enunciation of Athenian values in the Funeral Address includes praise of the Athenians' penchant for legally aiding persons being victimized.[102] Even where wrongdoing involved only allegation of financial mismanagement, third parties are known to have come to the victims' defense. In Demosthenes 38, under a statute permitting any willing person to intervene, a certain Nikidas, not otherwise involved, denounced a guardian for mismanagement of an estate intended to benefit minor children.[103] When Neaira, an ex-slave staying in Megara, had been subjected to *hybris* by the Athenian *politês* Phryniôn (who claimed to be her master), she sought assistance from the Athenian *politês* Stephanos whom she had only recently met. He responded to her appeal – for Stephanos the beginning of substantial litigation on her behalf, including defense of her freedom through a claim of *aphairesis* against Phryniôn.[104] Similarly the public slave Pittalakos was able to call on the influential *politês* Glaukôn to vindicate his legal rights against harassment by the prominent Hêgêsandros.[105]

The law against *hybris* clearly affected many aspects of Athenian behavior. Yet its prime impact was felt in sexual context, for eroticized misconduct was a

---

[100] 1968: 172. Cf. Humphreys 1993: 5.

[101] Τὸ ἐξεῖναι τῷ βουλομένῳ τιμωρεῖν ὑπὲρ τῶν ἀδικουμένων (Aristot. *Ath. Pol.* 9.4). See Plut. *Sol.* 18.3-8: ἐρωτηθεὶς γάρ, ὡς ἔοικε, ἥτις οἰκεῖται κάλλιστα τῶν πόλεων, ἐκείνη, εἶπεν, ἐν ᾗ τῶν ἀδικουμένων οὐχ ἧττον οἱ μὴ ἀδικούμενοι προβάλλονται καὶ κολάζουσι τοὺς ἀδικοῦντας. Cf. Plato, *Rep.* 462d.

[102] οὐ παρανομοῦμεν ... ἀκροάσει καὶ τῶν νόμων, καὶ μάλιστα αὐτῶν ὅσοι τε ἐπ' ὠφελίᾳ τῶν ἀδικουμένων κεῖνται ... (Thouk. 2.37.3).

[103] Dem. 38.23: οὐκ ἐμίσθωσαν ἡμῶν τὸν οἶκον, ἴσως ἐροῦσιν. οὐ γὰρ ἐβούλεθ' ὁ Θεῖος ὑμῶν Ξενοπείθης, ἀλλὰ φήναντος Νικίδου τοὺς δικαστὰς ἔπεισεν ἐᾶσαι αὐτὸν διοικεῖν· For *phasis* as a procedure against κάκωσις οἴκου ὀρφανικοῦ, see Harpokr., s.v. φάσις; Aristot., *Ath. Pol.* 56.6.

[104] Dem. 59.37-40: ἐπιδημήσαντα Στέφανον τουτονὶ εἰς τὰ Μέγαρα ... διηγησαμένη πάντα τὰ πεπραγμένα καὶ τὴν ὕβριν τοῦ Φρυνίωνος ... προΐσταται Στέφανον τουτονὶ αὐτῆς ... ἀφαιρουμένου δὲ τοῦ Στεφάνου κατὰ τὸν νόμον εἰς ἐλευθερίαν, κατηγγύησεν αὐτὴν πρὸς τῷ πολεμάρχῳ. Neaira's dependence on male juridical mediation is discussed at Johnstone 1998: 232-33.

[105] Aiskhin. 1.62: σκέψασθε μεγάλην ῥώμην Ἡγησάνδρου· ἄνθρωπον ... ἦγεν εἰς δουλείαν φάσκων ἑαυτοῦ εἶναι. Ἐν παντὶ δὲ κακοῦ γενόμενος ὁ Πιττάλακος προσπίπτει ἀνδρὶ καὶ μάλα χρηστῷ. Ἔστι τις Γλαύκων Χολαργεύς· οὗτος αὐτὸν ἀφαιρεῖται εἰς ἐλευθερίαν.

fundamental and frequent manifestation of *hybris*. Of approximately 500 occurrences of *hybris* or its cognates in the principal surviving Athenian prose authors, 82 incidents relate to sexual misconduct – more cases by far than of any other typology.[106] Even an ex-slave's marital bedding of his former mistress generated an action for "hybris" (Demosthenes 45.4). Rape is repeatedly denominated as *hybris*.[107] In fact, Aristotle specifically warns rulers that of the various manifestations of *hybris*, sexual abuse of boys and girls, and physical violation of individuals are most to be avoided.[108]

But how could one commit *hybris* against a brothel slave? Prostitution was lawful; owners could require slaves to work at such tasks as were assigned.[109] Yet the law against *hybris* could easily be interpreted as forbidding outrageous (mis)treatment of even a slave prostitute in his or her sexual labors: the statute was understood to forbid *hybris* "against the body of a slave."[110] Thus Neaira, allegedly a foreign whore born into slavery, charged the Athenian *politês* Phryniôn with *hybris* for forcing her to have sexual intercourse in public places.[111] In homoerotic situations, charges of *hybris* likewise arose from grossly abusive behavior. The public slave Pittalakos brands as *hybris* the actions of the well-connected Athenian *politai* Hêgesandros and Timarkhos who, as the dénouement of a sexual triangle, had sadistically tied Pittalakos to a column and whipped him during a nocturnal revel.[112] The linguistic anarchy inherent in the conceptualization of *hybris* explains

---

106 Even physical assault against free persons is reported less frequently. See D. Cohen 1991: 172-73; MacDowell 1976; Fisher 1976, 1979.

107 See D. Cohen 1991: 175; Doblhofer 1994, passim; Dover [1978] 1989: 36.

108 *Pol.* 1315a14-16: ἔτι δὲ πάσης μὲν ὕβρεως εἴργεσθαι, παρὰ πάσας δὲ δυεῖν, τῆς τε εἰς τὰ σώματα [κολάσεως] καὶ τῆς εἰς τὴν ἡλικίαν ... μὴ χρῆσθαι δεῖ τοῖς τοιούτοις, ἢ ... φαίνεσθαι ποιούμενον ... τὰς δὲ πρὸς τὴν ἡλικίαν ὁμιλίας δι' ἐρωτικὰς αἰτίας, ἀλλὰ μὴ δι' ἐξουσίαν.

109 See Garlan 1988: 60-73; Klees 1998: 109-116. Hence, the master's métier largely determined the slave's future opportunities: οἶμαι γὰρ ἅπαντας ὑμᾶς εἰδέναι, ὅτι τοῦτον, ἡνίκ' ὤνιος ἦν, εἰ συνέβη μάγειρον ἢ τινος ἄλλης τέχνης δημιουργὸν πρίασθαι, τὴν τοῦ δεσπότου τέχνην ἂν μαθὼν πόρρω τῶν νῦν παρόντων ἦν ἀγαθῶν. ἐπειδὴ δ' ὁ πατὴρ ὁ ἡμέτερος τραπεζίτης ὢν ἐκτήσατ' αὐτὸν ..., εὐδαίμων γέγονεν (Dem. 45.71-72).

110 Ἐάν τις εἰς δούλου σῶμα ὑβρίσῃ, γραφὰς εἶναι κατὰ τοῦ ὑβρίσαντος (Frag. *Mantitheos*).

111 Dem. 59.33-37: ἐκώμαζέ τ' ἀεὶ μετ' αὐτοῦ, συνῆν τ' ἐμφανῶς ὁπότε βουληθείη πανταχοῦ, φιλοτιμίαν τὴν ἐξουσίαν πρὸς τοὺς ὁρῶτας ποιούμενος. ... διηγησαμένη πάντα τὰ πεπραγμένα καὶ τὴν ὕβριν τοῦ Φρυνίωνος ... προΐσταται Στέφανον τουτονὶ αὑτῆς.

112 Although he had the support of *politai* who were prepared to act for him and who might have brought a public action for this *hybris*, the slave instead brought a private suit (*dikê*) on his own behalf against the two *politai*. (Aiskhin. 1.62: βαρέως δὲ φέρων τὴν ὕβριν αὐτῶν ὁ ἄνθρωπος, δίκην ἑκατέρῳ αὐτῶν λαγχάνει.) In P. Hamb. 133, a freedwoman's suit against Zoilos for killing her child was later undertaken by her former master. Cf. P. Oxy. 13.1606 (Lys. Fr. 1 [Gernet & Bizos]) where Lysias (or a

the exaggerated conclusion of Montuori – from the varied evidence of Aiskhinês 1 – that a charge of *hybris* could be brought against anyone who prostituted a male slave (1976: 12-14). Of course, not every possible accusation would have been made, and not every accusation made would have been successful. Each individual court case involving *hybris* against slaves would have had to resolve anew, in court or otherwise, the inherent conflict between Athenian commitment to protecting the authority of a slaveowner and Athenian social concepts mandating protection for dependent persons, the *philanthrôpia* in which Athens took pride.[113] But the law against *hybris might* have protected slave prostitutes in case of extreme abuse. The prevalence of prostitution in Athenian life and the absence of definition in Athenian law preclude any greater predictability.

BIBLIOGRAPHY

Adams, C. 1919. *The Speeches of Aeschines*. Cambridge, Mass.

Allen, D. 1997. "Imprisonment in Classical Athens." *Classical Quarterly* 47: 121-35.

Attalah, W. 1966. *Adonis dans la litterature et l'art grecs*. Paris.

Balot, R. 2001. *Greed and Injustice in Classical Athens*. Princeton.

Barberet, R. 1995. *Victimologia y Prostitucion: Informe de Resultados*. Madrid.

Beschi, L. 1967-68. "Contributi di topografia ateniese." *Annuario della Scuola archeologica di Atene* 45/46: 520-26.

Bloch, I. 1912. Die Prostitution. Vol. 1. Berlin.

Cairns, D. 1996. "*Hybris*, Dishonour, and Thinking Big." *Journal of Hellenic Studies* 116: 1-32.

Calame, C. 1996. *L'Éros dans la Grèce antique*. Paris. (English Translation: Princeton 1999.)

Camp, J. 2001. *The Archaeology of Athens*. New Haven.

Canfora, L. 1995. "The Citizen." In The Greeks, edited by J.-P. Vernant, pp. 120-52. (Translation of *L'uomo greco*. 1991).

Cantarella, E. 1991. "Moicheia. Reconsidering a Problem." In *Symposion 1990*, edited by M. Gagarin, pp. 289-96. Cologne.

— 2005. "Gender, Sexuality and Law." In *The Cambridge Companion to Greek Law*, edited by M. Gagarin and D. Cohen, pp. 236-53. Cambridge.

Carey, C., ed. 1992. *Apollodoros Against Neaira [Demosthenes] 59*. Warminster.

— 1993. "The Purpose of Aristophanes' Acharnians." *Rheinisches Museum* 136: 254-63.

— 1998. "The Shape of Athenian Laws." *Classical Quarterly* 48: 93-109.

Cartledge, P., P. Millett and S. Todd, eds. 1990. *Nomos: Essays in Athenian Law, Politics and Society*. Cambridge.

Cartledge, P., E. Cohen and L. Foxhall, eds. 2001. *Money, Labour and Land in Ancient Greece*. London.

Charles, J. 1938. *Statutes of Limitations at Athens*. Chicago.

Cohen, D. 1991. *Law, Sexuality and Society: The Enforcement of Morals in Classical Athens*. Cambridge.

colleague) defends a *therapaina* who had been sued by Hippothersês for her role in the effort to reclaim property confiscated by the Thirty and sold to Hippothersês.

[113] This tension is explored in detail in Fisher 1995.

— 1995. *Law, Violence and Community in Classical Athens.* Cambridge.

Cohen, E. 1973. *Ancient Athenian Maritime Courts.* Princeton.

— 2000a. " 'Whoring under Contract': The Legal Context of Prostitution in Fourth-Century Athens." In *Law and Social Status in Classical Athens*, edited by V. Hunter and J. Edmonson, pp. 113-47. Oxford.

— 2000b. *The Athenian Nation.* Princeton.

— 2003. "Athenian Prostitution as a Liberal Profession." In *Festschrift for Prof. Alan Boegehold*, edited by J. Sickinger and G. Bakewell, pp. 214-36. Oxford.

— 2006. "Consensual Contracts At Athens." In *Symposion 2003 (Akten der Gesellschaft für Griechische und Hellenistische Rechtsgeschichte,)* edited by H.-A. Rupprecht, pp. 73-84. Vienna.

— (forthcoming). *Athenian Prostitution: The Business of Sex.*

Corbin, A. 1998. *Women for Hire: Prostitution and Sexuality in France after 1850.* (Translation of *Les filles de noce: Misére sexuelle et prostitution aux 19ᵉ et 20ᵉ siècles.* Paris 1978.) Cambridge, Mass.

Cox, C. 1998. *Household Interests: Property, Marriage Strategies and Family Dynamics in Ancient Athens.* Princeton.

Davidson, J. 1997. *Courtesans and Fishcakes: The Consuming Passions of Classical Athens.* London.

Davies, J. 1971. *Athenian Propertied Families, 600-300 B.C.* Oxford.

Detienne, M. 1977. *The Gardens of Adonis. Spices in Greek Mythology.* Sussex. (First published in French as *Les Jardins d'Adonis.* Paris 1971.)

Doblhofer, G. 1994. *Vergewaltigung in der Antike. Beiträge zur Altertumskunde 46.* Stuttgart.

Dover, K. [1978] 1989. *Greek Homosexuality.* London.

Drerup, E. 1898. "Über die bei den attischen Rednern eingelegten Urkunden." *Neue Jahrbücher für Klassische Philologie*, Supplmentb. 24.

Fisher, N. 1976, 1979. "*Hubris* and Dishononour." *Greece & Rome* 23: 177-93 and 26: 32-47.

— 1990. "The Law of *hubris* in Athens." In *Nomos: Essays in Athenian Law, Politics and Society*, edited by P. Cartledge, P. Millett and S. Todd, pp. 123-45. Cambridge.

— 1992. *Hybris.* Westminster.

— 1993. "Multiple Personalities and Dionysiac Festivals: Dicaeopolis in Aristophanes' *Acharnians.*" *Greece and Rome* 41: 31-47.

— 1995. "*Hybris*, Status and Slavery." In *The Greek World*, edited by A. Powell, pp. 44-84. London.

— 2001. *Aeschines Against Timarchos.* Oxford.

Ford, A. 1999. "Reading Homer from the Rostrum: Poems and Laws in Aeschines' *Against Timarchus.*" In *Performance Culture and Athenian Democracy*, edited by S. Goldhill and R. Osborne, pp. 231-56. Cambridge.

Forsén, B. and G. Stanton (eds.). 1996. *The Pnyx in the History of Athens.* Helsinki.

Fox, R. 1994. "Aeschines and Athenian Democracy." In *Ritual, Finance, Politics: Athenian Democratic Accounts Presented to David Lewis*, edited by R. Osborne and S. Hornblower, pp. 135-55. Oxford.

Foxhall, L. 1989. "Household, Gender and Property in Classical Athens." *Classical Quarterly* 39: 22-44.

— 1991. "Response to Eva Cantarella." In *Symposion 1990*, edited by M. Gagarin, pp. 297-303. Cologne.

— 1996. "The Law and the Lady." In *Greek Law in its Political Setting*, edited by L. Foxhall and A. Lewis, pp. 133-152. Oxford.

Gagarin, M. 1979. "The Athenian Law against Hybris." In *Arktouros: Hellenic Studies presented to Bernard Knox*, edited by G. Bowersock, W. Burkert and M.C.J. Putnam, pp. 229-36. Berlin and New York.

Gagliardi, L. 2005. "The Athenian Procedure of Dokimasia of Orators." In *Symposion 2001*, edited by R. Wallace and M. Gagarin, pp. 89-97. Vienna.

Garlan, Y. 1988. *Slavery in Ancient Greece*. Ithaca, N.Y. (Originally published as *Les esclaves en grèce ancienne*. Paris 1982.)

Gernet, L. 1917. *Recherches sur le développement de la pensée juridique et morale en Grèce. Étude sémantique*. Paris.

Gofas, D. 1979. "Les 'emmenoi dikai' à Thasos." In *Symposion 1974*, edited by A. Biscardi, pp. 175-88 (Reprint: Gofas 1993: 71-77). Cologne.

— 1993. *Μελέτες ἱστορίας τοῦ ἑλληνικοῦ δικαίου τῶν συναλλαγῶν*. Athens.

Gulick, C. 1937. *Athenaeus*. Loeb Classical Library. Cambridge.

Halperin, D. 1990. *One Hundred Years of Homosexuality and Other Essays on Greek Love*. New York.

Halperin, D., J. Winkler and F. Zeitlin, eds. 1990. *Before Sexuality: The Construction of Erotic Experience in the Ancient Greek World*. Princeton.

Hamel, D. 2003. *Trying Neaira: The True Story of a Courtesan's Scandalous Life in Ancient Greece*. New Haven.

Hansen, M. 1976. *"Apagoge," "Endeixis" and "Ephegesis" against "Kakourgoi," "Atimoi" and "Pheugontes."* Odense.

— 1981. "Two Notes on the Athenian *dikai emporikai*." In *Symposion 1979*, edited by P. Dimakis, pp. 167-75. Cologne.

— 1991. *The Athenian Democracy in the Age of Demosthenes*. Oxford.

Hanson, A. 1990. "The Medical Writers' Woman." In Halperin, D., J. Winkler and F. Zeitlin, eds., pp. 309-37.

Hanson, V. 1995. *The Other Greeks: The Family Farm and the Agrarian Roots of Western Civilization*. New York.

Harris, D. 1995. *The Treasures of the Parthenon and Erechtheion*. Oxford.

Harris, E. 1992. Review of D.M. MacDowell, *Demosthenes against Meidias*. *Classical Philology* 87: 71-80.

— 2002. "Workshop, Marketplace and Household: The Nature of Technical Specialization in Classical Athens and Its Influence on Economy and Society." In P. Cartledge, E. Cohen and L. Foxhall, eds., pp. 67-99. London.

— (forthcoming). "Who Enforced the Law in Classical Athens?" In *Symposion 2005*, edited by E. Cantarella, pp. 159-76. Vienna.

Harrison, A. 1968, 1971. *The Law of Athens*. 2 Vols. Oxford.

Henriot, C. 2001. *Prostitution and Sexuality in Shanghai: A Social History, 1849-1949*. (Translation of *Belles de Shanghai: Prostitution et sexualité en Chine aux XIXe-XXe siècles*, Paris, 1997). Cambridge.

Henry, M. 2000. "Athenaeus the Ur-Pornographer." In Braund, D. and J. Wilkins, eds., *Athenaeus and His World*, , pp. 503-10. Exeter.

Humphreys, S. 1978. *Anthropology and the Greeks*. London.

— 1993. *The Family, Women and Death*. Second Edition. Ann Arbor.

Hunter, V. 1997. "The Prison of Athens: A Comparative Perspective." *Phoenix* 51.3-4: 296-326.

Isager S., and M. Hansen. 1975. *Aspects of Athenian Society in the Fourth Century B.C.* Odense

Jaggar, A. 1985. "Prostitution." In *Philosophy of Sex*, edited by A. Soble, pp. 349ff. Totowa, N.J.

Johnstone, S. 1998. "Cracking the Code of Silence: Athenian Legal Oratory and the Histories of Slaves and Women." In *Women and Slaves in Greco-Roman Culture*, edited by S. Murnaghan and S. Joshel, pp. 221-35. London.

Just, R. 1985. "Freedom, Slavery and the Female Psyche." In *Crux: Essays in Greek History presented to G.E.M. de Ste. Croix*, edited by P. Cartledge and F. Harvey, pp. 169-88. London.

Kapparis, K. 1999. *Apollodoros "Against Neaira" [D.59]*. Berlin.

Khatzibasileiou, B. 1981. *Τα δημοσιονομικά της Κω από μαρτυρίες αρχαίων επιγραφῶν* = *Vol. 8 of Κωακά*.

Klees, H. 1998. *Sklavenleben im klassischen Griechenland (= Vol. 30 of Forschungen zur antiken Sklaverei*, edited by H. Bellen). Stuttgart.

Kurke, L. 1999. *Coins, Bodies, Games, and Gold: The Politics of Meaning in Archaic Greece*. Princeton.

Lanni, A. (forthcoming). "Athenian Approaches to Legal Predictability in Contract Cases." In *Symposion 2005*, edited by E. Cantarella, pp. 225-36. Vienna.

Lape, S. 2004. *Reproducing Athens: Menander's Comedy, Democratic Culture, and the Hellenistic City*. Princeton.

— 2006. "The Psychology of Prostitution in Aeschines' Speech against Timarchus." In *Prostitution in the Ancient World*, edited by C. Faraone and L. McClure, pp. 139-60. Madison.

Lefkowitz, M. and M. Fant. 1982. *Women's Life in Greece and Rome*. Baltimore.

Lentakis, A. 1998. *Η πορνεία*. Vol. 3 of *Ο έρωτας στην αρχαία Ελλάδα*. Athens.

— 1999. *Οι εταίρες*. Vol. 4 of *Ο έρωτας στην αρχαία Ελλάδα*. Athens.

Leontsini, S. 1989. *Die Prostitution im frühen Byzanz*. Ph.D. diss., University of Vienna.

Lipsius, J. [1905-15] 1966. *Das attische Recht und Rechtsverfahren*. 3 Vols. Hildesheim.

MacDowell, D. 1976. "*Hubris* in Athens." *Greece & Rome* 23: 14-31.

— 1978. *The Law in Classical Athens*. London.

— ed. 1990. *Demosthenes Against Meidias*. Oxford.

— 1995. *Aristophanes and Athens*. Oxford.

— 2000. "Athenian Laws about Homosexuality." *Revue internationale des droits de l'antiquité*. 3rd Ser. 47: 13-27.

— 2005. "The Athenian Procedure of Dokimasia of Orators." In *Symposion 2001*, edited by R. Wallace and M. Gagarin, pp. 79-87. Vienna.

Martin, V. and G. de Budé. 1962. *Eschine, Discours*. Vol. 1. Paris.

McClure, L. 2003. *Courtesans at Table: Gender and Greek Literary Culture in Athenaeus*. London.

McGinn, T. 1998. *Prostitution, Sexuality and the Law in Ancient Rome*. Oxford.

— 2004. *The Economy of Prostitution in the Roman World: A Study of Social History and the Brothel*. Ann Arbor.

Meikle, S. 1996. "Aristotle on Business." *Classical Quarterly* 46: 138-51.

Millett, P. and S. Todd. 1990. "Law, Society and Athens." In Cartledge, Millett and Todd, pp. 1-18

Murray, O. 1990. "The Solonian Law of Hubris." In *Nomos: Essays in Athenian Law, Politics and Society*, edited by P. Cartledge, P. Millett and S. Todd, pp. 139-45. Cambridge.

Neils, J. 2000. "Others within the Other: An Intimate Look at Hetairai and Maenads." In *Not the Classical Ideal: Athens and the Construction of the Other in Greek Art*, edited by Beth Cohen, pp. 203-26. Leiden.

Ober, J. 1989. *Mass and Elite in Democratic Athens*. Princeton.

— 1991. "Aristotle's Political Sociology: Class, Status, and Order in the *Politics*." In *Essays on the Foundations of Aristotelian Political Science*, edited by C. Lord and D.K. O'Connor, pp. 112-35. Berkeley.

— 1996. *The Athenian Revolution: Essays on Ancient Greek Democracy and Political Theory*. Princeton.

O'Neill, M. and R. Barberet. 2000. "Victimization and the Social Organization of Prostitution in England and Spain." In R. Weitzer, ed., pp. 123-37.

Palmer, S. and J. Humphrey. 1990. *Deviant Behavior: Patterns, Sources and Control*. New York.

Paoli, U. [1930] 1974. *Studi di diritto attico*. Milan.

Parker, R. 1996. *Athenian Religion: A History*. Oxford.

Perrin, B. 1914. *Plutarch*. Loeb Classical Library. Vol. 1. Cambridge.

Pisano, I. 2002. *Io puttana: Parlano le prostitute*. Milan.

Rahe, P. 1992. *Republics Ancient and Modern: Classical Republicanism and American Revolution*. Chapel Hill.

Reinach, T. 1892. "L'impôt sur les courtisanes à Cos." *Revue des Etudes Grecques* 5: 99-102.

Rhodes, P. 1981. *A Commentary on the Aristotelian Athenaion Politeia*. Oxford.

Richlin, A. 1998. "Foucault's *History of Sexuality*: A Useful Theory for Women?" In *Rethinking Sexuality: Foucault and Classical Antiquity*, edited by D. Larmour, P. Miller and C. Platter, pp. 138-70. Princeton.

Roussel, P. 1960. *Isée*. Paris.

Ruschenbusch, E. 1965. "*Hybreos Graphe*: ein Fremdkörper in athenischen Recht des 4. Jahrhunderts v.Chr." *Zeitschrift der Savigny-Stiftung für Rechtsgeschichte. Romanistische Abteilung* 82: 302-309.

Scanlon, T. 2002. *Eros and Greek Athletics*. Oxford.

Schaps, D. 1998. "What Was Free about a Free Athenian Woman?" *Transactions of the American Philological Association* 128: 161-88.

Sealey, R. 1990. *Women and Law in Classical Greece*. Chapel Hill.

Shrage, L. 1994. *Moral Dilemmas of Feminism: Prostitution, Adultery, and Abortion*. New York.

Sissa, G. 1999. "Sexual Bodybuilding: Aeschines against Timarchus." In *Constructions of the Classical Body*, edited by J. Porter, pp. 147-68. Ann Arbor.

Stroud, R. 1998. *The Athenian Grain-Tax Law of 374/3 B.C.* Hesperia Supplement 29. Princeton.

Thompson, H. 1982. "The *Pnyx* in Models" In *Studies in Attic Epigraphy, History and Topography Presented to Eugene Vanderpool. Hesperia* Supp. 19, pp. 133-47.

Todd, S. 1993. *The Shape of Athenian Law*. Oxford.

Travlos, J. 1937. "Ἀνασκαφαὶ Ἱερᾶς ὁδοῦ." *Praktika*: 25-41.

Vélissaropoulos, J. 1980. *Les nauclères grecs*. Geneva.

Wallace, R. 1993. "Personal Conduct and Legal Sanction in the Democracy of Classical Athens." In *Questions de responsabilité*, edited by J. Zlinzsky, pp. 397-413. Miskolc (Hung.).

— 1994a. "Private Lives and Public Enemies: Freedom of Thought in Classical Athens." In *Athenian Identity and Civic Ideology*, edited by A. Scafuro and A. Boegehold, pp. 205-238. Baltimore.

— 1994b. "The Athenian Laws of Slander." In *Symposion 1993*, edited by G. Thür, pp. 109-24. Köln.

— 1997. "On Not Legislating Sexual Conduct in Fourth-Century Athens." In *Symposion 1995*, edited by G. Thür and J. Vélissaropoulos-Karakostas, pp. 151-66. Köln.

— 1998. "Unconvicted or Potential 'Atimoi' in Ancient Athens." *Dike* 1: 63-78.

Weitzer, R. 2000. "The Politics of Prostitution in America." In Weitzer, ed., pp. 159-80.

Weitzer, R. ed. 2000. *Sex for Sale: Prostitution, Pornography and the Sex Industry*. New York.

Winkler, J. 1990. *The Constraints of Desire: The Anthropology of Sex and Gender in Ancient Greece*. New York.

Wolff, H. 1944. "Marriage Law and Family Organization in Ancient Athens." *Traditio* 2: 43-95. (Reprinted in *Beiträge zur Rechtsgeschichte Altgriechenlands und des hellenistisch-römischen Ägypten* [Weimar 1961], pp. 155-242.)

Worthington, I. 1992. *A Historical Commentary on Dinarchus: Rhetoric and Conspiracy in Later Fourth-Century Athens*. Ann Arbor.

ADRIAAN LANNI (CAMBRIDGE, MA)

ATHENIAN APPROACHES TO LEGAL PREDICTABILITY IN CONTRACT CASES

Around the turn of the twentieth century the renowned legal scholar and jurist Oliver Wendell Holmes Jr. proposed what has become known as the "bad man" theory of the law.[1] Holmes described the function of law by imagining a "bad man" who viewed the law purely instrumentally and planned his behavior based on what he predicted he could (and could not) get away with under the existing rules. Under this theory, the law can only serve as an effective means of social control if legal rules are sufficiently certain and judicial decisions sufficiently predictable to allow individuals to conform their conduct to the law. More recently, scholars in the law and economics movement have pointed out that reduced legal certainty and predictability create inefficiencies, particularly in the field of private law.[2] The risk and cost of every transaction increase if sellers and buyers cannot be reasonably sure that they will be able, if necessary, to have the terms of a contract or the protections afforded them by law enforced by a court. If judicial decisions are highly unpredictable, parties may be forced to litigate even questions that would appear straightforward under the contract or governing statutes.

In this paper I examine the Athenians' unusual approach to legal predictability, focusing particularly on cases involving contracts. In most cases Athenian jurors were presented with a wide variety of information on which to base their decision, including not only the terms of the contract and any statutes the litigant chose to present but also the parties' reputation for honesty and fair dealing and general arguments from fairness. As a result, popular court verdicts were largely ad hoc determinations that might be difficult to predict at the time of the transaction. But the Athenians appear to have taken a different approach in one particular type of contract case: the *dikê emporikê* procedure governing maritime suits. In these cases, speakers focus more narrowly on the terms of the written agreement. I argue that the distinctive notion of relevance in the *dikai emporikai* was designed to enhance predictability in these cases and thereby to attract foreign merchants to Athens. I also offer some preliminary thoughts on why and how the Athenians tolerated a relatively unpredictable procedure for enforcing contracts in non-maritime suits.

---

[1] Holmes 1897.

[2] E.g., Rose 1988.

In modern American law, disputes concerning contracts are resolved by reference to (1) the terms of the contract agreed to by the parties; and (2) background rules found in statutes or case law that govern contract formation, interpretation, and enforcement. Some of these rules apply only when the contract is silent or ambiguous and can be contracted around by the parties; others, for example the rule that unconscionable contracts are void, apply regardless of the parties' agreement. In Athens, there were very few background contracting rules. With a few exceptions, such as the laws relating to the sale of slaves,[3] the general rule was that whatever agreements one man makes with another are binding.[4] Litigants could argue in individual cases that the jury should be influenced by considerations that a modern would think of as a background contracting rule – the speaker in Hyperides, *Against Athenogenes*, for example, argues that unjust contracts are void – but these arguments, even if successful, did not become legal rules that future contracting parties could rely on, since there was no doctrine of binding precedent in Athens. For this reason, enhancing legal certainty and predictability in Athenian contract cases boils down to trying to ensure that the jury will focus on interpreting and enforcing the terms of the contract and will ignore arguments based on extra-legal norms.

The different attitudes to contracts in maritime and non-maritime cases

I have argued elsewhere that jurors in most popular court cases considered a wide variety of both legal and extra-legal information in reaching their decision – including evidence based on the character of the parties, the background of the dispute, the effects of a likely fine or penalty, and general arguments from fairness – in an effort to reach a just verdict that took into account the broader context of the dispute and the particular circumstances of the individual case.[5] Even the relative importance of the various legal and extra-legal arguments in any individual case was open to dispute by the parties. It is impossible to draw firm conclusions based on the five maritime speeches (*dikai emporikai*) that survive,[6] but it appears that speakers in maritime cases are significantly more focused on the terms of the written contract and less likely to appeal to extra-legal argumentation than speakers in other popular court cases concerning contracts and wills. I will summarize the evidence for this argument[7] before turning to the reasons for these differences.

---

3 There was very little state regulation of private transactions, but there were some laws designed to protect buyers, such as a law prohibiting the making of false statements in the agora (Hyp. 3.14), a law regulating the process by which an Athenian official would declare silver coinage valid (Rhodes & Osborne 2003: No. 25), and various rules regarding the sale of slaves (Hyp. 3.14-15).

4 Hyp. 3.13: ὁ νόμος λέγει, ὅσα ἂν ἕτερος ἑτέρῳ ὁμολογήσῃ κύρια εἶναι.

5 Lanni 2005.

6 Dem. 32-35; 36.

7 For a more detailed discussion of the evidence for the differences, see Lanni 2006:149-171.

Dikai emporikai were exceptional in that (1) foreigners, metics, and perhaps even slaves were given standing in these suits equal to Athenian citizens[8] and (2) only disputes concerning written contracts could be heard through this procedure.[9] The requirement of written proof appears to have focused maritime suits on the terms of the written agreement: as several scholars have pointed out, one of the most distinctive features of these speeches is the importance of the terms of the agreement to the speakers' arguments.[10] In the three maritime cases in which the speaker is not challenging the existence of a contract, the written contract is recited in full within the first ten sections of the speech.[11] Of the 113 references to written contracts in the entire Demosthenic corpus, 100 occur in these three speeches alone.[12] Demosthenes *Against Lacritus* is most striking in this regard: the speaker discusses the contract in painstaking detail, "addressing in turn each of the provisions of the written contract,"[13] and then has the entire agreement read out a second time.[14]

The contract in Demosthenes *Against Dionydodorus* did not address the precise issue in dispute. The contract provided that the lender bear the loss if the ship was lost at sea, and that the borrowers pay a penalty if they did not return with their cargo to Athens. The contract made no provision for another contingency – rather than total loss of the ship, damage severe enough to preclude the return of the ship and require that her cargo be sold outside Athens. This is what the defendant claimed to have happened, if we can trust the prosecution's account.[15] Although the contract is silent on the crucial question of the rights of the parties in this contingency, the speaker quotes from the written contract four times and repeatedly refers the jurors to the terms of the agreement as the proper guide to their decision.[16] It is not only speakers who are pressing their contractual claims who emphasize that the terms of the written contract are decisive in maritime suits. The speaker in Demosthenes 33, the defendant in the original contract action, refers to a written contract as *akribês*[17] and states that contract disputes are to be resolved by reference to the written document.[18]

In stark contrast to the importance of the contractual terms in maritime suits, speakers in other suits involving written contracts or wills rarely dwell on the specifics of the legal instrument or suggest that the jurors should look only within

---

8 For discussion, see MacDowell 1978:234; Todd 1993:193; Gernet 1938.

9 On the debate over the jurisdiction of the maritime courts, see E. Cohen 1973:100-158; Gernet 1938:186; Carey & Reid 1985:233; Isager & Hansen 1975:86.

10 Carey & Reid 1985:200n.50; Christ 1998:220-221; D. Cohen 2003:94-95.

11 Dem. 34.7; 35.10; 56.6.

12 Carey & Reid 1985:200 n. 50.

13 Dem. 35.17.

14 Dem. 35.37.

15 Dem. 56.37.

16 Dem. 56.6, 36-38.

17 Dem. 33. 36.

18 Dem. 33.36.

the four corners of the contract.[19] Instead, speakers in non-maritime cases often appeal to general notions of fair dealing and argue that one or other of the parties has a superior moral claim to the money or property at issue.

Demosthenes 48, *Against Olympiodorus*, illustrates the diminished importance of the written instrument in non-maritime contract cases. The speaker is suing his partner in crime for breach of contract[20] for tricking him out of his share, and one would expect that the plaintiff would focus on the terms of the agreement in the absence of equitable sources of support for his claim. The speaker, Callistratus, and his brother-in-law, Olympiodorus, made a written contract to divide the estate belonging to Comon, a mutual relative, evenly between them and to exclude all other claimants. After the two managed to have the estate awarded to Olympiodorus by colluding in various misrepresentations to the court, Olympiodorus refused to give Callistratus half of the estate in accordance with their agreement. Predictably, Callistratus emphasizes that his opponent has breached their agreement. Callistratus does not rest his claim solely on the terms of the contract, however, but also includes a number of arguments rooted in fairness. He stresses that he offered Olympiodorus a fair settlement to avoid litigation but was rebuffed,[21] and he requests in the first instance not the enforcement of the contract as written but a compromise ruling.[22] He notes that he arranged for Comon's burial, a fact often cited by contestants in inheritance cases to show their personal connection to the deceased and right to a share of the estate.[23] Finally, Callistratus reports that Olympiodorus is unmarried and has been wasting all his money on his mistress, a former slave, while Callistratus has a wife and daughter to support.[24]

In keeping with the unusual emphasis on the written contract found in maritime suits, extra-legal arguments such as evidence based on the character or relationship of the litigants or appeals to pity play a smaller role in these cases than in non-maritime suits. One might expect that the presence of foreigners and metics in addition to citizens in *dikai emporikai* would lead to a plethora of arguments in which the litigant with the higher status would exploit his superior social standing to curry favor with jurors. With few exceptions, however, the social standing, character, and services of the litigants play little role in the arguments in the

[19] Compare, for example, the focus on the written contract in maritime suits such as Demosthenes 33, 35 and 56 to non-maritime contract cases such as Hyperides 3 or Demosthenes 48. In cases involving a will, litigants often appeal to a variety of arguments rooted in notions of fairness and justice unrelated to the issue of the formal validity of the will. (Avramović 1997:54-58; Hardcastle 1980).

[20] The suit was technically a *dikê blabês*, "an action for damage." There appears to have been no distinctive procedure for a breach of contract action (Todd 1993:266).

[21] Dem. 48.4.

[22] Dem. 48.3.

[23] Dem. 48.6.

[24] Dem. 48.54-55.

maritime suits.[25] Indeed, in several cases we are unsure of the legal status of the individuals involved in the transaction. A narrowed sense of relevance in *dikai emporikai* is also suggested by the complete absence of appeals to the jurors' pity, a well-known topos in our non-maritime cases.

The distinctive mode of argumentation in maritime cases, in which the character of the litigants and issues of fairness in light of the specific context of the transaction are played down in favor of the terms of the written agreement and the general principle that contracts should be binding, can be usefully compared to other commercial, non-maritime cases. Demosthenes 36 (*For Phormio*) and Demosthenes 37 (*Against Pantaenetus*) are promising candidates for comparison. These two cases are also speeches in the Demosthenic corpus dating from sometime in the middle of the fourth century that involve commercial transactions between litigants who are seasoned businessmen, but not political figures. Most important, they, like four of our five *dikai emporikai,* are part of *paragraphê* actions. These cases therefore suggest that the distinctive nature of maritime argumentation can be linked to a narrower notion of relevance in *dikai emporikai* rather than any unusual aspects of the *paragraphê* procedure.

Although the subject matter in Demosthenes 36 and 37 – the leasing arrangement of a banking business and a series of transactions involving mining property – is similar to that of maritime suits, the speeches are not as narrowly focused on the business transactions at issue. The speaker in Demosthenes 36, for example, disparages Apollodorus' performance of liturgies and ridicules his extravagant habits,[26] defends Phormio's career,[27] makes a standard appeal to win the juror's pity,[28] and argues that it is to the jurors' advantage to award the money to Phormio.[29] Similarly, in Demosthenes 37 Nicobulus repeatedly slanders his opponent's witnesses.[30] He also includes an extended discussion of his fear that his case will be prejudiced by the jury's dislike of money-lenders like himself, and the jury's disgust at what the speaker confesses are his unpleasant qualities: he apparently walks fast, talks loudly, and goes around with a walking stick.[31] Most striking is the use in these two speeches of witnesses to testify solely to the good character of the speaker or the villainy of his opponent. The speaker in Demosthenes 36 offers testimony both of Phormio's good character, uprightness, and generosity,[32]

[25] The one notable exception is Demosthenes *Against Lacritus*, in which the speaker slanders his opponents because they are from Phaselis. Nevertheless, the bulk of this speech is devoted to a close reading of the contract, which is twice read out in full in the course of the oration.

[26] Dem. 36. 42, 45, 52, 55-57.

[27] Dem. 36.56.

[28] Dem. 36.59.

[29] Dem. 36.58-59.

[30] Dem. 37.48.

[31] Dem. 37.52.

[32] Dem. 36.55.

and of the baseness of Apollodorus.[33] Nicobulus also presents character witnesses in Demosthenes 37, stating, "Please read the witness testimony regarding what sort of person I am toward men who lend money on bond and toward those who are in need."[34] Although speakers in our surviving popular court cases often boast of their character and slander their opponents, the use of character witnesses *stricto sensu* as in these two cases is quite rare. The emphasis of the litigants in both these cases on their reputation for fair business practices contrasts starkly with the narrow focus on the terms of the written contract typical in *dikai emporikai*. Matthew Christ has pointed out a similar difference between cases involving banking transactions and the *dikai emporikai*: while litigants in banking suits present their cases in terms of a breach of *philia*, parties in maritime cases emphasize a breach of contract.[35]

In sum, the speakers in non-maritime contract cases do not confine their arguments to the terms of the agreement or suggest, as speakers in *dikai emporikai* do, that the contract should be the sole guide to the jurors' decision. In non-maritime suits, a man's reputation for fair business practices and other issues beyond the specific terms of any written agreement, such as fairness and equity, become relevant to the jurors' decision. The narrow focus on the written contract unique to maritime suits presumably would facilitate business deals by increasing the predictability of verdicts, but would also hamper the jury's ability to take into account a wide range of factors in reaching its decision.

Explaining the approach to legal predictability in maritime suits

The *dikê emporikê* procedure was introduced in the middle of the fourth century, most likely as part of an effort to attract merchants, goods, and grain to Athens when its economy was flagging.[36] I think the unusual mode of argumentation in maritime cases can be traced to two interrelated causal factors: the common participation of non-citizens in *dikai emporikai*, and the need to facilitate trade and attract non-Athenian merchants by offering a predictable procedure based on the enforcement of contracts as written.

The desire to encourage lending and to facilitate trade by providing a predictable legal procedure to enforce contracts made the wide-ranging discretion wielded by juries in non-maritime suits counter-productive in the context of maritime cases.[37] A focus on the terms of the written contract reduced the legal uncertainty associated with the ad hoc approach taken in the Athenian popular courts

---

[33] Dem. 36.55-56.

[34] Dem. 37.54: λέγε δή μοι τὰς μαρτυρίας, τίς ἐγὼ πρὸς τοὺς συμβάλλοντας ἀνθρώπους καὶ πρὸς τοὺς δεομένους εἰμί.

[35] Christ 1998:180-191.

[36] See generally Cohen 1973; Gernet 1938; Paoli 1930:111-115.

[37] For speakers' statements regarding the importance of encouraging lending and facilitating trade by strictly enforcing written agreements, see Dem. 34.51; 35.54; 56.48-50.

and gave lenders and traders confidence that they would be able to enforce their contracts in court if necessary. The speaker in Demosthenes *Against Dionysodorus* makes precisely this argument in urging the jurors to strictly enforce the maritime contract in his suit:

> εἰ μὲν γὰρ ὑμεῖς τὰς συγγραφὰς καὶ τὰς ὁμολογίας τὰς πρὸς ἀλλήλους γιγνομένας ἰσχυρὰς οἰήσεσθε δεῖν εἶναι καὶ τοῖς παραβαίνουσιν αὐτὰς μηδεμίαν συγγνώμην ἕξετε, ἑτοιμότερον προήσονται τὰ ἑαυτῶν οἱ ἐπὶ τοῦ δανείζειν ὄντες, ἐκ δὲ τούτων αὐξηθήσεται ὑμῖν τὸ ἐμπόριον. ... τίς γὰρ ἐθελήσει τὰ ἑαυτοῦ προέσθαι, ὅταν ὁρᾷ τὰς μὲν συγγραφὰς ἀκύρους, ἰσχύοντας δὲ τοὺς τοιούτους λόγους, καὶ τὰς αἰτίας τῶν ἠδικηκότων ἔμπροσθεν οὔσας τοῦ δικαίου;
>
> For if you think that contracts and agreements made between men should be binding, and you will show no forbearance toward those who break them, then those men who lend their own money will do so more readily and as a result your market will flourish. ... For who will want to risk his money, when he sees written contracts having no effect, and arguments of this sort [i.e. contrary to the terms of the agreement] winning the day, and the accusations of criminals being placed before justice?[38]

This reassurance may have been particularly important in the maritime trade because it often involved doing business with men outside one's close-knit community, including foreigners whose reputation might not be well-known, who might not be repeat-players, and who might not be easily influenced by the informal norms of the marketplace. It is natural that merchants dealing with strangers would be less trustful, and therefore more likely to want well-defined commitments spelled out in written contracts and enforced in a more formal procedure. Strict enforcement of contracts is an easy – and ingenious – way to reduce legal uncertainty in a society without precise legal rules or legal experts because it does not involve the creation of a complex substantive law of contracting rules but permits the contracting parties to create their own law for each deal.

The narrower notion of relevance employed in *dikai emporikai* was also vital to attracting the foreign merchants who dominated maritime trade to Athens.[39] Foreigners would be at a distinct disadvantage in the ordinary Athenian popular courts, where they would be subject to judgment based on unwritten Athenian norms and values that they might not fully understand, let alone share. Few transient foreign merchants would have ready access to the witnesses necessary to present a contextualized account of their character, reputation, and manner of doing business.

---

[38] Dem. 56.48-50.

[39] Reed 2003:27-33.

Even those who could present such a case might not be sanguine about their chances of prevailing in an Athenian court against an Athenian citizen who could point to military service and other hallmarks of good character familiar to popular court juries. The *dikê emporikê* procedure, by focusing on the terms of the written contract and discouraging extra-legal information and argumentation, offered foreign merchants the chance to resolve their disputes on a truly equal footing with citizens based on a transparent, straightforward, and non-culturally specific standard: the terms of the written contract agreed to by the parties.

Explaining the approach to predictability in non-maritime cases

If a more formal, predictable legal procedure facilitated business deals, one might ask why the Athenians employed this approach only in maritime cases and did not adopt it in other business contexts such as banking and ordinary contract cases. In other words, why were the Athenians willing to tolerate the widespread legal uncertainty and resulting transaction costs that accompanied the discretionary, ad hoc approach of non-maritime popular court cases?

One potential answer is that when it came to interactions between citizens, jury verdicts were not so unpredictable after all because even in the absence of formal rules contracting parties would know how a jury would be likely to react to a particular case. Under this view, shared norms and values provided a sufficient amount of certainty regarding one's legal rights and responsibilities to facilitate transactions.

At first glance, this interpretation appears to have much to recommend it. Modern societies often have two separate sets of rules: legal rules known primarily by legal experts, and informal social norms that govern everyday interactions.[40] In Athens, by contrast, popular norms were often those at play in the courts, allowing potential litigants to draw on their cultural knowledge to predict the likely outcome of a lawsuit. Moreover, the homogeneity of the Athenian male citizenry (at least relative to modern societies) provides reason to believe that most Athenians would have a similar moral and emotional response to various types of cases.

Nevertheless, shared norms and values are not sufficient to foster predictability in a legal system that considers a vast array of factors relevant to any legal decision. While there may have been consensus on whether each type of legal or extra-legal argument favored the prosecutor or the defendant and which pieces of evidence were particularly damning for either side, it often must have been difficult to predict the interaction of all the evidence in a particular case. To take an example, most Athenians may have endorsed general values such as the importance of public service, family obligations, and honest fair dealing. Most Athenians also recognized many specific norms, such as the duty to care for and properly bury elderly relatives, the importance of respecting a man's wishes to will his money to whomever he

[40] Ellickson 1991:40-123.

wishes, and the immorality of forcefully seizing a disputed inheritance rather than pursuing legal avenues. But potential litigants in an inheritance case in which each side was supported by some of the values and norms listed above would find it difficult to predict a given jury's decision. It is important to distinguish here between predictability of outcomes as opposed to arguments. The types of arguments likely to be raised on either side of a particular case could easily be anticipated. Cultural knowledge can help predict the issues and arguments a jury will find relevant and how it is likely to react to each of those arguments, but cannot predict how the jury will weigh competing norms in any particular case. As far as we can tell, there was no clear hierarchy of norms in Athenian society that would permit a potential litigant to predict the outcome of a legal case.

Another, more promising, explanation is that many Athenians probably could have significantly reduced the effects of legal uncertainty by conducting their affairs with men with whom they had close ties whenever possible.[41] This would make it easier to settle their disputes through informal means without reference to the laws or recourse to the courts.[42] Members of the local community would be susceptible to informal pressures to stand by agreements and to conduct business honorably. Men who regularly did business together could be assured that each party had incentives to act fairly to preserve the ongoing relationship. This is what legal scholars call "relational contracting" – the tendency of market players to abandon short-term self-interest in individual exchanges for the sake of developing and maintaining an ongoing trading relationship.[43] Even when concluding single transactions with men outside the local community, one could expect that the fear of a tarnished reputation and negative gossip might prevent merchants and other businessmen from engaging in extremely unscrupulous behavior.[44]

But informal means of social control could not compensate completely for the high level of legal uncertainty surrounding contracting and other private law transactions in Athens. It has been found that informal norms are least effective in regulating conduct when the actors do not have close social ties or an ongoing business relationship, or when the stakes of a dispute are high.[45] It would be difficult for most Athenians to deal exclusively with members of one's small local community. Presumably Athenians would purchase some items from specialized venders whom they did not know (or know of) in the market of Athens or the

---

41 Examples of Athenians transacting with relatives, neighbors, or close friends: Dem. 33.6-7; 53.9; cf. Dem. 35.6-7.

42 Ellickson (1991) has shown that contemporary Americans in close-knit communities, who have imperfect access to predictable legal enforcements because of the high cost of litigation, are able to order their affairs effectively "without law," by reliance on trust and informal control over anti-social behavior.

43 Bernstein 1992; 1996.

44 On the importance of gossip as a means of informal social control, see Hunter 1994: 96-119.

45 Ellickson 1991:94, 250-51.

Piraeus.[46] Even when individuals had extremely close social ties, such as a family or neighborly relationship, informal means of social control would often prove inadequate to order private transactions if the stakes in the dispute were high. The surviving court speeches suggest, for example, that where a significant inheritance was in dispute, family members often turned to the formal legal rules and processes. Relational contracting must have helped to reduce the cost and burden caused by legal uncertainty, but it does not completely explain the Athenian approach to predictability in non-maritime cases.

The final explanation I can offer for why the Athenians tolerated less legal predictability in non-maritime than in maritime cases is the democratic commitment to jury discretion. Athenian jurors may have valued their ability to enforce unwritten norms of fair dealing and good conduct in reaching their verdicts in the popular courts. The adoption of a narrow relevance regime focusing on the terms of the contract in non-maritime cases would have detracted from the democratic juries' ability to wield their influence on Athenian life. In *dikai emporikai*, on the other hand, the common participation of foreigners may have isolated maritime business activity from the everyday social interactions in which the Athenian juror took great interest.[47] Regardless of the actual extent of citizen participation in maritime trade, the port of the Peiraeus was thought of as "a world apart" from city life, and commercial activity was always considered different and separate from more respected economic pursuits.[48] In this sphere, Athenian jurors probably saw less value in enforcing fair play and insuring a just resolution that took account of the particular circumstances of the case. On the other side of the ledger were the considerable economic advantages associated with the more narrow, legal approach of focusing on the written contract used in maritime cases. In this one area of law, the costs associated with discretionary justice outweighed the benefits, and steps were taken to narrow the range of evidence considered relevant to the jury in an effort to enhance the predictability of verdicts and thereby facilitate trade.

[46] Swords and shields for military service and other such items were unlikely to be produced in local areas and may have been obtained while visiting the city to attend festivals, the assembly, or to serve in the courts. Theophrastus' citizen *agroikos* (*Char.* 6) attends the Assembly while he is in the city shopping and running errands.

[47] The locus classicus for the (idealized) quality of these interactions is the *epitaphios* in Thucydides 2.37.2-3.

[48] von Reden 1995; Garland 2001:58-100.

BIBLIOGRAPHY

Avramović, S. (1997) *Iseo e il diritto attico.*

Bernstein, L. (1992) "Opting Out of the Legal System: Extralegal Contractual Relations in the Diamond Industry" *Journal of Legal Studies* 21:115-157.

—. (1996) "Merchant Law in a Merchant Court: Rethinking the Code's Search for Immanent Business Norms" *University of Pennsylvania Law Review* 144: 1765-1821.

Carey, C. & R.A. Reid (1985) *Demosthenes. Selected Private Speeches.*

Christ, M.R. (1998) *The Litigious Athenian.*

Cohen, D. (2003) "Writing, Law, and Legal Practice in the Athenian Courts" in H. Yunis, ed., *Written Texts and the Rise of Literate Culture in Ancient Greece*, 78-96.

Cohen, E.E. (1973) *Ancient Athenian Maritime Courts.*

Ellickson, R.C. (1991) *Order without Law: How Neighbors Settle Disputes.*

Garland, R. (2001) *The Piraeus.*

Gernet, L. (1938) "Sur les actions commerciales en droit athénien" *REG* 51:1-44.

Hardcastle, M. (1980) "Some Non-legal Arguments in Athenian Inheritance Cases" *Prudentia* 12:11-22.

Holmes, O.W. (1997) "The Path of the Law" *Harvard Law Review* 110: 991-1009 (reprint of 10:459 (1897)).

Hunter, V.J. (1994) *Policing Athens: Social Control in the Attic Lawsuits, 420-320 B.C.*

Isager, S. & M.H. Hansen (1975) *Aspects of Athenian Society in the Fourth Century B.C.*

Lanni, A. (2005) "Relevance in Athenian Law" in Cohen & Gagarin, eds., *Cambridge Companion to Ancient Greek Law*, 112-128.

—. (2006) *Law and Justice in the Courts of Classical Athens.*

Paoli, U.E. (1930) *Studi di diritto attico.*

Reed, C.M. (2003) *Maritime Traders in the Ancient Greek World.*

Rose, C.M. (1988) "Crystals and Mud in Property Law" *Stanford Law Review* 40:577-610.

Todd, S.C. (1993) *The Shape of Athenian Law.*

von Reden, S. (1995) "The Piraeus – A World Apart" *G&R* 42:24-37.

JEAN-MARIE BERTRAND (PARIS)

À PROPOS DE LA *RHÉTORIQUE* D'ARISTOTE (I, 1373b1-1374b23), ANALYSE DU PROCESSUS JUDICIAIRE

III. προαίρεσις

Devant un tribunal athénien, tout procès qu'il fût public ou privé, consistait en l'affrontement direct de deux individus. Le vaincu, qu'il fût reconnu coupable de ce dont il était accusé, ou qu'il n'ait pas réussi à convaincre de la validité de son accusation, se voyait touché, non seulement dans ses intérêts matériels, mais aussi dans sa dignité. Chacune des parties, quelque soucieuse qu'elle eût été d'éclairer le problème de fait et de droit touchant au fond de l'affaire, ne manquait pas de dénoncer, en termes souvent vifs, l'indignité de l'adversaire et de faire de celui-ci un portrait qui, dans le cas où le tribunal la suivait, devenait évidence publique. On passait ainsi, qu'il fût question de crime, de délit ou de simple conflit d'intérêt, de l'analyse matérielle de l'affaire à celle de la personnalité des plaideurs, aussi bien de l'accusé que de l'accusateur, remontant nécessairement de la «paire *quoi-pourquoi?*» à «la question-pivot *qui?*». On ne peut échapper à l'idée que le tribunal avait pour fonction, dans chaque procès, de connaître des personnes qui se présentaient devant lui et de faire savoir quelle appréciation il portait sur elles[1].

Si l'on considère la situation du condamné, on doit reconnaître que la validation du terme employé dans l'acte d'accusation et retenu par l'ordonnance de renvoi[2], varet reconnaissance de sa responsabilité dans l'acte incriminé ainsi que de la malignité qui l'a fait agir. Ainsi la sentence du tribunal va bien au-delà de la simple appréciation du fait et, si le juge reconnaît un accusé coupable d'une faute après avoir examiné l'événement soumis à son attention, les mots qu'il emploie qualifient non seulement le fait lui-même mais son auteur. Aristote montre comment le fait de désigner un acte du nom d'outrage, de vol ou d'adultère revient à condamner la *proairesis* de l'agent. C'est en elle que réside la malignité et le caractère injuste de

---

1 P. Ricœur, *Soi-même comme un autre*, Paris, 1990, p. 109-136 (Quatrième étude, «De l'action à l'agent»), les italiques sont de l'auteur.

2 Voir notre note «À propos de la *Rhétorique* d'Aristote, analyse du prcessus judiciaire, l'*epigramma,* l'*egklèma*», *DIKE*, 5, 2002, p. 161-185 et notre communication du *Symposion 2003*, p. 499-211, sur l'*epikrisis* et l'*erôtèsis.*

l'acte commis[3], le criminel révélant par l'usage qu'il en fait qu'il est mauvais et injuste[4]. En revanche, il peut arriver que le tribunal, considérant non pas l'acte seulement, mais la *proairesis* qui a conduit à le commettre ne souhaite pas prononcer un verdict de culpabilité, jugeant en équité[5].

Le mot *proairesis* a pu être considéré comme «rare» et de «sens indécis» dans la langue commune de l'époque, il semble qu'il soit devenu pour Aristote un «terme technique»[6]. L'étude la plus récente du terme est celle de J.-B. Gourinat[7] qui revient sur l'analyse du préverbe **pro* pour conclure, comme le faisait P. Aubenque[8], qu'il s'agit du choix d'une certaine action plutôt que de telle autre, un «choix préférentiel». Il faut se poser la question de savoir, si c'est uniquement dans le langage philosophique ou de théorie rhétorique qu'il atteint à cette signification et si cela induit quelque conséquence pour la construction du discours de la pratique judiciaire ou politique.

Platon avait montré comment le juge devait distinguer le dommage de la faute. Un procès devait aboutir à ce que les atteintes matérielles fussent intégralement réparées[9] et à ce que, dans le cas de violences corporelles dont les conséquences étaient moins faciles à évaluer le tribunal fixât une compensation qui parût juste[10]. Néanmoins, le dommage pouvant n'être pas le résultat d'une volonté mauvaise, si le législateur de la cité idéale devait imposer au juge d'apprécier le dommage subi par la victime indépendamment de toute autre considération, les lois «les plus belles»[11] lui enjoignaient d'apprécier quel était le degré d'injustice ayant fait agir le coupable d'une faute ou d'une simple erreur[12].

Aristote, de même, signifia nettement que le dommage infligé n'était pas la seule composante de l'acte délictuel ou criminel. Pour lui, le système judiciaire devait prendre en compte l'événement de façon globale dès qu'il en était saisi. Se présenter comme une victime impliquait, en effet, qu'on ait été lésé par quelqu'un qui l'avait fait de façon volontaire, le débat sur le dommage devant nécessairement se prolonger par un examen des modalités de l'acte dénoncé[13]. De façon symétrique,

---

[3] 1374a13, les références à la *Rhétorique* seront données ici sous cette forme simplifiée.
[4] 1382a35.
[5] Nous reviendrons sur ce problème.
[6] Voir le commentaire à l'*Éthique à Nicomaque* de R. Gautier et J.-Y. Jolif, p. 190.
[7] J.-B. Gourinat, «Délibération et choix dans l'éthique aristotélicienne» dans *L'excellence de la vie, sur l'*Éthique à Nicomaque *et l'*Éthique à Eudème *d'Aristote*, éd. G. Romeyer Dherbey et G. Aubry, Paris, 2002, p. 95-123.
[8] P. Aubenque, *La prudence chez Aristote*, Paris, 1963.
[9] Platon, *Lois* 933e.
[10] *Lois* 877b, l'enquête sur ce point est difficile, voir *Lois* 875e.
[11] *Lois* 862c.
[12] *Lois* 933e-934c, analysé de façon détaillée par T.J. Saunders, *Plato's penal code*, Oxford, 1991, p. 280-300.
[13] 1373b27.

commettre une injustice était infliger un dommage à quelqu'un en contrevenant volontairement aux prescriptions de la loi[14].

En parfait accord avec la pratique des Athéniens qui avaient souvent recours à la désignation fourre-tout d'une procédure pour dommage pour activer le processus répressif même quand l'évidence d'une volonté maligne n'apparaissait pas clairement[15], la *Rhétorique* montre comment la victime doit démontrer que le dommage subi résulte bien d'une faute de telle sorte que le responsable soit puni en tant que coupable d'avoir causé un dommage sciemment ou par l'effet d'une négligence inadmissible. Le défendeur doit, pour sa part, nier toute volonté maligne même s'il reconnaît la matérialité des faits et accepte de réparer les torts dont il admet qu'il les a causés, le tarif de la condamnation étant différent selon le degré de la responsabilité reconnue à son encontre[16].

Au cours des diverses étapes de la procédure, le défendeur peut essayer de démontrer que ce qu'il a fait est le produit d'une erreur, d'une malchance ou a été causé par une nécessité irrépressible[17]. L'accusateur, à l'inverse, présume le mauvais vouloir de la partie adverse car il veut, pour obtenir vengeance, que celui qu'il accuse d'avoir commis volontairement un crime subisse la colère du tribunal et soit puni[18]. Il peut lui suffire de montrer quel trait de caractère peut expliquer que l'accusé ait cédé à l'un de ses désirs pour se mal conduire[19]. Les raisons de faire du tort à quelqu'un sont, en effet, multiples. On est en droit d'imaginer que l'on peut avoir voulu s'en prendre à ses amis parce que c'est facile mais aussi à ses ennemis parce que c'est agréable[20]. Tel pourrait s'être laissé aller à la faute parce que, sa réputation étant excellente, nul ne le soupçonnerait jamais, tel autre, au contraire, parce qu'aucun nouveau crime ne changerait rien à l'idée que la société se fait de lui[21]. Le riche volerait par désir du superflu, le pauvre pour acquérir le nécessaire[22]. Le passage à l'acte serait facilité, sinon causé, par le sentiment que l'on pourrait avoir de ce que le crime resterait ignoré ou impuni[23], ou que, du moins, le châtiment serait moindre que le bénéfice escompté[24]. On peut imaginer, à l'inverse, que le fait

---

14 1368b6.

15 S. Todd, *The shape of Athenian law*, Oxford, 1993, p. 279-282.

16 Le droit athénien qui reste à l'horizon du traité avait établi que l'accusé convaincu devait payer au plaignant double indemnité si sa volonté coupable était établie mais que le plaignant recevait compensation au simple prorata du dommage si ce n'était pas le cas, Démosthène, *Contre Midias*, 43. Sur les fautes involontaires qui pouvaient être considérées avec une certaine indulgence, Antiphon, *Sur le meurtre d'Hérode*, 92.

17 1416a4.

18 Démosthène, *Sur la couronne*, 274.

19 1372a4 et suivantes.

20 1373a5.

21 1372b22.

22 1372b19.

23 1372b17.

24 1372a8.

d'agir ouvertement permettrait de n'être pas reconnu, nul ne pouvant penser que telle façon de faire est envisageable[25]. L'accusation pense être à même de démontrer qu'il n'est personne qui ne puisse faire ce qu'il veut quand il en a le pouvoir, si rien n'y met obstacle. Il suffit donc de démontrer que l'accusé a pu vouloir faire le mal et que rien n'est venu à la traverse de son désir[26]. Le discours peut jouer sur les deux versants de la personnalité de l'adversaire en lui reprochant sa capacité à raisonner en fonction de ses intérêts ou bien en stigmatisant son trop de facilité à se laisser aller à ses passions[27]. L'essentiel est de traiter de l'idée qu'il n'est pas de crime ou de délit qui ne soit l'expression d'un désir de transgresser les règles du droit et de la morale. La rhétorique peut insister sur les circonstances qui rendent cette transgression particulièrement condamnable[28], l'orateur revenant de façon récurrente à l'idée qu'une faute est d'autant plus grande qu'elle résulte d'une injustice plus grande[29].

Le juge est en tiers, il doit connaître des faits tels qu'ils lui sont présentés et leur donner sens. Il est seul habilité à mener cette analyse. Que le législateur se soit prononcé ou non, il ne doit pas s'en tenir à ce que les plaideurs peuvent en dire, si sa décision est connaître personnellement le droit et savoir fonder en lui sa décision[30]. Il doit trancher du mieux possible même s'il le fait nécessairement dans l'urgence et si les sentiments qu'il éprouve à l'audience peuvent influencer la décision qu'il prend[31]. Toute l'habileté du rhéteur est, en effet, de faire croire au tribunal qu'il va se prononcer en toute justice alors que tout son discours tend à le séduire, voire à le tromper[32].

Il faut, tout d'abord et de façon essentielle, que le tribunal examine si les actes incriminés ont été accomplis à contre-gré ou de bon-gré[33]. Cette distinction est essentielle, en effet, à la naissance du droit moderne puisque la loi de Dracon impose

---

25 1372a22.

26 1392a22.

27 1369a17.

28 1374b24-1375a20.

29 1374b24-26.

30 Il serait bon que le nomothète ait tout défini de façon précise mais cela est impossible, il existe nécessairement des lacunes ou des imprécisions dans le corpus législatif, 1374a20.

31 1354b1.

32 1354b31. Tout plaideur sait que le juge doit se prononcer en fonction de son intime conviction sans avoir, sauf dans la Magnésie platonicienne, à rendre des comptes, *Lois* 761e.

33 On lira sans trop d'illusion sur la pertinence de la doctrine énoncée, la dissertation de G.A. Rickert, Ekôn *et* Akön *in early geek thpought*, Harvard, 1985, voir, dans *Articles on Aristotle. 2. Ethics and politics* éd. J. Barnes et *alii*, D.J. Furley, «Aristotle on the voluntary» p. 47-60.

des modes de traitement différents des parties concernées par un homicide, en considérant les modalités de sa commission[34].

La *Rhétorique* sait qu'il faut distinguer la faute du crime. Dans la catégorie des fautes, il faut connaître ce qui relève de l'erreur, ce qui provient de la malchance et non de la méchanceté, quelles fautes ne sont pas le produit d'erreurs d'appréciation et ne procèdent pas du vice, lesquelles ne sont pas des erreurs mais sont l'effet d'une mauvaise nature[35]. Dans l'*Éthique à Nicomaque*, l'analyse est plus fouillée. Il y est admis qu'il existe trois modalités de la commission involontaire d'un dommage, l'ignorance, le mauvais calcul, la malchance. Dès que l'on sait ce que l'on est en train de faire, on est à même de se voir reprocher une injustice[36].

Aristote considère, en effet, que l'acte volontaire participe d'un savoir[37], l'involontaire se trouvant être défini comme ce qui est produit par l'effet de la violence ou de l'ignorance[38]. Ce qu'il définit comme acte commis en état de nécessité par l'effet d'une violence est restrictif car il ne veut considérer comme tel qu'un acte dont le principe est extérieur à son agent[39]. Il semble que nul ne puisse être exonéré de sa responsabilité au titre d'une violence irrépressible que s'il est mû par une force externe à laquelle il ne peut physiquement résister, qu'il s'agisse de celle d'une tornade qui détourne un bateau de sa destination, ou de celle de maîtres qui tiendraient l'agent en leur pouvoir, encore faudrait-il que son geste ait été contraint et que ses maîtres aient pris sa main pour lui faire porter le coup dont on lui demanderait compte[40]. Il est, donc, impossible d'admettre sans débat que doivent être tenus pour proprement involontaires les crimes que quelqu'un accomplirait pour obéir à un tyran qui retiendrait en otage ses parents et ses enfants, car le principe du mouvement qui l'a fait s'exécuter reste en lui[41]. De telles actions doivent donc être tenues pour mixtes[42]. Il ne faut pas penser que ce type de développement soit purement théorique et déconnecté de la casuistique. Platon, par exemple, traite de ce qu'il est possible pour un soldat de perdre son bouclier parce qu'il est pris dans un flot auquel il ne peut résister, et il démontre qu'il devrait être acquitté s'il était

34 Ce texte propose ainsi les éléments d'une véritable casuistique, s'il est bien vrai qu'il faille admettre qu'il traite différemment les meurtres sans préméditation, le meurtrier involontaire, les instigateurs d'un meurtre, l'exécutant, ou celui qui tue en état de légitime défense. E. Carawan, *Rhetoric and the law of Dracon*, Oxford, 1998, p. 38 et suivantes, met le texte en rapport avec *EE* 1226b30-1227a2.

35 1374b5- 9.

36 *EN* 1135b, 11-25.

37 1373b33.

38 *EN*, 1109b38-1110a, 1135α 25.

39 *EN* 1110a1.

40 *EN* 1135a27.

41 *EN* 110a16.

42 *EN* 111a11.

accusé de lâcheté[43]. Quant à la discussion sur la possibilité de choisir entre la mort et l'obéissance à un tyran criminel, elle fait le fond du discours *Contre Ératosthène* de Lysias qui, s'il récuse à son adversaire le droit de prétendre avoir agi sous la contrainte, admet néanmoins que l'on puisse envisager de pardonner à tout autre personne qui se serait trouvée dans ce type de situation sans l'avoir souhaité[44].

L'excuse absolutoire de la force majeure étant difficile à faire prévaloir en cette forme absolue, Aristote donne une large place à ce qu'il entend par ignorance, celle-ci pouvant, au même titre que la violence externe, donner à un acte le statut juridique d'acte involontaire[45]. Pour être absolutoire, elle ne peut porter que sur une erreur commise sur les moyens mis en œuvre de telle sorte que l'action ait abouti à un résultat différent de ce qu'il était raisonnable de prévoir en fonction des fins recherchées[46]. C'est alors le hasard qui frappe et non celui qui n'en est plus que le jouet et l'instrument[47]. Les exemples retenus par le philosophe appartiennent au domaine de ce que nul n'a les moyens de contrôler, celui du lapsus, celui de l'erreur qui fait prendre pour une arme d'exercice l'arme tranchante ou la potion mortifère pour un médicament[48]. Plusieurs cas de ce type sont connus par la littérature. Antiphon a traité du cas d'une belle-mère prétendant n'avoir empoisonné quelqu'un que pour avoir voulu le ramener à elle en lui administrant un philtre d'amour, de celui du chorège accusé d'avoir tué un choreute dont il voulait soigner la gorge en lui donnant à boire une potion[49]. Un autre des exemples proposés par. le philosophe renvoie de semblable façon à Antiphon[50] qui traite de façon contradictoire du fait d'avoir lancé un javelot lors d'un exercice et d'avoir tué quelqu'un[51]. L'essentiel est, pour lui, de faire comprendre qu'il ne faut pas, pour que le crime puisse être considéré comme involontaire, que l'on ait été soi-même cause de sa propre

43 Platon, *Lois* 944, J.-M. Bertrand, «Les lois sur la discipline militaire dans la cité platonicienne», *Quaderni*, Universita degli studi di Torino, 14, 2001, p. 9-27.

44 Lysias, *Contre Ératosthène*, 26-34.

45 *EN* 1109b38-1140a2, voir Pseudo-Aristote, *Rhétorique à Alexandre*, 1427a.

46 *EN* 1111a17

47 Antiphon, *Sur le meurtre d'Hérode*, 92, 2

48 Repris dans la *Grande morale* 1, 16, 2.

49 Antiphon, *Pour le choreute*. Le chorège se défend en prétendant n'avoir pas été présent lorsque le jeune homme a absorbé la potion, ce moyen de refuser toute responsabilité en l'affaire alors qu'on ne peut pas ne pas envisager l'éventuelle transmission d'un ordre à un subordonné peut paraître insuffisant mais il est sans doute plus commode de l'employer que de faire appel à la législation ou à la jurisprudence sur le meurtre non intentionnel (voir M. Gagarin, éd. Antiphon. *The Speeches*, Cambridge, 1997, p. 223). Seuls les médecins sont automatiquement exonérés de toute faute en cas de mort de leur patient par l'effet de leurs remèdes, la loi d'Athènes ne les poursuivant pas, Antiphon, *Tétralogie III*, 3, 5, aucune action, dans la Magnésie platonicienne, ne pouvant être intentée contre eux de ce chef, Platon, *Lois*, 865b.

50 Antiphon, *Tétralogie II*.

51 *EN* 1135b16.

ignorance[52]. Le juge doit punir ceux qui seraient par faute ou négligence cause de leur état de non-savoir[53]. Le buveur est, ainsi, par exemple, responsable de l'état d'inconscience dans lequel il s'est trouvé et qui lui a fait commettre tel ou tel crime ou délit car l'origine de l'acte en lui puisqu'il lui aurait été possible de ne pas boire jusqu'à l'ivresse[54]. De méme nul ne serait censé ignorer la loi[55] la pratique le sachant aussi[56]. Le Pseudo-Aristote va, pour sa part, jusqu'à dénoncer la bêtise de tel ou tel malfaisant comme essentiellement coupable[57]. Tout citoyen étant ainsi sommé de rendre compte de sa vigilance à vivre selon la norme sociale et politique, user d'une excuse fondée sur l'ignorance telle que la définit la théorie n'est pas fréquent chez les orateurs, Midias semble ne pas l'avoir fait pour s'excuser d'avoir frappé un thesmothète, il aurait eu, pourtant, trois éléments d'appréciation de son ignorance à invoquer, l'ignorance de l'ivresse, l'ardeur amoureuse et l'obscurité de la nuit[58]. Hypéride récuse tout recours à l'excuse d'ignorance et d'incompétence dès qu'il s'agit du cas d'un magistrat[59].

Outre la malchance et l'ignorance, la troisième cause d'un délit ou d'un crime dont on puisse envisager d'excuser la commission est le désir impétueux qui peut entraîner les gens à la faute sans que l'on doive qualifier leur acte d'involontaire[60]. La *Rhétorique* le sait parfaitement pour qui nombre de fautes sont commises par des personnes qui agissent en connaissance de cause mais le font sous l'empire de la passion[61]. *L'Éthique à Nicomaque* insiste sur le fait que si la faute est causée par ce type d'entraînement, on peut ne pas considérer que le coupable est injuste et vicieux[62], mais qu'il l'est, en revanche, lorsqu'elle a été commise *ek proaireseôs*[63].

---

[52] *EN* 1113b, 24.

[53] *EN* 1114a2.

[54] *EN* 1113b30. La *Grande Morale*, 1, 33, 25, reprend la formule de façon plus simple, «il lui était loisible de ne pas boire autant». Voir notre note, «La rhétorique de l'ivresse en Grèce ancienne», dans *The ways of life in classical political philosophy* (Studies in ancient philosophy, 5), éd. F. Lisi, Sankt Augustin, 2004, p. 33-41.

[55] *EN* 1113b35.

[56] Démosthène, *Contre Theocrinès*, 24,

[57] *Rhétorique à Alexandre*1426b31. Aristote va plus loin, encore, en dénonçant le mauvais orateur d'être coupable d'insuffisance rhétorique et considère qu'il est juste qu'il soit condamné, 1355a19sqq.

[58] Démosthène, *Contre Midias*, 38, 4

[59] Hypéride, *Contre Démosthène*, 6, 26, 2, Andocide, *Contre Alcibiade*, 19, 4

[60] *EN* 1111a24.

[61] 1373b36, par *pathos*, le texte de la *Rhétorique* entend surtout la colère qui est une faute car elle est un désir déraisonnable, 1369a4. Cette conception n'est pas étrangère à la loi athénienne car le nomothète n'y aurait pas prévu que le tribunal pût pardonner les manifestations de colère, Lysias, *Contre Théomnestos I*, 30, 5, *II*, 11, 2.

[62] Voir S. Vernières, «Akrasie et savoir pratique» dans *L'excellence de la vie*, *cit.* note 7, p. 253-268.

[63] *EN* 1135b11-25

Il semble bien, donc, que la mise en évidence de la *proairesis* d'un fautif est un élément essentiel dont le tribunal doit absolument tenir compte pour juger de la qualité d'un accusé dont la faute est avérée. Il serait hors de notre propos de vouloir décrire de façon complète quels sont les mécanismes mis en œuvre dans l'action humaine pour la philosophie aristotélicienne, le crime et l'exploit pouvant se révéler comparables sur ce point[64], car le mot, tel qu'il est employé dans le passage de la *Rhétorique* dont le commentaire nous occupe, peut être analysé pour lui-même.

Dans les textes de la pratique certains emplois d'aspect formulaire, comme *ek proaireseôs, kata proairesin*, semblent participer d'une certaine forme de langage technique et semblent qualifier des actes sciemment commis[65]. Néanmoins, l'usage du mot est parfois plus large quand il sert à évoquer la façon dont l'accusé mène sa vie[66].

La *proairesis* participe de la capacité réflexive[67], la pensée étant, dans l'action, associée au désir[68]. Les actes, volontaires ou involontaires, peuvent, ainsi, être évalués en fonction du désir qui les a suscités, de la *proairesis* qui a accepté de répondre à cet appel, de la pensée qui a fait appel aux moyens nécessaires à ce qu'ils fussent accomplis[69]. Le concept dépasse, ainsi, très largement le domaine intellectuel et participe de celui de la morale[70]. Tout orateur judiciaire, accusateur ou défendeur, doit conduire sa narration de telle sorte qu'elle soit «éthique»[71], ce qui signifie, pour Aristote, qu'il doit traiter essentiellement de ce qu'est la *proairesis* des parties en présence. Il doit parler non seulement des faits eux-mêmes dont on suppose que la matérialité a été établie lors de l'enquête préalable mais surtout montrer ce qu'est leur relation à la pratique ordinaire, *êthos*, de chacune des parties. C'est par ce biais que le tribunal peut être mis à même de juger de ce qu'est ou a été, dans le cadre de

[64] Il n'est pas de notre compétence de mener une analyse pertinente des problèmes posés par l'étude de la responsabilité telle que la conçoit Aristote, ni du concept plus large que C. Natali appelle «l'agentivité» dans un article «Actions humaines, événements naturels et la notion de responsabilité chez Aristote», *La querelle des normes, Cahiers de philosophie politique et juridique*, 27, Caen, 1995 (éd. J.-L. Petit) p. 193-213. J.-L. Petit a assuré la traduction du texte et assume donc, pour sa part qui le néologisme, les anglophones utilisant le terme d'*agency* (voir, par exemple, M. White, *Agency and integrality. Philosophical themes in the ancient discussions of determinism and responsability*, Dordrecht, 1985). La bibliographie récente du sujet est immense mais il n'est pas inutile de continuer à lire l'intéressante thèse de E. Kullmann, *Beiträge zum aristotelischen Begriff der «Prohairesis»*, Bâle, 1943.

[65] Démosthène, *Contre Léocharès, 57*. Lycurgue, *Contre Léocrate*, 38, 148.

[66] Eschine, *Contre Timarque*, 74.

[67] *EN*, 1112a20.

[68] *EE* 1225b 21.

[69] *EE* 1223a25.

[70] *EN*, 1139a34.

[71] 1417a17sqq. Kennedy traduit «indicative of character» qui est plutôt une glose.

sa saisine, la *proairesis* de ceux qui sont devant lui, car l'une et l'autre sont commensurables[72].

Si l'on reste, ainsi, dans le domaine de la morale, on peut distinguer les fins bonnes ou mauvaises et les moyens mis en œuvre pour les atteindre qu'ils soient légitimes ou inadmissibles. Une fin dont le sujet envisage la réalisation est affaire de souhait, la *proairesis* est affaire de moyens[73]. Le souhait peut porter sur des objectifs impossibles, la *proairesis*, faculté de délibération sur ce qui appartient à la sphère des possibles[74], ne concerne que ce qui dépend de chacun[75]. Elle est un désir impliquant délibération sur ce que le sujet sait pouvoir envisager de faire[76]. La délibération et l'action sont du ressort de chacun[77]. L'homme convenable choisit ce qui est véritablement bon, alors que nombre d'autres préfèrent aller à l'agréable qu'ils tiennent pour le bien. Sa vertu est de résister aux diverses formes de ses désirs. Il lui est toujours possible d'agir ou de ne pas le faire[78] et de montrer dans l'action ou l'abstention sa valeur[79]. Cela relativise, par un nouveau biais, la notion de force majeure car si certains peuvent s'imaginer avoir été contraints de commettre des indélicatesses, le philosophe et le plaideur savent que cela n'est vrai que pour celui qui ne possède pas en lui la force nécessaire pour mener à bien projet ou résister à des pulsions qui en rendraient fautif ou criminel la réalisation[80]. Dans le domaine intellectuel, par exemple, rhétorique et dialectique ne se distinguent que par la façon dont les pratiquants se situent, par l'effet de leur *proairesis*, au regard de leur compétence. Si tel ou tel peut choisir la sophistique et utiliser de façon fallacieuse la syllogistique, l'orateur dialecticien exerce son art de façon tout aussi efficace mais en honnête savant[81].

---

72 1417a20-25.

73 *EN* 1111b26, voir les commentaires de J. Tricot, *ad loc.*

74 *EE* 1226b17.

75 *EN* 1111b-1113a.

76 *EE* 1226b17.

77 *EN* 1226b33.

78 *EN* 1225b36.

79 *EN* 1113b8.

80 *EE* 1228a16.

81 1355b18-21. La rhétorique a pour fonction de persuader et elle est, en cela, utile est nécessaire, tout comme la médecine. Elle travaille sur les probabilités et le persuasif mais peut se contenter de ce qui n'en a que l'apparence tandis que la dialectique a pour objet la connaissance du système logique par la pratique raisonnée du syllogisme. La rhétorique a des rapports avec la dialectique mais aussi avec la sophistique, (1359b9-12), dont elle est parfois amenée à utiliser les méthodes (1419a14). Si la dialectique est forte de la compétence de celui qui l'exerce de façon savante, et que sa puissance se manifeste nécessairement dans le domaine qui est le sien, le rhéteur peut choisir de s'en servir pour la réussite d'un projet et il lui est possible de le faire de telle façon qu'il en pervertisse l'usage. On reconnaît le dialecticien à la puissance de sa compétence, on le reconnaît pour sophiste quand il la met au service d'une argumentation purement éristique par choix, *têi proairesei*.

Dans la vie courante, il semble que personne n'ait à délibérer sur ce que doive être la finalité de son activité sociale car elle est définie par sa position personnelle et professionnelle, le médecin sait qu'il doit guérir ses patients, l'orateur qu'il doit persuader, l'homme politique qu'il lui faut établir de bonnes lois. Il n'est personne qui ne soit dans la situation de ne pas considérer comme établi le projet de son existence, le sujet n'a pas autre chose à faire que de choisir quels moyens lui permettent de remplir la tache qui lui est impartie[82]. C'est à ce niveau que le juge peut être amené à intervenir. Il n'a pas à juger des fins poursuivies par les parties. Il sait que tout individu prétend remplir son rôle social, veut aussi être libre, aussi puissant et aussi prospère que possible. Il n'a pas à prendre position sur cette ambition mais doit faire savoir si les moyens mis en œuvre pour la remplir sont légitimes. L'escroquerie, le vol, la captation d'héritage ne sont pas des instruments d'enrichissement admissibles, ni la violence, l'assassinat des moyens convenables pour se venger d'un ennemi personnel, la dénonciation calomnieuse n'est pas non plus légitime quand il s'agit de se débarrasser d'un concurrent ou d'un gêneur. Le tribunal devant juger des seuls faits qui lui sont soumis[83], il lui est impossible de connaître de ce qu'est le projet des prévenus, mais, dans la mesure où la *proairesis* ne concerne pas le projet lui-même mais le choix des moyens, prononcer un jugement revient à la qualifier. Si l'appréciation se révèle avoir des liens étroits avec le jugement moral, il ne faut pas perdre de vue que le résultat obtenu doit être examiné objectivement plutôt que l'énergie employée et admettre que l'éthique ne régit pas le droit dans la mesure où le tribunal ne doit connaître que de la seule morale instituée par la loi positive. Aristote insiste sur le fait que la loi est un contrat garantissant la qualité des rapports interpersonnels mais non l'excellence individuelle, la cité aristocratique étant la seule à pouvoir, par un système qui lui est exclusif, faire se confondre l'éducation au métier de citoyen et l'éducation à la vertu[84]. Il suffit donc que citoyen convenable pratique l'excellence de son statut et de sa fonction[85], le tribunal siégeant en tant qu'institution politique et non en instance morale[86].

L'excellence, *aretê,* fait que celui qui en est doté ne peut se tromper dans le choix de ses fins[87] mais cela ne signifie pas que les moyens pour les atteindre soient prédéfinis. Si les *proaireseis* sont les choix que l'on fait en vue de les réaliser, elles sont en fait à l'origine même de l'excellence comme s'il existait une dialectique telle que c'est par l'action et les choix quotidiens que se construit l'*aretê*[88]. Le juge doit

[82] *EN* 1112b15.

[83] *EE* 1228a15.

[84] *EN* 1130b22.

[85] *Politique* 1276b34-1277a12, 1280a26-1280b10.

[86] P. Aubenque, «Politique et éthique chez Aristote», *Ktèma*, 5, 1980, p. 211-221 (p. 215-217, à propos de *EN* 1094a27sqq.).

[87] *EE* 1227b11-1228a1.

[88] *EN* 1111b7.

juger de la *proairesis* de ceux qui sont devant lui d'après la présentation qu'ils font l'un et l'autre de l'affaire, tout en considérant que leur valeur se manifeste par leur capacité à faire les bons choix[89]. Chaque orateur, donc, se doit, comme le sait bien le Pseudo-Aristote d'examiner ce qu'ont été les discours, les actions de son adversaire et ses choix dans la vie pour expliquer au juge, s'ils se révèlent êtres contradictoires dans leur logique et leur finalité, qu'il est susceptible d'écarts de conduite ou de pensée[90].

Il semble que l'on ait voulu considérer l'homme, accusateur ou accusé, comme une unité dont la cohérence dans le cours de sa vie devait être présumée. On admettait, en général, au moins implicitement, qu'il n'était pas ordinaire à un homme sage de se rendre coupable de délits qualifiés ou de crimes, de commettre l'adultère, donner des coups, jeter son bouclier, sinon par l'effet de l'imprévisible[91]. Cela correspond à une des idées essentielles de la rhétorique qui fonctionne sur les vraisemblances. Les orateurs le savent. Démosthène utilise ce genre d'argument dans le *Contre Euboulidês*, quand il évoque ceux qui ont fait le choix de vivre en travaillant[92], dans le *Contre Aristocrate* il reproche à ses adversaires d'avoir choisi de vivre d'orgueil[93]. Il existe, dit-il des vies que l'on construit par choix[94], la formule *proairesis tou biou* étant utilisée dans le discours *Contre Olympiodôros*[95]. Isocrate pour sa part prétend vouloir convaincre de ce qu'il n'avait jamais été, par choix, chicanier durant sa vie[96]. Le but de l'accusateur est de démontrer que son adversaire est un délinquant d'habitude, que ses amis ne valent pas mieux, le défendeur devant, évidemment démontrer le contraire[97].

Si l'accusateur présente la faute qu'il dénonce comme incontestable, toute personne qu'il accuse comme criminelle. Le défenseur, s'il lui arrive de devoir reconnaître la matérialité des faits et ne pas nier une certaine forme de responsabilité dans l'événement qu'on lui reproche, peut plaider l'ignorance excusable ou le malheureux

89 *EN* 1106a36.

90 *Rhétorique à Alexandre*, édition CUF par P. Chiron, p. XVI, voir l'index *s. v.* et surtout note 55 p. 9, celui-ci définit la *proairesis* comme une «option» sans que l'on sache très bien ce qu'il entend par ce mot qu'il qualifie de «délicat» «le mot désigne sans doute plus qu'une intention, purement intérieure, un choix de principe (par exemple, dans le domaine délibératif, la sympathie pour tel ou tel État, la préférence pour tel ou tel régime politique) qui se manifeste ensuite dans l'action». Le passage que nous évoquons est 1427b11sqq., voir aussi 1434a où l'on entre de façon plus évidente dans le domaine judiciaire.

91 *EN* 1137a18

92 Démosthène, *Contre Eubulidès*, 36.

93 Démosthène, *Contre Aristocrate*, 127.

94 Démosthène, *Contre Aristocrate*, 141.

95 Démosthène, *Contre Olympiodoros*, 56.

96 Isocrate, *Sur l'échange*, 4, 2.

97 Pseudo Aristote, *Rhétorique à Alexandre*, 1428a.

hasard. Le signe qui est censé pouvoir démontrer le caractère involontaire de ce qu'il a commis est qu'il en a éprouvé immédiatement remords et chagrin.

Devant le tribunal, le remords et le regret semblent avoir pu être acceptés comme des preuves du caractère involontaire de l'acte dénoncé comme faute. Pour le juge devrait être considérée comme ayant été non-volontaire l'action dont l'auteur regretterait de l'avoir commise ainsi que les conséquences. La théorie rhétorique, se fondant sur cette pratique, fait une place importante à cette argumentation quelque peu paradoxale car l'événement n'est plus jugé en fonction de ce qu'il a été ni de la façon dont il a été réalisé mais en fonction aussi des réactions de son auteur, l'analyse passant ainsi de la réflexion sur les antécédents, qu'elle ait dû porter sur la personnalité de l'agent ou sur ses mobiles éventuels, à celle qui porte sur les moments postérieurs à l'acte. Est réputé fait à contre-gré ce qui cause de la peine et du regret, celui qui ne regrette pas ce qu'il a fait peut ne pas avoir agi de son plein gré mais ne peut être considéré comme ayant agi à contre-gré[98], et cela se prolonge par l'affirmation positive de ce que le fait de ne pas avoir de sentiment de regret témoigne du bon gré. Cette idée n'a rien qui soit particulier à Aristote, puisque, par exemple, l'évidence du regret immédiat est prévue de façon explicite par la loi sur le meurtre de la Magnésie platonicienne qui distingue l'assassinat de l'homicide par colère, en donnant à celui-ci pour caractéristique d'avoir été suivi immédiatement de regret[99]. *L'Éthique à* Nicomaque reprenant ce thème à plusieurs reprises et l'enrichissant de telle sorte que l'on comprend bien que le fautif se révèle, n'a pas su se contrôler dans son incapacité à résister à l'appel de la passion, médiocre au plan moral[100]. La *Rhétorique* précise quelle est la fonction pratique de l'expression de ces remords qui désarme la partie lésée et partant de la cité[101]. L'idée se prolonge d'une façon qui montre que la personne se trouvant dans cette situation perd néanmoins toute dignité en se mettant de fait à la discrétion d'autrui puisqu'il se voit associé métaphoriquement à l'esclave qui n'est puni de façon sévère par son maître que s'il persiste à nier telle ou telle de ses fautes alors que s'il l'avoue son maître le punit sans colère. Quant au concept de remords, il s'enrichit de celui de honte puisque ne pas se désoler de ce que l'on a fait revient à manifester une manque de vergogne condamnable en soi[102].

Les orateurs de la pratique ne semblent pas récuser par principe cette idée. Il ne semble pas qu'ils aient argumenté sur ce qui pourrait passer pour une théorie

---

98 *EN* 1110b18.

99 Platon, *Lois*, 866e, voir 727c.

100 *EN* 1166b24.

101 1380a15.

102 Le terme *épilupos* n'est pas connu des orateurs et le lien que 1383b établit entre vergogne et chagrin de ce que l'on a fait mériterait d'être exploré.

juridique du remords[103]. Ils insistent néanmoins sur la nécessité pour l'accusé de manifester un repentir qui soit véritable et dénoncent ceux qui n'éprouvent pas le dégoût de leur faute ou de leur crime, ce qui veut bien dire que l'expression du remords a pertinence rhétorique. À la rigueur, il paraît possible d'accepter que l'on prenne pitié des faibles qui plaident l'état de nécessité et dont on peut penser que les fautes auraient été involontaires du fait même de leur faiblesse mais non pas de ceux qui auraient été assez forts pour pouvoir se conduire correctement[104]. Quand les discours en appellent au respect du droit, c'est en général pour signifier que l'application de la loi doit prévaloir sur la pitié et le pardon, deux concepts qui forment couple et appartiennent au domaine de la rhétorique d'émotion plus qu'à celui de l'argumentation proprement juridique. Accorder le pardon, sous quelque forme que ce soit, peut être considéré par Platon comme une entorse à la droite justice[105]. L'auteur de la *Rhétorique à Alexandre* prétend pouvoir convaincre de qu'il ne faut pas que le juge décide de façon non conforme à la lettre de la loi qui ne prescrit pas de pardonner[106]. Sa logique répressive lui fait, en effet, refuser d'envisager la possibilité du pardon[107] puisqu'il ne faut pas favoriser ou négliger la faute. Démosthène explique que le criminel ne doit pas imaginer pouvoir échapper au châtiment et conserver le bénéfice de son acte s'il n'est pas pris, espérer le pardon s'il est convaincu[108]. On peut se dire, en tout cas, que nul ne peut obtenir pardon s'il a été reconnu coupable de crimes dont on serait sûr qu'il auraient été commis, *kata proairesin*[109].

Dans la mesure où l'expression du regret et du remords peut suffire à convaincre le juge de ce que tel fait dénoncé n'a pas été commis sous l'action de la *proairesis* dont on accepte ou dont on prétend récuser le caractère moteur est plus complexe que ne le serait celui qu'il entretiendrait avec le volontaire ou le prémédité. Le remords, s'il est sincère, naît de la prise de conscience par le sujet de ce que l'acte dont il regrette qu'il l'ait commis ne correspond pas à l'idée qu'il se fait de lui-même. C'est ainsi toute sa vie antérieure qui se trouve déniée par ce qu'il vient de faire. En revanche, il est des façons d'être qui prédisposent à commettre des crimes

---

103 Sur l'*argumentum ad misericordiam*, dont il doit être admis qu'il ne peut être un aveu de culpabilité, voir D. Konstan «Pity and the law in greek theory and practicve» *Dike* III, 2000, p. 125-145.

104 Lysias, *Contre Philon*, 11. Cela ne va sans doute pas jusqu'à excuser les voleurs à la tire et autres petits malfaiteurs. On retrouve la même logique chez Démosthène, *Contre Midias*, 183, *Sur la couronne triérarchique*, 11.

105 Platon, *Lois*, 757e1.

106 Pseudo Aristote, *Rhétorique à Alexandre*, 19, 1, 7

107 Il faut citer ici, à nouveau, P. Ricœur, *La mémoire, l'histoire, l'oubli*,Paris, 2000, qui dans un épilogue sur le «pardon impossible» montre que «ce que les codes désapprouvent, ce sont les infractions à la loi, mais ce que les tribunaux punissent ce sont des personnes», le pardon permettant de «délier l'agent de son acte».

108 Démosthène, *Sur la Couronne triérarchique*, 15.

109 Lycurgue, *Contre Léocrate*, 148.

et rendent possible le passage à l'acte de telle sorte que l'on se reconnaît en celui-ci même si l'on n'est pas habitué à le commettre. C'est bien ce genre de disposition de l'âme ou du caractère ayant joué un rôle moteur en un moment donné qui constitue ce que les textes de la pratique judiciaire et Aristote, pour sa part, désignent comme la *proairesis*.

On peut s'en rendre compte, a contrario, de la façon dont la *Rhétorique* traite de l'éloge[110]. Comme pour une plaidoirie ou un réquisitoire, l'orateur doit tirer sa matière du récit des actions du sujet, pour mettre en évidence sa valeur éminente. Pour donner son, plein effet au discours, il faut convaincre de ce que chacune des actions de celui que l'on veut faire connaître pour un homme de bien est le résultat d'un choix de vie, *kata proairesin*, et que tout ce qu'il réalise est conforme en général à son programme, *kata proairesin*. Dans le cadre de cette rhétorique spécifique, le mot doit, dès qu'il est mis en rapport avec une action particulière, servir à indiquer qu'elle est conforme à cette façon de mener sa vie, même s'il faut parfois savoir biaiser et persuader que tel événement né de l'accident ou du hasard doit être considéré comme intentionnel. Ce qui vaut pour l'éloge est transposable à l'inverse dans le discours d'accusation, comme dans celui de la défense. Pour cette dernière, la façon dont l'accusé a mené sa vie témoigne de ce que ce qu'on lui reproche ne peut avoir été produit que par l'effet du hasard ou de la malchance. D'une certaine façon, quelles que soient les interrogations sur les modalités réelles de l'action, l'*aretè* comme la *proairesis* de l'agent conditionnent sa capacité à agir droitement dans la mesure où il possède une certaine force de caractère, *egkrateia*.

C'est par ce biais que l'on répond à la question posée par P. Ricœur, les tribunaux savent qu'au-delà des faits ils jugent des personnes. Les orateurs doivent savoir passer, sans sortir de la cause, des faits à leur auteur réel ou supposé. Les discours qui, dans le corpus des textes, se révèlent les plus habiles à passer de l'événement, sur la nature duquel chacun s'accorde, à l'homme à qui il faut que le juge l'impute, me paraît être la *Tétralogie II* d'Antiphon. C'est, paradoxalement, l'un de ceux qui traite le moins, pourtant, de la personnalité des protagonistes. On passe, de façon contrôlée, de l'idée selon laquelle on doit ne traiter pour sa défense que des faits, *ta pragmata*[111], à celle que les faits ont une vérité qui résulte de l'existence d'un acteur puisqu'ils sont commis[112], celui-ci devenant sujet potentiellement agissant quand le verbe d'action passe du passif à l'actif au moment même où le discours de défense dénie toute responsabilité dans le meurtre dont on l'accuse[113].

Pour en rester au passage de la *Rhétorique* qui nous a intéressé, Dufour pour la CUF rend le mot *proairesis* par «intention», Grimaldi propose «*deliberate choice*» (de même que Kennedy) ou «*deliberate purpose*». On ne sait pas très bien de quelle

---

110 1367b, 28.

111 Antiphon, *Tétralogie II*, 2, 1.

112 Antiphon, *Tétralogie II*, 2, 2 et 10; 3, 3; 4, 1 et 3.

113 Antiphon, *Tétralogie II*, 2.

façon, en tout cas, l'un ou l'autre de ces traducteurs distingue l'intention du mobile et s'il est souhaitable de le faire. Nous avons essayé de montrer que la signification du terme en était plus large. Le tribunal se prononce et juge de l'acte en globalisant la réflexion sur la personne. Ce qui frappe, donc, est que l'homme qui choisit de façon raisonnée, s'il n'est pas pris par telle ou telle passion, les actes qu'il commet, doit être responsable de sa forme de vie car c'est sur elle, surtout, qu'on le juge. Sur ce point, il n'y a pas de contradiction dans l'œuvre d'Aristote entre ce qui est du ressort de la rhétorique et ce qui appartient à la réflexion morale. Par ailleurs, si les praticiens du monde judiciaire sont peu soucieux de théorisation sans ce domaine, le développement des plaidoiries ou des réquisitoires répond bien, le plus souvent, à ce qui est proposé au juge comme mode de réflexion par la *Rhétorique*. Si l'on voulait élargir le débat à la rhétorique sumbouleutique, on pourrait montrer, comme le manifeste clairement Démosthène, que la *proairesis* est la politique elle-même d'une cité[114] dont les bons conseillers sont responsable en démocratie[115]. Elle est l'intention du législateur[116], c'est aussi l'esprit des institutions[117]. À l'époque hellénistique, mais les premières attestations en sont bien antérieures, le mot finit par qualifier une politique menée et continuée sciemment par un évergète, parfois souverain. Isocrate savait de quelle importance était la façon de vivre et de travailler des rois ou tyrans qu'il conseillait. Dans le discours des honneurs, à l'époque hellénistique, le choix de tel ou tel personnage de favoriser une cité qui l'en remercie est ainsi désigné[118]. C'est en fonction de cette évolution, je pense qu'il faut comprendre son usage dans la *Rhétorique* d'Aristote.

---

[114] Démosthène, *Sur la Couronne*, 206

[115] Démosthène, *Sur la Couronne*, 192. Eschine est du même sentiment, *Contre Ctésiphon*, 170.

[116] *Politique*, 1271a32.

[117] *Politique*, 1269b13

[118] Isocrate, *Démonicos*, 9, *Timothée*, 1.

STEPHEN C. TODD (MANCHESTER)

A RESPONSE TO JEAN-MARIE BERTRAND

[1] Setting the context

This is the third of a sequence of papers presented by Jean-Marie Bertrand, each expounding different facets of a single chapter of Aristotle's *Rhetoric* (1.13 = 1373b1-1374b23) and its relation to Athenian judicial procedure.[1] The first paper in the sequence (Bertrand 2002) dealt with Aristotle's double use in this chapter of the unusual term *epigramma*:[2] developing an idea put forward but only in passing by Lipsius,[3] Bertrand argued that we should read this not as an abstract term meaning "classification" or "designation," but instead to denote some concrete aspect of pre-trial procedures, and he suggested specifically that it refers to the prosecutor's *enklêma* or indictment. The next paper, with response by Andréas Helmis, was delivered at the previous meeting of the Symposion (Bertrand 2006): rather than covering a specific piece of Aristotelian terminology, this dealt instead with *erôtêsis* (cross-examination of the opposing litigant), and included the suggestion that occasional depictions of *erôtêsis* in our speeches may be a literary (re-)presentation of encounters which had already taken place at pre-trial proceedings such as the *anakrisis*, rather than reflecting the realities of a trial. By contrast, this third paper reverts methodologically to the starting-point of the sequence, in that it focuses on Aristotle's use of a single word (this time *proairesis*: broadly "moral choice"), and its use in philosophical texts as well as in oratory.

The task of the respondent is primarily to deal with the paper as delivered (or at least as pre-circulated), but in this case I have interpreted my responsibilities more broadly, so as to look at the present *proairesis* paper in the context of its predecessors in title. My justification is partly that the three papers together paint a broad picture of Athenian judicial and pre-trial procedure which I find stimulating though not wholly convincing, and I propose to explore some of my reservations in the final part of my response. But, firstly, the three papers together also raise some methodological issues about the language of Aristotle's *Rhetoric*.

---

[1] I understand that further papers in the sequence are planned on *pisteis* (traditionally "proofs") and on *epieikeia* ("equity" or "fairness").

[2] Arist., *Rhet.*, 1.13.9 = 1373b38-a2: ἐπεὶ δ' ὁμολογοῦντες πολλάκις πεπραχέναι ἢ τὸ ἐπίγραμμα οὐχ ὁμολογοῦσιν ἢ περὶ ὃ τὸ ἐπίγραμμα ... ("... since, while frequently acknowledging that they have committed the action, [defendants] refuse to acknowledge either the *epigramma* or else the thing that the *epigramma* is about ...").

[3] See n.5 below.

[2] Methodological issues of language

One of the things I have found most interesting about Bertrand's three papers (particularly the first and third in the sequence, with their close reading of Aristotelian terminology) is the striking unfamiliarity of the language under discussion. This is in part a simple difference of literary genre, in that my own background in Athenian law has approached the subject primarily from the perspective of the Orators rather than through philosophical treatments of justice. But if so, I seem not to be alone in this respect: it is notable that *proairesis* appears nowhere in the indices to either of the standard reference works on Athenian law (those of Lipsius and of Harrison),[4] while *epigramma* gets only one passing reference (in a Lipsius footnote).[5]

There seems to be a tendency for scholars working on Aristotle's *Rhetoric* and those working on Athenian forensic oratory to speak (as it were) a different language, both in the literal sense of using separate terminology but also in the metaphorical sense of non-communication: it is notable for instance that Grimaldi, in an otherwise excellent commentary on the *Rhetoric*, glosses the *epigramma* passage by asserting that the term has a technical legal meaning, but cites neither ancient text nor secondary literature to support this.[6] Against this background, one of the most valuable aspects of Bertrand's approach here is to bring the two languages together and highlight their discrepancies.

Whereas the problem with *epigramma* was the absence of parallels in any author for Aristotle's usage in this text, the word *proairesis* (as has been shown in Bertrand's current paper) recurs repeatedly in Aristotle's ethical treatises,[7] not

---

4 Harrison (1968-71.ii: 266) does have one index entry s.v. *epigrapheis*, but the passage in question deals only with the board of officials whose task was to assess individuals' liability to *eisphora* (1968-71.ii: 36).

5 Lipsius (1905-15: 997) presents one four-word index entry, prioritising the verbal phrase (ἐπιγράφειν or ἐπιγράφεσθαι τίμημα) over the noun (ἐπίγραμμα). The structure of this index entry is matched in the one passage to which it refers (1905-15: 252): here Lipsius' discussion focuses on the use of the verb with *timêma* whether in the active voice (as at Aristoph., *Wealth*, 480) or more commonly the middle (as at Isok. 18.33, 16.41, and elsewhere) to denote the prosecutor's appending of a proposed penalty (*Strafantrag*) to his writ (*Klageschrift*); and he continues with the supplementary point that the noun *epigramma* can on this basis be used as a synonym for the proposed penalty itself (as at Dem. 38.2). The only mention of *epigramma* as it is used in *Rhet.*, 1.13.9 = 1373a1-2 appears in a footnote to this passage (p. 252 n. 37), where Lipsius – like Bertrand, but without further discussion – suggests that it may be a synonym for *enklêma*.

6 Grimaldi (1980: 294): "The title or name given to an offence to classify it and to place it in a certain category as a violation of a specific law, and as subject to a certain court of law and certain penalty, is called τὸ ἐπίγραμμα."

7 My own TLG count finds the noun *proairesis* occurring 21 times in the *Rhetoric* (in each case denoting moral purpose, moral preference, or moral choice), 61 times in the *Nikomakhean Ethics*, 52 times in the *Eudemian Ethics*, 30 times in the *Magna Moralia*,

surprisingly given their focus on issues of moral responsibility. It is frequent also in the Orators, though here the pattern is more complex. Partly this is because the word can be used in other senses also (e.g. to denote personal predilection or public policy or even allegiance to a political faction, as well as the mental element in wrongdoing).[8] But there are in addition some oddities of distribution: *proairesis* as a noun is found nowhere in the forensic work of the five early Orators, where it appears only in the epideictic speeches of Isokrates (five times, plus once in the Letters attributed to him);[9] by contrast, it appears no fewer than forty-seven times in the work of four of the five later Orators (the exception being Deinarkhos), with thirty-eight of these examples being Demosthenic, and twenty-five being found in forensic speeches (obviously with some overlap).[10]

On the basis of the Orators' chronological distribution, it is tempting to suggest that discussion of *proairesis* as an abstract concept represented by a noun might have become fashionable first in the field of ethical philosophy,[11] and have been picked up from there by the Orators: initially by Isokrates, whose philosophical links and/or pretensions are well-attested, and in forensic contexts only from the second half of the fourth century. This hypothesis could account also for the rather mixed picture that one finds in the other probably contemporary rhetorical treatise (the pseudo-Aristotelian *Rhetorika Pros Alexandron*, now generally attributed to Anaximenes), which is regarded as a much more pragmatic (not to say amoral) handbook,[12] and is certainly much less influenced by Aristotelian ethical philosophy: at first sight, Anaximenes' frequency of usage (nine examples of the noun *proairesis* in a single-book treatise) would seem comparable to Aristotle's (twenty-one in three books of the *Rhetoric*) – until one notices that whereas Aristotle's passages nearly all denote a moral choice or preference, several of Anaximenes' refer instead to a private course of action or public policy with no overtones of moral intention.[13]

---

and only 48 times in the rest of the corpus. These figures do not take account of instances of the verb *proaireomai*.

8 As at Aiskh. 1.195 (predilection), Hyp., *Epitaph.*, §3 (public policy) and Dem., *Ep.*, 3.2 ("devote himself to the *proaireseis* of the *dêmos*").

9 The speeches in question are Isok. 1 *To Demonikos* (twice: 374-370 BC); Isok. 15 *Antidosis* (twice: 354-353); and Isok. 12 *Panathenaikos* (once: 342-339); the dramatic date of the *Letter to Timotheos* is 345.

10 It should however be noted that the distribution of the noun even among broadly similar categories of speech can be very uneven: there are for instance 18 examples in the public speeches of Demosthenes (only 2 in the private speeches), but 13 of these occur within the *Crown* speech. The pattern for the cognate verb *proaireomai* (overwhelmingly though not always middle) is broadly similar, but not identical: unlike the noun, for instance, it is found five times in Deinarkhos, and twice in Lysias.

11 The noun is found only 4 times in the corpus of Plato (contrast 34 examples of the verb), which might make him a transitional figure in this respect.

12 See e.g. Cope (1867: 402) on "the much higher moral tone" of Aristotle's *Rhetoric*.

13 E.g. a proposal of public policy (Anaxim. 33.3 = 1439b14), or a line of action or of speech (Anaxim. 1.3 = 1421b21-22, cf. sim. Anaxim. 20.4 = 1434a4 and 20.5 = 1434a9).

[3] Aristotle on juristic principles: some reservations

These observations would seem to raise questions not simply about the generic location of Aristotle's *Rhetoric* – what sort of work is this, and how therefore should we read it as evidence for legal history? – but also about the formation of a technical vocabulary of Athenian law. If we accept Bertrand's previous proposal that *epigramma* in this chapter of the *Rhetoric* is being used to mean *enklêma*, the question arises as to why Aristotle has chosen such an unfamiliar word: the unexpectedness of this usage is particularly striking given that Aristotle does use the (to us more obviously legal) term *enklêma* in the sense of "indictment" on two previous occasions in the *Rhetoric*, one of which occurs only six lines before the notorious *epigramma* (1.13.7 = 1373b33).[14]

One possible explanation, of course, would be that Athenian legal terminology may have been somewhat less technical in practice than is often assumed by modern handbooks. There is generally speaking some merit in explanations of this type, at least in my view, because of a linguistic point that was itself the subject of a famous Roman-law study by Daube (1969: 11-64), who pointed out that the use of what he called "action nouns" is characteristic of a more highly developed technical vocabulary than are phrases based on the corresponding verbs. Against this background, it is notable that modern discussions of Athenian legal procedure tend naturally but perhaps deceptively to use noun-based phrases like *graphê hubreôs* ("public prosecution for *hubris*") to denote ideas which in Greek are usually expressed by phrases with the verb *graphesthai*.[15]

In the case of *enklêma*, however, explanations of this type are less persuasive, precisely because this word is used in the Orators on 135 occasions specifically as a noun. So I am driven to the suggestion that Aristotle may be deliberately distancing himself from standard legal vocabulary, or perhaps even that he simply has a rather fuzzy understanding of Athenian law. There is certainly what looks suspiciously like an elementary legal howler in the *Rhetoric*, in that Aristotle chooses *moikheia* (either "adultery" or "seduction," depending on the view taken of a modern scholarly debate)[16] as one of his examples to illustrate the type of offence that is committed against an individual rather than against the community, despite the implications of its being an offence which seems to have given rise to a *graphê* but not a *dikê* (i.e. a

[14] The other use of *enklêma* with this meaning in the *Rhetoric* is at 1.12.5 = 1372a22. (The word is also used at *Rhet.*, 2.4.17 = 1381b5, but in the sense of "wrongs suffered".)

[15] I have discussed more fully in a previous paper (Todd 2000, at pp. 32-34) the significance of this point in the context of the formation of a technical vocabulary of law at Athens.

[16] For the minority view that *moikheia* was an offence that can be committed by a man only in situations where the woman is married, see D. Cohen (1991: 98-132, esp. at pp. 99-101); the traditional consensus, that she simply had to be a citizen, has been re-stated e.g. by Carey (1995: 407-408) and by Kapparis (1999: 297-298), each with refs. to earlier scholarship.

public prosecution that could be brought by any citizen, rather than a private prosecution that could be initiated only by the victim).[17]

It would be tempting, at least for rhetorical purposes and to stimulate discussion, to take an extreme position here: in other words, to argue that Aristotle's apparent lack of sympathy for the way in which the law of Athens was structured (as evidenced by his classification of *moikheia*) should make us wary of using any statement in the *Rhetoric* as evidence for Athenian thinking about law, unless independent confirmation can be found. But I am by no means sure how far I would want to go here, so I restrict myself to suggesting that although Bertrand has succeeded in showing that we do in the Orators find discussions of the mental element in wrongdoing, the question remains how far we can take Aristotle's interest in mental element as evidence for its being an established juristic principle underlying the structure of the whole of Athenian law.[18]

Obviously mental element does have an embedded status within the law of homicide, where the deliberate killing of a citizen has implications both for procedure and for jurisdiction which would have to be resolved through discussion before the case could come to trial.[19] A similar interest in motivation is implied by the name of the *trauma ek pronoias* procedure (lit. "wounding with intent"), though this perhaps should be regarded as an attenuation of homicide. But homicide could be a special case, since procedurally it is handled in rather unusual ways at Athens.

---

17 Arist., *Rhet.*, 1.13.3 = 1373b23-24 (ὁ μοιχεύων ["one who commits *moikheia*"] alongside ὁ τύπτων ["one who hits"] as offences against the individual, in contradistinction to ὁ μὴ στρατευόμενος ["one who fails to undertake military service"]); the public nature of the *graphê moikheias* is noted here by Grimaldi (1980: 291).

18 My following paragraph is not of course claiming that mental element was an issue that non-homicide courts might not find persuasive, as in the case of Polyeuktos of Kydantidai, who is said to have been acquitted of treason apparently on the basis that he had acted without treasonable intent (Dein. 1.58 [a reference I owe to Edward Harris], with Worthington 1992: 222-223). My point is simply that in the absence of established juristic principles, the issue would have to be argued afresh each time on the basis of e.g. popular views of morality. (Statements such as Lys. 10.31, which claim that the legislator makes no allowance for anger, are purely *ad hoc* – i.e. "my opponent will not be able to point to any statement in the *kakêgoria* law legitimising anger as an excuse" – and do not in my view constitute evidence for the existence of a juristic principle dealing with intent.)

19 I am not wholly unsympathetic to the argument of Carawan (1998) that homicide cases specifically may have seen the development of some quite sophisticated jurisprudence, either by the Basileus at preliminary hearings, or else by the Areiopagos or the ephetic courts who tried the case. It is worth bearing in mind that the Areiopagos at least had permanent membership, and we may presume that it was used to conducting debates in its capacity as a council. So even though we do not to my knowledge have evidence for there being any formal opportunity for debate during the trial of a homicide case, nevertheless the members of the Areiopagos will presumably have been able to chat through any legally interesting case informally and subsequently, to an extent that might have facilitated the development of a common mind among them.

Indeed, it is worth noting that Athenian law used different terminology to denote the preliminary hearings conducted by the Basileus in homicide proceedings on the one hand, and on the other hand those conducted by other officials presiding over other cases: we should therefore pause before assuming that the type of jurisprudence putatively developed through *prodikasiai* in the area of homicide can provide a model for how other officials would handle the *anakrisis*.[20]

As is often the case, one thing that this discussion has illuminated is the extent to which our knowledge of Athenian legal procedure, much of it derived from the Orators, is dominated by the events of the trial itself. To that extent, we need to play close attention to any evidence for the broader context of pre-trial proceedings or the juristic thinking that may underlie them, even if the status of that evidence is itself controversial.

BIBLIOGRAPHY*

Bertrand, J.-M. (2002), "À propos de la 'Rhetorique' d'Aristote (I, 1373b1-1374b23), analyse du processus judiciaire (τὸ ἐπίγραμμα – τὸ ἔγκλημα)," *Dike*, 5: 161-185.

Bertrand, J.-M. (2006), "À propos de la 'Rhetorique' d'Aristote (I, 1373b1-1374b23), analyse du processus judiciaire (ἀνάκρισις – ἐρώτησις)," in H.-A. Rupprecht *et al.*, eds., *Symposion 2003: Vorträge zur griechischen und hellenistischen Rechtsgeschichte*, pp. 191-202. Cologne & Vienna.

Carawan, E.M. (1998), *Rhetoric and the Law of Drakon*. Oxford.

Carey, C. (1995), "Rape and Adultery in Athenian Law," *CQ*, 45.2: 407-17.

Cohen, D. (1991), *Law, Sexuality and Society: the enforcement of morals in classical Athens*. Cambridge.

Cope, E.M. (1867), "On the *Rhetorika pros Alexandron*," in Cope, *An Introduction to Aristotle's Rhetoric*, pp. 401-464. London & Cambridge.

Daube, D. (1969), *Roman Law: linguistic, social and philosophical aspects*. Edinburgh.

Grimaldi, W.M.A. (1980), *Aristotle, Rhetoric 1: a commentary*. New York.

Harrison, A.R.W. (1968-71), *The Law of Athens*. 2 vols. Oxford.

Kapparis, K.A. (1999), *Apollodoros: 'Against Neaira' (Dem. 59)*. Berlin & New York.

Lipsius, J.H. (1905-15), *Das attische Recht und Rechtsverfahren*. 3 vols., Leipzig.

Todd, S.C. (2000), "The Language of Law in Classical Athens," in P.R. Coss, ed., *The Moral World of the Law*, pp. 17-36. Cambridge.

Worthington, I. (1992), *A Historical Commentary on Dinarchus*. Ann Arbor.

[20] I am not aware of any complaints in our speeches about partisan handling of the *anakrisis*, in the way that we do at times get hints that complaints were made about procedural impropriety on the part of an arbitrator (e.g. Meidias' charge against Straton in Dem. 21.83-96, where presumably Meidias had a much clearer – because successful – complaint than Demosthenes lets us hear).

* D. Allen's important discussion of proairesis in S. Goldhill/R.G. Osborne, Rethinking Revolutions through Ancient Greece, pp. 183-217 (Oxford, 2006), came to my notice only after I had received the proofs for the present volume.

ANDRÉAS HELMIS (ATHÈNES)

LA PRIVATION DE SÉPULTURE DANS L'ANTIQUITÉ GRECQUE

Les droits pénaux modernes n'infligent pas de châtiment aux défunts; la mort éteint aussi bien la responsabilité criminelle que la peine[1]. Il n'en était pas de même dans maintes sociétés du passé, dont celle de l'antiquité grecque, qui ne considérait pas que la mort fût une destruction complète de l'être.

L'existence d'une vie après la mort est déjà attestée dans les poèmes homériques. Ulysse, rendant visite au monde souterrain, assiste à une scène, où, Minos, le sceptre d'or à la main, rendait justice aux morts[2]. L'imaginaire poétique transpose dans l'au-delà une image familière du monde des vivants, l'administration de la justice. Il est vrai que n'avons pas ici à faire à des jugements posthumes, étant donné que la tâche du roi consistait à régler les différends qui surgissaient pour la première fois parmi ceux qui peuplaient la maison d'Hadès. Juste après, en revanche, dans le poème, Ulysse décrit les supplices de Tityos, Tantale et Sisyphe, qui, pour avoir, de leur vivant, porté atteinte, d'une manière ou d'une autre, à des divinités, avaient été condamnés à des châtiments atroces après leur mort[3]. On retrouve l'idée d'une punition posthume dans une invocation d'Agamemnon à Zeus, au Soleil, aux Fleuves et à la Terre, divinités qui «sous ce sol, [châtient] les morts parjures à un pacte»[4]. Chez Homère donc l'exécution d'une peine posthume a lieu dans un au-delà imaginé à l'instar du monde des vivants, alors que dans le monde des cités le théâtre d'exécution des châtiments posthumes est transféré sur terre.

De même que la cité souveraine peut administrer la peine de mort pour les crimes qu'elle considère comme particulièrement dangereux, de même elle peut

---

1 Le droit moderne connaît, en revanche, la réhabilitation de la mémoire d'un mort. Une récente loi française, relative à la révision des condamnations pénales, prévoit ainsi la possibilité d'un nouveau procès après la mort du condamné: la cour de révision, en présence des parties civiles et des «curateurs nommés par elle à la mémoire de chacun des morts», peut annuler une condamnation et décharge[r], s'il y a lieu, la mémoire des morts» (loi 89-431 du 23 juin 1989, dite loi Seznec).

2 Homère, *Odyssée*, XI, 568-571.

3 Homère, *Odyssée*, XI, 576-600; sur les supplices de ces trois figures mythiques, ainsi que sur celui, corollaire, de Prométhée, voir E. Cantarella, *Les peines de mort en Grèce et à Rome. Origines et fonctions des supplices capitaux dans l'Antiquité classique*, Paris 2000, p. 28-34; *Ithaque. De la vengeance d'Ulysse à la naissance du droit*, Paris 2003, p. 223-230.

4 Homère, *Iliade*, III, 276-280.

étendre son emprise après la mort du condamné, lui refusant la sépulture[5]. C'est la sanction la plus grave qui puisse être infligée à un citoyen. Priver quelqu'un des honneurs funèbres et de sépulture, c'est le priver de tous ces rituels qui visent à transformer sa disparition en une nouvelle forme d'existence, celle que peut lui conférer le statut de mort[6].

La privation de sépulture frappe tout d'abord ceux qui ont perdu la vie par décision de la cité, à savoir les condamnés à mort. Du temps de Socrate, l'attention de celui qui venait du Pirée à Athènes pouvait être attirée, juste avant d'entrer dans la ville, «au-delà de la partie nord des murs», par la vue des cadavres «jetés par les bourreaux»[7]; ce fossé était donc situé hors de la ville mais tout près, entre la porte du Pirée et les Longs Murs. Un autre témoignage nous amène à l'époque de Plutarque, qui nous apprend que l'endroit où Thémistocle avait fait construire un temple à Artémis Aristoboulè était près de sa maison, à Mélitè, dème au nord-ouest d'Athènes, où «les bourreaux jettent maintenant (νῦν) les corps des condamnés à mort»[8]. Les deux localités sont identifiées par les auteurs modernes; le «maintenant» de Plutarque se référerait à un changement survenu après le Ve siècle, à un moment où on aurait abandonné le vieux *barathron*, et le témoignage de Platon tiendrait déjà compte de cette nouveauté[9]. Cette «nouvelle» localité correspondrait à ce qui dans les sources postérieures au IVe siècle est qualifié d'*orygma*. Danielle Allen avance même une hypothèse séduisante: l'*orygma*, plus récent, est un gouffre artificiel, en l'occurrence entre la porte du Pirée et la partie nord des Longs Murs, dans lequel on jetterait les corps de ceux qu'on voulait expulser en dehors d'Athènes, alors que le *barathron*, attesté jusqu'au Ve siècle, serait un abîme naturel, situé plus loin, au

---

[5] On trouvera un aperçu des principales sources sur la privation de sépulture en Grèce ancienne, dans G. Glotz, *La solidarité de la famille dans le droit criminel en Grèce*, Paris 1904, p. 460-461; cf. aussi, du même auteur, l'article «poena», dans Ch. Daremberg-E. Saglio (éd.), *Dictionnaire des antiquités grecques et romaines*, t. IV/1, p. 531; sur l'importance de l'accomplissement des devoirs funéraires dans l'Égypte hellénistique, voir J. Mélèze-Modrzejewski, «Στέρησις θήκης. A propos du délit religieux dans l'Égypte grecque et romaine», dans: G. Thür (éd.), *Symposion 1993. Vorträge zur griechischen und hellenistischen Rechtsgeschichte*, Köln-Weimar-Wien 1994, p. 201-214.

[6] Sur cette fonction du rituel des funérailles, voir J.-P. Vernant, «Mort grecque, mort à deux faces», dans: J.-P. Vernant, *L'individu, la mort, l'amour. Soi-même et l'autre en Grèce ancienne*, Paris 1989, p. 81.

[7] Platon, *République*, IV, 439e.

[8] Plutarque, *Vie de Thémistocle*, 22.

[9] E. Cantarella, *Les peines de mort* (*op. cit.* [*supra*, n. 3]), p. 91; D. Allen, *The World of Prometheus. The Politics of Punishing in Democratic Athens*, Princeton 2000, p. 222. Il est tout de même étrange que le «maintenant» de Plutarque se réfère à une nouveauté dans la pratique du traitement des corps des condamnés à mort, survenue environ cinq siècles plus tôt.

nord-ouest, vers le Mont Parnès, et accueillerait les corps de ceux qui étaient expulsés en dehors de l'Attique[10].

Nous n'avons pas ici à traiter d'un autre problème, concernant la véritable fonction du *barathron* et de l'*orygma*, à savoir si dans ces endroits on jetait les corps des condamnés déjà mis à mort ou, au contraire, si on les y précipitait, afin de trouver la mort[11]. S'agissant toutefois des modalités de l'exécution capitale, nous devons évoquer l'*apotympanismos*, ce procédé qui consistait à attacher le cou, les mains et les pieds du condamné sur un poteau dressé sur le sol. On sait que A. Keramopoulos a pu reconstituer le procédé grâce à une découverte archéologique au Phalère, près du Pirée: dans une tombe on a retrouvé entassés, sans autre objets, dix-sept squelettes avec des pièces de fer autour du cou, des mains et des pieds[12]. C'étaient manifestement des corps des condamnés, à qui l'*apotympanismos* avait été appliqué. Or, il est intéressant de relever qu'un minimum de soins étaient réservés à ces cadavres, puisqu'ils avaient été inhumés, collectivement et sommairement, certes, mais inhumés, probablement par les soins de l'autorité publique[13].

Mis à part le sort réservé aux corps des condamnés à mort, le droit pénal grec connaît des cas, où la condamnation à la peine capitale est accompagnée d'une mesure prévoyant expressément la privation de sépulture, la sanction humaine s'étendant ainsi au mort; car, comme nous le dit une épigramme de Crinagoras, on ne doit pas dire «que la mort est le terme de l'existence. Il est pour les défunts, tout comme s'ils vivaient, des sources d'épreuves nouvelles»[14]. Ce sont notamment les condamnés pour trahison et sacrilège qui se voient refuser d'être ensevelis. Une loi athénienne, rapportée par Xénophon, prévoit que «si quelqu'un trahit la cité ou dérobe les objets consacrés, et si, après jugement devant le tribunal, il est condamné, il n'est pas enterré en Attique (μὴ ταφῆναι ἐν τῇ Ἀττικῇ) et ses biens sont confisqués». Nous trouvons un lointain écho de cette loi chez Dion Chrysostome, qui évoque la règle de la cité d'Athènes de «ne pas ensevelir les traîtres (μὴ θάπτεσθαι τοὺς προδότας)»; Diodore de Sicile, quant à lui, mentionne «une loi commune (κοινὸς νόμος) chez tous les Grecs», d'après laquelle «les sacrilèges sont jetés sans sépulture (ἀτάφους ῥίπτεσθαι τοὺς ἱεροσύλους)»[15]. On remarquera que dans les témoignages que nous venons de citer la condamnation à la peine capitale

---

[10] D. Allen, *op. cit.* (*supra*, n. 9), p. 222; nous reviendrons plus loin sur l'importance de la délimitation du territoire au-delà duquel doit être expulsé le cadavre indésirable.

[11] D. Allen, *op. cit.* (*supra*, n. 9), p. 218 s.

[12] A. Keramopoulos, L'apotympanismos. *Contribution archéologique à l'histoire du droit pénal et la laographie* [en grec], Athènes 1923; cf. L. Gernet, «Sur l'exécution capitale: à propos d'un ouvrage récent» (1924), repris dans: L. Gernet, *Droit et institutions en Grèce ancienne*, Paris 1982, p. 175-211.

[13] L. Gernet, *op. cit.* (*supra*, n. 12), p. 190.

[14] *Anthologie Palatine*, IX, 81.

[15] Xénophon, *Helléniques*, 1, 7, 22; Dion Chrysostome, *Discours*, 31, 85; Diodore de Sicile, 16, 25, 3.

n'est pas exprimée, elle résulte implicitement de la privation de sépulture qui l'accompagne et l'absorbe.

Une documentation relativement riche atteste l'application de cette sanction dans l'ensemble du monde grec, même si c'est pour Athènes que nous sommes le mieux renseignés. La privation de sépulture est une sanction qui est souvent corollaire de l'exil ou de l'atimie, dont elle prolonge, d'une certaine façon, les effets après la mort. Ainsi, par exemple, on avait interdit à Thémistocle, banni pour trahison, d'être enseveli dans l'Attique; un monument funéraire lui était élevé en Magnésie, en Asie, mais des parents ont transféré ses ossements en Attique où ils les ont enterrés, selon son vœu, à l'insu des Athéniens[16].

Ces transferts d'ossements n'étaient pas inhabituels. En 318 av. J.-C., un autre homme politique athénien, Phocion, avait été condamné à mort pour trahison. Après Socrate, c'est l'exemple le mieux connu d'exécution par la ciguë, ce «suicide légal, par tolérance», d'après l'expression de Louis Gernet. Ne se contentant pas de la seule condamnation capitale, les ennemis de Phocion, selon le témoignage de Plutarque, ont pris la décision «que son corps serait jeté hors des frontières et qu'aucun Athénien n'allumerait un bûcher pour ses funérailles»; aucun de ses amis n'a «osé toucher à son cadavre (οὐδεὶς ἐτόλμησεν ἅψασθαι τοῦ σώματος)»; celui-ci, confié à quelqu'un qui faisait cela avec rémunération, précise Plutarque, avait été transporté au-delà d'Éleusis, où il a été brûlé, avec du feu pris sur le territoire de Mégare. Ce détail, outre qu'il met l'accent sur l'importance de l'absence de contact du corps banni avec la terre attique, permet à Plutarque de faire une digression quasiment dramatique, introduisant le personnage de la femme de Phocion, originaire de Mégare. Comme une nouvelle Antigone, elle se rend sur place avec des servantes, elle fait des libations et y élève un tertre, puis «recueillant les ossements dans son sein, elle les emporte de nuit dans sa maison et les enfouit près de son foyer en disant: «c'est à toi, cher foyer, que je confie ces restes (λείψανα) d'un homme de bien; tu les rendras aux tombeaux de ses ancêtres (πατρῴοις ἠρίοις), quand les Athéniens seront revenus à la raison»[17]. Cette belle histoire de piété conjugale est d'une véracité peut-être douteuse; Plutarque a pu l'inventer de toute pièce, connaissant la réhabilitation de la mémoire de Phocion qui a dû se produire sous Démétrios de Phalère. Elle n'en est pas, pour autant, moins instructive, puisqu'elle fait ressortir, certes d'une manière plus prosaïque que Sophocle, l'acuité du conflit entre le devoir de sépulture et son interdiction.

Nous venons de voir, avec Phocion, l'expatriation du cadavre «au-delà d'Éleusis». Des éléments concernant la détermination de l'étendue que couvre l'interdiction d'inhumation nous sont également fournis par deux textes juridiques. Une fois la démocratie restaurée, après son renversement par les Quatre-Cents, deux

---

[16] Thucydide, *Guerre du Péloponnèse*, 1, 138, 6; cf. I. Koulakiotis, «Le monument funéraire de Thémistocle dans la côte du Pirée» [en grec], *Ναυτική Επιθεώρηση* 531 (sept.-oct. 2001), surtout p. 214.

[17] Plutarque, *Vie de Phocion*, 37.

oligarques, Archeptolémos et Antiphon, avaient été condamnés comme traîtres. Nous pouvons nous faire une idée du verdict par une reconstitution du texte que nous a conservé le pseudo-Plutarque: confiscation des biens, abattis de leurs maisons, atimie, privation de sépulture[18]. Or, l'étendue du territoire sur lequel s'appliquait l'interdiction d'inhumation comprend non seulement l'Attique, mais aussi les territoires sur lesquels Athènes, dans le cadre de la ligue de Délos, exerçait une pleine souveraineté: «il est interdit d'enterrer Archeptolémos et Antiphon à Athènes ou dans une possession d'Athènes». D'une manière analogue, le décret d'Aristotélès (377 av. J.-C.), qui établissait les règles de fonctionnement de la seconde Confédération athénienne, prévoyait à l'encontre de quiconque violerait les clauses du décret la confiscation des biens et l'atimie; si un procès devait avoir lieu, les peines auxquelles il s'exposait étaient le bannissement ou la peine capitale avec privation de sépulture; dans ce cas, les territoires que le condamné se voyait interdire, vivant ou mort, comprenaient non seulement l'Attique mais aussi les terres des cités alliées, dont les noms étaient gravés à la fin du décret[19]. L'étendue de l'interdiction sépulcrale varie ainsi en fonction de l'étendue du rayonnement politique d'Athènes.

Un autre texte législatif, daté du IIIe siècle av. J.-C., concerne la cité de Nisyros. Il s'agit d'une inscription qui contient des dispositions relatives à une interdiction d'inhumation, sans que nous sachions qui était visé par cette mesure, le début du texte faisant défaut; très probablement, il s'agit de mesures prises contre un tyran ou un aspirant à la tyrannie. Dans la partie du texte qui nous est conservée est prévue une amende contre celui qui transgresse l'interdiction; il est en plus obligé de déterrer le cadavre et de détruire la stèle commémorative; en cas de manquement, l'obligation d'exhumation incombe aux archontes, qui étaient également passibles d'une amende, s'élevant au dixième de l'amende du coupable, s'ils s'avéraient négligents; enfin, pour inciter les dénonciateurs, la moitié de l'amende perçue leur était promise[20]. Tout un arsenal pénal était ainsi mis en place, afin d'éviter que repose dans le sol le corps indésirable.

---

[18] Pseudo-Plutarque, *Vie des dix orateurs*, 834 A-B. En ce qui concerne l'atimie, elle frappe les deux coupables ainsi que leurs descendants, «tant légitimes qu'illégitimes (νόθοι)»; sur l'atimie héréditaire, cf. M. Youni, *Formes de peines dans le droit attique: ἄτιμος ἔστω-ἄτιμος τεθνάτω. Contribution à l'étude de l'atimie et la mise hors la loi dans le droit attique*, Thessalonique 1993, p. 88 [en grec]; S. Todd (*The Shape of Athenian Law*, Oxford 1993, p. 178) relève, à juste titre, le paradoxe d'infliger la peine d'atimie aux enfants «illégitimes» des coupables.

[19] *IG* II^2 43, 61-63 (=J. Pouilloux, *Choix d'inscriptions grecques*, Paris 1960, n° 27); nouvelle traduction française dans J.-M. Bertrand, *Inscriptions historiques grecques*, Paris 1992, n° 40.

[20] *Syll.*^{3} III 1220; cf. S.-Th. Stéphanopoulos, *La législation contre la tyrannie en Grèce. Contribution à l'étude des institutions des cités antiques*, Paris 1981 (thèse polyc.), t. II, p. 492-494.

L'interdiction d'ensevelissement peut se décider bien après l'inhumation, si c'est après sa mort et son enterrement que la cité se rend compte qu'un citoyen avait, de son vivant, nui aux intérêts de sa patrie. Le cas est assez fréquent après un changement de régime politique. Les nouveaux maîtres du pouvoir se tournent contre les anciens et s'en prennent à leurs tombes; cette exhumation, qui aurait été normalement considérée comme une violation de sépulture, peut parfois résulter d'un véritable procès contre les morts.

A Athènes, le plus ancien témoignage en la matière remonte à l'époque archaïque et concerne l'histoire bien connue de la mise à mort par l'archonte Mégaclès, membre de la famille des Alcméonides, des complices de Cylon, réfugiés près des autels sur l'Acropole. A en croire Plutarque, c'est bien des années plus tard, que Solon, fort de sa notoriété, «s'est avancé au milieu (εἰς τὸ μέσον)» et a pu persuader «ceux qu'on appelait les sacrilèges» d'être jugés par trois cents parmi les meilleurs citoyens. Les coupables furent condamnés: on a exilé ceux qui étaient encore en vie, alors qu'«on déterra les cadavres de ceux qui étaient morts et on les jeta au delà des frontières». Mise à l'écart, donc, des vivants comme des morts. D'après Thucydide, une nouvelle exhumation avec rejet hors des frontières a dû se produire quelque soixante-quinze ans plus tard[21]. Nous devons donc déduire que les parents de ceux qui avaient été déterrés avaient réussi, entretemps, à rapatrier pour un temps les ossements de leurs proches, comme ce fut le cas avec Thémistocle et Phocion.

Nous connaissons grâce à l'orateur attique Lycurgue un autre cas de procès posthume. Il s'agit de Phrynichos, oligarque, assassiné par les démocrates; après son assassinat, sur proposition de Critias, «le peuple décréta que le mort serait inculpé du chef de trahison (τὸν νεκρὸν κρίνειν προδοσίας) et que, si le crime démontré, il avait néanmoins reçu la sépulture en Attique, ses ossements seraient déterrés et rejetés hors du territoire (τά γε ὀστᾶ αὐτοῦ ἀνορύξαι καὶ ἐξορίσαι ἔξω τῆς 'Αττικῆς)»; ceux qui auraient pris sa défense devraient être mis à mort et privés, à leur tour, de sépulture, étant donné qu'«un secours apporté au traître équivalait à une trahison envers la cité». Un véritable procès était donc mis en place contre le défunt Phrynichos et la procédure à laquelle on a eu recours était celle de l'*eisangélie*, dénonciation publique à l'adresse de l'assemblée du peuple, qui rend une sentence préliminaire et peut, par la suite, se constituer en tribunal. Le mort a été condamné: «on déterra donc les ossements du traître et on les jeta hors de l'Attique (τὰ τοῦ προδότου ὀστᾶ ἀνορύξαντες ἐκ τῆς 'Αττικῆς ἐξόρισαν)». Par ailleurs, la peine capitale avec interdiction d'inhumation était infligée à Alexiclès et Aristarchos qui auraient pris la défense du mort; nonobstant la véracité de cette dernière information,

[21] Plutarque, *Vie de Solon*, 12; Thucydide, *Guerre du Péloponnèse*, 1, 126, 11-12; cf. aussi Aristote, *Constitution d'Athènes*, 1.

on notera l'idée d'une extension de la responsabilité à ceux qui défendent un criminel[22].

Grâce à Lycurgue, le cas de Phrynichos est le seul procès contre un mort dont nous puissions, dans une certaine mesure, suivre le déroulement[23]. D'autres témoignages, beaucoup plus succincts, nous laissent entendre la fréquence du procédé en dehors d'Athènes. D'après une source bien tardive, les Corinthiens avaient «jeté le cadavre de Cypsélos par delà la frontière, sans sépulture; ils ont violé les tombeaux de ses ancêtres et en ont vidé les ossements». Les Syracusains, selon Plutarque, «avaient jeté hors des frontières (ὑπεροριζόμενον) le cadavre de Denys», le tyran. Le même sort était réservé au corps de Nikias, tyran de Cos, qui, d'après la même épigramme funéraire que nous avons citée plus haut, «alors qu'il gisait dans sa tombe, vint mort à la lumière du soleil. Car ses concitoyens soulevèrent les verrous de son tombeau et traînèrent au châtiment le malheureux, qui ne mourut pas sans peine»[24].

Tous les cas de privation de sépulture dont il a été question, à Athènes comme ailleurs, concernent des crimes que nous aurions volontiers qualifié de politiques. Platon, de son côté, dans sa législation idéale pour la cité des Magnètes, réserve ce châtiment aux crimes censés être particulièrement odieux. Parmi ceux-ci, une place à part est accordée au meurtrier de ses proches parents (père, mère, frère, enfants): après être mis à mort, il devra être jeté, nu, à un carrefour déterminé, où convergent trois routes (τρίοδον), situé en dehors du centre de la ville; chaque magistrat est alors invité à jeter sur la tête du cadavre une pierre, pour purifier la cité tout entière; après cette étape de lapidation rituelle, «[les magistrats] le porteront hors des frontières du territoire et le laisseront dehors, sans sépulture»[25]. Le meurtrier d'une personne autre que ses parents est également mis à mort et son cadavre doit être «jeté, sans sépulture, hors du pays de la victime»[26]. De même, l'auteur d'un sacrilège est condamné à la peine capitale et «doit être fait disparaître hors des limites du territoire»[27]. Enfin, en cas de condamnation pour pratiques d'envoûtement et de

[22] Comme le dit un peu plus loin dans le même discours Lycurgue: «prendre la défense de ceux qui ont commis des injustices est une présomption (τεκμήριον) qu'on aurait participé aux actes incriminés» (*Contre Léocrate*, 138); cf. L. Rubinstein, *Litigation and Coopération: Supporting Speakers in the Courts of Classical Athens*, Stuttgart 2000, p. 160-161, qui met en doute la véracité du récit de Lycurgue concernant Alexiclès et Aristarque.

[23] Les procès contre les morts étaient très fréquents dans l'ancien droit français; il est intéressant de lire, sous la plume de Pierre Ayrault, jurisconsulte angevin du XVIe siècle, les principaux arguments pour et contre cette pratique (cf. J. Brégeault, «Procès contre les cadavres dans l'ancien droit», *R.H.D.* 3 [1879], p. 620-622).

[24] Corinthe: Nicolas de Damas (*F.G.H.*, III, fg. 60); Syracuse: Plutarque, *Sur les délais de la vengeance divine* [=*Œuvres morales*], 559 D; Cos: *Anthologie Palatine*, IX, 81.

[25] Platon, *Lois*, IX, 873b.

[26] Platon, *Lois*, IX, 874b.

[27] Platon, *Lois*, IX, 854e.

sorcellerie, l'emprisonnement à vie est prévu, accompagné de la défense d'inhumation, après la mort du condamné[28].

S'agissant du sort réservé au cadavre, nous devons mentionner un cas à part, qu'est celui du corps des suicidés. Pour Athènes, nous apprenons par Éschine que la main qui a commis l'acte meurtrier est enterrée séparément; c'est par cette atteinte à l'intégrité posthume du corps que la cité marque sa désapprobation[29]. Elle la marque aussi, à en croire Plutarque, par une autre pratique, qui consistait à jeter dans le *barathron* les cordes et tuniques des pendus, éliminant ainsi les objets qui avaient été en contact avec un acte maudit[30]. Quant à la législation platonicienne, elle stipule que «les tombes [des suicidés] seront d'abord isolées, sans qu'une seule autre les avoisine, puis placées dans les endroits déserts et sans nom sur les bordures des douze districts; là on les enterrera sans gloire, sans stèles ni noms pour désigner leurs tombes»[31].

Les cadavres des criminels sont ainsi le lieu, où s'inscrit toute une politique pénale de la cité. La mainmise sur la mort du citoyen n'a pas été sans poser des problèmes sérieux de justification. En témoignent notamment certaines pièces de tragédie, *Antigone*, bien entendu, mais aussi *Ajax* ainsi que les *Sept contre Thèbes*, où sont mis en question les fondements de l'interdiction d'inhumation et sont discutés les motifs de sa transgression. Nous trouvons également chez certains auteurs anciens des éléments explicatifs des mesures pénales comme celle de la privation de sépulture. Pour Platon, par exemple, une telle sanction, appliquée en cas de sacrilège, ne vise pas le mort, mais les vivants, à qui cela servira comme «exemple (παράδειγμα)», conception bien chère dans la théorie pénale platonicienne[32]. L'orateur Lycurgue précise qu'«il ne sied pas que la même terre recouvre ceux qui se sont signalés par leur valeur et le plus vil de tous les hommes», alors que dans Eschyle on évoque volontiers «la souillure à l'égard des dieux ancestraux»; le rejet symbolique du corps du malfaiteur est censé épargner la cité d'un danger de pollution[33]. Plutarque, quant à lui, fait valoir l'assouvissement d'un sentiment de vengeance, quand il écrit, se référant certainement à la deuxième expulsion des cadavres des Alcméonides, que «les enfants des enfants des victimes» n'étaient plus encore en vie pour profiter du spectacle[34]. Exemplarité, souillure, vengeance, voici trois modèles interprétatifs, d'ailleurs complémentaires, du châtiment infligé aux cadavres.

---

[28] Platon, *Lois*, IX, 909c.

[29] Éschine, *Contre Ctésiphon*, 244.

[30] Plutarque, *Vie de Thémistocle*, 22.

[31] Platon, *Lois*, IX, 873d.

[32] Platon, *Lois*, IX, 873b.

[33] Lycurgue, *Contre Léocrate*, 89; Eschyle, *Les Sept contre Thèbes*, v. 1017-1018. Sur l'ambiguïté de la notion de souillure en relation avec ce genre des pratiques, cf. R. Parker, *Miasma. Pollution and Purification in Early Greek Religion*, Oxford 1983, p. 46-47.

[34] Plutarque, *Sur les délais de la vengeance divine* [=*Œuvres morales*], 549 A.

Il en est encore un, évoqué d'une manière concise par Dion Chrysostome, qui introduit, nous semble-t-il, une dimension essentielle: on interdisait l'ensevelissement des traîtres, «afin qu'il n'y ait plus dans l'avenir aucun signe (μηδὲν σημεῖον) d'un homme méchant»[35]. Priver un citoyen de sépulture, c'est le rayer de la mémoire publique, lui enlever sa part d'immortalité que lui assurent la tombe et les rites funéraires. La cité grecque impose sur le cadavre du criminel un silence et elle diffère en cela d'autres sociétés, comme celle de la Rome impériale ou de la France de l'Ancien Régime, où l'on cherchait à inscrire sur la mémoire collective les supplices infligés sur le corps criminel[36]. Il faut donc éliminer, en Grèce, toute trace (σημεῖον) qui aurait pu évoquer aux survivants l'existence d'un citoyen ayant nui aux intérêts de sa cité. Louis Gernet a insisté sur cette tendance à l'élimination comme caractéristique d'une pénalité à sens religieux; elle se manifeste également dans les procès intentés à Athènes contre les animaux ou objets qui ont causé mort d'homme ou dans le procès intenté, lors de la fête des *Bouphonia*, contre le couteau avec lequel avait été tué l'animal sacrificiel[37].

La nécessité de l'oubli du corps va de pair avec une obligation de se souvenir de la volonté de sa disparition. En effet, comme le fait remarquer Danielle Allen, trois sont les possibilités de traitement d'un cadavre: il peut être rendu à la famille pour qu'il soit enseveli, il peut purement et simplement être rejeté pour être oublié ou, enfin, on peut chercher à remémorer ce rejet[38]. Le jeu entre mémoire et oubli est constant dans les sanctions posthumes que nous avons évoquées. D'un côté, en expulsant le cadavre on manifeste le désir ferme d'oublier; d'un autre côté, en déterrant les morts ou en leur intentant des procès, on veut garder présente à la mémoire la décision de leur élimination. Cette complémentarité entre mémoire et oubli se dégage bien dans le récit que donne Pausanias de la mise à mort du roi arcadien Aristocratès, qui, considéré comme traître, a été lapidé et jeté hors des frontières, sans sépulture; à la suite de quoi, on a consacré une stèle dans un sanctuaire de Zeus, dont le texte évoque l'épisode traumatique de l'histoire arcadienne, d'une manière cependant allusive: le nom d'Aristocratès n'y est pas mentionné, mais il y est question d'«un roi injuste», de «traître» et de «parjure»[39]. On garde ainsi en souvenir la punition pour trahison tout en vouant à l'oubli le nom du fauteur.

A cet égard, une inscription comme celle concernant le roi Aristocratès est aux antipodes de la pratique athénienne de la στηλίτευσις; elle se rapproche, en revanche, de la *damnatio memoriae* romaine. La στηλίτευσις consistait à graver sur des stèles exposées dans des lieux publics les noms des criminels ou des débiteurs de

---

35 Dion Chrysostome, *Discours*, 31, 85.

36 Cf. D. Allen, *op. cit.* (*supra*, n. 9), p. 223.

37 L. Gernet, «Quelques rapports entre la pénalité et la religion en Grèce ancienne» (1936), repris dans: L. Gernet, *Droit et institutions en Grèce ancienne*, Paris 1982, p. 159-160.

38 D. Allen, *op. cit.* (*supra*, n. 9), p. 217-218.

39 Pausanias, *Description de la Grèce*, IV, 22, 5; cf. Polybe, *Histoire universelle*, IV, 33, 3.

la cité; il est évident que ce qui était recherché par cet affichage des noms c'était la stigmatisation des citoyens fautifs[40]. Quant à la *damnatio memoriae*, elle consistait à anéantir la mémoire, notamment celle d'un empereur qui avait fait l'objet d'une condamnation sénatoriale posthume, en martelant son nom de toutes les inscriptions (monuments votifs, tombeaux) ou en le radiant de documents écrits sur papyrus.

En dehors d'un témoignage comme celui de Pausanias relatif au roi arcadien Aristocratès, il existe un autre document qui préfigure, d'une manière plus explicite, la *damnatio memoriae* romaine; il s'agit d'une loi du IIIe siècle av. J.-C. de la cité d'Ilion contre la tyrannie. Dans ce texte, il n'est plus question d'exhumer les restes d'un tyran, mort ou exécuté, ni de les expulser hors de la cité; c'est seulement son nom qui doit disparaître de toute inscription publique: «partout où l'on trouvera le nom d'un de ces hommes, soit parmi les prêtres soit sur un monument votif soit sur un tombeau, partout le nom sera martelé», de sorte qu'«il ne reste rien debout de ce que ces hommes ont érigé et qu'il ne subsiste d'eux aucun monument (μνημεῖον μηθὲν ἔσται)»[41].

Alors que l'interdiction de sépulture et l'éloignement des ossements hors des frontières s'inscrit dans l'espace, d'où elle élimine toute trace de matérialité corporelle, le martèlement des noms s'inscrit dans le temps, en gérant la mémoire collective. Dans un cas, on anéantit tout «signe» (σημεῖον) du criminel, dans l'autre on supprime tout support de sa mémoire (μνημεῖον). Cette deuxième solution se rapproche, nous semble-t-il, de la mentalité romaine, avec son goût particulier pour la temporalité. A cet égard, il est intéressant de constater qu'une fois encore le monde hellénistique préfigure la romanité.

[40] Cf. J.-M. Bertrand, «De l'usage de l'épigraphie dans la cité des Magnètes platoniciens», dans: G. Thür / J. Vélissaropoulos-Karakostas (éd.), *Symposion 1995*, Cologne-Weimar-Vienne 1997, p. 38-45; cf. aussi D. Allen, *op. cit.* (*supra*, n. 9), p. 203, 208.

[41] *IJG* II 22, l. 31-45.

LENE RUBINSTEIN (LONDON)

"*ARAI*" IN GREEK LAWS IN THE CLASSICAL AND HELLENISTIC PERIODS: DETERRENCE OR CONCESSION TO TRADITION?

In 1895 Ziebarth published the first systematic survey of the epigraphical evidence for *arai* as a deterrent in the legislation of the Greek cities. Primarily on the basis of the epigraphical material available at the time, Ziebarth arrived at three important conclusions. First, that the threat of the *ara* as a means of encouraging compliance with the *polis*' legislation was not confined to any particular region or regions of the Greek world. Ziebarth found several attestations in inscriptions from Mainland Greece and Sicily in addition to the more prolific evidence from the Aegean islands and the Greek and Hellenised communities in Asia Minor. Second, that this type of deterrent was not connected with any particular type of constitution: there is no evidence to suggest that it was more prevalent as a type of deterrent in legislation passed by narrow oligarchies or aristocracies than in *poleis* with a broader-based constitutional framework (including democracies). And, third, that the attestations of *arai* in various types of *polis* legislation are not confined to any one period: the evidence ranges from the earliest archaic inscriptions to legislation passed by *poleis* under Roman domination, although Ziebarth detected a higher frequency of attestation in the material from the earliest period.

However, Ziebarth himself added an important modification to his observations on continuity as evidenced in the inscriptions. In his view, the threat represented by the public curse declined gradually and continuously from the archaic period onwards, and he ascribed this decline to a 'general decline in religious sentiment'.[1] On Ziebarth's interpretation, the survival of the public *ara* in late classical and Hellenistic inscriptions should be interpreted primarily as a testimony to the conservatism that determined the framing of Greek legislation, long after the *ara* had lost its original significance and efficacy.

Ziebarth's general conclusions were later to provide the main point of departure for Latte's treatment of the *ara* in his *Heiliges Recht*. Like Ziebarth, Latte

[1] Ziebarth (1895: 70): 'Die Mehrzahl der Beispiele gehört freilich der alten und ältersten Zeit der griechischen Geschichte an, und das ist natürlich. Denn nur die äusserste Sucht nach Erhaltung alter Formen konnte gerade diese Rechtssitte in Zeiten hinein bewahren, *in welchen sie ihre Wirksamkeit mehr und mehr verlieren musste wegen des gänzlichen Schwindens des religiösen Sinnes*'.

interpreted the attestations of the public imprecation in texts dating from the late classical period and later as essentially empty formulae retained in legal systems that had in other respects undergone a process of secularisation, a 'Verweltlichung'.[2] Latte's general evolutionary schema was, like that of Ziebarth, informed by a wider scholarly consensus that the traditional religious structures and institutions of the Greek cities were declining throughout the classical period and had lost most of their significance by the end of the fourth century.

However, there was a second strand in Latte's argumentation, which had not been developed by Ziebarth: the decline in the importance of the *ara* as a legal deterrent was to be ascribed not only to changes in religious perceptions but should at the same time be interpreted also as a result of the increasing power of the political institutions within individual Greek communities. Originally, the reliance on the divine agency for the punishment of offenders reflected the weakness of the *polis*' institutions – that is, primarily, its courts and officials – which made it difficult to enforce sanctions against individual transgressors. As the power of these *polis* institutions grew, the protection offered by the *ara* gradually became redundant, so that in the Hellenistic period these sanctions had turned into 'mere ornaments with which even the most trivial honorary decree was lavishly adorned.'[3]

Since the publication of *Heiliges Recht*, there has not, to my knowledge, been any attempt to produce further comprehensive, diachronic discussions of the public *ara* as a form of legal deterrence. In more recent discussions, attention has tended to focus on archaic and early classical instances, although the continued importance of the public imprecation in the late classical and Hellenistic *polis* has also been asserted in discussions of individual inscriptions from these periods.[4] Important challenges to Latte's model of decline have been made especially in relation to individual inscriptions from the mid-fifth century. Examples are Thür (1998: 25-26) on *IP Ark* 8, and Koerner (1987: 460-461 and 467-468) on the *ara* in *IK Erythrai* 1 which regulated the terms of appointment of *grammateis* and on the famous *dirae*

[2] Latte (1920: 76): 'Um 300, wenn nicht schon früher, ist also die Rolle des Fluches als wirksamen Rechtsschutzes in der hellenischen Welt ausgespielt. Das hindert nicht daß die *leergewordene* Form namentlich auf Stiftungsurkunden immer wiederkehrt, bald allein, bald mit anderen Strafbestimmungen zusammen.' (my italics) Unlike Ziebarth, however, Latte made an exception in relation to the Greek communities of Asia Minor: here the threat of the *ara* retained its original force as a deterrent because of the influence of oriental religious perceptions and practices.

[3] Latte (1920: 87). *ibid.* on the redundancy of 'sakrale Strafformen': 'Abgesehen von wirklich religiösen Verbrechen treten sie in historischer Zeit ursprünglich nur ein, wo die Macht des Staates gegenüber dem einzelnen zur Ahndung noch nicht hinreichte. (...) Als der Staat an Geschlossenheit gewann, seine Macht gegenüber dem einzelnen Bürger immer mehr wuchs, da mußten diese Formen überlebt erscheinen, zumal der Glaube, den sie voraussetzten, seine zwingende Kraft für weite Kreise verlor.'

[4] See Lambrinudakis and Wörrle (1983: 310-313) on *SEG* 33.679 (Paros, C2), and Knoepfler (2001: 229-238) on *SEG* 51: 1105 (Eretria, C4).

Teiorum. While both scholars agree with the traditional proposition that the *ara* reflects a very ancient type of sanction, both of them also urge that the inscriptions testify to a continuous belief in the communities that produced the texts that the threat of divine punishment and divine intervention in the process of law enforcement was very real indeed.[5]

However, if the *ara* as a sanction has recently been interpreted as more than just an 'empty formula', especially as far as our fifth-century evidence is concerned, the Hellenistic attestations of its use still need to be reassessed in the context of a general survey. The call for such a reassessment is all the more urgent because of the development that has taken place generally in modern scholarship on Greek religion in the Hellenistic period, a development that has led to a fundamental revision of the 19th century model of decline.[6]

This paper will concentrate on evidence for public imprecations in inscriptions dating from the fourth century down to about 150 B.C., with reference to the archaic and early classical material primarily for the purposes of identifying areas of continuity as well as of change. In addition to the *arai* pronounced by officials of individual communities, sometimes with the assistance of priests, the discussion will take into account some of the evidence for the practice of self-imprecation as the confirmation of an undertaking made by oath. There are two reasons why this type of curse is relevant to the present discussion. First, although the *ara* is pronounced personally by the potential target of divine punishment for breach of the terms of the oath, its inclusion in oath formulae must, at least originally, have been based upon the same belief in the reality of divine intervention and divine sanctions as that which underpinned the pronouncement of *arai* at festivals and political gatherings. Second, there is a conspicuous overlap between the areas protected by *arai*

---

[5] On the basis of the evidence of *IP Ark* 8, Thür (1998: 26) concludes that 'Fluchtäfelchen oder "Orakeljustiz" funktionieren *aus dem festen Glauben, daß Gottheiten ständig in das menschliche Leben eingreifen*. In diesen neuerdings wieder mehr beachteten Texte ist zwar ἰνμενφές nicht mehr zu finden, wohl aber Formen des ἵλαος, und zwar meistens verneint: "nicht segensreich". *Eid und Fluch im griechischen Volksglauben bilden die Brücke zum offiziellen Prozeß der archaischen Zeit*.' (my italics). As far as the efficacy of the *ara* is concerned, the most monumental testimony to its survival in the postclassical era is the *ara epitymbios*, for which see, above all, *IK* 52 *Ἀραὶ Ἐπιτύμβιοι*. However, this evidence does not in itself undermine Latte's evolutionary model: as indicated in n. 2, Latte regarded Asia Minor, from which most attestations of this type of *ara* derive, as an exception to the rule.

[6] For continuity in patterns of religious observance and for the lack of a clear hiatus in the Hellenistic period, see e.g. Habicht (1997: 166-170), Mikalson (1998: 315-323 with references to studies of cults in other Hellenistic cities), Pakkanen (1996: 131-137), Parker (1996: 256-281), and Parker (2005), esp. 76-77 on the continued importance of the public imprecation 'persisting well down into the Hellenistic period'. It must be noted that the scholars cited all identify areas of change and development in religious practices and organisation, but change and development are not necessarily to be interpreted as signs of a 'crisis'.

pronounced on behalf of the community and those which were protected by prayers and curses in oaths to be sworn by individual members of the citizen body.

As noted earlier, part of the basis of Latte's contention that the public imprecation had been reduced to a mere formality by the end of the fourth century was his observation that, in the later period, even the most trivial decrees were sometimes 'adorned' with the threat of the *ara* directed against individuals who attempted to revoke or in other ways undermine the decision. However, closer inspection of the individual inscriptions in which the public imprecation is invoked as a deterrent does not in my view support the contention that such a trivialisation had indeed taken place.

It is an incontrovertible fact that the late classical and Hellenistic periods have not yielded any single piece of evidence for the contents of public *arai* that comes anywhere near the wealth of detail preserved in the *dirae Teiorum* from the fifth century. The scope of the two surviving Teian *arai* is also wider and more comprehensive than any other individual attestations of such public imprecations, be they archaic, classical or Hellenistic. Indeed, one of the Teian texts, Meiggs and Lewis 30, states explicitly that the text of the inscription contained the very words that were to be pronounced at the festivals of the Anthesteria, the Herakleia and of Zeus. The two Teian inscriptions are not entirely unique: one inscription from third-century Delos contains the wording of a public imprecation to be pronounced by priests and priestesses against individuals guilty of unlawful abduction of slaves as well as other offenders. But it is still fair to say that no other Greek community of any period has yielded comparable epigraphical evidence for the wording of such public imprecations.

On the other hand, as far as the specific contents of the Teian *arai* are concerned, that is, the individual areas to which the imprecations apply, there are a considerable number of parallels, including parallels dating from the late classical and early Hellenistic periods. In the appendix to this article I have set out for comparison the main themes of Meiggs and Lewis no. 30, the earlier of the two *dirae Teiorum*, along with a survey of the evidence for the application of the public *ara* in inscriptions from the fourth century and later. Apart from the first three inscriptions listed under heading a.i, which are entrenchment clauses of apparently trivial honorary decrees,[7] all of the other later attestations can be said with some justification to fall within the broad areas protected by the public *arai* in fifth-century Teos. Arguably, the categories from b. to f. were anything but trivial: the

[7] The decree honouring Thersippos of Pordoselene (*IK Adramyttion* 34) constitutes a warning that the political context of an honorary decision could render the decision itself highly controversial to the point of actually constituting a threat to the internal stability and the external safety of the community in question. The Pordoselenian decision, by elevating the political standing of Polyperchon's ally Thersippos, constitutes an unmistakeable token of loyalty to Polyperchon at a time when his position was clearly threatened by an alliance between Antigonos, Lysimachos, Ptolemy and Kassandros.

matters to which the imprecations relate range from actions that could potentially lead to destabilisation of the entire community to protection of ritual and sacred property to control of individuals whose actions might otherwise be difficult or, in some instances, impossible to prosecute and punish by other means.

The fact that the late classical and early Hellenistic *arai* are often applied to individual decisions with a narrowly defined scope is not in itself an indication of 'trivialisation' or change: indeed such applications are equally well attested in the archaic and early classical material, and again, there is a remarkable element of continuity in the types of decision that were secured by *arai*.[8] One area where continuity is especially noticeable is that of offences committed in relation to religious ritual, sanctuaries and sacred property. While this is not at all surprising, the continued reliance on the deterrent constituted by divine punishment, sometimes in combination with penalties administered by the institutions of the *polis*, does suggest that the public imprecation had not been emptied of its original religious significance.

However, if the elements of continuity are more conspicuous than have traditionally been recognised, there are also important indications of change in the application of the public imprecations. As noted earlier, Latte did not just explain the reduced significance of the public imprecations as a result of a general decline in traditional religious sentiment: he also pointed to the rise of the power of the political institutions of individual communities as a factor that contributed to making the reliance on divine sanctions increasingly redundant. This second strand of Latte's argumentation may indeed account for the low number of attestations in the late classical and early Hellenistic material of imprecations directed specifically at officials with the aim of limiting their powers and of making them comply with the terms of their office.

I have not been able to find a single late classical or Hellenistic parallel to the early classical examples of regulations in which the imprecation serves to ensure that officials impose penalties for individual offences committed within their area of responsibility.[9] As for the *ara* being used as a deterrent in order to force officials to step down from a position of power after a specified period, along the lines of *IK*

---

8 Examples of archaic and C5 decisions and regulations with *arai* in narrow context: Koerner no. 29, *IG* IV 506 (Argos C6): imprecation on persons who destroy the text of the law (a.), *IG* IX 1 (2) 609 = Koerner no. 47 (Naupaktos, C6/5): imprecation on persons who instigate redistribution of land or *stasis* with the aim of securing a redistribution of land (b.), *PEP Chios* 76c (Chios C5): imprecation on Pentekaideka who fail to impose penalty on other officials for failing to punish offences against *horoi* (c.), *IP Ark* 20 (North Arkadia C6): imprecation on female who fails to dedicate garment worn unlawfully in sanctuary (d.), *IK Rhodische Peraia* 251 (Lindos C5): imprecation on *strategoi* who fail to collect contribution from individual soldiers (e.), *PEP Chios* 76d (Chios C5): imprecation on any individual who attempts to render sale of land invalid (f.)

9 e.g. *PEP Chios* 76c (Chios, C5), *IP Ark.* 8 line 23 with commentary (Mantinea, C5) and more generally Koerner (1987: 467-485) on enforcement of the 'Strafpflicht' of officials.

Erythrai 1, I have as yet found only a single example.[10] A regulation from third century Teos, which concerns the merger of Teos and the smaller settlement of Kyrbissos, contains detailed regulations on the election of *phrourarchoi* to take charge of a stronghold in Kyrbissos, each for a period of four months. If a *phrourarchos* refuses to hand over the stronghold to his successor upon the expiry of his term of office, he is to 'flee Teos and Abdera and their territories under a curse, his property is to be confiscated and no blood guilt shall attach to the person who kills him'.[11] The following line of the inscription shows clearly that what the community was attempting to guard itself against was a real and immediate threat of *stasis*: 'if the *phrourarchos* dies fighting, his property is to be confiscated'.[12] The *phrourarchos*, like other military commanders, differed from even the most powerful officials in charge of the internal administration of a Greek community in that he had military resources at his immediate disposal, resources which might allow him to resist by armed force any attempt to force him to comply with the formal limitations imposed on his power. What is at stake here, then, is not just the question of accountability and limitation of the political powers of individuals: the curse along with the other penalties was most likely intended to guard the community against an outright armed conflict.

As for the more general problem of ensuring that officials carried out their tasks as specified, I have found only one instance of the public imprecation as a deterrent, namely in the law on educational provision in second-century Teos. The mention of the *ara* occurs towards the end of the text, and it is clearly aimed at the citizens generally as well as at officials in charge of the administration of the educational trust: 'The one who makes a proposal or acts in contravention of this law or who fails to carry out the tasks as stipulated in the law, let him and his *genos* be destroyed'. This is followed by further deterrents in the form of penalties as prescribed for persons guilty of *hierosylia*, along with an enormous fine of ten thousand drachmai payable to the *polis*, and prosecution by *ho boulomenos* by actions both public and private.[13]

---

[10] *IK Erythrai* 1 (C5): ὅσοι ἤδη ἐγραμμάτευσαν ἀπὸ Χαλκίδευ ἕκαθεν, τούτων μὴ ἐξεῖναι γραμματεῦσαι ἔτι μηδενὶ μηδεμιῆι ἀρχῆι, μηδὲ τὸ λοιπὸν γραμματεύεν ἐξεῖναι μηδενὶ πλέον ἢ ἅπαξ τῆι αὐτῆι ἀρχῆι, μηδὲ ταμίηι πλέον ἢ ἑνί μηδὲ δύο τιμαῖς τὸν αὐτόν· ὃς δ' ἂγ γραμματεύσηι ἤ ἀνέληται ἢ εἴπηι ἢ ἐπιψηφίσηι, κατάρητόν τε αὐτὸν εἶναι καὶ ἄτιμον καὶ ὀφείλεν αὐτὸν ἑκατὸν στατῆρας· For a detailed discussion and further references, see Koerner (1993: 451-463).

[11] *SEG* 26.1306: ὃς δ' ἂν παραλαβὼν τὸ χωρίον μὴ παραδῶ[ι τ]ῶι φρουράρχω[ι] τῶ[ι] ὑπὸ τῆς πόλεως ἀποσ[τελ]λομένωι ἀεὶ καθ' ἑκάστην τετράμη[νο]ν, φ[ε]ύγειν τε αὐτὸν ἀραιὸν ἐκ Τέω καὶ ἐξ 'Αβδήρων καὶ ἐκ τῆς χώρας καὶ τῆς Τηΐων καὶ τῆς 'Αβδηρ[ι]τῶν καὶ τὰ ὄντα αὐτοῦ δη[μό]σια ε[ἶ]ναι, καὶ ὃς ἂν ἀποκτείνηι αὐτὸν μ[ὴ] μιαρὸς ἔστω·

[12] *SEG* 26.1306: ἐὰν δὲ μαχόμενος [ἀποθάνηι, ὑπάρχ]ε[ι]ν αὐτοῦ δημόσια τὰ ὄντα·

[13] ὀφειλέτω δὲ καὶ τῆι πόλει ἕκαστος τῶν πρηξάντων τι παρὰ τόνδε τὸν νόμον περὶ τοῦ ἀργυρίου τούτου ἢ μὴ ποιούντων τὰ προστεταγμένα δραχμὰς μυρί[ας,] δικασάσθω δὲ αὐτῶι ὁ βουλόμενος καὶ ἐν ἰδίαις δίκαις καὶ ἐν δημοσίαις καὶ μετὰ τοῦ λόγου τοῦ

In this text, the Teian *arai* are directed as much against the ordinary citizen who might exercise his right in a legislative forum to make proposals in contravention of the law as against the individual officials who are charged with administering the money belonging to the trust, and it is significant that the officials are not highlighted as the main threat. Moreover, the elaborate specification of the procedural means by which offenders could be brought before the courts testifies to a confidence on the part of the community that its political and legal institutions would be capable of limiting the power exercised by its officials to a considerable degree. This text may, then, illustrate Latte's point that, as the central political institutions became increasingly powerful, the perceived need to invoke divine sanctions as penalties for specific offences decreased as a result, and it might be tempting to interpret the presence of the *ara* in the Teian regulations on their school trust as a concession to tradition.

However, matters may not be as simple as that. The powerful archaic official who, because of his personal prestige and resources, might use his office to ensconce himself in an impregnable position, *de facto* beyond the reach of the *polis*' laws, may have been perceived as less of an intractable problem in the late classical and early Hellenistic communities. Fifth century Chios relied on the gods as the last resort, at the top of a chain of accountability which prescribed punishment of individual offenders by a board of *horophylakes*, punishment of the *horophylakes* by the Fifteen, and punishment of the Fifteen through divine destruction invoked in an imprecation. In the later periods, most attested Greek communities would have replaced the gods with other institutions at the very top of their chains. But if the threat posed by the unaccountable individual official was perceived as less acute in the late classical and early Hellenistic *poleis*, the problem of political power exercised without accountability broadly defined arguably persisted in relation to judges who cast their votes in secret ballots and participants in large political gatherings. Likewise, persistent problems were posed by offences of omission, which were notoriously difficult to detect and prosecute.

The imprecations intended to guard the community against *stasis* and subversive activities are, like the imprecation in the Teian educational regulations, directed as much against ordinary citizens exercising their political privileges in large, collective decision-making bodies as against individuals who exercised power *ex officio*. Likewise, entrenchment clauses with imprecations were typically directed as much against individual proposers of motions that might undermine the decision in

---

ἐπιμηνίου τὴν ἀπήγησιν καὶ ἐγ καιρῶι ὧι ἂν βούληται, προθεσμίαι δὲ μηδὲ ἄλλωι τρόπωι μηθενὶ ἐξέστω τῶν δικῶν τούτων μηδεμίαν ἐγβαλεῖν, ὁ δὲ ἁλισκόμενος ἐκτινέτω διπλάσιον καὶ τὸ μὲν ἥμισυ ἔστω τῆς πόλεως, ἱερὸν Ἑρμοῦ καὶ Ἡρακλέους καὶ Μουσῶν, καὶ καταχωριζέσθω εἰς τὸν λόγον τὸν προγεγραμμένον, τὸ δὲ ἥμισυ τοῦ καταλαβόντος ἔστω... The final clauses of the law have recently been discussed by Fröhlich (2004: esp. 109-112) who does not, however, comment on the deterrent constituted by the public imprecation.

question as against those who presided over the political meeting and had responsibility for putting decisions to the vote. In many instances the imprecation would undoubtedly have been complemented by regular legal actions comparable to the Athenian procedures of the *graphe paranomon* and the *graphe nomon me epitedeion theinai*. Nevertheless, the deterrent offered by the public imprecation may still have been perceived as necessary – as indeed the Athenian evidence suggests that it was even as late as the fourth century – partly because of the unpredictability of the outcome of trials of this type, and partly because of the uncertainty surrounding the will of individual citizens to initiate the prosecutions.

Indeed, some of the public imprecations suggest that it was not the lack of power of the *polis*' courts and officials *vis à vis* individual offenders that was perceived as the problem in the fourth century and later: the weakest link in the process of law-enforcement was the individual citizen whose agency was required for setting the process of law-enforcement in motion. Hence, we find the public imprecation complementing the procedures and penalties that depended on individual prosecutors for their activation,[14] and, equally significantly, there are three attestations of the imprecation being directed against individuals who fail to

[14] In addition to *SEG* 26.1306, the following inscriptions provide examples: *PEP* Chios 80 (C4, imprecation combined with a sacred fine of a thousand drachmai), *IG* XII,2 526 = *RO* 83 (Eresos, C4; imprecation combined with prosecution warranted by law concerning the removal of stelai concerning tyrants and their descendants), *I di Cos* ED 53 (Kos, C4; imprecation combined with other *epitimia*), IK Adramyttion II 34 (Pordoselene, C4; imprecation combined with sacred fine of 300 stateres, hereditary *atimia* and prosecution warranted by law on *katalysis tou demou*), *IP Ark.* 2 (Tegea, C4; imprecation combined with fine of a hundred drachmai), *SEG* 25.447 = *IP Ark* 24 (Alipheira, C3; imprecation combined with sacred fine of ten thousand drachmai), *IK Ephesos* 4 (Ephesos, C3; imprecation combined with prosecution for insubordination and plotting against collective interests), *Labraunda* III 8 (Mylasa, C3; imprecation combined with *atimia*, fine and confiscation of property as well as prosecution by *ho boulomenos*), *SEG* 44.949 (Teos, C3; imprecation combined with confiscation of precious metal unlawfully withheld and *phasis* by *ho boulomenos*), *ID* 1520 (local association at Delos, C2; imprecation combined with information lodged by *ho boulomenos*), *SEG* 33.679 (Paros, C2; imprecation combined with *agon timetos* initiated by *ho boulomenos*). The co-existence in such text of the threat of the curse and provision for regular court procedures and punishment has long been regarded as an indication that communal trust in the efficacy of divine sanctions was waning (see recently Lambrinudakis and Wörrle (1983) 313: 'Die Kombination ist auch sonst – und schon im 5. Jahrhundert – zu beobachten und verrät natürlich mangelndes Vertrauen in die praktische Verbindlichkeit religiöser Vorstellungen und Normen, die man deswegen doch nicht für verzichtbar gehalten hat.' See also, more recently, Horster (2004: 44-46)). For a different interpretation of the co-existence of divine and human sanctions as deterrents see Parker (2005: 77) who comments on the fifth-century *dirae Teiorum* that 'it is inconceivable that the Teians would simply have left traitors, for instance, to be punished by the gods. (...) There is no incompatibility, no tension, between threatening the same offender with both punishment and curses.'

report an offence that they have witnessed (see Appendix, heading c). Failure by a witness to report an offence – sometimes an offence so serious that it might threaten the very existence of the community as a whole – is an offence of omission that must have been exceedingly difficult to detect and almost impossible to prove before a court.

In an earlier context, I have commented on the question of how individual communities attempted to combine the volunteer principle with the desire to ensure maximum efficiency in the actual process of law-enforcement. While the incentives offered to volunteers in the form of financial rewards as well as the political prestige to be derived from a successful high-profile prosecution are well known, I was able to find only one attestation, from fifth-century Chios, of a penalty threatened against an individual who failed to report on a criminal act that he had observed.[15] I failed to discover any other examples of pressure being placed on potential volunteer informers comparable to the responsibilities placed on officials to take action in connection with offences committed within their area of jurisdiction. I was therefore tempted to conclude that, while the stick was frequently employed against officials who in some contexts clearly could be taken to task for failing to initiate a legal process when required, the carrot was not only the preferred method but normally the *only* method by which other citizens might be spurred into action.

However, if it is assumed that the threat of divine punishment for failing to report to the *polis*' authorities was perceived as both real and serious in the fourth century and later, the Chian example is not as exceptional as I first thought. Although the three inscriptions documenting the application of the public imprecation against reluctant informers cannot, with the best will in the world, be said to be overwhelming, the notion that failure to act was punishable – not with fines, *atimia* or death, but with destruction through divine intervention – recurs in the formulae of self-imprecation pronounced with certain types of oaths. In the appendix to this article I have set out examples of the kind of undertakings that were confirmed with compulsory oaths sealed by *euchai* and *arai*.[16]

As was the case of the public imprecations, the material pertaining to compulsory self-imprecations shows a remarkable affinity to the contents of the fifth-century *dirae Teiorum*, but the attestations of divine destruction invoked by individual citizens on themselves for failing to report on acts of treason, planned revolutions and other serious offences constitutes a conspicuous difference. Where the fifth-century Teian *arai* invoked divine retribution on the offender directly, a

[15] *PEP Chios* 1 = *LSAG* 116 (Chios, C4): the individual who observes unlawful herding, depositing of manure or removal of sacred equipment from sacred groves is obliged to report the offence to the *basileis* under the threat of a sacred fine of five stateres.

[16] I have not included examples from inter-state treaties (which merit a discussion of their own), except those that concern acts of *sympoliteia*, where the oaths sworn by members of the merging communities bear as strong resemblance to attested citizen oaths. Nor have I included evidentiary oaths that serve to corroborate specific facts.

number of self-imprecations, particularly those associated with citizens' oaths, recognise the crucial role played by the individual citizen in the process of law enforcement. In those contexts the passivity of an individual is equated with his condoning the offence and leaves him open to divine retribution.

Like the public imprecation, the Hellenistic self-imprecation of course has a long and distinguished pedigree. And it might still be possible to argue with both Ziebarth and Latte that its preservation in texts from the fourth century and later simply reflects a traditional ritual that was perceived as essential in defining the identity of the community, but which had nonetheless lost its real religious significance, and with that its significance as a legal deterrent. This, however, runs counter to the evidence, which suggests that individual communities took particular steps and sometimes invested considerable resources to ensure that everybody required to swear oaths with imprecations actually did so at specified times.

In fourth-century Eretria, for example, all individuals who had sworn the oath confirming their arrangements with an individual contractor were registered by name, and a similar practice is attested for third-century Ioulis.[17] At Dreros, the responsibility for administering the oath to the new cohorts of young citizens rested with an official who would be liable to prosecution before the *boule* if he failed to carry out his duty.[18] At Teos it seems that individuals who refused to swear the required oaths upon the merger with Kyrbissos would be liable to penalties,[19] although perhaps not as severe as that attested for third-century Itanos: here the penalty for refusing to swear the citizen's oath was loss of citizen privileges and complete exclusion from all communal activities sacred and profane.[20]

These are but a few examples taken from a very rich body of material which deserves further systematic investigation. I hope, however, that they may prove sufficient to establish a plausible case for seeing the religious sentiment that lent a

---

[17] *IG* XII, 9 191 (Eretria, C4) ὀμόσαι τοὺς πολίτας π]άντας Χαιρεφάνει ἐν Ἀπόλλωνος Δαφνηφόρου· ὃς δ' ἂν μ[ὴ ὀμόσει, ἄτιμος ἔστω· ἐξορκούντων δὲ] οἱ πρόβουλοι, ἐξορ[κ]ούντων δὲ καὶ οἱ στρατηγοὶ κατὰ [ἔτος τοὺς ἐφήβους· ὅπως οὖ̣ν τὴν γῆν] καρπίζηται τὰ ἔτη τὰ σ[υ]γκείμενα Χαιρεφάνης, ἀναγ[ράφειν καὶ τὸ ψήφισμα καὶ τὸν ὅρκον ἐν στήλει λιθ]ίνει καὶ στῆσαι ἐν τῶι ἱερῶι τοῦ Ἀπόλλωνος τοῦ Δα[φνηφόρου· ἀ̣ναγράφειν δὲ κα]ὶ τοὺς ὀμόσαντας· ἀ]ναγράφειν δὲ καὶ τῶ[ν] ἐφήβων τοὺς ὀμόσαντ[ας ἐν στήλει... Although some of the restorations proposed by the editors are very doubtful indeed, the main point about the registration of oathtakers seems secure. cf. *IG* XII Suppl. 235 (Ioulis, C3), and *IK* Magnesia Sip. 1.

[18] *IC* I ix 1: part of the citizen's oath was the undertaking: ἦ μὰν ἐγὼ τὸγ κόσμον, αἴ κα μὴ ἐξορκίξοντι τὰν ἀγέλαν τοὺς τόκα ἐγδυομένους τὸν αὐτὸν ὅρκον τόνπερ ἁμὲς ὀμωμόκαμες, ἐμβαλεῖν ἐς τὰν βωλὰν, ἆι κα ἀποστᾶντι τοῦ μηνὸς τοῦ Κομνοκαρίου ἢ τοῦ Ἁλιαίου· ἁ δὲ β[ω]λὰ πραξάντων ἕκαστον τὸν κοσμίοντα στατῆρας πεντακοσίους ἀφ' ἇς κα ἐμβάληι ἁμέρας ἐν τριμήνωι·

[19] *PEP Teos* 48 (C3): ἐὰν δέ τις μὴ ὀμόσηι, [ζημίαν ψηφίσαι κα]τ' αὐτοῦ τὸν δῆμον ὡς ἀδικοῦντος·

[20] *IC* III iv 7: ὃς δέ κα ἐπίδαμος ἐὼν τῶν πολιτᾶν μὴ λῆι ὀμόσαι μὴ ἔστω πολίτας ἀλλὰ ἐργέσθω καὶ θίνων καὶ ἀνθρωπίνων.

force of deterrence to the publicly imprecations as well as the self-imprecations incorporated in oaths of various types as being still very much alive in the Hellenistic period. They lend additional force to Thür's observation in relation to *IP Ark* 8 that 'oath and curse in Greek popular religion constitute the bridge back to the official procedures of the archaic period', a bridge, moreover, that reaches well into the Hellenistic period and beyond.

To sum up. The continuity attested in the material in regard to the areas that were wholly or partially protected by the threat of divine sanctions suggests that the trivialisation of such imprecations, as suggested by Latte, must be rejected. As for the question whether the threat of divine punishment was taken seriously in the fourth century and later, the adaptations that appear to reflect changing political realities and power structures within individual communities do together point to the conclusion that they continued to matter.[21]

BIBLIOGRAPHY

Fröhlich, P. (2004): *Les cités grecques et le contrôle des magistrats (IVe-Ier siècle avant J.-C.)*. Genève.

Gschnitzer, F. (2003): 'Bemerkungen zum Zusammenwirken von Magistraten und Priestern in der griechischen Welt' in *Kleine Schriften zum griechischen und römischen Altertum*, 145-152, Stuttgart.

Habicht, C. (1997): *Athens from Alexander to Antony*. Cambridge MA.

Horster, M. (2004): *Landbesitz griechischer Heiligtümer in archaischer und klassischer Zeit*. Berlin.

Knoepfler, D. (2001): 'Loi d'Érétrie contre la tyrannie et l'oligarchie (première partie)', *BCH* 125, 195-238.

Koerner, R. (1987): 'Beamtenvergehen und deren Bestrafung nach frühen griechischen Inschriften', *Klio* 69, 450-498.

Koerner, R. (1993): *Inschriftliche Gesetzestexte der frühen griechischen Polis*. Köln.

Lambrinudakis, W. and M. Wörrle (1983): 'Ein hellenistiches Reformgesetz über das öffentlichen Urkundenwesen von Paros', *Chiron* 13, 283-368.

Latte, K. (1920): *Heiliges Recht*. Tübingen.

Mikalson, J.D. (1998): *Religion in Hellenistic Athens*. Berkeley, Los Angeles, London.

Pakkanen, P. (1996): *Interpreting Early Hellenistic Religion*. Helsinki.

Parker, R. (1996): *Athenian Religion. A History*. Oxford.

Parker, R. (2005): 'Law and Religion' in M. Gagarin and D. Cohen [eds], *The Cambridge Companion to Ancient Greek Law*. Cambridge, 61-81.

Rubinstein, L. (2003): 'Volunteer Prosecutors in the Greek World', *Dike* 6, 87-113.

Thür, G. (1998): 'IPArk 8: "Gottesurteil" oder "Amnestiedekret"? (Nochmals zu IG V 2,262)', *Dike* 1, 13-26.

Vallois, R. (1914): ''Αραί', *BCH* 38, 250-271.

Ziebarth, E. (1895): 'Der Fluch im griechischen Recht', *Hermes* 30, 57-70.

[21] I am grateful to the Leverhulme Trust for granting me a research fellowship in 2004-2005, during which period this article was written.

APPENDIX
The public imprecation in the late classical and Hellenistic periods

Themes in ML 30: areas of protection (thematic, not following the order of the stone)

a. protection of the stelai bearing the words of the *ara* itself

b. protection against installation of *aisymnetes* (i.e. narrowing of constitution/tyranny)

c. protection against betrayal of the city and its territory, including protection against individuals knowingly giving bad advice to the Teians in matters of foreign policy

d. protection against *timouchoi* failing to pronounce the *ara* at specified times

e. protection against magic (φάρμακα δηλητήρια) employed against individuals or the community as a collectivity

f. protection against undermining of grain supply to the city

Areas of application

a. Entrenchment clauses

i. entrenchment clauses in (apparently) straightforward honorary decrees

***IK Ilion* 24** (Ilion, C4/3): entrenchment of a decree granting extensive *ateleia* to four Tenedian honorands and anyone who trades with them. The political background and significance of this decision cannot be assessed. The decree may be trivial, but is not necessarily so.

***TAM* III 1** (Termessos, C2): honorary decree, apparently straightforward, but note that neither the name of the honorand, nor any indication of the decree's original political context have survived.

***SEG* 41.1379** (Limyra, *koinon* of Pernitai, C4): simple honorary decree for Pyrimatis Masatos. The background is unknown: the decree appears to have been straightforward.

***IK Ilion* 36** (Ilion, C3/2): entrenchment clause protecting against reversal of decisions made in favour of royal family. Potentially of high political significance with implications for the collective safety of the community.

***SEG* 45.1876** (unidentified *polis* in Kolchis, C4/3)?: context lost, possibly entrenchment clause, but restoration is uncertain.

ii. entrenchment clauses in decisions likely to have serious implications for the community as a whole

***FD* III 1.294** (Delphi, C5/4): entrenchment clause with imprecation on anyone who, in his capacity as *damiourgos* or ordinary citizen (*damoteumenos*), abolishes the law on lending.

***PEP Teos* 41** (Teos, C2): entrenchment of law on administration of educational trust set up by Polythros, and imprecation on anyone who is in breach of its terms whether by omission or commission.

***SEG* 4.58, *IG* XIV 432** (Tauromenion, C2): entrenchment of law pertaining to admission of new members of the gymnasion. Imprecation most likely also on those who violate its stipulations.

b. Protection against treason, *stasis* or actions that may lead to *stasis*

***FD* III 1.294** (Delphi, C5/4): imprecation on individuals who propose redistribution of land or cancellation of debts, along with entrenchment clause pertaining to the law on lending in its entirety.

***SEG* 51.1105** (Eretria, C4): imprecation on individuals who attempt to abolish the law against tyranny and oligarchy or act in contravention of its stipulations.

IK **Mylasa 1** (Mylasa, C4): prohibition against overturning the sentence passed on individuals convicted of treason against Mausollos. Corrcsponds closely to *IG* XII,2 526 = *RO* 83 (Eresos, C4)

IK **Mylasa 2** (Mylasa, C4): prohibition against overturning the sentence passed on individuals convicted of treason against Mausollos. Corresponds closely to *IG* XII,2 526 = *RO* 83 (Eresos, C4)

IK Mylasa **3** (Mylasa, C4): prohibition against reversing sale of property confiscated from individuals convicted of treason against Mausollos. Corresponds closely to *IG* XII,2 526 = *RO* 83 (Eresos, C4) which places a curse on anyone who attempts to restore confiscated property to the descendants of Agonippos.

IG **XII,2 526 =** ***RO*** **83** (Eresos, C4): imprecation on judges voting against the *polis*' interests in trials of Eresian tyrants.

IG **XII,2 526 =** ***RO*** **83** (Eresos, C4): imprecation on anyone who assists in returning the exiled descendants of Agonippos, if the latter is convicted, or attempts to restore conficated property to them.

IK Adramyttion **II 34** (Nasos/Pordoselene C4): being an honorary decree for a prominent citizen, Thersippos, this appears on the surface to be one of Latte's trivial decisions, the entrenchment of which is secured by a curse. But it appears from lines A23-29 that Thersippos had sided decisively with Polyperchon and that his policy in this regard had implications for the entire *polis* vis à vis the king and, equally importantly, the King's rivals. The honours voted for Thersippos were thus anything but trivial: they were an important token of allegiance to an outside potentate and at the same time potentially contentious within Nasos/Pordoselene itself. Within the *polis*, there was undoubtedly a risk that a rival faction might attempt to undermine Thersippos' position (and with that, the position of Polyperchon) by bringing about a shift in the *polis*' allegiance to Polyperchon's enemies and using this a stepping stone to gaining power for themselves. It is indicative that the curse upon individuals who attempt to reverse the decision is accompanied by another deterrent, namely that such individuals may also be prosecuted for *katalysis tou demou*! On this interpretation, this instance may be grouped with other examples of the *ara* as a protection against *stasis*.

SEG **50.1304** (Sagalassos, C4/3): clearly connected with on-going *stasis*. Divine destruction is invoked against a faction which has occupied stronghold in the city's territory.

SEG **25.447 = IP Ark 24** (Alipheira, C3): protection against breach of amnesty following *stasis*.

SEG **26.1306** (Teos, C3): imprecation on garrison commander at fortress in Kyrbissos if he fails to hand over fortress to his successor (the following clause 'if he dies fighting, his property shall be confiscated' suggests a clear perceived threat of internal armed conflict).

c. Ensuring that offence is reported and/or punished

FD **III 1.294** (Delphi, C5/4): failure by anyone knowing of offence to report it (text lacunose).

IG **XI,4 1296** (Delos, C3): failure by anyone witnessing the abduction of slaves from Delos or any sanctuary belonging to the god to the detriment of the slave's master to report the offence to the *astynomoi*.

SEG **33.679** (Paros, C2): failure by anyone witnessing damage or destruction of documents in public archive, deposited in sanctuary, to report the offence to the relevant officials (cf. heading d.).

d. Protecting ritual and/or sacred property and precincts

IP Ark. **2** (Tegea, C4): the law contains regulations of herding within the sanctuary. The priest is obliged to tie and lead away (*inphorbiein*?) small livestock. Failure to do so results in his becoming *katarwos*. In so far as the priest incurs the penalty if he fails to take action against an offence that he has witnessed, the text may be regarded as belonging also under heading c.

***I di Cos* ED 53** (Kos, C4): the contents of the law are lost, but most likely relate to sanctuary.

***PEP Chios* 80** (Chios, Klytidai, C4): protection against unauthorised use of building constructed in sanctuary for storage of *ta koina hiera*.

***IK Tralles* 3** (Tralles, C4): protection of supplicants.

***IK Ephesos* VII,1 3401** (pertains to the sanctuary of Meter Gallesia in Metropolis, C4): protection of supplicants.

***SEG* 27.942** (Xanthos, C4): entrenchment of decision relating to the construction of an altar to Basileus Kaunios and regulations for sacrifices.

***IG* XI,4 1296** (Delos, C3): abduction of slaves from Delos or any sanctuary belonging to the god to the detriment of the slave's master and imprecation on anyone who generally offends against *ta patria*.

***Syl.* (3) 1219 = *LSAM* 16** (Gambreion, C3): protection of funerary legislation. The ten-year ban on transgressors sacrificing as 'guilty of *asebeia*' suggests that the curse is first and foremost intended as a protection of ritual, but individual funerals would obviously have been difficult to control in practice (heading e).

***TAM* II i-iii 1** (Telmessos, C3): imprecation on ordinary citizens and officials if they fail to perform annual sacrifices at altar to Zeus Soter, constructed at the behest of King Ptolemy.

***SEG* 9.73, *SEG* 13.618** (Kyrene, C2/1): protection against unauthorised use of equipment of Apollo sanctuary.

***I Priene* 201** (Priene, C2): entrenchment of terms of sale of priesthood and its privileges.

***I Priene* 203** (Priene, C2): entrenchment of terms of sale of priesthood and its privileges.

***SEG* 33.679** (Paros, C2): imprecation on individuals who damage or destroy documents deposited in public archive in sanctuary of Apollon, Artemis and Leto. Note that imprecation applies only to acts of destruction or damage to documents that have been carried out *after* the transfer of the archive to the sanctuary: εἴ τις τῶν γραμμάτων τῶν ἐν τῷ ἱερῷ τῶν μνημονικῶν τῶν ἀνενηνειγμένων ἠδίκηκέ τι ἢ ἐξαλήλιφέ τι ἢ ἐγγέγραφε <u>ἀφ' ὃ ἀνηνείχθη εἰς τὸ ἱερόν</u>, ἐξώλη εἶναι αὐτόν κτλ.

<u>e. Protecting against offences that are difficult or impossible to detect and prosecute</u>

i. directed against officials:

***Labraunda* III 8** (Mylasa, C3): protection of ban on *euthynai*: ἐὰν δὲ ἢ] παραλάβηι τις τὴν εὔθυναν ἢ εἰσαγάγηι ἢ δικα[στὴς δικάσηι ἢ δῶι παρὰ] τὰ δεδογμένα παρευρέσει ἡιτιν⟨ι⟩οῦν, ἐξώλης [ἔστω αὐτὸς καὶ οἱ ἐξ αὐ]τοῦ καὶ ἐπικατάρατος καὶ ἄτιμος καὶ προσαπο[τεισάτω δραχμὰς .....] ας καὶ ἔστω τὰ ὑπάρχοντα αὐτοῦ ἱερὰ Διὸς 'Οσ[ογω καὶ ἐξέστω τῶι βου]λομένωι εὐθύνειν τὸν μὴ ἐμμείναντα ἄνευ π[ροθεσμίας παρευρέσει μη]δεμιᾶι ἐκκλειομένωι· Context is unclear, but there is a clear parallel to Koerner no. 27 (Halieis?, C5): αἴ τιστις [ἒ τὰ]ν βολὰν τ[ὰ]ν ἀνφ' Ἀρίσστονα ἒ τὸν⟨ς⟩ συναρτύοντας [ἒ ἄ]λλον τινὰ ταμίαν εὐθύνοι τέλος ἔχον ἒ δικάσ[ζο]ι ἒ δικάσζοιτο τõν γρασσμάτον Ηένεκα τᾶς καταθέσιος ἒ τᾶς ἀλιάσσιος κτλ. In this text, the *boule* collectively αὐτοὶ ἔνοχοι ἔντο ἐνς Ἀθαναίαν which is conventionally interpreted as 'incurring a sacred fine', if they fail to enforce the penalties of exile and confiscation of property against offenders. May in fact belong under heading b.

***PEP Teos* 41** (Teos, C2): protection against maladministration or unauthorised diversion of funds by officials reponsible for the educational trust set up by Polythros.

ii: directed against individuals who will cast votes in collective decision-making processes
***IG* XII,2 526 = *RO* 83** (Eresos, C4): imprecation on judges voting in secret ballot against the *polis*' interests in trials of Eresian tyrants. See also b. above.

***Syl.* (3) 577** (Miletos, C3/2): imprecation on individuals who vote to elect *paidotribai* and teachers against their better judgement. That such appointments were potentially contentious in political terms is suggested by the phrase καὶ μηδεμιᾶι φιλοτιμίαι παρὰ τὸ δίκαιον προσνέμοι τὴν αὑτοῦ γνώμην.

***IC* III iv 7** (Itanos, C3): public imprecation combined with self-imprecation in oath sworn by the entire citizen body of Itanos. The undertaking in the oath itself has not been preserved, but most likely corresponds to that of *IC* III iv 8 protecting against *i.a.* treason, conspiracy to overthrow the constitution, failure to report conspiracies, cancellation of debts.

iii: directed against individuals generally who by omission may cause harm to the collectivity
***SEG* 44.949** (Teos, C3): imprecation (combined with self-imprecation in oath) on residents in Teos who withhold precious metals and objects required for payment of ransom to pirates. The inscription as a whole suggests that the entire community was under a serious threat.

***IC* II xii 22** (Eleutherna, C2): imprecation on individuals who fail to report to the *kosmoi* of Eleutherna on leaving the πολ[ι]τήιαν τῶν Ἀρτεμιτᾶν.

f. protecting property of individuals or the community
***SEG* 28.1224** (Telmessos, C3): imprecation on individuals who request a *polis* or *kome* belonging to Termessos as a gift from King or Queen.

***IK Ephesos* 4** (Ephesos, C3): imprecation on individuals who give or receive, without authorisation, documentation relating to individual compromises in connection with post-war settlement of debts.

Self imprecation

Affinity with publicly pronounced arai:
Koerner (1993: 166) noted the close correspondence with the oath formula in the public imprecation of IG IX 1(2) 609 = Koerner no. 47 ('Bronze Pappadakis'), Naupaktos, ca. 500 B.C.: ἔμεν τõι τα]ῦτα παρβαίνοντι ἐξξόλειαν αὐτõι καὶ γενεᾶι καὶ πάντ̣εσιν, τõι δ' εὐσεβέοντι Ηίλαος ἔσστο. For a parallel, see *SEG* 9.3 = *ML* 5.46-51.

SEG 31.985 = Koerner no. 79 (Teos, 480-450) combines text of imprecation against officials (τιμὴν ἔχων) with the text of an oath the main objective of which was clearly to protect against *stasis*. It is not absolutely clear whether the oath was to be sworn by all citizens of Teos or specifically by incoming officials only:

ἐπανά̣σ̣τα[σ]ιν οὐ̣ βολεύσω οὐδὲ π̣οιήσω οὐδὲ λυ[ή]σ̣ω ο[ὐ]δ̣ὲ̣ διώξω ο[ύ]δ̣ὲ [χρ]ή̣μ[α]τ̣α δημιώσ[ω οὐ]δὲ δήσω. οὐδὲ κατ̣[ακ]τ̣ε̣[ν]έω ἂμ̣ μ̣ὴ σ[ὺ]ν [........]Ι[ ]ΙΣΙΝ ἐ̣ν Τ̣έωι [ἢ] π̣λέο̣σ[ι]ν [κ]α̣ὶ ἂμ̣ μ̣ὴ ὐ̣π[ὸ] πόλε̣ω[ς] ν̣[ό]μ̣ο̣ καταλαφθέν[τ]α̣ ἐν δὲ Ἀβδή[ρ]οισιν [σ]ὺμ πεντακ̣ο̣[σ]ίοισιν ἢ πλ[έο]σιν αἰσυμνήτην οὐ στήσω̣ [ο]ὔτε σὺμ πολλοῖσι[ν]; the rest is lost.

Areas of application
a. Entrenchment clauses (very widespread in treaties throughout the period)
***IG* XII,9 191** (Eretria, C4): self-imprecation by all citizens undertaking not to alter agreement with contractor and his heirs in draining project.

b. Protection against treason, *stasis* or actions that may lead to *stasis*

***RFIC* 70:15** (Telos, C4/3): citizen oath with undertaking not to engage in subversion and to abide by post-*stasis* settlement.

***IC* I ix 1** (Dreros, C3/2): citizen oath with undertaking not to betray *polis*, not to initiate *stasis* or participate in conspiracy.

***IG* XII Suppl. 235** (Ioulis, C3): undertaking not to form ties with enemies of the community.

***Tit. Cal.* pp.9-10 T xii** (merged community of Kos and Kalymna, C3): undertaking to remain loyal to democracy and to abide by its laws and decrees, to remain loyal to King Ptolemy, not to support tyranny or oligarchy or any conspiracy that may destabilise the constitution.

***IK Magnesia Sip.* 1** (Magnesia on merger with Smyrna, C3): undertaking to stay loyal to King Seleukos and the *polis* of Smyrna, to abide by *sympoliteia* agreement and the laws and decrees of Smyrna, to uphold *autonomia*, *isonomia* and *dêmokratia* of Smyrna.

***IK Magnesia Sip.* 1** (Smyrna on merger with Magnesia, C3): undertaking to abide by agreement with residents of Magnesia Sip. and to stay loyal to King Seleukos. Undertaking to co-exist with new citizens on equal terms and admit them to relevant civic subdivisions.

***PEP Teos* 48** (Teos, C3): undertaking not to demolish the nucleated settlement of Kyrbissos by Teian citizens upon merger of Teos and Kyrbissos.

***IosPE* 1(2) 401 = *Syl.* (3) 360** (*koinon* of Taurian Chersonnese, C3): citizen oath undertaking not to betray the *koinon* or its territory, to remain an enemy of those who plot against or betray the *koinon*, to serve as *damiourgos* and *bouleutês* in the best interests of the community, without taking bribes or engaging in harmful activities against any individual citizen, and not to participate in any *synômosia* against the *koinon* or any individual citizen who remains loyal to the *koinon*.

***IC* III iv 8** (Itanos, C3): citizen oath with undertaking not to betray *polis* or to engage in any conspiracy against the *polis* or any individual citizen, not to engage in *anadasmos gês* or cancellation of debts, and to live as a citizen according to the *polis* laws.

***Labraunda* III 47** (Mylasa, C2): citizen oath with undertaking not to overthrow democracy or any of its decisions.

c. Ensuring that offence is reported and prosecuted

***IG* II(2) 1196** (Athens, Aixone, C4): undertaking by *dêmotai* to uphold decision and to report any transgressions to fellow demesmen. καὶ ἐς τὸν λοιπὸν χρόνον ἀποφανῶ τοῖς δημόταις, ἐάν τινά τι εἰδῶ ποιοῦντα τούτων ἐν τοῖς [ἀ]γροῖς.

***RFIC* 70:15** (Telos, C4/3): citizen oath with undertaking to lodge information with *polis* officials about revolutionary activities or conspiracies: αἰ δέ κα αἴσθωμαί τινα νεωτερίζοντα ἢ συλλόγους συνάγοντα ἐπὶ καταλύσει τοῦ δάμου, δηλωσέω τοῖς ἄρχουσιν·

***IC* I ix 1** (Dreros, C3/2): citizen oath with undertaking to lodge information about conspiracy with *polis* officials, and to report *kosmos* to *boule*, if *kosmos* fails to exact oath from members of the *agela* who have escaped the oath on the stipulated occasion. εἰ δέ τινάς κα πύθωμαι συνομνύοντας, ἐξαγγελίω τοῦ κόσμου τοῖς πλίασιν·

***PEP* Teos 48** (Kyrbissos on merger with Teos, C3): undertaking to report conspirators against territory or phrourarchos to the Teian *polis* (?) and phrourarchos: καὶ ἂν [εἰδῶ τινα] ἐπιβουλεύοντα τῶι χωρίωι ἢ τῶι φρου[ρ]άρχωι δηλώσω τῆ[ι πόλει] καὶ τῶι φρουράρχ[ω]ι καὶ οὐκ [ἐπ]ιτρέψω κατὰ δύναμιν τὴν [ἐμήν].

***IK Magnesia Sip.* 1** (Magnesia on merger with Smyrna, C3): undertaking to report conspiracies against *polis* and its territory as well as conspiracies to overthrow *dêmokratia* or *isonomia* to the Smyrnaian Assembly. καὶ ἐάν τινα αἰσθάνωμαι ἐπιβουλεύο[ντα] τῆι πόλει ἢ τοῖς χωρίοις τοῖς τῆς πόλεως, ἢ τὴν δημοκρατίαν ἢ τὴν ἰσονομίαν καταλύοντα, μηνύσω τῶι δήμωι τῶι Σμυρναίων καὶ βοηθήσω ἀγωνιζ[όμ]ενος μετὰ πάσης φιλοτιμίας, καὶ οὐκ ἐγκαταλείψω κατὰ δύναμιν τὴν ἐμαυτοῦ·

***IK Magnesia Sip.* 1** (Smyrna on merger with Magnesia, C3): undertaking to report any plan to harm the Magnesians admitted as Smyrnaian citizens or their descendants or their property, and to assist the victims. καὶ ἐάν τινα αἰσθάνωμαι ἐπιβουλεύοντα αὐτοῖς ἢ τοῖς ἐκγό[νοις] αὐτῶν ἢ τοῖς ὑπάρχουσιν αὐτῶν, μηνύσω ὡς ἂν τάχιστα δύνωμαι, καὶ βοι[ηθήσ]ω μετὰ φιλοτιμίας·

***IosPE* 1(2) 401 = *Syl.* (3) 360** (*koinon* of Taurian Chersonnese, C3): citizen oath with undertaking to report any conspiracy to betray *koinon* or undermine its institutions to the *damiourgoi kata polin*. οὐδὲ τῶι προδιδόντι καὶ καταλύοντι ἐπιτρεψῶ οὐδὲ συγκρυψῶ, ἀλλὰ ἐξαγγελῶ τοῖς δαμιοργοῖς τοῖς κατὰ πόλιν·

***IosPE* 1(2) 401 = *Syl.* (3) 360** (*koinon* of Taurian Chersonnese, C3): citizen oath with undertaking to report and judge any offence causing harm to an individual citizen of the *koinon*. οὐδὲ ἐπιβουλευσῶ ἄδικον πρᾶγμα οὐθενὶ οὐθὲν τῶμ πολιτᾶν τῶμ μὴ ἀφεστακότων, οὐδὲ τῶι ἐπιβουλεύον[τι ἐπιτρεψῶ οὐδὲ συγκρυψῶ οὐθὲν οὐθε]νί, ἀλλ' εἰσαγγελ[ῶ] καὶ κρινῶ ψά[φωι] κατὰ τοὺς νόμους·

***IosPE* 1(2) 401 = *Syl.* (3) 360** (*koinon* of Taurian Chersonnese, C3): citizen oath with undertaking to report on any *synômosia* threatening the *koinon* to the *damiourgoi*. καὶ εἴ τινά κα συνωμοσίαν αἴσ[θ]ωμαι ἐοῦσαν ἢ [γι]νομέναν, ἐξαγγελῶ τοῖς δαμ[ιορ]γοῖς·

***IC* III iv 8** (Itanos, C3): citizen oath with undertaking to report any *synômosia* or *syllogos* set up to betray the *polis* of Itanos to the *polis* officials. πόλιν τὰν Ἰτανίων οὐ πρ[οδ]ωσέω, οὐδὲ χώραν οὐδὲ νά[σ]ου[ς] τὰς τῶν [Ἰ]τανίων, οὐδὲ [πολ]εμίους ἐπαξέω, οὐδὲ ναῦ[ς τὰς] τῶν Ἰτανίων προδωσέω, [οὐδὲ] τῶν πολιτᾶν προδωσέω [οὐδέν]α, οὐδὲ χρήματα πολιτ[ᾶν, ο]ὐδὲ σύλλογον οὐδὲ συνωμο[σίαν] ποιησέω ἐπὶ τῶι κακίονι τ[ᾶς πόλ]ιος ἢ τῶν πολιτᾶν, οὐδὲ ἄλ[λω]ι συνεσσέομαι οὐδενί, αἴ τί[ς κα χ]ρήιζηι τούτων τ[ι π]οιεῖν, ἀλ[λ'] ἐρέω ποτὶ τοὺς ἄρχοντας·

***Milet* I,3 150 = *Syl.* (3) 633** (Miletos and Herakleia, C2): in principle, the oath to be taken by *all* citizens of the two communities constitutes an entrenchment of a treaty, but the effect of the treaty is the merger of the *poleis*. One undertaking to which the self-imprecation relates is to report any breach of the agreement to the *boulê* and the Assembly. καὶ ἐάν τινα ἄλλον πυνθάνωμαι παραβαίνοντα τὰς ὁμολογίας, οὐκ ἐπιτρέψω κατὰ δύναμιν τὴν ἐμήν, ἀλλὰ δηλώσω τῆι βουλῆι καὶ τῶι δήμωι.

***Milet* I,3 149** (Miletos and Pidasa, C2): in principle, the oath to be taken by *all* citizens of the two communities constitutes an entrenchment of a treaty, but the effect of the treaty is the merger of the *poleis*. One undertaking to which the self-imprecation relates is to report any breach of the agreement to the *boulê* and the Assembly. καὶ ἐὰν τινα ἄλλον πυν[θά]νωμαι αἱρούμενον παραβαίνειν τὰς ὁμολογίας, οὐκ ἐπιτρέψω κατὰ δύναμιν τὴν ἐμήν, ἀλλὰ δηλώσω τῆι βουλῆι καὶ τῶι δήμωι.

d. Protecting ritual and/or sacred property and precincts

Unattested, except in very general contexts of certain citizen's oaths.

e. Protecting against offences that are difficult or impossible to detect and prosecute

i. self-imprecation by officials or quasi officials

***CID* I.9 = *RO* 1** (Delphi, Labyadai, C4): protection against maladministration of funds, undertaking to administer oath to successors in office.

***IG* II(2) 1183** (Athens, Myrrhinous, C4): self-imprecation by *logistai* and individuals acting as *synêgoroi* in accounting procedure.

***SEG* 26.136** (Athens, Thorikos, C4): self-imprecation by *euthynos* and his *paredroi.*

***CID* I.10, *SEG* 28.100, *IG* II(2) 1126** (Delphi, C4): self-imprecation by *grammateus* (?) undertaking to draw up records according to the instructions of *hieromnamones*, parallel undertaking by *kêrykes*.

***Syl.* (3) 577** (Milet, C3): self-imprecation by candidates for elected office undertaking not to rig election.

***I di Cos* ED: 196** (Kos, C3): self-imprecation by official undertaking not to engage in maladministration (particularly embezzlement).

***PEP Teos* 48** (Teos, C3): undertaking to propose only the most suitable candidate for the elected office of phrourarchos (corresponds closely to Syl. (3) 577 (Miletos, C3/2) relating to election of *paidotribai* and teachers).

***IG* II(2) 1243** (Athens, Tetrapoleis, C3): undertaking by officials to obey instructions and to administer same oath to successors in office.

***IG* XII, 207** (Eretria, C3): undertaking by individuals appointed to assign contracts to *technitai* to make the awards without bribes or any regard to *charis* or individual enmity.

***IC* III vi 7** (Praisos, C3): undertaking by official to administer oath with self-imprecation to the citizens generally within specified time. The rest of the oath relates to entrenchment of treaty with Stalitai.

***IG* XII,7 515** (Aigiale, C2): undertaking by officials to designate *epimelêtês* from among *euergetai* and *aleitourgetoi* (the first part of the oath is 'evidentiary', confirming integrity of the officials' own past conduct in office).

***FD* III 1:362 + 4:354** (Halai and Boumeliteia, C2): undertaking by quasi officials (= guides who will show judges round disputed territory and point out *horoi*) only to show them the original *horoi* and not to fabricate any new ones.

***FD* III 1:362 + 4:354** (Halai and Boumeliteia, C2): undertaking by quasi officials (= *dikastagôgoi*) not to exert undue influence on judges, their secretary or their slaves or to bribe them prior to the hearing of the dispute.

***SEG* 43.381** (Beroia, C2): undertaking by gymnasiarchoi to discharge their duties according to laws, and not to be influenced by *charis* or enmity.

ii. self-imprecation by individuals who will cast votes in collective decision-making processes
***IG* II(2) 1183** (Athens, Myrrhinous, C4): self-imprecation by individuals who will assume decision-making role in accounting process of officials.

***CID* I.10, *SEG* 28.100, *IG* II(2) 1126** (Delphi, C4): self-imprecation by amphiktyons acting in a judicial capacity as well as agents of implementation of penalties.

***IK Knidos* I 221** (Knidos, C4/3): self-imprecation by individuals judging dispute between Kalymna and the descendants of a Koan citizen.

***Tit. Cal.* pp.9-10 T xii** (merged community of Kos and Kalymna, C3): undertaking by citizens of the merged community to cast votes (openly as well as in secret ballots) that will benefit the *polis*, without regard to *charis*.

***FD* III 4:278** (Delphi, C2): undertaking to judge without regard to *charis*, *philia* or enmity, to restore property to Apollon immediately after verdict, and not to accept bribes or engage in embezzlement.

f. Protection of grain imports

***IosPE* 1(2) 401 = *Syl.* (3) 360** (*koinon* of Taurian Chersonese, C3): citizen oath with undertaking not to import grain except to the Taurian Chersonese (close correspondence with ML 30, public imprecation, Teos C5: ὅστις ἐς γῆν τὴν Τηΐην κωλύοι σῖτον ἐσάγεσθαι ἢ τέχνηι ἢ μηχανῆι ἢ κατὰ θάλασσαν ἢ κατ' ἤπειρον ἢ ἐσαχθέντα ἀνωθεοίη, ἀπόλλυσθαι καὶ αὐτὸν καὶ γένος τὸ κένο).

ADELE C. SCAFURO (PROVIDENCE)

A RESPONSE TO LENE RUBINSTEIN

Using with admirable dexterity all the varied corpora of Greek inscriptions as primary evidence, Lene Rubinstein presents a sample of her on-going research, viz., legal institutions in the Greek world outside of Athens; her essay on *arai* in Greek laws is a companion piece to her recent and seminal work on volunteer prosecutors in the Greek World.[1] Here, in the essay on *arai*, she focuses on evidence for public curses used as legal deterrents in inscriptions dating from the fourth century down to about 150 B.C.; she supplements this with some of the evidence for the practice of self-imprecation as the confirmation of an undertaking made by oath. Her purpose is, ostensibly, to examine the curses against the model provided for the most part by K. Latte in 1920: according to Latte, attestations of public curses in texts dating from the late classical period and later are 'essentially empty formulae retained in legal systems that had in other respects undergone a process of secularization.'[2] Again, according to Latte, the decline in the importance of the *ara* as a legal deterrent was due not only to changes in religious perceptions but also to 'the increasing power of political institutions within individual Greek communities.'[3] With the exception of Asia Minor where the *ara* retained religious substance, these sanctions in the Hellenistic period had turned into 'mere ornaments with which even the most trivial honorary decree was lavishly adorned.'[4] Rubinstein asks, is Latte's evolutionary model correct? Does it fit the inscriptions we now possess from the fourth century and later?

In dealing with the vast corpora of evidence, Rubinstein follows Latte's method in part: just as he had listed the offences subjected to curses in the famous fifth century Teian inscription to show their nature – that the offences all caused serious threat to public welfare, so too Rubinstein lists the Teian offences. She uses them, however, to provide a comparative taxonomy: many though not all the offences appear to be subject to public imprecation in later inscriptions and almost all 'were anything but trivial.'[5] One area where Rubinstein perceives

[1] Rubinstein 2003.

[2] Rubinstein's paraphrase of Latte 1920: 76.

[3] Rubinstein's paraphrase of Latte 1920: 87.

[4] Rubinstein's translation of Latte 1920: 76.

[5] Rubinstein tends to qualify a decree or a category of a decree as 'trivial' or 'apparently trivial' (with irony, of course). The leit motif promotes an argument: a decree which is not trivial and which is accompanied by an imprecation is using that imprecation as an important aid to carrying out the law (cf. Koerner 1987: 468). The leit motif slightly distorts Latte's argument. While Rubinstein is right to contest the use of the adjective

great continuity with archaic inscriptions is that of offences committed in relation to religious ritual and sacred property. An area of apparent difference is manifested in the post-archaic texts by the absence of imprecations for officials who do not impose penalties and by the near absence of imprecations for officials who do not step down from office after a specified period or for officials who do not carry out specified tasks. The absence of imprecation in the last category appears to buttress Latte's argument that the strengthening of political institutions resulted in a decreased need to invoke divine sanctions.

Rubinstein appears to follow Latte in this argument but at this point, using her more extensive evidence, she makes her first real departure and original point: there were numerous gaps in developed legal systems that might be and were in fact remedied by public imprecation. Whereas 'the threat posed by the unaccountable individual official' may have been perceived as 'less acute in the late classical and early Hellenistic *poleis*' and so may not have required imprecation, there were other areas of accountability where an imprecation might help out – e.g., in regard to 'judges who cast their votes in secret ballots and participants in large political gatherings' – citizens who might render a decree invalid by proposing its abolition or something contrary to its provisions. Imprecation might be useful in this last case – especially, according to Rubinstein, since imprecation 'would undoubtedly have been complemented by regular legal actions' similar to the Athenian *graphê paranomôn* and the outcome of such trials would be unpredictable.[6] Moreover, problems posed 'by offences of omission' persisted – such as failing to report an offence. In fact, the imprecation texts suggest that 'the weakest link in the process of law-enforcement was the individual citizen whose agency was required for setting the process of law-enforcement in motion.' This is the reason, Rubinstein tells us, that 'we find the public imprecation complementing the procedures and penalties that depended on individual prosecutors for their activation.'[7]

I want to stop at this point and focus on Rubinstein's last point and the trend of her argument in general. Rubinstein has galloped through thousands of inscriptions from all over the Greek world and over a very wide period. In the process of this gallop, she has left Latte's argument and model far behind. Most importantly, she has decided, perhaps heuristically, to assume what had to be proved, at least

(*gleichgültigsten*) to describe certain honorary decrees, even the very ones to which Latte had attached the word or the concept, yet Latte's method was *not* first to measure a decree's importance and then to allow the criterion of 'significance' to determine whether an accompanying curse was 'real' or 'ornamental' (so that a curse accompanying a trivial honorary decree would necessarily be 'ornamental'); his method (granted, not always pellucid) was to question whether the curse was imbued with religious meaning in the first instance.

6 Rubinstein provides no evidence for 'regular legal actions that would be similar to the Athenian *graphê paranomôn*.'

7 A long note (14) is attached to this statement, citing twelve examples – one of which is too fragmentary for any claim (I di Cos 53), and two others are decisions of corporate bodies that are independent of the *polis* (the decree of the Klytidai, PEP Chios 80 and an honorary decree of merchants and sea captains in Delos, ID 1520).

according to Latte's conceptual framework, namely, that the threat of divine punishment was perceived 'as both real and serious in the fourth century.' Once a religious belief is assumed, everything falls into place. But religious belief had been the crux of the matter. Rubinstein has changed the game plan: Latte was concerned with the religious basis of a curse's efficacy; Rubinstein is concerned with the law's efficiency. For Latte, one criterion of efficacy was whether the curse stood by itself or was accompanied by legal procedures – e.g., if someone commits a particular offence, he is to be cursed *and* a volunteer prosecutor is to pursue him. Such a blending, according to Latte, demonstrates a waning in a belief in the gods' efficacy.

But Rubinstein has assumed belief and her focus are those very decrees or regulations that blend imprecation with legal aids as remedies for offences and as goads in law enforcement. As I've mentioned already, she thinks the imprecation texts suggest that 'the weakest link in the process of law-enforcement was the individual citizen whose agency was required for setting the process of law-enforcement in motion.' Hence we find the combination of imprecation and legal remedy. Rubinstein may be right, but if so, then a possible implication should be made explicit: the inclusion of imprecations in such decrees is not accidental; it is a rational decision to use the gods, to manipulate the conduct of society's members – it is a matter of 'social control' – if a witness does not turn up to prosecute the offender, we can curse him and that will encourage others to take up the slack. There is probably no need to point out that such manipulation of religious belief does not signify belief in the gods' efficacy; it might better signify cynical exploitation on the part of the makers of the laws.[8] I do not think that is correct, and Rubinstein certainly hasn't proved that is correct – but I do believe it is the conceptual framework she has presented – a rational legal system where lawmakers insert imprecations in their laws when citizens need an extra spur to motion or where the chain of hierarchical chastisers comes to a halt.

Rubinstein has made an important contribution to the study of Greek law by pointing out the diverse legal deterrents used by different Greek *poleis*. That contribution, however, has been obscured by a line of argument that has used Latte as a straw man; if Rubinstein were to see that argument to its conclusion, then she should have clearly demarcated the imprecation texts of Asia Minor (which Latte saw as retaining religiosity) from texts elsewhere in the Greek world. More importantly, she should have demonstrated how the religiosity of a curse can be

[8] An alternative view is possible: the imprecations in these inscriptions may be rhetorical: they are not mere ornaments, but they signify, 'this penalty is really awful and there is nothing worse possible.' It is possible to interpret some texts cited in Rubinstein n. 14 in this way; this is especially true of texts that present numerous offences and only one is to be cursed; such an offence is surely the worst; and sometimes it is presented last (ID 1520, Delos, second century) and sometimes the offender is the highest magistrate in a series, though not necessarily in a series presented in a growing crescendo (IPArk 2 Tegea, fourth century).

proven. That, of course, is the hardest task and one that probably cannot be accomplished on such a broad scale. Surely curse tablets, appeals to justice at oracles, 'judicial prayers' all attest to vibrant religious belief in classical and Hellenistic cities throughout the Greek world.[9] A method to determine religiosity of curses in the texts cited by Rubinstein might require a data base for all the other kinds of texts just mentioned (curse tablets, appeals to justice at oracles, etc.) dated and located in their home *poleis*. To assume religious efficacy only on the basis of texts that combine legal deterrents with curses is a weak foundation.

It is not an easy matter to measure religious belief. But in this instance, the stones themselves might speak to us – on a micro-level. Here I call attention, very briefly, to the *editio princeps* by Wörrle and Lambrinudakis in *Chiron* 1983 of the text mentioned by Rubinstein in n. 14 as SEG 33.679, a law from second century Paros that provides protection for documentary archives. The editors, by situating the law in its rhetorical shape on the stone, by drawing comparisons with the measure of attention given to imprecations on other stones – whether a curse stands by itself as a law or decree or is isolated from the rest of the text – make very convincing arguments for the use of curses that are religiously based in times of crisis (as they suppose for Paros) and for the continuity of curses in Teos. This is a different approach from Rubinstein's, yet one that follows the line of Ziebarth and Latte – who had taken into account changes in geographical place, changes in religious climate – and one that argues for and does not assume religious belief.

Although I am critical of the logical disposition of Rubinstein's essay, I think it is a valuable contribution to the study of legal deterrents in the Greek world.

BIBLIOGRAPHY

Chaniotis, A. (1997) 'Tempeljustiz im kaiserzeitlichen Kleinasien: Rechtliche Aspekte der Sühneinschriften Lydiens und Phrygiens,' in G. Thür and J. Velissaropoulos-Karakostas (eds.) *Symposion 1995, Vorträge zur griechischen und hellenistischen Rechtsgeschichte* (Köln, Wien), 353-84.

Cohen, D. (2002) Ed., *Demokratie, Recht und soziale Kontrolle im klassischen Athen* (München).

Faraone, C. (2002) 'Curses and Social Control in the Law Courts of Classical Athens,' in D. Cohen 2002: 77-92.

Koerner, R. (1987) 'Beamtenvergehen und deren Bestrafung nach frühen griechischen Inschriften,' *Klio* 69, 450-498.

Lambrinudakis, W./Wörrle, M. (1983) 'Ein hellenistisches Reformgesetz über das öffentliche Urkundenwesen von Paros,' *Chiron* 13, 283-368.

Latte, K. (1920) *Heiliges Recht* (Tübingen).

Rubinstein, L. (2003) 'Volunteer Prosecutors in the Greek World,' *Dike* 6, 87-113.

Versnel, H. (2002) 'Writing Mortals and Reading Gods. Appeal to the Gods as a Dual Strategy in Social Control,' in D. Cohen 2002: 37-76.

Ziebarth, E. (1895) 'Der Fluch im griechischen Recht,' *Hermes* 30, 57-70.

[9] See, e.g., Chaniotis 1997; Faraone 2002; Versnel 2002.

II. DIRITTO ELLENISTICO, GRECO-ROMANO E BIZANTINO

BERNARD LEGRAS (REIMS)

LES TESTAMENTS GRECS DANS LE DROIT HELLÉNISTIQUE: LA QUESTION DES HÉRITIÈRES ET DES TESTATRICES

Il y a dix ans, lors du *Symposion 1995* réuni à Corfou, Livia Migliardi Zingale s'était posée la question de la «césure ou de la continuité» entre les testaments d'époque ptolémaïque et d'époque romaine d'Égypte[1]. Nous voudrions revenir aujourd'hui sur ce vaste champ d'étude de la *diathêkê* grecque, dont Joseph Mélèze Modrzejewski relevait en 1993 qu'il s'agissait d'une «matière négligée par les historiens du droit depuis les travaux, déjà anciens de Kreller»[2]. Nous poserons ici la question de la place et du rôle des femmes de statut grec dans l'Égypte grecque et romaine à la lumière de la documentation papyrologique grecque[3]. Cette enquête reposera sur la republication de deux corpus qui sont loin d'avoir été suffisamment exploités par les jusgrécistes, en 1991, la série des trente «testaments Petrie» par Willy Clarysse[4], et en 2002, les trois testaments de Drytôn par Katelijn Vandorpe[5]. Il convient cependant d'ajouter à ces trente-trois documents, neuf testaments isolés: P. Eleph. 2; P. Lond VII 2015; SB XII 10859; SEG IX 7 (testament de Ptolémée VIII); P. Grenf. I, 24; *Archiv f. Pap.* 1 (1901), p. 63-65; P. Lond. II 219a verso; P. Lond. II 219b;

---

1 Livia Migliardi Zingale, «Dal testamento ellenistico al testamento romano nella prassi documentale egiziana: cesura o continuità», dans *Symposion 1995* (Corfou, 1er-5 septembre), Cologne, Weimar, Vienne, 1997, p. 303-312.

2 Joseph Mélèze Modrzejewski, «Chronique», *RHD* 71 (1993), p. 281.

3 Cf. Terry G. Wilfong éd., *Women and Gender in Ancient Egypt from Prehistory to Late Antiquity*, Ann Arbor, Kelsey Museum of Archaeology, 1997 (bibliographie p. 97-103); Jane Rowlandson éd., *Women and Society in Greek & Roman Egypt. A Sourcebook*, Cambridge,1998; Henri Melaerts et Leon Mooren éd., *Le rôle et le statut de la femme en Égypte hellénistique, romaine et byzantine* (Actes du colloque international, Bruxelles-Leuven, 1997), Paris, Louvain, 2002. Nous dressons un rapide état des recherches sur le genre dans l'Égypte hellénistique dans notre article «Les contrats de mariage grec dans l'Égypte ptolémaïque: de l' histoire des femmes à celle du genre», dans *Genre et Antiquité* (Actes de la table-ronde, Paris, 2005), à paraître aux Publications de la Sorbonne.

4 Willy Clarysse, *The Petrie Papyri*, Second edition (P. Petrie²), Vol. I, *The Wills*, Bruxelles, 1991.

5 Katelijn Vandorpe, *The Bilingual Family Archive of Dryton, his Wife Apollonia and their Daughter Senmouthis* (P. Dryton), Bruxelles, 2002.

BGU VI 1285[6]. Ces éditions permettent de reprendre l'étude du corpus des testaments grecs d'Égypte ptolémaïque qui compte donc une trentaine de documents en les rapprochant d'autres textes documentaires de la Grèce et de l'Orient hellénistique. Des travaux importants portant globalement sur les femmes dans le monde hellénistique ont de fait marqué la recherche la plus récente, ainsi ceux de Sarah B. Pomeroy, d'Anne Bielman ou d'Inés Calero Secall[7]. Seuls les documents mentionnant des femmes dans les testaments seront ici pris en compte[8].

Cette étude sera ainsi l'occasion d'aborder deux problématiques déjà étudiées dans les précédents *Symposia*[9]*:* les rapports entre le masculin et le féminin analysés – entre autres – par Eva Cantarella ou David Cohen[10], et le testament grec, au sujet duquel Alberto Maffi a montré qu'il ne saurait exister avant Solon contrairement à l'opinion d'Eberhard Ruschenbusch[11].

Notre réflexion portera sur le sexe des légataires et des bénéficiaires, en partant du constat que les testaments grecs d'Égypte mentionnent de fait l'accès des enfants des deux sexes à l'héritage, mais ignorent, dans l'état actuel de notre documentation, tout exemple de testatrice agissant seule, avec ou sans *kyrios*[12].

---

6 Cf. Willy Clarysse, «Ptolemaic Wills», dans *Legal Documents of the Hellenistic World,* Markham J. Geller et Herwig Maehler éd., Londres, 1995, p. 88-105.

7 Sarah B. Pomeroy, *Families in Classical and Hellenistic Greece,* Oxford, 1997; Anne Bielman, *Femmes en public dans le monde hellénistique, IV*[e]*-I*[er] *s. av. J.-C.*, Paris, 2002; Inés Calero Secall, *La Capacidad Jurídica de las Mujeres Griegas en la Época Helenística. La epigrafía como fuente*, Malaga, 2004.

8 Cf. Hans-Albert Rupprecht, «Das Ehegattenererbrecht nach den Papyri», *BASP* 22 (1985), p. 291s.; id., «Ehevertrag und Erbrecht», dans *Miscellania Papirologica Ramon Roca-Puig en el seu vuitantè aniversari*, S. Janeras éd., Barcelone, 1987, p. 307s.

9 On peut aussi rappeler que la ville de Salerne où s'est réuni ce *Symposion 2005* a été le sujet d'une importante recherche sur les contrats de mariage et les testaments pour la période médiévale: Antonio Marongiu, *Matrimonio e famiglia nell'Italia meridionale, sec. VIII-XIII,* Bari, 1976. L'ouvrage a été utilisé pour établir des comparaisons par Anne-Marie Vérilhac et Claude Vial, *Le mariage grec, du VIe siècle av. J.-C. à l'époque d'Auguste,* Athènes, Paris, 1998, p. 135 (26) (BCH Suppl. 32).

10 Cf. Eva Cantarella, «Moicheia. Reconsidering a Problem», dans *Symposion 1990* (Pacific Grove, Californie, 24-26 septembre 1990), Cologne, Weimar, Vienne, 1991, p. 289-296; David Cohen, «Women in Public: Gender, Citizenship, and Social Status in Classical Athens», dans *Symposion 2001* (Evanston, Illinois, 5-8 septembre 2001), Vienne, 2005, p. 33-45.

11 Alberto Maffi, «Adozione e strategie successorie a Gortina e ad Atene», dans *Symposion 1990* (Pacific Grove, Californie, 24-26 septembre 1990), Cologne, Weimar, Vienne, 1991, p. 205-231 (bibliographie p. 230-231).

12 La bibliographie sur la question est donnée par Hans-Albert Rupprecht, *Kleine Einführung in die Paépyruskunde,* Darmstadt, 1994, p. 111-112. Les deux ouvrages de synthèse pour la période grecque et romaine demeurent: V. Arangio-Ruiz, La *successione testamentaria secondo i papiri greco-egizii,* Naples, 1906, et H. Kreller, *Erbrechtliche Untersuchungen aufgrund der graeco-aegypt. Papyrusurkunden*, Leipzig, 1919 (rééd. Aalen, 1970). La question avait retenu l'attention de Paul Collinet, «La Papyrologie et

1. Les femmes héritières

Les sources papyrologiques font apparaître une réelle diversité du statut social et juridique de l'héritière. Dans la majeure partie des cas, celle-ci est l'épouse légitime du testateur. Cette part réservée à l'épouse dans le testament est un «douaire», puisqu'il s'agit des biens propres du mari que celui-ci laisse à son décès à son épouse survivante. On sait que cette pratique hellénistique trouve des précédents dans l'Athènes des orateurs où trois cas sont attestés[13], et dans d'autres cités, en particulier à Gortyne et à Krimisa[14]. À Athènes, ces biens laissés à la veuve portent le nom de *proïx:* cette dot indirecte est donc désignée du même terme que la dot directe remise par le père de la mariée à son futur gendre. De fait ce legs avait pour but à Athènes de permettre un remariage de la veuve, dont le futur époux avait été choisi par le légataire lui-même[15].

Le partage des biens du testateur entre des héritiers des deux sexes est mis exemplairement en valeur, dans le testament du clérouque lycien Peisias (P. Petrie^2 13)[16]. En 238/237 av. n.è., Peisias, probablement un officier, envisage une division de ses biens *post mortem* entre d'une part son fils Peisikratês, né d'un premier mariage avec dame Nikô, et d'autre part sa seconde épouse, Axiothea. Peisikratês recevra un immeuble (*sunoikia, i.e. insula*) à Alexandrie, le mobilier qu'elle contient et quatre esclaves (deux hommes et deux femmes). Axiothea héritera d'une maison (*oikia*) dans le village fayoumique de Boubastos, et d'une esclave (une femme). Le mobilier de la maison de Boubastos restera en indivision avec Peisikratês. Il est clair que la valeur de ce douaire est inférieure point pour point à la part qui échoit au fils. Mais les biens propres d'Axiothea devenue veuve seront plus considérables, puisque le mari inscrit scrupuleusement les objets constituant sa dot. Celle-ci devra lui être restituée intégralement, à sa valeur au moment du mariage. Une telle clause prévoyant que les objets usés ou détériorés devaient être remplacés procédaient peut-être de la générosité du mari. En tout cas au Moyen Âge, à Salerne (et à Amalfi) il n'était ainsi pas prévu de telles clauses compensatoires pour la restitution du trousseau[17]. La *phernê* illustre l'appartenance d'Axiothea, qui vient de Lycie comme Peisias, à un milieu d'élite tant par son montant élevé (230 dr).) que par son contenu, où figurent, en sus des espèces monétaires, des vêtements définis par leur qualité et leur diversité, des bijoux et des instruments de cuisine. La présence de vêtements

l'Histoire du Droit», dans *Internationaler Papyrologentag. Papyri und Altertumswissenschaft* (Munich, 4-7 septembre 1933), Munich, 1934, p. 219-221.

13 Démosthène, *Contre Aphobos*, I, 4-5; *Contre Stéphanos*, I, 28; Lysias, *Contre Diogiton* 6.

14 Code de Gortyne, col. X, l. 15-20; *Nomima* II, 57. Des legs à l'épouse sont peut-être mentionnés dans d'autres d'inscriptions: *Nomima* II 55 (Métaponte), *Nomima* II 56 (Locres) et *Nomima* II 58 (Pételia),

15 Un cas serait aussi attesté à Syracuse, Diodore, XX, 3, 2. Cf. Anne-Marie Vérilhac et Claude Vial, *op. cit.*, p. 133 (22).

16 Cf. Annexe (Texte 1).

17 Antonio Marongiu, *op. cit.*, p. 157 et 161.

masculins dans ce trousseau (l. 18: une tunique d'homme, χιτών ἀνδρεῖος, l. 19-20: une ceinture d'homme, ζωή ἀνδρεῖα), pourrait s'expliquer – sous réserve d'hypothèses plus pittoresques – comme un indice du fait qu'Axiothea était veuve au moment de son mariage avec Peisias, et qu'elle avait conservée quelques effets de son précédent mari. Mais le texte est muet sur la possession d'autres biens plus substantiels, comme des biens fonciers ou immobiliers. On ne peut guère douter que si cela avait été le cas leur existence aurait été mentionnée, pour que ceux-ci ne puissent être accaparés par Peisikratês. On soulignera aussi que Nikô, la première épouse, ne reçoit rien. Mais elle est peut-être décédée.

Un parallèle à ce type de partage qui se règle entre les enfants d'un premier mariage et l'épouse actuelle se rencontre probablement dans un papyrus grec de Pathyris daté de 123 av. n.è. publié par B.P. Grenfell et A.S. Hunt (Gizeh Museum Inv. Nr. 10388 = *Arch.f. Pap.* 1, 1901, p. 63-65). Pakhnoubis fils de Taskos divise ses biens entre Tathôtês sa femme légitime vivante, et les fils qu'il a eu «d'une autre femme (ἐξ ἄλλης γυναικός)». Cette dernière ne peut guère être qu'une précédente épouse du testateur, morte ou divorcée. Tathôtês, Perse par son ethnique, recevra l'essentiel des biens de son mari: un cheptel bovin, une maison et douze aroures de terres. Chaque fils devra se contenter d'un lit et de son matelas (l. 5). Les fils de Pakhnoubis sont donc clairement désavantagés, en fait quasiment déshérités, à la différence de Peisikratês ou d'Esthladas, le fils du cavalier clérouque Drytôn qui est l'un des témoins de ce testament (l. 27) dont nous verrons *infra* la part substantielle dans l'héritage de son père.

Cependant, dans la plupart des testaments la légataire du défunt est la mère (ou une des mères) des enfants du défunt. Elle hérite avec ses enfants, ce qui est signifié par la formule «Je transmets tous mes biens à ma femme et à mes enfants». Cette formule désigne ordinairement l'objet de la transmission à l'accusatif, et les bénéficiaires au datif (καταλείπω τὰ ὑπάρχοντα μοι πάντα τῆι ἐμαυτοῦ γυναικὶ καὶ τοῖς ὑπάρχουσί μοι τέκνοις). Mais il existe des exceptions tant dans la construction grammaticale que dans l'ordre dans lequel sont nommés les ayants-droits, ainsi pour le P. Petrie² 3, l. 18-19: τὰ ὑπάρχοντα ἃ ἔχουσιν οἱ υἱοὶ καὶ ἡ γυνή μου ἐχέτω[σαν]). Un père, N fils de Philôn laisse ses biens à sa femme Artemidôra, ainsi qu'à ses deux fils et à ses deux filles (P. Petrie² 25). Menandros d'Amphipolis les transmet à sa femme Agatharkhis et à ses «enfants» des deux sexes (P. Petrie² 17, l. 15-40). Diôn d'Herakleia les laisse à «ses fils et à sa femme» (P. Petrie² 3, l. 8-37). Un père, dont le nom n'est pas conservé, laisse, de même ses biens à sa femme Eteandra et à ses fils dont le nombre, trois, est ici précisé (P. Petrie² 4). Philôn fils d'Hêrakleidês les transmet à sa femme Eirênê et à leur fille (P. Petrie² 14). Kalas les transmet de même à sa femme N et à leur fille (P. Petrie² 16, l. 67-96). Des cas restent douteux ainsi pour la succession de N destinée à sa femme Ammônia et à un enfant dont l'état du papyrus ne permet pas de déterminer s'il s'agit d'une fille ou d'un garçon (P. Petrie² 15).

L'épouse peut aussi hériter seule des biens du mari. C'est le cas d'une Macédonienne fille de Pyrrhos qui hérite de son mari l'Illyrien Meleagros (P. Petrie^2 6, l. 27-47); de Dionysia qui hérite d'Antipatros de Cyrène (P. Petrie^2 16, l. 12-40); de la Perse N fille d'Hêrakleidês qui hérite de l'Agrien Ptolemaios (P. Petrie^2 16, l. 41-66); une épouse dont le nom est probablement Thaleia recevra de même les biens de son époux, le Cyrénéen Euphronios P. Petrie^2 17, l. 41-49); Anaxila hérite de son mari, un Oitaien, dont le nom est perdu (P. Petrie^2 22, 1-14); Hagemona recevra ceux de son mari dont le nom est perdu (P. Petrie^2 28); une disposition semblable est également présente dans le P. Petrie^2 23 dont les noms du couple ne nous sont pas parvenus.

Les testaments peuvent aussi ne pas mentionner l'épouse. L'unique héritier peut être le fils du testateur. C'est indéniablement le cas dans le P. Petrie^2 9, l. 8-19, et très probablement dans le P. Petrie^2 1, l. 1-26 où Xenoklês bénéficie de l'annulation des testaments précédents. Dans trois testaments, il s'agit de femmes dont le statut n'est pas mentionné. Le Libyen Marôn fils d'Euphranôr lègue des espaces sacrés, des maisons et des cours à Musta et à Meneia (P. Petrie^2 1, l. 33-68). Le Béotien N lègue tous ses biens à Arist[...], *astê* alexandrine. Axiothea fille de Dizoulas recevra de même tous les biens d'Aphrodisios (P. Petrie^2 24, l. 15-38). On peut évidemment supposer que certaines de ces femmes sont en fait les épouses légitimes du testateur et que cette qualité a été omise par le scribe. L'hypothèse en a été formulée pour Axiothea et Arist[... qui reçoivent la totalité des biens du testateur. Mais cette hypothèse ne peut convenir pour Musta et Meneia dont le lien avec le testateur, Marôn, n'est pas désigné par une des formules habituelles (par ex. τῆι ἐμαυτοῦ γυναικί, θυγατρί), et qui sont chacune accompagnée par leur *kyrios*, Artemidôros pour Musta et Kleandros pour Meneia. Le statut de ces deux femmes, des Alexandrines (*astai*) ne peut que faire l'objet d'hypothèses. Eugène Revillout, qui ne manquait pas d'imagination, en avait formulé plusieurs voyant en elle des «fiancées», des «maîtresses» ou des femmes bénéficiant d'«adoptions déguisées»[18]. Mais aucune ne peut être raisonnablement prouvée.

La volonté du testateur peut évoluer comme le montrent les trois testaments de Drytôn[19]: le deuxième testament prévoit un partage des biens entre sa nouvelle épouse Apollônia alias Semnonthis et son fils Esthladas né du premier mariage, ce fils recevant en outre l'armure et le cheval de guerre de son père (P. Dryton 2)[20]. Le

[18] Eugène Revillout, *Mélanges*, p. 398-400. Une approche plus prudente est adoptée par H. Kreller, *op. cit.*, p. 256, et W. Clarysse, *op. cit*, p. 36. Sur les travaux d'Eugène Revillout, cf. Sophie Sagay, «Eugène Revillout: un étrange cas de '*damnatio memoriae*' moderne?», dans *IXe Congrès International des Études démotiques* (Paris, 31 août-3 septembre 2005), à paraître.

[19] Cf. Annexe (Texte 2, 3 et 4).

[20] Le mariage avec Apollônia intervenu le 4 mars 150 marque la deuxième période de la vie de Drytôn qui le fait entrer dans la sphère culturelle égyptienne, tout en lui donnant une postérité élargie. Cf. Willy Clarysse, «Le mariage et le testament de Dryton en 150 avant J.-C.», *Chron. d'Ég.*, t. 61 (1986), p. 99-103, en part. p. 100 (1).

troisième testament (P. Dryton 4), rédigé après la naissance de cinq filles de ce mariage avec Apollônia (I), modifie ces dispositions, les biens étant désormais partagés entre son fils Esthladas et les cinq filles. Esthladas conserve dans ce testament le cheval de bataille et l'équipement militaire (τὸν μὲν ἵππον ἐφ'οὗ στρατεύομαι καὶ τὰ ὅπλα [πάντα, l. 3-4). La règle proportionnelle adoptée est clairement exprimée pour les esclaves – Esthladas en reçoit quatre (mais il y a trois enfants parmi eux), alors que les cinq filles doivent se contenter à elles-toutes de deux esclaves – ainsi que pour les biens fonciers situés à Diospolis-la-Grande – Esthladas reçoit une part égale à celle Apollônia (II) et de ses quatre soeurs réunies. Ce partage qui assure à l'héritier une part égale à ses cinq sœurs peut certes être interprété comme assurant au fils la part du lion selon un principe bien attesté dans le droit égyptien ancien[21]. Mais on peut aussi le comprendre dans la perspective de donner une part égale aux enfants issus des deux mariages. Dans le premier cas, le partage exprimerait bien évidemment une inégalité testamentaire des sexes; dans le second cette interprétation ne serait plus acceptable, le principe étant une division des biens selon chaque mariage quel que soit le sexe et le nombre d'enfants nés de chacun. Cette seconde hypothèse, proposée par Jane Rowlandson, est séduisante dans le cadre d'une étude du genre puisqu'elle introduit une «neutralité sexuelle» dans le principe du partage[22].

La possibilité pour les femmes grecques d'Égypte d'hériter n'était pas limitée aux milieux clérouchiques. Si la plupart des testaments Petrie émanent bien de ceux-ci, il existe cependant des actes émanant d'autres habitants de l'Égypte ptolémaïque[23]. Willy Clarysse a lui-même souligné combien la désignation de ce dossier comme des «testaments de clérouques» était inadéquate, puisque dans ce corpus de trente documents, quatre émanent d'hommes issus «de l'épigone » (*tês epigonês*) et un texte d'un «étranger résident» (*parepidêmos*)[24]. Aphrodisios qui lègue tous ses biens à sa femme Axiothea est précisément ce *parepidêmos* (P. Petrie^2 24, l. 15-38), qui a le même statut que Zénon de Kaunos lorsque ce dernier quitte le service du dioecète Apollonios. La documentation est donc assez diversifiée socialement, et les parallèles extérieurs à l'Égypte ne sauraient se limiter aux autres milieux clérouchiques connus à savoir la loi sur les successions de Doura-Europos (300-150 av. n.è.). Ce texte dont l'origine royale et séleucide ne semble pas faire de doute pose qu'hérite «Si le défunt n'a pas laissé de postérité ou s'il n'a pas adopté de

[21] Erwin Seidl, «La preminente posizione successoria del figlio maggiore nel diritto dei papiri», *Rend. Ist. Lombardo, Cl. Lett.* 99 (1965), p. 185s.

[22] Jane Rowlandson, *op. cit.*, p. 110.

[23] Il faut joindre au dossier des testaments non clérouchiques le P. Ent. 19 = C.P. Jud. I 127b (Magdôla, 243-221 ou 221-203 av. n.è.) où une femme, Damasippa, prétend avoir des droits sur l'héritage de son parent Diogenês et conteste à Diodôros le droit à héritage d'un Thesmophorion de Déméter. La *Propopographia Ptolemaica* les range tous trois dans la catégorie des pastophores. Fritz Übel, *Die Kleruchen Ägyptens unter den ersten sechs Ptolemäern*, Berlin, 1968, n'utilise de fait pas ce document.

[24] Willy Clarysse, *op. cit.*, p. 32-33.

fils conformément aux lois, le père ou la mère à condition qu'elle ne soit pas remariée, l. 3-6»[25].

L'impression se dégage donc, au total, que le droit et les usages sociaux de l'Égypte grecque offrait au testateur une indéniable liberté qui lui permettait de choisir ses héritiers qui pouvaient être des héritières, dans un cadre où le droit des femmes a connu par rapport à celui de la cité grecque une singulière évolution.

La question se pose cependant de savoir si la femme héritière ne jouissait pas en fait sur cet héritage, non d'une pleine propriété mais d'un simple usufruit, les vrais héritiers étant les enfants du mari. Une clause, que l'on rencontre dans certains contrats, et qui figure également dans la loi de Doura-Europos, stipulait en effet l'impossibilité pour l'épouse survivante de se remarier, ainsi pour Apollônia alias Semmonthis qui devra «rester à la maison et vivre de manière irréprochable, P. Dryton 4, l. 18)». La solution apportée à la question d'une éventuelle capacité testamentaire des femmes peut fournir à ce sujet une réponse décisive: le testateur pouvait-il être une testatrice?

2. Des femmes testatrices?

La documentation issue de l'Égypte ptolémaïque ne nous a livré – à ce jour – aucun testament féminin. Le fait est connu. Willy Clarysse le soulignait encore dans son introduction aux P. Petrie^{2}: «Egyptians and woman are absents»[26]. Le P. Lond. Inv. 2850 publié en 1969 par Pieter W. Pestman sous le titre «A Greek Testament from Pathyris» est en fait une cession (*parakhôrêsis*) de biens d'une mère à sa fille[27]. Ce papyrus grec qui appartient aux riche dossier des «archives (grecques et démotiques) de Pathyris» est une homologie où dame Tathôtis cède de son vivant une partie de ses biens à sa fille Kobaetêsis, elle-même mère de Peteharsemtheus dont les archives privées ont été étudiées par Pestman en 1965[28]. Le formulaire de cette cession réalisée devant un agoranome ne reproduit pas celui des testaments[29], et le verbe utilisé pour désigner cette cession, παρακεχωρηκέναι (l. 16), ne permet pas de trancher la question essentielle, à savoir si cette transmission intervient

[25] Bernard Haussoullier, «Une loi grecque inédite sur les successions 'ab intestat'», *RHD* 1923, p. 515-553 (p. 519): ἐὰ[ν] μὴ [τέκ]να λείπῃ ἢ υἱοποιήσητε κατὰ τοὺς νόμους, πατὴρ ἢ μήτηρ μὴ ἄλλῳ ἀνδρὶ συνοικοῦσα· Cf. Paul Koschaker, «Griechische Rechtsurkunden aus Dura in Mesopotamien», *ZSS. RA*, t. 51 (1931), p. 427-430; Maurice Sartre, *D'Alexandre à Zénobie. Histoire du Levant antique (IVème av J.-C.-IIIème ap. J.-C.*), Paris, 2001, p. 210-211.

[26] Willy Clarysse, *op. cit.*, p. 33.

[27] Pieter W. Pestman, «A Greek Testament from Pathyris (P. Lond. Inv. 2850)», *JEA*, t. 55 (1969), p. 129-160.

[28] Pieter W. Pestman, «Les archives privées de Pathyris à l'époque ptolémaïque. La famille de Pétéharsemtheus, fils de Panebkhounis», dans *Studia Papyrologica Varia*, E. Boswinkel, P.W. Pestman et P.J. Sijpesteijn éd., Leyde, 1965 (Papyrologica Lugduno-Batava 14), p. 47-105.

[29] L. 14: ὁμολογία, ἥν ἑκοῦσα καὶ συνχωρήσασα...

immédiatement du vivant de Tathôtis ou éventuellement plus tard, par exemple après sa mort. L'éditeur du texte reconnaît lui-même un souci de «simplification» dans l'intitulé de son article et admet qu'il faudrait au moins ouvrir les guillemets pour parler d'un «testament»[30].

La question qui se pose est d'interpréter cette lacune des sources. Pour Willy Clarysse celle-ci ne saurait s'expliquer «probablement» que par un malheureux hasard des trouvailles. Il invoque deux faits, auxquels nous ajouterons un troisième terme pour justifier cette hypothèse.

En premier lieu, l'existence de testaments féminins dans l'Égypte romaine, qui permettraient d'invoquer des continuités hellénistico-romaines. Orsolina Montevecchi avait relevé dès 1931 l'importance des quatorze documents alors connus dans son étude sociologique parue dans *Aegyptus,* en concluant qu'en règle générale ces femmes transmettent leurs biens dans la famille de leur mari[31]. Toutes agissent sous le contrôle d'un *kyrios*[32].

En second lieu, la documentation épigraphique d'époque hellénistique extérieure à l'Égypte, fait connaître plusieurs testatrices, ainsi pour la fondation religieuse d'Agasikratis à Calaurie au IIIe siècle (IG IV 840), les fondations testamentaires d'Epiktêta à Théra au tournant du IIIe et du IIe siècle (IG XII 3, 330) ou d'Ekhenikê à Délos vers 250 (IG XI 2, 287A, l. 122-123; IG XI 2, 288, l. 9; IG XI 2, 289, l. 45...) ou bien encore la donation d'Aretê de Mégare au IIe siècle (IG VII, 43). Les analogies entre ces fondations et donations hellénistiques qu'elles émanent d'hommes ou de femmes ont souvent été relevées, ainsi par Andreas Helmis dans son étude de la fondation à la mémoire d'Aleximakhos fils de Kritolaos instituée à Aigialé, une cité d'Amorgos (IG XII.7, 515) lors du *Symposion 1999*[33]. L'absence de mention de *kyrios* uniquement attestée dans l'inscription sur laquelle est gravé le testament d'Agasikratis est probablement due au fait qu'elle soit une version abrégée du testament, le nom de son tuteur étant sans doute cité dans la version complète, en tête du texte. Comme pour les testaments grecs dans l'Égypte romaine, la présence d'un *kyrios* apparaissait donc très probablement indispensable.

En troisième lieu, l'existence d'un type de document où les conjoints définissent d'un commun accord les principes successoraux en cas de décès en faveur des

[30] Pieter W. Pestman, «A Greek Testament from Pathyris (P. Lond. Inv. 2850)», *op. cit.,* p. 141-142.

[31] Orsolina Montevecchi, «Ricerche di sociologia nei documenti dell'Egitto greco-romano. I.-I testamenti», *Aegyptus* 13 (1931), p. 103.

[32] Cf. désormais Livia Migliardi Zingale, *I testamenti romani nei papiri e nelle tavolette d'Egitto. Silloge di documenti dal I al IV secolo d.C.,* Turin, 1991.

[33] Andreas Helmis, «Entre les vivants et les morts. La fondation à la mémoire d'Aleximachos fils de Critolaos (IG XII.7, 515; IIe siècle av. J.-C.), dans *Symposion 1999* (Pazo de Mariñan-La Corogne, 6-9 septembre), Cologne, Weimar, Vienne, 2003, p. 463-480.

enfants ou de tiers, la *syngraphodiathêkê*[34]. Il est attesté dès le début de la période grecque à Éléphantine par un contrat conclu entre un couple de Temnites installés dans l'île nilotique, Dionysios et Kallista (P. Eleph. 2 = M. Chr. 311, 285/3 av. n.è.). Il reste en usage durant l'époque romaine (BGU I 183 = M. Chr. 313 ; BGU I 251; BGU I 252; CPR 28). Cette *diathêkê* est bien un acte juridique, un contrat (*Erbvertrag*) «écrit en commun» puisqu'il se définit comme une homologie et une *syngraphê* (l. 1-2 et 16). Le préverbe συν indique sans ambiguïté que le couple se définit dans la συνγραφοδιαθήκη comme testateur et testatrice.

De ces trois évidences documentaires, la plus importante nous semble être la troisième puisqu'elle est la seule à mettre en évidence la volonté d'une testatrice dans l'Égypte ptolémaïque. Mais elle ne saurait – à notre avis – constituer un indice décisif permettant d'avancer que la femme grecque peut alors tester seule.

Il est en effet évidemment tentant d'invoquer d'éventuels antécédents ptolémaïques aux testaments d'époque romaine écrits par des femmes en dehors des documents conservant les *syngraphodiathêkai*. Mais on peut rétorquer que sur bien des points le droit régissant le statut des femmes a évolué sous les deux dominations, grecque et romaine. Qu'il suffise ici de citer l'admission des femmes grecques des métropoles dans l'ordre des «gens du gymnase». On chercherait en vain un équivalent ptolémaïque à ces femmes «du gymnase» *ai apo gymnasiou*, dont l'institution résulte de la mise en place du statut augustéen de l'Égypte[35].

Les parallèles d'époque hellénistique extérieurs à l'Égypte doivent de même être invoqués avec prudence. Il faut souligner qu'ils concernent une zone géographique précise, la Grèce propre avec Mégare, le Golfe Saronique avec Calaurie, l'Égée avec Théra et Délos. Toute extrapolation géographique dans l'Orient hellénistique est par principe périlleuse tant le monde hellénistique est marqué par la diversité des situations régionales. Les fondations testamentaires sont le fait de riches veuves âgées et influentes dans un cadre social marqué par une éthique aristocratique[36]. La question est de savoir si l'on peut trouver l'équivalent d'un tel cadre aristocratique dans le milieu des immigrants grecs d'Égypte. Celui-ci semble ne pouvoir résider que dans la maison royale et la vie de cour. Mais si nous voyons des reines gérer en toute autonomie leurs biens, les sources littéraires et

---

[34] Cf. Ludwig Mitteis, *Grundzüge der Papyruskunde*, Leipzig, 1912, p. 242; Hans-Albert Rupprecht, *art. cit.* (n. 5); et en dernier lieu Uri Yiftach-Firanko, *Marriage and Marital Arrangements. A History of the Greek Marriage Document in Egypt. 4th century BCE-4th century CE,* Munich, 2003. Orsolina Montevecchi, *La papirologia*, Milan, 1988, p. 205, ne cite curieusement que les *syngraphodiathêkai* d'époque romaine.

[35] Joseph Mélèze Modrzejewski, «Entre la cité et le fisc: le statut grec dans l'Égypte romaine», dans *Symposion 1982* (Santander, 1er-4 septembre 1982), Cologne, Vienne, 1989, p. 241-280; Peter van Minnen, «Ai apo gymnasiou. 'Greek' Women and the Greek 'Elite' in the Metropoleis of Roman Egypt», dans *Le rôle et le statut de la femme en Égypte hellénistique, romaine et byzantine,* p. 337-353.

[36] Anne Bielman, *op. cit.,* p. 26-27.

documentaires restent muettes sur une éventuelle capacité de tester de la *basilissa* et des femmes de la cour.

L'existence de *syngraphodiathêkai* dans l'Égypte ptolémaïque ne saurait non plus faire foi. S'il s'agit bien d'un contrat, la formulation des clauses fait en effet apparaître une indéniable primauté masculine puisque l'on lit aux lignes 2 et 3: «Τάδε διέθετο Διονύσιος Τημνίτης Καλλίται Τημνίτει τῆι αὑτοῦ γυναικί. Il n'est pas inutile de rappeler que les témoins de ce contrat sont – comme pour les contrats de mariage – tous des hommes. Il est par ailleurs hautement probable que ce type de contrat avait pour résultat d'empêcher la femme d'agir seule, après la mort éventuelle de son mari. Elle n'a alors aucun pouvoir pour le modifier de sa propre initiative. Une disposition semblable se lit dans le P. Petrie² 25 (226/225 av. n.è.) où le testateur règle en détail les dispositions testamentaires que devra respecter son épouse Artemidôra pour la transmission des biens à leurs enfants si elle lui survit.

La volonté de la femme ne semble donc – d'après la documentation existante – pouvoir s'exprimer que dans un accord contractuel avec son mari. Ceci ne signifiait nullement que dans la réalité sociale et humaine la volonté féminine ne soit la plus forte et que celle-ci ne prime sur celle du mari. Les femmes grecques de l'Égypte ptolémaïque d'un certain niveau social prenaient de véritables décisions dans l'ordre économique, qu'elles soient par exemple propriétaires foncières ou propriétaires de navires[37]. Sur le plan juridique, la question de la femme testatrice a en fait beaucoup à voir avec celle de la tutelle. Il est aujourd'hui en effet souvent admis que le pouvoir du tuteur (*kyrios*) dans le monde hellénistique semble plus relever d'un formalisme juridique, que d'une foncière inégalité entre les sexes[38]. Cette position trouve une illustration saisissante dans le dossier de la Syrienne Elaphion (P. Eléph. 4 et 3, 283/282 av. n.è.) cher à Joseph Mélèze qui a montré que loin d'être une «fille ou une femme facile», une concubine, une courtisane ou une prostituée, Elaphion est une «femme libre» qui rémunère ses trois *kyrioi* successifs, Diôn, Pantarkês puis Antipatros et se sépare des deux premiers quand ils ne lui donnent plus satisfaction pour des raisons que nous ignorons[39]. La Macédonienne Olympias (P. Giss. 2, 16 septembre 176) qui se donne «elle-même en mariage» par *auto-ekdosis* est elle aussi accompagnée d'un tuteur.

Nous admettrons donc, pour conclure, que la femme grecque d'Égypte – en l'état actuel de notre documentation – n'avait pas la capacité de tester – à l'inverse des Grecques de Calaurie, de Théra ou de Mégare – et que l'inégalité entre les sexes

[37] Cf. Hans Hauben, «Femmes propriétaires et locataires de navires en Égypte ptolémaïque», *JJP* 23 (1993), p. 61-74.

[38] Une bibliographie sur la question est donnée par Anne Bielman *ibid.*, p. 30. Cf. l'analyse globale d'Inès Calero Secall, *op. cit.*, p. 30-37.

[39] Cf. Séminaire de l'EPHE (IVe Section), Paris, «Papyrologie et droits de l'Antiquité». 2004-2005 où fut reprise la vaste question de l'*epitropos* et du *kyrios* en droit grec et hellénistique. Le domaine d'intervention de l'un ou de l'autre n'exige pas de réponse unique. Le droit grec est caractérisé par une grande souplesse du vocabulaire.

serait alors sur ce point patente. Il nous apparaît cependant certain que la femme grecque d'Égypte pouvait intervenir dans les partages successoraux de manière active. Elle intervenait conjointement avec son mari dans la *syngraphodiathêkê*. Et elle disait probablement son mot dans la répartition des biens qu'elle était chargée d'assurer entre les enfants après la mort de l'époux. On peut aussi imaginer qu'elle pouvoit peser – de différentes manières – sur les choix testamentaires faits par son mari. L'analyse des expressions et du vocabulaire juridique exige donc prudence et acribie si l'on veut vraiment percevoir à l'arrière-plan de termes qui pourraient paraître transparents (Κύριος, Τάδε διέθετο Διονύσιος...) la réalité des rapports sociaux, ici des rapports entre les sexes. En dépit de la richesse des sources juridiques, les alcôves des *oikoi* des Grecs d'Égypte gardent bien des mystères.

Les femmes recevaient en revanche des parts d'héritages qui pouvaient être substantielles, la documentation papyrologique révélant des situations très variées dans la volonté du testateur. Mais l'impossibilité probable pour la femme de disposer librement de ces biens paraît les assimiler en fait à un usufruit et non à une pleine propriété. L'interdiction faite à l'épouse héritière de se remarier dans de nombreux contrats de mariage, une clause qui se lit aussi dans la loi de Doura-Europos, apparaît comme une innovation de l'époque ptolémaïque. Dans l'Athènes des orateurs, le legs fait à l'épouse était de fait expressément lié au remariage de la veuve. Le douaire qui était, pour les Athéniennes du IVe siècle av. n.è., une dot indirecte est donc devenu un legs à caractère usufruitier. Mais son but reste le même: assurer à son épouse (ou à une autre femme) un niveau de vie correct après la mort du légataire[40].

ANNEXE

Quatre contrats de mariage

Texte 1 – Le contrat de mariage du clérouque lycien Peisias
P. Petrie^{2} 13 (238/237 av. n.è.). Éd. Willy Clarysse, *The Petrie Papyri*, Second edition, Vol. I, *The Wills*, Bruxelles, 1991.

«Voici les dispositions testamentaires de Peisias, Lycien, du détachement de Leontiskos, [... clérouque], l'un de ceux dotés de terres dans l'Arsinoïte, environ [.] ans, la peau couleur de miel (?), aux cheveux en broussailles, de taille moyenne, au visage allongé, une cicatrice sous le menton, étant conscient et sain d'esprit.

Qu'il me soit possible, étant en bonne santé, de gérer moi-même mes biens. Mais si je suis frappé par le destin humain, je lègue [mes biens] d'Alexandrie à Pisikratês, le fils que j'ai eu de Nikô: un immeuble et tous les équipements que j'y possède et les esclaves Dionysios et Eutykhos, Syriens, et l'esclave féminine Abisila et sa fille Eirênê, Syriennes; à Axiothea fille d'Hippias, Lycienne, mon épouse, l'esclave féminine syrienne Libuseion et la maison que je

[40] L'analyse de genre qui recherche des convergences ou des identités entre des personnes de sexe génétique opposé est donc ici relativement mise en échec, le sexe des testateurs et les héritiers différenciant dans le droit grec de l'Égypte hellénistique de manière fondamentale les hommes et les femmes.

possède dans le village de Boubastos dans l'Arsinoïte; les autres équipements de Boubastos (je les lègue) en commun à Pisikratês et à Axiothea. Tout ce qu'Axiothea a apporté en dot et qui est intact, doit lui rester et ne pas être dévolu à Pisikratês.

Tout ce qui n'est plus intact ou est usé, Pisikratês en restituera le prix inscrit ci-dessous pour le montant de leur perte de valeur:

Pour une tunique de femme en laine: 40 (drachmes)
Pour un vêtement d'été: 6 (drachmes)
Pour une tunique d'homme: 12 (drachmes)
Pour un vêtement usé d'été: 10 (drachmes)
Pour une tunique neuve: 10 (drachmes) 2 (oboles)
Pour une ceinture d'homme: 1 (drachme)
Pour un vêtement neuf d'été: 32 (drachmes)
Pour un vêtement d'intérieur: 8 (drachmes)
Pour un couvre-lit: 12 (drachmes)
Pour un vase en bronze: 4 (drachmes)
Pour des vases à rafraîchir le vin en bronze: 6 (drachmes)
Pour deux tissus de lin: 4 (drachmes)
Pour deux sandales de femmes: 4 (drachmes)
Pour [...]: 30 (drachmes)
Pour un couteau et une broche: 1 (drachme)
Pour de la laine moelleuse: [...]
Pour [...]
Pour un bracelet: 18 (drachmes)
Pour des pendants d'oreille: 12 (drachmes)
Pour un bracelet (?) d'or: 20 (drachmes)
Pour de la laine [...]».

Texte 2 – Le premier testament du clérouque crétois Drytôn fils de Pamphilos
P. Dryton 1 (Diospolis-la-Petite, 31 mai-29 juin 164 av. n.è.). Éd. Katelijn Vandorpe, *The Bilingual Family Archive of Dryton, His Wife Apollonia and theid Daughter Senmouthis*, Bruxelles, 2002.

«Sous le règne de Ptolémée (VI), de Ptolémée (VIII), son frère, et de Cléopâtre (II), sa sœur, enfants de Ptolémée (V) et de Cléopâtre (II), les dieux Épiphanes, l'an 6; le prêtre d' Alexandre, des dieux Sôter, des dieux Adelphes, des dieux Évergètes, des dieux Philopatôr, des dieux Épiphanes, et des dieux Philomêtôr étant Polukritos fils d'Aristodêmos; l'athlophore de Bérénice Évergetis étant Aristonikê fille de <u>*Nwl3ts;*</u> la canéphore d'Arsinoé Philadelphe étant Hermokrateia fille d'Hermokratês; la prêtresse d'Arsinoé Philopatôr étant Dêmarion fille de Mêtrophanês: les prêtresses qui sont en fonction à Alexandrie; à Ptolémaïs de Thébaïde, le prêtre de Ptolémée Sôter étant Noumênios fils d'Hêrakleodôros; celui du roi Ptolémée Philomêtôr étant [...] fils d'Eurumakhos; celui de Ptolémée Philadelphe étant Aristôn fils de Kalliklês; la prêtresse de la reine Cléopâtre étant Agathokleia fille de Noumênios; celle de Cléopâtre, la mère de Ptolémée dieu Épiphane Eukharistos, étant Thaïs fille de <u>*3pr*</u>[...]; la canéphore d'Arsinoé Philadelphe étant Eukharistê fille de Ptolemaios, fils de Ptolemaios: les prêtresses qui sont en fonction à Ptolemaïs; au mois de Pakhôn, le [...] jour, à Diospolis-la-Petite de Thébaïde, devant Dionysios, l'agoranome.

Voici les dispositions testamentaires de Drytôn fils de Pamphilos, du dème Philoteris, un des cavaliers de[...], âgé de [...] ans, de taille moyenne, [...], une cicatrice au-dessus du sourcil gauche, ayant de bonnes sensations, conscient et sain d'esprit. Qu'il me soit possible, étant en bonne santé, de rester maître de mes biens. Mais si je suis frappé par le destin humain, je lègue et je donne mes biens[...] à Sarapias fille d'Esthladas, fils de Theôn, une *astê*, l'épouse avec laquelle j'ai vécu légalement, [...] et grâce à moi [...]. Je ne lègue ni ne donne rien d'autre à quiconque. Je laisse comme *epitropos* Herm[a/o]philos fils de Pamphilos, [...], (un parent) de Drytôn fils de Pamphilos, un des misthophores de la cavalerie[...], l'an 6, mois de Pakhôn[...]

Verso (en démotique)

[...] que Drytôn fils de Pamphilos a rédigé pour sa femme Sarapias fille d'Esthladas.»

Texte 3 – Le deuxième testament de Drytôn fils de Pamphilos
P. Dryton 2 (Latopolis, 4 mars 150 av. n.è.). Éd. Katelijn Vandorpe, *op. cit.*

«Sous le règne de Ptolémée (VI) et de Cléopâtre (II), sa sœur, enfants de Ptolémée (V) et de Cléopâtre (I), dieux Épiphanes, l'an 31; durant la charge du prêtre qui est en fonction à Alexandrie, d' Alexandre, des dieux Sôter, des dieux Adelphes, des dieux Évergètes, des dieux Philopatôr, des dieux Épiphanes, du dieu Eupatôr et des dieux Philomêtôr; durant la charge de l'athlophore de Bérénice Évergetis; durant la charge de la canéphore d'Arsinoé Philadelphe; durant la charge de la prêtresse d'Arsinoé Philopatôr: les prêtresses qui sont en fonction à Alexandrie; à Ptolémaïs de Thébaïde, le prêtre de Ptolémée Sôter étant [...]ios fils de Lukophrôn; celui du roi Ptolémée Philomêtôr étant Antipatros fils d'Antipatros; celui de Ptolémée Philadelphe étant[...] fils de [...]ôros; celui de Ptolémée Évergète étant Ptolemaios fils de Prôtarkhos[...]; celui de Ptolémée Philopatôr étant Diodôros fils de Di[...]; celui du dieu Épiphane Eukharistos étant Nikias fils de Dêmêtrias; celui de Ptolémée Eupatôr étant Zénôn fils de [...]; la prêtresse de la reine Cléopâtre étant Theodôra fille de [...]agros; celle de Cléopâtre, sa mère, étant [...]tê fille de Diognêtos; la canéphore d'Arsinoé Philadelphe étant [...]ais, fille de [...]*thwns*, fils de *Tywgls* (Dioklês?): les prêtresses qui sont en fonction à Ptolémaïs, au mois de Mekheir, le 6ème jour, à Latopolis de Thébaïde, devant Ptolemaios, l'agoranome.

Voici les dispositions testamentaires de Drytôn fils de Pamphilos, du dème Philoteris, un des cavaliers de Diodotos, âgé de [...] ans, de taille moyenne, de peau couleur de miel, aux cheveux longs, au visage allongé, aux cheveux en broussailles, au nez crochu, une cicatrice au-dessus du sourcil gauche, étant en bon santé, conscient et sain d'esprit. Qu'il me soit possible, étant en bonne santé, de rester maître de mes biens, c'est ce que je préfère. Mais si je suis frappé par le destin humain, je lègue et je donne mes biens, meubles et immeubles, à Esthladas, le fils que j'ai eu de Sarapias, fille d'Esthladas, une *astê*, l'épouse avec laquelle j'ai vécu, (donc) à Esthladas, mon fils sus-mentionné, la moitié de mon héritage, les armes et le cheval avec lequel je fais la guerre; le reste ira aux enfants qui me naîtront d'Apollônia. Je laisse comme *epitropos* Herm[a/o]philos fils de Pamphilos, du dème Philoteris, un parent de Drytôn fils de Pamphilos, ainsi que d'Esthladas fils d'Esthladas. Je ne lègue ni ne donne rien d'autre à quiconque.

Suit la liste des six témoins

Moi Ptolemaios je me suis occupé de cette affaire.

Verso

Le mariage d'Apollônia avec Drytôn a eu lieu à Latopolis devant Ptolemaios, l'agoranome, l'an 31, le 6 Mekheir».

Texte 4 – Le troisième testament de Drytôn fils de Pamphilos
P. Dryton 4 (Pathyris, 29 juin 126 av. n.è.). Éd. Katelijn Vandorpe, *op. cit.*

«L'an 44, le 9 du mois de Payni, à Pathyris, devant Asklêpiadês l'agoranome.

Voici les dispositions testamentaires de Drytôn fils de Pamphilos, Crétois, un des «diadoques» et hipparque à la tête des hommes incorporés dans la réserve, étant en bon santé, conscient et sain d'esprit.

Qu'il me soit possible, étant en bonne santé, de rester maître de mes biens. Mais si je suis frappé par le destin humain, je lègue et je donne mes biens, meubles et immeubles, bétail et tout ce que j'acquerrais: le cheval avec lequel je fais la guerre et tout mon équipement militaire, à Esthladas mon fils que j'ai eu de Sarapias fille d'Esthladas, fils de Theôn, une *astê*, à laquelle j'ai été uni par le mariage légalement et conformément au testament qui a été rédigé dans le bureau de Diospolis-la-Petite, devant l'agoranome Dionysios, l'an 6 du règne de Philomêtôr, (un testament) qui précise, entre autres dispositions, la désignation d'Herm[a/o]philos comme *epitropos,* un parent; des quatre esclaves domestiques, (je lègue à Esthladas) celle dont le nom est Mursinê et ses enfants (?) [...]; mais les deux autres esclaves féminines dont le nom est Eirênê et Ampelion (je les lègue) à Apollônia et à ses sœurs, mes cinq filles; et (je lègue à Esthladas) le vignoble situé dans la zone sèche et caillouteuse sur la rive est du Pathyrite, ainsi que les puits de brique cuite qui s'y trouvent et les autres dépendances, et le char avec son équipement, et le colombier, ainsi qu'un autre à moitié terminé, ainsi qu'une cour dont le voisinage est constitué au sud par des terrains vagues dudit Esthladas, au sud par la maison voûtée d'Apôllonia la Jeune, à l'est par le terrain de Petras[...] fils d'Esthladas, à l'ouest par le terrain vague d'Esthladas, jusqu'à la porte qui s'ouvre vers l'ouest. Les autres bâtiments avec leurs dépendances, ainsi qu'un vieux [...], ainsi que le terrain vague affecté au colombier au-dessous de la porte d'Esthladas et à l'ouest de la maison voûtée, je les donne à Apôllonia, à Aristô, à Aphrodisia, à Nikariôn et à Apollônia la Jeune, les cinq filles que j'ai eues d'Apôllonia alias Senmônthis, la femme avec laquelle je suis uni légalement; elles posséderont aussi deux esclaves féminines et la vache, en parts égales, conformément au partage que j'ai fait. Esthladas cèdera (à ses sœurs?), sur le terrain à lui donné face à la porte qui s'ouvre sur l'ouest, quatre coudées carrées pour l'emplacement d'un four. Pour ce qui est des immeubles et des terrains vagues à Diospolis-la-Grande dans le quartier de l'Ammôneion et dans le quartier des Potiers, Esthladas en aura la moitié, Apollônia et ses sœurs l'autre moitié. Ils partageront, également à part égale, le reste de ma fortune consistant en créances de blé et d'argent et les meubles. Esthladas ainsi qu'Apollônia et ses sœurs fourniront ensemble les sommes pour l'achèvement du colombier qui doit être construit dans l'emplacement prévu; (ils fourniront) à Apôllonia alias Senmônthis, ma femme, pendant une période de quatre ans, si elle reste à la maison et vit de manière irréprochable, pour sa subsistance et celle de ses deux filles, chaque mois, 9,5 artabes de blé, 1/12 (d'artabe) de croton et 200 (drachmes) de cuivre. Après quatre ans, ils donneront les mêmes montants aux deux plus jeunes filles durant onze années. Ils donneront à Takhratis pour sa dot 12 talents en monnaie de cuivre sur les fonds communs. Tous les biens possédés par Senmônthis qu'elle aura acquis pour elle-même pendant la durée du mariage avec Drytôn, resteront sa propriété. Ceux qui intenteraient des poursuites contre elle au sujet de ces acquisitions [serait débouté].

L'an 44, mois de Payni».

BARBARA ANAGNOSTOU-CANAS (PARIS)

LA RÉPARATION DU PRÉJUDICE DANS LES PAPYRUS GRECS D'ÉGYPTE

Lorsque le dommage subi revêt un caractère extrapatrimonial, sa réparation peut susciter des objections, tant il est difficile pour les uns de la solliciter sans avoir l'air de monnayer leur douleur et pour les autres de l'accorder d'une façon adéquate. C'est à ce sujet qui n'a jamais cessé d'être à l'ordre du jour que sera consacrée cette communication sur la réparation du préjudice dans les papyrus grecs d'Égypte. Je me propose d'étudier les sanctions réparatrices du préjudice moral telles qu'elles ont pu être appliquées dans la réalité juridique de l'Égypte hellénistique et romaine et leurs précédents dans le monde grec.

De tout temps la codification de la réparation du préjudice moral a été très limitée et de nos jours son application en France dépend de l'extension que le juge donnera aux articles 1382 et 1383 du Code Napoléon régissant la responsabilité civile[1]. Or, aussi bien dans le droit grec ancien que dans celui de l'Égypte hellénistique et romaine, la réparation du préjudice moral n'était pas prévue d'une façon explicite par la loi. Cependant, si l'intention explicite des législateurs de prévoir la réparation du dommage moral faisait défaut, l'idée de cette réparation avait pris du relief depuis l'époque archaïque.

Ainsi, le plus ancien exemple d'exercice de la justice qui nous soit parvenu pour la Grèce antique, à savoir la scène judiciaire représentée sur le bouclier d'Achille[2],

---

1 Sur l'article 1382 du code civil relatif au délit civil, c'est-à-dire au fait illicite et dommageable commis avec l'intention de nuire:«Tout fait quelconque de l'homme, qui cause à autrui un dommage, oblige celui par la faute duquel il est arrivé à le réparer» et sur l'article1383 relatif au quasi-délit civil, c'est-à-dire au fait illicite dommageable commis sans intention de nuire: «Chacun est responsable du dommage qu'il a causé, non seulement par son fait, mais encore par sa négligence ou par son imprudence», voir Fr. Terré, Ph. Simler, Y. Lequette, *Droit civil. Les obligations*, 6e éd., 1996, p. 535sq. Sur la réparation du préjudice revêtant un caractère extrapatrimonial, voir *ibidem*, p. 562-563; cf. Fr. Givord, *La réparation du préjudice moral*, Thèse pour le doctorat, Grenoble, 1938, 293 p. et P. Kayser, «Remarques sur l'indemnisation du droit moral dans le droit contemporain», *Mélanges J. Macqueron*, Aix-en-Provence, 1974, p. 411-424.

2 Homère, *Iliade XVIII, 497-508*. Sur l'interprétation de cette scène voir E. Cantarella, «Lo scudo di Achille: Considerazioni sul processo in età omerica», *Riv. Ital. Sc. Giur., 3e sér., 16*, 1972, p. 246-267; Eadem, *Les peines de mort en Grèce et à Rome. Origines et fonctions des supplices capitaux dans l'Antiquité classique*, Paris, 2000, p. 59-60.

présente deux hommes qui se disputaient au sujet d'un *wergeld*, le prix du sang (*poinê*) qui était dû à l'occasion d'un homicide. Cette transaction permettait à l'auteur du meurtre de ne pas s'exiler et interdisait au vengeur de s'attaquer au coupable car il était censé se satisfaire et abandonner son désir de vengeance en recevant une indemnité[3]. Dans un autre passage de l'Iliade[4], pour infléchir la colère d'Achille, provoquée à la suite de l'outrage (*hybris*) subi par le Péléide quand Agamemnon lui a enlevé sa récompense de guerrier, à savoir la captive Briséis[5], et pour l'inciter à accepter les cadeaux offerts par Agamemnon en réparation du préjudice subi et à reprendre le combat, Ajax rappelle au fils de Thétis le principe de ces compositions volontaires: «on accepte pourtant du meurtrier d'un frère une compensation (*poinê*) – on en accepte même pour un enfant mort! – et, de cette façon, l'un reste dans son bourg, puisqu'il a largement payé, l'autre retient son âme et son cœur superbe, puisqu'il a reçu sa compensation». [6]

A Athènes, la loi sur l'homicide attribuée à Dracon, datée de 621/620, recopiée sur pierre en 409/408 et conservée dans l'*IG I³, 104*[7], réglementait l'*aidesis*, à savoir le pardon que les parents de la victime avaient la possibilité d'accorder à l'auteur d'un homicide en contrepartie d'une compensation. La loi, dont le contenu a été l'objet de nombreuses analyses juridiques[8], prévoyait l'exil comme sanction pour celui qui avait été reconnu coupable d'homicide involontaire non prémédité (*mê ek pronoias*[9]). En ce qui concerne l'*aidesis*, trois groupes étaient appelés les uns après les autres à accorder ce pardon: d'abord le père, le frère et le fils du défunt; ensuite les parents plus éloignés jusqu'aux enfants des cousins; enfin, s'il s'agissait d'un homicide involontaire par imprudence (*akôn*) dont le caractère avait été reconnu par un arrêt des éphètes, en l'absence de parents de la victime, le pardon pouvait être accordé par dix membres de la phratrie choisis par les éphètes[10]. Sans entrer dans

---

3 Cf. G. Glotz, *La solidarité de la famille dans le droit criminel en Grèce*, Paris, 1904, p. 94sq.

4 *IX, 626-642.*

5 *Iliade IX, 367-369.*

6 *Iliade IX, 632-636* (trad. P. Mazon, Paris, 1937). Cf. E. Cantarella, *Norma e sanzione in Omero. Contributo alla protoistoria di dirito greco*, Milan, 1979, p. 231sq., et Eadem, *Les peines de mort en Grèce et à Rome*, Paris, 2000, p. 57-58.

7 *=Nomima I, 02*: H. Van Effenterre-Fr.Ruzé, *Nomima. Recueil d'inscriptions politiques et juridiques de l'archaïsme grec, t. I, no 02*, Rome, 1994, p. 16-23.

8 Voir les travaux cités dans H. Van Effenterre-Fr.Ruzé, *Nomima I, 02*, p. 18 et 21; cf. les travaux recensés par A. Maffi et M. Faraguna, «Monde grec», *RHD 66*, 1988, p. 111-116, *68*, 1990, p. 125 et *71*,1993, p. 647-649.

9 Sur cette notion dans la loi de Dracon, cf. les interprétations d' E. Cantarella, «Φόνος μὴ ἐκ προνοίας. Contributo alla storia dell'elemento soggetivo nell'atto illecito», *Symposion 1971, Vorträge zur griechischen und hellenistichen Rechtsgeschichte*, Cologne,Vienne, 1975, p. 293-319, Eadem, *Studi sull'omicidio in diritto greco e romano*, Milan, 1976, p. 79-127 et celles de M. Gagarin, *Drakon and the Early Athenian Homicide Law*, New Haven et Londres,1981, p. 30sq.

10 *IG I³*, 104, *l.13-19*; cf. Démosthène, *Contre Macartatos 57;*

l'interprétation des détails de la loi, nous retiendrons ici que, même si l'homicide avait été commis sans intention de donner la mort, c'est aux proches parents de la victime qu'appartenait la décision de pardonner au coupable et d'accepter la composition. Certes, le but premier de l'*aidesis* était d'arrêter la poursuite du crime; pour autant, elle avait également une fonction compensatoire du dommage qu'avaient éprouvé les parents de la victime[11], un dommage qui pouvait aussi être patrimonial mais dont le caractère moral prévalait. Par la consécration des compositions volontaires, la loi de Dracon consacrait donc implicitement aussi l'indemnisation du préjudice d'affection accompagnant la mort, en l'occurrence de la douleur éprouvée en raison d'un lien de parenté avec la victime. Au demeurant, la rançon de l'homicide[12] compensait la frustration forcément éprouvée par les parents du mort, lesquels, en dépit de l'offense qu'ils avaient subie, accordaient le pardon en faisant preuve de beaucoup d'humanité[13] mais se trouvaient privés de la satisfaction que leur procurait l'exécution du châtiment infligé au coupable, fût-ce une peine légale comme l'exil et non plus une vengeance privée.

Si les textes des orateurs athéniens de l'époque classique nous informent sur les peines publiques prévues par la cité contre les auteurs d'homicide[14], dans l'Égypte ptolémaïque la seule intervention de l'État connue au sujet de la répression de l'homicide est le *prostagma* de Ptolémée VIII Évergète II, Cléopâtre II et Cléopâtre III, par lequel ces souverains, après une période de guerre civile, désirant effacer un passé caractérisé par l'arbitraire et par la corruption, ont accordé une amnistie pénale générale dont ils ont exclu les gens coupables de meurtres et de sacrilèges[15]. Aucune loi royale ne nous parle d'une sanction étatique de l'homicide. Cependant, un petit nombre de documents de la pratique, dont la plainte conservée par le *P. Köln VI 272*[16], montrent qu'une procédure judiciaire était prévue afin que les suspects de meurtre dénoncés par les parents de la victime soient traduits en justice et proclamés coupables par l'autorité publique. Dans une autre plainte pour homicide sur la voie

---

[11] Cf. A.R.W. Harrison, *The Law of Athens. Procedure*, Oxford, 1981, p. 78.

[12] *Ὑποφόνια* (*Harpocration*, éd. J.J. Keaney, Amsterdam, 1991, p. 257,Y13) εἰκοσάβοιον (*Pollux 9, 60-61*: F. Jacoby, *F GR HIST III, b Suppl., t. I*, Leyde, 1954, *568, l. 10-11*). Sur les termes utilisés à l'époque classique pour désigner la somme que l'auteur d'un homicide payait aux parents de la victime afin que ces derniers arrêtent les poursuites légales contre lui cf. M. Gagarin, *op. cit.*, p. 139, et E. Heitsch «Aidesis im attischen Strafrecht», *Abhandlungen der Geistes- und sozialwissenschaftlichen Klasse / Akademie der Wissenschaften und der Literatur* 1, 1984, p. 11-12.

[13] Cf. Démosthène, *Contre Midias* 43.

[14] La sanction tenait compte de l'intention de l'auteur du crime – peine de mort pour meurtre, exil pour homicide involontaire – Démosthène, *Contre Midias 43* et *Contre Aristocrate 72*; cf. E. Karabélias, «La peine dans l'Athènes classique», *La peine. Recueils de la Soc. J. Bodin 55*, Bruxelles, 1991, p. 77-132.

[15] *P. Tebt. I 5, l.1-5=C. Ord. Ptol. 53*, daté de 121/0-118 av. n. è.

[16] Datée du milieu du IIe s. av. n. è.

publique[17], déposée par le frère de la victime, celui-ci demande la recherche des coupables en vue non seulement de leur punition mais aussi de la réparation du préjudice matériel subi, en l'occurrence la perte d'un âne qui accompagnait la victime et d'une somme d'argent que celle-ci portait sur elle. Dans sa liste de documents[18], Andrea Jördens cite cinq papyrus qui contiennent des plaintes pour coups et blessures si forts qu'ils ont mis la victime en danger de mort[19]. Les plaignants y demandent soit au roi, soit aux fonctionnaires auxquels ils ont adressé leur plainte de prendre des mesures afin d'assurer la comparution en justice de l'auteur des coups[20]. En l'occurrence, il s'agissait pour les juges sollicités ou bien d'énoncer un mandat d'amener ou d'arrêt[21] ou bien de demander une caution de la part de l'accusé; ce dernier devait soit déposer une somme d'argent, soit fournir des répondants qui garantiraient sa présence[22]. Les plaignants tenaient donc à ce que, s'ils trépassaient à la suite de leurs blessures, l'accusé fût jugé pour homicide[23]. Cela est dit clairement dans le *P.Tebt. III 2 960* où l'on trouve une phrase quasi identique à celle formulée par l'auteur du *P. Köln VI 272*[24]. Dans les *P. Ent. 81*, *P. Tebt. III 1 800* et *I 44* les plaignants disent agir pour que l'agresseur ne s'échappe pas impuni (*athôos*), si ses victimes mouraient. Quant à la plaignante du *P. Ryl. II 68*, elle demande à l'épistate des phylacites que, si elle décédait des suites de l'agression qu'elle a subie, la décision soit conforme aux dispositions des ordonnances applicables aux cas de coups et blessures pouvant entraîner la mort[25]. Toutefois, nous ignorons le contenu de ces lois royales et les formules des demandeurs exprimant le désir que l'accusé soit puni ne nous informent pas sur la nature de la sanction attendue. J. Mélèze-Modrzejewski[26] pense que, en cas de meurtre, la justice

---

17 *BGU VIII 1857*, sans date.

18 «Die Ahndung von Übergriffen auf Leib und Leben im griechischen Ägypten. Liste de références avec extraits des documents cités: I. Belege aus ptolemäischer Zeit, B. Nur Sanction, ohne Erwähnung einer Summe».

19 *P. Ent. 81* (221 av. n. è.), *P. Tebt. I 44, III 1 800, III 2 960* (114, 142 et IIe s. av. n. è.) et *P. Ryl. II 68* (89 av.n. è.).

20 Διεγγυᾶσθαι et ἀσφαλίζεσθαι. Dans deux documents (*P. Ent. 81* et *P. Ryl. II 68*), il est question d'un délai légal au terme duquel l'auteur de l'agression devait être jugé; ce délai devait commencer le jour de l'enregistrement de la plainte. Cet enregistrement ἐν χρηματισμῶι est expressément requis dans le *P. Tebt. I 44*.

21 Cf. R. Taubenschlag, *The Law of the Greco-Roman Egypt in the Light of the Papyri, 332 B.C.-640 A.D.*, 2e éd. (*Law²*), Varsovie, 1955, p. 439 et H.J. Wolff, *Das Justizwesen der Ptolemäer*, Munich, 1962, p. 164, n. 15.

22 Cf. le commentaire d'O.Guéraud ad *P. Ent. 81, l. 17-23.*

23 Selon toute vraisemblance par les agents administratifs auxquels ils adressaient la plainte; cf. H.J. Wolff, *op. cit.*, p. 115-122 et 123sq., qui pense que ces derniers pouvaient infliger une peine en vertu de leur pouvoir coercitif.

24 Ἵν', ἐάν τι πάθῃ, ἔνοχος εἴη τῶι φόνωι et ὅπως ἔνοχος γένηται περὶ τοῦ φόν[ο]υ.

25 *L. 22-25=C. Ord. Ptol. All. 86.*

26 «La sanction de l'homicide en droit grec et hellénistique», *Symposion 1990, Papers on Greek and Hellenistic Legal History*, Cologne, 1991, p. 3-16 et *Mélanges Pierre*

lagide pouvait proclamer la culpabilité de l'accusé mais qu'elle ne pouvait prononcer à son encontre aucune peine afflictive. Tout au plus elle pouvait reconnaître à la famille du défunt le droit d'obtenir la réparation du dommage subi. Pour H.-A. Rupprecht l'homicide faisait l'objet d'une sanction étatique et celle-ci relevait des attributions juridiques des fonctionnaires du roi[27]. A partir du *P. Tebt. I 14* (114 av. n. è.), il admet aussi que cette sanction pouvait être la confiscation des biens du condamné. Cependant, on y voit le comogrammate Menchès ordonner la mise sous séquestre jusqu'à la fin de son procès des biens d'un accusé pour homicide qui était convoqué à comparaître trois jours plus tard. Dans sa réponse à H.-A. Rupprecht, R.S. Bagnall[28] pense qu'il ne s'agit pas d'une peine de confiscation mais d'une mesure de sûreté en vue d'une somme à verser à la suite d'une condamnation par le tribunal. S'agissait-il d'une amende à verser à l'État donc d'une peine patrimoniale ou d'une composition pécuniaire fixée par l'autorité publique en faveur des parents de la victime ou bien encore, dans ce dernier cas, d'un partage de la somme? La question de la nature de la condamnation reste ouverte mais le fait est que, quel que fût le degré de distinction de la répression et de la réparation en matière d'homicide dans l'Égypte des Ptolémées, en dehors du règlement de ce délit dans un cadre judiciaire, la documentation ne nous a livré ni de cas de vengeance privée, ni d'acceptation d'une compensation de la part des proches parents de la victime.

Sous les Romains, l'homicide en Égypte était un délit public (*crimen*) qui entraînait les peines de l'exil et de la confiscation des biens du coupable[29]; les documents de la pratique judiciaire font état de poursuites judiciaires engagées sur l'initiative des proches de la victime[30] et, dans le cas spécial du meurtre d'un officier, d'une poursuite *ex officio* par l'État[31]. Nonobstant, une lettre privée, le *P. Mich. VIII, 473*, daté du début du IIe siècle de notre ère, révèle qu'un homicide ne donnait pas toujours lieu à une action judiciaire[32]. En marge du droit positif, Tabatheus, une pérégrine de Karanis, envisageait la composition avec la famille de la victime d'un homicide commis par son fils Saturnilus. Elle a écrit à son frère, le soldat romain Claudius Tiberianus, afin de lui réclamer une somme d'argent de 1200 drachmes qui lui était due à titre d'indemnité à la suite d'un dommage matériel

---

Lévêque, M.-M. Mactoux et E. Geny (dir.), t. 7, *Société et anthropologie*, Besançon-Paris, 1993 (Centre de rech. d'hist. anc. 121; Annales littér. de l'Univ. de Besançon 491), p. 245-259.

27 «Straftaten und Rechtschutz nach den griechischen Papyri der ptolemäischen Zeit», *Symposion 1990*, p. 139-141 et 146-147.

28 «Response to Hans-Albert Rupprecht», *ibidem*, p. 151.

29 *Gnômôn de l'Idiologue § 36=BGU V 1210;* cf. R. Taubenschlag, *Law²*, p. 434.

30 *P. Amh. 66* (123/124)*; P. Oxy. XVII 2111*(entre 133 et 137); *P. Oxy. III 472* (130), *P. Tebt.* II *333=M. Chrest. 115* (216).

31 *P. Brem. 37* (vers 118).

32 Cf. J. Modrzejewski, «Quelques remarques à propos de l'homicide et de la rançon dans le droit d'Egypte romaine. Note sur *P. Mich.* VIII 473», *IURA* 8, 1957, p. 93-101.

(*blabê*) et pour lui demander que cette somme serve de rançon (*peripsêma*[33]) en réparation de l'homicide qui semble ne pas avoir été prémédité. Si la famille de la victime acceptait cette solution illégale, c'est très probablement parce qu'elle estimait que la somme qui lui était offerte à titre de rançon servirait à réparer le tort moral et éventuellement aussi patrimonial qu'elle avait subi avec la perte de son proche parent, tandis que les peines de l'exil et de la confiscation de ses biens qui menaçaient l'assassin jugé coupable, mis à part leur satisfaction morale, ne procureraient pas de compensation en argent aux parents de la victime. Au demeurant ces derniers, s'ils y tenaient, pouvaient aussi suivre en plus la voie légale et engager un procès pénal contre l'auteur du crime. Cette éventualité ne semble pourtant pas hanter l'auteur de la lettre, qui paraît persuadée que les parents, en acceptant la rançon, renonceraient à leur droit de poursuite légale du coupable.

*

Un délit qui à Athènes aurait pu donner lieu à une réparation du préjudice moral est celui d'*hybris*[34]. Une loi rapportée par Démosthène dans son discours *Contre Midias*, 47[35] nous apprend qu'il pouvait être commis sur la personne d'un homme, d'une femme ou d'un enfant, libre ou esclave, mais le texte ne donne pas de définition de la notion d'*hybris* qui était censée être connue de tous mais qui n'avait pas une extension limitée à un certain nombre d'actes. D'après les discours des orateurs, les actes générateurs du délit de l'*hybris* variaient mais leur trait commun était que leur auteur portait délibérément atteinte à l'honneur (*timê*) d'une autre personne[36]. Bien qu'en eux-mêmes ces actes fussent contraires au droit, le législateur athénien avait ajouté la mention «ou tout comportement contraire à la loi», afin d'élargir le champ d'application de la loi sur l'*hybris*. C'était un délit public qui donnait lieu à une action publique (*graphê hybreôs*) dont l'initiative appartenait à tout citoyen athénien (*pas boulomenos*) et qui était sanctionné par une peine. Mais la démonstration de l'outrage était loin d'être inattaquable; en effet, il ressort des discours des orateurs

---

33 Cf. la note de l'éditeur du *P. Mich. VIII 473* ad *l. 18*.

34 Sur le sens de la notion d'*hybris* dans le monde homérique avant que ce terme n'ait acquis un sens juridique précis, voir E. Cantarella, «Spunti di riflesione critica su ὕβρις e τιμή in Omero», *Symposion 1979. Akten der Gesellschaft für griechische und hellenistische Rechtsgeschichte*, Cologne, Vienne, 1983, p. 85-96.

35 Cf. Eschine, *Contre Timarque 15*.

36 Cf. N. Fisher, «The Law of *hubris* in Athens», *Nomos. Essays in Athenian Law, Politics and Society*, Cambridge, 1990, p. 126. Dans son ouvrage fondamental sur l'*hybris*, N.R.E. Fisher, *Hybris. A Study in the Values of Honour and Shame in Ancient Greece*, Warminster, 1992, p. 36-82, étudie les actes considérés comme constitutifs du délit d'*hybris* dans la pratique judiciaire mais aussi, p. 151sq, l'emploi du terme d'*hybris* en dehors de la sphère du droit, à savoir dans des sources littéraires, d'Homère à Platon et à Aristote, en passant par Solon, les poètes archaïques, les trois tragiques athéniens, et les historiens Hérodote et Thucydide, qui reflètent la pensée morale commune à ce sujet.

qu'il fallait démontrer que les faits, les paroles ou les agissements de l'accusé avaient porté atteinte à l'honneur de la victime en insistant aussi bien sur les circonstances que sur la personnalité de l'auteur du délit et, très probablement aussi, sur sa *proairesis* à outrager sa victime[37]. L'action étant estimable, c'est le tribunal qui se prononçait sur la peine, afflictive ou pécuniaire, que l'auteur de l'*hybris* devait subir ou acquitter, et, dans le cas d'une peine pécuniaire, après avoir choisi entre les «estimations», les *timêseis*, proposées par les deux parties en présence[38]. Le préjudice moral pour atteinte à l'honneur ou à la considération d'un individu était donc reconnu par le droit attique mais comme le montrent les dires de Démosthène[39], la cité, qui se sentait atteinte par l'outrage autant que la victime d'*hybris*[40], considérait que le châtiment du coupable donnait à sa victime une pleine satisfaction et que cette dernière n'avait pas à réclamer pour elle une indemnité. Mais, étant donné qu'un nombre de faits illicites qui avaient généré le délit d'*hybris* comme par exemple les voies de fait, les actes de violence ou les injures verbales, constituaient des délits privés, les personnes lésées pouvaient intenter une action privée (*dikê*) contre l'auteur, ce qui leur permettait d'obtenir une indemnité[41]. C'est ce que fit le jeune et timide Athénien Aristôn qui avait été attaqué outrageusement par Conon et sa bande mais qui a renoncé à la *graphê hybreôs* pour n'intenter contre son agresseur qu'une action privée pour voies de fait (*dikê aikeias*)[42]. Dans son plaidoyer civil *Contre Conon, 1*, Démosthène fait dire à Aristôn que, en dépit de l'outrage qu'il avait subi, il lui a été conseillé par ses amis et parents de ne pas recourir à une action aussi grave que la *graphê hybreôs* et de ne pas montrer une présomption au-dessus de son âge[43]. Il était également plus prudent pour Aristôn de ne pas risquer de payer l'amende de mille drachmes qui frappait l'auteur perdant d'une action publique ou ayant renoncé à son accusation[44]. Démosthène lui-même a choisi une solution extrajudiciaire lorsque, pour une raison ou pour une autre, il a renoncé à poursuivre son vieil ennemi Midias qui l'avait frappé en pleine figure au théâtre en présence des Athéniens assemblés, quand l'orateur était chorège, lors de

37 A ce propos voir la contribution de J.-M. Bertrand, «A propos de la *Rhétorique* d'Aristote (I, 1373b1-1374b23), analyse du processus judiciaire», *supra*, p. 237-252 et la réponse de S.C. Todd, *supra*, p. 253-258.

38 Sur le déclenchement de la procédure de l'action publique pour *hybris* et sur les sanctions prévues par la loi voir A.R.W. Harrison, *op. cit.*, p. 74-82 et D. MacDowell, *The Law in Classical Athens*, Londres, 1978, p. 129-132.

39 *Contre Midias 45*.

40 Sur l'exercice réel de l'action publique d'*hybris* pour outrage commis sur la personne d'un ou d'une esclave et plus particulièrement dans un contexte sexuel, cf. la contribution au présent volume de E.E. Cohen, «Laws affecting Prostitution in Athens», *supra*, p. 201-224.

41 Cf. A.R.W. Harrison, *op. cit.*, p. 76, n. 1.

42 Cf. N.R.E. Fisher, *Hybris*, p. 39-40.

43 Cf. D.M. MacDowell, «Hybris in Athens», *Greece & Rome 23*, 1976, p. 28sq.

44 Cf. Démosthène, *Contre Midias 47*.

la fête des Grandes Dionysies en 347 av. n. è. Ces circonstances particulières ont permis à Démosthène de déclencher la *probolê* qui était une procédure spéciale destinée à mettre en cause les auteurs d'outrage à la fête et a obtenu du peuple un vote (*katacheirotonia*) qui déclarait Midias coupable à l'égard de la fête (*adikein tê heortê*)[45]. Cependant cette victoire était purement morale et il fallait que le tribunal prononçât un second jugement pour le délit commis. Dans le virulent discours qui nous est parvenu, Démosthène accuse Midias d'*hybris* envers lui mais il ne l'a jamais prononcé car il a préféré en rester là. Dix-sept années plus tard, son ennemi politique Eschine nous apprend[46] qu'un arrangement a eu lieu et que Démosthène a vendu pour trente mines et l'injure subie et la sentence préalable prononcée par le peuple contre Midias

*

Il faut se transporter en Égypte au IIIe siècle avant notre ère pour trouver une législation comparable à la loi athénienne sur l'*hybris*. Il s'agit d'une loi alexandrine conservée dans le *P. Hal. 1, ll. 210-213* et intitulée «sur l'*hybris*» qui clôt une série de dispositions concernant les agressions physiques telles que les menaces avec un instrument, les coups et blessures entre un esclave et un homme libre ou entre hommes libres, punies par des peines pécuniaires fixées par le tribunal suivant des tarifs établis par la loi (*P. Hal. 1, ll. 186-209*). La disposition «sur l'*hybris*» établissait les modalités d'exercice de l'action accordée à la personne qui avait subi un outrage (*kathybrizein*) qui n'était pas prévu par la loi dans ses précédentes dispositions (*agrapha*). En dehors des actes violents portant atteinte à l'intégrité corporelle d'autrui, le droit alexandrin faisait donc un délit de tout acte qui portait atteinte à l'honneur de quelqu'un[47]. Mais ce n'était pas une disposition qui reposait sur une simple réception du droit athénien[48]. En effet, contrairement à ce qui se

---

45 Au sujet de la *probolê* voir A.R.W. Harrison, *op. cit.*, p. 59-64 et D.M. MacDowell, *The Law in Classical Athens*, p. 194-197; cf. G.O. Galen, «The Charge against Meidias», *Hermes 122*, 1994, p. 55-63.

46 *Contre Ctésiphon 52.*

47 Les *agrapha* ne se réfèrent pas à des agressions physiques autres que celles prévues dans les *ll.186-209* comme le pensaient les éditeurs du *P. Halensis*, p. 117, commentaire ad *l. 210;* cf. J. Vélissaropoulos, 'Αλεξανδρινοὶ νόμοι. Πολιτικὴ αὐτονομία καὶ νομικὴ αὐτοτέλεια τῆς πτολεμαϊκῆς 'Αλεξάνδρειας, Athènes-Komotini, 1981, p. 128

48 L'identité des lois alexandrines et athéniennes a été affirmée par un martyr païen alexandrin devant un empereur romain qui devait être Trajan ou Hadrien (*P. Oxy. XVIII 2177*=H.A. Musurillo, *The Acts of Pagan Martyrs*, Oxford, 1954, *X, Acta Athenodori, l. 12-17*). Pour F. Pringsheim, *The Greek Law of Sale*, Weimar, 1950, p. 8, n. 1, cette affirmation est une hyperbole rhétorique sans valeur juridique et, d'après lui, il s'agirait d'une coïncidence partielle entre les deux droits, notamment en matière d'*hybris*. J. Partsch, «Die alexandrinischen Dikaiomata», *Arch. f. Pap. 6*, 1920, p. 54sq, pense que les Alexandrins se seraient inspirés pour leur loi sur l'*hybris* de dispositions en vigueur dans le monde grec ailleurs qu'à Athènes et reconnaissant une action privée (*dikè*) à la

passait à Athènes, l'action envisagée était privée, reconnue à la victime d'un outrage et réservée aux Alexandrins mais ne concernant pas les esclaves. Le procès était estimable et la disposition alexandrine énonce que le perdant devait acquitter le double de la condamnation pécuniaire, du *timêma*, fixée par le tribunal. Cependant une loi royale lagide conservée également dans le *P. Hal.1, ll. 115-118* qui porte sur l'organisation judiciaire à Alexandrie dispose que le perdant d'un procès pour *hybris* devait verser à la victime le dixième du montant déterminé par le tribunal. Le droit alexandrin ne pouvait pas se prétendre aussi «poliade» que le droit athénien, produit de la cité la plus policée selon Solon, car «sans être lésé soi-même, on y mettait autant de zèle à poursuivre et à punir une injustice que ceux qui en étaient victimes»[49]. Nonobstant, la disposition alexandrine s'avérait aussi moins intimidante que la loi athénienne pour le déclenchement d'un procès pour *hybris* puisque d'une part, au moins une partie de la peine pécuniaire était allouée à la victime et d'autre part, le plaignant ne risquait pas de payer une amende s'il décidait d'abandonner son procès ou si sa plainte n'était pas jugée recevable. Le manque de définition de la matérialité des actes qui étaient compris dans le terme d'*agrapha* donne à l'action privée née de cette loi alexandrine, datée du IIIe s. av. n. è., le caractère d'une formule générale qui rappelle celui de l'*actio iniuriarum aestimatoria* de l'édit du préteur à Rome[50]: après avoir protégé le droit à l'intégrité physique dans les paragraphes précédents, le législateur alexandrin défendait les biens moraux que sont la considération, la réputation et la pudeur contre tout affront. Afin d'éviter les imprécisions et les abus mais aussi dans le but d'obtenir du tribunal un montant de compensation plus élevé pour la victime, la loi stipulait que le plaignant devait décrire sur sa demande minutieusement les faits constitutifs de l'outrage et le temps où celui-ci a eu lieu.

On ne dispose pas de textes de la pratique judiciaire alexandrine pour vérifier le respect de ces prescriptions dans la formulation des plaintes pour *hybris*. En ce qui concerne celles qui nous sont parvenues de la *chôra* ptolémaïque, la distinction alexandrine entre les actions pour agressions corporelles et celles pour *hybris* n'est pas toujours évidente. L'étude de H.-A. Rupprecht sur le délit d'*hybris* dans les papyrus[51] porte sur le sens du terme d'*hybris* du point de vue juridique, à savoir de

---

victime de l'injustice mais qui ne nous sont pas parvenues. N.R.E. Fisher, *Hybris*, p. 84, pense que la loi en question est d'inspiration athénienne, l'essence des deux lois sur l'*hybris* étant la même, à savoir l'atteinte à l'honneur ou à la considération d'autrui.

49 Plutarque, *Solon 18, 6-7*.

50 Celle-ci aurait été instituée à l'imitation du droit grec (Labéon assimilait l'*iniuria* à l'*hybris* du droit attique: *Coll. 2, 5, 1*); cf. R. Monier, *Manuel élémentaire de droit romain, t. II*, 5e éd., réimpr. Paris, 1970, p. 42-44. Pour J. Partsch, *op. cit.*, p. 62-64, l'*actio iniuriarum aestimatoria* serait plus proche du droit alexandrin en la matière que du droit athénien.

51 «Hybris. Anmerkungen zu einem Delikt in den Papyri der ptolemäischen und römischen Zeit», *Überlieferung, Bewahrung und Gestaltung in der rechtsgeschichtlichen*

sa spécificité en tant que délit, et sur la nature de la sanction imposée, à savoir s'il s'agissait d'une peine ou d'une condamnation à l'indemnisation d'un dommage subi. Dans la plupart des cas, l'*hybris* était associée à une agression corporelle ayant provoqué des blessures (*plêgai*), l'accusation pour *hybris* et *plêgai* correspondant à celle contemporaine pour «coups et blessures»[52]. Cependant, les éléments constitutifs de la plainte pour *hybris* pouvaient être d'autres comportements outrageants, comme par exemple les menaces, la violation de domicile avec vol[53] et des actes insultants tels que, des propos injurieux, le crachement, la destruction de vêtements ou la mise à nu en public de quelqu'un[54]. Par ailleurs, la documentation a conservé des plaintes dans lesquelles des victimes d'agressions de la même nature, notamment des *plêgai*, n'ont pas accusé leur agresseur d'*hybris*[55]. Si donc on considère l'acte, il n'est pas possible de trouver le fondement d'une distinction juridique dans la matérialité des actes de *plêgai* tout court et de celle d'*hybris* et *plêgai* ou des autres agressions dans la définition juridique desquelles intervenait la notion d'*hybris*[56]. En revanche, si l'on considère le résultat de l'acte, les textes laissent entendre que le terme d'*hybris* dans les documents de la pratique judiciaire de la *chôra* ptolémaïque désignait une atteinte à la considération de la personne, perçue comme telle par les victimes.

L'initiative du dépôt de la plainte appartenait à la victime. Soumises au régime procédural lagide, les demandes en justice pour *hybris* revêtaient la forme d'une *enteuxis* quand elles étaient adressées au roi ou d'une plainte quand elles étaient adressées à ses fonctionnaires et, en cas d'échec de la conciliation proposée, l'affaire

---

Forschung, Paderborn, Munich, Vienne, Zurich, 1994, p. 269-275; cf. Idem, «Straftaten und Rechtschutz» (cité *supra*, n. 27), p. 143-144 et 146.

52 Comme dans les *BGU X, 1903* et *1904* (IIIe s. av. n. è.), *BGU VI 1249* (148/147 av. n. è.), *UPZ II 170-171* (126 av. n. è.), *P. Coll. Youtie 16* (109 av. n. è.) et *P. Fay.12= M. Chrest. 15* (vers 103 av. n. è.); cf. H.-A. Rupprecht, «*Hybris*», p. 272, n. 12. A. Di Bitonto, «Le petizioni al re», *Aeg. 47*, 1967, p. 22sq. et Eadem, «Le petizioni ai funzionari nel periodo tolemaïco. Studio sul formulario», *Aeg. 48*, 1968, p. 75sq., inclut dans les paragraphes consacrés au délit d'*hybris* les plaintes pour violences physiques dans lesquelles ce terme ne figure pas.

53 Comme dans les *UPZ I, 12* (158 av. n. è.), *BGU VIII 1855* (Ier s. av. n. è.), *P. Tebt. I 16* (114 av. n. è.) et *P. Col. Youtie 16* (109 av. n. è.). Une agression particulièrement violente est celle faite μετὰ σκυλμοῦ comme lors de l'attaque à main armée avec violation de domicile dont il est question dans le *P. Tebt. I 16;* cf. A. Passoni dell'Acqua, «ΣΚΥΛΜΟΣ», *Aeg. 54*, 1974, p. 201.

54 Comme dans les *P. Gourob 2=CP. Jud. 19* (226 av. n. è). et *P. Ent. 79* (222 et 218 av. n. è.).

55 Cf. H.-A. Rupprecht, «*Hybris*», p. 272 et Idem, «Straftaten und Rechtschutz», p. 141-143.

56 Au sujet du même problème concernant les actes d'*hybris* et d'*aikia* en droit athénien cf. L. Gernet, *Recherches sur le développement de la pensée juridique et morale en Grèce*, Paris, 1917, p. 181.

était jugée soit par le fonctionnaire soit renvoyée par lui devant les tribunaux[57]. Les plaignants s'y présentaient comme des victimes d'illégalités sans se référer à une loi quelconque[58]. Dans huit cas, c'est à dire pratiquement la moitié des cas d'*hybris* connus pour l'époque ptolémaïque[59], la prétention des plaignants portait sur un *timêma*, à savoir sur une condamnation de leur adversaire au paiement d'une somme estimée par eux-mêmes. Comme les plaignants le disent clairement dans le *P. Ent.74* et le *P. Fay. 12=M. Chrest. 15*, la somme versée par l'auteur de l'*hybris* était perçue par la victime. A. Jördens remarque qu'il arrivait que la mention de l'*hybris* et la prétention du plaignant au *timêma* soient ajoutées entre les lignes[60] après que la plainte eut été rédigée, signe d'une part que cette référence pouvait n'avoir qu'un effet rhétorique et d'autre part que le plaignant lui-même et le rédacteur de l'acte avaient peu d'espoir qu'une condamnation pécuniaire puisse leur donner satisfaction, les accusés pouvant être insolvables. Deux documents font état de l'aboutissement de procès introduits par des plaignants pour *hybris* prétendant à un *timêma*. Le premier est le *P. Gourob 2=CPJud. I, 19* qui relate le procès-verbal d'audience d'une affaire portée devant le dicastère grec de Crocodilopolis en 226 av. n. è.. Ce document contient l'estimation du dommage par la victime, en l'occurrence Dosithéos, un Juif d'Égypte qui accusait Hérakleia, Juive elle aussi, de l'avoir «insulté» (*eloidorêsas*)[61] en lui ayant prêté des paroles qu'il aurait dites à certaines

---

57 Cf. H.J. Wolff, *Das Justizwesen*, p. 133sq.; cf. H.-A. Rupprecht, «*Hybris*», p. 274, n. 26.

58 Que ce soit dans les plaintes adressées au roi ou à ses fonctionnaires ou dans les procès-verbaux d'audience, aucune allusion n'est faite à des dispositions normatives qui prévoiraient, selon le schéma de R. Taubenschlag, *Das Strafrecht*, p. 18-21 et *Law²*, p. 435-438, par analogie avec le droit alexandrin, une action spéciale pour coups et blessures(*dikè plêgôn*), une action spéciale pour «conduite injuste (*adikos agôgê*)», et une action générale pour toute autre forme d'agression ou pour outrage, actions sanctionnées, selon les cas, soit par des amendes fixées par la loi soit d'une somme estimée par le juge. Une *dikê plêgôn* est mentionnée dans le *P. Petrie III 21(d)* (225/224 av. n. è.) au sujet d'une affaire qui a été portée devant le dicastère de Crocodilopolis. Par ailleurs, A. Helmis, «Despotisme et répresion: les limites du pouvoir ptolémaïque», *Symposion 1988*, *Comunicazioni sul diritto greco ed ellenistico*, Cologne, 1990, p. 314, signale un document, le *BGU XIV 2371*, daté du Ier s. av. n. è., qui contient un extrait des statuts d'une association religieuse prévoyant des sanctions contre ses membres qui échangeraient des injures ou qui se battraient. Mais la portée de ce code était restreinte puisqu'il ne concernait que les membres de l'association et que sa validité était annuelle.

59 *P. Hib. I 32* (246/245 av. n. è.), *P. Gurob 2=CPJud I, 19* (226 av. n. è.), *P. Ent. 73* et *74* (222 et 221 av. n. è.), *BGU X 1903* (IIIe s. av. n. è.) et *VI 1249* (148/147 av. n. è.), *UPZ II, 171* (126 av. n. è.) et *P. Fay. 12=M. Chrest. 15* (vers 103 av. n. è.); cf. H.-A. Rupprecht, «Straftaten und Rechtschutz», p. 143, n. 42 et 144, n. 44; Idem, «Hybris», p. 273, n. 20 et. A. Jördens, «Die Ahndung von Übergriffen», I. A. τίμημα.

60 *BGU X 1903, l. 5* (vers le milieu du IIIe s.av. n. è.).

61 Sur l'injure verbale ayant pour cible le roi lagide et qui constituait une offense au souverain, punie de la peine de mort, cf. J. Mélèze-Modrzejewski, «Paroles néfastes et vers obscènes. A propos de l'injure verbale en droit grec et hellénistique»,

personnes et, après que lui aussi l'eut contre-insulté (*antiloidorountos*), d'avoir craché sur lui dans un lieu public et de lui avoir déchiré son manteau. Dosithéos réclamait 200 drachmes comme prix de l'*hybris,* mais étant donné qu'il n'a pas comparu à l'audience, il a perdu son procès par défaut. Le deuxième est le *P. Hibeh I 32*, où il est question de la séquestration des biens de quelqu'un accusé d'*hybris*, condamné par contumace à verser un *timêma* estimé aussi à 200 drachmes par la victime. Cette somme est proche de celle établie par les lois alexandrines pour coups et blessures[62], lesquelles, comme les deux documents cités, datent du IIIe s. av. n. è. En revanche, la plainte du *P. Fayoum 12*, datée de 103 av. n. è., montre un clérouque hécatontaroure réclamant 420 drachmes comme prix de l'*hybris* qu'il a subie pour avoir été agressé, séquestré, dénudé et dépouillé de son manteau par deux Perses de l'épigone, mais le montant de ces sommes de même que celles réclamées dans deux autres pièces judiciaires relatives à l' *hybris* datées du IIe s. av. n. è.[63], s'expliquent par la dévaluation de la monnaie lagide intervenue entre-temps[64]. Certains plaignants demandaient la punition du coupable sans la préciser en utilisant les termes et expressions suivants: «la peine appropriée[65]» ou «afin que j'obtienne justice[66]» ou «un jugement[67]» du stratège, auquel le plaignant demandait le renvoi de l'affaire.

On en vient à la question de la nature de la sanction imposée à l'auteur des actes constitutifs du délit d'*hybris*, à savoir peine ou dédommagement? H.-A. Rupprecht pense que non seulement l'homicide mais aussi le vol et le brigandage étaient des infractions donnant lieu à des peines infligées par les autorités publiques[68]. Pour ce qui est de l'*hybris*, il considère le *timêma* comme une amende infligée la suite d'une

---

Anthropologies juridiques. Mélanges Pierre Braun, Limoges, 1998, p. 569-585 et *Dike* 1, 1998, p. 151-169

62 *P. Hal. 1, l. 186-193.*

63 *BGU VI 1249* (148/147 av. n. è.) et *UPZ II 171* (126 av. n. è.).

64 Cf. Cl. Préaux, *Le monde hellénistique. La Grèce et l'Orient (323-146 av. J.-C.), t. I*, p. 383.

65 Ζημία, ἁρμόζουσα ἐπίπληξις, προσήκουσα μισοπονηρία: *P. Ent. 79* (218 av. n. è.), *UPZ I 8* (161/160 av. n. è.), *P. Tebt. I 16* (114 av. n. è.).

66 Τυχόντες ὧν προσήκει, ou ὅπως τύχω τῶν δικαίων: *BGU VIII 1855* (sans date), *UPZ I 12* (158 av. n. è.), *BGU VI, 1247* (149/148 av. n. è.).

67 Περὶ δὲ τῆς ὕβρεως Διοφάνην διαγνῶναι: *P. Ent. 75* (222 av. n. è.). Sur tous ces documents cf. H.-A. Rupprecht, «*Hybris*», p. 273, n. 22 et A. Jördens, *Die Ahndung von Übergriffen, B.* und *D.* Au sujet du *P. Ent. 75*, A. Jördens, *ibidem, A.*, signale que la partie pour *hybris* de la plainte de ce régisseur de *klêroi*, que des bergers ont roué de coups parce qu'il leur reprochait d'avoir causé des dommages aux pâturages pour avoir fait paître leurs brebis sur une tenure dont il avait la garde, n'a probablement pas été retenue puisque sur la note figurant au *verso* (*l.3*) du document on lit περὶ κλήρων. Selon O. Guéraud, *Enteuxeis*, p. 182, pour lequel le régisseur avait déposé plainte pour «obtenir le paiement des dégâts et une réparation pour les violences qu'il a subies», il n'est pas certain «que la note se termine avec κλήρων: il a pu y avoir une quatrième ligne courte, contenant par exemple [καὶ ὕβρεως]. Mais les résumés des verso sont si peu précis que le scribe peut s'être contenté de περὶ κλήρων» (Idem , *Enteuxeis*, p. 186).

68 Avec restitution de la chose dérobée; cf. «Straftaten und Rechtschutz», p. 141-147.

estimation. Il admet aussi que la demande en justice pouvait avoir comme but de faire reconnaître par l'État à la victime le droit à la *praxis* sur les biens du coupable pour toucher le montant infligé à titre d'amende[69]. Dans le cas des lois alexandrines sur l'*hybris*, l'État percevait les neuf dixièmes de cette amende[70], tandis que dans les procès intentés dans la *chôra* il n'en percevait aucune part. En ce qui concerne les peines demandées par les plaignants se considérant comme des victimes d'*hybris*, la nomenclature utilisée dans leurs demandes est floue et ne révèle pas la nature de la privation qui frappait le condamné[71]. Au demeurant, nous ne disposons d'aucun document faisant état de l'application de la peine sollicitée, tandis que le *P. Hibeh I 32* montre que la condamnation au versement à la victime du montant estimé par elle-même était effective. En outre, la conciliation, dont des documents sous forme d'homologie[72] ou de retrait de plainte[73] montrent que ce pouvait être réellement l'aboutissement d'une introduction d'instance pour *hybris* et *plêgai*, est une phase procédurale non appropriée à un procès à caractère exclusivement criminel[74]. Présent du début au dénouement du litige, l'État ne prenait pas pour autant l'initiative de l'introduction de l'instance et, dans les cas jugés dans la *chôra*, il ne profitait pas de la condamnation pécuniaire. Son appareil judiciaire et le droit en vigueur, légal ou coutumier, étaient à la disposition des particuliers pour que ceux-ci obtiennent justice s'ils se trouvaient lésés, la conciliation des litigants étant toutefois une étape envisageable et très souvent recommandée par le fonctionnaire auquel les plaintes étaient adressées[75].

A partir du moment où l'action privée était introduite, la répression du délit contre un particulier revêtait un caractère étatique. Le verbe *adikeisthai*[76] utilisé par les plaignants dénonce certes l'acte illégal[77], à savoir les violences dont ils ont été les

---

69 «*Hybris*», p. 274.

70 Évaluée librement par le tribunal alexandrin qui jugeait l'affaire: *P. Hal. 1, ll. 210-213* et *113-117*; cf. *supra*, p. 315.

71 Le terme de *zêmia* par exemple pouvait désigner une peine patrimoniale mais aussi la peine de mort; cf. H.-A. Rupprecht, «Straftaten und Rechtschutz», p. 147, n. 71-73.

72 *BGU VI 1249* (148/147 av. n. è.).

73 *P. Tebt. III, 1 821* (209 av. n. è.?).

74 R.S. Bagnall, «Response to Hans-Albrecht Rupprecht», p. 152.

75 *P. Ent. 73* et *74* (222 et 221av. n. è.); cf. O. Guéraud, *Enteuxeis. Requêtes et plaintes adressées au roi d'Egypte au IIIe siècle av. J.-C*, Le Caire, 1931, p. LVsq.

76 La formule introductive de leurs plaintes «ἀδικοῦμαι ὑπὸ τοῦ δεῖνος» («je suis lésé par quelqu'un») le signale d'une manière abstraite avant l'exposé des faits; cf. O. Guéraud, *Enteuxeis. Requêtes et plaintes adressées au roi d'Egypte au IIIe siècle av. J.-C.*, p. XXII-XXIV. Par ailleurs, dans son analyse de la pensée du législateur athénien au sujet du délit d'*hybris*, Démosthène emploie le verbe *adikein* pour qualifier son trait d'atteinte d'ordre à la cité; cf. H.J. Wolff, «Le droit hellénistique d'Egypte dans le kosmos des droits grecs: réception ou formation originale?», *Studi in onore di A. Biscardi, t. I*, Milan, 1982, p. 337-338.

77 En l'occurrence contraire aux dispositions soit d'une loi royale, soit d'une loi d'une cité grecque d'Egypte, soit d'une règle coutumière en vigueur dans la campagne égyptienne,

victimes mais constate également le tort subi[78]. La sanction pour le délit d'*hybris* était imposée par un jugement rendu par l'État à l'égard d'une personne en vertu d'une règle légale à Alexandrie et sans doute coutumière dans la *chôra*. Mais il appert qu'elle n'était pas imposée seulement en vue de punir l'acte socialement dangereux que la personne avait commis mais aussi en vue de réparer le préjudice subi par la victime. La peine pécuniaire qui est la seule dont le prononcé soit attesté dans les cas des violences à la personne qualifiées d'*hybris* contient, nous semble-t-il des éléments de réparation. Une réparation qui, dans un contexte juridique et judiciaire où le civil se dégageait à grand' peine du pénal, ne pouvait pas être obtenue par une action purement civile.

Or, le préjudice subi n'était pas seulement d'ordre corporel et matériel. D'après l'exposé des faits par les plaignants, l'injustice subie par eux, qui consistait à une atteinte à leur intégrité et/ou à leur honneur et à leur considération, combinée parfois avec la violation de leur domicile et avec une atteinte à leurs biens, revêtait aussi un caractère extrapatrimonial. On est en présence de cas de dommages moraux de différents degrés de gravité tels que les préjudices d'agrément consécutifs aux violences physiques[79], le sentiment d'humiliation après une atteinte à l'honneur, à la considération ou à la pudeur[80] ou au sentiment de supériorité ethnique des plaignants que ces derniers indiquaient pour accentuer le caractère outrageant de l'acte[81]. Le vocable d'*hybris*, certes bien enraciné dans le champ du droit afin de qualifier ces attaques à la personne, n'avait pas pour autant perdu sa place dans la norme morale

---

qui étaient les composantes du droit positif du royaume selon la hiérarchie des règles juridiques énoncée dans le *diagramma* conservé dans le *P. Gourob 2=CPJud I, 19, l. 40-45* (226 av. n. è.). Sur la toile de fond du pluralisme juridique dans l'Egypte lagide voir H.J. Wolff, *Das Justizwesen der Ptolemaër*, p. 196-197, n. 14 et Idem, *Das Recht der griechischen Papyri Agyptens in der Zeit der Ptolemäer und des Prinzipats, t. I, Bedingungen und Triebkräfte der Rechtsentwicklung*, éd. H.-A. Rupprecht, Munich, 2002, p. 29sq.; cf. J. Mélèze-Modrzejewski, «Droit et justice dans l'Egypte des premiers Lagides», *L'Orient méditérranéen de la mort d'Alexandre au Ier siècle avant notre ère. Anatolie, Chypre, Egypte, Syrie* (coord. M.-Th. Le Dinahet), Nantes, 2003, p. 281-302 et J. Vélissaropoulos-Karakostas, Λόγοι ευθύνης. Ιστορική γένεση και σύγχρονη αμφισβήτηση των πηγών της ενοχικής δεσμεύσεως, Athènes, Komotini, 1993, p. 95-96.

[78] Dans le langage des documents papyrologiques, officiels ou privés, la notion d'*adikia* était utilisée pour constater une illégalité dans des situations relevant aussi bien du domaine de la responsabilité civile que de celui de la responsabilité pénale; à cet égard cf. J. Modrzejewski, «La notion d'injustice dans les papyrus grecs», *IURA 10*, 1959, p. 67-85, notamment, p. 71-75.

[79] *P. Ent. 74* (221 av. n. è.), *BGU VI 1247*(149/148 av. n. è.), *BGU* V*III 1855*(sans date).

[80] *P. Ent. 79* (218 av. n. è.) et *P. Fayoum 12* (vers 103 av. n. è.).

[81] Tels les plaignants grecs des *P. Ent. 79* (218 av. n. è.) et *UPZ I 8* (161/160 av. n. è.), qui ont été violentés ou agressés et injuriés par des Egyptiens et qui font part de leur indignation.

de l'époque[82]. Comme à Athènes il ne se cantonnait pas à désigner des violences pénalement sanctionnées mais aussi l'arrogance, le non-respect voir le mépris d'autrui et, par conséquent, la douleur morale associée à l'outrage subi dont il était devenu le signifiant.

En ce qui concerne les plaintes pour *plêgai* qui ne comportaient pas d'accusation pour *hybris*, dans la *P. Ent. 72*, datée de 218 av. n. è., où il est question d'échange de propos blessants (*loidoria*), la prétention du plaignant porte sur un *timêma* de 200 drachmes[83]. Dans le reste de ces plaintes les plaignants demandent la punition de leurs agresseurs en se servant de locutions abstraites qui ne laissent pas deviner la forme de la sanction sollicitée et dans aucun cas nous ne possédons de sentences rendues à cet égard[84].

Enfin, au IIIe s. av. n. è., un *timêma* réglementaire, qui visait à empêcher les perquisitions arbitraires mais qui était perçu par celui chez lequel on avait perquisitionné à tort, était prévu dans le cahier contenant les conditions d'affermage du monopole des huiles[85]. Après sa fabrication surveillée, l'huile devait être vendue et l'administration prévoyait des perquisitions chez les personnes soupçonnées de détenir de l'huile volée ou de posséder des ateliers de fabrication clandestine[86]. L'initiative en revenait au fermier et si ce dernier ne découvrait pas ce qu'il avait soupçonné et si, à la demande de la personne chez laquelle il avait perquisitionné, il n'attestait pas sous serment que sa perquisition n'avait pas d'autres motifs que ceux

---

82 Cf. H.-A. Rupprecht, «Hybris», p. 271. Dans les clauses contenues dans six contrats de mariage d'époque ptolémaïque et dans huit du début de l'époque romaine, dont des *synchôrêseis* alexandrines destinées à régler la vie commune, on lit les engagements réciproques des époux et les sanctions d'un manquement à ces engagements (*ibidem* n. 10). Ces clauses protégeaient la femme contre l'infidélité de son époux, contre sa faculté à la répudier, contre un mauvais traitement matériel et contre l'attitude outrageante du mari (*hybrizein*) à l'égard de sa femme. La sanction prévue dans le *P. Eléph. 1* était double: le mari qui manquerait à ses engagements était privé de la dot déposée en ses mains et il était passible d'une amende qui était fixée à un montant égal à celui de la dot. Dans les autres contrats où figure la clause du comportement outrageant du mari, la sanction consiste à payer une fois et demie le montant de la dot (*hêmiolion*). Mais étant donné que nous manquons de documents (plaintes ou actes de divorce) démontrant les conséquences juridiques de l'inobservation de ces engagements, elles paraissent comme des «clauses de bonne conduite», reflétant la morale de la patrie d'origine, notamment Athènes, et dépourvues d'importance juridique; cf. H.-A. Rupprecht, «Ehevertragliche Regelungen und urkundliche Praxis», *Mélanges en l'honneur de P.D. Dimakis. Droits antiques et société*, Athènes, 2002, p. 543-563 et U. Yiftach-Firanko, *Marriage and Marital Arrangements: a History of the Greek Marriage Document in Egypt: 4th century BCE-4th Century CE*, Munich, 2003, p. 185sq.

83 Cf. *supra*, p. 317 et 318, au sujet des *P. Gourob 2=CPJud I 19* et *P. Hibeh I 32*, datés aux aussi du IIIe s. av. n. è.

84 Cf. H.-A. Rupprecht, «Straftaten und Rechtschutz», p. 141-143.

85 *P. Rev. Laws, col. 38-72*; cf. Cl. Préaux, *L'économie royale des Lagides,* Bruxelles, 1939, p. 65-93.

86 *P. Rev. Laws, col.55, l. 18-26.*

qui avaient été exposés dans une plainte écrite[87] et qui relevaient de l'exercice de la ferme, il devait payer à cette personne «le double de la valeur à laquelle il avait estimé la fraude, avant la perquisition[88]».

*

A l'époque romaine le vocable d'*hybris* est assez fréquent dans les plaintes pour désigner les coups et blessures, associé ou non au terme de *plêgai*[89] mais il est également présent dans des plaintes pour violation de domicile avec enlèvement d'esclave ou pour vol[90], pour menaces, usage de contrainte et extorsion de signature[91] ou pour des insultes[92]. La notion d'*hybris* continue à embrasser non seulement les injures de fait que représentent les atteintes portées au corps d'autrui[93], mais également celles portées à son honneur et à sa condition juridique[94]. Ainsi, pour un requérant qui, en 147, s'adresse au préfet au sujet des abus de pouvoir d'un fonctionnaire, «la pire des injustices qui puisse arriver dans la vie d'un homme libre est d'être victime d'*hybris*»[95], pour un père au IIe s., déjà victime d'une escroquerie

---

87 *P. Rev. Laws, col. 56, l. 9-10*: προσαγγελέντων: il s'agissait d'un προσάγγελμα ou d'une προσαγγελία c'est à dire d'une dénonciation à la police.

88 *P. Rev.Laws, col. 56, l. 7-13*; cf. Cl. Préaux, *op. cit.*, p. 89.

89 Comme par exemple dans le *SB I 5235* (12) et le *BGU XI 2069* (292); cf. H.-A. Rupprecht, «Hybris», p. 272, n. 12.

90 Comme dans le *P. Oxy. VIII 1120* (début du IIIe s.); cf. H.-A. Rupprecht, *ibidem*, n. 13.

91 Ainsi dans les *P. Fouad I 26* (157), *Mich. III 174* (145) et *Lond. II 358* (150); cf. H.-A. Rupprecht, *ibidem*, n. 14.

92 Des mots tels que *loidoria, anaideia* et *thrasos* y sont utilisés pour indiquer le dépassement de la mesure ordinaire, comme dans les *P. Mil. Vogl. I 24* (117), *SB VI 9421* (IIIe s.) et *BGU XI 2069* (292), datés des IIe et IIIe s.; cf. H.-A. Rupprecht, *ibidem*, n. 15.

93 Les *P. Oxy. XII 1405* et *XLIII 3105* (IIIe s.) contiennent deux rescrits de l'empereur Septime Sévère relatifs à la *cessio bonorum* en matière de liturgies, c'est- à-dire à la possibilité donnée à celui qui avait été désigné comme liturge de livrer une partie de ses biens à celui qui l'avait désigné pour qu'il accomplît la liturgie à sa place. Apparemment les gens étaient battus ou emprisonnés par les autorités locales pour les dissuader de procéder à cet abandon et l'empereur, qui accepte cette cession, leur garantit qu'ils ne seraient ni déchus de leur condition civique ni maltraités physiquement: οὐδὲ εἰς τὸ σῶμα ὑβρισθήσει.

94 Le *SB XII 11012* (55), contient une lettre de Néron dans laquelle l'empereur, après avoir refusé les honneurs divins qui lui avaient été proposés par une ambassade de Grecs d'une métropole du nome arsinoïte, leur confirme les privilèges qui leur avaient été accordés par ses prédécesseurs et qu'ils pourront en jouir de façon pacifique et sans être dérangés: col. II, l. 2-3: ἀνηβρίστους (lire ἀνυβρίστους) καὶ ἀνηπερεάστους (lire ἀνεπηρεάστους); cf. O. Montevecchi, «Nerone a una polis e ai 6475», *Aeg. 50*, 1970, p. 5-33, notamment p. 28-29. On trouve la même locution dans une demande adressée au IIIe s. à un haut fonctionnaire par un corvéable qui demande de bénéficier d'une mesure impériale et d'avoir τὸ σῶμα ἀνεπηρέαστον καὶ ἀνύβριστον: *PSI IV 292, l. 19.*

95 *P. Wisc I, 33, l. 11-12* (147).

de la part d'un imposteur, la suprême *hybris* commise fut le fait que l'homme en question ait en plus dépouillé ses filles de leurs vêtements en public et qu'il ait voulu les monnayer[96], et pour le père d'une fille égarée qui s'adresse à un centurion en 312, «il n'y a rien de plus horrible et de plus difficile à supporter que l'*hybris*»[97]. Contrairement à ce qui se passait à l'époque ptolémaïque et qui serait en accord avec l'action estimatoire d'injures du droit romain, les conclusions des plaintes d'époque romaine en Égypte, dans lesquelles les actes contraires au droit subis par le plaignant sont qualifiés par lui d'*hybris*, ne portaient pas expressément sur une peine pécuniaire. On y voit les plaignants exprimer le souhait que leurs adversaires subissent «la peine appropriée[98]» ou que «ceux-ci soient traduits en justice[99]».

Le matériel papyrologique concernant les affaires qui entrent dans le concept d'*hybris* et qui sont appelées par ce nom ne reproduisent pas de sentences jugeant le fond du litige. Notons que dans le *P. Oxy. XXXIII 2672* (218), le plaignant Aurelius Aphynchis semble exiger que lui soit versée une somme d'argent: celui-ci, père d'un mineur dont l'esclave a été attaquée et blessée à la lèvre par un pâtissier qui a également agressé et insulté le plaignant (*[e]xybrisen kai dieloidorêsato moi*), demandait que l'agresseur fût amené devant le stratège afin qu'il répondît de ses actes et que la fille pût se faire soigner[100]. En fait, agissant non seulement en tant que maître de l'esclave blessée mais aussi en tant que victime lui aussi du délit d'*injuria*, il y avait dans la formulation de sa pétition la demande non seulement d'obtention d'une peine à la mesure du ressentiment subi mais aussi que celle-ci fût calculée matériellement de façon à tenir compte des frais médicaux (leur remboursement, le *damnum emergens*) qu'il allait verser pour soigner l'esclave.

Les plaintes pour ces agissements étaient adressées à de hauts fonctionnaires, tels que l'épistratège, le stratège et des officiers de police qui, de par leurs fonctions avaient des pouvoirs d'arbitrage et de coercition. Les justiciables savaient qu'ils pouvaient en obtenir la solution du litige même s'il leur arrivait de solliciter le renvoi de leur affaire à un fonctionnaire hiérarchiquement supérieur tel que le préfet[101], source de tout pouvoir judiciaire dans la province. C'est peut-être ce

---

96 *SB VI 9458, l. 16-20* (2e moitié du IIe s.).

97 *P. Graux 4=SB IV 7464* (248).

98 Ạṿτοὶ δ̣ὲ τύχωσι ὧν προσήκει: *SB XVIII 13087* (4), *I 5235* (12); καταστῆσαι ou ἐκπέμψαι τὸν ἐνκαλούμενον ἐπὶ σὲ πρὸς τὴν ἐσομένην ἐπέξοδον, ou ἵνα τῆς ἐπ' ἄκρον ἐγδικίας (lire ἐκδικίας) τύχω: *Ryl. II 136* (4), *P. Mich. V 228* (47), *229* (48) et *230* (48), *P. Wisc. I 33* (147), *P. Graux 4=SB IV 7464* (248); cf. H.-A. Rupprecht, «Hybris», p. 273-274, n. 22-25.

99 'Αξιῶν σε] κελεῦσαι ἀχθῆ[ναι αὐτὴν ἐπί] σε; cf. dans ce sens *P. Mich. VI 365* (194), *PSI III 222* (IIIe s.), *SB VI 9421*(IIIe s.) et *P. Coll Youtie I 77*(324), où le plaignant, qui s'adresse au *praepositus* du 5ème *pagus*, demande que ses deux causes, à savoir la destruction de ses plantations par les animaux (περὶ τῆς σπορᾶς) des accusés et leurs violences envers lui (περὶ τ̣ῆ̣ς̣ ὕβρεως) soient portées devant le tribunal préfectoral.

100 L. 23-25: πρὸς τὸ δύνασθαι ἐκδικίας καὶ θαραπείας τὴν παῖδα τυχεῖν.

101 Comme dans le *P. Coll.Youtie I 77*; cf. *supra*, n. 99.

dernier qui s'est occupé de l'agression abjecte que nous révèle le *P. Mich. V 228* (47): à la suite d'un différend avec son mari, un éleveur d'Oxyrhyncha a roué de coups une femme enceinte qui perdit l'enfant qu'elle portait et se trouva de surcroît en danger de mort. Le mari adresse sa plainte au stratège et demande que l'affaire puisse être promptement jugée mais s'agissant d'un cas d'*anêkestos hybris* c'est à dire d'*iniuria atrox* on peut supposer qu'elle fut renvoyée devant le tribunal préfectoral. En effet, selon un édit du préfet M. Petronius Mamertinus[102], l'*anêkestos hybris* faisait partie des cas qui, en raison de leur gravité, étaient jugés en premier et dernier ressort par le gouverneur de la province[103]. On ne sait pas non plus si, le cas échéant, l'affaire a été jugée selon le droit romain et quelle fut la peine infligée à l'agresseur[104].

*

Le propos de cet exposé a été de chercher les façons implicites de compenser la perte de la vie d'un homme ou de choses inestimables dans la vie d'un homme, à travers la sanction pénale imposée aux délits d'homicide et d'*hybris* dans l'Égypte hellénistique et romaine. Certes, quand on intentait une action délictuelle, on cherchait à obtenir une satisfaction morale à travers la souffrance que la peine corporelle ou pécuniaire prononcée par le juge devait faire subir au coupable[105]. Concernant plus particulièrement les infractions contre la personne, lesquelles, selon la documentation de l'époque hellénistique, étaient sanctionnées par un *timêma*, nous nous sommes demandée si ces peines, en même temps qu'elles punissaient l'auteur de l'acte, n'opéraient pas aussi une réparation de fait du dommage moral éprouvé par la victime. Ce dommage était évoqué par le vocable d'*hybris*, lequel désignait l'atteinte morale causée par un comportement illégal. Mais, aucun texte n'accordant à la victime la réparation d'un tel préjudice causé par un acte illicite, la satisfaction légale par le versement d'une somme d'argent ne pouvait avoir lieu qu'à travers les actions délictuelles sanctionnées par une amende pénale. C'était aussi

102 *SB XII 10929* (133-137); cf. N. Lewis, «Un nouveau texte sur la juridiction du préfet d'Egypte», *RHD 50*, 1972 p. 5-12 et *51*, 1973, p. 5-7; Idem, «Emperor or Prefect?», *Le monde grec. Hommages à Cl. Préaux*, Bruxelles, 1975, p. 760-765 et J.H. Oliver, «Greek Applications for Roman Trials», *American Journal of Philology 100*, 1979, p. 549-551.

103 Sur le renvoi des affaires d'*anêkestos hybris* cf. *SB XIV 11707* (212). Une affaire d'empoisonnement, dont il est question dans le *P. Oxy. III 472, l.21-22* (130) a été renvoyée devant le préfet T. Flavius Titianus par l'épistratège Claudius Quintianus, comme cela résulte du *P. Oxy. III 486=M. Chrest. 59, l. 18-22* et *8-9* (131); cf. G. Foti-Talamanca, *Ricerche sul processo nell'Egitto greco-romano II 1. L'introduzione del giudizio*, Milan, 1979, p. 299sq. et plus particulièrement p. 313-314, n. 778 au sujet de l'édit de Petronius Mamertinus (*SB XII 10929, l. 14:* περὶ φαρμακείας).

104 Cf. H.-A. Rupprecht, «Hybris», p. 275.

105 Cf. R. Taubenschlag, *Das Strafrecht*, p. 21.

l'un des résultats des conciliations vers lesquelles la justice officielle orientait les adversaires dans les affaires d'*hybris*. A Athènes aussi, où la loi sur l'*hybris* prévoyait une peine pécuniaire contre le coupable mais où celle-ci était encaissée par la cité, les victimes de l'outrage n'ayant aucun droit sur la somme versée, cette douleur morale pouvait être monnayée, car les victimes recouraient à l'action privée pour voies de fait ou à des arrangements afin de pouvoir toucher, en compensation, le montant d'une peine pécuniaire ou d'une composition qui, par ces voies biaisées, leur procurerait le prix de leur honneur ou considération «perdus»[106].

A l'époque romaine, l'*hybris* est resté un délit privé au contenu vaste s'appliquant à diverses attaques personnelles et dont le support légal restait selon toute vraisemblance le droit local. Nous ignorons la forme que prenait la sanction mais, qu'elle ait été prononcée selon les précédents ptolémaïques ou selon le droit romain, elle pouvait être patrimoniale. R. von Jhering avait soutenu que la condamnation à une somme d'argent en droit romain, à côté de sa fonction d'équivalent et de peine, avait aussi une fonction satisfactoire du sentiment juridique lésé du demandeur, quand le défendeur avait porté atteinte à un de ses intérêts non-économiques en n'exécutant pas un contrat ou en commettant un délit[107]. J. Macqueron a rétorqué qu'il n'a jamais été possible en droit romain d'accorder à la victime la réparation du préjudice moral ou d'affection causé par un acte illicite, mais il a admis une spécificité de la fonction de la peine dont bénéficiait la victime du délit d'injure. Il a admis aussi que la fonction répressive de cette peine n'excluait pas l'idée d'une sorte de satisfaction accordée à la victime pour le ressentiment qu'elle avait éprouvé[108]. Ce dernier ayant été primitivement un délit qui autorisait la victime à recourir à la vengeance privée, la peine pécuniaire que le préteur lui a substituée avait aussi pour fonction d'assouvir une vengeance[109]. Rappelons aussi qu'à la suite de la loi *Cornelia de iniuriis*, votée en 81 pendant la dictature de Sylla et soumettant à un jury criminel les coups et blessures et la violation de domicile, la question a été posée sous l'Empire de savoir si les victimes des faits prévus par cette loi ou des faits qui constituaient une injure grave et qui étaient punis *extra ordinem*, pouvaient obtenir successivement la prononciation d'une peine par les tribunaux criminels et la condamnation du défendeur, par les tribunaux civils, à une indemnité

---

106 Cf. *supra*, p. 312-314 et D.M. MacDowell, *The Law in Classical Athens*, p. 132.

107 R.von Jhering, «De l'intérêt dans les contrats, et de la prétendue nécessité de la valeur patrimoniale des prestations obligatoires(1880)», *Œuvres choisies. VII*, Paris, 1893, trad. par O. De Meulenaere, p. 145-211, notamment p. 155 no 6, 163 no 11, 175 no. 17 et 178 no 19.

108 «L'intérêt moral ou d'affection dans les obligations délictuelles en droit romain», *Etudes offertes à André Audinet*, Paris, 1968, p. 173-188; cf. P. Kayser, «Remarques sur l'indemnisation du dommage moral dans le droit contemporain» (cité *supra*, n. 1), p. 412 et G. Cardascia, «Réparation et peine dans les doits cunéiformes et le droit romain», *La responsabilité à travers les Âges*, 1989, p. 23sq.

109 Ulp. *D. 47, 10- de iniuriis-, 7 § 1*; cf. J. Macqueron, *op. cit.*, p. 174-177.

pécuniaire. Il a été décidé que la victime aurait le choix entre l'action prétorienne estimatoire et la poursuite criminelle[110].

De ce parcours historique qui nous a conduits du droit athénien à celui de l'Égypte hellénistique et romaine et au droit romain, il nous semble qu'on peut dégager les remarques suivantes quant au préjudice moral: inhérent aux actes qui constituent l'élément matériel des crimes et des délits tels que l'homicide, l'*hybris* et l'*iniuria*, sa satisfaction n'a pas été distinguée des compositions volontaires et des mesures répressives. Il ne paraît pas absurde de reconnaître au versement de sommes payées à titre de peines et à titre d'exécutions pécuniaires par les auteurs d'actes illicites générateurs de dommages non patrimoniaux une fonction satisfactoire de fait des victimes d'un dommage non patrimonial. A Athènes la somme de la condamnation pour *hybris* bénéficiait à la cité mais les victimes avaient aussi la possibilité de s'y prendre autrement pour toucher une somme versée par l'auteur de l'outrage à titre de peine. A Alexandrie, la somme de la condamnation était perçue en partie par la cité et en partie par la victime, en vertu d'une loi poliade, mais pour ce qui est de la *chôra*, dans le silence des textes normatifs, ce sont les documents de la pratique judiciaire, notamment les plaintes, qui montrent une justice fonctionnarisée s'occuper d'infractions qui, en plus d'attaques personnelles de toute sorte, avaient causé des dommages moraux. Enfin, l'affaire du *P. Mich. VIII 473*[111], dont les protagonistes appartenaient au milieu des pérégrins qui servaient dans l'armée romaine, montre que, au IIe s. de n. è., l'idée que l'on pouvait transiger et se racheter même pour un homicide était bien présente dans les mentalités.

---

[110] Paul. *D. 47, 10, 6;* cf. R. Monier, *op. cit., t. 2*, p. 45 et M. Kaser, *Das römische Zivilprozessrecht*, Munich, 1966, p. 118, n. 9 et 347-348, n. 44.

[111] Cf. *supra*, p. 311 et 312.

ANDREA JÖRDENS (HEIDELBERG)

ANTWORT AUF BARBARA ANAGNOSTOU-CANAS

Der reichhaltige Vortrag von Barbara Anagnostou-Canas zu strafrechtlichen Fragen, insbesondere zur Verfolgung und Ahndung von Tötung und schwerer Körperverletzung in der griechischen Welt hat ein weites Panorama vor uns ausgebreitet und dabei viele verschiedene Punkte berührt, die ich hier unmöglich alle würdigen kann. Schon aus Zeitgründen muß ich mich vielmehr im folgenden auf einen einzigen Aspekt beschränken, nämlich die Sanktionen solcher Delikte im Ptolemäerreich[1]. Dabei wird es mir vor allem um die Frage gehen, wie weit es dort noch ein Fortleben der aus dem Mutterland vertrauten Formen gab, und zwar insbesondere des Sühnegelds, von dem auch schon in den Vorträgen von Laura Pepe und Michael Gagarin die Rede war. Hier scheinen mir doch gewisse Zweifel am Platze, was die einheitliche Konzeption unter den Ptolemäern betrifft. Dazu habe ich im Anhang noch einmal die verschiedenen Sanktionen zusammengestellt, wie sie in den Papyri begegnen.

Die Quellenproblematik als solche ist bekannt: einerseits die geringe Zahl der einschlägigen Dokumente, andererseits die oft formelhaften und insofern wenig aussagekräftigen Anträge, so etwa ganz allgemein auf Gerechtigkeit (Beispiele hierfür unter **I D**). Nach Barbara Anagnostou erkannten die Richter bei den hier in Rede stehenden Delikten stets auf ein *timêma*, was bei den unter **I A** aufgelisteten Fällen auch das Richtige trifft.

Dort habe ich nun, soweit ersichtlich, sämtliche Belege für ein Sühnegeld aus ptolemäischer Zeit aufgeführt. Auffallend ist dabei, daß darunter die Tötung überhaupt nicht erscheint, sondern nur *plêgai* oder *hybris*, teilweise auch beide zusammen. Schaut man auf die Entstehungszeit, so ergibt sich, daß im III. Jhdt. in der Regel *plêgai* oder *hybris* allein als Delikt benannt werden, während sie seit dem II. Jhdt. vorzugsweise kumuliert erscheinen. Offenbar wollte man damit die Aussage verstärken, was auf eine gewisse Verwässerung der Termini deuten mag.

Unter **I B** sind dagegen diejenigen Anträge auf Sanktionen für *plêgai* oder *hybris* gegeben, die keine ausdrückliche Erwähnung eines Sühnegeldes enthalten. Im III. Jhdt. ist dies nur bei dem berühmten Fall der Ägypterin anzutreffen, die dem

[1] Alle hier genannten Daten liegen folglich, soweit nicht ausdrücklich anders angegeben, vor Christi Geburt.

Herakleides den Nachttopf über Kopf und Kleider gießt[2], im II. Jhdt. finden sich dafür bereits drei Belege. In diesen letzten Fällen wird durchweg auf die *harmozousa epiplêxis* abgestellt, wie es auch aus den zweiteiligen Bitten geläufig ist, die bei Raub oder Diebstahl zusätzlich noch Schadensersatz begehren (vgl. unter **I C**). Die klare Zweiteilung läßt erkennen, daß es hier um eine Bestrafung des Täters geht, wie *epiplêxis* denn auch die Prügelstrafe bezeichnen kann[3]. Dazu paßt, daß eine solche Strafe abschreckend wirken kann, wie es sich jedenfalls der Antragsteller in P. Tebt. III.1 784 erhofft (letzter Text unter **I B**)[4].

Die ersten sechs Zeugnisse unter **I B** betreffen dagegen die Tötung bzw. solche Fälle von Körperverletzung, bei denen das Opfer noch in Lebensgefahr schwebt. Entgegen den Erwartungen ist hier jedoch nirgends eine Summe oder der Begriff *timêma* erwähnt, anders als bei den unter **I A** gesammelten Belegen für *plêgai* und/oder *hybris*. Dem Antragsteller ist es hier vielmehr darum zu tun, daß der Täter für die Tat haftet[5] – ἔνοχος εἴη – bzw. nicht straflos davonkommt – μὴ ἀθῷος δια-

---

[2] Hierzu auch H.J. Wolff, Das Justizwesen der Ptolemäer (MB 44), München 1962. ²1970, S. 133 Anm. 37.

[3] So zumindest A. Helmis, Crime et châtiment dans l'Égypte ptolémaïque. Recherches sur l'autonomie d'un modèle pénal, Diss. masch. Paris X-Nanterre 1986, S. 201ff., was durch die hier in Rede stehenden Belege eine Stütze erfährt. Zu beachten ist insbesondere die Kennzeichnung der *epiplêxis* als *harmozousa* ‚passend, angemessen, gebührend', wie es auch für den Begriff *timôria* belegt ist, der schon Wolff, Justizwesen (wie Anm. 2), S. 116f. Anm. 4 als einschlägig galt. Zweifellos war dies nicht die einzige mögliche Bedeutung, wie bereits P. Tebt. I 41 (zitiert unter **I C**) zeigen mag. Die von H.-A. Rupprecht, Straftaten und Rechtsschutz nach den griechischen Papyri der ptolemäischen Zeit, in: Symposion 1990. Vorträge zur griechischen und hellenistischen Rechtsgeschichte [Pacific Grove, Cal., 24-26. Sept. 1990], hrsg. v. M. Gagarin, Köln/Weimar/Wien 1991, S. 139-148, bes. S. 147 Anm. 74 geäußerte grundsätzliche Skepsis wird man gleichwohl kaum aufrechterhalten wollen.

[4] Zum Abschreckungsgedanken vgl. auch BGU VIII 1816 (60/59a), wo der malträtierte Bewohner eines Pastophorion offenbar sogar die Todesstrafe für seine Widersacher fordert:] θανατηφόροις εὐθύναις π̣ρ̣ὸ̣ς̣ ἑ̣τ̣έρων ἀνεν̣[(Z. 27). Ob dabei der – wohl strafverschärfend zu wertende – Vorwurf der Hierosylie eine Rolle spielte (dazu später), ist aufgrund des fragmentarischen Zustandes nicht mehr zu erkennen. In diesem Sinne sind vermutlich auch die Bitten um ein unnachsichtiges Durchgreifen bzw. ein Urteil πρὸς ἐπίστασιν ἄλλων/ἑτέρων zu deuten, vgl. etwa P. Amh. II 35, 44ff. mit BL III 4 (132a); BGU IV 1187, 29ff.; VIII 1832, 15ff.; 1855, 16ff.; 1858, 18f.; P. Oxy. XII 1465, 12ff. (alle Ia); SB XIV 11274, 14ff. (4a).

[5] Wenn das persönlich konstruierte *enochos* hier mit ‚haftbar, verantwortlich', *enechesthai* mit ‚haftbar, verantwortlich gemacht werden' wiedergegeben wird, geschieht dies allein aus sprachlichen Gründen, da das Deutsche ansonsten stets eine Ergänzung (etwa ‚schuldig <gesprochen>') erfordert, während ‚strafbar' allein die Tat, nicht der Täter ist. Eine wie auch immer geartete rechtliche Einordnung soll damit ausdrücklich nicht verbunden sein. – Maro Schäfer verdanke ich den freundlichen Hinweis, daß die Begriffe *enochos* und *athôios* auch noch im modernen Griechisch den Gegensatz von Schuld und Unschuld in strafrechtlichem Sinne kennzeichnen.

φύγῃ[6]. Deswegen wird auch um seine vorläufige Festsetzung[7] gebeten, bis klar ist, ob das Opfer überlebt; nur für diesen Fall bittet man mit der üblichen Formel um Gerechtigkeit. Es wird also zwischen zwei Sanktionen unterschieden, was kaum nur auf Differenzen bei der Höhe des Sühnegeldes abzielen kann. Offenbar gab es sogar eine gesetzlich vorgeschriebene Frist, innerhalb derer das Opfer verstorben sein mußte, um eine Klage auf Tötung zu rechtfertigen. Die Existenz zweier verschiedener Verfahren für Tötung und Körperverletzung sollte folglich außer Zweifel stehen.

Klarheit über die Form der Sanktion herrscht damit zwar immer noch nicht, doch spricht meines Ermessens grundsätzlich nichts gegen nichtmaterielle Strafen, wie sie Barbara Anagnostou erst unter den Römern vermutete. In dieser Hinsicht sind die kaiserzeitlichen Zeugnisse (gesammelt unter **II**) kaum aussagekräftiger als ihre ptolemäischen Vorgänger. So vermag ich etwa zwischen dem von Anagnostou angeführten Beispiel – ὅπως τύχωσι ὧν προσήκει, hier unter **II A** – und denen in **I C** – ὅπως τύχωσι τῆς ἁρμοζούσης ἐπιπλήξεως – keinen grundsätzlichen Unterschied zu erkennen. Die beantragte *epexodos* des Gegners tritt nunmehr an die Stelle der ptolemäischen *epiplêxis*, soll aber wie diese allein den Täter treffen; von dem Geschädigten selbst, gar einer wie auch immer gearteten Kompensation zu seinen Gunsten, ist nirgends die Rede. Dies deutet eher auf bloße Varianten im Ausdruck ohne wesentliche Änderungen des Sachverhalts. Hier wie dort dürfte damit letztlich eine körperliche Strafe gemeint gewesen sein.

Die Entwicklung in Richtung einer Bestrafung des Täters scheint demnach bereits unter den Ptolemäern eingesetzt zu haben[8]. Möglicherweise orientierte man sich hierbei an der Behandlung des Raubes, wo man – wohl vor allem aus praktischen Gründen, da die wirtschaftliche Lage nur allzu selten eine angemessene finanzielle Satisfaktion erwarten ließ – offenbar relativ rasch zu nichtmateriellen Strafen übergegangen war. Wenn derartige Anträge seit dem II. Jhdt. auch bei Tötung und schwerer Körperverletzung zunahmen, spricht dies dafür, daß das Konzept des *timêma* sich auch allgemein schon sehr viel früher als vermeint zugunsten der Strafe auf dem Rückzug befand. Dies könnte etwa auch die Bedeutungsverschiebung des Begriffes in römischer Zeit erklären, wo *timêma* kaum mehr als den bloßen ‚Schätzwert' bedeutet.

---

[6] Eine Ausnahme bildet bislang nur der späte P. Ryl. II 68 (89a), wo lediglich um ein *dialêmphthênai* (in diesem Zusammenhang wohl prägnant, ähnlich dem deutschen ‚Durchgreifen') gebeten, allerdings ausdrücklich auf festgelegte Fristen (*diêgoreumenai hêmerai*) und bestehende Vorschriften (*ta peri toutôn prostetagmena*) verwiesen wird.

[7] Dies betraf außer der Person offenbar auch das Vermögen, vgl. nur P. Tebt. I 14 = M. Chr. 42 (114a) mit den Bemerkungen von L. Wenger, Rechtsurkunden aus Tebtynis, in: APF 2, 1902, 483-514, bes. S. 498ff.

[8] So auch schon H.-A. Rupprecht, Hybris. Anmerkungen zu einem Delikt in den Papyri der ptolemäischen und römischen Zeit, in: Überlieferung, Bewahrung und Gestaltung in der rechtsgeschichtlichen Forschung (FSchr E. Kaufmann), hrsg. v. S. Buchholz/P. Mikat/D. Werkmüller, Paderborn u.a. 1993, S. 269-275, bes. S. 273ff.

Falls demnach aber Strafen für Schwerstdelikte schon im II. Jhdt. häufiger wurden und nicht erst ein Phänomen der Kaiserzeit sind, bliebe freilich noch zu fragen, wieso sie sich gegenüber den traditionellen griechischen Auffassungen durchzusetzen vermochten. Vielleicht ist hier doch auch den Interessen der Geschädigten ein stärkerer Einfluß zuzubilligen, deren Aussicht auf Wiedergutmachung zumeist wohl vergeblich war. Gerade auch bei schwerer wiegenden Schäden verschaffte sich so neben dem grundlegenden Bedürfnis nach Satisfaktion der Wunsch nach einer fühlbaren Sanktion immer mehr Raum, bis wir endlich sogar auf den Abschreckungsgedanken treffen. Bekanntlich folgte das *timêma* anderen Vorstellungen, wie schon seine vermutete Herkunft aus einem Friedensvertrag zwischen Familienverbänden zeigt. Am ehesten für Gesellschaften anzunehmen, wo staatliche Strukturen für andere Formen der Bestrafung nicht vorhanden waren, war es letztlich ein aristokratisches Konzept, das mit den zentralistischen Tendenzen einer starken Königsmacht zwangsläufig konkurrierte[9] und insofern in mehrfacher Hinsicht in den Verhältnissen der ägyptischen Chora fehl am Platze war.

Strafen mußten dagegen dort angemessen erscheinen, wo umgekehrt eine Bußzahlung aufgrund der sozialen oder wirtschaftlichen Lage nicht zu befriedigen vermochte; dies gilt für die den Nachttopf ausleerende Ägypterin, deren Beleidigung durch Geld ohnehin nicht gutzumachen war, ebenso wie für den mittellosen Badewächter, der Philista mit heißem Wasser verbrüht[10], oder jetzt auch den jüngeren Bruder aus P. Phrur. Diosk. 7. Vor allem bei Eigentumsdelikten, aber auch bei Übergriffen auf Leib und Leben mochte sich insofern eine Kombination von Schadensersatz und körperlicher Bestrafung empfehlen, und zwar zur Befriedigung der Interessen der Opfer wie vielleicht nicht minder der Täter. Denn anders als materielle Sanktionen, die kaum ohne Auswirkungen auf die gesamte Familie bleiben konnten – und dies durchaus langfristig –, hatten solche körperlicher Art immerhin den Vorteil, begrenzt zu sein, indem sie sich zumindest physisch, unter Umständen aber auch sozial auf seine Person beschränkten. Zugleich mußte dies auch den Interessen des Staates entgegenkommen, dessen Autorität durch die öffentlich vollzogenen Strafen stets aufs neue gestärkt wurde. Zu berücksichtigen ist zudem, daß ein solches System der ägyptischen Bevölkerung, der ein Gutteil der Täter wie der Opfer entstammte, offenbar seit alters vertraut war und daher einen hohen Akzeptanzgrad besaß[11].

---

[9] Vgl. auch bereits Rupprecht, Straftaten (wie Anm. 3), S. 141 mit dem Verweis auf die Herrschaftsstruktur als „allgemeines Argument gegen eine rein private Strafverfolgung" bei Tötungsdelikten.

[10] P. Ent. 82 = M. Chr. 39 (221a); der Antrag geht auf Erlangung des *dikaion*, Gegenstand der Klage ist die Verbrennung (vgl. Verso Z. 3f.: *peri tou katakekausthai*). Nach Wolff, Justizwesen (wie Anm. 2), S. 125f. u.ö. handele es sich um eine „reine Strafsache" (S. 146).

[11] Vgl. nunmehr R. Müller-Wollermann, Vergehen und Strafen. Zur Sanktionierung abweichenden Verhaltens im alten Ägypten, Leiden u.a. 2004, bes. S. 200ff.

Andererseits sind auch im I. Jhdt. noch gelegentliche Zeugnisse für das Sühnegeld zu finden. Die bisher kaum je erörterte Frage, ob nicht je nach Zugehörigkeit zu bestimmten Rechtskreisen unterschiedliche Formen der Sanktion gebräuchlich gewesen sein könnten, folglich Indizien für einen auch in diesem Bereich herrschenden Rechtspluralismus vorliegen, wäre insofern eine eingehendere Untersuchung wert[12].

Daß es auch in der Chora im übrigen mehr unnatürliche Todesfälle gab, als es die üblichen Quellen verraten, zeigt jetzt ein Mailänder Papyrus aus der frühen Kaiserzeit. Dort ist eine Reihe von Verhandlungen, zumeist *peri phonou*, vor einem gewissen Cornelius belegt[13]. Wie weit aus diesem vereinzelten Zeugnis Rückschlüsse auf die Organisation der Strafjustiz unter den Ptolemäern zu ziehen sind – etwa zur Frage der Existenz vergleichbarer, offenbar regulär zuständiger Beamter –, sei freilich noch dahingestellt.

Bedeutsamer erscheint insofern jedoch ein kürzlich publizierter Leipziger Papyrus aus der Wende vom II. zum I. Jhdt., der erstmals einen Antrag auf Strafverfolgung wegen Hierosylie enthält. Wie unter **III** zu sehen ist, zielt diese Eingabe wie bei den *plêgai* mit möglicher Todesfolge vor allem darauf, daß der Täter nicht *athôios* entkommt. Dies läßt natürlich sofort an die gemeinsame Behandlung von Tötung und Hierosylie in den großen Indulgenzdekreten des II. Jhdts. denken, wo dies die beiden einzigen von der Amnestie ausgenommenen Delikte blieben[14]. Wie bekannt, entspann sich hierüber auf dem Symposion vor 15 Jahren eine lebhaft geführte Kontroverse, wie diese Bestimmung zu deuten sei[15]. Die unverkennbare Verwandtschaft der Anträge bei beiden Delikten legt nun doch ein einheitliches staatliches Verfahren auf gesetzlicher Grundlage für beide nahe, das mit dieser Klagformel von den Betroffenen in die Wege geleitet werden konnte: Jeder Anspruch auf Gnade war demnach verwirkt angesichts der Schwere der Tat.

---

12 Von A. Helmis, Despotisme et répression: les limites du pouvoir ptolémaïque, in: Symposion 1988. Vorträge zur griechischen und hellenistischen Rechtsgeschichte [Siena – Pisa, 6-8 Giunio 1988], hrsg. v. G. Nenci/G. Thür, Köln/Wien 1990, S. 311-317 wurde dies im Fall der Tötung noch verneint, wenngleich er mit Verwunderung bemerkt „Il est toutefois étrange qu'un tel système de régulation de la pathologie sociale, qui se caractérise par l'absence d'une punition étatique des délits privés, trouve sa place dans l'Égypte lagide, un État par définition autoritaire et ‚despotique'" (S. 317).

13 SB XX 14085 (13/12a oder 31/32p).

14 Vgl. außer P. Tebt. I 5 = C. Ord. Ptol. 53, 5 [π]λ̣ὴν τ̣[ῶν φόν]ους (l. φόνοις) ἑκουσίοις καὶ ἱεροσυλίαις ἐνεχομ̣[ένων (118a) auch bereits P. Köln VII 313 A, 4ff. πλ]ὴ̣ν τῶν [. . . . . φό]ν̣[ο]υς ἑκουσίους καὶ τῶν ἐκ τ̣[ῶν ναῶν καὶ τ]ῶ̣ν ἄλλω[ν ἱερῶν καὶ ἱ]ε̣ρῶν ἀποδοχίων σεσυληκό[των (ehem. P. Kroll = C. Ord. Ptol. 34; 186a).

15 Nach J. Mélèze Modrzejewski, La sanction de l'homicide en droit grec et hellénistique, in: Symposion 1990 (wie Anm. 3), S. 3-16 seien Tötung und Hierosylie demzufolge nicht staatlich verfolgt worden, da sie als Domäne von Familie bzw. Sakralrecht nicht durch den Staat zu ahnden waren; dagegen erkannte H.-A. Rupprecht, Straftaten (ebda.) in solchen Fällen ein eigenständiges Verwaltungshandeln, das ggf. auch die Konfiskation des Vermögens nach sich zog, zumal von einem *timêma* nie die Rede sei.

ANHANG

I. Belege aus ptolemäischer Zeit (vollständig)

A. *timêma*

• bei *plêgai*:

– P. Hib. I 32, 7ff. (246/45a): πρὸς καταδίκην ἔρημον ὕβρεως πρὸς (δρ.) σ καὶ τοῦ ἐπιδεκάτου (δρ.) κ

– P. Ent. 72, 8 (218a): πραχθῆναί μοι αὐτὸν τῶν π[λ]ηγ[ῶ]ν (δρ.) σ; Verso, 3: περὶ πληγῶν (δρ.) σ

– P. Straßb. I 91, 30f. (86a?): πρὸς τὸν ἐσόμενόν μοι πρὸς αὐτοὺς ἀργυ(ρίου) (ταλ.) μ[ ] λόγον; zum Delikt Z. 14f. δόντες αὐτῶι πληγὰς πλείους

• bei *hybris*:

– CPJ I 19 = P. Gurob 2, 27 (226a): τὴν ὕ]βριν (δρ.) σ. τίμημα δίκης (δρ.) [xy.]

– P. Ent. 73 Verso, 3 (222a): περὶ ᾿Α (δρ.) ὕβρεως

– P. Ent. 74, 12f. (221a): ὑβρ]ίζων καὶ ἄρχων εἴς με χειρῶν ἀδίκων· διὸ τ[ι]μῶμαι τὴν ὕβριν [; Z. 17f. γράψας τῶι ξενικῶι πράκτορι πρᾶξαι Πειθίαν τὸ τίμημα τῆς ὕβρεως καὶ ἀποδοῦναί μοι

– *P. Ent. 75 (222a) trotz eindringlicher Schilderung (vgl. auch Z. 11 ἀνόμως ὑβρισμένον, Z. 13 κἀμὲ ὑβρικότες, Z. 14 περὶ δὲ τῆς ὕβρεως ... διαγνῶναι) offenbar nicht anerkannt, vgl. Verso, 3 περὶ κλήρων!*

• bei *plêgai + hybris*:

– BGU X 1903, 5 (IIIa): μὴ περιιδεῖν με ἠνομημένον ᾿καὶ ὑβρισμέ[νον΄ ὑπ᾿ αὐτῶν, [ἀλλὰ] ᾿τιμῶμαι δὲ τὰς πληγὰς καὶ τὴν ὕβριν΄ [(jeweils nachgetragen)

– BGU VI 1249, 6ff. (148/47a): (ἐντεύξεως) δι᾿ ἧς ἐνεκάλει αὐτοῖς [περὶ] ὕβρεως κ[αὶ] πλ[η]γῶν ἃ ἐτιμήσατο [χ]αλκοῦ ταλά[ν]των δύο καὶ ἀργυρί[ο]υ δραχμῶν [ἑκατ]όν

– P. Tor. Choach. 9 = UPZ II 171, 15f. (126a): Zurückziehung einer früheren Eingabe (nämlich P. Tor. Choach. 8 = UPZ II 170 A und B) περὶ ὕβρεως καὶ πληγῶν καὶ ἀδικίου χαλκ(οῦ) ταλάντων πέντε

– P. Fay. 12 = M. Chr. 15, 30ff. (nach 104/03a): πραθχῆναί (l. πραχθῆναί) μοι ... τῆς ἀδίκου ἀγωγῆς ἀργυ(ρίου) (δρ.) ρ καὶ τῆς ὕβρεως χα(λκοῦ) υκ; zum Delikt Z. 17 ἤγαγον μεθ᾿ ὕβρεως καὶ πληγῶν

B. nur Sanktion, ohne Erwähnung einer Summe

• bei Tötung:

– P. Köln VI 272, 15ff. (Mitte/2. H. IIIa): ὅπως ἔνοχος γένηται περὶ τοῦ φόν[ο]υ; zum Delikt Z. 6ff. ἐλάκτισεν αὐτὴν καὶ ἔτυπτεν πυγμαῖς ... ὥστε ... πεσοῦσαν παραχρῆμα τελευτῆσαι

• bei *plêgai* mit möglicher Todesfolge:

– P. Ent. 81, 21ff. (221a): ἀποστεῖλαι ὅπως διεγγυηθῆ καί, ἐὰν ἐν ταῖς κατὰ τὸν νόμον ἡμέραι[ς τι πάθω, μὴ ἀθῶιος δι]αφύγῃ, ἐὰν δὲ διαναστῶ, λάβω παρ᾿ αὐτοῦ τὸ δίκαιον; zum Delikt Z. 12ff. ἐ]πάτ[αξε ... ξύλ]ωι ἑκὼν εἰς τὸν δεξιὸν πῦχυν (l. πῆχυν) τῆς χειρὸς καὶ κατέαξ[ε] ... [... εἰς] ὃ [ἂν] τύχοι μου μέρος τοῦ σώματος, ἄρχων εἴς μ[ε χειρῶν ἀ]δίκων

– P. Tebt. III.1 800, 35ff. (153a oder 142a, mit BL IV 99): ἀσφαλισθῆι ἡ ᾿Ιωάννα μέχρι τοῦ τὰ κατ᾿ αὐτὴν (sc. das Opfer) ἀποβῆσαι καὶ μὴ συμβῆι ἀτόπ[ου] τινὸς πράγματος γενομένου διαφυγεῖν τὴν Ἰωάνναν ἀθῳιαν; zum Delikt Z. 25ff.] ὑπὸ τῶν πληγῶ[ν] καὶ τ[ο]ῦ πτώματος δεινῶς κακοπ[α]θεῖν, mit Gefahr einer Fehlgeburt

– P. Tebt. III.2 960 descr., 7ff. (IIa): ἀσφαλισάμενον αὐτὸν ἐξαποστεῖλαι ἐφ' οὓς καθήκει, ἵν' ἐάν τι πάθῃ (sc. das Opfer) ἔνοχος εἴη τῶι φόνωι; Delikt größtenteils verloren, endet Z. 3ff. ὥστ' ἂν κλινοπετῆ αὐτὸν εἶναι ⟨καὶ⟩ κινδυνεύειν τῶι βίωι

– P. Tebt. I 44, 26ff. (114a): μή ποτε ἐξ ὑστέρου παθόντος τί μου ἀθῶιος διαφύγηι; zum Delikt Z. 18ff. ἐπιπηδήσας ἔδωκεν πληγὰς πλείους ἧι [ε]ἶχεν ῥάβδωι. ἐπε[ὶ] οὖν ὑ[πὸ τ]ῶν πληγῶν κινδυν[εύω]ι τῶι ζῆν

– P. Ryl. II 68, 18ff. (89a): ὅπως ... ἀσφαλισθῆι μέχρι τοῦ ἐπιγνωσθῆναι τὰ κα[τ'] ἐμ[ὲ] ἐν ταῖς διηγορευμέναις ἡμέραις, ἵν' ἐὰν μέν τι πάθω, δ[ια]ληφθῆι π[ερὶ] αὐτῆς κα[τ]ὰ τὰ περὶ [τούτων] προστεταγ[μένα,] ἐὰν δὲ περιγένωμαι, λάβω παρ' αὐτῆς τὸ δίκαιον ὡς καθήκει; zum Delikt Z. 10ff. ἔ[πληξέν] με ταῖς αὐτῆς χερσὶν [πλη]γαῖς πλεί[στα]ις ..., ὥ[στε] διὰ τὰς πληγὰς ἀρρωστήσασα⟨ν⟩ κατακεῖσ⟨θ⟩αι κινδυνεύουσα⟨ν⟩ τῶι βίωι, mit Gefahr einer Fehlgeburt

• bei <u>*plêgai*</u>:

– PSI V 542, 27ff. (um 185-165a, mit BL III 223): ὅπως τύχῃ ὁ ἄνθρωπος δι' αὐτοῦ τῆς ἁρμοζούσης ἐπιπλέξεως (l. ἐπιπλήξεως); zum Delikt Z. 7ff. ἔτυπτεν ἡ[μᾶς π]ληγαῖς τε καὶ λακ[τίσ]μασιν

• bei <u>*hybris*</u>:

– P. Ent. 79, 11f. (218a): ὅπως διακρι]θῆι πρός [μ]ε περὶ το[ύτων καὶ ...] ... τύχηι ζημίας ἧς ἂν ὁ στρατηγὸς συνκρ[ίνηι; zum Delikt Z. 7f. ὑβρίζουσά με καὶ ἄρχουσα εἴς με χερῶν ἀδίκων; Z. 9f. μὴ περιιδεῖν με οὔ]τως ἀλόγως ὑπὸ Αἰγυ[πτίας ὑβρισμέ]νον, Ἕλλην[α ὄν]τα καὶ ξένον (u.a. Übergießen mit Inhalt des Nachttopfs)

– P. Phrur. Diosk. 7, 21ff. (um 153a?): προνοηθῆναι ὡς τεύξεται τῆς ἁρμοζούσης ἐπιπλήξε[ω]ς; zum Delikt Z. 11ff. προσαλόμενός μοι ὕβρισεν τύπτων πληγαῖς πλείοσιν (Beschuldigter ist jüngerer Bruder)

– P. Tebt. I 16, 23f. (114a): οἷς κα(θήκει). προ(νοήσατε) ὡς αὐτοὶ κατασ[ταθέντες τύχωσι] τῆς ἁρμοζούσης ἐπιπ[λήξεως; zum Delikt Z. 7 ὡς ἦν ὑβρισμένος οὐ μετ[ρίως]

• vgl. auch P. Tebt. III.1 784, 6ff. (IIa in.): ὅπως ἐν [τῶι συν]εδρίωι ἐπιπλη[χθῆι] περὶ τούτων, ἀ[πὸ δὲ τῆς] ἐπιπλήξεως κ[ωλύσηις] ἑτέρους τὸ ὅμοιο[ν ἐπιτη]δεῦσαι; Delikt größtenteils verloren, erhalten lediglich Z. 2f. ᾤχητ[αι ἔχων] τὸ ἱμάτιον

C. Sanktion + Schadensersatz

• bei <u>*plêgai* nebst Vermögensschäden</u>, offenbar Ausnahme:

– P. Tebt. III.1 797, 24ff. (IIa): ὅπως ... τύχωσ[ι τῆς] ἁρμοζούσης ἐπιπλήξεως, [ἐγὼ δὲ ἀνα]κομίσω[μαι τὰ δεδη]λω[μένα; zum Delikt Z. 16ff. πληγάς] μοι πλείους ἐνέκοψαν u.a.

– BGU VI 1253, 18ff. (IIa): ἵνα τύχωσιν τῆς ἁρμοζούσης ἐπιπλήξεως [και]ει ἐπαναγκασθῶσιν ἐκτεῖ[σ]αι τὸ βλάβος; zum Delikt Z. 3ff. προσεμαστίγωσαν αἷς εἴχ[ο]σαν ῥάβδοις ... \`ὥστ' ἂν δεινῶ[ς] διακε[ῖ]σθαι ὑπὸ τῶν πληγῶ(ν)´ (nachgetragen) ... τά τε κτήνη ἀπεβιάσαντο

• bei <u>Raub bzw. Diebstahl</u> dagegen üblich, etwa ἵνα τῶν ἐγκαλουμένων κατασταθέντων ἐγὼ μὲν κομίσωμαι τὰ ἐμαυτοῦ, αὐτοὶ δὲ τύχωσι τῆς ἁρμοζούσης ἐπιπλήξεως

– so z.B. in BGU VI 1252; P. Phrur. Diosk. 11; P. Tebt. I 183 (alle IIa); 45; 46; 47; IV 1095; 1096 (alle 113a); BGU IV 1138 (19/18a)

– beides offenbar identisch in P. Tebt. I 41, 22f. (um 119a): εἰσπραχθέντος τὰ σείσματα τύχηι τῆς ἁρμοζούσης ἐπιπλήξεως

• vgl. auch P. Tebt. IV 1098, 14ff. (um 114a): ἵνα ἐγὼ μὲν τὰ ἐμαυτοῦ \`κομ[ίσ]ωμαι´, αὐτὸς δὲ μὴ ἀθῶιος διαφύγη[ι]; Delikt verloren

D. einfaches ἵνα/ὅπως τύχω τῶν δικαίων o.ä.
vgl. nur A. Di Bitonto, Le petizioni al re. Studio sul formulario, in: Aegyptus 47, 1967, 5-57, bes. S. 52f.; dies., Le petizioni ai funzionari nel periodo tolemaico. Studio sul formulario, in: Aegyptus 48, 1968, 53-107, bes. S. 103f.; vgl. auch Rupprecht, Straftaten (wie Anm. 3), S. 142 Anm. 30. Darunter zu schwerer Körperverletzung:
- UPZ I 7, 19f. 21f. (163/62a): ἐπαναγκάσαι αὐτοὺς τὰ δίκαιά μοι ποιῆσαι, andernfalls ὅπως διαλάβηι⟨ς⟩ περὶ αὐτῶν μισοπονήρος (l. μισοπονήρως), mit Hypogr. Z. 23 προνόησον ὅπως τεύξεται τῶν δικαίων; zum Delikt u.a. Z. 17 ἔτυπτον τοῖς χαλκοῖς ξυστῆρσιν
- UPZ I 8, 29ff. (161/60a): ὅπως περὶ ἁπάντων τούτων τύχωσι τῆς προσηκούσης μισοπονηρίας; zum Delikt Z. 21f. ὑβρίζοντας καὶ τύπτοντας
  Z. 23ff. zudem Verweis auf τὰ ὅμοια bereits früher (nämlich wie in UPZ I 7 dargelegt), aber ἀνεπιπλήκτων αὐτῶν ὄντων (Z. 27)
- UPZ I 12, 52 (158a): ὅπως τύχω τῶν δικαίων; zum Delikt Z. 38f. ὕβριζάν με καὶ 'ṃαστίκου (l. ἐμαστίγουν)

II. Belege aus römischer Zeit (Beispiele nach Anagnostou-Canas)

A. „peine appropriée"
- SB XVIII 13087, 25ff. (4a): ὅπως ἐγ̣ὼ μὲν τὸν χόρτον καὶ τὸν πυρὸν κομίσωμαι καὶ τὸ ἡμέτερον ἱμάτιον, α̣ὐ̣τοὶ δ̣ὲ τύχωσι ὧν προσήκει; zum Delikt Z. 11 συντελεσαμένου μοι ὕβριν̣, woraufhin erste Dialysis; diese jedoch als gescheitert zu betrachten, denn Z. 21 ἐτραυμ̣ά̣τ̣ισαν μεθ' ὕβρεως πλείστης καὶ πληγῶν

B. „traduit en justice"
- SB I 5235, 13ff. (12p): ὅπως ἐγὼ [τυγχά]νωι ἀν[τει]λημμένος, ὁ δ' ἐγκαλούμενος [τὴν πρ]ὸς ἑτέρων ἐπίστασιν τύχηι ὧν προσήκει; zum Delikt Z. 6 ὕβρισέν̣ με καὶ [π]λείους μοι πληγὰς ἐνέτεινε[ν]; zur Rolle des Richters Z. 11ff. σοῦ οὖν ... [ἀπα]γο[ρ]εύ-[σαντος] μί[σ]γεσθα[ι τὰς] τοιαύτας ὕ[βρεις] καὶ [πληγάς]
- P. Mich. V 228, 25f. (47p): ἐκπέμψαι τὸν ἐνκαλούμενον ἐπὶ σαὶ (l. σὲ) πρὸς τὴν ἐσομένην ἐπέξοδον; zum Delikt Z. 15f. ὕβριν μοι ἐπετέλεσον; Z. 18f. ἔτι δὲ καὶ ἔδωκεν ... πληγὰς πλήρους, mit Gefahr einer Fehlgeburt

ebenso Anträge P. Mich. V 229, 32ff.; 230, 25ff. (beide 48p)

III. Zur Hierosylie

- P. Lips. II 126, 15ff. (II/Ia): ὅπως μὴ διαφύγωσιν ἀθῷοι ἱερόσυλο̣ι ὄντας (l. ὄντες); zum Delikt Z. 9ff. ἐπιβαλόντες ἐπὶ τοὺς θησαυροὺς καὶ λύσαντες ᾤχοντο ἔχοντες εἰς χα(λκοῦ) τά(λαντα) ι ἀργυρίου ἐπ[β̣λ̣]`ι̣σ´ήμ̣ου (δραχμὰς) μ

KAJA HARTER-UIBOPUU (WIEN*)

ZUM GERICHTSWESEN IM KAISERZEITLICHEN SPARTA

Der Inschriftenkomplex IG V 1,18-20 enthält drei Inschriften, die sich mit den Leonidaia in Sparta beschäftigen und wird an die Wende vom 1. zum 2. Jh. n.Chr. datiert[1]. Davon dürften IG V 1,18 und 20 zu dem selben Stein gehört haben, sie enthalten den Anfang und das Ende eines spartanischen Dekretes, IG V 1,19 ist in seiner Zuordnung unsicher. Die Leonidaia waren ein jährlich wiederkehrender Agon in Sparta – zu Ehren des berühmten Feldherren und an dessen Grab – von dem Pausanias berichtet, daß nur spartanische Bürger zur Teilnahme berechtigt waren[2]. Inhalt der beiden vorliegenden Inschriften ist die Neuordnung dieser Spiele im Rahmen einer Stiftung durch T. Flavius Charixenos und C. Iulius Agesilaos, zwei spartanische Euergeten, die auch das römische Bürgerrecht hatten. Beide sind nicht nur als eponyme *patronomoi* überliefert, sondern waren auch *athlothetai* im Jahr 97 n.Chr. bei den ersten *megista Ourania Sebasteia Nervanideia*, die Agesilaos gestiftet hatte[3].

Der Text enthält, wie die Fragmente zu Beginn von IG V 1, 18 A erkennen lassen, das eigentliche Stiftungsdekret, also die Annahme der Stiftung und ihrer Bestimmungen durch die Stadt (A 1: ... καθὰ] καὶ οἱ γέροντẹ[ς ἐπέκρειναν])[4]. Dabei geht es vor allem um eine finanzielle Aufwertung der Spiele, 10.500 Denarii Kapital werden zusätzlich gestiftet und sollen von der ἀμειπτική τράπεζα (Wechselbank) betreut werden, die ansonsten in Sparta nicht erwähnt wird. A 4-9 und B 12-15 enthalten wohl die genaueren Bestimmungen zur Verwaltung der Gelder durch diese Bank[5]. Die jährlichen Einkünfte aus den Zinsen sollten zur Verdoppelung der Preisgelder

---

* Die Forschungsarbeiten zum Gerichtswesen in der römischen Provinz Achaea werden von der Österreichischen Akademie der Wissenschaften im Rahmen eines APART-Stipendiums unterstützt.

1 Editionen: H.J.W. Tillyard, ABSA 12, 1906, 445ff.; A.M. Woodward, ABSA 15, 1909, 98ff., Lesungen in den IG auch von A. Wilhelm und F. Hiller v. Gaertringen.

2 Paus. 3,14,1; IG V 1,660 belegt, daß dabei auch des Feldherrn Pausanias und anderer Heroen gedacht wurde.

3 C. Iulius Agesilaos: IG V,1 19; 378; 667; SEG 11,559; T. Flavius Charixenos: IG V 1,19; 34; 667; vgl. A.S. Bradford, A Prosopography of Lacedaemonians from the Death of Alexander the Great 323 BC to the Sack of Sparta by Alaric, AD 396, Vestigia 27, München 1977, 11 und 450.

4 P.J. Rhodes/D.M. Lewis, The Decrees of the Greek States, Oxford 1997, 81f.

5 R. Bogaert, Banques et Banquiers dans les cités grecques, Leiden 1968, 99f.

aufgewandt werden (A 8-9). Der Verwaltung liegen die Bestimmungen eines *hieros nomos* und eines nicht näher benannten *psephismas* zugrunde (A 5-6). Bereits hier wird die Zustimmung der Stadt zu den Regelungen der Verwaltung der Spiele, wie sie von den Stiftern vorgesehen waren, deutlich. Für das Prozeßrecht spannend ist dann Seite B der Inschrift Nr. 18, die ich hier mit einer Übersetzung wiedergebe.

IG V 1,18 B 1-12

[– – – – –]μα[̣... ὁ] μὲν [δα]νε̣ιζόμενος – – – – –αν̣... ν[– – – – –]ν ἐφορ̣[– – – – – – –]
[– – – – – – – – – –] ἀγωνιζομ[εν – – – – – – – – – – – – – – – – – –]ΤΟ̣Π̣[– – – – – ζημι]-
[ωθ]ήσεται μέχρι ʒφ΄. εἰ δέ τις ἀντιλέγοι τῶν ζημιωθέντων, κρινοῦσιν ὀμόσαντε[ς ἐν]
[ἱερ]ῷ̣ οἱ πεπατρονομηκότες τῆς τρίτης ἡμέρας, καὶ τὸν κατακριθέντα πρά[ξουσιν]
[οἱ ταμ]ιευ̣σ[ό]μενοι[6] τὴν διοίκησιν ἢ ἄλλος ὁ βουλόμενος τῶν πολειτῶν μετ' αὐ[τῶν]
[ἡμ]ι̣όλιο[ν], ὃ ἔσται τοῦ πράξαντος, τὰ δὲ προσγεινόμενα χωρήσει εἰς ἃ ἂν ὁ δῆμος
[θ]ελήσῃ καὶ οἱ ἄρχοντες κρείνωσι· τῆς δὲ ἐσομένης κατ' ἔτος πανηγύρεως ἀπὸ
Ἀ̣γριανίου ιϛ΄ μέχρι Ὑακινθίου ε΄ ἱσταμένου ἐπιμελήσονται οἱ νομοφύλακες
κ̣αὶ οἱ ἀθλοθέται, οἵτινες διαγνώσονται περὶ τῶν γεινομένων τισὶν ἐν τῇ πα-
νηγύρει ζητήσεων, ἃς εἶναι ἐκεχειρίας πᾶσι πρὸς πάντας ἐκύρωσεν ὁ
δῆμος, τῶν εἰσαγόντων τι ἐν ταῖς τῆς πανηγύρεως ἡμέραις ἐχόντων
ἀτέλειαν τῆς τε εἰσαγωγίμου καὶ πρατικῆς· ...

... soll bestraft werden bis zu 500 Den. Wenn aber einer Einspruch erhebt von den Bestraften, so sollen im Heiligtum die ehemaligen *patronomoi* am dritten Tag unter Eid entscheiden. Und beim Verurteilten vollstrecken die, (5) die *tamiai* sein werden für die Finanzgebarung, oder ein anderer Freiwilliger von den Bürgern mit ihnen auf das *hemiolion*, das dem Eintreibenden gehören soll. Der Zuwachs soll dafür ausgegeben werden, wofür es das Volk will und die Amtsträger beschließen. Um die kommende jährliche Festveranstaltung, die vom 17. Agrianios bis zum 5. Hyakinthios stattfindet, sollen sich die *nomophylakes* und die *athlothetai* kümmern. Diese entscheiden über die während der Festveranstaltung unter irgendwelchen (Teilnehmern) entstehenden Untersuchungen, von denen der *demos* eine *ekecheiria* für alles gegenüber allen beschlossen hat. Die Einführenden haben an den Tagen der Festveranstaltung Abgabenfreiheit von dem Einfuhrzoll und der Verkaufssteuer. ...

Die erste erhaltene Klausel handelt von der Strafgewalt von Amtsträgern, gegen deren Strafaussprüche eine Einspruchsmöglichkeit vorgesehen ist (B 2-4). Dabei

---

[6] Zur Neulesung ταμ]ιευ̣σ[ό]μενοι statt ταμ]ιευ̣σ[ά]μενοι siehe unten bei Anm. 24.

stellt die Frage nach der Identität der strafenden Amtsträger eine erste Hürde dar, da der Text oberhalb abgebrochen und nicht erhalten ist. Zu denken ist aber am ehesten an die *athlothetai*, unter deren Ägide die Leonidaia durchgeführt wurden (IG V 1, 19, 2.4.15), sie veranstalteten die *panegyris* gemeinsam mit den *nomophylakes* (IG V 1, 18 A 10), die ebenfalls als strafende Behörde in Frage kämen. Möglich wäre auch die Annahme von *epimeletai*, die für die Veranstaltung zuständig waren. (IG V 1, 20 A 1-2).

IG V 1, 20 A 1-3

[ἀ]γωνιζομένων καθεδοῦνται ἐν ᾧ ἂν οἱ ἐπιμελούμενοι τοῦ ἀγῶνος
κελεύ⟨σ⟩ωσι τόπῳ,
[ὁ] δὲ μὴ πειθόμενος ἐκτείσει ≺ σʹ. ἔσται δὲ ὁ γυμνικὸς ἀγὼν κατ' ἐνιαυτὸν
κατὰ τὴν ῥή-
τραν τῇ κζʹ · ...

... der Wettkämpfer sollen sich dort aufhalten, wo es die Verantwortlichen für den Agon anweisen. Wer aber nicht Folge leistet soll 200 Den. zahlen. Der gymnische Agon soll jährlich gemäß dem Gesetz am 27. stattfinden.

Für diese ist ebenfalls eine Strafgewalt vorgesehen, Strafen von 200 Denarii werden verhängt, wenn die Wettkämpfer sich nicht an den für sie bestimmten Orten aufhalten. Bei der Zahl 200 in Z.2 handelt es sich um eine Neulesung, bislang wurde im Text jeweils εʹ angegeben, für 5 Den. K. Hallof konnte aber in einer Untersuchung des Abklatsches feststellen, daß es sich um einen Schwalbenschwanz, also ein um 90 Grad verdrehtes Y mit starken Serifen, die nach innen stehen, handelt, welches wohl als Denarzeichen zu deuten sei und auch in Kos vorkommt[7]. Als Zahlzeichen folgt ein Sigma, der Strafsatz betrug also 200 Den.

Jedenfalls hatten die unbekannten Amtsträger in IG V 1, 18 B die Möglichkeit, Strafen bis zu einer Höhe von 500 Denarii zu verhängen. Ein Einspruch gegen diesen Strafausspruch war möglich und sollte von den πεπατρονομηκότες entschieden werden, den ehemaligen *patronomoi*. Die Frage nach der Identität dieses Richtergremiums ist von größtem Interesse. Die *patronomoi* wurden in Sparta erst unter Kleomenes III im Rahmen seiner Verfassungsreformen eingeführt. In der Kaiserzeit traten sie als eponyme Amtsträger der Polis auf, erhalten sind Listen mit jeweils 6 Namen für jedes Jahr. Das jährlich zu besetzende Amt hatte sicher liturgischen Charakter und war prestigereich, aber nicht mit großen Kompetenzen versehen. Einigkeit herrscht in der Forschung darüber, daß der Aufgabenbereich im Rahmen der staatlichen Erziehung, der *agoge* zu sehen sein wird, da die *patronomoi* oft gemeinsam mit dem Gymnasiarchen genannt werden. Auf die laufenden Diskussionen zu diesem Amt werde ich in diesem Beitrag nicht weiter eingehen, denn für das Prozeßrecht ist daraus lediglich die Frage interessant, wie viele *patronomoi* in Sparta

---

[7] Segre, Iscr. di Cos ED 258,5

jedes Jahr tätig waren[8]. Ich möchte mich hier der Ansicht Kennells anschließen, der von einem *patronomos* und fünf *synarchontes* ausgeht, ihm stellt sich Bradford entgegen, der sechs *patronomoi* annimmt, von denen nur einer *eponymos* sei[9]. Diese Überlegung hat natürlich Auswirkungen auf die angenommene Größe der Gruppe, die während der Leonidaia richterliche Entscheidungen treffen sollte, auch wenn diese Frage weder von Kennell noch von Bradford in ihre Untersuchungen einbezogen wurde. Geht man von M.H. Hansens Berechnungen für die Größe des athenischen Areopags aus (145-175), kommt man für das Gremium der „ehemaligen *patronomoi*" nach Kennell auf 16-19 Personen, während nach Ansicht Bradfords 96-116 Personen anzunehmen wären[10]. Diese Angaben scheinen meines Erachtens für die Theorie Kennells zu sprechen, da die anderen Ratsversammlungen Spartas, die Gerousia und die Boule (Gerousia und Ephoren) ebenfalls die Zahl 30 nicht überschreiten. Hier nun für die Leonidaia ein Gremium anzunehmen, das so deutlich größer ist, als es in Sparta je üblich war, und an einen demokratischen Gerichtshof erinnert, scheint mir verfehlt.

Als Besonderheit ist natürlich darauf hinzuweisen, daß hier Amtsträgern nach Ablauf ihrer Amtszeit eine eigene Funktion zugewiesen wird, ein Phänomen, das sich in Griechenland so nicht oft findet. Natürlich wird man bei den Vorbildern zunächst vor allem an den Areopag in Athen denken, der gerade in der Kaiserzeit zur bedeutendsten Institution der Stadt wurde[11]. Allerdings wäre dazu die Parallele in Sparta sicher die Gerousia, die zwar im Unterschied zur klassischen Verfassung Spartas nunmehr jährlich neu besetzt wurde, aber doch deutlich den mächtigsten Rat der Stadt bildete[12]. Ich glaube nicht, daß der – nur einmal erwähnte – Rat der ehemaligen *patronomoi* politischen Einfluß irgendeiner Art hatte, zumal wohl bereits den aktiven Amtsträgern kaum eine politische Rolle zukam. Auch kann man aus dieser

---

8 B. Shimron, The Original Task of the Spartan Patronomoi. A Suggestion, Eranos 63, 1965, 155-158; N.M. Kennell, The Public Institutions of Roman Sparta, Diss Toronto 1985, 73-105; P. Cartledge/A. Spawforth, Hellenistic and Roman Sparta, London ²2002, 201-202.

9 N.M. Kennell, The Size of the Spartan Patronomate, ZPE 85, 1991, 131-137; A.S. Bradford, The Synarchia of Roman Sparta, Chiron 10, 1980, 413-425; dazu auch: L. Pareti, La Patronomia Spartana, Studi Spartani Turin 1910. Der Meinung Kennells schließen sich auch P. Cartledge und A. Spawforth an (Hellenistic and Roman Sparta, 201f.)

10 M.H. Hansen, The Size of the Council of the Areopagos and its Social Composition in the Fourth Century B.C., ClMed 41, 1990, 73-77.

11 D.J. Geagan, The Athenian Constitution after Sulla, Hesperia Suppl. XII, Princeton N.J. 1976, 41ff.

12 V.a. K.M.T. Chrimes, Ancient Sparta. A Re-Examination of the Evidence, Manchester 1949, 142-149; N.M. Kennell, IG V 1,16 and the Gerousia of Roman Sparta, Hesperia 61, 1992, 193-202; ders., The Spartan Synarchia, Phoenix 46, 1992, 342-351.

Stelle nicht auf allgemeine Kompetenzen der *patronomoi* im Rahmen der Jurisdiktion in Sparta schließen, wie dies in der Forschung geschehen ist[13].

Dem römischen Denken ist die ausschließliche Berechtigung „ehemaliger" Amtsträger zur Übernahme weiterer besonderer Funktionen wesentlich näher als dem griechischen Denken. Hier sei nur exemplarisch auf die Rolle der Rangklassen des Senats im Rahmen der Rechtssprechung hinweisen, auch wenn ich nicht ein eindeutig römisches Vorbild für die vorliegenden spartanischen Verhältnisse konstatieren möchte. Wie auch die Quellen aus anderen griechischen Städten zeigen, ist eine Entscheidung zwischen rein römischem oder rein griechischem Vorbild zumeist gar nicht notwendig. In den meisten Fällen läßt sich festhalten, daß eine Institution, die in einer griechischen Stadt neu eingerichtet oder modifiziert wurde, oft beiden Rechtskreisen bekannt war, und damit sowohl von der Stadt als auch der römischen Verwaltung leicht akzeptiert werden konnte. Wichtig scheint mir an dieser Stelle auch, daran zu erinnern, daß im Rahmen einer Stiftung jedwede Regelung der Organisation einer Festlichkeit oder eines Agones denkbar war, also auch neue Gremien geschaffen werden konnten, die nicht nur die städtischen Einrichtungen zum Vorbild haben konnten. Sobald die Stiftungsbestimmungen von der Stadt angenommen waren – und genau diesen Akt überliefert die vorliegende Inschrift –, waren diese Gremien fester Bestandteil der städtischen Verwaltung geworden[14].

Ein nahes Vergleichsbeispiel liefert eine Inschrift aus Oinoanda, die Stiftung des C. Julius Demosthenes, die 1988 von M. Wörrle publiziert und kommentiert wurde[15]. Hier treten in Zeile 87 die ehemaligen Agonotheten auf, die gemeinsam mit dem amtierenden Agonotheten den Vorsitz in der Festversammlung übernehmen:

SEG 38,1462, 87

[Καὶ το]ὺς ἠγωνοθετηκότας ἤδη συνπροεδρεύειν τῷ ἀγωνοθέτῃ ἐν τῇ πανηγύρει.

Und die, die schon Agonotheten gewesen sind, sollen mit dem Agonotheten zusammen beim Fest das Präsidium einnehmen.

Wenn auch in der komplett erhaltenen Stiftung des Demosthenes in Oinoanda den ehemaligen Agonotheten keine weiteren Kompetenzen zugewiesen werden, ist es doch bemerkenswert, daß in der Kaiserzeit hier erstmals Amtsträgern ihre Vorgänger im Amt gleichsam als Unterstützung zur Seite gestellt werden. Auch eine In-

---

13 K.M.T. Chrimes, Ancient Sparta, 144f.

14 Vgl. z.B. die detaillierten Regelungen der Stiftung des Aristomenes und der Psylla in Korkyra, IG IX 1^2 4,798 und B. Laum, Stiftungen in der griechischen und römischen Antike I, Berlin 1914, 227ff.

15 M. Wörrle, Stadt und Fest im kaiserzeitlichen Kleinasien. Studien zu einer agonistischen Stiftung aus Oinoanda, Vestigia 39, München 1988

schrift aus Kyzikos aus dem 1. Jh. n.Chr. zeigt ein Auftreten des eponymen Amtsträgers gemeinsam mit seinen Amtsvorgängern, dort allerdings in rein repräsentativer Rolle[16]. Hadrian wiederum rät der Stadt Pergamon in Rechtsfragen, die die Geschäften der Geldwechsler betreffen, die ehemaligen Strategen zu einem Gerichtshof zusammenzufassen, da diese größere Erfahrung hätten und im Unterschied zu den zuständigen *tamiai* nicht selbst in die Angelegenheiten verwickelt seien. Hierbei wird das Motiv deutlich, das auch den Regelungen in Oinoanda und in Sparta zugrunde liegen dürfte: die Erfahrung der ehemaligen Amtsträger soll – nicht nur im Gerichtsverfahren – genützt werden[17].

OGIS 484, 52-56

... [τὰς μέντ]οι κρί-
σεις γείνεσθαι μὴ ἐπὶ τῶν ταμιῶ[ω ἀλλ]ὰ ἐπὶ τῶν ἐστρατη[γηκ]ότων
ἀνδρῶν ἐξ ἀπολογῆς εὔλο[γον εἶ]ναι νομίζω, ἔτι δὲ το[ὺ]ς μὲν τα-
μίας μετέχειν τῆς χρε[ίας κ]αθῆκον, το[ὺς] δὲ ἐσ[τρα]τη[γηκ]ότας
καὶ ἐμπείρους εἶνα[ι ...

... daß Verfahren jedoch nicht vor den *tamiai* sondern vor den ehemaligen Strategen stattfinden sollen, halte ich für vernünftig wegen der Auswahl, da die *tamiai* an dieser Sache beteiligt sind, und die ehemaligen Strategen Erfahrung haben ...

Als Vergleich zu den Regelungen in Sparta läßt sich auch der *hieros nomos* von Andania heranziehen. Auch dort haben verschiedene Amtsträger Strafbefugnisse während der Mysterienfeiern, diese unterlagen allerdings einer Kontrolle durch die *hieroi*, eines eigens für diese Veranstaltung gebildeten Rat[18]. An einen derartigen „Rat der Festveranstaltung" könnte man parallel auch bei den πεπατρονομηκότες der Leonidaia denken.

IG V 1, 1390, 110-11

ἂν δέ τις τῶν ἐγδεξαμένων ἢ τῶν βαλανέων μὴ ποιεῖ καθὼς γέγραπται, τὸν
μὲν δοῦλον μαστιγούτω ὁ ἀγορ̣α̣νό-
[μος, τ]ὸν δὲ ἐλεύθ⟨ε⟩ρον ζαμιούτω καθ' ἕκαστον ἀδίκημα εἴκοσι δραχμαῖς·
καὶ τὸ κρίμα ἔστω ἐπὶ τῶν ἱερῶν.

Wenn aber einer der Unternehmer oder der Bader nicht gemäß dem Vorgeschriebenen handelt, soll der *agoranomos* den Sklaven züchtigen, den Freien für jedes einzelne Unrecht zu zwanzig Drachmen bestrafen. Die Entscheidung liegt bei den *hieroi*.

16 M. Sève, BCH 103, 1979, 329, Z.43f.

17 J.H. Oliver, Greek Constitutions of Early Roman Emperors from Inscriptions and Papyri, Memoirs of the American Philosophical Society 178, Philadelphia 1989, Nr.84, 208-215; A.N. Macro, Imperial Provisions for Pergamum: OGIS 484, GRBS 17, 1976, 169-179.

18 K. Harter-Uibopuu, Strafklauseln und gerichtliche Kontrolle in der Mysterieninschrift von Andania (IG V 1,1390), in: Dike 5 (2002), 138f.

Abschließend sei kurz auf die zahlreichen Karriereinschriften hingewiesen, die aus dem kaiserzeitlichen Sparta erhalten sind und in denen die spartanischen Bürger stolz von den innegehabten städtischen Ämtern berichten. Hierin zeigt sich eine generelle Änderung im Ansehen der Leistung einzelner Bürger für ihre Städte, die ihrerseits natürlich vermehrt auf diese Leistungen angewiesen waren[19]. Die vorgestellte Einführung eines kleinen Rates von ehemaligen Amtsträgern hat meines Erachtens dieser allgemeinen Entwicklung folgend Eingang in die spartanische Rechtspflege zumindest für die Leonidaia gefunden.

Der generelle Ablauf der Kontrolle von Strafaussprüchen von Gremien ist aus verschiedenen Inschriften der Poleis und einzelner Stiftungen recht gut bekannt, der spartanische Text stellt hier keine Ausnahme da[20]. Wichtig ist dabei, die Verteilung der Parteienrollen im Auge zu behalten und die Frage zu beantworten wer in der Verhandlung als Kläger auftrat und wer als Beklagter. Das klassische Vergleichsbeispiel aus hellenistischer Zeit ist die Bestätigung einer Strafe, die gegen den Bauunternehmer Philon von Korinth durch die Boule von Epidauros verhängt wurde.

IG IV 1^2 98, 1-8

[ἐπ' ἱαρ]εῦς Θιοκύδευς, μηνὸς Ἀπελλαίου
ὀφείλει τῶι θεῶι ὁ ἐργώνας τᾶς ὕσπλα-
κος Φίλων Κορίνθιος τᾶς ζαμίας ἇς ἐ-
ζαμίωσε αὐτὸν ὁ ἀγωνοθέτας τοῦ γυ-
μνικοῦ Τρίτυλλος καὶ οἱ ἑλλανοδίκαι καὶ
ἐπέκρινε αὐτὸν παρεόντα ἁ βουλὰ δι-
καίως ἐζαμιῶσθαι δραχμαῖς Ἀλεξαν-
δρείαις πεντακοσίαις·

Unter dem Priester Thiokydeus, im Monat Apellaios. Der Unternehmer, der die Arbeiten an der Startanlage übernommen hat, Philon aus Korinth, schuldet dem Gott die Strafsumme, die ihm der *agonothetes* des gymnischen (Agons) Trityllos und die *hellanodikai* auferlegt hatten und die Boule hat in seiner Anwesenheit durch Urteil bestätigt, daß er rechtmäßig bestraft ist zu 500 alexandrinischen Drachmen.

Hier verhängen Amtsträger, die für die Spiele zuständig sind (*agonothetes* und *hellanodikai*) eine Strafe, die durch die städtische Behörde überprüft werden kann. Philon hat sicher die Rolle des Beklagten, da speziell auf seine Anwesenheit bei dem Verfahren hingewiesen wird (6: αὐτὸν παρεόντα) – Kläger waren entsprechend die Amtsträger. Philon hatte wohl die Zahlung verweigert und durch seine Weigerung

---

19 F. Quass, Die Honoratiorenschicht in den Städten des griechischen Ostens. Untersuchungen zur politischen und sozialen Entwicklung in hellenistischer und römischer Zeit, Stuttgart 1993, 184ff.

20 P. Fröhlich, Les cités grecques et le contrôle des magistrats (IVe-Ier siècle avant J.-C.), Genf 2004, 287ff. und 292ff.

konnte er selbst die Amtsträger zwingen, eine Kontrolle herbeizuführen. Als zweites Vergleichsbeispiel soll hier die Gymnasiarcheninschrift aus Beroia herangezogen werden, die die Rechte und Pflichten des Gymnasiarchen um die Mitte des 2. Jh. v.Chr. beschreibt[21].

Z. 101-107

ταῖς δὲ ζημίαις ἁπάσαις ἐπιγραφέτω τὴν αἰτίαν ὁ γυμνασίαρχος δι' [ἣν]
[ἐζ]ημίωσεν κα[ὶ] ἀ̣ν̣ακηρυσσέτω ἐν τῶι γυμνασίωι καὶ ἐκτιθέτω τοὺς ἐζημιωμένους π[άν]-
[τα]ς ἐν λευκώματι καὶ παραγραφέτω τῶι πολιτικῶι πράκτορι, ὁ δὲ πράκτωρ εἰσπράξας ἀποκ[α]-
[τ]αστησάτω τῶι ἐνεστῶτι γυμνασιάρχωι. ἐὰν δέ τις φήσῃ μὴ δικαίως ἐζημιῶσθαι, ἐξέ-
[στ]ω ἀντείπαντι αὐτῶι διακριθῆναι ἐπὶ τῶν καθηκόντων ἀρχείων καί, ἐὰν νεικήσῃ τῆι κρίσει ὁ ζη-
[μι]ωθείς, ἀποτινέτω ὁ γυμνασίαρχος τὸ ἡμιόλιον τῶι νικήσαντι προσα ποτινέτω τὸ ἐπίπεμ-
π̣τον καὶ ἐπιδέκατον.

Bei allen Geldstrafen soll der Gymnasiarch den Grund aufschreiben, weshalb er die Buße verhängte, und er soll dies im Gymnasion ausrufen lassen und von allen, die mit einer Geldbuße belegt wurden die Namen bekanntgeben auf einer weiß getünchten Tafel und durch eine Notiz den *praktor* der Stadt benachrichtigen; der *praktor* soll nach der Vollstreckung zurückleiten an den im Amt befindlichen Gymnasiarchen. Wenn jemand behauptet, zu Unrecht mit einer Geldbuße belegt worden zu sein, soll er Widerspruch einlegen können und von den zuständigen Behörden eine Entscheidung erhalten. Obsiegt in dem Verfahren derjenige, der mit einer Geldbuße belegt worden war, soll der Gymnasiarch dem Erfolgreichen das *hemiolion* bezahlen und dazu ein Fünftel und ein Zehntel entrichten.

Hier liegt die Verteilung der Pateienrollen eben umgekehrt: der Bestrafte selbst hatte die aktive Möglichkeit, den Gymnasiarchen anzuzeigen, und die Kontrolle des Strafausspruches zu erzwingen. (104f.) Für den Fall der Verurteilung des Gymnasiarchen war vorgesehen, daß er nicht nur das Hemiolion dem siegreichen Kläger, sondern darüber hinaus noch anteilige Strafen an die Stadt oder die Kasse des Gymnasiums bezahlen mußte (105-107). Wie sieht nun die Verteilung der Parteienrollen in Sparta aus? Grundsätzlich wären beide eben vorgestellten Modelle denkbar, genaue Angaben dazu macht der Text leider nicht. Die Inschrift spricht allerdings von der aktiven Möglichkeit dessen, der mit einer Strafe belegt worden war, Einspruch zu erheben (ἀντιλέγειν, IG V 1, 18 B 3). Dies würde ihm auf den ersten Blick die Klägerrolle zuweisen und damit wäre der Amtsträger der Beklagte. Dagegen spricht allerdings die im nächsten Satz angesprochene Verurteilung. Diese wird wohl zu-

[21] P. Gauthier/M. Hatzopoulos, La loi gymnasiarchique de Beroia, Meletemata 16, Athen 1993, 134-138.

nächst gegen den ursprünglich Bestraften zu erwarten sein und nicht gegen den Amtsträger, daher müßte der ursprünglich Bestrafte in dem Verfahren Beklagter gewesen sein und wiederum – ähnlich wie in Epidauros – durch die Weigerung, die Strafsumme zu bezahlen, die Kontrolle in Gang gesetzt haben. Kläger wären dann die Amtsträger. Allerdings ist es wichtig zu bemerken, daß in der Verweigerung der Zahlung im vorliegenden Text eine legitime Möglichkeit der Bestraften festgehalten und mit ἀντιλέγειν bezeichnet wurde. Trotzdem soll die eingangs erwähnte Möglichkeit der Verteilung der Parteienrollen nicht außer Acht gelassen werden. Meines Erachtens ließe der Text auch diese Annahme zu: Nach dem Beispiel von Beroia könnte der Bestrafte auch als Kläger auftreten, im ursprünglichen Sinn des ἀντιλέγειν, dann wären in den Verurteilten die Amtsträger zu sehen. Auffallenderweise wäre dann allerdings keine Strafe *expressis verbis* für denjenigen Bestraften vorgesehen, dessen Einspruch ungerechtfertigt war. Eine ausschließliche Entscheidung für eine der beiden Möglichkeiten ist nach dem erhaltenen Text nicht möglich, der in dieser Hinsicht ungewöhnlich ungenau ist.

Die Verhandlung vor den πεπατρονομηκότες sollte im Heiligtum und innerhalb von drei Tagen stattfinden, das Gremium ist angehalten, nach der Ableistung eines Richtereides zu urteilen. Auch die Frist von drei Tagen hat einige Forscher dazu bewogen, hier einen eindeutig römischen Einfluß anzunehmen (*comperendinatio*)[22]. Sie ist aber im griechischen Bereich ebenso geläufig, wenn auch selten im Gerichtswesen[23]. Nach dem Urteil der πεπατρονομηκότες sollte die Vollstreckung erfolgen, allerdings bestehen an dieser Stelle meines Erachtens Schwierigkeiten mit dem Text (IG V 1,18 B 5). Den Ergänzungen Woodwards folgend, hätten die ehemaligen *tamiai* ([οἱ ταμ]ιευσ[ά]μενοι) für die Verwaltung die Pflicht, das Strafgeld einzutreiben[24]. War schon der Einsatz ehemaliger *patronomoi* eine Besonderheit, kann ich im Rahmen der Finanzverwaltung nicht an einen Einsatz ehemaliger Amtsträger, deren Rechenschaftsablage wohl schon erfolgt war, glauben. Der Text scheint an dieser Stelle generell schlecht zu lesen, ich würde aber vorschlagen, [οἱ ταμ]ιευσ[ό]μενοι parallel zu anderen Ämtern in der Inschrift im Futur zu halten[25]. Als Hinweis darauf,

---

22 Z.B. K.M.T. Chrimes, Ancient Sparta, 144. Bereits in den XII Tafeln ist die *comperendinatio* zwingend festgehalten, die Frist von drei Tagen wird erst in der *lex Iulia iudiciorum privatorum* verlängert, um den veränderten räumlichen Verhältnissen Rechnung zu tragen. Vgl. Gai. Inst. 4,15; M. Kaser, Das Römische Zivilprozeßrecht, HdAW 10,3,4, München 1966, 83 Anm. 4 und 274.

23 Vgl. z.B. aus Oiantheia IG IX 1^2 706 A 17: δίκαν τὸν ἄρχοντα δόμεν ἀμερᾶν τριῶ[ν τῶν Αἰαντείων τῶι ἐγκαλέσαντι] | καὶ ἐκκπρᾶξαι δέχ' ἀμερᾶν τὸ κατὰ ξένον· Ein Verfahren soll der *archon* eröffnen innerhalb von drei Tagen demjenigen Aianteier, der Klage erhebt, und die Vollstreckung vornehmen innerhalb von zehn Tagen nach dem Gastrecht (?).

24 A.M. Woodward, ABSA 15, 1909, 101f.

25 Eine Einordnung der in der Inschrift auf 17. Agrianios bis 5. Hyakinthios festgesetzten Feier in das spartanische Amtsjahr ist aufgrund der fehlenden Informationen zu den Mo-

daß die *tamiai* wohl die städtischen Amtsträger sein müssen, und nicht eine eigens für die Stiftung geschaffene Behörde, mag die Vorschrift, herangezogen werden, daß die eingetriebenen Gelder dafür verwendet werden sollten, „wofür es das Volk will und die Amtsträger beschließen“, also in die städtische Kasse übergeleitet wurden (IG V 1,18 B 6-7)[26].

Festzuhalten ist also, daß zunächst die Pflicht von Amtsträgern bestand, die Strafgelder beim Verurteilten einzutreiben. Zusätzlich war vorgesehen, daß sie dieser Pflicht auch gemeinsam mit einem *boulomenos* aus den Reihen der Bürger nachkommen konnten. Die Betonung des Bürgerrechtes des *boulomenos* findet eine Parallele in den Vorschriften des *hieros nomos* von Gytheion aus dem 1. Jh. n.Chr., den Regelungen zur Durchführung des Kaiserkultes. Dort steht es nur den Gytheaten zu, die Amtsführung des *agoranomos* zu beeinspruchen[27].

SEG 11, 923, 17f.

ἐξέστω δὲ τῷ βουλομένῳ Γυθεατῶν παντὶ περὶ τῶν ἱερῶν ἐκδικεῖν χρημάτων ἀθῴῳ ὄ[ν]-
τι. ...

Jedem Bürger von Gytheion, der betreffs der heiligen Gelder Klage erheben will, soll es erlaubt sein, ohne daß ihm daraus Schaden erwächst.

Eine erweiterte Möglichkeit findet sich in dem etwa zeitgleichen Stiftungsdekret aus Gytheion über eine Ölstiftung durch Phaenia Aromation. Dort ist gerade jedem griechischen und römischen Freiwilligen anheim gestellt, die Mißachtung der Stiftungsvorschriften anzuzeigen, wie auch generell die Bestimmungen dieser Inschrift auf das Zusammenleben der beiden Bevölkerungsgruppen in Gytheion zielen[28]. Die Leonidaia aber sind – wie auch dieser Passus zeigt – eine rein spartanische Angelegenheit, daher ist ein Eingreifen fremder *boulomenoi* nicht vorgesehen. Der Einsatz des *boulomenos* hier in Sparta stellt zusätzlich insofern eine Besonderheit dar, als

natsabfolgen ebenfalls nicht möglich, also kann auch die Möglichkeit eines Festes zum Jahreswechsel, bei dem etwa die erst vor kurzem amtierenden *tamiai* noch eine Rolle spielten, nicht überprüft werden.

26 Neben der Eingliederung in die staatliche Ordnung bestand auch immer die Möglichkeit, eine Stiftung durch eigens dafür gewählte Amtsträger, die den städtischen Behörden nachgebildet waren, verwalten zu lassen, vgl. B. Laum, Stiftungen, 227-231. Auch in Teos (Syll.[3] 578, 3. Jh. v.Chr.) und Kalaureia (IG IV 840) sind derartige Vorgänge zu beobachten.

27 L. Wenger, Griechische Urkunden zum Kaiserkult und zum Grabrecht, ZRG 49 (1929), 323ff.; K. Harter-Uibopuu, Kaiserkult und Kaiserverehrung in den Koina des griechischen Mutterlandes, in: H. Cancik/K. Hitzl, Die Praxis der Herrscherverehrung in Rom und seinen Provinzen, Tübingen 2003, 219f.

28 K. Harter-Uibopuu, *The Trust Fund of Phaenia Aromation (IG V,1 1208) and Imperial Gytheion*, in SHT 5 (2004), http://www.ut.ee/klassik/sht/2004/harter-uibopuu1.pdf

dieser deutlich an der *praxis* selbst beteiligt war. Die Vollstreckung ist normalerweise die Angelegenheit von Amtsträgern, auch wenn sie durch eine Anzeige eines *boulomenos* in Gang gebracht werden konnte. Häufig finden sich Beispiele für eine Verantwortlichkeit der Amtsträger, wenn sie die *praxis* nicht durchführten, die dann mit Anzeigen durch Privatpersonen verbunden war[29]. In seltenen Fällen aber wird die Verantwortung für das eigentliche Herbeischaffen des Geldes Privatleuten oder Privatleuten gemeinsam mit den Amtsträgern übergeben. Das folgende hellenistische Beispiel aus Delphi beschäftigt sich ebenfalls mit einer Eintreibung von Strafgeldern, wiederum sind die Amtsträger der *polis* aufgerufen, dazu die *hieromnamones* der Amphiktyonie und griechische *boulomenoi*, die in diesem Fall aber deutlich dazu angehalten sind, entweder vor einem Urteil bereits die Gelder zu erhalten, oder in einem Verfahren als Kläger aufzutreten und ein Urteil über die Strafe herbeizuführen[30].

CID IV 51, 9-12

... τὴν δὲ πρᾶξι̣ν̣ καὶ τῆ̣[ν ἐπιμέ]-
[λ]ειαν ὑπὲρ αὐτῶν ποιεῖσθαι τήν τε πό[λιν ἢ τὴ]ν̣ ἀρχὴν [καὶ]
τοὺς ἱερομνήμονας τοὺς ἀντιτυ[γχάνοντας καὶ τῶν]
ἄλλων Ἑλλήνων τὸν βουλόμ̣[ενον. ...

Die *praxis* und die Verantwortung für sie übernehmen die *polis*, oder das Amt oder die anwesenden *hieromnamones* oder jeder andere von den Griechen, der das möchte.

In der Kaiserzeit finden sich ebenso Belege für die Beteiligung von Privatpersonen an der *praxis*, welche nunmehr auch alleine vorgehen können. Ein Beispiel für derartiges Vorgehen ist ein Stiftungsdekret aus Aphrodisias aus dem beginnenden 1. Jh. n.Chr., in dem folgendes vorgesehen ist.

McCabe, Aphrodisias 32 (SEG 13, 491), 40-46

ἐὰν δέ τις τῶν ὀφειλόντων πρᾶξαι τὸ ἀρ-
γύριον μὴ πράξῃ, ἢ μὴ ποήσηται τὴν
διάδοσιν ὡς προγέγραπται, ἀποτεισά-
τω ἱερὰ Ἀφροδείτῃ δη(νάρια) τρισχείλια, ἃ καὶ
πράσσεσθαι ἐπάνανκες ὑπὸ τοῦ βου-
λομένου τῶν πολειτῶν ἐπὶ τρίτῳ
μέρει·

Wenn einer von denen, die das Geld eintreiben müssen, nicht eintreibt oder die Spende nicht durchführt, wie es vorgeschrieben ist, soll er 3000 Denare zahlen, die der Aphrodite

---

29 Vgl. z.B. IG XII 7,515 (Aigiale, 2. Jh. v.Chr.); P. Gauthier/M. Hatzopoulos, Beroia, B Z. 94-96; P. Fröhlich, Cités Grecques, 126ff.

30 Zur *epimeleia* vgl. G. Thür, Prozeßrechtliches in der Mauerbauinschrift IG II2 244, in: M. Kandler (Red.), Lebendige Altertumswissenschaft, Festschrift Hermann Vetters, Wien 1985, 66-69.

verfallen, und diese müssen eingetrieben werden von jedem Bürger, der das möchte, gegen den dritten Teil.

Allerdings handelt es sich dabei nicht um Strafgelder, sondern um Summen, die zu zahlen bestimmte Personen regelmäßig verpflichtet waren, damit die in einem Testament festgesetzten Geldspenden durchgeführt werden können. Auch hier wurde dem *boulomenos* eine Beteiligung an den eingetriebenen Geldern versprochen, um einen Anreiz zu schaffen. Ebenso sahen die Bestimmungen in Sparta vor, daß dem *boulomenos* das Hemiolion zufallen sollte, also der 50% Aufschlag auf die Strafsumme, der Rest des einzutreibenden Geldes stand der Polis Sparta zur Verfügung[31].

Auch die Beschreibung des Festes, das rund um die Leonidaia gefeiert wurde, enthält für den Rechtshistoriker Interessantes. Wir erfahren, daß für die Zeit der *panegyris* – immerhin mit 20 Tagen eines der längsten bekannten Feste – eine *ekecheiria* ausgerufen wurde, πᾶσι πρὸς πάντας, also zwischen allen Beteiligten[32]. Diese Formulierung taucht auch in anderen Inschriften immer wieder auf, es handelt sich dabei natürlich nicht um die zwischenstaatliche Waffenruhe, sondern den „Rechtsfrieden", der für die Tage der *panegyris* herrschen sollte. Zahlreiche epigraphische Beispiele belegen die Existenz dieser Institution, aufschlußreich ist vor allem ein Text aus Lampsakos aus dem 2. Jh. v.Chr., zur Stiftung der Asklepieia, der etwas detaillierter berichtet, worum es in der *ekecheiria* geht.

IK Lampsakos 9, 24-28

... μὴ εἶναι δὲ μηθεν[ὶ μηθὲν]
[ἐ]νεχυράσαι ἐν̣ [τ]αῖς ἡμέραις τῶν Ἀσκληπιείων, εἰ δὲ μή, ὁ̣ ἐνεχυράσας
ἔ̣ν̣[οχος]
[ἔ]στω τῷ νόμῳ τῷ περὶ τῶν παρανόμως ἐνεχυρασάντων· μὴ κ⟨ρι⟩ν[έτωσαν]
[δ]ὲ μηδὲ οἱ ἐπιγνώμονες ἐν ταῖς ἡμέραις ταύταις, μηδὲ οἱ εἰσαγωγ⟨εῖ⟩ς
συ[λλε]-
[γ]έ̣τωσαν [δικ]α[σ]τ⟨ή⟩ρι⟨ον⟩·

Es soll keinem erlaubt sein, an den Tagen der Asklepieia etwas zu pfänden. Wenn aber doch, soll der, der pfändet, dem Gesetz über widerrechtliche Pfandnahme unterworfen sein. Weder sollen die *epignomones* in diesen Tagen Entscheidungen fällen, noch die *eisagogeis* einen Gerichtshof versammeln.

---

31 Diese Vorschrift verlangt es auch, über die Ergänzung in A Z. 8 erneut nachzudenken, die annimmt, daß auch die Strafgelder automatisch zur Erhöhung der Preisgelder verwendet werden sollten.

32 Während für die Olympia, Pythia und Soteria jeweils nur fünf Tage angenommen werden, sind für das Fest zu Ehren des Kaiserhauses in Gytheion acht Tage vorgesehen (SEG 11,923). Die Ptoia und Kaisareia in Akraiphia dauern zehn Tage (IG VII 2712, 55ff.), ebenso die Panegyris des Sisyphos in Attaleia in Pamphylien (IGR III 785). Einzig die Demostheneia in Oinoanda übertreffen mit einer Dauer von 23 Tagen das Fest in Sparta. Vgl. M. Wörrle, Stadt und Fest, 245ff.

Interessant ist allerdings am spartanischen Text, daß es doch zumindest zu Untersuchungen gekommen ist, über die die *nomophylakes* und *athlothetai* im Rahmen ihrer Amtsgewalt eine Entscheidung wohl über Verstöße gegen die Festordnung zu treffen hatten. Διαγιγνώσκειν wird hier wohl in der Form des römischen *cognoscere* für die Verfügung eines Amtsträgers verwendet und hat keinen Zusammenhang zur Entscheidung eines Gremiums[33]. Darüber hinaus ist es auch fraglich, ob sich die *ekecheiria* auch auf die notwendigen Entscheidungen über die Rechtmäßigkeit der verhängten Strafen erstreckt hatte. Die Vorschrift, daß eine Entscheidung der πεπατρονομηκότες innerhalb von drei Tagen zu erfolgen hatte, verweist meines Erachtens eben auf das Gegenteil. Möglicherweise hängt diese Ausnahme auch mit dem Status des entscheidenden Gremiums zusammen, das – wie oben angedeutet – eine Art Festausschuß gebildet haben könnte.

Der vorgestellte Text enthält die ausführlichsten und interessantesten Bestimmungen zur Rechtspflege im kaiserzeitlichen Sparta. Wenn sie auch kaum allgemeine Aussagen zum staatlichen Gerichtswesen erlauben, lassen sie sich doch gut in die späthellenistische und kaiserzeitliche griechische Tradition der Städte einreihen und zeigen keine direkten Eingriffe oder Einflüsse des römischen Rechts. Abgesehen von dieser Inschrift besitzen wir kaum weitere Quellen zu rechtlichen Fragen in Sparta. Erwähnung verdient hier aber in aller Kürze eine Episode die Philostrat aus dem Leben des Apollonios von Tyana schildert.

Philostr. VA 4,32

Ἐτύγχανε δὲ περὶ τὸν χρόνον τοῦτον νεανίας Λακεδαιμόνιος αἰτίαν ἔχων παρ' αὐτοῖς, ὡς ἀδικῶν περὶ τὰ ἤθη· ... "ἀγὼν" εἶπεν "ἐπήγγελταί μοι δημόσιος, ἐπειδὴ πρὸς ναυκληρίαις εἰμὶ καὶ τὰ κοινὰ οὐ πράττω." ... καθεστῶτα δὲ αὐτὸν ἰδὼν ὁ Ἀπολλώνιος καὶ τὴν γῆν ἀσπαζόμενον κατήγαγε παρὰ τοὺς ἐφόρους καὶ παρῃτήσατο τῆς δίκης.

Zu dieser Zeit war zufällig gerade ein junger Lakedämonier angeklagt wegen angeblicher Verletzung der Vätersitten. ... „Man hat einen öffentlichen Prozeß gegen mich angeregt", erwiderte jener, „weil ich die Seefahrt betreibe und mich nicht der Politike widme." ... Als Apollonios dann sah, daß er sich gebessert hatte und das Land zu lieben begann, führte er ihn zu den Ephoren und erwirkte seinen Freispruch.

Apollonios kümmert sich um einen jungen Mann, der wegen Seehandels angeklagt ist und erreicht durch seine Unterweisung nicht nur, daß er sich in Hinkunft der Politik zuwenden wird, sondern auch vor den Ephoren seinen Freispruch. N. Kennell bemerkt richtig, daß derartige Handelstätigkeiten im kaiserzeitlichen Sparta selbst in

---

[33] Den entgegengesetzten Fall, in dem eben eine Entscheidung eines Gremiums angesprochen wird, findet man zum Beispiel in den tegeatischen Inschriften IPArk 1 und 3, dazu G. Thür/H. Taeuber, IPArk, 7 und 38, zur späteren Terminologie H.J. Mason, Greek Terms for Roman Institutions. A Lexicon and Analysis, Toronto 1974, 35.

den archaisierendsten Perioden durchaus gängig waren und keinesfalls den Grund einer Anklage gebildet haben können. Daher verwirft er die Episode als Quelle für die Tätigkeiten der einzelnen dort erwähnten Magistrate völlig. Vor dem Hintergrund der übrigen Nachrichten zu den Ephoren allerdings, die – abgesehen von der Abgabe der Eponymie an die *patronomoi* – immer noch die bedeutendsten Amtsträger Spartas waren und die Außenbeziehungen leiteten, kann man meines Erachtens doch annehmen, daß sie in der Gerichtsbarkeit auch weiterhin eine Rolle spielten[34].

Die einzelnen Ämter, die aus den Karriere-Inschriften und den Ämterlisten und Ehrungen bekannt sind, beziehen sich wohl zumeist auf das Verhältnis Spartas zu Rom und der Provinzialverwaltung[35]. Das gleiche gilt für die Inschrift IG V 1,21, deren Kolumne II Vorschriften zur Appellation an den Kaiser enthält[36]. Dieser Kaiserbrief dürfte sich an die ganze Provinz gerichtet haben und nicht nur an die Stadt Sparta, ihm kann man entnehmen, daß allgemein die *synedroi*, also die Ratsversammlung, im Falle Spartas wohl die Gerousia, für Entscheidungen über die Möglichkeit der Weiterleitung einer Klage im Rahmen der Appellation zuständig waren. Somit wird man davon ausgehen können, daß die Gerousia ihre Rolle als Gerichtshof, die sie in klassischer Zeit ausübte, auch in römischer Zeit nicht völlig aufgegeben hat[37]. Ein großer Teil der anhängigen Gerichtsverfahren wurde ja durch die kaiserliche Einschränkung eben gerade nicht der römischen Gerichtsbarkeit überantwortet, sondern in den jeweiligen Städten der Provinz selbst entschieden[38]. Das Verhältnis zwischen der lokalen Gerichtsbarkeit und der römischen Provinzialverwaltung wird wohl auf der Basis der epigraphischen Evidenz noch einer genauen Untersuchung unterzogen werden müssen, die dann auch weitere Rückschlüsse auf die Verhältnisse innerhalb der Polis Sparta zulassen kann.

[34] Vgl. Xen. Lak. Pol. 8,4; Aristot. Pol. 1270b; 1275b; D.M. MacDowell, Spartan Law, Edinburgh 1986, 128ff.; K.M.T. Chrimes, Ancient Sparta, 161f.; N.M. Kennell, Public Institutions, 50f.

[35] N.M. Kennell, Public Institutions, 219f. zu den *syndikoi* und dem *epimeletes epi ton dikon*.

[36] J.H. Oliver, Constitutions, Nr. 91, 229-232.

[37] D.M. MacDowell, Spartan Law, 127ff.

[38] Auch das sogenannte „Ölgesetz" des Hadrian aus Athen (IG II^2 1100) zeigt eine gleichartige Entwicklung: Appellation war möglich, wurde aber zugunsten der eigenen Gerichte eingeschränkt: D. Nörr, Imperium und Polis in der hohen Prinzipatszeit, Münchner Beiträge zur Papyrusforschung und Antiken Rechtsgeschichte 50, München 1969, 31ff.

MARIO AMELOTTI (GENOVA)

RISPOSTA A KAJA HARTER-UIBOPUU

La relazione della Harter-Uibopuu merita vivo apprezzamento per la disamina attenta e minuziosa dell'iscrizione di Sparta e delle altre iscrizioni richiamate e in generale per l'interesse rivolto al materiale testuale non proveniente da Atene. Entro questi limiti essa fornisce validi argomenti per la ricerca di basi comuni ai diritti greci. E' necessario comunque – se lo propone la stessa relatrice – tornare anche e soprattutto al materiale ateniese per un giudizio sulla giurisdizione in Acaia al tempo del principato. Un giudizio sui rapporti non tanto col diritto romano – la relatrice esclude, e a ragione, una diretta influenza di principii romani presi a modello per ritoccare istituti locali – quanto con la politica romana, cioè della potenza dominante.

Questa politica si fonda sull'adesione dei notabili locali, come ha ben dimostrato per l'Egitto il Modrzejewski. Ciò può spiegare il fenomeno del ricorso agli exmagistrati per costituire collegi giudicanti. Nessuna imitazione del senato romano, ma uno stringere le fila da parte dei notabili, che numericamente in minoranza si scambiano le cariche. Non si può certamente parlare di democrazia nel senso nostro, ma di oligarchia di un ristretto ceto sociale.

La dominazione di Roma porta all'immobilismo nell'attività legislativa. Le città non decidono più sovranamente delle loro costituzioni e non fanno più leggi. Magari sono gli imperatori (in particolare Adriano) che risuscitano antiche leggi (quella, ad esempio, sugli *astynomoi* di Pergamo) o ne creano di nuove, assumendo il compito della *nomothesia*: così Adriano dà ad Atene una nuova legge sul commercio dell'olio. Lo stesso Adriano, nell'*oratio de Italicensibus*, si meraviglia che città chiedano di diventare colonie, rinunciando ai loro ordinamenti, perché le colonie possono solo servirsi del diritto romano. Richieste che hanno però motivi concreti (rifondazione della città con privilegi imperiali), ma esprimono al contempo un atteggiamento, che riconosce la sovranità di Roma e la assume a modello. Di questo atteggiamento dà testimonianza, per l'età degli Antonini, Elio Aristide nel suo Elogio di Roma.

Quanto alla giurisdizione è inevitabile la contrapposizione tra giustizia locale e intervento del governatore o addirittura dell'imperatore, specie attraverso l'appello. Assistiamo a comportamenti diversi: di governatori e imperatori che tendono a lasciare alle città il compito di sbrigare le loro controversie e di altri governatori o imperatori che tendono a richiamarle al proprio giudizio. Possono essere anche le parti a preferire la giustizia di Roma a quella dei notabili locali, con l'appello all'autorità romana o la richiesta di un rescritto imperiale. Dipende anche dal genere delle controversie, perché la remissione alle città è più probabile per le questioni di minor rilievo, specie di carattere amministrativo oppure attinenti, come nell' iscrizione di Sparta, a feste e agoni.

Si viene lentamente ad oscurare quella visione ideale dell'impero come federazione di *civitates* e *poleis* che è stata accennata dal Luzzatto per raffigurare la situazione, di una parte almeno dell'impero, per un paio di secoli tra la fine della repubblica e il principato. L'autonomia di *civitates* e *poleis*, su cui il Luzzatto insiste, si va perdendo di fronte ad un controllo imperiale sempre più rigoroso, non tanto politico – Roma non ha sotto questo profilo molto da temere, anche se ci sono città ribelli e rissose, come Gerusalemme od Alessandria – quanto economico, per l'esaurimento delle risorse locali, dissestate anche dagli eccessivi campanilismi in edifici e giuochi. Le città si trasformano progressivamente in centri di amministrazione, nel quadro di un ordinamento che tende all'uniformità sotto la potestà di Roma. Tutto ciò prelude all'azione dei Severi: municipalizzazione generalizzata anche là dove, come in Egitto, i municipi non erano conosciuti, e *constitutio Antoniniana* che livella anche gli abitanti, più sudditi che cittadini dell'impero.

Della nuova realtà, quale si presenta nella seconda metà del III secolo, dà questa volta testimonianza Menandro di Laodicea. Per svolgere l'elogio di una città è sterile far appello alla sua costituzione e alle sue leggi. Resta solo il richiamo ai costumi, agli *ethê*. Ma qui non voglio entrare nella questione se si tratti di usanze formalmente illecite, tutt'al più tollerate, nell'unitario ordinamento romano, o di consuetudini locali che invece sussistono come fonti sussidiarie di diritto.

Per concludere, la relazione della Harter-Uibopuu è un importante contributo allo studio della sopravvivenza, sempre più tenue fino a scomparire, degli ordinamenti cittadini greci sotto la dominazione romana: uno studio in gran parte ancora da fare.

FEDERICO MORELLI (VIENNA)

GRAMMATÊPHOROI E VIE DELLA GIUSTIZIA NELL'EGITTO TARDO ANTICO[*]

Oggetto di questo lavoro è una serie di – per usare il termine estremamente vago con il quale testi del genere sono normalmente definiti – 'lettere bizantine', o tardo antiche, accomunate dal fatto di menzionare *grammatêphoroi*, "portatori di lettere" o "latori della presente", secondo la interpretazione del termine che qui viene proposta.

L'esame di questi testi ha per scopo, attraverso la definizione da un lato del significato del termine γραμματηφόροϲ, dall'altro della funzione, del ruolo di queste persone, di inquadrare questi documenti in un contesto di tipo giuridico, e di trarne alcune conclusioni sulle vie seguite dalla giustizia nell'Egitto – ma verosimilmente in generale anche nel resto del mondo greco-romano – della fine del tardo antico.

1. I grammatêphoroi

Per il termine γραμματηφόροϲ si trovano a partire dal II secolo poco più di 70 attestazioni, in un numero di documenti di poco inferiore. Il *Wörterbuch* di Preisigke[1], senza dare una interpretazione del termine rimanda al vol. III Abschn. 8, relativo a uffici e funzioni amministrative, nel quale vengono semplicemente elencate le attestazioni. Lo stesso rimando all'Abschn. 8 si trova nei supplementi al *Wörterbuch* di Preisigke editi successivamente[2]. Soltanto nel Suppl. III, di

---

[*] Questo lavoro è un risultato del progetto "Von der Spätantike zum Islam. Edition des Senuthios-Archives" (http://www.fwf.ac.at/de/abstracts/abstract.asp?L=D&PROJ=P17897), da me condotto e finanziato dal *Fonds zur Förderung der wissenschaftlichen Forschung* (FWF).
Per i criteri di citazione delle edizioni dei papiri e degli strumenti di lavoro papirologici, cfr. J.F. Oates *et al.*, *Checklist of Editions of Greek, Latin, Demotic and Coptic Papyri, Ostraca and Tablets*, accessibile all'indirizzo http://odyssey.lib.duke.edu/papyrus/texts/clist.html

[1] F. Preisigke, *Wörterbuch der griechischen Papyrusurkunden mit Einschluß der griechischen Inschriften, Aufschriften, Ostraka, Mumienschilder usw. aus Ägypten*, Berlin 1925-1931, I 307.

[2] E. Kießling, *Wörterbuch der griechischen Papyrusurkunden, mit Einschluss der griechischen Inschriften, Aufschriften, Ostraka, Mumienschilder usw. aus Ägypten.* Supplement 1 (1940-1966). Unter Leitung des Herausgebers bearbeitet von Winfried Rübsam, Amsterdam 1969-1971, p. 60; A. Jördens, *Wörterbuch der griechischen Papyrusurkunden. Mit Einschluss der griechischen Inschriften, Aufschriften, Ostraka,*

A. Jördens, p. 66, si trova, accanto al solito rimando all'Abschn. 8, la citazione di due documenti del VI secolo, per i quali viene dunque sottointeso un significato diverso: P. Rainer Cent. 79.7[3] e SB XVI 12943.4[4]. Tolte queste due eccezioni, le attestazioni del termine sono dunque trattate nel *Wörterbuch*, come generalmente dagli editori, come se fossero tutte riferite a una professione, una funzione, un ufficio: in particolare alla funzione liturgica di messaggero.

In verità per questo significato del termine esistono solo 8 attestazioni in 7 documenti, quasi tutti relativi a nomine liturgiche e databili non oltre l'inizio del V secolo[5]. Si tratta di una minoranza delle attestazioni, che sono poi anche le più antiche. Questi casi qui non interessano.

Nella documentazione più tarda i *grammatêphoroi* sono menzionati sempre e solamente in lettere. Mai in altre tipologie documentarie, come sarebbe da aspettarsi se si trattasse di una qualifica professionale, indipendente dal tipo di documento nel quale essa si trova. Il ricorrere del termine a partire dal V secolo in una sola tipologia documentaria, e cioè le lettere, fa pensare che esso fosse usato non come una qualifica di valore assoluto, ma piuttosto per definire una persona proprio in relazione al testo nel quale essa viene menzionata.

E di fatti, prendendo in considerazione queste 'lettere' bizantine o tardo antiche, si constata che il *grammatêphoros* è *grammatêphoros* solo occasionalmente, in maniera contingente; in relazione cioè alla lettera nella quale egli è menzionato e che evidentemente egli porta a destinazione, indipendentemente da quale fosse la sua professione.

Si dovrà dunque tradurre più propriamente non "messaggero", o "portalettere", ma "latore della lettera", "latore della presente"[6].

Mumienschilder usw. aus Ägypten. Supplement 2 (1967-1976), Wiesbaden 1991, p. 43; A. Jördens, Supplement 3 (1977-1988), Wiesbaden 2001, p. 66.

3 Per il quale la interpretazione corretta "der Überbringer dieses Briefes" risale all'editore del documento H. Maehler.

4 L'editore P.J. Sijpesteijn, *Drei Wiener Papyri aus byzantinischer Zeit*, JÖB 34 (1984), p. 44, intendeva invece – conformemente alla norma degli editori – il termine nel senso di "Briefträger".

5 P. Panop. Beatty 1.61, 253 (Panopoli 298), P. Oxy. XXXIII 2675.9-10 (318), LI 3623.8-9 (359), PSI X 1108.8 (Ossirinco 381), Chr. Wilck. 405.6-7 (Ossirinco 396), P. Oxy. LV 3796.9 (412); posteriore sarebbe P. Prag. II 196.2 (?), datato dall'editore al VI secolo, ma la cui scrittura fa pensare piuttosto ad una datazione anteriore, V se non fine IV. Anche la presenza della formula di saluti ἐρρῶϲθαί ϲε εὔ|χομαι a ll. 21-22 fa preferire una datazione anteriore al VI. Sulla liturgia dello ἁλιαδίτηϲ ἤτοι γραμματηφόροϲ τοῦ ὀξέωϲ δρόμου cfr. da ultimo A. Kolb, *Transport und Nachrichtentransfer im Römischen Reich*, Berlin 2000 (Klio Beih. NF 2), pp. 203-204, 282.

6 Una discussione del significato del termine γραμματηφόροϲ con la conclusione esplicita che esso non sempre doveva riferirsi a una funzione all'interno dell'amministrazione, è a quanto mi risulta soltanto in A. Papathomas, P. Heid. VII 411.4 n.: "Als γραμματηφόροϲ wird hier die Frau bezeichnet, welche dem Adressaten den vorliegenden Brief überbracht hat. Der Terminus könnte theoretisch auch als amtilche Bezeichnung aufgefaßt werden.

Ora, lasciando da parte una serie di casi nei quali una persona si trova a recapitare una lettera senza avere una qualche connessione particolare con il suo contenuto[7], ce ne sono altri nei quali la relazione tra il *grammatêphoros* e la missiva

In diesem Fall hätte di Frau, von der die Rede ist, das byzantinische liturgische Amt des ἀλιαδίτηϲ ἤτοι γραμματηφόροϲ bekleidet. Dies ist allerdings nicht wahrscheinlich (...). Daß die Bezeichnung γραμματηφόροϲ sich nicht nur auf die das Amt ausübenden Personen beschränkte, zeigen Papyri, in denen die jeweiligen γραμματηφόροι ausdrücklich einen anderen Beruf, Stand, oder ein anderes Amt haben; vgl. z.B. P.Apoll. 24,1-2: (...); ferner P.Fouad. 88,1; P.Oxy. XVI 1857,1; 1858,3-4; 1861,1 und SB VI 9376,2." In realtà i casi nei quali il termine non indica affatto una qualifica professionale o amministrativa, ma semplicemente colui che – per lo più occasionalmente – si trova a portare e a consegnare una missiva, sono la stragrande maggioranza. E cioè tutte le altre attestazioni al di fuori dei pochi documenti citati sopra alla n. 5.

7 I *grammatêphoroi* sono menzionati in apertura di lettera per sottolineare l'opportunità che si è presentata al mittente di inviare la lettera in SB XIV 11881.4-5 (? IV): καιρὸν εὑροῦϲα τοῦ | γραμματηφόρο[υ]; o P. Apoll. Anô 54.1 (seconda metà VII, cfr. J. Gascou/K.A. Worp, *Problèmes de documentation apollinopolite*, ZPE 49 [1982], pp. 83-89): εὑρὼν τὴν εὐκαιρείαν (*sic*) τῶν παρόντων γραμματηφόρων; dello stesso genere P. Fouad. 88.1 (Afrodito ? Cfr. J. Gascou, *P. Fouad 87: Les monastères pachômiens et l'État byzantin*, BIFAO 76 [1976], pp. 159-163, VI), 89.1 (Afrodito ? Cfr. J. Gascou, *cit.*, VI), P. Oxy. XVI 1861.1 (VI o VII). La menzione del *grammatêphoros* può anche precisare in qualche modo le circostanze o il modo in cui è stata inviata la lettera, senza per questo avere un valore determinante nell'economia del discorso: P. Cairo Masp. III 67323.9-10 (Afrodito 540, cfr. C. Zuckerman in J.-L. Fournet, *Un nouvel épithalame de Dioscore d'Aphrodité adressé à un gouverneur civil de Thébaïde*, AnTard 6 [1998], p. 81): καὶ τὰ τοιαῦτα γράμματα ἀπέϲτειλα διὰ τοῦ γραμματηφ[όρου | τῇ ϲῇ ἀδελφότητι; BGU IV 1039.10-11 (? biz.): τὴν δὲ ῥύϲιν τοῦ οἴνου οὐκ ἐδυνήθην δηλῶϲαι | ὑμῖν διὰ τὸ πρὸ τοῦ τὸν οἶνον ἀντληθῆναι ὅλον ἐξελθεῖν τὸν γραμματηφόρον; P. Ross. Georg. III 21.8 (? VII): κατὰ ϲπουδὴν γὰρ ἀπέλυϲαν τὸν γραμματηφόρον. Talvolta la menzione dell'invio di un *grammatêphoros* equivale più o meno a dire che si è inviata la lettera, se mai con un valore rafforzativo: come dire, "ho mandato una persona appositamente": P. Alex. inv. 439.2-3 (p. 15) (? biz.): ὥϲτ' ἐμὲ | ἀναγκαϲθῆναι πέμψαι τὸν γραμματηφόρον πρὸϲ τὴν ὑμετέραν ἀδελφικὴν εὐλάβειαν. Dello stesso genere P. Grenf. I 66.2-3 (Apollonopolis ? Prima metà VI, cfr. *BL* XI p. 86): διὰ τ[οῦτο | ἀπέϲτειλα τὸν γραμματηφόρον παῖδα. In altri casi il *grammatêphoros* viene nominato perché egli deve svolgere una qualche altra funzione oltre quella di portare la lettera: così in CPR XIV 49 (Eracleopolite VI-VII) il mittente chiede al destinatario di inviargli degli indumenti tramite il *grammatêphoros* che consegna la lettera (lo stesso CPR XIV 49). O in PSI XIV 1426.7-8 (? VI cfr. R.S. Bagnall, *Five Problematic Fourth-Century Pieces*, BASP 27 [1990], p. 90), nel quale il destinatario deve consegnare alla persona che ha consegnato la lettera un *nomisma*, perché lo riporti al mittente (il denaro può, in alternativa, essere inviato anche tramite altre persone menzionate subito dopo). Così anche in P. Bodl. I 63.6-7 (? VII; ed.: "Late Byzantine period") il *grammatêphoros* deve portare non si sa cosa al mittente; documenti, cfr. D. Hagedorn, *Bemerkungen zu Urkunden*, ZPE 151 (2005), pp. 131-132, in P. Wash. Univ. I 8.6-7 (Ossirinco VI); lino in SB XIV 11881.23-25 (? IV); un *phialion* in SB XIV 12123.1-2 (? V/VI); del grano in SB XVI 12943.3-4 (Arsinoite VI), e a quel che sembra P. Ness. III 158.8 (periodo arabo). Analoga la situazione di SPP XX 262.9 (?

che egli porta è meno casuale. Il *grammatêphoros* porta la lettera cioè non per il semplice fatto che, recandosi da una località A a una località B, egli può svolgere questa funzione, bensì perché la missiva che egli recapita lo riguarda direttamente. Egli ha insomma un interesse diretto al contenuto della lettera, ed altrettanto diretto è l'interesse che egli ha a recapitarla. Il fatto di aver portato la lettera, ossia il fatto di esserne in possesso e di presentarla al destinatario, conferisce alla persona qualificata – sempre soltanto in relazione a quella situazione contingente e occasionale – come "portatore della lettera" o "latore della presente", dei diritti o dei privilegi. La lettera con il suo contenuto è il documento che conferisce diritti o privilegi a chi ne è in possesso: come ad esempio nel caso di una lettera di raccomandazione[8].

Tra questi documenti, un gruppo abbastanza nutrito è costituito da comunicazioni che lasciano intravedere con maggiore o minore chiarezza una serie di vicende – in senso lato – giudiziarie: liti, controversie, ricorsi alla e interventi

---

VII), nel quale senza usare il termine γραμματηφόροϲ si chiede comunque l'invio di denaro διὰ τοῦ ἀποδιδοῦντοϲ τὴν ἐπιϲτολήν. Il *grammatêphoros* insomma fa un viaggio di andata e ritorno: porta la lettera e riporta indietro qualcos'altro. Assimilabile P. Alex. inv. 439.6 (p. 15s.), nel quale lo scrivente chiede al destinatario di inviargli, tramite il *grammatêphoros*, notizie sulla sua salute. Un po' diverso P. Oxy. VII 1071.8 (prima metà VI, cfr. F. Mitthof, *Korr. Tyche 436*, Tyche 17 [2002], p. 250), nel quale si chiede al destinatario di inviare una lettera ad altre persone tramite lo stesso *grammatêphoros*. In altri documenti il *grammatêphoros* è menzionato perché insieme alla lettera deve consegnare al destinatario anche qualcos'altro: in P. Cairo Masp. I 67068.6 (Afrodito VI), due *keratia*; in P. Laur. II 45.13 (Ermopolite, cfr. J. Rea, JEA 71 [1985] Suppl., p. 70, VI/VII) una quantità di vino; in P. Ness. III 47.2-3 (Nessana prima del 605?) del pesce; pesce anche in P. Oxy. XVI 1857.1 (VI o VII), da un *grammatêphoros* (correttamente tradotto: "who brings this letter") che di mestiere era un *hippokomos*. Di lui il mittente non doveva fidarsi troppo, se dopo aver indicato con precisione la quantità del pesce inviato, chiede anche al destinatario di scrivergli per confermare che la quantità arrivata a destinazione è la stessa di quella inviata. Ancora, un *nomisma* in P. Oxy. XVI 1939.2 (VI o VII); dell'oppio in PSI I 49.4 (? VI) da un *grammatêphoros* che di mestiere è un guardiano; sei fichi o meloni in SB XIV 11492.12 (? VI). Nominati nel discorso in altri contesti, senza che comunque essi abbiano una rilevanza particolare, o in contesti non ricostruibili con una qualche chiarezza, in P. Apoll. Anô 55.1 (seconda metà VII, cfr. J. Gascou/K.A. Worp, *art. cit.*, pp. 83-89), P. Cairo Masp. I 67073.2 (Afrodito VI), III 67356.1 (Afrodito VI), P. Fouad. 87.34 (Afrodito ? Cfr. J. Gascou, *cit.*, VI), P. Haun. III 52.3 (? VI-VII) – il termine γραμματηφόροϲ è qui usato in riferimento alla persona che ha recapitato una lettera allo scrivente – P. Rainer Cent. 79.7 (Ermupoli VI).

8 Così in P. Oxy. I 156 (VI) i due *grammatêphoroi* – tradotto dagli editori come "letter-carriers" – devono essere arruolati come buccellari; per evitare equivoci o scambi di persona, ne vengono indicati – cosa inusuale in questo genere di documenti – anche i nomi. SB VI 9376.2 (Skithi, Wâdi Natrûn ? VI/VII) è una richiesta di riservare (o di marchiare ?) tre animali per i monaci latori della lettera (qui correttamente tradotto come "the bearers of this letter"). SPP VIII 1036 (Ermupoli 592, cfr. P.J. Sijpesteijn, *Ein weiterer Magistor-Text*, ZPE 49 [1982], p. 117 n. 1): ordine di consegnare al *grammatêphoros* 30 *pholleis*.

della autorità. Questi testi mostrano per lo più una struttura unitaria e si distinguono per alcuni termini, espressioni, e formule ricorrenti.

2. Un esempio

Tra i non pochi testi inediti di questo genere che ho potuto individuare nella *Papyrussammlung* della *Österreichische Nationalbibliothek*, un esempio rappresentativo è P. Vindob. G 40259[9], che illustra chiaramente quanto accennato finora.

P. Vindob. G 40259 11,4 x 17,7 cm metà VII
Ermopolite

↓ 1 † ὁ παρὼν γραμματηφόροϲ ἦλθεν λέγων ὡϲ
2 ϲυναλλαγὴν ἔχει μετά τινων ἀπὸ τῆϲ κώμηϲ Ϲιρ[
3 κ̣[α]ὶ τ̣ο̣ῦ̣ ἐ̣π̣ο̣ικείου Πταλ. δ̣ια̣λ̣άβη̣ [ο]ὖν τὸ πρᾶγμα ἡ μ̣ε̣γαλο(πρέπειά)
4 ϲου ἀ̣λλὰ καὶ διοι̣κ̣ήϲη̣ μετὰ τοῦ δικα̣ίου. εἰ δέ τί ποτέ
5 ἐϲτι π̣έ̣μ̣ψ̣ο̣ν̣ μο̣ι αὐ̣τ̣ο̣ὺ̣ϲ̣ ἐνταῦθα καὶ διοικήϲω τὸ πρᾶγμα
6 αὐτ̣ῶν † tracce

verso

→ 7] ̣ ̣ τ[ῷ] τὰ πά(ντα) περι̣βλ̣έ̣(πτῳ) (κ̣α̣ὶ̣) τι(μῆϲ) ἀξίῳ Ϲεν̣ο̣υ̣θίῳ διο̣ι̣κ̣(η)τ(ῆ̣)
† Τ̣α̣[υρ]ῖ̣[νοϲ

3. l. ἐποικίου

"Il presente latore della lettera è venuto dicendo che ha una controversia con alcuni del villaggio di Sir... e dell'abitato di Ptal. La tua magnificenza dunque esamini la cosa, ma anche la regoli con giustizia. Se poi ci fosse qualche problema, mandameli qui, e regolerò io la loro questione."
verso: "al sotto ogni aspetto notabile e degno di stima Senouthios *dioikêtês* † Taurinos"

La ricostruzione dei fatti: un tale si è recato dallo scrivente, per lamentarsi di una controversia che egli ha con alcune persone di due villaggi. L'istanza che ha ricevuto le sue lamentele scrive dunque la comunicazione conservata nel papiro per incaricare il *dioikêtês* Senouthios di esaminare la cosa e di risolvere la questione, come egli dice, secondo giustizia. Nel caso ci dovessero essere problemi, e cioè se Senouthios non dovesse essere in grado di risolvere la controversia, i contendenti dovranno essere mandati dallo scrivente, che si occuperà personalmente della cosa.

P. Vindob. G 40259 fa parte di un archivio, per la gran parte ancora inedito[10]. Sulla base di altri documenti dello stesso archivio è possibile stabilire che il mittente, Taurinos, è un funzionario di grado elevato dell'ufficio del pagarco.

---

[9] Ringrazio Cornelia Römer per il permesso di pubblicazione.

[10] Si tratta dell'archivio di Senouthios *anystês*, per il quale vedi sopra n. *.

L'ἐνταῦθα di l. 5 deve allora riferirsi alla città, Ermupoli, capitale della pagarchia e sede degli uffici della amministrazione regionale.

Il destinatario Senouthios porta il titolo di *dioikêtês*: come è da intendere questo titolo, e come deve egli risolvere la questione ? Ha egli un potere coercitivo che gli permette di imporre una decisione ? È il titolo di *dioikêtês* da intendere semplicemente come "amministratore", o si tratta piuttosto di una funzione pubblica, come aveva concluso Steinwenter[11] sulla base dei documenti copti di Jeme ?

In questo caso il *dioikêtês* avrebbe "als erste und wichtigste ihrer Funktionen (...) die Mitwirkung an der Beilegung privater Rechtsstreitigkeiten"[12]. "Vermittlung der Dialysis ist also das Wesen der «richterlichen» Funktion des Dioiketen. (...) Er kann aber auch selbst das Richteramt an sich nehmen und auf der Abschluß der Dialysis unmittelbaren Einfluß nehmen"[13]. Il *dioikêtês* "als Dialysisrichter entfaltet (...) die einflußreiche Tätigkeit eines Rechtsschutzorganes, genießt offenbar das Vetrauen der ihr Recht suchenden Bevölkerung und vermag durch Streitabwendung, bezw. Streitlösung die Zahl der Prozesse zu vermindern und dadurch den ordentlichen Richter, den Pagarchen, zu entlasten."[14]

Per quel che riguarda il ruolo del *grammatêphoros*, esso è facile da definire: egli ha portato le sue lamentele all'ufficio della pagarchia, e ne riceve in risposta P. Vindob. G 40259 con istruzioni per una istanza inferiore alla quale viene trasmesso il caso. Con questa risposta in mano egli deve presentarsi al funzionario delegato a risolvere la controversia per ottenere il suo diritto. Solo in questo contesto egli è *grammatêphoros*, in relazione alla comunicazione che lo riguarda direttamente e che egli deve consegnare per difendere i suoi interessi.

3. La struttura e il contenuto

Confrontando P. Vindob. G 40259 con gli altri documenti che mostrano *grammatêphoroi* in contesti analoghi, è possibile metterne in evidenza gli elementi comuni, e chiarire ulteriormente il procedimento all'origine di questi testi. La maggior parte di queste comunicazioni trasmette il caso da una istanza superiore ad una inferiore; in altre è invece un sottoposto che invia (o reinvia) il *grammatêphoros* ad un superiore; oppure si tratta di comunicazioni tra persone di ambiti diversi, tra le quali è impossibile riconoscere un rapporto di gerarchie definito. La sostanza comunque – come la forma e la struttura – di questi testi è la stessa: una persona che ha ricevuto una lamentela trasmette ad un'altra la soluzione del caso.

---

11 A. Steinwenter, *Studien zu den koptischen Rechtsurkunden aus Oberägypten*, Leipzig 1920 (SPP XIX), pp. 19-25.

12 Steinwenter, *cit.*, p. 20.

13 Steinwenter, *cit.*, p. 22.

14 Steinwenter, *cit.*, p. 33.

3.a L'inizio del procedimento

Il primo passo è la lamentela che il *grammatêphoros* ha portato davanti una qualche istanza – non necessariamente un funzionario –. I testi sembrano lasciare intendere che almeno in un buon numero di casi ciò fosse fatto di persona, oralmente: senza cioè una lamentela scritta, una petizione.

P. Vindob. G 40259: ὁ παρὼν γραμματηφόροϲ ἦλθεν λέγων ὡϲ, "il presente latore della lettera è venuto dicendo che ".

Analoga la apertura di altri documenti:

P. Ross. Georg. V 12*a*1 (? VI/VII)] ὁ̣ γρα[μμ]ατηφόροϲ λέγει;

PSI VII 824.1 (? VI) ὁ γραμματηφόροϲ ἦλθεν λέγων ὅτι;

SB XXIV 16116.1 (? VII) ὁ γραμματηφόροϲ πρεϲβύτεροϲ ἦλθεν ἐγγύϲ μου λ[έγων[15];

SPP X 152 *r*.1 (Arsinoite VII invece del VI-VII dell'edizione) ὁ γραμ]μ̣ατηφόροϲ γεωργὸϲ[16] προϲῆλ[θεν;

P. Vindob. G 16199.1 (? VII) (inedito[17]): οἱ γραμματηφόροι ἀμπελο̣υ̣ργοὶ (...) ἤλθαν ἐνταῦθα̣ λέγο[ντεϲ ὅτι[18]; un richiamo a questa azione iniziale dei *grammatêphoroi* lo si ritrova anche più avanti nello stesso documento: διότι ἦλθαν καὶ προϲῆλ[θ]ά̣ν μ̣ο̣ι. Un analogo riferimento è in CPR XXV 20.3 (? VII) ἐπειδὴ ὁ ἀπελθὼν εἶπεν ὅτι;

P. Oxy. VIII 1164.1 (VI o VII) οἱ γραμματηφόροι ἦλθαν πρὸϲ ἐμέ[19];

P. Lond. III 1073.1 (p. 251) (? VII invece del VI dell'edizione) οἱ γραμματηφόροι[20] γεωργοὶ λέγουϲιν;

A questa categoria di documenti potrebbe essere ricondotto anche P. Apoll. Anô 3 (seconda metà VII[21]), la cui apertura è (l. 1): ἐπειδ[ὴ ὁ παρὼν γραμ]ματηφό[ροϲ ὁ Μ]ω̣αγαρίτηϲ εἶπεν [[22].

---

15 Invece del λα̣λ̣[ῆϲαι dell'edizione. Oggetto della lamentela del *grammatêphoros* doveva essere qui l'invio di una persona, invalida – per il significato da dare a ἀδύναμον, cfr. P. Oxy. LVIII 3960.23 (621) – a *Babylôn* (ε̣ἰ̣ϲ̣ Βαβυλῶνα da leggere dopo le prime tre lettere dal senso ancora oscuro di l. 2), al-Fusṭâṭ, evidentemente per prestazioni di lavoro coatto. Sul *verso* è da leggere διοικ(η)τ(ῇ) invece di διοικητῇ; [Π]έ̣τ̣ροϲ ἐλ(ά)χ(ιϲτοϲ) † invece di [Πέ]τροϲ ἐλ(έει). L'indirizzo doveva finire qui, né ci sono elementi per ipotizzare la completamente perduta l. 5 trascritta nell'edizione. Nel papiro non c'è niente che possa far pensare che il mittente fosse un vescovo, come invece supposto dall'editore.

16 Cfr. N. Gonis, *Korr. Tyche 337*, Tyche 14 (1998), p. 331.

17 Edizione in preparazione da parte di Federico Morelli.

18 Per evitare scambi di persona i nomi dei *grammatêphoroi* sono indicati in questo documento, come anche in P. Oxy. I 156.

19 In questo caso i *grammatêphoroi* si sono recati dallo scrivente non per presentare la loro lamentela, ma per consegnare la risposta già avuta da un'istanza superiore, vedi più avanti punto 3.*d* e n. 60.

20 Per la lettura, Grenfell/Hunt in APf 4 (1907), p. 558.

21 Per la datazione di tutto l'archivio, J. Gascou/K.A. Worp, *art. cit.*, pp. 83-89.

22 Dopo la prima linea, con la esposizione del problema – relativo a un acquisto di legna da ardere e al suo prezzo – perduta in lacuna, seguirebbero a l. 2 le istruzioni sulle misure da prendere: οὖν παράϲχετ[ε] ̣ του ξυλοκα[ϲίμου; a ll. 3-4 ci sarebbe la motivazione per le misure prescritte: in particolare cfr. il χρεωϲτεῖ di l. 4. Il διοικήϲῃ μετὰ του[di l.

Dello stesso tipo, per quanto il termine γραμματηφόροϲ vi sia sostituito dalla perifrasi ὁ ἀποδιδοὺϲ ὑμῖν τὴν παροῦϲάν [μου ἐπιϲτολήν], PSI Congr. XI 14.3-4, 7 (Apollonos Anô seconda metà VII[23]): ὁ ἀποδιδοὺϲ ὑμῖν τὴν παροῦϲάν [μου ἐπιϲτολὴν (...)] (...) καὶ ὡϲ εἶπέν μοι (...) εἶπέν μοι δὲ καὶ τοῦτο, ὡϲ.

Riferimenti in forma diversa a ciò che è stato detto dai *grammatêphoroi* e alla loro iniziativa di presentare il loro caso allo scrivente, si trovano in P. Strasb. IV 279.6 (Afrodito[24] VI) τῶν [λ]εγομένων παρὰ τοῦ γραμματηφ[ό]ρου; SPP XX 212.1-2 (? VI-VII), ἐὰν ἀληθεύει[25] ἡ γραμματηφόροϲ (...) αὐτὴν προϲελθεῖν μοι, nel quale il riferimento al προϲελθεῖν si trova, come anche in CPR VIII 55.2 (Arsinoite[26] VII invece del V/VI dell'edizione) ἔν τινι προϲελθεῖν, più avanti nel corpo del documento e in un contesto che si discuterà più avanti.

Il verbo che viene usato, oltre al semplice ἔρχομαι, è προϲέρχομαι, più volte attestato anche in epoche precedenti per il "rivolgersi" con una petizione o una richiesta a un'autorità[27].

3.b L'esposizione del caso

Segue quindi l'oggetto della lamentela. In P. Vindob. G 40259 è genericamente questione di una non meglio precisata controversia: ὡϲ | ϲυναλλαγὴν ἔχει μετά τινων.

In altri testi la natura della controversia o dei problemi viene meglio specificata: in questi casi è l'istanza che ha ricevuto la lamentela a esporre o almeno a introdurre il problema al destinatario delegato a risolvere il caso. Se ciò implichi in qualche modo una presa di posizione dello scrivente a favore del *grammatêphoros* – o

4 richiama il διοικήϲῃ μετὰ τοῦ δικαίου di P. Vindob. G 40259.4, e potrebbe anch'esso essere un invito a risolvere la questione secondo giustizia.

23 Per la datazione di tutto l'archivio, J. Gascou/K.A. Worp, *art. cit.*, pp. 83-89.

24 J. Gascou/J.-L. Fournet in *BL* XI 255.

25 Il concetto espresso ed anche il formulario sono gli stessi che si ritrovano più volte in petizioni: per l'età tolemaica, A. Di Bitonto, *Le petizioni al re. Studio sul formulario*, Aegyptus 47 (1967), pp. 47-48; *Le petizioni ai funzionari nel periodo tolemaico. Studio sul formulario*, Aegyptus 48 (1968), p. 98; *Frammenti di petizioni del periodo tolemaico. Studio sul formulario*, Aegyptus 56 (1976), p. 136.

26 Cfr. J. Gascou in BiOr 42 (1985), p. 336.

27 Cfr. ad esempio BGU II 614.12 (Arsinoite 217): προϲελήλυθα διὰ βιβλιδίων τῷ λαμπροτάτῳ ἡγεμόνι; P. Oslo II 62.6-7 (? prima metà IV, cfr. P. Oslo III p. 277): τ]ῷ λαμπροτάτῳ | ἡγεμόνι π[ρο]ϲῆλθον; SB VI 9194.13s. (Alessandria III): προϲῆλθεϲ τῷ ἐπ[ι]ϲτρα|τήγῳ; P. Rainer Cent. 99 *r.* 5 (Ermopolite 451): διὰ λιβέλλου δόϲεωϲ προϲελθὼν τῷ λαμπ[ροτάτῳ ἡγεμόνι; P. Cairo Masp. I 67002 II 10 (Antinoe 567, cfr. J. Maspero, *Les papyrus Beaugé*, BIFAO 10 [1912], p. 137 ss.): καί τινεϲ ἐξ ἡμῶν τοτε προϲῆλθαν τῷ εἰρημ(ένῳ) ἐνδοξ(οτάτῳ) δουκί; SB VI 9616 *v.* 18 (Antinoe 550-8?): προϲελθεῖν τῷ ἐνδοξοτάτῳ [δο]υκί; per il rivolgersi a un ufficiale con la risposta ottenuta in seguito ad una petizione già presentata a un'autorità superiore, in Chr. Mitt. 93.18 (Ermupoli c. 250): προϲῆλθεν κατὰ τ[ὴ]ν ὑπογραφὴν τῆϲ ἡγεμονίαϲ τῷ ἐπιϲτρατήγῳ.

comunque in merito alla controversia – più netta rispetto a testi nei quali, come in P. Vindob. G 40259, si parla in maniera più neutrale di una controversia e l'esposizione del caso è lasciata al *grammatêphoros* stesso, è difficile dire.

Testi di questo tipo sono:

P. Ross. Georg. V 12*a*1 (? VI/VII) λέγει ἐν τῇ πεδιά[δι διαπ]εφωνηκέναι λινοκαλάμηϲ π[;

PSI VIII 938.2 (Afrodito VI) παρεκράτηϲεν εἰκοϲιδύο κεράτια τῶν γραμματηφόρων;

P. Lond. III 1162 *r*.12 (VII)[28] καὶ ἐπὶ τοῦ παρόντοϲ ἠναγκάϲθηϲαν κτλ.;

P. Lond. III 1073.1-2 (? VII) κωλύεϲθαι (οἰκοδομῆϲαι, come risulta da l. 3[29]) ἀκαίρωϲ παρά τινων | γιτόνων (*sic*) αὐτῶν ἐκ τῇ κώμῃ;

P. Strasb. IV 279.6-7 (Afrodito VI) παθόντοϲ οὐ μ̣ ̣ [| παρὰ τῶν ποιμένων τοῦ λαμπροτάτ[ου κ]αὶ ψευδοτυρ[άν]νου.

In diversi casi i *grammatêphoroi* si sono rivolti a una autorità per lamentarsi di abusi da parte della amministrazione, come nel caso della indebita riscossione di tasse di P. Cairo Masp. II 67194.3-6 (Afrodito c. 570[30])[31] ὡϲ τῆϲ ὑμετέραϲ | ἀδελφότητοϲ ἀπαιτούϲηϲ τὸν εἰρημένον | γραμματηφόρον ἄνδρα φα̣ν̣ερὸν χρυ̣ϲ̣ί̣[ον ? | ὑπ[ὲρ ἀρουρῶ]ν̣ μὴ οὐϲ̣ῶν ὑπ' α[ὐ]τό[ν[32]. Alcuni di questi documenti riguardano incarcerazioni – almeno dal punto di vista del *grammatêphoros* – illegittime:

PSI VII 824.1-2 (? VI) ὅτι ἔχειϲ τὴν γυναῖκ[α αὐτοῦ | εἰϲ τὴν φυλακὴν καὶ ἔλαβεϲ τὰ ἄλ⟨λ⟩α τὰ αὐτοῦ;

P. Vindob. G 16791.2[33] (Ermopolite VII) μᾶλλον[34] ἐκράτηϲαν τὸν μιϲθογεωργὸν αὐτοῦ οἱ ἀπὸ Ϲιγκερή;

---

[28] Edito in *BL* I 294, e mai ripreso in SB. La datazione al VII-VIII indicata nell'edizione è da precisare al VII (comunicazione di N. Gonis). Anche in questo documento, analogamente a PSI Congr. XI 14 (vedi sopra al punto 3.*a*), il termine γραμματηφόροι è sostituito dalla perifrasi (ll. 5-6) τοὺϲ (...) ἀ̣ν̣α̣δ̣ι̣δ̣οῦ̣ντ̣αϲ (*l.* ἀναδίδονταϲ) (...) τὴν παροῦϲάν μου ἐπιϲτολήν.

[29] Fatti dello stesso genere, e cioè l'impedimento di costruire, sono all'origine di petizioni al re nel periodo tolemaico: P. Ent. 13.5 κεκώλυκεν οἰκοδομεῖν; P. Ent. 102.4 κωλύ]ειν με οἰκοδ[ομεῖν.

[30] Datazione di F. Reiter nello *Heidelberger Gesamtverzeichnis der griechischen Papyrusurkunden Ägyptens*: http://aquila.papy.uni-heidelberg.de/Hauptregister/FMPro?-db=hauptregister%5f&Nummer=67194&-format=DFormVw.htm&-lay=Einzel&-max=1&-skip=0&-token=25&-find

[31] In questo caso lo scrivente espone il caso sulla base non delle dichiarazioni dirette del *grammatêphoros*, bensì secondo quanto gli è stato scritto dal suo superiore, il *topotêrêtês*, al quale è stata presentata la lamentela.

[32] Altri casi analoghi sono riconoscibili dalle misure che il destinatario della lettera dovrà prendere: CPR XXV 20.2, ἢ μὴ ἀπαιτήϲῃϲ αὐτόν. Faccende di imposizioni o di riscossioni fiscali sono probabilmente all'origine anche di SB VI 9208 (? VI/VII) e P. Heid. VII 411. Per SB XXIV 16116, cfr. sopra n. 15.

[33] Ringrazio A. Papathomas per avermi comunicato il testo di questo documento, che egli prevede di pubblicare nel 2006.

CPR XXV 20.4-5 (? VII) καὶ ὅτι τὸν ὅμηρον αὐτοῦ |] εἰς φυλακήν;
e forse anche in P. Heid. VII 411.4 (Ermopolite VII) μ̣ᾶλλον γὰρ τὰ τέκνα τῆς γυ̣[ναικός, se nella lacuna destra è da integrare una forma di κρατέω[35].

3.c *L'ordine o richiesta di intervento*

Dopo queste premesse, lo scrivente dà gli ordini che sono propriamente l'oggetto e il fine della sua comunicazione. P. Vindob. G 40259: δ̣ια̣λά̣βῃ [ο]ὖν τὸ πρᾶγμα ἡ μ̣ε̣γαλο(πρέπειά) | σου ἀλλὰ καὶ διο̣ι̣κ̣ήσῃ μετὰ τοῦ δικα̣ίου: il destinatario deve esaminare la questione e risolverla secondo giustizia.

Analogamente in altri documenti:
P. Apoll. Anô 61.4-6 (seconda metà VII[36]) ἀπελθέτωσαν | ἐκ δευτέρου εἰς δί[αι]ταν, καὶ π[οίη]σον αὐτοὺς (...) ἐμμεῖναι τὰ κριθησόμενα;
P. Oxy. VIII 1164.8 s. (VI o VII) ἐπιτρέψατε αὐτοῖς ἐλθεῖν εἰς δίαιταν (...) καὶ τὰ ἀπὸ διαίτης ποιῆσαι;
P. Oxy. XVI 1839.1 (VI) [παρασκευά]σ̣ον Κυριακὸν τὸν υἱὸν Βάμου ἀπελθεῖν εἰς δίαιταν μετὰ τ̣ῆς γραμματηφό[ρου];
verosimilmente P. Ross. Georg. V 10.4 (Arsinoite VII) καὶ ἀπάλλαξον (?)[37] τὸ πρᾶγμα τοῦ γραμματηφ[όρου;
P. Ross. Georg. V 12*a* 2 (? VI/VII)] . [.] π̣[. . .] . . . . . ἀπαλλαγῆναι;
CPR XXV 20.1 s. (? VII) ἵνα ἢ δικάσῃ τὸ πρᾶγμα αὐτοῦ (...) ἢ μὴ ἀπαιτήσῃς αὐτόν;
P. Lond. III 1162 *r.* 6-8 (VII) ἱλαρῶς | ἀκουσθῆναι καὶ δι[ακρι]θῆναι τὸ κατ' αὐτοὺ̣ς | πρᾶγμα;
PUG I 34.3-6 (? VI)[38] θελ̣ήσατε τοίνυν | μεταξὺ αὐτῶν | γενέσθαι καὶ δ[ι]α̣λ̣ύ̣ε̣ι̣ν̣ | μετὰ τοῦ δ̣ι̣κ̣αίου;
CPR VIII 55.1 (Arsinoite VII) θελήσῃ σου ἡ καθοσίωσις ἀπαλλᾶξαι τὸ πρᾶγμ̣α̣;
P. Grenf. II 93.1 ss. (Apollonos Anô ?[39] VI/VII) παρασκευάσαι Φοιβ[ά̣μμονα τὸν | πρεσβύτερον τὸ δίκαιον φυλάξῃ (*l.* φυλάξαι) τῷ γραμματηφόρῳ (...) νουθετῆσαι αὐτὸ[ν . . . . | πρὸς τὸ δίκαιον;
P. Strasb. IV 279.5-6 (Afrodito VI) καταξιωσάτω τοίνυν ἡ ὑμετέρα εὐδοκίμησις ἀκροάσα̣[σθαι] τ̣ῶ̣ν̣ [λ]εγο̣μ̣ένων.

---

[34] Per il significato da attribuire a μᾶλλον, "illegittimamente", "ingiustamente", cfr. J. Gascou, *Trois ordres de libération d'époque arabe (à propos de P.Strasb. G 329)*, di prossima pubblicazione nella *Gedenkschrift* P.J. Sijpesteijn.

[35] Un altro testo che riguarda imprigionamenti illegittimi di persone da impiegare per prestazioni di lavoro coatto, è P. Vindob. G 30067 (Ermopolite VII) (inedito): ἐκρατήθη ὁ ἀδελφὸς αὐτοῦ (...) καὶ χθὲς πάλιν ἐκρατήθη ὁ ἄλλος ἀδελφὸς αὐτο̣ῦ.

[36] Per la datazione di tutto l'archivio, J. Gascou/K.A. Worp, *art. cit.*, pp. 83-89.

[37] Una lettura ἀπάλλαξον κτλ., "e risolvi la faccenda del latore della lettera", è probabilmente da preferire alla lettura καὶ ὑπάλλαξον τὸ πρᾶγμα τοῦ γραμματηφ[όρου, "und verpfände den Besitz des Briefträgers", dell'edizione.

[38] Di questa lettera è conservata soltanto la parte finale. Per contenuto e struttura essa è comunque analoga agli altri testi qui presi in esame. La menzione dei *grammatêphoroi* può bene essere andata perduta con l'inizio del documento.

[39] Cfr. K.A. Worp, *A Checklist of Bishops in Byzantine Egypt (A.D. 325-c. 750)*, ZPE 100 (1994), p. 289 n. 36.

Tra questi documenti alcuni fanno esplicitamente riferimento ad una *diaita*, un arbitrato, come via per risolvere la controversia: P. Apoll. Anô 61, P. Oxy. XVI 1839, P. Oxy. VIII 1164; così anche in PUG I 34, con il verbo διαλύειν, che rimanda appunto ad una *dialysis*. Lo stesso potrebbe essere ancora in altri casi, nei quali però i verbi ἀπαλλάϲϲω[40], διακρίνω[41], δικάζω[42], ἀκροάομαι[43] non sono univoci o discriminanti.

È evidente comunque, che anche in quei casi nei quali la soluzione della controversia deve essere ricercata attraverso un arbitrato, una mediazione, o comunque un procedimento extragiudiziario, le parti devono trovare un accordo in seguito a una decisione presa da un'istanza superiore; nel caso specifico dalla persona che avendo ricevuto una lamentela ordina ad un sottoposto di prendere determinate misure. In P. Apoll. Anô 61, che pure indica l'arbitrato come via per la soluzione della controversia, l'affermazione che uno dei due contendenti è un bugiardo predetermina già l'esito del procedimento. L'arbitrato è dunque solo una via per dare una forma giuridica ad una decisione che di fatto è già stata presa[44].

---

40 Accanto a significati più specifici – cfr. ad esempio P. Apoll. Anô 61.2-3 n.: "faire une tentative de conciliation", F. Preisigke, *Fachwörter des öffentlichen Verwaltungsdienstes Ägyptens*, Göttingen 1915, p. 25 *s. v.* 3 –, il verbo ha anche il significato più generico di "risolvere, sistemare una questione".

41 Le attestazioni del verbo nei papiri superano di poco la decina. Per il verbo in contesto arbitrale, J. M. Modrzejewski, *Private Arbitration in the Law of Greco-Roman Egypt*, JJP 6 (1952), p. 253 n. 145, e T. Varie 1.10 (? VII); in contesto giudiziario e.g. in P. Tor. Choach. 12 VII 3 (Tebe 118 a.C.), P. Oxy. XLVI 3285.30 (II/III) (?), XLVII 3366.33 (258, cfr. W.H.M. Liesker, *The Dates of Valerian Caesar and Saloninus*, in B.G. Mandilaras [ed.], *Proceedings of the XVIII International Congress of Papyrology (Athens 25-31 May 1986)*, Athens 1988, II p. 460 n. 23).

42 Il verbo è attestato solo in contesto giudiziario: ad esempio BGU I 288.7 (Arsinoite 144-147), IV 1024 V 5, 14 (Ermupoli dopo il 360, cfr. F. Mitthof, *Annona Militaris*, Firenze 2001, p. 480 e n. 869), VII 1567 B 14 (Arsinoite III), XV 2492.8 (? II), etc. Va detto però che soltanto tre sono le attestazioni posteriori al IV secolo, e cioè CPR XXV 20, SPP XX 212 (? VI-VII), e SPP XX 255.4 (Menfi VI) (leggere qui πρὸϲ ὧ ἐδηκαϲάμην per πρὸϲ ὃ ἐδικαϲάμην, invece del τρόπῳ ἐδηκαϲάμην dell'edizione): non è chiaro in questi casi se si tratti di contesto giudiziario o arbitrale. In contesto arbitrale sono d'altra parte attestati il termine δικαϲταί e il verbo δικαιόω: Modrzejewski, *art. cit.*, pp. 248 e n. 85, 253 e n. 149.

43 Per ἀκροάομαι in contesto di giudizio arbitrale ma non solo, Modrzejewski, *art. cit.*, p. 253 n. 133, e da ultimo P. Paramone 16.5 n.

44 La lettera è inviata da Liberios al pagarco Papas, suo figlio. In che qualità Liberios scriva al figlio – con il tono di dare ordini piuttosto che di chiedere un favore – non è chiaro. Egli è ex-pagarco, cfr. J. Gascou/K.A. Worp, *art. cit.*, pp. 84 e n. 8, 89, e pare ben introdotto negli ambienti amministrativi. Nella sua lettera egli fa riferimento ad un testimone che ha già fatto la sua deposizione – a favore di una delle due parti – al *dikastês*, ed invita energicamente il figlio a non permettere più che siano commesse ingiustizie.

Casi di questo genere non sono nella sostanza molto differenti da quelli nei quali al destinatario viene soltanto demandata la applicazione di una decisione già presa, come in:

P. Apoll. Anô 23.2 (seconda metà VII[45]): παραϲκευάϲατε πέμψαι τὸ τριμήϲιν;

P. Apoll. Anô 24.4 s. (seconda metà VII[46]) ἀπαίτηϲον αὐτῷ τὸ | χρέοϲ αὐτοῦ;

PSI VII 824.2-3 (? VI) θέληϲ[ον οὖν | ἀπολῦϲαι τὰ ἄλλα τὰ αὐτοῦ καὶ φυλαχθῆ⟨ναι⟩ τὴν γυναῖκα α[ὐτοῦ;

PSI VIII 938.3-4 (Afrodito VI) θέληϲον οὖν π[ᾶϲ]ιν τρόποιϲ ἀπαιτῆϲαι | αὐτοῖϲ (*sic*) ὅϲα χρεωϲτοῦϲιν (...) καὶ δοῦναι τοῖϲ γραμματηφόροιϲ; e ancora sul *verso*, come riepilogo del contenuto della lettera, ἀπάλλαξον δὲ αὐτοὺϲ καὶ ὧν χρεωϲτοῦνται περὶ αὐτῶν;

SPP X 152 *r*. 3 (Arsinoite VII) παραγγείλῃ οὖν [ἡ ϲή[47];

SPP XX 212.1-2 (? VI-VII) ἐὰν ἀληθεύει ἡ γραμματηφόροϲ ὅτι ἐδικάϲθη μετὰ τ[οῦ] ἀντιδίκου αὐτῆϲ πρὸϲ τὴν δίκην ἀπάλλαξων (*sic*) αὐτούϲ[48];

PSI Congr. XI 14.9 (Apollonos Anô seconda metà VII) παραϲκευάϲαι τὸν χρεωϲτοῦντα αὐτῷ ἀπαλλάξαι αὐτοῦ τὸ χρέοϲ;

P. Cairo Masp. II 67194.7 (Afrodito c. 570) καταξιώϲατε οὖν φυλάξαι τὸ δίκαιον τῷ γρ[α]μμ[ατ(ηφόρῳ);

P. Lond. III 1073.2-4 (? VII) καταξιώϲατε οὖν γράψαι τοῖϲ πρωτοκωμήτ(αιϲ) | ἐφιδεῖν (*l.* ἐπ-) τὸ κτίϲμα καὶ ϲυγχωρῆϲαι αὐτοὺϲ οἰκοδομῆϲαι ἐὰν τὸ δίκαι[ον | οὐ κωλύει αὐτούϲ;

P. Vindob. G 16791.4-7[49] (Ermopolite VII) γράψατε | (...) ἀπιλιτικὰ (*sic*) γράμματα πρῶτον μὲ⸢ν⸣ | ἵνα ἀπολῦϲαι (...), ἔπιτα δὲ ἵνα μὴ | παρελθῶϲιν δι' αὐτὸν τοῦ λοιποῦ.

Si tratta in questi casi di procedimenti amministrativi[50] o di misure di tipo poliziesco o comunque di interventi di autorità[51].

---

45 Per la datazione di tutto l'archivio, J. Gascou/K.A. Worp, *art. cit.*, pp. 83-89.

46 Per la datazione di tutto l'archivio, J. Gascou/K.A. Worp, *art. cit.*, pp. 83-89.

47 Seguito da una delle usuali *abstrakten Anredeformen* come ad esempio ἀδελφότηϲ: "dia dunque ordine la tua ...". Wessely trascriveva soltanto παραγγείλη οὖν[, corretto tacitamente in παράγγειλαν οὖν [in DDBDP PHI7: correzione da non accettare. A l. 5 Wessely trascriveva ἀπελ^{θ}, lasciando insoluta la abbreviazione anche nell'*index verborum*; la abbreviazione è riportata come ἀπελθ( ) in DDBDP PHI7, che farebbe pensare a un aoristo di ἀπέρχομαι. La abbreviazione è da sciogliere in realtà in ἀπελ(ύ)θ(η), a indicare il momento in cui è stato emesso il documento, secondo la formula ricorrente in comunicazioni amministrative di questo periodo, cfr. ad esempio CPR XXII 1.13.

48 La procedura in questo caso è più complessa: la latrice della lettera ha già ottenuto una sentenza (arbitrale o giudiziaria ?) relativa ad una controversia che ella ha con il suo *antidikos*. Ella si reca quindi dallo scrivente di SPP XX 212 esponendo il contenuto della sentenza – ma evidentemente senza mostrarne un testo scritto: la lettera si apre con ἐὰν ἀληθεύει –. Né riceve quindi SPP XX 212, con il quale si incarica un *archisymmachos* di risolvere la questione secondo quanto deciso nella sentenza, πρὸϲ τὴν δίκην. Lo scrivente si limita dunque a ordinare di dare applicazione a una sentenza emessa da una istanza a lui superiore.

49 Vedi sopra n. 33.

50 P. Cairo Masp. II 67194, PSI VII 824, P. Vindob. G 16791; cfr. anche P. Vindob. G 30067 (Ermopolite VII): παρακαλῶ οὖν (...) κελεῦϲαι τοῦτον ἀπολυθ⸢ῆναι⸣ κτλ.

Al destinatario di P. Lond. III 1073 viene richiesto di scrivere un'ulteriore lettera ai responsabili del villaggio, i *prôtokômêtai*, ai quali dunque viene di fatto demandata la soluzione del problema. Lo stesso si verifica in P. Vindob. G 16791 e verosimilmente anche in SPP X 152 *r.* 3 (Arsinoite VII), παραγγείλῃ οὖν [ἡ ϲή, con il quale si chiede di trasmettere ulteriori ordini a una istanza inferiore.

Lettere come quelle che avrebbero dovuto scrivere il destinatario di P. Lond. III 1073, P. Vindob. G 16791, e probabilmente anche quello di SPP X 152, sono di fatto conservate: CPR VIII 55 (Arsinoite VII)[52], P. Cairo Masp. II 67194 (Afrodito c. 570)[53], P. Grenf. II 93 (Apollonos Anô ? VI/VII)[54].

---

[51] P. Apoll. Anô 23, 24, P. Lond. III 1073, PSI VIII 938, PSI Congr. XI 14, SPP XX 212. Il tipo di intervento non è definibile in P. Cairo Masp. I 67085.3 (Afrodito VI) κ̣ατα̣ξ̣ίωϲο̣ν̣ ο̣ὖ̣ν̣, δέϲπο[τα, e SPP X 152 *r.*

[52] Gli editori intendevano il documento come un "Auftrag an eine Person, (...) um eine nicht näher angedeutete Sache eines Briefträgers namens Julius zu erledigen. Ein Comes hat Auftrag gegeben, dass Julius sich absolut nicht in die Sache einmischen soll". In realtà la parte conclusiva della comunicazione καὶ μὴ ϲυγχωρῆϲαι αὐτὸν ἕν τινι προϲε̣λθεῖν, ἐπειδὴ | τοῦτο αὐτὸ ᾔ̣τηϲέν με γράψαι τῇ ϲῇ καθοϲιώϲει καὶ ὁ̣ μεγα̣λοπρ(επέϲτατοϲ) κόμε(ϲ) – per la cui interpretazione vedi più avanti, n. 63 – lascia intendere che il mittente scrive la sua lettera in seguito a istruzioni dategli dal *komes*, che deve essere in una posizione a lui superiore. Se il *komes* si preoccupa di dare istruzioni sul modo in cui deve essere regolata la faccenda, deve essere perché a lui si era rivolto il *grammatêphoros* con le sue lamentele.

[53] . . . . . . Ἑλλάδ̣ι̣οϲ [ὁ] τ̣οποτηρ̣[η]τὴϲ τῆ̣ϲ̣ Ἀ̣ν̣τ̣[α]ί̣ο̣υ̣ (?) | ἔγρ̣αψέν μοι διὰ το(ῦ) γραμματηφόρο̣(υ), ὡ̣ϲ τῆϲ ὑμετέραϲ | ἀ̣δ̣ελφότητοϲ ἀπαιτούϲηϲ τὸν εἰρημένον | γραμματηφόρον ἄνδρα φα̣ν̣ε̣ρὸν χρ̣υ̣ϲ̣ί̣[ον (?) | ὑπ[ὲρ ἀρουρῶ]ν̣ μὴ οὐϲ̣ῶν ὑπ' α[ὐ]τό[ν. | καταξ̣ιώϲατε ο̣ὖν φυλάξα̣ι̣ τὸ δίκαιον τῷ γρ̣[α]μμ[ατ(ηφόρῳ̣) | διὰ τὴν κέλευϲιν τοῦ λαμπ̣ρ̣[ο]τ̣ά[το(υ)] ἀν̣δ̣[ρ]ό̣ϲ. Una persona, dalla quale sono state riscosse delle tasse per dei terreni che non erano suoi, è andata ad esporre il caso al *topotêrêtês.* Questi scrive una lettera (ormai perduta) con la sua decisione, e la affida al petente che – in qualità di *grammatêphoros* – la consegna ad una istanza inferiore. È questa istanza inferiore che scrive P. Cairo Maspero II 67194 e lo affida ancora al petente che, di nuovo fungendo da *grammatêphoros*, dovrà consegnarlo alla persona responsabile della riscossione illegittima per ottenere il suo diritto. Il mittente della prima comunicazione (quella perduta), è Helladios, noto da P. Cairo Masp. III 67279 *r.* 16, 24-25 e P. Coll. Youtie II 92.4-5, come *topotêrêtês*, rappresentante, del duca della Tebaide ad Anteopoli. All'ufficio ducale – per quanto, a quel che sembra, a livello decentrato tramite il suo rappresentante nella capitale della pagarchia – era stata presentata dunque la lamentela. Da rilevare che proprio lo stesso Helladios che in P. Cairo Masp. II 67194 interviene contro una esazione di imposte illegittima, è egli stesso accusato di esazioni illegittime in P. Cairo Masp. III 67279, una petizione al duca della Tebaide Kallinikos.

[54] † ὁ μεγαλοπρεπέϲτατοϲ ὑμῶν υἱὸϲ ὁ κόμεϲ ἔγραψέν μοι πάντωϲ παραϲκευάϲαι Φοιβ̣[άμμονα τὸν | πρεϲβύτερον τὸ δίκαιον φυλάξῃ̣ (*l.* φυλάξαι) τῷ γραμματηφόρῳ̣ αὐτοῦ ἀνυψιῷ̣ (per ἀνε-; l'ed. lo intendeva come nome proprio, ma cfr. W. Crönert, *Zur Kritik der Papyrustexte*, SPP IV p. 90)· καὶ ἐπειδὴ πρ[. . . . . . . | αὐτὸν ἐξευτελέϲαι (*l.* ἐξευτελίϲαι), παρακαλῶ τὴν ὑμετέραν πατρικὴν θεοφιλίαν νουθετῆϲαι αὐτὸ[ν . . . . . | πρὸϲ τὸ δίκαιον· ἐπεὶ ἐὰν μηδὲ ὑμῖν πείθεται ἀναγκάζομαι παραϲκευάϲαι αὐτὸν θέλοντα καὶ μὴ θ̣[έλοντα] | πρὸϲ τὰ γραφέντα μοι παρὰ τοῦ αὐτοῦ προειρημένου

3.d Istruzioni in caso di impossibilità a risolvere il caso

Infine, viene considerata la possibilità che l'istanza inferiore delegata non sia in grado di risolvere il caso. P. Vindob. G 40259: εἰ δέ τί ποτέ ἐϲτι πέμψον μοι αὐτοὺϲ ἐνταῦθα καὶ διοικήϲω τὸ πρᾶγμα αὐτῶν.

È evidente, che se anche il *dioikêtês* Senouthios dovesse risolvere il caso attraverso un arbitrato, un tale procedimento non è altro che una via, un tentativo, una possibilità che viene offerta ai contendenti per impedire che la cosa sia risolta attraverso il potere coercitivo dello scrivente.

Questa funzione del *dioikêtês* Senouthios si accorda perfettamente con quella che Steinwenter aveva proposto per i *dioikêtai* di Jeme: "durch Streitabwendung, bezw. Streitlösung die Zahl der Prozesse zu vermindern und dadurch den ordentlichen Richter, den Pagarchen, zu entlasten."[55]

Conclusioni simili sono in PSI Congr. XI 14.12-13 (Apollonos Anô seconda metà VII): λοιπόν, ἔργον ὑμῖν γένηται περὶ τούτου καὶ γρ[ά]ψ[ατέ μοι ἵνα μάθω τὸ πρᾶγμα τοῦ]το πῶϲ ἀπηλλάγη· εἰ δὲ μὴ | ἀνάϲχωνται ἀπαλλαγῆναι πρὸϲ αὐτὸν πέμψον μοι αὐτοὺϲ μετ[ὰ πάϲηϲ ϲυντομίαϲ[56].

E in due altri documenti che, per quanto non menzionino esplicitamente i *grammatêphoroi* – tale menzione può bene, nel secondo, essere perduta –, sono comunque dello stesso genere:

P. Vindob. G 16047 (Ermopolite VII) εἰ δὲ καὶ ἔχει τι εἰπεῖν πέμψατε ἀμφοτέρουϲ πρόϲ με ἐν τῇ | πόλει;

PUG I 34.6-9 (? VI) [ἢ | ἀντιλέγονταϲ | παραπέμψατε | ἐπὶ τὴν πόλιν.

μεγαλοπρεπεϲτάτου ἀνδρὸϲ δεϲ[πότου ἐμοῦ. *Verso*: † τῷ ἁγ]ιωτ(άτῳ) πατρ(ὶ) κυρίῳ (cfr. U. Wilcken in APf 3 [1906], p. 126) ἀββ(ᾷ) † Cενούθῃ ἐπιϲκόπ(ῳ) † Cαραπάμμων υἱόϲ. †. Il *grammatêphoros* è andato dal *komes* a lamentarsi di ingiustizie che gli fa il *presbyteros* Phoibammôn suo parente (αὐτοῦ di l. 2 è da riferire a ἀνεψιῷ e a πρεϲβύτερον o meno probabilmente a κόμεϲ: il *grammatêphoros* è parente del *presbyteros* Phoibammôn, o più difficilmente del *komes*; gli editori intendevano erroneamente "his letter-carrier", del *komes*). Il *komes* – forse un pagarco ? – affida al petente una lettera – perduta – per un suo sottoposto, sempre un funzionario civile, con l'incarico di risolvere la questione. Il *grammatêphoros* consegna la lettera del *komes* allo scrivente di P. Grenf. II 93, che per sistemare la faccenda scrive al vescovo, in quanto superiore del *presbyteros*. Questa seconda lettera – P. Grenf. II 93 – viene affidata allo stesso *grammatêphoros*, che la consegnerà al vescovo. Lo scrivente cerca insomma di aggiustare la cosa ricorrendo alle gerarchie ecclesiastiche, perché la faccenda sia sistemata all'interno della chiesa. Se questa via non darà risultati, lo scrivente penserà lui ad aggiustare la cosa, voglia il *presbyteros* o no, verosimilmente mettendo in atto le vie della giustizia civile. Il fatto che egli minacci, qualora il *presbyteros* non voglia ubbidire al vescovo, di agire di forza, mostra che egli rappresenta un potere parallelo e indipendente da quello ecclesiastico: e cioè il potere dello stato.

55 Steinwenter, *cit.*, p. 33.

56 Quest'ordine di reinviare i contendenti dallo scrivente contrasta con la minaccia formulata dallo stesso scrivente subito prima alle ll. 11-12: ἐὰν γὰρ ὑ]ποϲτρέψῃ πρὸϲ ἐμὲ ἀναπόκρ[ι]τοϲ | οὐ βαϲτάϲηϲ με, vedi oltre 3.*e*.

Ciò accade effettivamente in P. Oxy. VIII 1164 (VI o VII): i *grammatêphoroi* hanno presentato il loro caso al destinatario di P. Oxy. VIII 1164. Dopo che il caso era stato delegato con uno scritto, *grammata*, alla istanza inferiore – il mittente dello stesso documento –[57], entrambe le parti hanno portato testimoni a loro favore[58], e perciò (ll. 7-8) οὐκ ἐδυνήθην αὐτοὺϲ | ἀπαλλάξαι. Lo scrivente dunque li rimanda indietro, con una lettera di accompagnamento e di spiegazioni[59], al suo superiore, che in un (secondo ?) arbitrato dovrà risolvere la faccenda[60].

Come, negli altri casi, l'istanza superiore (probabilmente il pagarco in P. Vindob. G 16047 e PUG I 34, avendo egli la sua sede nella città), intendesse

---

[57] ll.1-2: οἱ γραμματηφόροι ἦλθαν πρὸϲ ἐμὲ φέροντέϲ μοι γράμματα τῆϲ ὑμετέραϲ | πατρικῆϲ μεγαλοπρεπείαϲ ἕνεκεν καμήλου.

[58] ll. 4-7: προήνεγκαν οὐκ ὀλίγουϲ | ἄνδραϲ μαρτυροῦνταϲ ὡϲ αὐτῶν ἐϲτιν ἡ κάμηλοϲ· οὐ μὴν δὲ ἀλλὰ καὶ οἱ | γραμματηφόροι ἤνεγκαν ἄλλουϲ μαρτυροῦνταϲ πάλιν ὡϲ αὐτῶν ἐϲτιν ἡ αὐτὴ | κάμηλοϲ, καὶ τῶν ἀμφοτέρων ἐνεγκόντων μάρτυραϲ κτλ. Riferimenti espliciti a *martyres*, testimoni, come elemento decisivo per la formulazione del giudizio, sono ancora in P. Apoll. Anô 24 e 61.

[59] Appunto P. Oxy. VIII 1164, che fa di queste persone – e in relazione al quale esse sono – dei *grammatêphoroi*. Gli editori Grenfell e Hunt consideravano invece queste persone come dei "letter-carriers", cfr. la traduzione del papiro.

[60] Gli editori riconducevano il documento ad ambienti privati – esso è classificato tra la "private correspondence" – e lo intendevano come "letter to a comes from a minor local magnate concerning a dispute for the possession of a camel, which was claimed by their respective subordinates. The writer proposes arbitration and promises that the sentence should be respected." Ad ambienti privati sembra ricondurre il documento anche Modrzejewski, *art. cit.*, p. 244: "Theodosius, "a minor local magnate", suggests to comes Petros to let the dispute about a question of possession which had arised among their dependants be settled by arbitration; he assures in advance that he will do his best to get the arbiter's decision carried into effect." Ma nel papiro non c'è niente che possa far pensare che il secondo gruppo di contendenti, gli *antidikoi* dei *grammatêphoroi*, avesse un rapporto di dipendenza diretto – e privato – con il destinatario Petros. Questi dunque può bene avere una posizione istituzionale ed agire in qualità di funzionario dell'apparato statale. Quanto al mittente della lettera Theodosios, il fatto che egli parli dei *grammatêphoroi* come dei "suoi" (τῶν | ἐμῶν a ll. 8-9, τοὺ⟨ϲ⟩ ἐμούϲ a l. 10), non esclude comunque che egli potesse avere su di loro una autorità di tipo istituzionale, o come responsabile di un villaggio, o almeno in forza della "conciliation d'interêt" tra stato e proprietari terrieri che faceva di questi ultimi dei rappresentanti e degli agenti dello stato sulle loro proprietà: cfr. lo studio classico di J. Gascou, *Les grands domaines, la cité et l'État en Égypte byzantine*, T&MByz. 9 (1985), pp. 1-90, in particolare pp. 3-60; e da ultimo, dello stesso J. Gascou, *Les pétitions privées*, in D. Feissel/J. Gascou (édité par), *La pétition à Byzance*, Paris 2004, pp. 96-103. Ad un contesto di tipo pubblico, non privato, è ricondotto P. Oxy. VIII 1164 anche da D. Simon, *Zur Zivilgerichtsbarkeit im spätbyzantinischen Ägypten*, RIDA 3e s., 18 (1971), p. 650s. Se si trattasse invece soltanto di una questione tra i dipendenti di due diversi patroni – i *grammatêphoroi* sotto il patronato del Theodosios mittente della lettera, i loro *antidikoi* sotto il patronato del destinatario Petros – e né Theodosios né Petros avessero funzioni istituzionali, sarebbe difficile capire perché i dipendenti di Theodosios vadano a lamentarsi da Petros, invece di recarsi dal loro patrono ed affidare a lui la difesa dei loro interessi.

intervenire – con misure poliziesche, come giudice di pace, o in maniera giurisdizionale – è difficile dire.

In ogni caso, anche quando l'intervento non è di tipo giudiziario-arbitrale, ma consiste soltanto in un "Auftrag oder Vorschlag, durch Schiedsmänner eine διάλυϲιϲ herbeizuführen"[61], è questo "Vorschlag" da considerare come una sorta di imposizione.

3.e Intimazione a risolvere definitivamente il caso

In altri testi il mittente scrive che i *grammatêphoroi* non devono più recarsi da lui per la stessa questione. Una simile intimazione non è da intendere come un divieto ai *grammatêphoroi* di ripetere le loro lamentele, ma come un rafforzamento dell'ordine di risolvere la questione dato all'istanza inferiore: la controversia deve essere risolta definitivamente e secondo giustizia, senza lasciare alle parti motivo di ulteriori querele.

P. Oxy. XVI 1839.2-3 (VI) ἐὰν ἔτι ἔλθῃ πρὸϲ ἐμ̣ὲ [| καὶ μὴ ἀ]πηλλάγηϲαν[62], οὐκ ἔχειϲ μου βαϲτάξαι.

Molto simile il concetto espresso – ed anche il vocabolario usato – in PSI Congr. XI 14.11-12 (Apollonos Anô seconda metà VII): ἐὰν γὰρ ὑ]ποϲτρέψῃ πρὸϲ ἐμὲ ἀναπόκ̣ρ̣[ι]τ̣ο̣ϲ | οὐ βαϲτάϲῃϲ με.

Simili anche SPP XX 212.2 (? VI-VII): καὶ μηκέτι ϲυγχωρήϲῃϲ αὐτὴν προϲελθεῖν μοι περὶ τούτου; CPR VIII 55.2 (Arsinoite VII): καὶ μὴ ϲυγχωρῆϲαι αὐτὸν ἔν τ̣ινι προϲ̣ελθεῖν[63]; qualcosa di questo genere si trovava probabilmente anche nel lacunoso P. Cairo Masp. I 67085.4, προϲέλθῃ[64] τῷ δεϲπότ(ῃ) τῷ μ̣[, dove il congiuntivo fa pensare a qualcosa come ἵνα μὴ προϲέλθῃ oppure ἐὰν προϲέλθῃ seguito da una qualche minaccia.

In qualche modo paragonabile è anche P. Apoll. Anô 24.6 (seconda metà VII): λοιπὸν μὴ δεηθῇ ἄλληϲ ἐπιϲτολῆϲ μου περὶ αὐτοῦ. Anche in questo caso, la frase "per il resto, che non ci sia bisogno di un'altra mia lettera a proposito di lui!", implica un'intimazione al destinatario a risolvere la questione con equità e una volta per tutte, in modo che le parti in causa non debbano di nuovo rivolgersi allo scrivente e costringerlo a rioccuparsi della cosa.

[61] Steinwenter, *cit.*, p. 12.

[62] La lettura ἀ]πηλλάγηϲαν invece del ϲυ]ν̣ηλλάγηϲαν degli editori, è sicura: cfr. la immagine del papiro all'indirizzo http://163.1.169.40/gsdl/collect/POxy/index/assoc/HASH339c.dir/POxy.v0016.n1839.a.01.hires.jpg

[63] Gli editori traducevano: " ... und nicht gestatten, dass er sich auf irgendwelche Weise der Sache zuwendet"; cfr. anche introd. al papiro: "Ein comes hat Auftrag gegeben, dass Julius sich absolut nicht in die Sache einmischen soll." Il verbo προϲέρχομαι ha qui in realtà – come risulta dai paralleli – il significato tecnico di "rivolgersi" a qualcuno con una richiesta, una petizione, e la frase è da intendere "e non permettere che egli presenti una (altra) lamentela per un qualche motivo".

[64] Secondo una proposta di R.H. Horn, *The Use of the Subjunctive and Optative Moods in the Non-Literary Papyri*, Diss. Philadelphia 1926, p. 123, riportata in *BL* VI 25, il congiuntivo potrebbe qui essere un errore per l'infinito. Ma il testo del papiro è frammentario e la sua struttura sintattica rimane poco chiara.

3.f Interventi coercitivi

E se i problemi che hanno dato origine alle lamentele, non possono essere risolti pacificamente, non si rinuncia all'impiego della forza: lo scrivente di PSI VIII 938 (Afrodito VI) minaccia, qualora il destinatario non riesca a riscuotere una somma della quale alcune persone sono debitrici ai *grammatêphoroi*, di inviare a riscuotere il capo delle guardie (ll. 5-6): ἀλλὰ πάντωϲ ἀπαιτήϲατε αὐτούϲ, ἐπεὶ θεὸϲ οἶδεν πέμπω τὸν ἀρχίφρουρον[65] | ἀπαιτοῦντα αὐτοὺϲ μετὰ δαπάνηϲ.

Analogamente lo scrivente di P. Grenf. II 93 (Apollonos Anô ? VI/VII) minaccia di ricorrere alle maniere forti qualora il *presbyteros* che ha fatto un torto al *grammatêphoros* non voglia dare ascolto al vescovo al quale è diretta la lettera (l. 4): ἐπεὶ ἐὰν μηδὲ ὑμῖν πείθεται ἀναγκάζομαι παραϲκευάϲαι αὐτὸν θέλοντα καὶ μὴ θ̣[έλοντα.

4. Le vie della giustizia: 'petizioni orali' e arbitrato come soluzione imposta

Dopo averne messo in evidenza la struttura e gli aspetti comuni, e aver chiarito il contesto e la successione dei fatti dei quali esse sono il prodotto, è possibile parlare di queste 'lettere bizantine' quasi come di una tipologia documentaria di ambito giuridico, con la sua funzione, la sua struttura, e le sue formule. Sulla natura più precisa di questa tipologia documentaria, che si riallaccia ad antecedenti del periodo romano, si ritornerà più avanti.

Prima però, alcune osservazioni sulle procedure che questi documenti mostrano o sottointendono. Anche nei casi nei quali la decisione dell'istanza interpellata consiste nel rimandare la controversia ad un arbitrato, a una mediazione, o ad una qualche altra via extragiudiziaria, ciò sembra essere non una semplice proposta, ma piuttosto una misura coercitiva.

Ancora, e conseguentemente, ciò che normalmente si legge in compromessi e *dialyseis*, e cioè che le due parti volontariamente, insieme e di comune accordo, hanno deciso di venire a un arbitrato o una mediazione[66], non deve necessariamente corrispondere alla realtà dei fatti.

---

[65] Per *l'archiphrouros*, G. Rouillard, *L'administration civile de l'Égypte byzantine*², Paris 1928, pp. 45-46.

[66] BGU I 309.6-8 (Arsinoite 602): τόδε τὸ κομπρόμιϲϲον ποιούμ(εθα) | πρὸϲ ἀλλήλουϲ ἑκουϲίᾳ γνώ-|[μῃ; idem in BGU I 315.5-6 (Arsinoite 627, cfr. P. Heid. V 361.38 n.), SB I 5271.6-7 (Arsinoite 615), cfr. R.S. Bagnall/K.A. Worp, *Christian Invocations in the Papyri*, CdÉ 56 (1981), p. 121 n. 1, SB I 5681.4-5 (Arsinoite, cfr. R.S. Bagnall/K.A. Worp, *CSBE*¹ p. 61 n. 52, 654 o 669, cfr. D. Hagedorn/K.A. Worp, *Papyri aus der Sammlung Gradenwitz im Kloster Beuron*, ZPE 134 [2001], p. 176), XIV 12194.7-8 (Arsinoite VII), XXIV 15899.5-6 (Arsinoite 608); BGU I 315.12-13 (Arsinoite 627): ἔδοξεν αὐτοὺϲ αἱρήϲαϲθαι (*sic*) κατὰ | κοινὴν γνώμην; κοινῇ γνώμῃ in P. Iand. III 41.14 (Ossirinco seconda metà VI, cfr. N. Gonis, *An Unrecognised (Post)Consular Date of 383*, ZPE 147 [2004], p. 164 n. 1); P. Lond. III 992.11-12 (p. 253) (Ermupoli cfr. *BL* I 295, 507): καὶ πρὸ δίκηϲ καὶ φιλονικείαϲ (*sic*) | ἔδοξεν ἡμῖν κοινῇ γνώμῃ ἀπαντῆϲαι εἰϲ δίαιταν; P. Lond. V 1707.5 (Antinoe 566) ἔδοξεν αὐτοῖϲ διαίτῃ χρήϲαϲθαι καὶ

È invece la persona che ha subito – o ritiene di aver subito – un'ingiustizia, che si rivolge a un ufficiale o a un personaggio influente per avere giustizia: si potrebbe dire che questi presenta una sorta di petizione orale. Da rilevare che proprio nel periodo coperto da questo genere di documenti, le petizioni propriamente dette, ed anche in buona misura le lettere di petizione, regrediscono notevolmente, fino a scomparire del tutto[67].

In diversi casi sembra che l'istanza interpellata abbia già preso una decisione – per lo più a favore del petente – e si limiti a ordinare di darle applicazione, anche se attraverso la forma di un arbitrato.

Il procedimento che si lascia intravedere attraverso queste comunicazioni mette in una luce più corretta il così frequente ricorso all'arbitrato o altri procedimenti extragiudiziari testimoniato dai numerosi compromessi e *dialyseis*; esso chiarisce come in realtà si arrivasse ad una soluzione arbitrale e quali vie seguisse la amministrazione della giustizia.

Compromessi e *dialyseis* sono solo – come del resto già risulta chiaramente da alcuni di questi documenti[68] – la conclusione del problema, la fine della storia; il punto di arrivo di una vicenda sul cui procedere siamo il più delle volte del tutto privi di informazioni. Questa mancanza di informazioni sulle vie attraverso le quali si poteva arrivare ad una soluzione arbitrale o comunque extragiudiziaria di una controversia, può portare ad una sopravvalutazione del ruolo dell'arbitrato – da un punto di vista non della frequenza con la quale tale procedimento poteva essere impiegato, ma del valore e significato che a tale procedimento può essere attribuito –, e in particolare a una sopravvalutazione della volontarietà della scelta di una simile via per risolvere una controversia[69]. Con quel che ne consegue per il significato da attribuire a questa presunta volontarietà[70].

εἵλαντο κατὰ κοινὴν cυναίνεcιν; P. München I 6.4 (Siene ? 583): κατὰ κοινὴν γνώμην μεcιτείᾳ τινῶν cυνελθεῖν αὐτούc; cfr. anche l. 23; SB I 5681.28-29: ἔδοξεν αὐτοῖc αἱρήcαcθ[αι | κοινῇ γνώμῃ; BGU I 317.2 (Arsinoe 580/581): [τήνδε τὴν ἔγγραφον] (cfr. *BL* I 435) ὁμολογίαν τῆc διαλύcεωc καὶ τελείαc ἀπαλλαγῆc ποιο[ῦμαι ἑκουcίᾳ γνώμ]ῃ (cfr. *BL* I 38) καὶ αὐθαιρέτῳ βουλήcει; P. München I 7.6-8 (Antinoe 583): τάcδε τὰc ἀντιcυγγράφουc διαλύcειc τίθενται καὶ ποιοῦνται | πρὸc ἀλλήλουc ἑκόντεc καὶ πεπειcμένοι πάcηc ἀπάτηc | καὶ βίαc χωρίc; P. Par. 20.4 (Panopoli 600): ταύτην τίθεντο (*sic*) καὶ ποιοῦνται πρὸc ἑαυτοὺc τὴν αἰώνιον διάλυcιν ἑκόντεc καὶ πεπειcμένοι.

67 J. Gascou, *Les pétitions privées*, in D. Feissel/J. Gascou (édité par), *La pétition à Byzance*, Paris 2004, pp. 93-94 e J. Gascou/J.-L. Fournet, *Liste des pétitions sur papyrus des Ve-VIIe siècles*, *ibid*., pp. 141-196.

68 Cfr. T. Gagos/P. van Minnen, *Settling a Dispute. Toward a Legal Anthropology of Late Antique Egypt*, Ann Arbor 1994, pp. 37-38 e i documenti ivi citati. Cfr. anche P. Lond. V 1708, con la lunga e complessa serie di vicende, anche giudiziarie, che vengono narrate come antefatto dell'arbitrato.

69 Secondo la analisi di *dialyseis* e compromessi condotta da Gagos e van Minnen, l'intervento di ufficiali per la scelta di una soluzione extragiudiziaria di una controversia sarebbe ampiamente documentato fino alla fine del V secolo, ma cesserebbe nel periodo

In verità una *dialysis* è spesso solo la via che viene scelta dall'autorità e che viene imposta alle parti – o piuttosto, come sembra, alla parte accusata – per risolvere una controversia, o anche addirittura per imporre una soluzione già decisa e darle una forma giuridica.

Chi ha subito un'ingiustizia e – come è presumibile per buona parte della popolazione egiziana – non ha un'idea chiara di diritto e procedimenti giudiziari, si rivolge semplicemente e in maniera ingenua ad un personaggio influente, spesso – anche se non necessariamente – a un ufficiale. Questi, dopo aver ascoltato la lamentela e spesso anche dopo aver già preso una decisione – se mai condizionata all'accertamento di alcuni elementi –, sceglie la via che gli appare la più veloce, la più semplice, la più efficace e la più economica, per sistemare la questione[71].

L'istanza presso la quale è stata presentata la querela ordina dunque – se la cosa non è da risolvere con misure amministrative o poliziesche, o ancora in altro modo – di far venire le due parti ad un arbitrato, il cui esito può essere già deciso[72].

Tutto ciò ha poco a che fare con il supposto desiderio della popolazione egiziana di evitare traumatici – da un punto di vista sociale e antropologico – procedimenti giudiziari, o con una presunta sfiducia e diffidenza nei confronti dello stato bizantino ortodosso[73]: in definitiva, gli ufficiali che comunque – tanto in un procedimento giudiziario che di altro genere – avrebbero dovuto risolvere il caso, altro non erano che egiziani e copti, quanto quelli che sarebbero intervenuti in un arbitrato.

In che misura potesse essere volontaria la scelta di un tale modo di procedere risulta chiaramente da intimazioni quali "mandali da me, e deciderò io" di cui al punto 3.*d*, o "e non lasciare che vengano da me un'altra volta" di cui al punto 3.*e*; o ancora meglio, da un testo come P. Grenf. II 99a (? VI/VII):

† Δαυεὶτ ἀνεδέξατο Θαηςίαν ὥςτε αὐτὴν ἀπελθῖν (*sic*) εἰς δίαιταν (pap.: διαίτην) καὶ τὰ ἀπὸ διαίτης ποιήςῃ (*l.* ποιήςειν)· εἰ δὲ μὴ ποιήςῃ ἐπὶ τῷ ἐμὲ βαλεῖν αὐτὴν εἰς τῆν φυλακήν.

---

successivo: T. Gagos/P. van Minnen, *op. cit.*, p. 41. Le nostre 'lettere bizantine' attestano invece ampiamente tale intervento ancora per i secoli VI e VII.

70 Cfr. ad esempio A.A. Schiller, *The Courts are no more*, in *Studi in onore di Edoardo Volterra*, Milano 1971, I pp. 500-502: in particolare le considerazioni relative al 'nazionalismo' della popolazione egiziana, per cui i copti avrebbero evitato (p. 501) "all unnecessary contact with government officials". Essi invece (p. 502) "would turn to the respected members of their own communities – and not in their capacity as minor local officials, but as trusted co-religionists – for aid as arbiters or as mediators in settling their little disputes". Contro la ancora diffusa idea del 'nazionalismo egiziano', cfr. E. Wipszycka, *Le nationalisme a-t-il existé dans l'Égypte byzantine?*, JJP 22 (1992), pp. 83-128. Motivazioni di ordine religioso sono escluse anche da T. Gagos/P. van Minnen, *op. cit.*, p. 43.

71 Cfr. D. Simon, *Zur Zivilgerichtsbarkeit im spätbyzantinischen Ägypten*, RIDA 3e s., 18 (1971), p. 654. Cfr. anche T. Gagos/P. van Minnen, *op. cit.*, pp. 42-43.

72 Cfr. anche Simon, *art. cit.*, p. 650, che rilevava come in P. Oxy. VIII 1164 "das Schiedsverfahren gerade nicht auf private Initiative durchgeführt wird."

73 Vedi sopra, n. 70.

"David ha garantito per Thaesia, che ella si presenterà all'arbitrato e che adempirà alla decisione arbitrale. Se non lo farà, la getterò in prigione !"

Analogamente, almeno in alcuni casi l'istanza incaricata di far venire le parti a un arbitrato viene anche esplicitamente richiesta di far sì che esse si attengano al verdetto arbitrale: P. Apoll. Anô 61.5-6: καὶ π[οίη]cον αὐτοὺc (...) ἐμμεῖναι τὰ κριθηcόμενα; P. Oxy. VIII 1164.9 (VI o VII) καὶ τὰ ἀπὸ διαίτηc ποιῆcαι. Con quali mezzi non viene precisato; difficilmente però con l'esclusione di misure di coercizione[74].

Il ricorso all'arbitrato o ad altre soluzioni extragiudiziarie insomma non implica affatto la rinuncia – e ancor meno il rifiuto – all'intervento di un rappresentante dell'apparato statale nella la soluzione di una controversia.

5. *La natura dei documenti e i loro precedenti*

Infine, la questione della natura di questi documenti, che, in seguito ad una querela rivolta a una autorità, vengono diretti di regola ad un sottoposto ed affidati alla persona che ha presentato la lamentela. Attraverso queste comunicazioni viene delegata un'istanza inferiore a prendere una decisione per la soluzione di una controversia, o ad applicare una decisione già presa.

Non si tratta, è evidente, di semplici 'lettere'. Si tratta invece di risposte a persone che sono andate a lamentarsi, che hanno in un certo modo, presentato oralmente e personalmente una petizione: un genere documentario che, come si è già detto, in questo periodo scompare.

Queste comunicazioni hanno in definitiva la stessa funzione e le stesse caratteristiche delle *hypographai* delle petizioni di età romana, o ancora meglio, delle comunicazioni che in certi momenti del periodo romano venivano affidate al petente in risposta ad una petizione, e con le quali si delegava un'istanza inferiore a risolvere una questione[75].

Così R. Haensch, *Die Bearbeitungsweisen von Petitionen in der Provinz Aegyptus*, ZPE 100 (1994), p. 489: "Im 1. und beginnenden 2. Jh. (Phase I) reagierte

---

[74] Il potere coercitivo dell'apparato statale entra comunque in gioco – anche in assenza di riferimenti espliciti – per garantire la applicazione di una decisione arbitrale. Come osserva D. Simon, *art. cit.*, pp. 624, 652-653, anche nei casi in cui le parti ricorrono all'arbitrato per la soluzione di una controversia, esse non possono comunque evitare di ricorrere al potere coercitivo dello stato: se non per la soluzione della controversia, almeno per la applicazione della decisione presa uguale attraverso quale procedimento: (p. 653) "Zusammenfassend haben wir festzustellen, daß aus den vorhandenen Schiedsurkunden und Vergleichen ein Hinweis auf eine *gesteigerte* Zurückhaltung der Bevölkerung gegenüber den staatlichen Gerichten nicht zu entnehmen ist und daß von einem Verzicht auf den staatlichen Zwangsstab nicht die Rede sein kann."

[75] Per una dettagliata trattazione di queste comunicazioni con le quali il prefetto comunicava ad un sottoposto i provvedimenti di carattere sostanziale da prendere, o lo delegava a prendere egli una decisione, cfr. G. Foti Talamanca, *Ricerche sul processo nell'Egitto greco-romano*, II, *L'introduzione del Giudizio* 1., Milano 1979, pp. 164-196.

der Statthalter auf eine überreichte Petition anscheinend in der Form, daß er einen kurzen Brief verfassen ließ. In ihm erläuterte er dem Administrationsträger, an den er den Bittsteller verwies, wie er das Gesuch behandelt wissen wollte. Diesem Schreiben fügte man die urspüngliche Petition in Abschrift oder als abgezeichnete Beilage hinzu. Beide Dokumente zu überbringen, war dann Aufgabe des Bittstellers."

Queste 'lettere bizantine' acquistano così un significato particolare per l'esame da un lato delle vie che nella tarda antichità venivano scelte dalla popolazione egiziana per la presentazione delle proprie lamentele; dall'altro, del procedimento avviato dalle diverse istanze per la soluzione di queste controversie, si potrebbe dire quasi per la elaborazione di queste 'petizioni orali'[76].

[76] Questo esame dovrebbe naturalmente prendere in considerazione anche quelle comunicazioni trasmesse direttamente all'istanza richiesta di risolvere il caso, senza essere cioè affidate al 'petente', o almeno senza che egli venga menzionato nel testo come *grammatêphoros*. Casi di questo genere – pur non essendo qui stati trattati – possono in effetti per contenuto e struttura essere molto simili ai testi con *grammatêphoroi*, allo stesso modo in cui *hypographai* ed *epistulae* dei prefetti possono esser tra loro simili indipendentemente dalle modalità della trasmissione all'istanza incaricata. Così ad esempio in P. Vindob. G 16047 (Ermopolite VII), la cui edizione è in preparazione per un prossimo volume di CPR e che si è già avuto modo di citare sopra, si trova il riferimento a ciò che è stato detto dal petente e alla sua iniziativa di presentare il caso allo scrivente (punto 3.*a*), ὡϲ λέγει; l'esposizione del caso: ἦλθεν τίϲ ποτε (...) καὶ ἐκώλυϲεν αὐτ̣ὸν (punto 3.*b*); l'ordine di intervento: μὴ ϲυγχωρήϲητε οὖν αὐτὸν κωλῦϲαι (...) ἀλλὰ πάντωϲ (punto 3.*c*); le istruzioni qualora non fosse possibile risolvere il caso: ε̣ἰ̣ δ̣ὲ καὶ ἔχ̣ε̣ι τι εἰπεῖν πέμψατε ἀμφοτέρουϲ πρόϲ με ἐν τῇ | π̣όλει (punto 3.*d*).

LIVIA MIGLIARDI ZINGALE (GENOVA)

RISPOSTA A FEDERICO MORELLI

Nella relazione dal suggestivo titolo, *Grammatêphoroi e vie della giustizia nell'Egitto tardo antico*, il giovane studioso presenta i risultati della minuziosa indagine da lui condotta sul termine *grammatêphoros*, che fino ad oggi è stato comunemente interpretato nei dizionari della lingua greca nel significato tecnico di "portalettere", "messaggero", "corriere", un addetto cioè del servizio postale, vuoi privato vuoi pubblico.

Secondo il Morelli proprio questa accezione specifica, che è ampiamente testimoniata nelle fonti letterarie – mi vengono in mente i *grammatêphoroi* citati da Plutarco nella vita di Galba, cui è affidato da parte dei consoli il delicato compito di consegnare *ta dogmata* all'imperatore[1] – e che pure è confortata dalla documentazione papirologica di provenienza egiziana, a partire almeno dal II secolo fino a tutto il V secolo della nostra éra, si sarebbe in seguito perduta e il vocabolo avrebbe assunto nelle attestazioni del VI e del VII secolo il significato assai più generico di mero "latore di una lettera", che è d'altronde il suo significato originario.

Si tratta di testi sempre redatti in forma epistolare, che il Morelli con puntuale riferimento all'età cui appartengono, qualifica più semplicemente come "lettere bizantine", nelle quali il *grammatêphoros* che materialmente consegna la missiva nella maggior parte dei casi non ha un qualche rapporto diretto con il contenuto della lettera stessa, ma che in alcuni interessanti esempi, specificamente indagati dallo studioso, appare invece coinvolto di persona.

Sono documenti, questi ultimi, che – ripeto le parole del Morelli – "lasciano intravedere con maggiore o minore chiarezza una serie di vicende … giudiziarie, liti, controversie, ricorsi alla e interventi della autorità" e che – prosegue il Morelli – "mostrano per lo più una struttura unitaria e si distinguono per alcuni termini, espressioni e formule ricorrenti": in essi il *grammatêphoros*, cioè il portatore della missiva, ha subìto una qualche ingiustizia ed inizialmente si è rivolto proprio a chi ora ha scritto la lettera, indirizzata a sua volta a chi dovrà in qualche modo tentare di comporre la controversia.

Nella più gran parte di essi il *grammatêphoros* rimane per noi ignoto (vedi ad esempio P. Vindob. G. 40259, P. Oxy. VIII 1164, PSI Congr. XI 14, PSI VII 824, ecc.) e solo raramente è possibile conoscerne il nome, come nel caso piuttosto eccezionale di un tal Ioulios in CPR VIII 55 o di un certo Anypsios in P. Grenf. II 93. In pochi casi è possibile apprenderne almeno il mestiere (*ampelourgos* in P. Vindob. G 16199, *gheôrgos* in P. Lond. III 1073 e SPP X 152 r., *nautês* in P. Apoll. Ano 23 e 24) o la posizione giuridica (*misthotês*

---

[1] Plut., *Vita Galbae* 8: "…I consoli designarono degli schiavi pubblici con il compito di portare i decreti all'imperatore e diedero loro i cosiddetti diplomi con i contrassegni, riconoscendo i quali i capi delle singole città nei cambi dei veicoli affrettavano le operazioni per far procedere il viaggio dei messaggeri (*grammatephoroi*)".

in P. Strasb. IV 279) o la funzione (*presbyteros* in SB XXIV 16116) o il sesso (*hê parousê grammatêphoros* in P. Apoll. Ano 61, *hê grammatêphoros gynê* (?) in P. Oxy. XVI 1839).

Anche per quanto riguarda il mittente e il destinatario di queste comunicazioni epistolari mancano in molti casi più precisi elementi per una sicura identificazione, ma in alcuni documenti, che per curiosità ho voluto rapidamente controllare – così come ho fatto per il *grammatêphoros* –, si può invece conoscerne le mansioni. Per esempio, in SB XXIV 16116 chi scrive è un *episkopos* e il destinatario è un *dioikêtês*, mentre in SPP XX 212, dove rimane ignoto il mittente, il destinatario è un *archisymmachos*. In PSI Congr. XI 14 mittente è un emiro e destinatario è un pagarca. Anche in P. Apoll. Ano 23, 24 e 61 il destinatario è un pagarca. In CPR VIII 55 se invero resta sconosciuto il mittente, il destinatario è certamente un personaggio influente alla cui *devotio* ci si rivolge. In P. Oxy. VIII 1164 è una qualche autorità locale che invia la lettera ad un *comes* non altrimenti noto. In P. Lond. III 1073 il destinatario è addirittura il *comes* d'Arcadia..

Tra queste numerose testimonianze l'attenzione del Morelli si sofferma specificamente su P. Vindob. G 40259, un breve documento epistolare di provenienza ermopolitana, databile alla metà del VII secolo d.C., che viene indirizzato da un certo Taurinos, il quale – come risulta dall'archivio in gran parte inedito che di lui ci è conservato – sembra essere un alto funzionario della pagarchia, anche se il titolo non compare esplicitamente nel testo in esame.

Destinatario della lettera è un *dioikêtês* di nome Senouthios, cui il mittente si rivolge, chiedendo espressamente di esaminare la questione che vede in lite l'ignoto latore dell'*epistolê* con alcune persone, anch'esse non meglio identificate: lo stesso Taurinos insiste poi, domandando che la cosa sia regolata con giustizia, altrimenti sarà egli stesso ad occuparsi del caso.

Secondo il Morelli l'intera vicenda può essere così ricostruita: l'ignoto *grammatêphoros*, che ha subìto un qualche sopruso, si è rivolto ad un funzionario della pagarchia, Taurinos appunto, per esporgli oralmente le proprie lamentele ed il funzionario è intervenuto demandando la questione ad altro funzionario, il *dioikêtês* Senouthios, cui egli affida attraverso questa lettera la risoluzione della lite.

Si tratterebbe quindi, se si accetta la terminologia squisitamente tecnica adoperata dallo studioso nel suo commento al testo, quando – sono le precise parole da lui utilizzate – scrive di "istruzioni per un'istanza inferiore alla quale viene trasmesso il caso" o ancora "di funzionario delegato a risolvere la controversia", di una comunicazione ufficiale, inviata da un giudice superiore delegante ad un giudice inferiore delegato.

Ma questa interpretazione sembra trovare alcuni ostacoli. In primo luogo il mittente non si qualifica con il suo titolo e questo poco si comprende in un formale procedimento giudiziario. In secondo luogo sembra strano che sia lo stesso interessato ad avere il compito assai delicato di trasmettere gli atti processuali, che normalmente era attribuito proprio a quei portalettere, corrieri, messaggeri, nunzii – cioè *grammatêphoroi* in senso tecnico –, che ricoprivano siffatta funzione liturgica a servizio dello stato nel *cursus* cosiddetto *velox* – l'*oxys dromos* ampiamente attestato nei papiri – e che erano appunto presenti nell'apparato amministrativo della giustizia. Si aggiunga poi che all'ufficio della pagarchia, cui secondo le risultanze dell'archivio appartiene lo scrivente, non sembrano competere funzioni giurisdizionali vere e proprie, se non limitatamente ed esclusivamente all'ambito fiscale, dove addirittura potevano essere utilizzate polizia e carceri private [2].

Si potrebbe allora pensare – come d'altra parte lo stesso Morelli propone nel prosieguo della sua ricerca, in contrasto con quanto ha prima affermato – ad una comunicazione, con la quale Taurinos chiede informalmente ad un *dioikêtês* di comporre in modo stragiudiziale, e non attraverso un regolare processo, la lite in cui è coinvolto l'anonimo latore della missiva.

Ancora una volta verrebbe così documentato il ricorso alla giustizia privata piuttosto che alla giustizia statale, che se pure non del tutto morta – lo aveva prospettato A.A. Schiller[3] in un suo famoso saggio – certamente più non funzionava a pieno ritmo come nelle epoche precedenti: un'ulteriore conferma che si aggiunge agli altri esempi citati dal relatore, che consistono in analoghe comunicazioni, in cui si fa specifico riferimento a queste procedure stragiudiziali assai diffuse in età tardo-antica, cui l'amico Modrzejewski ha dedicato un ampio saggio in tempi ormai lontani[4], e che in anni anche successivi sono state oggetto di rinnovata indagine da parte di altri studiosi quali K.-H. Ziegler, D. Simon o S. Allam.

Ma su queste diverse "vie della giustizia", nelle quali si può plausibilmente inquadrare il documento viennese esaminato dal Morelli e che dagli editori di testi papirologici vengono spesso indicate genericamente sotto il nome di "arbitrati", è necessaria forse maggiore cautela, dal momento che si ha un arbitrato solo quando le parti coinvolte in una lite sono d'accordo nel demandare a terze persone di loro fiducia – gli arbitri appunto – la risoluzione della controversia.

Al riguardo, ancora S. Allam in un interessante saggio pubblicato anni addietro[5], sulla scia già tracciata da altri storici dei diritti antichi e in particolare dal già citato Schiller, richiama accanto all'arbitrato almeno altri due diversi modi utilizzati nell'Egitto tardo antico per risolvere una lite al di fuori del processo, che nella terminologia giuridica inglese vengono rispettivamente qualificati come

---

2 Per quanto riguarda i dubbi sulle funzioni giurisdizionali del pagarca, sostenute da parte della dottrina più risalente, si veda almeno D. Simon, *Zur Zivilgerichtsbarkeit im spätbyzantinischen Ägypten*, in *RIDA* 3e s., 18, 1971, 623-658, più specificamente 638. Vedi anche di recente, R. Mazza, *Ricerche sul pagarca nell'Egitto tardoantico e bizantino*, in *Aegyptus* 75, 1995, 169-242, in particolare 226, dove la studiosa così si esprime: "... I compiti giudiziari e di ordine pubblico sono incerti e paiono comunque essere connessi con questioni riconducibili al fisco".

3 Cfr. *The Courts are no more*, in *Studi in onore di E. Volterra*, I, Milano 1971, 469-502.

4 Cfr. *Private Arbitration in the Law of greco-roman Egypt*, in *JJP* 6, 1952, 239-256.

5 Cfr. *Observations on civil Jurisdiction in late byzantine and early arabic Egypt*, in *Life in a Multi-Cultural Society: Egypt from Cambyses to Constantine and beyond*, a cura di J.H. Johnson, Chicago 1992, 1-8.

"negotiation" e "mediation" o "conciliation": in italiano diremmo "negoziato" o "trattativa" precontrattuale nel primo caso, "mediazione" o "conciliazione" nel secondo caso.

Ora per gli esempi raccolti dal Morelli, che rinviano più o meno direttamente a queste differenti soluzioni stragiudiziali delle liti, bisognerebbe riesaminare con attenzione ogni singolo caso e questo non spetta certo a chi vi parla quale semplice respondente.

Dal canto mio mi limito ad osservare che, almeno per quanto concerne il documento viennese inedito che il Morelli ci ha presentato, si possa escludere qualsiasi riferimento diretto ad un arbitrato, dal momento che a questo punto della vicenda non risulta ancora alcun accordo tra le parti per la scelta di un terzo quale risolutore della controversia, che vede protagonisti l'ignoto *grammatêphoros* e gli altrettanto sconosciuti suoi avversari. Ciò non significa che il *dioikêtês* Senouthios non possa in seguito avere indicato tale via ai contendenti – come d'altronde suggerisce lo stesso Morelli in altro punto della sua relazione –, tanto più che proprio al *dioikêtês* spesso sono demandati in questa tarda età compiti di tipo arbitrale, ma questa rimane soltanto un'ipotesi, dal momento che non conosciamo ciò che poi è accaduto.

In conclusione, penso piuttosto – come già ho detto all'inizio – ad una comunicazione non ufficiale inviata da Taurinos, che può ben essere un alto esponente della pagarchia, ma che agisce in questo contesto non tanto come funzionario dell'amministrazione statale bensì quale persona di certo assai influente, cui si è rivolto per esporre le proprie lagnanze il latore della missiva, che con questa lettera di raccomandazione potrà trovare giustizia presso il *dioikêtês* Senouthios o forse no.

Il fatto poi che Taurinos, in caso di fallimento da parte di Senouthios, chieda di occuparsi direttamente del caso, forse vuol dire soltanto che dalla sua posizione di potere egli sarà comunque in grado di risolvere in un modo o nell'altro l'intera questione.

Un'ultima osservazione, del tutto collaterale e che nulla vuol togliere all'interesse e alla rilevanza dell'indagine, riguarda il termine "istanza", che in un linguaggio curialesco può indicare il grado di giurisdizione, appunto in riferimento all'autorità giudicante, e che il nostro papirologo continua ad adoperare nelle espressioni, "istanza superiore" e "istanza inferiore", anche se nei casi da lui esaminati in realtà di giurisdizione non si tratta: invero questo significato, che pure era contenuto nel codice del 1865, non è più utilizzato nel codice vigente e rimane pertanto la sola accezione tecnica di "richiesta", "domanda", e quindi "domanda giudiziale" propriamente detta.

JAKUB URBANIK (VARSAVIA)

COMPROMESSO O PROCESSO? ALTERNATIVA RISOLUZIONE DEI CONFLITTI E TUTELA DEI DIRITTI NELLA PRASSI DELLA TARDA ANTICHITÀ[*]

Il tema del presente articolo tocca un problema su cui ho cominciato a lavorare solo da poco tempo: in particolare, ho intenzione di analizzare l'opera di Dioskoros d'Aphrodité sotto il profilo giuridico, con la speranza che questo lavoro potrà contribuire alla comprensione dell'esperienza giuridica dell'Egitto tardo antico. M'è sembrato probabile che i litigi tra privati risolti in maniera stragiudiziale, e, quindi, *prima facie*, meno formale, rivelino quale fosse l'uso comune e, per così dire, l'immagine del diritto e dei meccanismi legali tra la gente 'normale'. Dagli archivi attribuiti a Dioskoros, provengono al meno ben cinque interessantissimi documenti relativi alla risoluzione "amichevole" di conflitti[1]; studiandoli, mi è parso naturale esaminarli in un contesto più ampio, quale promana dalla generale tematica delle risoluzioni stragiudiziali dei conflitti nella tarda antichità. Pertanto, i risultati che mi accingo a presentare in questa sede, hanno carattere preliminare; questo articolo è destinato a presentare al lettore, e a me stesso, un ampio panorama – ossia il contesto

---

[*] Ringrazio di cuore Raffaele D'Alessio (Napoli) per aver reso il moi italiano più comprensibile; Petra M. Sijpesteijn (Christ Church, Oxford) per le informazioni sulla prassi islamica e, soprattutto, Bernhard Palme (Vienna) per la Sua critica Risposta alla mia presentazione. Ne ho approfittato tanto durante il *Symposion 2005* a Salerno. Ho tratto profitto anche dei critici appunti di José Luis Alonso (San Sebastian) e del Prof. Józef Mélèze Modrzejewski (Parigi), ai quali sono pertanto grato; v. infr. [ad1]. Tutti gli errori e le incongruenze restano naturalmente miei.

[1] *P. Lond.* v 1707; 1708; 1709; *P. Mich.* XIII 659 + *P. Vat. Aphod.* 17; *P. Mich. Aphrod.* Un altro documento arbitrale copto è stato pubblicato da Leslie S.B. MacCoull, "A Coptic Cession of Land by Dioscorus of Aphrodito: Alexandria Meets Cairo", [in:] T. Orlandi & F. Wisse (Edd.), *Acts of the Second International Congress of Coptic Studies, Roma, 22-26 September 1980*, Roma, 1985, pp. 159-166, 2 pll. [= eadem, *Coptic Perspectives on Late Antiquity,* Aldershot 1993, art. VII]. L'autrice non ha visto in questo documento però un verbale di un arbitrato ma una cessione di terreno, tra altro la congiunzione di due papiri non pare molto sicura. Sull'uso di plurale nel riferimento ai papiri di Dioskoros, Vedi articolo di J.-L. Fournet, "Archive ou archives de Dioscore?" che sarà pubblicato in *Atti* del colloquio svoltosi a Strasburgo in dicembre 2005: *Les archives de Dioscore d'Aphrodité cent ans après leur découverte. Histoire et culture dans l'Égypte byzantine.*

in cui si trovano i papiri di Dioskoros – piuttosto che uno studio dettagliato ed approfondito.

1. Introduzione – compromesso: alternativa al processo[2]?

Spesso, quando si tratta di conflitti tra privati, si pensa che questi debbano necessariamente sfociare in un processo e che la meta naturale di ogni dibattito giuridico sia il giudizio del pretore e, soprattutto per le epoche successive all'età classica, dei diversi funzionari giusdicenti. Sennonché, tale presunzione limita la propria ottica al livello più alto della risoluzione dei conflitti, allorché, nel litigio tra le parti, interviene lo Stato. In molti casi, però, non si giunge a questo stadio, e il conflitto termina nel modo – sembrerebbe – più pacifico: in seguito ad un accordo tra i litiganti.

Ed, infatti, antropologia giuridica e sociologia giuridica – forse anche in modo troppo elaborato – distinguono vari gradi della risoluzione dei conflitti tra gli individui. A un livello più elementare conflitto cessa d'esistere qualora una delle parti abbia deciso di ignorarlo, o sfugga al problema (per es. lasciando il luogo del conflitto), o per rapporti di forza (godendo una delle parti di una posizione dominante sull'altra di modo che sia in grado di imporre a quest'ultima la sua soluzione).

Vi sono, poi, altre tre modalità che c'interesseranno di più in questa sede: (1) la negoziazione, quando le parti trovino, da sole, la soluzione del problema; (2) la mediazione, che richiede l'aiuto di un terzo per trovare la risoluzione. Infine, (3) l'arbitrato, quando le parti si obblighino a sottomettersi alla soluzione proposta da terzi. Il livello più formale è il ricorso al processo: la richiesta d'aiuto al potere giurisdizionale[3].

---

[2] Il problema esposto è stato già trattato da diversi punti di vista da diversi autori, sia giuristi che papirologi; vedi sopratttutto, J. Mélèze-Modrzejewski, "Private Arbitration in the Law of Graeco-Roman Egypt", *JJurP* 6 (1952), pp. 239-256 con una descrizione approfondita dei tipi dei documenti, loro formulazione, procedimento arbitrale. Vedi anche il classico R. Taubenschlag: *Law*², pp. 402-406; K-H. Ziegler, *Das private Schiedsgericht im antiken römischen Recht*, München 1971, in part. capitolo quarto sul diritto giustinianeo e le pp. 263-272 consacrate a *Rechtspraxis*, da ultimo P. van Minnen & T. Gagos, *Settling a Dispute: Toward a Legal Anthropology of Law Antique Egypt*, Ann Arbor 1994, *passim* ma in part. pp. 30-46. Si consultino anche opere che descrivono la figura di arbitrato nel mondo greco ed ellenistico: A. Steinwnewter, *Die Streitbeedigung durch Urteil, Schiedsspruch und Vergleich nach griechischen Rechte*, München 1971 (2ed), §§ 8, 9 e 13; E. Karabélias, "L'arbitrage privé dans l'Athènes classique" [in:] *Symposion* 1995, pp. 135-149 [= *L'assistance dans la résolution des conflits*, *Recueils de la société Jean Bodin* 63, pp. 9-35) e Julie Vélissaropoulos-Karakostas, "L'arbitrage dans la Grèce antique. Époque archaïque et classique", *Revue de l'arbitrage* 46 (2000), pp. 3-26.

[3] Cf. N. Rouland, *Antropologia giuridica*, Milano 1992 (trad. it. dell'originale francese), pp. 298-299; Deborah W. Hobson, "The impact of Law on Village Life in Roman Egypt", [in:] B. Halpern & Deborah W. Hobson, *Law Politics and Society in the Ancient*

La questione che si può porre riguarda i motivi per cui le parti possano preferire una risoluzione del conflitto che non preveda il ricorso all'ausilio del potere istituzionale. Di questo problema vorrei occuparmi nel presente saggio, ribadendo in premessa che i risultati, che ho intenzione di presentare, sono solamente preliminari; la mia ricerca si limita al periodo tardo-antico, e, in particolare, a quello giustinianeo e post-giustinianeo. Le ragioni che giustificano una tale circoscrizione del tema sono varie: in primo luogo, come già accennato, questo studio dovrebbe dare sfondo alla ricerca sugli archivi di Dioskoros. L'altro argomento è anche ovvio: Ugo Zilletti, non senza ragione, chiamò l'ultimo capitolo del suo noto libro *Giustiniano legislatore sul processo*[4]. La tendenza unificante e riformatrice dell'imperatore s'evidenzia non solo tramite lo sforzo interpolatorio verificabile nei testi del *Digesto* e nelle vecchie costituzioni collocate nel *Codice*, ma anche tramite una serie di testi legislativi da lui stesso voluti. Il *corpus* giustinianeo ci offre, pertanto, un punto di riferimento abbastanza omogeneo e ben definito. Infine, la maggioranza dei papiri che documentano questo tipo di soluzione dei conflitti proviene proprio da quell'età. Gran parte degli oltre ottanta documenti che, in qualche maniera, riguarda il problema delle transazioni, come più avanti sarà specificato, (fra poco cercherò di definire che cosa intendo con questo termine generico) proviene dal periodo postclassico. Di questi ultimi, la maggior parte è databile tra il sesto e il settimo secolo dopo Cristo. Bisogna chiedersi se mai si sia verificato qualche cambiamento che abbia causato questo numero elevato di convenzioni.

1.1. Questioni terminologiche

Prima di proseguire, vorrei chiarire brevemente i problemi terminologici sulle questioni dogmatiche in materia. Per il diritto romano *compromissum* / compromesso ed anche la *transactio conventio* ovvero convenzione / accordo, sono figure giuridiche diverse. Il primo si concreta nell'accordo con cui le parti si obbligano a risolvere la loro controversia amichevolmente mediante l'aiuto di qualche arbitro scelto da loro[5]; mentre l'altra figura descrive il finire della

---

MediterraneanWorld, Sheffield 1993, pp. 193-219 sulle pp. 199-120; P. van Minnen & T. Gagos, *Settling a Dispute* (cit. n. 2), in part. 30-32; S. Allam, "Observations on Civil Jurisdiction in Late Byzantine and Early Arabic Egypt", [in:] Jannet H. Johnson (ed.), *Life in the Mutli-cultural Society: Egypt from Cambyses to Constantine and Beyond*, Chicago 1992, pp. 1-9, sulla p. 3.

4 U. Zilletti, *Studi sul processo civile giustinianeo*, Milano 1965.

5 Il diritto classico presuppone l'uso delle reciproche stipulazioni penali per assicurare l'adempimento dei doveri assunti nel *compromissum* (cf. le parole dell'editto "*pecuniam compromissam*" attestate dal commento ulpianeo, D. 4.8.11.2, Ulpianus 13 *ad ed.*). Questa struttura del negozio è ancora molto ben visibile in diritto dioclezianeo. Un esempio significativo ne dà un rescritto di Diocleziano e Massimiano indirizzato a Petronia, C. 2.55(56).3 (a. 290 o 293): *Arbitrorum ex compromisso sententiae non obtemperans, si sordes vel evidens gratia eorum qui arbitrati sunt intercessit, adversus filiam tuam agentem ex stipulatu exceptione doli mali uti poteris. sed et ex doli clausula,*

controversia, tramite rinuncia alle azioni spettanti ad entrambe le parti. In particolare, la *transactio,* che, in tempi remoti si realizzava attraverso reciproche stipulazioni[6], in epoca classica, poteva, almeno teoricamente, tradursi in un patto[7]. Ci porterebbe, però, fuori dal tema scelto tentare di trattare queste due figure in modo molto preciso[8]. Queste forme invero manifestano lo stesso fenomeno socio-giuridico, cioè l'*iter* dell'accordo tra i litiganti che non si rivolgono al potere dello Stato. Visto che mi accingo a presentare il materiale della prassi, userò sia il termine compomesso, che transazione nel loro significato comune – corrispondenti all'inglese *settlement* o tedesco *Vergleich* – senza volere alludere all'accezione tecnica appena esposta. Tale premessa facilita il mio compito permettendomi di esaminare questi documenti in un'ottica d'insieme. Una ragione che potrebbe ancora giustificare questa semplificazione sembra anche consentita dal fatto che i regolamenti di Giustiniano in materia non abbiano trovato applicazione nella prassi, soprattutto perché egli, nella sua passione per la 'classicizzazione' del diritto, voleva resuscitare il *compromissum* e la *transactio* nella loro forma classica, ed invece la prassi già da secoli era andata oltre.

Al fine di indicare la persona del mediatore, il terzo che aiuta a risolvere la controversia, ricorrerò al termine 'arbitro'. E, come si vedrà più avanti, quest'apparente semplificazione non è immotivata.

2. Transazioni evidenziate dalla prassi giuridica

Occorre, ora, definire la base delle fonti documentali nella ricerca. Hanno suscitato il mio interesse tutti gli atti che in qualche maniera forniscono informazioni relative alle transazioni tra privati.

---

quae compromissi stipulationi subici solet, filiam tuam convenire non vetaberis. Il passo non solo conferma l'uso delle stipulazioni reciproche, ma anche che la loro formulazione coincideva ancora con quella delle *Tabulae Herculanenses* al meno per quanto riguarda l'incisione della *clausola doli* (*cf. TH* 76; 81; 86 e M. Talamanca, *Ricerche in tema di compromissum*, Milano 1958, pp. 7-17, su questa fonte in part. p. 82sq.).

6 Un perfetto esempio si vuole citare *TPSulp.* 27, *conventio finiendae controversiae.* Quando le parti raggiungono accordo stragiudiziale, il procedimento per la via giudiziaria era già avvanzato: i *cognitores* nominati dagli contendenti avevano già garantito la sua comparazione davanti al magistrato con un *vadimonium.* In questo momento dunque reciproche stipulazioni penali garantivano nel modo migliore che nessuno di loro avrebbe cominciato il processo, o proceduto per esecuzione di *vadimonium.*

7 Così per es. M. Kaser, *Das Römische Privatrecht*², vol. I p. 641-642. Nella prassi documentale però tutte le transazioni furono garantite dalle stipulazioni penali o persino dedotte in stipulazione.

8 Si consultino a questo uopo gli auterovoli lavori romanistici, cfr. per es. *NNDI*, *s.vv.*; M. Talamanca, *Ricerche in tema di compromissum*, Milano 1958, *passim*; M. Kaser *Das Römische Privatrecht*², vol. I p. 584-585; 641-642; diritto postclassico: vol. II, p. 384-385; 445-447.

2.1. *Kompromissa*

Il primo gruppo di documenti viene costituito dai cd. compromessi[9]. La loro caratteristica più evidente è l'applicazione del termine greco-latino *kompromisson* che appare solitamente nella clausola concernente l'accordo e l'indicazione delle parti che l'avevano concluso: τόδε τὸ κομπρόμισσον ποιοῦν[ται πρὸς ἀλλήλους] | ἑκουσίᾳ γνώμῃ ἐκ μὲν τοῦ ἑνὸς μ[έρους Αὐρήλιος Κοσμᾶς] (...) ἐκ δὲ ἑτέρου μέρους Αὐρηλία Μα[ροῦς] (*SB* XXIV 15899 = *SB* I 5266, ll. 5-6 e 9, Arsinoites, 8 agosto 608)[10]. Con questa espressione viene sottolineata la libera volontà di entrambe le parti in contesa, volta a porre fine alla loro controversia e a sottomettersi alla decisione di un arbitro. Le parti solitamente dichiarano di volersi 'processare' (ὁμολογοῦμεν δικάσασθαι ἐπὶ ..., cf. per es. *P. Prag.* I 49.15, Arsinoites 21-22 sett. 628 o 643) davanti alle persone che nominano come arbitri della loro causa[11]. La formulazione dell'atto non lascia più spazio alla narrazione sulla natura e sulle circostanze della controversia.

Infine, i documenti continuano con una clausola importante con cui le parti si vincolano al verdetto pronunciato dall'arbitro scelto. La chiusa "ἐμμεῖναι" (per. es. *SB* XIV 12194, ll. 19-20: ὁμολογοῦμεν ἐμμεῖναι τῇ διδομένῃ ἡμῖν παρ' αὐτῶν δίκῃ)[12] è anche ben attestata nelle fonti giuridiche. Giustiniano nell'anno 529 prometteva l'esecuzione dell'arbitrato tramite un'*actio in factum/actio in rem utilis* o *condictio ex lege*, a condizione che nel documento di compromesso le parti avessero usato il verbo attestato dai papiri, cioè appunto ἐμμεῖναι o simili[13]. È ovvio che

---

[9] Vedi soprattutto J. Modrzejewski, "Private Arbitration" (cit. n. 2), pp. 241-243 con una descrzione del formulario tipico del *kompromisson*. Una breve introduzione è contenuta anche nell'articolo di L. Migliardi & K.-H. Ziegler, "Un nuovo compromesso dall'Egitto romano: PUG inv. N. 1126", *RIDA* 18 (1971), pp. 554-555.

[10] Su questo papiro vedi d'ultimo, B. Palme, "Die Witwe und der Grundherr,. Aurelia Marous in *SB* I 5266 und 5271", *Aegyptus* 76 (1996), pp. 93-99. Altre clausole di compromesso, cf. *BGU* I 309.6-7 (20.03.602, Arsinoites); 315.5-7 (22.07.627, Arsinoites); *SB* XIV 12194.7-9 (Arsinoites, prima metà del VII); SB I 5681.4-10 (Arsinoites, 8.06.654 o 669). Una ricchissima formulazione piena di sinonimi, pleonasmi e ornamentazioni, davvero 'dioskoriana': *P. Lond.* V 1707.2-3 (5.10.566, Antinoopolis).

[11] Cf. anche *SB* XIV 12194.16; *BGU* I 315.10-11 (22.07.627, Arsinoites), con una formulazione un poco diversa.

[12] Altri papiri conservanti l'intera formula usano applicano anche il verbo στέργω vedi *BGU* I 315.15-17 (22.07.627, Arsinoites) *P. Prag.* I 49 (Arsinoites, 21.09.623 o 22.09.643); *SB* I 5681.32-34 (Arsinoites, 8.06.654 o 669): καὶ ὁμολογοῦσιν στέρξαι καὶ ἐμμέναι τῇ διδομένῃ αὐτοῖς παρ' αὐτῶν δίκῃ.

[13] C. 2.55(56).4 (Iustinianus Demostheni p.p. (a. 529): 4. *Et in his omnibus casibus liceat vel in factum vel condictionem ex lege vel in rem utilem instituere, secundum quod facti qualitas postulaverit.* (...) 6. *Si quis autem post arbitri definitionem subscripserit* ἐμμένειν *vel* στοιχεῖν *vel* πληροῦν *vel* πάντα ποιεῖν *vel* διδόναι *(graecis enim vocabulis haec enarrare propter consuetudinem utilis visum est), etsi non adiecerit* ὁμολογῶ, *et sic omnimodo per actionem in factum eum compelli ea facere quibus consensit. qualis enim differentia est, si huiusmodi verbis etiam* ὁμολογῶ *adiciatur vel huiusmodi vocabulum*

l'imperatore è ricorso alla comune prassi giuridica: questo è messo in evidenza dal fatto che la costituzione venne indirizzata al prefetto del pretorio, Demosthenes. Evidentemente, però, il riconoscimento da parte del *Reichsrecht* non ha bastato. Tutti i compromessi sono rafforzati da una *poena compromissi*, dal valore solitamente elevato, che sarebbe gravata sulla parte che non avesse obbedito al verdetto degli arbitri[14]. Questo fatto dipende naturalmente dalla solita articolazione pregiustinianea del *compromissum*, per la quale era essenziale la *stipulatio poenae*, ma conferma anche il fatto, invero noto, che la prassi giuridica avrebbe fatto ricorso a tutti i modi possibili per garantire l'esecuzione del negozio giuridico.

Allo stesso modo si lascia interpretare un'ulteriore garanzia in forma di giuramento alla santa Trinità e al Genio e alla Vittoria dell'imperatore. Queste promesse solenni, in ogni caso, ricorrono, come vedremo più avanti, ancora nel periodo in cui erano già state proibite da Giustiniano. L'imperatore ha ordinato alle parti di accontentarsi della stipulazione della pena contrattuale per evitare un possibile spergiuro laddove una delle parti del compromesso non avesse voluto ottemperare alla sentenza dell'arbitro[15]. Abbiamo, dunque, ancora una volta, una testimonianza di quanto i privati, nell'intessere i loro rapporti giuridici, non si fidassero della normativa della legge, preferendo rimettere l'efficacia di quanto convenuto alla protezione del divino.

2.2. *Dialyseis*

Il secondo gruppo delle testimonianze viene costituito dalle transazioni vere e proprie: a differenza dei *kompromissa* appena presentati, essi certificano una soluzione del problema già consolidatasi con o senza il tramite di una mediazione. Gli atti stessi si chiamano solitamente *dialysis* o *homologia dialyseon*, *vel sim.*[16] e dal punto di vista giuridico costituiscono delle *transactiones*. Segnatamente, alcuni

---

transmittatur? Cf. D. Simon, *Untersuchungen zum justinianischen Zivilprozeß*, München1969, pp. 207-211.

[14] Sulla *poena compromisi* in generale vedi il classico libro di M. Talamanca, *Compromissum* (cit. n. 2) pp. 139-152.

[15] Nov. 82.11.1 (a. 539): *Et quia cognovimus ex rerum esperimento incautum hoc esse, sancimus de cetero nullum fieri omnino iudicem arbitralem et cum iurisiurandi cautione indicare, ne ex hoc in periurium invitum incidant homines propter iudicum ignorantiam peierare compulsi, se omnino qui iudicem aut iudices eligunt cum poena eligant eos, quantenus partes adinvicem coeant et necessitatem habeant aut contentae esse iudicio, aut si retractare voluerit alter, det multam, et sic licentiam habeat discendere ab his quae iudicata sunt et ad aliud venire auditorium.*

[16] Vedi per es. *P. Dublin* 34 (Arsinoe, 511), *P. Mich.* XIII 659 + *P. Vat.* 17 (Aphrodité, seconda quarta del VI sec.) o eseguiti negli ultimi decenni del sesto secolo: *P. Münch.* I 1 (Syene); 7 (Antinoopolis) e 14 (Syene); altri formulazioni: *CPR* IX 11 (Hermoupolis, VI sec.) and *SB* VI 8988 (Apollonopolis Magna, 16.07.647): διαλυτικὴ ὁμολογία; *P. Münch.* I 7: ἀντισυγγράφη διαλύσεις; *P. Lond.* V 1731 (Syene, 585): ὁμολογία ἀμεριμνείας; Sul formulario vedi A. Steinwenter, "Das byzantinische Dialysis Formular", [in:] *St. Albertoni* I, pp. 73-94.

di questi papiri, in linguaggio bizantino ricco ed iperbolico, raccontano la storia del conflitto, mostrando le radici della controversia, la sua lunga durata, l'impossibilità di trovare una soluzione, gli sforzi delle parti di convenire in giudizio, e infine, il felice intervento di uno o più arbitri, che possono restare anonimi o essere menzionati. Questa è la mediazione, o in greco *mesiteia*, di buoni uomini, o amici. Qualche documento viene stilizzato come un protocollo di udienza davanti all'arbitro, con l'"attore" che presenta le sue pretese e il "convenuto" che vi si oppone[17].

Infine, naturalmente, i documenti riportano l'arbitrato, che le parti accettano e si obbligano ad eseguire. Il suo adempimento è sempre garantito da una pena convenzionale e spesso anche da un giuramento. A questo fa seguito la reciproca (se il documento è redatto in plurale) o l'unilaterale (quando solo una parte della controversia scrive all'altra) rinuncia alle azioni, con cui convenzionalmente, qualche volta in modo molto elaborato, le parti abbandonano ogni pretesa ed azione legale, piccola e grande che sia, prevista o imprevista, attuale e futura, nel foro e fuori la corte, non solo tra di loro ma anche a nome dei successori, eredi e subentranti[18]. Occorre ricordare a questo punto che, in senso lato, potremmo includere nel gruppo anche transazioni avvenute senza esplicito arbitrato o mediazione. Tale allargamento della categoria accoglierebbe tutti i papiri in cui le parti promettono di abbandonare ogni azione o pretesa riguardo a cause nei confronti della loro controparte. La differenza consisterebbe nella funzione preventiva di

---

17 Cf. soprattutto la serie dei documenti provenienti dall'archivio di Patermouthis (*P. Münch.* I 1; 6; 7; 11; 14).

18 V'è sempre la promessa di non procedere in giudizio contro l'altra parte dell'accordo: ὁμολογῶ [μὴ ἐγκαλεῖν πρός σε καὶ μηδ]ένα λὸγον ἔχειν με ... cf. per. es. *SB* VI 9456 ll. 16-17 (Arsinoe, 20.09.594) o una simile μὴ ἐξεῖναί μοι ποτε κ(αι)ρ[ῷ] [ἢ χρό]νῳ ἐνάγειν σοι, *P. Lond.* V 1728.15-16; Syene; 8.03.584 o 585). Una formulazione particolarmente ricca ed illustrativa si trova in *P. Münch.* I 1.32-42: ἔπειτα δὲ ὁμολογοῦμεν μηδένα λόγον ἔχειν πρὸς σὲ τὸν προειρημένον Ἰάκωβον τὸν ἀδελφὸν ἡμῶν μηδὲ ἕξειν περὶ τῆς προχρείας τῆς ὑπολειφθείσης παρὰ τοῦ μνημονευθένος Δίου πατρὸς ἡμῶν μηδὲ περὶ οἱουδήποτε πράγματος προσήκοντος τῇ πατρῴᾳ ἡμῶν κληρονμίᾳ μικροῦ ἢ μεγάλου νοηθέντος ἢ μὴ νοηθέντος λεχθέντος ἢ μὴ λεχθέντος ἐλθόντος εἰς μέσον ἢ μὴ ἐλθόντος ταγέντος ταύτῃ τῇ διαλύσει ἢ μὴ ταγέντος. ἁπλῶς οὐκ ἐπελευσόμεθά σοι οὐχ ἡμεῖς αὐτοὶ κληρονόμοι ἡμῶν οὐ διάδοχοι οὐ διακάτοχοι μηδὲ ἐνάξωμέν σοι μηδὲ κληρονόμοις σοῖς ἢ διαδόχοις ἢ διακατόχοις μηδὲ ἐγκαλέσωμεν μηδὲ παραβαίνωμεν ἢ παρασαλεύσωμεν ταύτην τὴν διάλυσιν ἐν τῷ νῦν καὶ ἐν μηδενὶ καιρῷ κατὰ μηδένα τρόπον ἢ ἀφορμὴν ἢ μέθοδον ἢ εὑρεσιλογίαν ἐν δικαστηρίῳ μηδέ ἐκτός δικαστηρίου ... Un'altra bella parallela si trova in un documento di mezzo secolo anteriore: *P. Mich.* XIII 659.241-256. Giova anche osservare assomiglianza di questa con l'intero *P. Lond.* V 1717 (periodo antinopolitano di Dioskoros); tutto il testo conservato costituisce, infatti, una lunghissima clausola di rinuncia, rafforzata da un giuramento. È possibile dunque questo documento costituisce di una transazione vera e propria. Forse appunto la l'"iperbolazione" della clausola del documento originale aveva convinto il noto poeta d'Afrodité di farsene una copia, un possibile modello per la sua prassi notarile.

questi atti. Mentre la *dialysis* vera e propria viene fatta per porre fine ad una controversia, questi atti – che, tra l'altro, in età bizantina utilizzano la stessa formula di rinuncia delle pretese delle transazioni in senso stretto (chiamandosi anche loro *dialysis* o *homologia dialyseos*) – sono tese ad evitare una controversia futura. Basta ricordare in proposito i cosiddetti contratti di divorzio che non erano fatti allo scopo – o, comunque, non allo scopo primario – di attestare l'avvenuto divorzio, ma per regolare i conti tra gli ex-sposi, e come prova della rinuncia delle reciproche pretese[19].

2.3 Altre testimonianze

Infine, si devono richiamare alla memoria tutti gli altri papiri che ci danno informazioni sulla risoluzione pacifica di conflitti tra privati. Innanzitutto, questo terzo gruppo accoglierà i documenti connessi direttamente con il procedimento arbitrale. Tra quelli posto speciale tengono le sentenze degli arbitri. Dallo studio di Federico Morelli a loro dedicato nell'introduzione a *P. Paramone* 16 e 17 (entrambi di Herakleopolites, VII sec.) risulta che di questo tipo di documenti restano sorprendentemente pochi esempi. In realtà oltre i due papiri appena citati ci resterebbero solo atri due, *SB* I 4674 e 4712[20], più forse la decisione degli arbitri conservata in *SB* XXII 15764 (Arsinoites, VII sec.). Ma ci sono sentenze arbitrali che sono pervenute ai nostri tempi nel seno di altri atti[21]. Basta ricordare due

[19] Del problema ho trattato nella mia tesi di dottorato (in corso di pubblicazione) sul divorzio nell'Egitto greco-romano e in diritto romano. A tal proposito vedi, per es. *P. Cair. Masp.* II 67154 (Antinoopolis, 527-65): ὁμολογοῦσιν ἀλλὴλοι̣ς (...) μηδένα λόγον ἔχειν μ[ή]τ̣ε ἕξειν ἑκάτερον μέρος πρὸς τὸ ἕτερον μὴ περὶ ἕδνων μὴ περὶ προικὸς μὴ περὶ ἀναλωμά̣[των] γ̣άμων μὴ περὶ σκευῶν ἢ εἰδῶν, μὴ περὶ ἄλλου οἵο̣υ δήπο[τε] πράγματος ἀνήκοντος τῷ̣ κο[ιν]ῷ̣ αὐ[τ]ῶν συνοικεσίῳ̣ τὸ σύνολον, μικροῦ ἢ μελάλου, ἐγγράφου ἢ ἀγράφου, νοηθέντος ἢ μὴ νοηθέντος, ε̣ἰ̣ς̣ νοῦν ἐλθόντος ἢ μὴ ἐλθόν̣[το]ς, ἐνταγέντος ἐν ταύτ̣ῃ τῇ διαλύσει ἢ μὴ ἐντ̣α̣γέν̣το̣[ς]. Cf. anche Modrzejewski, "Private arbitration" (cit. n. 2), p. 256 con gli esempi di altri atti negoziali contenenti la clausola rinunciatoria in nota 171. Possiamo a tal proposito osservare che la clausola presente nei tardo-bizantini atti di vendita svolge però una funzione ben diversa: mentre nelle *dialyseis* proprie questa attesta un finito litigio, in atti di vendita il venditore rinuncia alla proprietà del terreno venduto, rafforzando - si potrebbe dire - la trasmissione del dominio della re venduta al compratore.

[20] Vedi *P. Paramone*, pp. 175-176 dove l'autore analizza i documenti che sono stati ritenuti in dottrina sentenze degli arbitri, generalmente, e non senza ragione, squalificandole come tali. Morelli insiste sulla natura dubiosa di *P. Oxy.* VI 893 (tardo VI-VII sec. = *Chr. Mitt.* 99), un τύπος, in cui gli uomini caratterizzati come μείζονες possono agire "nell'ambito delle loro funzioni istituzionali", non neccesariamente come arbitri tra i privati, vista soprattutto la natura del loro verdetto: si decide che una delle parti potrà chiedere giuramento dall'opponente (coglie attenzione il fatto che l'"attore" è rappresentato dalla figlia, Sophia). Non è neanche chiara la sostanza di *P. Oxy.* VII 1026 (V sec.) che sembra, *prima facie* una sentenza e rapporto della sua esecuzione.

[21] F. Morelli, *P. Paramone* 16-17, p. 175-176, riportando l'opinione di K.-H. Ziegler, *Das private Schiedsgericht* (cit. n. 2), pp. 136 e 256 sostiene che le sentenza parziale, che

protocoli verbali delle udienze davanti all'arbitro. Il primo, *P. Münch.* I 6 (Syene, 7.06.583 ?), è stato originariamente pubblicato come *Zivilurteil* ma, dopo una ampia discussione in dottrina, e più plausibilmente da interpretare, come verbale con la sentenza di un arbitrato. L'altro esempio è costituito da dioskoriano *P. Lond.* V 1708 (Antinoopolis, 567-568).

Alla comprensione del fenomeno della popularità della risoluzione pacifica dei conflitti in tarda antichità si prestano anche i tardo-bizantini documenti menzionanti *gramatophoroi* discussi da Federico Morelli in questo volume[22]. In queste lettere il mittente, solitamente un ufficiale ammistrativo, come *dioketes* in papiro discusso, chiede al ricevente di render giustizia al latore, che s'era recato da lui per presentare le sue lamentele. Se il destinatario non riuscirà a regolare la controverisa tra le parti, le dovrà rimandare allo speditore, a cui spetterà risolvere finalmente la causa. Tale pratica attesta argutamente reintrepretato da Morelli, *P. Oxy.* VIII 1164 (VI/VII secolo). Theodosios, non avendo trovato esito della controversia su un cammello, rimanda le parti al *comes* Petros.

Infine, occorre anche citare le lettere private contenute in *SB* XX 14987 (Oxyrynchos, prob. sesto secolo), attestante un'epistola del vescovo Leontios che aveva pronunciato il verdetto per una lite concernente l'uso delle tombe. Da pendant

---

"non risolve definitivamente la controversia" non costituisce *sententia arbitri* secondo il diritto classico e poi giustinianeo". Ma i due passi citati del *Digesto* non sopportano una opinione tanto critica. Sia D. 4.8.19.1 (Paulus, 13 *ad ed.*: *Dicere autem sententiam existimamus eum, qui ea mente quid pronuntiat, ut secundum id discedere eos a tota controversia velit, sed si de pluribus rebus sit arbiterium receptum, nisi omnes controversias finierit, non videtur dicta sententia, sed adhuc erit a praetore cogendus*, che D. 4.8.37 (Celsus, 2 *dig.*: *Quamvis arbiter alterum ab altero petere vetuit, si tamen heres petit, poenam committet: non enim differendarum litium causa, sed tollendarum ad arbitros itur.*) non hanno valore assoluto. Il primo passo concerne responsabilità nascente dal *receptum arbitri*. Paolo discute il caso in cui l'arbitro s'era obbligato a risolvere tutte le controversie tra le parti, se non lo fa – come leggiamo nei passi successivi – la sentenza non ha valore, e lui stesso può esser citato in tribunale per non adempimento dell'obbligo accetato. Nel secondo frammento Celso dà solamente una regola interpretativa: anche se la sentenza dell'arbitro nomina solo le parti del dibattito, la si ritiene vincolante pure nei confronti di loro eredi. Nessuno di questi passi, quindi, ostacola la possibilità di una risoluzione parziale della controversia tramite sentenza arbitrale. Quando le parti accettano una soluzione parziale, che è proprio successo nei casi di questi papiri, tale soluzione è perfettamente eseguibile grazie ai giuramenti e le stipulazioni penali prestati (un bel esempio ne troviamo in *P. Münch.* I 7, su di cui vedi *infra*). Comunque una tipologia documentale dipende dal contenuto del documento voluto dalle parti e non dalla validità giuridica dell'atto. E così K.-H. Ziegler confonde categorie nella sua affermazione che "neben dem in P. Lond. 1708 Z. 185ff. wiedergegeben Schiedsspruch ist eine private *sententia arbitri*, deren *Rechtsnatur* zweifelsfrei feststünde, nicht überliefert" (*op. cit.* p. 267): i dubbi non rigaudano infattii la *Rechtsnatur*, ma tutt'al più la *Rechtskraft*.

[22] F. Morelli, "Γραμματοφόροι e le vie di giustizia nell'Egitto tardo antico", pp. 351-372.

fa una clausola documentale di un contratto di matrimonio, *P. Lond.* V 1711 (Antinoopolis, 566-573, altra versione *P. Cairo Masp.* III 67310) dove si menziona appunto che eventuali colpe della moglie avrebbero dovuto essere provate da almeno tre uomini di fiducia[23].

3. Anatomia di un compromesso

Come sarebbe stata conseguita la risoluzione extra-processuale di un conflitto? La storia delle individuali controversie può esser ricavata da diversi documenti. Come introduzione al problema ci servirà, un modest sommario di un intero set dei papiri che presenta una lite sin dalla sua preistoria. Questo archivio bilingue (pare probabile che i documenti fossero accumulati nei tempi antichi e separati solo dai scavatori di *sebakh*), studiato da Arthur A. Schiller nel secolo scorso[24], consiste di un lungo arbitrato copto tra diacono Ioannes ed un certo Tsokar da un lato, e Thekla e Philemon d'altro (*P. Bu.* = *KSB.* I 36), nonché due documenti greci (*SB* VI 8987, Oxyrynchos – 644-645: trasferimento della proprietà della casa – oggetto della controversia – a Thekla e Philemon, e VI 8988, Apollonopolis Magna – 16.07.647: *dialysis* risultante dal menzionato arbitrato copto)[25].

Vediamo, dunque, come venticinque anni prima dell'esecuzione degli atti, una certa Thekla figlia di Iakobos Kana aveva ipotecato la propria casa a favore di Philemon e sua moglie, Thekla figlia di Apa Dios, per garantire la restituzione da loro ottenuto prestito di un *holokottinos* d'oro. Negli anni successivi, Thekla figlia di Iakobos Kana, trasferitasi a nord, morì affidando la cura del proprio patrimonio e

[23] Cf. ll. 29-33, e commento di J. Modrzejewski, "Private arbitration" (cit. n. 2), p. 243 e le note 37 & 38. Si deve però notare la differenza tra il compito di arbitri in casi soliti e questi tre (o più*) axiopistoi andres.* Qua si tratta non di mediatori tra i litiganti ma piuttosto di inspettori del morale della donna.

[24] Vedi il sommario in A.A. Schiller, "The Interrelation of Coptic and Greek Papyri: *P. Bu.* and P. BM Inv. Nos. 2017 and 2018" [in:] H. Braunert, *Studien zur Papyrologie und Antiker Wirtschaftsgeschichte Friedrich Oertel zur 80. Geburstag gewidmet*, Bonn 1964, pp. 107-117; nonché l'altra versione del saggio "The Budge Coptic Papyrus of Columbia University and Related Greek Papyri of the British Museum" [in:] J. Wolski, *Actes du Xe Congrès International de Papyrologues, Varsovie-Cracovie, 3-9 septembre 1961*, Wrocław - Varsovie - Cracovie, 1964, pp. 193-200; l'*editio princeps* del papiro in: "The Budge Papyrus of Columbia University", *JARCE* 78 (1968), pp. 79-118, with plates (*http://wwwapp.cc.columbia.edu/ldpd/app/apis/item?mode=item&key=columbia. apis.p1842*), abbreviato come *P. Bu.* (= P. Col. Inv. 600). Sfortunatamente Schiller non scrisse mai il promesso studio sull'arbitrazione e aggiudicazione nell'Egitto bizantino (cf. "The interrelation", p. 108). Sulla possible storia della scoperta, vedi *P. Bu.*, p. 79 e la n. 4; a questo piccolo *dossier* appartiene ancora *SB* VI 8986 (26.01-24.02.641), contratto di matrimonio eseguito ad Apollonopolis Magna tra un certo Herakleides e figlia di Thekla e Phoibammon (cf. *Leuven Homepage of Papyrus Archives*, *http://www.trismegistos.org/ arch_detail.php?tm= 190&i=1*); su archivio di Philemon e Thekla vedi anche S. Allam, "Observations on Civil Jurisdiction" (cit. n. 3), *passim.*

[25] L'edizione originale dei documenti greci: H. Zilliacus, "Griechische Papyrusurkunden des VII. Jahrhunderts n. Chr.", *Eranos* 38 (1940), pp. 84sq.

della figlia al nipote, il diacono Ioannes. Tempo dopo, la coppia dei creditori, essendosi recata ad Ossirinco, concluse un accordo di compravendita con gli eredi della debitrice (la figlia e la vedova del figlio defunto che agivano anche al nome del terzo figlio di Thekla figlia di Iakobos Kana, ancora minorenne), aggiungendo alla somma originariamente prestata altri tre solidi. Ciò nonostante, al ritorno ad Edfou di Philemon e Thekla figlia di Apa Dios, il diacono Ioannes non cedette a loro il possesso della casa, di talché la controversia si aprì ufficialmente. Così arriviamo al protocollo verbale dell'udienza arbitraria tra le parti, il *KSB*. I 36. L'udienza assomiglia a un vero processo: le parti produssero documenti e testimonianze, chiamarono testimoni e s'opposero ai mezzi istruttori della controparte. Gli arbitri, i cui nomi apprendiamo solamente della *dialysis* posteriore, *spectabiles* Marinos e Markianos, interrogarono le parti, e furono da loro indirizzati con orazioni piene di topica retorica processuale. Merita attenzione, per esempio, l'auto-rappresentazione di Philemon come contadino poco pratico di cose giuridiche. Il malvagio diacono, secondo Philemon, voleva sfruttare questa sua deficienza. Allo stesso tempo, le abili argomentazioni dell'"attore" rivelano una sua relativa esperienza del diritto. Ai precisi argomenti legali contro l'affidabilità delle prove presentate dal diacono, vengono aggiunte esortazioni bibliche contro la falsità del chierico, una diretta citazione dal 1 *Tim.* 3.8 (cf. *KSB*. I 36.85-95). Qualche tempo dopo l'udienza, gli arbitri pronunciarono la loro decisione che, però, non ci è pervenuta, ma il suo esito viene realizzato con una transazione che fortunatamente possediamo (*SB* VI 8988). Con questa *dialysis* il diacono rinunciò a tutte le pretese sulla casa, che viene restituira a Thekla figlia di Apa Dios e Philemmon, riconoscendo allo stesso tempo la validità della compravendita.

3.1. La controversia

Vediamo ora come complessa diventa la storia di una controversia, quanto diventa lunga la sua durata e anche i problemi che un dibattito antico porta al lettore moderno. Pure in un caso, come questo, in cui la documentazione è abbondante e quasi completa, restano interrogativi insoluti. Soprattutto, ignoriamo perché le parti hanno scelto la maniera arbitrale di risolvere la loro lite. Nella parte che segue, cercherò di dare alcuni spunti per la questione, premettendo che però, sul tema, almeno per il momento, non è possibile maturare alcuna opinione definitiva.

È teoricamente plausibile che, ancora prima del sorgere dell'eventuale litigio, le parti ne avessero concertato la risoluzione stragiudiziale; ma la nostra documentazione presenta, piuttosto, casi in cui la soluzione pacifica dell'eventuale argomento non fosse stata prederminata: le parti attestano spesso gli sforzi di presentarsi in un giudizio ordinario; né mancano riferimenti al linguaggio tecnico affine al lessico solitamente adoperato per le citazioni in giudizio. Sovente quei litigi nascono da cause lecite (negozi, succesioni, matrimoni); ma si rinvengono anche controversie originate da un illecito, come *SB* VI 9456 (Arsinoe 20.09.594), nel quale si attesta un accordo tra un cuoco, Paulos, accusato di furto da Petros, figlio di

Epimachos, oppure il misterioso caso di un'accusa criminale del vescovo di Lykopolis Kyros e dei suoi due fratelli preti, promossa da parte del diacono Theophilos, e ritirata dopo un arbitrato (*P. Princ.* II 82, Lykopolis – 481)[26].

Tantissimi casi emergenti dalle fonti ebbero una lunghissima durata. Capita che la *dialysis* avrebbe dovuto risolvere controversie accumulatesi per generazioni: a questo proposito basta ricordare alcuni lunghissimi papiri: *P. Oxy.* LXIII 4397 (545), relativo a un accordo tra il monastero di Apa Hierax e la *domus gloriosa* degli Apioni; un documento proveniente dall'archivio di Dioskoros: *P. Lond.* V 1709 (in copto)[27], ed anche i due papiri connessi con suo padre, Apollos, *P. Mich.* XIII 659 + *P. Vat. Aph.* 17 e *P. Mich. Aphrod*[28]. Anche altri documenti copti testimoniano la lunga durata del conflitto: *P. KRU* 39, in cui si parla genericamente di una lunghissima controversia; *KSB* I 36, appena citato, nonché *P. KRU* 45: in quest'ultimo si narra di due sorelle, Abesa e Takum, che conclusero una disputa sulla successione solo dopo 8 anni, allorché, le parti decisero di porre termine alla controversia pacificamente; restava dunque da trovare il modo per farlo.

3.2 I modi di risoluzione

3.2.1 Negoziazione

La soluzione si può trovare ricorrendo a negoziazioni. Anche se le parti non lo ammettono esplicitamente, questa era probabilmente la maniera con cui si scioglievano le controversie finanziarie degli ex-sposi. Pare anche plausibile che così si regolassero i conti tra coeredi[29]; tra altro, anche la dottrina ufficiale raccomandava come soluzione naturale delle cause ereditarie, appunto, quella stragiudiziale, tanto è vero che le *Istituzioni giustinianee* 2.18.3 e Teofilo nella loro *Parafrasi* greca suggerivano di procedere a completare la mancata legittima ἀνδρὸς ἀγαθοῦ μεσιτείᾳ, *arbitratu boni viri*, evitando il ricorso alla *querela ad supplendam legitimam* o *inofficiosi testamenti*. Sia il matrimonio che la cerchia di parenti più

---

[26] Vedi anche il commentario del primo editore del papiro: H.B. Dewing, "A Dialysis of the Fifth Century A.D. in the Princeton Collection of Papyri" *TAPA* 53 (1922), pp. 113-127, nonché il saggio di W. Ensslin, "Ein Prozeßvergleich unter Klerikern vom Jahre 481 (Zu Papyrus Princeton 55)", *Rheinisches Museum für Philologie* 75 (1926), pp. 422-446; correzioni: P.J. Sijpesteijn, "Corrections on Some Princeton Papyri", *ZPE* 68 (1987), pp. 143-148. Per una vicenda simile, vedi Nov. 115 *praef.* che attesta un litigio tra il vescovo di Tloa, Eustathius e Pistus diacono della chiesa di Telmissena. In questo caso però il procedimento si svolse in processo ordinario davanti al tribunale del governatore della provincia, contro di cui sentenza una della parti (o forse tutte le due?) si appellarano.

[27] Cf. commentario a questo papiro W.C. Till, "Erbrechtliche Untersuchungen auf Grund der koptischen Urkunden", *SBWien* 229.2 (1954), p. 216.

[28] A cui è stato dedicato libro di T. Gagos e P. van Minnen, *Settling a Dispute* (cit. n. 2).

[29] Cf. i più significativi: *SB* XXIV 15957 (Oxyrinchites, sesto sec.): una *dialysis* sulla eredità materna (cf. *AfP* 42 [1996]); *P. Ness.* III 22 (2.11.566): divisione dell'ereditià di nonno paterno; *P. Cair. Masp.* III 67314 (Antinoopolis, 569-570): un accordo tra fratelli, con la clausola di rinunciazione: fr. 2 ll. 14-16; *P. Par.* 20 (Panopolis, 14.07.600): accordo tra due fratelli e sorella riguardo il patrimonio di loro genitori.

stretti, spesso fratelli, sembrano disposti ad accordarsi in maniera meno invasiva[30] (il che non esclude delle controversie molto violente anche in quest'ambito familiare, come quelle documentate nell'archivio di Patermouthis). Tra le transazioni proprie, un ottimo esempio di tale *iter* è fornito dal caso del monastero di Apa Hierax e Fl. Apiones, *P. Oxy.* LXIII 4397 (545). L'assenza di terze persone, come arbitri di questa lunghissima disputa su un'ipoteca potrebbe esser spiegata dalla grande discrepanza tra le posizioni delle parti. Un altro caso che probabilmente ebbe termine in modo simile era il litigio tra la monaca Aurelia Tsone e sua madre, forse la donna più litigiosa del tempo, Aurelia Tapia (*P. Lond.* V 1731, Syene, 20.09.585) – anche se in questo caso la presenza di personaggi importanti come testimoni della transazione (due preti, un arcidiacono, un diacono, due *strategoi arithmou*) potrebbe suggerire una loro intromissione già nella ricerca di una soluzione.

3.2.2 Mediazione/Arbitrato

Nella maggioranza dei documenti però, si allude all'intervento di persone estranee, di amici (come in *P. Münch.* I 7), uomini virtuosi (*axiopistoi andres*: *SB* VI 9456, Arsinoe 20.09.594), o spettabili cittadini (*KSB* I 36 + *SB* VI 8988) e alla loro *mesiteia*, mediazione. Quale era veramente il ruolo di queste persone? Chi avanzava l'iniziativa di conciliazione? Ci si può chiedere quanto informale fosse questo intervento? Possiamo formulare solo supposizioni.

Qualche notizia sui meccanismi di individuazione degli arbitri e sulla scelta dell'arbitrato come metodo della risoluzione del conflitto ci è consegnata da diversi documenti. Vediamo, in particolare, che, talvolta, l'iniziativa avrebbe potuto esser intrapresa da una parte della controversia, non esclusa quella che avesse commesso l'illecito da cui fosse nata la controversia. In questo modo, in *P. Ness.* III 57 (sett. 689), il prete Ioannes, marito di Nonna, propone alla moglie di scegliere di commune accordo gli arbitri per giudicare una causa instauratasi tra loro, laddove la moglie, mossa dall'irrefrenabile desiderio di divorziare, si ostinava a rifiutare l'offerta[31]. Similmente, ancora prima di procedere contro suoi fratelli un certo Sousneus in *P. Oxy.* I 131 (sesto secolo) cercò aiuto nella controversia sull'eredità

---

[30] Vedi anche altri atti conclusi sempre nel cerchio famigliare: *P. Lond.* III 997 = *M.Chr.* 365 = *Sel. Pap.* I 61 = *FIRA* III 182 (Hermopolis, 507) – un *kompromisson* per risolvere una disputa tra due fratelli e sorella a riguardo di certe somme pecuniarie (forse risalente ad controversia ereditaria?); *P. Mich. Aphrod.* (*ca.* 537) – una lunga controversia famigliare: *P. Iand* III 41 (Oxyrynchos, nel verso di N. Gonis, *ZPE* 147 [2004], p. 164 eseguito in seconda metà del VI sec.), un *kompromisson* tra due fratelli; : *P.Heid.* VII 404 (Arsinoiton Polis, 5. ott. 629 - 4. ott. 630), sfortunatamente mutilato ma conservando notizia su un disputa tra madre e figlio.

[31] Su questo papiro vedi d'ultimo con la bibliografia mio articolo „A Priestly Divorce in the Seventh Century Palestine: Various Legal Orders at Work (the Case of P. Nessana III 57, a. 689)" [in:] Z. Służewska & J. Urbanik [ed.], *Marriage: Ideal – Law – Practice. Proceedings of a Conference Held in Memory of Henryk Kupiszewski*, Warsaw 2005, pp. 199-218.

paterna e una somma di 110 solidi che, pur dovendo essere divisa tra lui, i suoi fratelli e le sue sorelle, era stata data alla sorella Elisabeth. È, forse, immaginabile che l'ignoto adresato della lettera, che viene indicato come "signore", fosse designato da Sousneus come arbitro nella causa tra lui e suoi fratelli. Ma è anche possibile che il "signore" fosse stato già nominato come arbitro dalle parti. Più spesso, comunque, i litiganti dichiarano d'aver scelto i loro arbitri di comune accordo. Si può ipotizzare anche che, talora, volta le mediazioni avessero luogo grazie all'intromissione di altre persone. Un esempio molto significativo ci viene fornito – anche se datato a un'epoca anteriore a quella di cui mi sto occupando in questa sede – da *P. Oxy* VI 903 (tardo IV sec.). Questo papiro ci conserva la denuncia d'una cristiana maltrattata dal marito. Nel documento vengono ricordati gli anteriori tentativi di riconciliazione promossi dal vescovo. In seguito, lo sposo, promettendo, per il futuro, di mostrare maggior riguardo nei confronti la vittima, aveva dato seguito al contratto nuziale, finché, dopo qualche tempo, non tornò a consumare nuove violenze ai danni della moglie. La storia della fallita mediazione ci viene appunto tramandata dal papiro[32].

Atteso, comunque, che tutti i *kompromissa* pervenuti finora contengono l'obbligo di sottomissione al verdetto del mediatore, azzarderei l'ipotesi che, laddove si riscontra la collaborazione da parte di terzi alla soluzione di conflitto, i litiganti erano formalmente obbligati a seguire il verdetto dell'arbitro. Questo dovere, in particolare, è accettato dalle parti tramite pene pecuniarie e giuramenti, atteso che Giustiniano in *Nov.* 82.11 lascia alla parte insoddisfatta dalla decisione, la possibilità *ad aliud venire auditorium*. Dunque – in una terminologia di antropologia giuridica – tutti questi casi saranno stati arbitrati e non mediazioni.

3.2.2.1 Arbitri

Il numero degli arbitri varia. Da uno fino a sei (come in *SB* I 5681 [Arsinoites, 654/669], che comunque doveva essere un caso eccezionale). Spesso ce ne sono due o tre. Chi veniva scelto come arbitro? La prassi giuridica ci offre un ampio panorama di tipi di mediatori. In casi estremi di "informalità" il compito di arbitro poteva, forse, essere assunto anche da donne; invero, il gentil sesso non appare mai nei documenti; ma è verosimile che esse si intromettessero nei conflitti degli altri: lo dimostra lo sforzo legislativo di Giustiniano che ne proibì la presenza[33]. La scelta di

[32] Vedi tra altri D. Monseratt, *Sex and Society in Graeco-Roman Egypt*, London 1996, pp. 99-100, ed mio articolo in corso di stampa in *Studi Labruna* (Napoli 2007): "La repressione constantiniana dei divorzi: la libertà dei matrimoni trafitta con una forcina".

[33] C. 2.55.6: *Sancimus mulieres suae pudicitiae memores et operum, quae eis natura permisit et a quibus eas iussit abstinere, licet summae atque optimae opinionis constitutae arbitrium in se susceperint vel, si fuerint patronae, inter libertos suam interposuerint audientiam, ab omni iudiciali agmine separari, ut ex earum electione nulla poena, nulla pacti exceptio adversus iustos eorum conventores habeatur. Iust. A. Iohanni pp.* (a. 531 d. k. sept. Constantinopoli post consulatum Lampadii et Orestae).

personaggi molto comuni è confermata, quantomeno in modo indiretto, dal divertente passo di Ulpiano, D. 4.8.21.11, che esclude la responsabilità di quella parte che, essendosi obbligata ad apparire innanzi all'arbitro, non lo abbia fatto, dal momento che l'arbitro aveva scelto come sede d'udienza un luogo poco dignitoso (una *popina* o persino un *lupanar*)[34]. Il valore meno conviviale hanno "buoni amici" (*philoi agathoi*, *P. Mich. Aphrod.*, 537) o "virtuosi uomini" (*SB* VI 9456, Arsinoe, 20.09.594), ed ancora di meno *spectabiles cives* (*SB* VI 8988, Apollonopolis Magna: 646). Con i chierici (come Apa Ol in *BGU* I 315 [22.07.627, Arsinoites], vescovo Leontios, due apa – oltre 4 altri arbitri – in *SB* I 5681 [Arsinoites, 654/669], presbyteros Seren in *P. Münch.* I 14), passiamo a personaggi più formali che coprivano anche incarichi semi-ufficiali o ufficiali. Talvolta, la mediazione viene affidata a giuristi di professione: *P. Lond.* III 992 (Hermopolis, 25.06-24.07.507) and in *P. Lond.* V 1707 (Antinoopolis, 5.10.566): curiosamente in entrambi i casi si parla di σοφώτατοι σχολαστικοὶ καὶ (συνηγόροι) φόρου Θηβαΐδος. Dioskoros stesso era autore di *P. Lond.* V 1709 (*ca.* 570, Antinoopolis), redatto in copto. In *P. Münch.* I 6 la mediazione viene amministrata dallo scholastikos Markos. In *P. Münch.* I 1, invece, le parti scelgono il collegio dei *devoti priores*, quindi dei militari, per definire la loro contesa. I documenti copti spesso hanno come arbitro un impiegato: *dioiketes* (questi appare anche in documenti greci con *grammatophoroi*) o *lašane*, in alcuni, come *P. KRU* 36, vengono menzionati *nog rôme*, "grandi uomini", che in qualche modo impongono la conciliazione tra le parti; *P. KRU* 44 nomina come *meizontes*: *lašane* and due *nog rôme*. Alla stessa tipologia di arbitri appartengono gli *horistoi* del villaggio che decidono la causa in *SB* XIV 12194 (Arsinoe, 619-629 o 640). Questi personaggi non appaiono normalmente nel mezzo delle controversie tra i privati nella carica del loro impiego; sono piuttosto investiti della fiducia comune, autorevoli nella comunità locale. A volte, nondimeno, leggendo i documenti, si ha l'impressione che gli arbitri, allo stesso tempo, rivestissero una qualche carica ufficiale e che agissero quasi "ufficialmente"[35]. Un

---

[34] D. 4.8.21.11 (Ulpianus 13 *ad ed*). *Sed si in aliquem locum inhonestum adesse iusserit, puta in popinam vel in lupanarium, ut Vivianus ait, sine dubio impune ei non parebitur: quam sententiam et Celsus libro secundo digestorum probat. unde eleganter tractat, si is sit locus, in quem alter ex litigatoribus honeste venire non possit, alter possit, et is non venerit, qui sine sua turpitudine eo venire possit, is venerit, qui inhoneste venerat, an committatur poena compromissi an quasi opera non praebita. et recte putat non committi: absurdum enim esse iussum in alterius persona ratum esse, in alterius non.* Su l'importante problema problema giuridico discusso nella seconda parte della fonte vedi Talamanca, *Compromissum* (cit. n. 2), pp. 92ss. Che il passo era ancora rilevane nei tempi dei compilatori e dopo dimostrano bene gli *Scholia* alla sua parafrasi in *Basilika*.

[35] Ancora di più: pare che ai *dioketai* dei documenti pubblicati e citati da Morelli in questo volume, gli arbitrati siano stati affidati da parte del superiore amministrativo appunto per la loro carica ufficiale. Cf. anche A. Steinwenter, *Studien zu den koptischen Rechtsurkunden aus Oberägypten* (*SPP* XIX), Leipzig 1920, p. 22.

perfetto esempio di ciò è *P. Münch.* I 6:[36] in esso il procedimento assume quasi la fisionomia di un vero processo, al punto che i primi editori lo hanno ritenuto tale. Atteso che Scholastikos Markos, forse identificabile con il *dikastes* Markos presente nel *P. Lond* V 1732 di qualche anno posteriore, chiamato a decidere sulla causa, si comportava come un vero giudice all'atto di ascoltare le parti, condurre l'istanza probatoria ecc. Uguale sembra la posizione di spettabili cittadini Marinos e Markianos che conducono l'istanza documentata da *KSB* I 36. Abbandono, per ora, questo aspetto dell'esposizione, per poi tornarvi al termine della mia presentazione.

3.2.2.2 Le prove in procedimento arbitrale

I documenti rivelano la partecipazione di testimoni, e la loro presenza sembra, talvolta, regolata quasi formalmente. In *P. Münch.* I 6, la testimonianza di un teste unico non venne ammessa, perché, secondo quanto afferma il giudicante, "la legge non ammette la testimonianza di un solo testimone"[37]. Le parti avrebbero potuto servirsi di documenti, e come vediamo dal *KSB* I 36 contendevano l'uso di atti redatti contro le regole giuridiche (Philemon protesta contro l'introduzione delle scritture non sottoscritte, senza testimoni, non registrate ufficialmente). Lo strumento probatorio che venne maggiormente usato era il "giuramento corporale", *sacramentum corporaliter praestitum. P. KRU* 44, per esempio, documenta la conclusione di un litigio tra fratelli per questioni di successione, a mezzo di giuramento pronunciato dal marito dell'"attrice"; questi dichiara che il suocero aveva legato la casa a lei. Così, prestata la promessa solenne, finisce il procedimento arbitrale al pari dei procedimenti giudiziali ordinari.

Un caso interessante è la delega del potere dell'arbitro. *SB* XXII 15764, pubblicato da Klaas A. Worp e Piet Sijpesteijn[38], racconta la storia di un preteso debito: in particolare si narra di Phib e Kiamul provenienti da Pelkeesis che scelsero come arbitri due uomini di Antinoe, obbligandosi con pena a sottostare al loro giudizio. I due arbitri però, nominarono altresì tre concittadini dei contendenti, ai quali venne delegata la decisione su chi avesse ragione, presumibilmente in forza del convincimento che la comune provenienza li avrebbe resi più adatti degli altri due arbitri originari, a scoprire la verità.

[36] Cf. K-H. Ziegler, *Das private Schiedsgericht* (cit. n. 2), p. 267-277; A.A. Schiller, "The Courts are no More", *Studi Volterra*, vol. I , Milano 1971, pp. 469-502; D. Simon, "Zur Zivilgerichtsbarkeit im spätbyzantinischen Ägypten", *RIDA* 18 (1971), pp. 629-657.

[37] *P. Münch.* I 6.59-60: καὶ τὰ παρ' ἑνὸς δὲ μαρτυρούμενα ὁ νόμος παντελῶς οὐ προσίεται. Si deve osservare però che è difficile trovare tale regola in corpus giurisprudenziale giustinianeo, cf. D. Simon, *Untersuchungen zum justinianischen Zivilprozeß*, München 1969, p. 253

[38] P. Sijpesteijn & K.A. Worp, '*Tres faciunt collegium*', *ZPE* 104 (1994), p. 256 (= *SB* I 4672 + 4868 + 4862).

3.3. Arbitrato forzato?

Un meccanismo molto diverso dal modello di accordo commune in arbitrato presentano le lettere menzionati *grammatophoroi* discusse di Federico Morelli in questo volume, che a cui mi sono già riferito in § 2.3. Alla luce di questi papiri quasi non si può parlare di una "risoluzione" pacifica dei conflitti. L'"arbitro" viene scelto dall'ufficiale a cui era venuto qualcuno con una petizione orale di rendere giustizia. In verità non si tratterebbe in questi casi di un compromesso, ma piuttosto di surrogato della giurisdizione ordinaria che potesse esser anche forzata sulle parti (o al meno su una di loro), come dimostra perfettamente *P. Gren.* II 99a (? VI/VII sec.) citato e commentato da Morelli, dove si minaccia Thaesia con incarcerazione se non si presenterà all'arbitrato e poi non adempierà il verdetto dell'arbitro.

3.4 Le soluzioni

Quali erano i fondamenti dei verdetti pronunciati dagli arbitri e delle soluzioni trovate dalle parti da sole in processo di negoziazione? Quanto questi erano conformi alle leggi allora vigenti? Più volte, i documenti fanno riferimento alle norme legislative. E così depone per esempio *P. KRU* 36 in base al quale l'originaria *dialysis* in lite tra Stephanos, Chareb, Abigaia e Elisabeth venne fatta in accordo al *nomos* del *castrum*, tanto è vero che questa *dialysis* sarebbe stata poi contestata da una delle parti, e la controversia avrebbe avuto termine solo col presente documento. Ho già citato il riferimento alle norme legali presente in *P. Münch.* I 6. Anche *P. Mich. Aphrod.* presenta un deciso sapore legale. Nello stesso tempo, però, troviamo nell'opera legislativa di Giustiniano alcune disposizioni che suggeriscono il contrario. In primo luogo, ci ricordiamo della già menzionata disposizione *Nov. 82.11*[39]. Con questa normativa, Giustiniano proibisce il giuramento di obbedienza alla sentenza dell'arbitro, lasciando come unica garanzia la *poena compromissi*. La *ratio legis* per la norma viene presentata nel *principium*: la legge è provocata dai molti casi in cui le parti scelgono, sotto giuramento, *iudices penitus ignorantes leges et experimentum*. La stessa argomentazione può essere dedotta dalla preventiva di Nov. 113.1 che ordina a tutti i giudici (ma anche agli arbitri privati) di seguire solamente le norme generali, non sanzioni pragmatiche o il proprio parere. In caso contrario, le decisioni degli arbitri sarebbero state nulle e le parti non sarebbero state obbligate ad ubbidirle.

3.4.1 Conformità con la legge vigente delle soluzioni pacifiche dei conflitti

Come si confrontano queste notizie con la prassi? Quanto "legali" erano i verdetti? Quando legali erano le transazioni? Possiamo supporre che una delle ragioni per cui le parti preferivano l'arbitrato al processo fosse la speranza di trovare una soluzione conciliatrice non conforme alle disposizioni della legge. Un esempio eloquente di

[39] Cf. anche Talamanca, *Studi* (cit. n. 2), pp. 144-146.

tale comportamento si trova in *POxy*. LXIII 4397. Non va obliterato che la controversia sedata in questo papiro risultava dalla doppia ipoteca costituita da un Diogenes su propri beni: prima a favore di Fl. Strategios II, e poi come garanzia del credito dato a nome del santo monastero di Apa Hierax. Secondo la ben affermata regola giuridica, *prior tempore, potior iure*, i monaci, portando la causa nel tribunale, non avrebbero ottenuto un quattrino dei centocinquanta solidi prestati al disonesto concittadino[40]. La *dialysis*, invece, li sodisfa in pieno. Ugualmente in tante vicende ereditarie troviamo decisioni degli arbitri che mai sarebbero pronunciate dai giudici. Laddove le *dialyseis* definiscono contese familiari tra i figli del defunto e la vedova (spessa genitrice dei suoi contendenti), la madre viene ammessa alla successione al pari dei figli[41]. Particolarmente istruttive sono le vicende di diversi litigi ereditari in cui prese parte Aurelia Tapia, la quale, dopo essersi impossessata illegittimamente dell'intero patrimonio ereditario del marito morto intestato, riuscì nondimeno ad ottenere, attraverso una serie di accordi, una quota ereditaria pari a quella dei figli Kako e Ioannes, all'eredità di Iakobos. Nello stesso archivio la disputa ereditaria tra Kako, Patermouthis e il loro fratello-cognato Ioannes viene risolta in *P. Münch*. I 7 + *P. Lond*. V 1860 (23.06.583, Antinoopolis = *Pap. Eleph. Eng*. D36) senza troppo accurata considerazione delle regole giuridiche. Ricordiamo che l'oggetto di questa lite era, tra altro, la proprietà di un terzo di una casa a Syene. Questo palazzo fu originariamente venduto dalle sorelle Aureliai, Tsone e Tsere a Patermouthis e Kako (*P. Lond*. V 1724 = *Pap. Eleph. Eng*. D32, Syene). Successivamente, la coppia avrebbe trasferito il dominio dell'immobile Iakobos, rispettivamente padre e suocero dei due coniugi, come garanzia di un prestito da lui compiuto. In ogni caso, dopo la morte di quest'ultimo, Ioannes trovò tra le carte del padre defunto il titolo di proprietà e chiese la resitituzione della casa. In un processo civile, il documento avrebbe costituito una prova abbastanza forte per consentirgli l'aggiudicazione di metà della casa in questione. Sennonché l'arbitro denegata ogni pretesa di Ioannes sull'edificio, a suo carico dispose, altresì, l'ordine di consegna dell'atto attestante il titolo di proprietà in favore di Kako e di suo marito Patermouthis[42].

---

[40] Cf. mio articolo "*P. Oxy*. LXIII 4397: Monastery Comes First, or Pious Reasons Before Earthly Securities" [in:] J. Clackson, Anne Boud'hors & Petra Sijpesteijn, *Studies in Memory of Sarah J. Clackson*, in print; su questo documento ed Apioni vedi d'ultimo Roberta Mazza, *L'archivio degli Apioni. Terra, lavoro e proprietà senatoria nell'Egitto tardoantico*, Bari 2001, su *P. Oxy*. LXIII 4397: pp. 134-135; su Fl. Strategios II e Fl. Apion II che sono protagonisti del papiro: pp. 53-68; con la mia recenzione e commento al *P. Oxy* 4397 in *JJurP* 34 (2004), pp. 271-274.

[41] Joëlle Beaucamp, "La transmission du patrimoine: legislation de Justinien et pratiques observables dans les papyrus", *Subseciva Groningana. Studies in Roman and Byzantine Law* 7 (2001) pp. 1-13.

[42] In più largo contesto, vedi le mie considerazioni su questa vicenda: "Tapia's Banquet Hall and Eulogios' Transfer of Ownership as a Security in Byzantine Papyri" che sarà

Un altro esempio di risultati difformi alla legge vigente è dato dall'ammissione di fratellastri e sorellastre, al pari di fratelli e sorelle di pieno sangue, all'eredità dei beni dei fratelli spesso presente nei documenti copti di divisione d'eredità.

3.4.2 L'effettività dei compromessi

Si potrebbe pensare che un accordo concluso con il consenso delle parti dovesse essere più duraturo e che le parti lo rispettassero più volentieri. E forse era così in numerosi casi; ma non dobbiamo dimenticare le lunghe controversie familiari raccontate dai documenti provenienti dall'archivio di Patermouthis[43]. Nonostante i molteplici accordi rafforzati da sanzioni e giuramenti, le parti continuavano a litigare per anni, citandosi anche in un giudizio ordinario. La fine di questo conflitto avvenne solamente con *P. Münch.* I 14, forse a causa dell'aggravamento di salute di uno dei protagonisti (Ioannes dichiara di esser malato) piuttosto che per un'ulteriore mediazione. Lo stesso documento ci fa vedere che le pene pecuniarie per inadempimento delle condizioni del compromesso erano veramente eseguite: si racconta che Ioannes avrebbe dovuto pagare a suo cognato sette solidi d'oro per averlo citato davanti Kallinkos, *vicarius* di Hermonthis, contro i patti delle "*dialyseis* scritte tra Patermouthis, Kako e Ioannes" in cui l'ultimo aveva già rinunciato a tutte pretese verso la sorella e il suo marito. Anche *P. KRU* 36 narra di una fallita mediazione.

4. Perché compromesso?

Arrivando al termine di questa – lo ribadisco – preliminare presentazione, occorre tornare alla domanda posta all'inizio. Per quale motivo il compromesso, la convenzione e la transazione diventano così diffusi nel sesto secolo dopo Cristo? È impossibile dare una risposta semplice, questa situazione era sicuramente dovuta ai diversi fattori.

4.1 La spiegazione di Arthur Schiller e la sua refutazione

Diversi autori hanno cercato di trovare la soluzione, con la proposta più radicale di A. Arthur Schiller. Questi, studiando il materiale papiraceo dell'epoca bizantina, arrivò alla conclusione che, poco prima dell'età di Giustiniano, le corti civili cessarono di esistere in Egitto. Schiller presentò cinque argomenti per suffragare la sua teoria[44]:

---

pubblicato negli Atti di *Recht – Geschichte. Internationales Symposion zum 65. Geburtstag von Peter E. Pieler.*

43 Su questo archivio vedi, oltre la classica introduzione a *P. Mon.* I (ripresa nella ristampa *P. Münch.* I), H.I. Bell, "The Syene Papyri in the British Museum", *Klio* 13 (1913), pp. 160-74; J.J. Farber, "Family Financial Disputes in the Patermouthis Archive", *BASP* 27 (1990), pp. 111-122 (e la bibliorafia ivi citata).

44 A.A. Schiller, "The Courts are no More" (cit. n. 35), pp. 469ss.

1. Non ci sono tracce di processo civile o *per libellis* nei papiri;
2. non ci sono prove che avvocati agissero nelle loro funzioni professionali, e ugualmente è dubbia la loro professionalità ed educazione legale;
3. le decisioni "giurisdizionali" dei magistrati in verità fanno parte del procedimento amministrativo;
4. i rescritti imperiali non sono mai usati (tranne in un caso amministrativo, cioè l'autopragia di Aphrodité);
5. la clausola di rinuncia presente nei documenti bizantini, in ordine alla rinuncia al ricorso delle vie legali (nella corte e fuori la corte), è meramente retorica.

Agli argomenti contrari già presenti in dottrina (l'argomento *e silentio* non è mai abbastanza forte; alcuni papiri potrebbero decisamente essere interpretati come prove d'esistenza del processo)[45], se ne potrebbero aggiungere due circa la professionalità degli avvocati e il loro impiego professionale. Sul punto è eloquente l'archivio di Dioskoros i cui documenti ci forniscono una prova contraria. Possiamo ancora allegare la recente scoperta dell'università tardoantica ad Alessandria dove – come sappiamo dalla vita di Severo di Antiochia scritta da Zacharias Rhetor – s'insegnava anche diritto: se non ci fossero state le corti in Egitto, l'esistenza di questa università con la cattedra di giurisprudenza[45a(v. infr.)], nonché il fenomeno di Dioskoros, sarebbero inspiegabili.

Anche il fatto che nel diritto giustinianeo ci sono tantissime norme sui giudici – che tra l'altro sembrano esser stati provocati dalla prassi – depone contro la tesi di Schiller. È utile ricordare in questo luogo come il legislatore nelle costituzioni giustinianee che stabiliscono le regole per la risoluzione stragiudiziaria dei conflitti, tiene sempre presente un possibile ricorso al tribunale corte. Un perfetto esempio di tale pensiero è consentito da CI. 2.55.(56).5.4. Con questa costituzione si permette di accettare davanti al giudice ordinario il matierale probatorio prodotto già in procedimento arbitrale[46].

Non mi convince il quinto argomento di Schiller. È possibile che in tanti documenti la frase "nel tribunale o fuori tribunale" potrebbe puramente topica. Lo scriba, senza dare un secondo pensiero avrebbe usato le clausole convenzionali che aveva imparato dai vecchi formulari. In alcuni casi si può immaginare che le parti parlando del procedimento "nel tribunale o fuori tribunale" avessero in mente un proprio collegio giudicante. Così in *P. Köln* III 156 (582-602, Antinoopolis ?), un prestito con ipoteca, un asinario Aurelios Psais, prendendo a mutuo 4 solidi, si

---

[45] Vedi soprattutto l'importante critica promossa D. Simon, "Zur Zivilgerichtsbarkeit" (cit. n. 36), pp. 624ss. Colgono attenzione i suoi argomenti circa rilevanza per il processo civile del *defensor civitatis* e *riparius*. Di tale funzione dell'ultimo funzionario convince anche (oltre esempi citati da Simon), *P. Cairo Masp.* I 67092 (Aphrodité 21.09.553). Su questo foglio dioskoriano Irene depone contro un Makarios che aveva rotto promessa di matrimonio e contro la sua madre per ingiurie subite, chiedendo giudizio; v. infr. [ad45].

[46] Vedi K.-H. Ziegler, *Das private Schiedsgericht* (cit. n. 2), pp. 211-215.

obbliga a pagare i costi dell'eventuale litigazione, sia nel tribunale che risolta per strada non giudiziaria (cf. ll. 8-9: ἑτοίμως ἔχω καὶ τὰ [σ]υμβησόμενά σοι διὰ ταύτην τὴν αἰτιαν ἀναλώματα ἢ [κ]αὶ ζημιώματα ἐν δικαστηρίοις [ἢ] ἐκτ[ὸ]ς δ[ι]καστηρίων ὁμολογῶ). Per ricordare un'altro esempio significativo: in *P. Cairo Masp.* II 67161 (28.09.566, Antinoopolis): Aurelia Athanasia autorizza Dioskoros a rappresentarla per la causa ereditaria contro lo zio Theodoros, figlio di Psoios, sia nelle negoziazioni stragiudiali che nei tribunali: εἴ[τε ἐν δικαστερτηρίοις εἴτε καὶ ἐκτὸς δικαστηρίων.

Ci sono tracce del procedimento *per cognitionem* nei papiri tardo-bizantini. Dieter Simon[47] ha letto in *P. Oxy.* VIII 1164 allusioni al processo davanti al *comes,* previa offerta di arbitrato. Anche l'interpretazione di Morelli (vedi *supra* pp. 384-385) di questo papiro concede ricostruzione dell'istanza giuridica davanti al *comes*. Contro l'inesistenza della corti depone anche *P. Münch.* I 14 dove si racconta sulla citazione davanti al tribunale del *vicarius* effettuata da Ioannes contro Patermouthis. L'altro esempio di uguale significato ci è fornito da *PSI* I 76 (Alessandria ma trovato ad Oxyrynchos, 3.05.572 o 573)[48], in cui Flavia Christodote, trovatasi in problemi finanziari, ed avendo meditato di avviare una causa presso il tribunale imperiale, intraprende un processo avverso il banchiere Eustathios davanti al *defensor civitatis* di Alexandria. Durante il suo viaggio a Costantinopoli Dioskoros ottenne per suoi clienti dei rescritti imperiali. La permamenza dei monaci di Apa Hierax nella Capitale (*P. Oxy.* LXIII 4993) poteva anche avere come scopo ottenere verdetti o verdetto della corte imperiale.

In definitiva, la supposta penuria di corti non basta a spiegare l'abbondanza dei compromessi – almeno fino all'invasione Araba in Egitto che naturalmente abolì le corti bizantine.

Anche la seconda ipotesi di Schiller circa la popolarità dei compromessi: gli Egizi – monofisiti – avevano sfiducia delle corti imperiali – melchite, alla luce delle più recenti ricerche sui rapporti tra le confessioni in Egitto, deve essere abbandonata. Le delimitazioni religiose in tarda antichità non erano così rigide e forti, come si supponeva fino a un cinquantennio fa. E basti ricordare a tale proposito alcuni esempi delle transazioni "interreligiose". In primo luogo, il piccolo dossier di *P. Dublin* 32-34 che conserva transazioni tra monaci ortodossi e meliciani dimoranti – occorre ricordare – nella stessa laura[49]. Si possono citare ancora altri esempi. In una transazione, *SB* I 2137 (= *I. Louvre* 9, VI-VII, Thebes) appaiono, senza

---

47 D. Simon, "Zur Zivilgerichtsbarkeit" (cit. n. 36), p. 650.

48 Si consultino gli studi J.G. Keenan, "The Case of Flavia Christodote: Observations on PSI I 76", *ZPE* 29 (1978) pp. 191-209; idem, "On the Law and Society in Late Roman Egypt". ZPE 17 (1975), pp. 245-246; Simon 645. Una nuova traduzione con commento vedi Jane Rowlandson, *Women and Society*, no. 151.

49 Su questi documenti, vedi Ewa Wipszycka, "Monks and Monastic Dwellings. *P. Dublin* 32-34, KRU 105 and BL Ms. Or. 6201-6206 Revisited" [in:] *Studies in Memory of Sarah J. Clackson* nonché il mio "Tapia's Banquet Hall" (cit. n. 38).

discriminazione, come testimoni, personaggi dai nomi ebraici accanto ad un certo Apa Petros. Molto interessante è anche un testo pubblicato come liberazione di *paramone*, ma con funzione di compromesso, *P. Ness.* III 56 (18.01.687). In papiro bilingue (greco-arabo) Al-Aswad ibn Adi libera della servitù figlio di abba Kyrin per 50 solidi: ne 30 Kyrin aveva pagato all'ufficiale arabo, e 20 sono definiti come elemosina (il testo arabo usa l'espressione tecnica: *sadaqa*: a causa di Dio) di Al-Aswad ad abba Kyrin.

4.2 Altre spiegazioni

In qualche istanza, sicuramente, la scelta del compromesso, quale strada più veloce, e forse, anche più definitiva, dipendeva dalla situazione personale di una o di entrambe le parti, così per due volte è la malattia a causare la soluzione dei litigi tra le parti (vedi *SB* VI 9456 e *P. Münch.* I 14). Sicuramente è anche giusta la tesi di Morelli che ha individuato arbitrati forzati in alcuni casi dei compromessi tardo-antici. In queste vicende l'economia processuale portava al devolvere giudizio ordinario, statale, al livello più basso, che forse era più semplice, più veloce, più effettivo. Se supponiamo che gli arbitri delegati avessero conosciuto meglio la situazione delle parti, sarebbe stato più facile per loro che per un ufficiale di livello superiore emanare una sentenza (come *comes* Petros in *P. Oxy.* 1164 o alto funzionario dell'ufficio di pagarcha in P. Vindob. G. 40256).

Ci restano però numerosi casi in cui l'arbitrato è stato sicuramente l'esito di una decisione "amichevole" delle parti. Forse sarebbe meglio guardare più da vicino il contenuto delle controversie risolte in via di compromesso. La maggioranza riguardava problemi patrimoniali familiari, soprattutto le successioni. L'ambito "famigliare" sembra naturalmente, come ho già detto all'inizio, predisposto a risolvere i problemi fuori della corte. Troviamo tormentate vicende concernenti il patrimonio familiare nell'archivio di Patermouthis, o nel piccolo dossier *P. KRU* 34-36. Forse lo stesso si potrebbe dire di tanti compromessi in cui prendono parte gli ecclesiastici, che, in tal modo, evitavano di comparire davanti a un giudice secolare. È vero che la predilezione per l'arbitrato e la mediazione, come metodi di risoluzione dei conflitti, sarebbe persistita nei tempi di dominazione araba, trovando autorità anche nel *Corano*[50]. Il che testimonia che la strada conciliatoria esisteva nei costumi dei popoli arabi: a proposito si può ricordare il già menzionato celebre caso Nonna e il suo marito, presbitero Ioannes (*P. Ness.* III 57), ed esempi nei papiri arabi collezionati da Gladys Franzt Murphy[51].

---

[50] Vedi *Corano* 4:114; 4:127; 2:280 e il saggio (in corso di pubblicazione) di Petra M. Sijpesteijn, "Family Tsorus – A Settlement from the Cairo Geniza (*TS* 24.81)" che serve anche come testimonianza della popularità di soluzione amichevole dei conflitti tra la minorità ebrea e popolazione araba in tempi molto posteriori ai Copti e Bizantini in Egitto.

[51] Gladys Franzt-Murphy, "Settlement of Property Disputes in Provincial Egypt: Early Islamic Period", *Al-Masâq Studia Arabo-Islamica Mediterranea* 6 (1993), pp. 95-105.

La mediazione o l'arbitrato sarebbero stati molto più convenienti del processo, che, invece, avrebbe potuto durare anni, esser molto impegnativo e comportare gravi costi (con il solito ricorso all'appello e alla *retractatio*[52], e con il viaggio alla capitale imperiale). Era quindi più facile proseguire in modo meno formale senza doversi spostare in un'altra sede.

Il compromesso che portava all'arbitrato poteva sembrare la soluzione più naturale anche perché, negli anni, il procedimento arbitrale andava vieppiù formalizzandosi; sicché l'arbitrato poteva risultare – almeno nella percezione delle parti – un'applicazione della giustizia comparabile alla via processuale, e quindi poteva garantire una tutela dei diritti più certa e sicura dell'ordinamento processuale. La visione del tutto informale del procedimento arbitrale che troviamo in *Epitrepontes* di Menandro, di cui copia come è ben noto, s'era trovata nel possesso di Dioskoros, risulta lontanissima dai documenti della prassi tardoantica. È poco probabile che Dioskoros nei suoi compromessi si fosse servito delle immagini che gli offriva questa opera comica. L'arbitro del gioco gioioso, Smikrines, è ugualmente del tutto incomparabile nel suo ufficio con nomikos Markos di *P. Münch.* I 6.

Ed è anche senz'altro importante rendersi conto che l'arbitrato poteva risultare più discreto che il processo pubblico. Sul carattere tendenzialmente intimo e segreto dei problemi portati davanti all'arbitro rifletteva già un passo di Ulpiano nel commentario all'editto pretorio, per spiegare perché il pretore si sarebbe impegnato a constringere l'arbitro a pronunciare la sentenza in una causa pendente davanti a lui[53].

---

[52] Vedi T. Derda & J. Urbanik, "P. Naqlun inv. 27 + 28: a Document Concerning ἀναψηλάφησις / *retractatio* from Fayum Monastery" [in:] J. Krzynówek, Z. Służewska, J. Urbanik & M. Zabłocka, *Au-delà des frontières. Mélanges de droit romain offerts à Witold Wołodkiewicz*, Warszawa 2000, pp. 197-205 con la letteratura ivi citata.

[53] D. 4.8.3.1 (Ulpianus 13 *ad ed.*): *Tametsi neminem praetor cogat arbitrium recipere, quoniam haec res libera et soluta est et extra necessitatem iurisdictionis posita, attamen ubi semel quis in se receperit arbitrium, ad curam et sollicitudinem suam hanc rem pertinere praetor putat: non tantum quod studeret lites finiri, verum quoniam non deberent decipi, qui eum quasi virum bonum disceptatorem inter se elegerunt. finge enim post causam iam semel atque iterum tractatam, post nudata utriusque intima et secreta negotii aperta, arbitrum vel gratiae dantem vel sordibus corruptum vel alia qua ex causa nolle sententiam dicere: quisquamne potest negare aequissimum fore praetorem interponere se debuisse, ut officium quod in se recepit impleret?*

[ad1] La prima versione del presente saggio era promunciata durante il convegno "Discipline cotrattuali e le forme di tutela" a Soverato in settembre 2005: esprimo riconoscenza ai partecipanti per la stimolante discussione.

[ad45] Due altri esempi ancora testimonianti processo in Egitto bizantino nella tarda antichità cita Joëlle Beaucamp, "Difficile et dissimulée: La rébelion contre la famille à Byzance

(4e-7e siècle)" [in:] Marie Theres Fögen (ed.), *Ordnung und Aufruhr im Mittelalter. Historische und juristische Studien zur Rebellion (Iur commune. Sonderhefte: Studien zur Europäischen Rechtsgeschichte* 70), p. 266 e la n. 2. Tutti i due provengono dalle carte dioscoriane. Il primo papiro è un protocollo greco-latino del dibattito processuale davanti al *comes militum* (*P. Mich.* XIII 660+661 + *SB* XVI 12542, Aphrodité o Antinoopolis, prima metà del VI sec.); l'altra testimonianza troviamo in *P. Mich. Aphrod.* dove come luogo dell'accordo viene menzionato in l. 9 κατὰ χώραν πολιτικὸν δικαστήριον.

[45a] Su questo ateneo vedi T. Derda, T Markiewicz & Ewa Wipszycka, Alexandria and the Late Antique Education: Proceedings of a Colloquium in Alexandria, April 2005, Warsaw 2007 (in part. l'articolo di Elżbieta Szabat).

BERNHARD PALME (WIEN)

ANTWORT AUF JAKUB URBANIK

Das Verhältnis zwischen statthalterlicher Gerichtsbarkeit und außergerichtlicher Streitbeendung (Schiedsgericht und Vergleich) im byzantinischen Ägypten ist seit langem Gegenstand kontroverseller Diskussionen in der juristischen Papyrologie. Ausgehend von der Beobachtung, daß die im 4. und 5. Jh. n.Chr. in größerer Zahl überlieferten bilinguen Prozeßprotokolle seit justinianischer Zeit fast völlig ausbleiben, hat Arthur Schiller die provokante These aufgestellt, daß die ordentlichen Gerichtshöfe der Statthalter praktisch aufgehört hätten zu existieren und die private Schiedsgerichtsbarkeit an ihre Stelle getreten sei[1]. Dieter Simon hat dieser These vehement widersprochen und für die Existenz der Statthaltergerichte auch im späten 6. und frühen 7. Jh., solange Ägypten dem byzantinischen Reich angehörte, plädiert[2]. Dennoch: Die merkwürdige Koinzidenz, daß um etwa 530 die Prozeßprotokolle verschwinden, aber gleichzeitig die Zeugnisse außergerichtlicher Streitbeendung, insbesondere Kompromisse und Dialysis-Urkunden, stark an Zahl zunehmen, bleibt ein bislang nicht befriedigend erklärtes Faktum. Die Frage scheint sogar virulenter denn je, da auch bis heute, 35 Jahre nach der Publikation von Schillers Studie, kein Prozeßprotokoll aus nachjustinianischer Zeit aufgetaucht ist, während weitere Kompromisse und Dialyseis publiziert wurden. Es geht dabei nicht um die Beobachtung, wann alte Urkundstypen verschwinden oder neue aufkommen; vielmehr geht es einerseits um Ansichten, wie man sich die Rechtspraxis in einer Provinz des früh-

---

[1] A. Schiller, The Courts Are No More, in: Studi in onore di Eduardo Volterra I, Milano 1971, 469-502, bes. S. 471: „... that state litigation was absent and private arbitration paramount for the settlement of civil disputes"; und S. 502: „... factual disappearence of the courts in Egypt". – Auf das Phänomen hatte vor Schiller bereits E. Seidl, Die Jurisprudenz ägyptischer Provinzialrichter byzantinischer Zeit, Festschrift E. Rabel, Tübingen 1954, II, 235-261 hingewiesen, freilich ohne einen Kollaps des staatlichen Justizsystems zu postulieren.

[2] D. Simon, Zur Zivilgerichtsbarkeit im spätbyzantinischen Ägypten, RIDA 18 (1971) 623-657. Am Rande sei angemerkt, daß auch die früharabischen Papyri amtliche Gerichte und Klageschriften an Beamte bezeugen, s. G. Frantz-Murphy, Settlement of Property Disputes in Provincial Egypt: Early Islamic Period, Al-Masâq. Studia Arabo-Islamica Mediterranea 6 (1993) 95-105. Eine Kontinuität zu den byzantinischen Verhältnissen ist plausibler als ein vorübergehendes Aussetzen staatlicher Jurisdiktion, vgl. auch S. Allam, Observations on Civil Jurisdiction in Late Byzantine and Early Arabic Egypt, in: Life in a Multi-cultural Society: Egypt from Cambyses to Constantine and Beyond, Chicago 1992, 1-8.

byzantinischen Reiches vorzustellen hat, andererseits um die grundsätzliche Frage, wie die papyrologische Evidenz zu werten sei – beides Fragen von nicht geringer Tragweite.

Jakub Urbanik nähert sich dem Thema von der sozialhistorisch-juristischen Seite her. Seine Kernfrage ist: Was sind die Gründe, daß streitende Parteien sich anscheinend nicht mehr an die institutionalisierten Gerichte wenden, sondern in Vergleichen oder Schiedsgerichten eine Lösung des Konflikts suchen? Er untersucht dazu folgende Urkundengruppen, die in den Papyri klar zu fassen sind:

1) Die Schiedsgerichtsvereinbarung (κομπρόμισσον, *compromissum*): Zwei streitende Parteien einigen sich aus freiem Willen vertraglich auf einen oder mehrere Schiedsrichter, verpflichten sich zur Einhaltung des Schiedsspruches und widrigenfalls zu einer *poena compromissi*. Die Schiedsrichter können den Fall durch Spruch entscheiden oder aber einen Vergleich vermitteln. Dies alles entspricht dem im Reichsrecht verankerten *pactum compromissi*. Zur Zeit kennt man etwa zwei Dutzend Papyri, die als *compromissa* (oder eng verwandte Urkunden) gelten dürfen. Sie folgen einem recht stereotypen Formular mit Klauseln, die zum Teil dem römischen Recht entlehnt sind[3].

2) Der Schiedsvergleich (διάλυσις, *transactio*): Die streitenden Parteien einigen sich auf eine einvernehmliche Lösung des Konfliktes, die vertraglich niedergelegt und durch eine Konventionalstrafe gesichert wird. Dialyseis können auf Eigeninitiative oder durch Vermittler (z.B. Mediatoren, Schiedsrichter) herbeigeführt werden. In den Papyri präsentieren sich diese *transactiones* häufig als protokoll-artige Niederschriften stilisiert, die den Konflikt und seine Genese wortreich erzählen. Bislang sind über 40 Dialysis-Urkunden in den Papyri bekannt geworden[4].

3) Der Schiedsspruch (ὅρος, *sententia arbitri*): Ein oder mehrere Schiedsrichter entscheiden die ihnen übertragene Streitsache und legen ihre Entscheidung schrift-

[3] Urkundenliste bei H.-A. Rupprecht, Tyche 12 (1997) 267f. – Literatur zu den Kompromissen: A. Berger, Die Strafklauseln in den Papyrusurkunden, Leipzig 1911, 212-217; J. Modrzejewski, Private Arbitration in the Law of Greco-Roman Egypt, JJP 6 (1952) 239-256; A. Steinwenter, Studien zu den koptischen Rechtsurkunden aus Oberägypten, (SPP XIX), Leipzig 1920, *passim* (s. Index), S. 22-25; ders., Das Recht der koptischen Urkunden, (HdAW X.4.2), München 1955, 53-56.

[4] Urkundenliste bei T. Gagos – P. van Minnen, Settling a Dispute. Toward a Legal Anthropology of Late Antique Egypt, Michigan 1994, 121-127 sowie die Bemerkungen S. 36, Anm. 74-76; hinzu kommen: P.Petra 1, P.Stras. V 494, SB XXII 15768; 15801, SB XXIV 15957; 15958; 16039; 16040; 16126, SB XXVI 16415; 16564. – Literatur zu den Dialyseis: A. Steinwenter, Das byzantinische Dialysis-Formular, in: Studi in memoria di Aldo Albertoni, Padova 1932, I, 73-94; G. La Pira, La stipulatio aquiliana nei papiri, in: Atti del IV Congr. Internaz. di Papirologia, Milano 1936, 479-484; R. Taubenschlag, The Law of Greco-Roman Egypt, Warszawa [2]1955, 403-406. Nicht heranzuziehen sind für unsere Fragestellung die koptischen Vergleiche, die durchwegs aus arabischer Zeit stammen, vgl. W. C. Till, Erbrechtliche Untersuchungen auf Grund der koptischen Urkunden, Wien 1954, 14-27.

lich nieder. Bislang sind acht derartige Schriftstücke bekannt geworden (s. dazu unten). Hinzu treten noch:

4) Indirekte Erwähnungen von Schiedsgerichtsbarkeit in Privatbriefen, Dokumenten des privaten Rechtsverkehrs etc. Hier gibt es wenige Beispiele. Auf diesen Befund wird noch zurückzukommen sein.

Schiedsgericht und Vergleich waren Gegenstand eingehender Studien führender Rechtshistoriker wie Artur Steinwenter, Karl-Heinz Ziegler, Joseph Modrzejewski, Dieter Simon, Arthur Schiller und Mario Talamanca[5]. Von papyrologischer Seite sind etliche Kompromiß-Urkunden ausführlich kommentiert[6] und insbesondere die Dialyseis oft besprochen worden[7]. Zuletzt haben Traianos Gagos und Peter van Minnen auch einige sozialgeschichtliche und rechts-anthropologische Aspekte behandelt[8]. Urbanik greift diesen Ansatz auf und verfolgt ihn weiter, indem er folgenden Fragen nachgeht: Wie kommt man zur außergerichtlichen Einigung? Welche Personen treten als Vermittler auf? Wie groß ist die Zahl der Schiedsrichter und aus welchem Personenkreis rekrutieren sie sich? Wie gesetzeskonform waren die Schiedssprüche? Welche Fälle kamen vor den Schiedsrichter und wie erfolgreich war die Konfliktlösung. Alle Antworten, die Urbanik anbietet, sind zwar plausibel, aber wenig überraschend.

In der zentralen Frage, warum Vergleich und Schiedsgericht im späten 6. und im 7. Jh. anscheinend so beliebt wurden, liegt Urbanik sicherlich richtig, wenn er nach einer multikausalen Erklärung sucht. Überzeugend ist auch sein Ansatz, daß tatsächliche Streitfälle, wie sie die Urkunden überliefern, am ehesten Aufschlüsse über die Rechtswirklichkeit und allfällige Entwicklungen wie ein Vordringen der Schiedsgerichtsbarkeit geben können. Zunächst schließt er sich – wie ich meine, zu Recht – der Meinung Dieter Simons an, daß die Nichtexistenz von ordentlichen

[5] Über die in Anm. 3 und 4 genannte Literatur hinaus seien hervorgehoben: Zur griechischen Schiedsgerichtsbarkeit: A. Steinwenter, Die Streitbeendigung durch Urteil, Schiedsspruch und Vergleich nach griechischem Rechte, (MB 8), München 1925 (ohne Papyri); D. Roebuck, Ancient Greek Arbitration, Oxford 2001, bes. S. 300-343 zu den (ptolemäischen) Papyri (vgl. dazu G. Thür, SZ 100 [2003] 209-211). – Zum römischen Schiedsgericht: M. Talamanca, Ricerche in tema di „compromissum“, Milano 1958; K.-H. Ziegler, Das private Schiedsgericht im antiken römischen Recht, (MB 58), München 1971; D. Roebuck, Roman Arbitration, Oxford 2004 (sehr allgemein).

[6] Vgl. etwa die Bemerkungen in den Editionen folgender *compromissa*: L. Migliardi – K.-H. Ziegler, RIDA 18 (1971) 553-560; P.J. Sijpesteijn – K.A. Worp, ZPE 31 (1978) 127-130; J.G. Keenan, ZPE 75 (1988) 267-271; D. Hagedorn, ZPE 84 (1990) 27-29 zu T.Varie 1; A.B.J. Sirks – K.A. Worp, ZPE 104 (1994) 256-260; M. Amelotti – L. Migliardi-Zingale, PUG I 23; S. van Lith, CPR VI 7.

[7] Ausführlichere Kommentare finden sich in den Editionen folgender Dialyseis: H.B. Dewing, TAPhA 53 (1922) 113-127; B.C. McGing, Tyche 5 (1990) 85-91; T. Gagos – P.J. Sijpesteijn, ZPE 105 (1995) 245-252; F.A.J. Hoogendijk, ZPE 107 (1995) 105f.; A. Papathomas, P.Heid. VII 404.

[8] Gagos – van Minnen, Settling a Dispute (o. Anm. 4) 30-46; vgl. aber die Bemerkungen von H.-A. Rupprecht, Tyche 12 (1997) 264-269.

Gerichtshöfen unbewiesen sei und daher nicht als Grund für die Inanspruchnahme von Schiedsgerichten gelten kann. Überzeugend sind auch Urbaniks Argumente, daß *contra* Schiller nicht von einem allgemeinen Niedergang der Rechtswissenschaft im spätantiken Ägypten auszugehen sei (Dioskoros, Alexandrinische Juristenschule), und daß, gleichfalls *contra* Schiller, der monophysitische Teil der Bevölkerung die Gerichte der orthodoxen Statthalter und die kaiserliche Gesetzgebung keineswegs abgelehnt habe[9].

Allerdings scheinen die Argumente, die Urbanik ins Feld führt, um die Entwicklung zu erklären, auch nicht schlagend:

Argument 1: Der Streitgegenstand bei Vergleich und Schiedsgericht ist oft eine Familiensache (Erbschaftsfragen etc.); deshalb habe man vermieden, ein öffentliches Gericht zu involvieren[10]. – Dann fragt sich aber, warum man in ptolemäischer und vor allem in römischer Zeit, in der diesbezüglich dieselben Voraussetzungen galten, nicht ebenso gehandelt hat? Warum käme man erst im 6. Jh. auf die Idee, Familienzwist „privat" zu regeln?

Argument 2: Das Schiedsgericht sei einfacher und kostengünstiger gewesen als der reguläre Prozeß, der durch Appellation jedenfalls theoretisch bis an den Kaiserhof gehen konnte. – Auch dieses Argument wird durch einen Verweis auf die frühe-

---

[9] Kenntnis, Anwendung und Akzeptanz insbesondere des justinianischen Gesetzeswerkes in Ägypten wurden von R. Taubenschlag, Geschichte der Rezeption des römischen Privatrechts in Ägypten, in: Studi in onore di Pietro Bonfante, Milano 1930, I, 367-440 (repr.: Opera minora, I, Warszawa, Paris 1959); ders., The Legislation of Justinian in the Light of the Papyri, Byzantion 15 (1940-41) 280-295 (repr.: Opera minora, II, Warszawa, Paris 1959) sehr positiv eingeschätzt; vorsichtiger äußerten sich V. Arangio-Ruiz, Applicazione del diritto giustinianeo in Egitto, Aegyptus 1 (1920) 21-36 und A. Steinwenter, Was beweisen die Papyri für die praktische Geltung des justinianischen Gesetzgebungswerkes, Aegyptus 32 (1952) 131-137; dagegen meinte A. Schiller, The Fate of Imperial Legislation in Late Byzantine Egypt, in: J.N. Hazard – W.J. Wagner (Hgg.), Legal Thought in the United States of America, Bruxelles 1970, 41-60 und ders., Courts (o. Anm. 1), daß die kaiserliche Gesetzgebung in Ägypten praktisch ignoriert worden wäre. Neuere Arbeiten schätzen sowohl die Wirkung des „kaiserlichen Rechts" als auch die juristischen Fachkenntnisse der ägyptischen Notare günstig ein, vgl. etwa P. van Minnen, Dioscorus and the Law, in: A.A. MacDonald – M.W. Twomey – G.R. Reinink (Hgg.), Learned Antiquity, Leuven 2003, 115-133. – Ausdrückliche Verweise auf „kaiserliches Recht" sind in den Papyri der byzantinischen Zeit mehrfach zu finden, vgl. etwa P.Bodl. I 47 (nach 535); P.Cair.Masp. I 67028, 7. 21f. (ca. 551); I 67006 verso 14. 114. 142 (566-570); III 67312, 27f. (567); II 67151, 26. 149f. (570); CPR I 30 Kol. II = M.Chr. 290 Kol. II 23-25 (6.-7. Jh.); vgl. ferner die Zitate der *lex Falcidia* in P.Cair.Masp. I 67097 und III 67353, die sog. „Kairener Kaiserreskripte" P.Cair.Masp. I 67024-67029 und die Drohung, das Kaisergericht anzurufen, in PSI I 76 (572/3).

[10] Die Beobachtung, daß bestimmte Arten von Konflikten besonders für die Schiedsgerichtsbarkeit prädestiniert sind, findet sich schon bei Simon, Zivilgerichtsbarkeit (o. Anm. 2) 649f., J.J. Faber, Disputes in the Patermuthis Archive, BASP 27 (1991) 111-122 und Gagos – van Minnen, Settling a Dispute (o. Anm. 4) 38f.; sie gilt nicht nur für die byzantinische Zeit.

re Kaiserzeit entkräftet. Prozesse waren auch im 2. Jh. langwierig und teuer. In der Spätantike trat hier sogar eine Verbesserung für die Bevölkerung ein, weil man seit der diokletianischen Provinzteilung nicht unbedingt zum *praefectus* nach Alexandreia reisen oder auf den nächsten *conventus* warten mußte, sondern in jeder der bis zu sieben Teilprovinzen des Landes ein Statthalter zu Gericht saß. Die Zugänglichkeit der Gerichte war einfacher, ihre terminliche Überlastung nicht mehr so drückend wie früher. Zudem stand mit dem Libellprozeß, der sich seit der Mitte des 4. Jh. in Ägypten nachweisen läßt, ein Verfahren zur Verfügung, das eine sehr einfache und schnelle Prozeßeinleitung hatte[11].

Argument 3: Wenn Kleriker in einen Streit verwickelt waren (was öfters der Fall war), wollte man das weltliche Gericht umgehen. – Dies rührt an eine andere mysteriöse Frage bezüglich der Gerichtsbarkeit im spätantiken Ägypten: Warum ist nach wie vor P.Lips. I 43 (Lykopolis?, 4. Jh.) unser einziges halbwegs sicheres Zeugnis für die *episcopalis audientia*? Obwohl das Bischofsgericht in der Gesetzgebung so prominent vorkommt, hat es in den Papyri so gut wie keine Spuren, nicht einmal indirekter Art (etwa durch Erwähnungen in Briefen), hinterlassen[12]. Diese Erklärung könnte zudem nur jene Fälle betreffen, in denen Kleriker als Kläger auftraten.

Argument 4: Mit einer voranschreitenden Formalisierung des Schiedsgerichtes und einer perfektionierten schriftlichen Niederlegung sei das Schiedsgericht immer attraktiver geworden. – Dagegen läßt sich einwenden, daß bereits die früheste Kompromiß-Urkunde, P.Giss. I 104 vom 30. Juni 399, ein entwickeltes Formular aufweist und auch das nächste gut erhaltene Beispiel, M.Chr. 365 vom Juni/Juli 507, hinsichtlich seiner formalen Ausgestaltung den *compromissa* des späteren 6. Jh. in nichts nachsteht. Außerdem hat auch die perfektionierte Ausgestaltung der Urkunde kaum einen anderen, empfindlichen Nachteil des Schiedsgerichtes gegenüber dem mit staatlicher Autorität ausgestatteten Statthaltergericht aufgewogen: Einem

[11] Zum Libellprozeß s. M. Kaser – K. Hackl, Das römische Zivilprozeßrecht, München [2]1996 (HdAW X 3.4), bes. 570-576; ausführlicher D. Simon, Untersuchungen zum Justinianischen Zivilprozeß, (MB 54), München 1969, bes. 37-63; und A. Steinwenter, Zur Frage der Gliederung des Libellprozesses, Festschrift L. Wenger, I (MB 34), München 1944, 180-203. Der früheste papyrologische Beleg für einen Libellprozeß ist derzeit SB XVIII 13769 = ChLA XLV 1337 (Herm., 345-352). Zu den Libellpapyri vgl. zuletzt B. Palme, Spätrömische Militärgerichtsbarkeit in den Papyri, in: H.-A. Rupprecht (Hg.), Symposion 2003, Wien 2006, 375-408, bes. 395-399 mit weiterführender Literatur in Anm. 62 und 63.

[12] Zur *episcopalis audientia* s. etwa J. Lammeyer, Die ‚audientia episcopalis' in Zivilsachen der Laien im römischen Kaiserrecht und in den Papyri, Aegyptus 13 (1933) 193-202; F. Cuena, La Episcopalis Audientia, Valladolid 1985; W. Selb, Episcopalis audientia von der Zeit Konstantins bis zur Nov. XXXV Valentinians III., SZ 84 (1967) 162-217, bes. 166-168 zu den Papyri.

Schiedsrichter stehen keine Mittel zur Rechtsdurchsetzung zur Verfügung, falls ein Kontrahent sich nicht an den Spruch hält[13].

Welche Gründe wären aber dann maßgeblich, um die vermehrte Inanspruchnahme der Schiedsgerichte und Vergleiche zu erklären? Ich frage mich, ob es denn diese drastische Vermehrung wirklich gab, oder ob wir nicht vielmehr einem Trugbild der derzeit vorliegenden Evidenz aufsitzen. Allzu leicht erliegt man ja angesichts der Menge und der Buntheit des Papyrusmaterials der Versuchung, zu glauben, die erhaltenen (bzw. die edierten) Papyri seien repräsentativ und vermitteln ein einigermaßen vollständiges Bild der Verhältnisse. Doch in Wahrheit sind sie Zufallsfunde, die trotz aller Fülle nur einen schmalen Ausschnitt der Wirklichkeit beleuchten. Nehmen wir die papyrologische Evidenz also etwas genauer unter die Lupe:

Beginnen wir bei den Kompromissen[14]: Ohne Zweifel gibt es eine steigende Zahl an Belegen aus dem 6. Jh. und vor allem eine merkliche Häufung im 7. Jh., während der vorjustinianischen Zeit nur vier *compromissa* zweifelsfrei zuzuordnen sind[15]. Allerdings ist dabei in Rechnung zu stellen, daß die Gesamtzahl der Papyri aus dem sog. „spätbyzantinischen“ Zeitabschnitt tendenziell dieselbe Häufung – wenngleich nicht so extrem – aufweist, während das 5. Jh. bekanntermaßen unterrepräsentiert ist[16]. Schwerer noch wiegt die völlig ungleiche räumliche Streuung der Belege. Die Texte aus der Mitte des 6. Jh. stammen überwiegend aus Antinoopolis; sie gehören zum Dioskoros-Archiv. Die Belege zwischen 575 und 650 kommen dagegen fast ausschließlich aus dem Arsinoites und Herakleopolites – jenen Gauen, die durch den 1. und 2. Fayumer Fund gerade für diese Zeitspanne so reiche Dokumentation haben. Zu denken gibt, daß andere Fundorte, die im Untersuchungszeitraum gleichfalls sehr gut dokumentiert sind, fast gar nicht aufscheinen: Aus Oxyrhynchos kommt nur ein Beleg (P.Iand. III 41, [2. Hälfte 6. Jh.]), aus Hermupolis stammen nur zwei Zeugnisse (P.Giss. I 104 [399] und M.Chr. 365 mit BL I 295 [507]). Darf man daraus ableiten, daß die Schiedsgerichte nur in bestimmten Gauen beliebt waren, in anderen dagegen nicht? Ich meine, daß sich hierin eher die Zufälligkeit der Funde – und damit unserer Evidenz – widerspiegelt.

Sodann die Dialyseis: Die ca. 50 vorliegenden Urkunden zeigen ein deutlich anderes Bild als die Kompromisse. Die räumliche Streuung ist einigermaßen ausgewo-

---

13 Diese Schwierigkeit und ihre Implikationen hat schon Simon, Zivilgerichtsbarkeit (o. Anm. 2) 624f. aufgezeigt.

14 Nur in Parenthese sei angemerkt, daß in der Forschungsliteratur mehr als die oben angeführten ca. zwei Dutzend Texte als ‚Kompromiß‘ bezeichnet sind. Aber die Identifizierung mancher fragmentarischer Urkunde als Kompromiß ist fragwürdig, und man müßte tiefer in die Textkritik einsteigen, um erst einmal eine gesicherte Quellenbasis zu gewinnen.

15 P.Giss. I 104 (399), PUG I 23 = SB X 10733 (4.-5. Jh.), M.Chr. 365 (507), CPR VI 8 (509?).

16 W. Haberman, Zur chronologischen Verteilung der papyrologischen Zeugnisse, ZPE 122 (1998) 144-160, bes. 150f. mit Abb. 5.

gen und auch in ihrer zeitlichen Verteilung präsentieren sich die Belege viel breiter gefächert: Etwa ein Drittel der Testimonien stammt aus vorjustinianischer Zeit, zwei Drittel aus der besser dokumentierten nachjustinianischen. Ein markantes Schwergewicht gibt es auch da, doch es fällt in die 2. Hälfte des 6. Jh., also um ca. ein halbes Jahrhundert früher als bei den Kompromissen. Aber auch diese Steigerung fällt mit dem angesprochenen, generellen Anstieg der (publizierten) Papyrustexte in byzantinischer Zeit zusammen. Wollte man genaue statistische Auswertungen machen, dann müßte man alle Zahlen mit der Gesamtzahl der Papyri aus dem jeweiligen Zeitabschnitt und Herkunftsort konfrontieren, um zu verläßlichen Aussagen zu gelangen. Die bloßen Belegzahlen, mit denen man bislang operiert, verzerren allzu leicht das Bild.

Schließlich die Schiedssprüche (*sententiae*) selbst, die doch die zentralen Zeugnisse sein müßten, falls Schiedsgerichte tatsächlich die institutionellen Gerichte verdrängt hätten. Urbanik hat drei Testimonien dieser höchst seltenen Textgattung beigebracht[17]. Einer der Texte (SB XXII 15764) stammt wohl schon aus arabischer Zeit, als es kein byzantinisches Statthaltergericht mehr gab[18]. Zu diesen Beispielen lassen sich sechs andere hinzufügen[19]. Insgesamt halten wir demnach bei acht Belegen für Schiedssprüche – nicht eben eine Zahl, die geeignet wäre, eine völlige Ablösung der Gerichte durch die Schiedsgerichtsbarkeit zu postulieren. Hinzu kommt eine weitere Beobachtung: Von den Dialysis-Urkunden geben nur drei ausdrücklich an, daß sie durch einen Schiedsrichter vermittelt wurden[20]. Die meisten Dialyseis wurden durch Verhandlung der Parteien oder Vermittlung von Vertrauenspersonen zustande gebracht.

Kurzum: Die vielfach geortete Zunahme der Schiedsgerichte und Dialyseis zwischen ca. 550 und 650 n.Chr. scheint nur so drastisch. Die steigende Anzahl einschlägiger Urkunden korreliert mit der generell ansteigenden Zahl der erhaltenen Papyri im

---

17 P.Münch. I 6 (Syene, 583), P.Oxy. VI 893 = M.Chr. 99 (Oxy., Ende 6./7. Jh.), und SB XXII 15764 (Ars., ca. 630-660).

18 Abgesehen davon wird in diesem Text kein definitives Urteil gefällt, sondern die Entscheidung an drei andere Schiedsrichter delegiert. Somit sind die in Dig. 4, 8, 19, 1 formulierten Bedingungen einer echten *sententia arbitri* nicht erfüllt: *nisi omnes controversias finierit, non videtur sententia dicta.*

19 P.Paramone 16 (Herakl., 616) und P.Paramone 17 (Herakl., Anf. 7. Jh.), die Federico Morelli kürzlich ediert hat, sowie die sehr fragmentarischen SB I 4674 (Ars., 6./7. Jh.) und SB I 4712 (Ars, ca. 630-640), die er ebenda als *sententiae* identifiziert hat. In koptischer Sprache: P.Lond. V 1708 (566/7) und 1709 (ca. 570), beide aus Antinoopolis; eine Übersetzung findet sich bei Till, Erbrechtliche Untersuchungen (o. Anm. 4) 216-220. Um keinen Schiedsspruch handelt es sich – entgegen der Überschrift in der Edition – bei BGU XIX 2771 (Herm., 3./4. Jh.): Die knappe Notiz bezieht sich zwar auf ein Schiedsgericht, ist aber nicht von den Schiedsrichtern formuliert und daher keine *sententia arbitri*.

20 P.Mich. XIII 659 + P.Vat.Aphrod. 17 (Aphrod., 564/5); P.Münch. I 14 (Syene, 594); SB VI 8988 (Apollonopolis, 647).

6. Jh., ist also weitgehend auf die Überlieferungslage zurückzuführen. Allenfalls darf die etwas vermehrte Anzahl von Dialyseis als Indiz für ein moderates Anwachsen der außergerichtlichen Streitbeendung gewertet werden. Sie beweisen aber keineswegs ein derart massives Überhandnehmen dieser Formen der Streitbeendung, daß schließlich die regulären Gerichte verdrängt worden wären.

Umso virulenter wird jedoch die Frage nach demjenigen Phänomen in der papyrologischen Evidenz, das ursprünglich den Anlaß zur These vom Ende der Gerichtshöfe gegeben hatte: Das Ausbleiben der Prozeßprotokolle nach der Regierungszeit Justinians[21]. Zunächst ist freilich festzuhalten, daß auch die Zahl der aus dem 5. Jh. überlieferten Protokolle nur auf den ersten Blick groß scheint. Wenn man von dem Komplex P.Oxy. XVI 1876-1879 aus dem *officium* des *praeses Arcadiae* absieht, bleibt kaum noch eine Handvoll solcher Urkunden über – nicht mehr als aus dem 6. Jh. Vor allem aber ist, wie bereits Dieter Simon hervorgehoben hat, die Frage nach der Gerichtsverfassung Ägyptens zwischen ca. 540 und 640 keinesfalls allein auf der Basis der Urkundstypen ‚Prozeßprotokoll' einerseits und ‚Dialysis und Compromissum' andererseits zu entscheiden[22]. Zum einen ist auch die jurisdiktionelle Tätigkeit des *defensor civitatis* – er nimmt Petitionen entgegen und trifft Entscheidungen *cognitionaliter* (PSI VII 790) – eine Form der staatlichen Gerichtsbarkeit. Durch die Aufnahme von Beweisurkunden (διαμαρτυρίαι) leistet er Vorarbeit für Gerichtsverfahren vor dem Statthalter oder sogar dem Kaiser (P.Cair.Masp. II 67131, PSI I 76). Im dörflichen Bereich erfüllt der *riparius* ganz ähnliche Aufgaben (etwa in P.Cair.Masp. I 67091-67093).

Zum anderen sind auch indirekte Zeugnisse für den Fortbestand von Gerichten zu berücksichtigen: In Privatbriefen wie P.Fouad III 85 (6./7. Jh.) wird von einem Prozeß vor dem Statthalter (*praeses* oder *Augustalis*) gesprochen. Das Edikt eines *dux Thebaidis* aus den Jahren 543-545 beschränkt die Sporteln bei Libellprozessen *cum scriptis* und *sine scriptis* (P.Cair.Masp. I 67031)[23]. Ferner ist zu bedenken, daß auch mittels Petitionen ein Kognitionsverfahren in Gang gesetzt werden konnte, in

[21] Eine Liste der bilinguen Prozeßprotokolle aus der nachdiokletianischen Zeit gibt J.D. Thomas, P.Ryl. IV 654: the Latin Heading, CdÉ 73 (1998) 132f. Dort ist auch verzeichnet, welcher Magistrat die Verhandlung geführt hat. Ergänzungen zur Liste finden sich bei U. & D. Hagedorn, P.Thomas S. 217, Anm. 1. Seither sind folgende Urkunden hinzugekommen: P.Harrauer 46 = ChLA XLI 1188 + SPP XX 283 (= ChLA XLV 1325), mit einem weiteren Fragment neu ediert von F. Mitthof, JJP 33 (2003) 205-211 (Herm./Antin., 332); P.Bodl. I 170 *descr.* (Herk. unbek., 4. Jh.); P.Thomas 24 (Herk. unbek., Ende 4./5. Jh.); P.Thomas 25 (= ChLA III 217) (Herk. unbek., 437?); CPR XXIV 3 (Ars. oder Herakl., Ende 4., Anf. 5. Jh.); P.Acad. 56/1+2 + 57/1 (ed. J. Gascou, T&MByz 14 [2002] 269-277 [Antin., Mitt 5. Jh.]).

[22] Simon, Zivilgerichtsbarkeit (o. Anm. 2), bes. 639-651.

[23] Die Bezeichnung *sine scriptis* bezieht sich lediglich auf die bloß mündliche Ladungsform, s. A. Steinwenter, Das Verfahren sine scriptis im justinianischen Prozessrechte, SZ 76 (1959) 306-323 und Simon, Zivilgerichtsbarkeit (o. Anm. 2) 641f. Hierin liegt also nicht der Grund für das Verschwinden der Verhandlungsprotokolle.

dem Beamte auf Gau- und Provinzebene in straf-, zivil- und verwaltungsrechtlichen Angelegenheiten entschieden. Vom 5. bis zum 7. Jh. liegen nicht weniger als ca. 120 Petitionen vor[24]. Mit den Tabellionenurkunden, die im 5. Jh. aufkamen und im 6. Jh. weit verbreitet waren, hatte man vollstreckbare Dokumente, welche diese Form der Jurisdiktion erheblich erleichterten. Erkenntnisverfahren und Vollstreckungsverfahren konnten rasch durchgeführt werden und lagen in der Hand desselben Beamten, der zudem auch über die Autorität verfügte, den Rechtsentscheid sofort durchzusetzen. Bis um 550 richteten sich Petitionen auch an *defensores* und Statthalter; aus den Jahren 565-570 überliefert das Dioskoros-Archiv eine ganze Reihe von Petitionen an den *dux Thebaidis*, danach vorwiegend an δεσπόται, in denen wohl zumeist die lokalen Grundherren zu erblicken sind[25]. Schließlich wurde zu bedenken gegeben, daß auch die Bestimmung der Novelle 149 des Kaisers Justin II. vom Jahre 569, nach welcher die Provinzialen ihre Statthalter hinfort selbst aus den Reihen ihrer Notablen auswählen sollten, zu einem Rückgang der statthalterlichen Autorität geführt und sich dies auch in einer verminderten Gerichtstätigkeit bemerkbar gemacht habe[26].

All diese Faktoren mögen dazu geführt haben, daß streitige Verfahren im 6. und 7. Jh. seltener angestrengt wurden als früher, doch dies ist nicht als Zusammenbruch der staatlichen Justiz zu werten. Nach wie vor entschieden die Organe der staatlichen Gerichtsbarkeit, nur hatte sich mit vollstreckbarer Tabellionenurkunde und Petition mit anschließendem Kognitionsverfahren ein noch schnellerer Weg der Entscheidungsfindung aufgetan, als dies auch der Libellprozeß bieten konnte. Daneben wurden Schiedsgericht und Vergleich wie eh und je in Anspruch genommen, vielleicht sogar öfter als früher[27]. Sie waren aber keine Gegenspieler der staatlichen Jurisdiktion und haben nicht die Auflösung der Statthaltergerichte bewirkt.

---

24 J.-L. Fournet – J. Gascou, Liste des pétitions sur papyrus des Ve-VIIe siècles, in: D. Feissel – J. Gascou (Hgg.), La pétition à Byzance, (Centre de recherche d'histoire et civilisation de Byzance, Monographies 14), Paris 2004, 141-196.

25 J. Gascou, Les pétitions privées, in: Feissel – Gascou, Pétition (o. Anm. 24) bes. 93f., wobei allerdings zu fragen wäre, ob angesichts der Einbindung der Grundherrn in das staatliche Verwaltungssystem die an sie gerichteten Bittschriften tatsächlich als „pétitions privées" zu werten sind. Wie bei der Steuereintreibung verschwimmen auch hier die Grenzen zwischen staatlicher und privater Gewalt. Zudem wird auch bei dieser Urkundengruppe die Zufälligkeit der Überlieferung sehr deutlich: Ohne das Dioskoros-Archiv wäre keine einzige Petition an den *dux Thebaidis* erhalten.

26 C. Zuckerman, Les deux Dioscore d'Aphroditè ou les limites de la pétition, in: Feissel – Gascou, Pétition (o. Anm. 24) bes. 90f.

27 Doch selbst das ist schwer zu beweisen; Gagos – van Minnen, Settling a Dispute (o. Anm. 4) 40 erwägen, daß in den früheren Jahrhunderten die Schiedsgerichte und Vergleiche vielleicht genauso häufig gewesen seien wie im 6. und 7. Jh., aber nicht schriftlich niedergelegt wurden: Die früheste sicher datierte Dialysis-Urkunde ist derzeit P.Oxy. XII 1562 (276-282).

Die Alternative „compromesso o processo“ hat sich in vielen Streitfällen wohl gar nicht gestellt. Wann immer nämlich eine vollstreckbare Urkunde existierte, stand dem Kläger ein rascher und leichter Weg offen, sein Recht zu erlangen: Man wandte sich (durch Petition) an ein staatliches oder semi-staatliches Organ, das nach Prüfung des Sachverhaltes und der Urkunde sofort die darin angedrohten Konsequenzen (z.B. Vollstreckung in das gesamte Vermögen, andernfalls Schuldhaft) durchsetzen konnte. Dadurch gelangten nur mehr jene Streitfälle, bei denen man sich auf keine Urkunden stützen konnte (wie etwa Erbangelegenheiten, familieninterne Vermögensfragen), vor den Richter oder Schiedsrichter.

Die von Jakub Urbanik vorgebrachten Argumente und Beobachtungen, weshalb und unter welchen Umständen streitende Parteien ein Schiedsgericht in Anspruch nahmen, sind deshalb nicht hinfällig, im Gegenteil: Sie erhellen trefflich die Konstellationen, in denen Schiedsgericht und Vergleich stattfanden. Vermutlich dürften sie aber nicht nur für die byzantinische, sondern wohl mindestens auch schon für die römische Zeit Gültigkeit beanspruchen.

RIFLESSIONI FINALI

JOSEPH MÉLÈZE MODRZEJEWSKI (PARIS)

DE RHEDA À SALERNO – QUINZE SYMPOSIA

Chères amies, chers amis jusgrécistes,

Il y a deux ans, au château de Rauischholzhausen, j'ai eu le privilège d'ouvrir les travaux de notre XIVe Symposion d'histoire du droit grec et hellénistique[1]. Ce fut surtout l'occasion d'évoquer quelques souvenirs personnels liés à l'histoire de notre Société, mais j'ai réussi à glisser dans mon *Eröffnungsrede* quelques mots sur un sujet qui me tient à cœur, à savoir le besoin de bons manuels modernes de droit grec et hellénistique, pour nos collègues et pour nos étudiants, sinon pour nous-mêmes. Sur ce point, nos vœux sont déjà exaucés dans une certaine mesure grâce aux récents travaux collectifs publiés sous la responsabilité de nos collègues britanniques[2] et américains[3]. Mais ces ouvrages, si précieux et utiles qu'ils soient, n'annulent pas la nécessité d'un traité systématique qui reste à faire.

Pour notre XVe Symposion, qui s'achève en ce moment, c'est un discours de clôture que notre gracieuse hôtesse a bien voulu me confier. Cette fois-ci la tâche était plus rude. J'ai cherché des antécédents pour m'en inspirer. J'en ai trouvé deux, à une vingtaine d'années d'intervalle (ce qui montre bien qu'il ne s'agit nullement d'un usage invétéré): le discours d'Arnaldo Biscardi à l'issue du Symposion de Gargnano-sur-Garde en 1974 et l'«Épilogue» de Julie Vélissaropoulos-Karakostas clôturant le Symposion de Corfou en 1995[4]. Ne possédant ni les ressources d'art oratoire qui donnaient tant de finesse et d'élégance aux propos florentins du regretté Biscardi, ni le don de concision quasi attique de notre amie Julie, j'ai renoncé à cette forme de synthèse finale. Laissons cette tâche aux auteurs des comptes rendus que notre rencontre ne manquera pas de générer, espérons-le, dans des revues intéressées par les antiquités juridiques grecques.

J'ai pensé ensuite à un «flash» sur l'état actuel des études de droit grec, dont notre *Symposion* est un brillant reflet. Comme exemple, le bilan dressé par Mario

---

1 «Eröffnung», in *Symposion 2003* (Rauischholzhausen, 30 septembre-3 octobre 2003), Vienne, 2006, p. 3-7.

2 Edward M. Harris & Lene Rubinstein, Eds., *The Law and the Courts in Ancient Greece*, Londres, Duckworth, 2004.

3 Michael Gagarin & David Cohen, Eds., *The Cambridge Companion to Ancient Greek Law*, Cambridge/New York, Cambridge University Press, 2005.

4 Arnaldo Biscardi, «Sintesi conclusiva», in *Symposion 1974* (Gargnano, 5-8 juin 1974), p. 393-401; Julie Vélissaropoulos-Karakostas, «Épilogue», in *Symposion 1995* (Corfou, 1-5 septembre 1995), p. 385-387.

Talamanca à Athènes, à l'ouverture du centre de recherches créé pour Panayotis Dimakis, s'imposait pas ses orientations et par son ampleur. Mais ce bilan, publié en 1994[5], avait déjà trouvé son double prolongement dans deux récents articles d'Alberto Maffi sur les études de droit grec depuis le premier *Symposion* et sur leur état actuel[6]. Le rapport d'Eva Cantarella sur l'enseignement du droit grec, présenté à notre précédent *Symposion* et enrichi par la discussion qu'il avait suscitée, complétait le tableau[7]. Mon «flash» perdait sa raison d'être.

C'est alors qu'une idée, que certains d'entre vous jugeront sans doute téméraire, me vint à l'esprit: puisqu'on me demande un «rapport de synthèse», pourquoi ne pas tenter la synthèse des quinze volumes de *Symposia,* depuis notre premier colloque au château de Rheda en Westphalie au début de septembre 1971 jusqu'à notre présente rencontre? Je n'avais certainement pas la vaine ambition de résumer les quatre centaines de communications étalées sur environ 5700 pages dans ces quinze volumes de nos Actes; plus exactement, treize volumes déjà publiés, avec un total de 4844 pages, un volume sous presse, celui du XIVe *Symposion*, avec ses 475 pages, et un volume qui réunira les travaux de la rencontre qui s'achève aujourd'hui et qui gravitera, d'après le calcul que j'ai fait sur les textes informatisés qui nous avaient été communiqués, autour de 400 pages. Je pensais qu'il ne serait peut-être pas inutile d'essayer de dégager quelques grandes lignes thématiques qui ont orienté notre curiosité pendant ces trente et quatre années, de mesurer l'étendue du champ de recherches traversé par nos enquêtes, de souligner l'importance de leur apport aux études grecques et à la science historique du droit.

Je me plongeais donc, avec un mélange de délectation et de mélancolie, dans ces pages oh combien évocatrices pour quelqu'un (je sais que je ne suis pas le seul dans ce cas) qui avait assisté assidûment à toutes nos rencontres – à une seule exception près (Altafiumara, 1997), bien contre mon gré. Pour ne pas rester dans le vague, il m'a paru utile de confectionner un index général à partir des tables des matières des volumes publiés (ou, pour Marbourg, sous presse) et du programme de Salerno. Il correspond à un vœu qui s'était quelquefois fait entendre au cours de nos réunions. J'aurai pu m'arrêter là. Ma charge de «synthétiseur» m'imposait cependant – du

---

[5] Mario Talamanca, «Gli studi di diritto greco dall'inizio dell'ottocento ai nostri giorni», in *Studi in memoria di Gino Gorla,* Milano 1994, p. 889-949.

[6] Alberto Maffi, «Hans Julius Wolff e gli studi di diritto greco a trent'anni dal I Symposion», *Dike* 4, 2001, p. 269-291; Idem, «Gli studi di diritto greco oggi», dans D.F. Leão, L. Rossetti, M do Céu G.Z.Fialho (Ed.), Nomos. Direito e sociedade na Antiguidade Clássica, Coimbra 2004, p. 33-49. Pour l'information courante, je rappelle les chroniques que Michele Faraguna et Alberto Maffi publient régulièrement dans *Dike* et dans la *Revue historique de droit français et étranger* (la dernière en date: RHD 83, 2005, p. 487-516).

[7] Eva Cantarella, «L'insegnamento del diritto greco a trent'anni dal primo Symposion: diffusione, approcci e prospettive di sviluppo», *Symposion 2003* (Rauischholzhausen, 30 septembre-3 octobre 2003) p. 435-442.

moins était-ce ainsi que je la concevais – le devoir de partager avec vous quelques réflexions que j'ai pu faire pendant la confection de cet index.

Dans un cadre géographique qui s'étend des Balkans aux confins orientaux de l'Empire d'Alexandre à l'Est, aux cataractes du Nil au Sud, à la Grande Grèce et à la Sicile à l'Ouest, nous avons sillonné un espace deux fois millénaire, englobant les tablettes en linéaire B, les poèmes homériques, les écrits des philosophes, les discours des orateurs, les inscriptions et les papyrus, les notices des lexicographes, jusqu'au *Corpus Juris* de Justinien et sa postérité byzantine. Il n'était pas facile d'imaginer une construction qui permette d'engranger une moisson aussi riche et aussi variée dans le temps et dans l'espace. La division chronologique tripartie – droit archaïque et classique, droit hellénistique, droit grec dans l'Empire romain (mieux que «droit gréco-romain», formule trompeuse pour les profanes qui ne connaissent pas l'œuvre mémorable de Zacharie von Lingenthal[8]), bien commode pour les programmes de nos colloques et les tables des matières de leurs actes, était indubitablement trop étroite pour mon inventaire. De plus, toute division chronologique m'aurait imposé des doublets et des redites, écueil auquel se heurtent les auteurs de manuels qui décident de traiter à plusieurs endroits la même question pour les périodes successives d'une histoire de longue durée, et les lecteurs qui doivent les consulter. Le schéma du *Companion*, qui combine le critère spatio-temporel pour le corps de l'ouvrage (Athènes – droit grec hors d'Athènes) avec un critère thématique pour le chapitre introductif (unité, écriture, religion, origines) et pour la conclusion (rapports avec le théâtre, théorie politique et le binôme «légal/naturel» dans la pensée grecque) ne paraissait pas non plus assez opératoire.

J'ai fini par opter pour un traitement thématique global, sans division selon les régions ou les périodes. Le vieux débat sur l'unité du droit grec, dont Michael Gagarin vient de proposer une brillante mise au point dans le *Companion*[9], se profilait à l'arrière-plan. Nos réunions qui associent les spécialistes des diverses périodes, venant de divers horizons – juristes, historiens, épigraphistes, papyrologues – sont, par l'active participation de tous à tous les débats et par l'entente qui les anime, la meilleure preuve que les jusgrécistes forment une famille par nature, *physei*, sans qu'il soit nécessaire de les agréger au moyen d'une *klarographie* ou d'une *adelphothetie*. Pour reprendre la célèbre formule de Louis Gernet, nous collectionnons, au gré de nos enquêtes, des «variantes sur le même thème»[10].

Les thèmes étant nombreux, leur classement n'allait pas de soi. Que les schémas traditionnels des romanistes ne soient pas recommandables, nous le savons depuis

---

[8] Zacharie von Lingenthal, *Geschichte des griechisch-römischen Rechts*, 3e éd. corrigée, Berlin, 1892.

[9] Michael Gagarin, «The Unity of Greek Law», in *Companion, op. cit.*, p. 1-28.

[10] Louis Gernet, «Introduction à l'étude du droit grec ancien», dans *AHDO* 2, 1938, p. 261-292, citation textuelle: p. 278.

longtemps[11]. Cela ne nous empêche pas de continuer à utiliser une terminologie dérivée du latin juridique, dont les défauts sont connus, mais dont la principale vertu est de rendre nos travaux lisibles aux historiens et aux juristes qui n'ont pas eu la chance d'avoir reçu une formation «jusgrécistique» spécifique. Les efforts déployés pour gréciser, ou au mois pour «déromaniser», notre vocabulaire au moyen de périphrases et de néologismes tirés de racines grecques sont souvent vains. Remplacer «propriété» par «maîtrise réelle des choses» (la «Sachherschaft» allemande) ne suffit pas pour faire comprendre aux profanes la différence entre ce que nous appelons «propriété» en droit grec, notion autrefois magistralement scrutée par le même Gernet, et le *dominium ex iure Quiritium* romain[12]. Parler d'une «Frauenkyrieia» à propos de la tutelle des femmes, en introduisant dans la famille sémantique de *kyrios* un terme (*kyrieia*) qu'on ne trouve dans aucun dictionnaire, ne vaut guère mieux. Les romanismes qui nous guettent ne sont en fin de compte pas plus redoutables que les fautes d'accent grec dans les citations textuelles ou les lacunes de nos bibliographies.

Conscient de ces pièges, je vous propose un tableau en dix parties qui correspondent aux grandes orientations des recherches consignées dans nos quinze volumes. Dans une première partie, pour laquelle je n'ai trouvé, pour l'instant, que l'intitulé banal (I) L'HISTOIRE DU DROIT GREC ET SES ARTISANS, je groupe les travaux qui concernent la vie de notre discipline, ses méthodes, ses rapports avec d'autres branches des études grecques ainsi que de l'histoire juridique et institutionnelle de l'Antiquité classique et orientale. On y trouvera (a) les notices bio- et bibliographiques consacrées à nos confrères vivants et disparus à l'occasion des dates qui ont marqué leur parcours scientifique (38, 102, 248, 271, 248); (b) des réflexions sur les limites de notre discipline, les différentes manières de la pratiquer (1, 2, 19, 65, 103, 122, 157) et l'état actuel de son enseignement (367); (c) des réflexions sur ses rapports avec les disciplines-sœurs, dans le domaine grec: la philologie (40, 200), la papyrologie et l'épigraphie (52, 85), et même la sigillographie (352, 353), et dans le domaine de l'histoire comparée des droits de l'Antiquité: Orient cunéiforme (129, 331, 332), droit égyptien (51, 319, 320), droit juif (162), droit romain (59, 60, 63, 100, 101, 323, 324). Je note au passage, dans nos rapports avec les études grecques, l'absence de la numismatique, mais je profite de cette lacune pour y glisser la chronologie, ne sachant pas où fourrer ma propre

[11] Sur la persistance de ces schémas en droit civil moderne, voir Witold Wołodkiewicz, *Les origines romaines de la systématique du droit civil contemporain*, Wroclaw, Varsovie, Cracovie, Gdansk, Ossolineum, 1978, 39 p. (Accademia pollaca delle scienze, Biblioteca e centro di studi a Roma, Conferenze e studi, 76).

[12] Louis Gernet, «La notion de propriété en droit grec», conférence à l'Institut de Droit Romain de Paris le 6 février 1959 (inédit). Une liste des conférences inédites de Louis Gernet faites à l'Institut de Droit Romain de Paris, et qui peuvent être, pour la plupart, consultées sous forme dactylographiée, est donnée à la fin de la bibliographie qui accompagne son recueil *Anthropologie de la Grèce classique*, 1968, p. 436.

prestation relative au calendrier égyptien adopté et obstinément conservé par les Grecs (321). Je constate aussi avec un certain soulagement que nous avons échappé à l'emprise d'idéologies tyranniques, comme le marxisme ou le structuralisme. Quant à la philologie, il est clair qu'un jusgréciste doit être un bon helléniste et polyglotte par-dessus le marché; inversement, on ne dit pas assez à quel point la connaissance du droit est indispensable aux philologues que «la vérité juridique» – je cite encore Louis Gernet – «ne tourmente guère»[13]. Un philologue sérieux doublé d'un paléographe averti – je prends au hasard un exemple parmi tant d'autres possibles – qui traduit *systêma politikon* par «constitution»[14], alors qu'il s'agit de toute évidence de *corps civique*, commet une imprudence qu'une plus attentive prise en compte des données courantes de l'histoire institutionnelle grecque aurait permis d'éviter.

La deuxième partie est celle des (II) SOURCES, au double sens que ce mot revêt pour l'historien droit: facteurs de formation de règles juridiques et textes qui nous permettent de les connaître. Dans le premier volet (a), outre les lois de cités grecques (3, 33, 83, 165, 197, 198, 222, 331, 332), notamment Athènes (90, 372, 384-387) et Gortyne (71, 107, 187, 188, 200-203, 223, 275, 394, 395), on trouvera quelques témoins de la législation royale des Lagides (53, 268) et de la législation provinciale des préfets d'Égypte (245). Dans le second volet (b), les poèmes homériques se taillent la part du lion (20-22, 39, 69, 79, 87, 195, 196, 249, 272), suivis de penseurs politiques – Platon (8, 18, 32, 45, 98, 178, 179, 225), Aristote (34, 347, 348, 378, 379), le Vieil Oligarque (254), et des orateurs attiques – Démosthène (119), Isée (139), Lysias (209); l'historiographie étant représentée par Xénophon (228), le théâtre tragique l'est par Euripide (253) et le roman grec par Chariton d'Aphrodisias (166). Un troisième volet est réservé aux (c) sources documentaires; il regroupe des études, essentiellement papyrologiques, concernant la forme de documents (30, 43, 123, 158, 360, 361) et les archives (266), ainsi que des articles suscités par des trouvailles nouvelles: la lettre de Berezan (27), des tablettes de Pompéi (220) et de Nakone (93, 144).

Ma troisième partie, (III) CITES ET MONARCHIES, ressortit, d'après nos catégories modernes, au domaine du droit public. On y trouvera des recherches qui ont pour objet (a) les rouages du régime politique: constitutions et hiérarchie des lois (73, 237), citoyenneté (368, 369), magistratures (77, 145, 324); (b) les Etats fédéraux (79, 94, 148) et la monarchie hellénistique (160); (c) les relations interpoliades et internationales (4, 5, 44, 72, 81, 84, 120, 154, 234), y compris la guerre et le droit militaire (130, 143, 238, 362, 363); (d) les finances, la fiscalité, la banque et la circulation monétaire (131, 189, 190, 260, 374, 375). Dans la partie

[13] Article précité (ci-dessus, note 10).

[14] Jean Scherer, «Le Papyrus Fouad Ier Inv. 211», *Bulletin de l'Institut français d'archéologie orientale* 41, 1942, p. 43-73 (texte réédité comme SB VI 9016; cf. C.Ord.Ptol., All. 121); pour *systêma politikon*, voir p. 66. Dans le tirage à part de cet article qu'il m'a offert, l'auteur avait lui-même corrigé son erreur.

suivante figurent les contributions ayant trait au (IV) STATUT PERSONNEL: (a) citoyens (49, 144, 259, 228, 229); (b) métèques et étrangers (11, 153); (c) affranchissements et affranchis (13, 14, 78, 87, 95, 224), et notamment la mystérieuse loi des *ateknoi* à Bouthrotos (54, 236); (d) Grecs et indigènes dans l'Egypte romaine (99, 163).

Le centre du tableau est investi par deux vastes ensembles qui traditionnellement mobilisent l'attention des jusgrécistes: la justice et la délinquance. Dans le premier, (V) PROCES ET JUSTICE, Athènes se place en tête de liste : (a) les formes de procédure (7, 9, 42, 113, 182-185, 256, 280, 380, 381); les actions (26, 74); les accusateurs (335, 336); les juges (88, 109, 231, 246, 279, 284); les synégores (282, 307); le régime des preuves (25), les sentences (23, 24, 108, 156). En deuxième position, viennent (b) l'organisation de la justice et le déroulement des procès dans l'Orient hellénisé, en Egypte (36, 62, 241, 388-391) et dans d'autres régions du monde hellénistique (356, 357). Quant au (VI) CRIMES ET DELITS, cette partie comprend, d'une part, des enquêtes sur (a) divers types d'infractions: homicide (15, 16, 169-171, 254, 258, 273); adultère (193, 194); vol (128, 146, 276); impiété et d'autres formes d'atteintes au sacré (41, 161, 214, 215, 350, 351); injure verbale (239); malfaisance (132, 281), à quoi s'ajoute une vue d'ensemble de l'Egypte criminelle sous les Lagides (180, 181); d'autre part, en font partie les études examinant les (b) réactions à des comportements délictueux, individuelles, comme la vengeance (48), et collectives: peine capitale (110, 132, 145, 345, 346, 370, 371), atimie (46), malédiction publique (376, 377).

Avec la septième partie, (VII) FAMILLE, nous passons au domaine du droit privé. Nous y trouverons d'abord tout ce qui concerne (a) le mariage et la condition féminine: rites nuptiaux (235); lien conjugal et filiation (67, 92, 115, 118, 358, 359, 388, 389); régime dotal (29, 55, 135); concubines (191, 192); épiclères (12, 50, 56, 75, 136-138) et patroôques (200, 201); adoption (187, 188); grossesse et avortement (97, 285); situation juridique de la femme à Athènes et à Sparte (117, 150). Autour de la famille, se déploie le délicat espace de la (b) sexualité qui, chez les Grecs comme chez nous, c'est le moins qu'on puisse dire, ne s'identifie pas à la vie conjugale: comportements sexuels et leur réglementation (232, 339, 340); homosexualité (114, 267); prostitution (240, 398). A la famille est lié le droit des (VIII) SUCCCESSIONS, notre huitième partie: testaments (66, 243, 397); successions ab intestat (89, 104, 127); survie de la mémoire (167, 270, 396); évolution des droits successoraux sur les terres dans l'Egypte ptolémaïque (217, 218).

Les deux dernières parties regroupent les recherches relatives aux droits réels et aux opérations contractuelles. Sous la rubrique des (IX) BIENS figurent les travaux relatifs à (a) l'acquisition et à la protection de la propriété (80, 105, 151); aux servitudes (276); aux sûretés réelles (17, 125, 242); aux droits des copropriétaires et des voisins (82, 168); à l'emphytéose (64). Une place à part revient au (b) droit minier (341-344) et au (c) droit de l'environnement (292). Notre dernière partie est réservée aux (X) CONTRATS, au sens que les jusgrécistes donnent à ce terme:

d'abord, (a) quelques questions générales, à savoir la structure de l'obligation contractuelle (16, 86, 399), et notamment le problème du consensualisme (337, 338), représentation (164), rupture du rapport contractuel (76) et sa protection par le serment (232), réparation du préjudice moral (392, 393); ensuite, (b) des contrats spécifiques, comme vente (31, 47, 126, 246, 269, 279, 366), cession (96, 124), prêt (68, 140) et la *misthôsis* sous quelques-uns de ses nombreux aspects, en l'occurrence bail et location (58, 61, 68) et contrat d'ouvrage (226).

Le temps nous manque pour essayer d'évaluer en détail notre apport au progrès des études grecques et de l'histoire des droits de l'Antiquité. Contentons-nous de relever quelques points saillants.

Premièrement, nos travaux prouvent à l'évidence la maturité de notre discipline. Affranchie des schémas romains, forte d'une documentation aussi riche que variée, la jusgrécistique est aujourd'hui une science adulte, parfaitement autonome et sa place propre parmi les sciences de l'Antiquité n'est pas contestable. Le temps où elle n'était qu'une *ancilla philologiae* est loin derrière nous.

En second lieu, le bilan qui vient d'être dressé atteste l'unité de notre discipline et, à travers elle, celle de son objet: le droit grec dans toute son étendue, comme je l'indiquais plus haut en prenant le risque de dresser un panorama thématique plutôt que de suivre une démarche chronologique et régionale. Des études «transversales», qui avec succès retracent l'évolution d'une institution depuis Solon à l'édit de Caracalla, sinon jusqu'à Justinien, traduisent cette unité substantielle du droit grec dans sa permanence comme dans ses mutations. Chercher dans l'expérience des cités classiques ou de la monarchie macédonienne le point de départ de phénomènes juridiques dont on veut saisir la nature est une règle élémentaire dans la démarche du juriste-papyrologue. La démarche inverse, qui tend à affiner l'interprétation d'une notion classique en remontant le chemin de son évolution à partir d'un point atteint par celle-ci à l'époque hellénistique, est tout aussi instructive, bien qu'elle soit moins souvent pratiquée.

Troisième et dernier point: notre dynamisme. La jusgrécistique est une science en constante et rapide progression. Il suffirait de relever l'extension et l'approfondissement du concept de responsabilité: fondé par Wolff sur la notion de dommage matériel, il s'est enrichi par l'idée d'une autorisation modale comme corolaire de la «Zweckverfügung», disposition à finalité déterminée, dans la conclusion des contrats, pour déborder ensuite du domaine contractuel vers le domaine du «délit religieux» et celui du préjudice moral.

Au total, notre bilan est franchement positif et encourageant. Sa visualisation décimale étant loin de satisfaire vos esprits critiques (j'en suis parfaitement conscient), je serais comblé si vous acceptiez, en dehors de son emploi pratique comme inventaire bibliographique, de lui reconnaître une potentialité que j'aperçois en filigrane à travers ses rubriques: celle d'un canevas sur lequel pourraient se greffer un jour les chapitres d'un traité de droit grec ancien à l'usage de nos confrères et de nos étudiants, toujours attendu, non pas pour remplacer, mais pour compléter utilement les recueils que je citais au début de ce rapport. Mais en exprimant ce vœu je ne fais que réitérer celui que je formais à notre précédent colloque. La boucle est donc bouclée et je peux arrêter ce discours auquel vous avez bien voulu prêter votre indulgente attention.

SYMPOSIA 1971-2005

I. *Symposion 1971. Vorträge zur griechischen und hellenistischen Rechtsgeschichte* [Rheda bei Bielefeld, 1.-4. September 1971], In Gemeinschaft mit Josef Modrzejewski und Dieter Nörr herausgegeben von Hans Julius Wolff; Cologne et Vienne, Böhlau, 1975, X + 382 pages (Akten der Gesellschaft für hellenistische und griechische Rechtsgeschichte 1),

II. *Symposion 1974. Vorträge zur griechischen und hellenistischen Rechtsgeschichte (Gargnano am Gardasee, 5.-8. Juni 1974).* In Gemeinschaft mit Hans Julius Wolff, Josef Modrzejewski und Panayotis Dimakis herausgegeben von Arnaldo Biscardi, Athènes-Milan, 'Panteios', 1978, et Cologne-Vienne, Böhlau, 1979, VIII + 418 pages (Akten der Gesellschaft für griechische und hellenistische Rechtsgeschichte 2).

III. *Symposion 1977. Vorträge zur griechischen und hellenistischen Rechtsgeschichte (Chantilly, 1.-4. Juni 1977).* Herausgegeben von Joseph Modrzejewski und Detlef Liebs. Cologne et Vienne, Böhlau, 1982, XXVIII + 446 pages, frontispice (Akten der Gesellschaft für griechische und hellenistische Rechtsgeschichte 3).

IV. *Symposion 1979. Vorträge zur griechischen und hellenistischen Rechtsgeschichte (Ägina, 3.-7. September 1979).* In Gemeinschaft mit Hans Julius Wolff, Arnaldo Biscardi und Joseph Modrzejewski herausgegeben von Panayotis Dimakis. Annuaire scientifique de l'École des Hautes études politiques 'Panteios' 1978/1979, 2e partie, Athènes 1981, et Cologne et Vienne, Böhlau, 1983, 363 pages (Akten der Gesellschaft für griechische und hellenistische Rechtsgeschichte 4).

V. *Symposion 1982. Vorträge zur griechischen und hellenistischen Rechtsgeschichte (Santander, 1.-4. September 1982).* Herausgegeben von Francisco Javier Fernández Nieto, Cologne et Vienne, Böhlau, 1989, VI + 317 pages (Akten der Gesellschaft für griechische und hellenistische Rechtsgeschichte 5).

VI. *Symposion 1985. Vorträge zur griechischen und hellenistischen Rechtsgeschichte. (Ringberg, 24.-26. Juli 1985).* Herausgegeben von Gerhard Thür. Cologne et Vienne, Böhlau,1989, XIV + 468 pages, 2 pl. (Akten der Gesellschaft für griechische und hellenistische Rechtsgeschichte 6).

VII. *Symposion 1988. Vorträge zur griechischen und hellenistischen Rechtsgeschichte (Siena – Pisa, 6.-8. Juni 1988). Comunicazioni sul diritto greco ed ellenistico (Siena – Pisa, 6-8 giugno 1988).* Herausgegeben von/a cura di Giuseppe Nenci – Gerhard Thür. Cologne et Vienne, Böhlau, 1990, IX + 448 pages (Akten der Gesellschaft für griechische und hellenistische Rechtsgeschichte 7).

VIII. *Symposion 1990. Vorträge zur griechischen und hellenistischen Rechtsgeschichte. Papers on Greek and Hellenistic Legal History (Pacific Grove, California, 24.-26. September 1990).* Herausgegeben von/edited by Michael Gagarin. Cologne, Weimar et Vienne, Böhlau, 1992, X + 314 pages (Akten der Gesellschaft für griechische und hellenistische Rechtsgeschichte 8),

IX. *Symposion 1993. Vorträge zur griechischen und hellenistischen Rechtsgeschichte (Graz-Andritz, 12.-16. September 1993).* Herausgegeben von Gerhard Thür, Cologne, Weimar et Vienne, Böhlau, 1994, X + 287 pages (Akten der Gesellschaft für griechische und hellenistische Rechtsgeschichte 10).

X. *Symposion 1995. Vorträge zur griechischen und hellenistischen Rechtsgeschichte (Korfu, 1.-5. September 1995).* Herausgegeben von Gerhard Thür et Julie Vélissaropoulos-Karakostas, Cologne, Weimar et Vienne, Böhlau, 1997, X +

414 pages (Akten der Gesellschaft für griechische und hellenistische Rechtsgeschichte 11).

XI. *Symposion 1997. Vorträge zur griechischen und hellenistischen Rechtsgeschichte (Altafiumara, 8.-14. September 1997). Comunicazioni sul diritto greco ed ellenistico Rechtsgeschichte (Altafiumara, 8-14 Settembre 1997).* Herausgegeben von/a cura di Eva Cantarella – Gerhard Thür, Cologne, Weimar et Vienne, Böhlau, 2001, X + 341 pages, 1 frontispice (Akten der Gesellschaft für griechische und hellenistische Rechtsgeschichte 13)

XII. *Symposion 1999. Vorträge zur griechischen und hellenistischen Rechtsgeschichte (Pazo de Mariñán, La Coruña, 6.-9. September 1999). Comunicaciones sobre Historia de Derecho Griego y Helenístico (Pazo de Mariñán, La Coruña, 6-9 septiembre 1999).* Herausgegeben von/editadas por Gerhard Thür – Francisco Javier Fernández Nieto, Cologne, Weimar et Vienne, Böhlau, 2003, XXX + 579 pages, 1 frontispice (Akten der Gesellschaft für hellenistische und griechische Rechtsgeschichte 14).

XIII. *Symposion 2001. Vorträge zur griechischen und hellenistischen Rechtsgeschichte (Evanston, Illinois, 5.-8. September 2001). Papers on Greek and Hellenistic Legal History (Evanston, Illinois, September 5-8, 2001).* Herausgegeben von / edited by Robert W. Wallace – Michael Gagarin, Vienne, Verlag der Österreichischen Akademie der Wissenschaften, 2005, X + 369 p. (Österreichische Akademie der Wissenschaften, Philosophisch-historische Klasse, Kommission für Antike Rechtsgeschichte; Akten der Gesellschaft für hellenistische und griechische Rechtsgeschichte 16).

XIV. *Symposion 2003. Vorträge zur griechischen und hellenistischen Rechtsgeschichte (Rauischholzhausen, 30. September-3. Oktober 2003).* Herausgegeben von Hans-Albert Rupprecht, Vienne, Verlag der Österreichischen Akademie der Wissenschaften, 2006, X + 468 pages (Österreichische Akademie der Wissenschaften, Philosophisch-historische Klasse, Kommission für Antike Rechtsgeschichte; Akten der Gesellschaft für hellenistische und griechische Rechtsgeschichte 17).

XV. Salerno, 14-18 septembre 2005 (*le présent volume*).

SUJETS

I. L'HISTOIRE DU DROIT GREC ET SES ARTISANS: (a) bio- et bibliographie (38, 102, 248, 271, 248); (b) jusgrécistique, ses limites et méthodes (1, 2, 19, 65, 103, 122, 157); enseignement (367); (c) rapports avec les disciplines-sœurs: philologie (40, 200), papyrologie et épigraphie (52, 85), sigillographie (352, 353), chronologie (321); rapports avec l'histoire des droits de l'Antiquité: Orient cunéiforme (129, 331, 332), droit égyptien (51, 319, 320), droit juif (162), droit romain (59, 60, 63, 100, 101, 323, 324).

II. SOURCES: (a) sources normatives: lois de cités (3, 33, 83, 165, 197, 198, 222, 331, 332), Athènes (90, 372, 384-387), Gortyne (71, 107, 187, 188, 200-203, 223, 275, 394, 395); législation royale des Lagides (53, 268); édits des préfets d'Égypte (245); (b) sources littéraires: Homère (20-22, 39, 69, 79, 87, 195, 196, 249, 272); Platon (8, 18, 32, 45, 98, 178, 179, 225); Aristote (34, 347, 348, 378, 379); le Vieil Oligarque (254); orateurs: Démosthène (119), Isée (139), Lysias (209); historiens: Xénophon (228); théâtre: Euripide (253); roman: Chariton d'Aphrodisias (166); (c) sources documentaires: forme de documents (30, 43, 123, 158, 360, 361); archives (266); tablettes: Berezan (27), Pompéi (220), Nakone (93, 144).

III. Cités et monarchies: (a) constitutions et lois (73, 237); citoyenneté (368, 369); magistratures (77, 145, 324); (b) Etats fédéraux (79, 94, 148); monarchie hellénistique (160); (c) relations interpoliades (4, 5, 44, 72, 81, 84, 120, 154, 234); guerre et droit militaire (130, 143, 238, 362, 363); (d) finances, fiscalité, banque, circulation monétaire (131, 189, 190, 260, 374, 375).

IV. Statut personnel: (a) citoyens (49, 144, 259, 228, 229); (b) métèques et étrangers (11, 153); (c) affranchissements et affranchis (13, 14, 78, 87, 95, 224); *ateknoi* (54, 236); (d) Grecs et indigènes en Egypte (99, 163).

V. Procès et justice: (a) Athènes: formes de procédure (7, 9, 42, 113, 182-185, 256, 280, 380, 381); actions (26, 74); accusateurs (335, 336); juges (88, 109, 231, 246, 279, 284); synégores (282, 307); régime des preuves (25); sentences (23, 24, 108, 156); (b) justice et procès dans l'Orient hellénisé: Egypte (36, 62, 241, 388-391); autres régions (356, 357).

VI. Crimes et délits: (a) homicide (15, 16, 141, 169-171, 254, 258, 273); adultère (193, 194); vol (128, 146, 276); impiété et atteintes au sacré (41, 161, 214, 215, 350, 351); injure verbale (239); malfaisance (132, 281); Egypte criminelle sous les Lagides (180, 181); (b) sanctions: vengeance (48); peine capitale (110, 132, 145, 345, 346, 370, 371); atimie (46); malédiction publique (376, 377).

VII. Famille: (a) mariage et condition féminine: rites nuptiaux (235); lien conjugal et filiation (67, 92, 115, 118, 358, 359, 388, 389); régime dotal (29, 55, 135); concubines (191, 192); épiclères (12, 50, 56, 75, 136-138) et patroôques (200, 201); adoption (187, 188); grossesse et avortement (97, 285); situation juridique de la femme à Athènes et à Sparte (117, 150); (b) sexualité: comportements sexuels et leur réglementation (232, 339, 340); homosexualité (114, 267); prostitution (240, 398).

VIII. Succcessions: testaments (66, 243, 397); successions ab intestat (89, 104, 127); survie de la mémoire (167, 270, 396); évolution des droits successoraux sur les terres dans l'Egypte ptolémaïque (217, 218).

IX. Biens: (a) acquisition et protection de la propriété (80, 105, 151); servitudes (276); sûretés réelles (17, 125, 242); droits des copropriétaires et des voisins (82, 168); emphytéose (64); (b) droit minier (341-344); (c) droit de l'environnement (292).

X. Contrats: (a) structure de l'obligation contractuelle (16, 86, 399); consensualisme (337, 338); représentation (164), rupture du rapport contractuel (76); serment (232); réparation du préjudice moral (392, 393); (b) vente (31, 47, 126, 246, 269, 279, 366); cession (96, 124); prêt (68, 140); misthôsis: bail et location (58, 61, 68); contrat d'ouvrage (226).

I. Symposion 1971 (Rheda/Bielefeld, 1-4 septembre 1971)

1. Hans Julius Wolff, Juristische Graezistik – Aufgaben, Probleme, Möglichkeiten: I, 1-22
2. Johannes Triantaphyllopoulos, Rechtsphilosophie und positives Recht in Griechenland: I, 23-65
3. Eberhard Ruschenbusch, Die Quellen zur älteren griechischen Geschichte. Ein Überblick über den Stand der Quellenforschung unter besonderer Berücksichtigung der Belange des Rechtshistoriker: I, 67-77

4. Fritz Gschnitzer, Ἐπὶ τοῖσδε ἔδωκαν Πραισίοι Σταλίταις τὰν χώραν. Zu einem Geschäftstyp des griechischen Völkerrechts: I, 79102
5. Georges Daux, Traité entre le roi Attale Ier de Pergame et la Cité de Malla (Crète) (résumé): I, 103
6. Giuseppe Ignazio Luzzatto, Sulla condizione delle città suddite nelle cosiddette ἀρχαί durante il principato: I, 105-123
7. Mario Talamanca, Giudizio paragrafico ed amissibilità dell'azione nel sistema processuale attico: I, 125-129
8. Diederich Behrend, Die ἀνάδικος δίκη und das Scholion zu Plato *Nomoi* 937d: I, 131-156
9. Gerhard Thür, Komplexe Prozessführung. Dargestellt am Beispiel des *Trapezitikos* (Isokr. 17): I, 157-188
10. Harald Meyer-Laurin, Zur Entstehung und Bedeutung der καθάπερ ἐκ δίκης-Klausel in den griechischen Papyri Ägyptens: I, 189-204
11. Claude Mossé, Métèques et étrangers à Athènes aux IVe-IIIe siècles avant notre ère: I, 205-213
12. Evanghélos Karabélias, L'épiclérat dans la Comédie Nouvelle et dans les sources latines: I, 215-254
13. Arnold Kränzlein, Die attischen Aufzeichnungen über die Einlieferung von φιάλαι ἐξελευθερικαί: 255-264
14. Benjamin Nadel, Actes d'affranchissement des esclaves du Royaume de Bosphore et les origines de la *manumissio in ecclesia*: I, 265-291
15. Eva Cantarella, φόνος μὴ ἐκ προνοίας. L'elemento soggetivo dell'atto illecito nei logografi e nei filosofi: I, 293-319
16. Johannes Herrmann, Verfügungsermächtigungen als Gestaltungselemente verschiedener griechischer Geschäftstypen: I, 321-332
17. Louis R. F. Germain, Les *horoi*: I, 333-346
18. Eberhard Klingenberg, Bemerkungen zum platonischen Bienenrecht (Lg. 843d7-e1): I, 347-354

II. Symposion 1974 (Gargnano-sur-Garde, 5-8 juin 1974)

19. Arnaldo Biscardi, Diritto greco e scienza del diritto: II, 1-22 (et discussion 23-31)
20. Alberto Maffi, Rilevanza delle 'regole di scambio' omeriche per la storia e la metodologia del diritto: II, 33-62 (et discussion 63-68)
21. Eva Cantarella, Aspetti del fenomeno processuale in Omero: II, 69-83
22. Stefano Nespor, Spunti sui rapporti fra diritto e religione in Omero: II, 85-96 (et discussion 96-101)
23. Mario Talamanca, Δικάζειν e κρίνειν alle origini dell'attività giurisdizionale in Grecia: II, 103-133 (et discussion 133-135)
24. Diederich Behrend, Dike nach Émile Benveniste: II, 137-145 (et discussion 145-152)
25. Gerhard Thür, Die πρόκλησις zur βάσανος: II, 153-164 (et discussion 165-173)
26. Dimitri Gofas, Les *emmenoi dikai* à Thasos: II, 175-186 (et discussion 186-188)
27. Henryk Kupiszewski, La lettera di Berezan: 189-195 (et discussion 195-199)
28. Evanghélos Karabélias, Contribution à l'étude de l'épidikasie attique: II, 201-222 (et discussion 223-225)
29. Panayotis Dimakis, A propos du droit de propriété de la femme mariée sur les biens dotaux d'après le droit grec ancien: II, 227-240 (et discussion 240-243)

30. Maria Grazia Bianchini, La συγγραφή e il problema delle forme contrattuali: II, 245-258 (et discussion 258-262)
31. Harald Meyer-Laurin, Die Haftung für den *noxa non solutus* beim Sklavenkauf nach griechischem Recht: II, 263-279 (et discussion 279-282)
32. Eberhard Klingenberg, La legge platonica sulle fontane pubbliche: II, 283-303 (et discussion 303-305)
33. Luisa Lepri Sorge, Ai confini fra *nomos* e *psephisma*: II, 307-322 (et discussion 322-326)
34. Alain Houlou, Eté 330 avant Jésus-Christ: aux origines du droit constitutionnel: II, 327-356 (et discussion 356-359)
35. Mario Amelotti, Conoscibilità degli altri diritti ellenistici rispetto al diritto tolemaico: II, 361-365 (et discussion 365-374)
36. Joseph Modrzejewski, Chrématistes et laocrites: II, 375-388 (et discussion 388-391)
37. Arnaldo Biscardi, Sintesi conclusiva: II, 393-401

III. Symposion 1977 (Chantilly, 31 mai-3 juin 1977)

38. Bibliografie Hans Julius Wolff: III, XVII-XXVIII
39. Eberhard Ruschenbusch, Der Ursprung des gerichtlichen Rechtsstreits bei den Griechen: III, 1-8
40. Haiim B. Rosén, Questions d'interprétation de textes juridiques grecs de la plus ancienne époque. La contribution de la philologie à la compréhension juridique: III, 9-32
41. Alberto Maffi, Τὰ ἱερὰ καὶ τὰ ὅσια. Contributo allo studio della terminologia giuridico-sacrale greca: III, 33-53
42. Gerhard Thür, Kannte das altgriechische Recht die Eigentumsdiadikasie?: III, 55-69
43. Julie Vélissaropoulos, Les symbola d'affaires. Remarques sur les tablettes archaïques de l'île de Corfou: III, 71-83
44. Henri van Effenterre, 'Ανδιχάζω dans le traité Oiantheia-Chaleion: III, 85-97
45. Eberhard Klingenberg, Das Zinsrecht in Platons *Nomoi*: III, 99-112
46. Mogens Herman Hansen, Atimia in Consequence of Private Debts: III, 113-120
47. Dimitri Gofas, La vente sur échantillon à Athènes d'après un texte d'Hypéride: III, 121-129
48. Benedetto Bravo, *Androlēpsíai*. La 'prise d'hommes' comme vengeance d'un meurtre commis dans une cité étrangère: III, 131-156
49. Claude Mossé, Citoyens 'actifs' et citoyens 'passifs' à Athènes au IVe siècle avant J.C.: III, 157-160
50. Naphtali Lewis, *Aphairesis* in Athenian Law and Custom: III, 161-178
51. Erwin Seidl, Das Grundsteuerkataster in Ägypten vor der Ptolemäerzeit: III, 179-182
52. Georges Daux, Un mot-fantôme ou les méfaits d'une erreur de lapicide: III, 183-188
53. Livia Migliardi Zingale, Richiamo ad un prostagma tolemaico nel papiro genovese PUG II Nr.54: III, 189-195
54. Pierre Cabanes, La loi des atecnoi dans les affranchissements d'Épire: III, 197-213
55. Arnaldo Biscardi, *Proix* e *pherne* alla luce di un nuovo papiro fiorentino: III, 215-221
56. Evanghélos Karabélias, La situation successorale de la fille unique du défunt dans la koiné juridique hellénistique: III, 223-234
57. Hans-Albert Rupprecht, Βεβαίωσις und Nichtangriffsklausel. Zur Funktion zweier Urkundenklauseln in den griechischen Papyri bis Diocletian: III, 235-245

58. Johannes Herrmann, Prodoma-Leistungen in Urkunden der Ptolemäerzeit: III, 247-257
59. Jean Triantaphyllopoulos, *Varia Graeco-Romana* IV (I. Une loi grecque dans Cicéron; II. Lucrèce et le folklore byzantin; III. Cassia; IV. Δευτερολόγος; V. Lucullus): III, 259-268
60. Dieter Nörr, Cicero, Topica 4, 22: Zur Anwendung der *cautio damni infecti* bei einer Kommunmauer und zum rhetorisch-philosophischen Topos ἀπὸ τοῦ αἰτίου: III, 269-305
61. Arnold Kränzlein, Zu den Privatpacht-Hypomnemata der ersten zwei nachchristlichen Jahrhunderte: III, 307-324
62. Herwig Maehler, Neues vom Prozeß der Drusilla gegen Agrippinus: III, 325-333
63. Joseph Modrzejewski, Ménandre de Laodicée et l'Édit de Caracalla: III, 335-363
64. Dieter Simon, Das frühbyzantinische Emphyteuserecht: III, 365-422

IV. Symposion 1979 (Égine, 3 -7 septembre 1979)

65. Hans Julius Wolff, Zum Problem der dogmatischen Erfassung des altgriechischen Rechts: IV, 7-20
66. Arnaldo Biscardi, Osservazioni critiche sulla terminologia διαθήκη, διατίθεσθαι: IV, 21-35
67. Joseph Modrzejewski, La structure juridique du mariage grec: IV, 37-71
68. Mario Amelotti – Livia Migliardi-Zingale, Un mutuo ipotecario di diritto ellenistico in un papiro di età traianea: IV, 73-81
69. Eva Cantarella, Spunti di riflessione critica su ὕβρις e τίμη in Omero: IV, 83-96
70. Pierre Cabanes, Les Etats fédéraux de Grèce du nord-ouest: pouvoirs locaux et pouvoir fédéral: IV, 97-111
71. Henri van Effenterre, Le droit et la langue. A propos du code de Gortyne: IV, 113-128
72. Marta Giacchero, Il trattato di unione monetaria fra Mitilene e Focea (IG XII, 2, 1): IV, 129-139
73. Fritz Gschnitzer, Zur Normenhierarchie im öffentlichen Recht der Griechen: IV, 141-164
74. Mogens Herman Hansen, Two Notes on the Athenian *dikai emporikai*: IV, 165-175
75. Evanghélos Karabélias, Homère, Platon et survivances littéraires de l'épiclérat: IV, 177-196
76. Photios P. Katzouros, Pollux et la δίκη συνθηκῶν παραβάσεως: IV, 197-215
77. Eberhard Klingenberg, Die Aufgaben der städtischen Verwaltungsbeamten in Griechenland: IV, 217-235
78. Arnold Kränzlein, Bemerkungen zu den griechischen Freilassungsinschriften: IV, 237-247
79. Alberto Maffi, 'Ατιμάζειν e φεύγειν nei poemi omerici: IV, 249-260
80. Claude Mossé, La démocratie athénienne et la protection de la propriété: IV, 261-271
81. Francisco Javier Fernández Nieto, Die Abänderungsklausel in den griechischen Staatsverträgen der klassischen Zeit: IV, 273-286
82. Hans-Albert Rupprecht, Zu Voraussetzungen, Umfang und Herkunft des Vorkaufsrechts der Gemeinschafter nach den Papyri: IV, 287-301
83. Eberhard Ruschenbusch, Die Polis und das Recht: IV, 303-326
84. Gerhard Thür, Bemerkungen zum Zeugenbeweis im Rechtshilfevertrag aus Stymphalos IG 5/2, 357: IV, 327-342

V. Symposion 1982 (Santander, 1-4 septembre 1982)

85. Henri van Effenterre, Préliminaires épigraphiques aux études d'histoire du droit grec: V, 1-8
86. Gábor Hamza, Quelques aspects de l'idée du contrat au [dans le] domain[e] des droits antiques en Méditerranée: V, 9-20
87. Francisco Javier Fernández Nieto, Die Freilassung von Sklaven in Homerischer Zeit: V, 21-29
88. Eberhard Ruschenbusch, Drei Beiträge zur öffentlichen Diaita in Athen (I. Der öffentliche Schiedsrichter und die Paragraphe; II. Schriftlichkeit bei Zeugnis, Klage und Klagenbeantwortung; III. Das Wirken der öffentlichen Schiedsrichter vor dem Hintergrund ihrer sozialen Herkunft): V, 31-40
89. Evanghélos Karabélias, La succession ab intestat en droit attique: V, 41-63
90. Douglas M. MacDowell, Athenian Laws about Choruses: V, 65-77
91. Ángel Sánchez de la Torre, Un derecho sin violencia: el mito de Crono en *Leyes* de Platon: V, 79-128
92. Claude Mossé, Quelques remarques sur la famille à Athènes à la fin du IVe siècle: le témoignage du théatre de Ménandre: V, 129-134
93. David Asheri, Formes et procédures de réconciliation dans les cités grecques: le décret de Nakone: V, 135-145
94. Pierre Cabanes, Le Koinon des Prasaiboi: institutions et société d'après les inscriptions de Bouthrôtos: V, 147-183
95. Arnold Kränzlein, Fragen der Rechtsverfolgung in Delphi zur Zeit der Freilassungsinschriften [résumé]: V, 185-186
96. Hans-Albert Rupprecht, Parachoresis und Ekchoresis. Abtretung und Rechtsübertragung in den griechischen Papyri: V, 187-193
97. Sophia Adam, La femme enceinte dans les papyrus: V, 195-203
98. Eberhard Klingenberg, Διακωλύειν ἀνταγωνιστήν. Eine platonische Bestimmung des griechischen Wettkampfrechts: Pl. Lg. 955a2-b4: V, 205-239
99. Joseph Modrzejewski, Entre la cité et le fisc: le statut grec dans l'Égypte romaine: V, 241-280
100. Naphtali Lewis, A Roman Law of Hellenistic Origin?: V, 281-289
101. Armando Torrent, Pap. Oxy. II 237. A propósito de *accusatio falsi*: V, 291-300

VI. Symposion 1985 (Ringberg, 24-26 juillet 1985)

102. Gerhard Thür, Hans Julius Wolff und sein Symposion: VI, XI-XII
103. Henri van Effenterre, Droit et prédroit en Grèce depuis le déchiffrement du linéaire B: VI, 3-6
104. Arnaldo Biscardi, La successione legittima degli ascendenti nel diritto ereditario panellenico: uno spunto epigrafico del VI o V secolo a.C.: VI, 7-13
105. Eberhard Klingenberg, Griechisches Fundrecht in der 'Vita Aesopi'?: VI, 15-21
106. Micheline van Effenterre, Ein neues Gesetz aus dem archaischen Kreta: VI, 23-27
107. Michael Gagarin, The Function of Witnesses at Gortyn: VI, 29-54
108. Gerhard Thür, Zum δικάζειν im Urteil aus Mantineia (IG V 2, 262): VI, 55-69
109. Ernst Heitsch, Der Archon Basileus und die attischen Gerichtshöfe für Tötungsdelikte: VI, 71-87

110. John Whitehorne, Punishment under the Decree of Cannonus: VI, 89-97
111. David Cohen, The Prosecution of Impiety in Athenian Law: VI, 99-107
112. Laurens Winkel, Das sokratische Paradoxon οὐδεῖς ἐξαμαρτάνει und strafrechtliche Zurechnung im Lichte neuerer Literatur: VI, 109-117
113. Photios P. Katzouros, Origine et effets de la παραγραφή attique: VI, 119-151
114. Eva Cantarella, L'omosessualità nel diritto ateniese: VI, 153-175
115. Alberto Maffi, Matrimonio, concubinato e filiazione illegittima nell'Atene degli oratori: VI, 177-214
116. Claude Mossé, Le *Contre Spoudias* de Démosthène et les droits économiques des femmes d'Athènes au IVe siècle: VI, 215-219
117. Panayotis D. Dimakis, Quelques remarques à propos de la position juridique des Athéniennes ('Ατθίδες) à l'époque classique (tentatives en vue de l'effondrement d'un mythe): VI, 221-231
118. Evanghélos Karabélias, Inceste, mariage et stratégies matrimoniales dans l'Athènes classique: VI, 233-251
119. Douglas M. MacDowell, The Authenticity of Demosthenes 29 (*Against Aphobos III*) as a Source of Information about Athenian Law: VI, 253-262
120. Martin Dreher, Zu IG II[2] 404, dem athenischen Volksbeschluß über die Eigenstaatlichkeit der keischen Poleis: VI, 263-281
121. Sophia Adam, Aspects de la sécurité de la navigation dans l'Antiquité grecque: VI, 283-291
122. Eberhard Ruschenbusch, Über die rechte Art, das Recht Athens zu studieren: VI, 293-296
123. Mario Amelotti – Livia Migliardi Zingale, Osservazioni sulla duplice scritturazione nei documenti: VI, 299-309
124. Naphtali Lewis, Why *Parachoresis*?: VI, 311-315
125. Johannes Herrmann, Zur ὠνή ἐν πίστει des hellenistischen Rechts: VI, 317-324
126. Arnold Kränzlein, Probleme kaiserzeitlicher Tierveräußerungsverträge auf Papyrus: VI, 325-335
127. Joseph Mélèze-Modrzejewski, 'Ιουδαῖοι ἀφῃρημένοι: la fin de la communauté juive d'Égypte (115-117 de n.è.): VI, 337-361, pl. I
128. Adam Łukaszewicz, Zur ἀναζήτησις in Diebstahlsanzeigen aus dem römischen Ägypten: VI, 363-368
129. Joachim Hengstl, Altassyrisches und gräko-ägyptisches Eherecht. Eine rechtsvergleichende Skizze: VI, 369-374
130. Francisco Javier Fernández Nieto, Zur Problematik der Kriegskostenentschädigung in der Alten Welt (mit besonderer Berücksichtigung der griechischen Verhältnisse): VI, 375-388
131. Fritz Gschnitzer, Beurkundungsgebühren im römischen Kaiserreich. Zu IvE I a 13: VI, 389-403
132. Julie Vélissaropoulos-Karakostas, Ὕπαιπα: VI, 405-413, pl. II
133. Johannes Triantaphyllopoulos, Griechische Parallelen zur lex Aquilia: VI, 415-423
134. Dimitri C. Gofas, *Epiplous*: une institution du droit maritime grec, antique, hellénistique, byzantin et postbyzantin: VI, 425-444

VII. Symposion 1988 (Sienne et Pise, 6-8 juin 1988)

135. Arnaldo Biscardi, Sulla cosiddetta consensualità del contratto dotale in diritto attico: VII, 3-13
136. Eberhard Ruschenbusch, Bemerkungen zum Erbtochterrecht in den solonischen Gesetzen: VII, 15-20
137. Alberto Maffi, E' esistita l'aferesi dell'epikleros?: VII, 21-36
138. Luisa Lepri Sorge, Per una riprova storica dell'ἀφαίρεσις τῆς ἐπικλήρου (con una replica di A.Maffi): VII, 37-40
139. Sima Avramović, Plaidoyer for Isaeus, or. IX: VII, 41-55
140. Edward Cohen, A Study in Contrast: 'Maritime Loans' and 'Landed Loans' at Athens: VII, 57-79
141. Michael Gagarin, 'Bouleusis' in Athenian Homicide Law: VII, 81-99
142. Eberhard Klingenberg, Eigentumserwerb durch Fund: VII, 101-110
143. Francisco Javier Fernández Nieto, La competencia penal de los estrategos: VII, 111-122
144. Claude Mossé, Les hippeis athéniens au IVème siècle: classe censitaire ou ordre privilégié?: VII, 123-128
145. Salvatore Alessandrì, I dieci probuli ad Atene: aspetti giuridico-costituzionali: VII, 129-147
146. Martin Dreher, Ein athenischer Synhedros im Zweiten Athenischen Seebund. Κλοπή in Dem. 24, 127: VII, 149-177
147. Giuseppe Nenci, *Klarographia* e *adelphothetia*. Osservazioni sul decreto di Nacona (ASNP, s. III, XII, 1982, pp. 776-777; SEG, XXX, nr. 1119): VII, 173-177
148. Silvio Cataldi, Il giuramento al ϱοϱolo dei re molossi: VII, 179-192
149. Felice Costabile, Πολιτεία ed οἰκονομία a Locri Epizefiri: VII, 193-200
150. Panayotis D. Dimakis, La posizione inferiore delle donne nella Sparta classica: VII, 201-212
151. Mαuro Corsaro, Qualche osservazione sulle procedure di recupero delle terre pubbliche nelle città greche: VII, 213-229
152. Diederich Behrend, Die Pachturkunden der Klytiden: VII, 231-250
153. Henri et Micheline van Effenterre, Le contrôle des étrangers dans la cité grecque: VII, 251-259
154. Giangiacomo Panessa, La *philia* nelle relazioni interstatali del mondo greco: VII, 261-266
155. Andreas Wittenburg, Il ritorno degli esuli a Mitilene: VII, 267-276
156. Gerhard Thür, Nachträge zum Urteil aus Mantineia (IG V 2,262): VII, 277-282
157. David Cohen, Late Sources and the 'Reconstruction' of Greek Legal Institutions: VII, 283-293
158. Mario Amelotti – Livia Migliardi Zingale, Συγγραφή, χειρόγραφον – *testatio, chirographum*. Osservazioni in tema di tipologie documentali: VII, 297-304
159. Remo Martini, Di alcuni prestiti ai naviganti nella prassi ellenistica: VII, 305-309
160. Andréas Helmis, Despotisme et répression: les limites du pouvoir ptolémaïque: VII, 311-317
161. Joseph Mélèze-Modrzejewski, Les tourments de Paul de Tarse: VII, 319-336
162. Benjamin I. Nadel, Jewish Freedmen and 'Semi-Proselytes' in the Roman Empire: A Socio-Religious Appraisal and the Problem of Hellenistic Legal Influences: VII, 337-340

163. Adam Łukaszewicz, Quelques remarques sur l'expulsion des Aigyptioi d'Alexandrie: VII, 341-347
164. Gábor Hamza, Zur Frage der Stellvertretung im Willen anhand der P.Amh. 90 und P.Oxy. 501: VII, 349-360
165. Carlo Castello, Sulla legislazione attribuita a Caronda nel secondo Mimiambo di Eroda: VII, 361-368
166. Evanghélos Karabélias, Le roman de Chariton d'Aphrodisias et le droit. Renversements de situation et exploitation des ambiguïtés juridiques: VII, 369-396
167. Dimitri C. Gofas, Observations sur une inscription de Sparte contenant des *damnationes memoriae* (SEG XXXIV, 309): VII, 397-412
168. Julie Vélissaropoulos-Karakostas, Συνεπαινοῦντες. Aux origines du droit de préemption: VII, 413-424

VIII. Symposion 1990 (Pacific Grove, Californie, 24-26 septembre 1990)

169. Joseph Mélèze Modrzejewski, La sanction de l'homicide en droit grec et hellénistique: VIII, 3-16
170. Sally Humphreys, A Historical Approach to Drakon's Law on Homicide: VIII, 17-45
171. Stephen C. Todd, Response to Sally Humphreys: VIII, 47-51
172. Gerhard Thür, The Jurisdiction of the Areopagos in Homicide Cases: VIII, 53-72
173. Robert W. Wallace, Response to Gerhard Thür: VIII, 73-79
174. Henri van Effenterre, Criminal Law in Archaic Crete: VIII, 83-86
175. Michael Gagarin, Response to Henri van Effentene: VIII, 87-91
176. Julie Vélissaropoulos-Karakostas, Νεποινεὶ τεθνάναι: VIII, 93-104
177. Edwin M. Carawan, Response to Julie Vélissaropoulos: VIII, 107-114
178. Trevor J. Saunders, Penal Law and Family Law in Plato's Magnesia: VIII, 115-132
179. Edward Harris, Response to Trevor Saunders: VIII, 133-148
180. Hans-Albert Rupprecht, Straftaten und Rechtschutz nach den griechischen Papyri der ptolemäischen Zeit: VIII, 149-152
181. Roger S. Bagnall, Response to Hans-Albert Rupprecht: VIII, 149
182. David Cohen, Demosthenes' *Against Meidias* and Athenian Litigation: VIII, 155-164
183. Alan Boegehold, Three Court Days: VIII, 165-182
184. Ronald Stroud, Response to Alan Boegehold: VIII, 183-185
185. Douglas M. MacDowell, The Athenian Procedure of *phasis*: VIII, 187-198
186. Mogens H. Hansen, Response to Douglas MacDowell: VIII, 199-201 [*addendum*: Symposion 1999, 167 n. 1]
187. Alberto Maffi, Adozione e strategie successorie a Gortina e ad Atene: VIII, 205-231
188. Sima Avramović, Response to Alberto Maffi: VIII, 233-237
189. Edward E. Cohen, Banking as a 'Family Business': Legal Adaptations Affecting Wives and Slaves: VIII, 239-263
190. Josiah Ober, Response to Edward Cohen: VIII, 265-271
191. Claude Mossé, La place de la *pallakè* dans la famille athénienne: VIII, 273-279
192. Cynthia Patterson, Response to Claude Mossé: VIII, 281-287
193. Eva Cantarella, *Moicheia*. Reconsidering a Problem: VIII, 289-296
194. Lin Foxhall, Response to Eva Cantarella: VIII, 297-304

IX. Symposion 1993 (Graz-Andritz, 12-16 septembre 1993)

195. Henri et Micheline van Effenterre, Arbitrages homériques: IX, 3-10
196. Gerhard Thür, Diskussionsbeitrag zum Referat Henri und Micheline van Effenterre: IX, 11-15
197. Peter Siewert, Eine archaische Rechtsaufzeichnung aus der antiken Stadt Elis: IX, 17-32, 1 pl.
198. Fritz Gschnitzer, Diskussionsbeitrag zum Referat Peter Siewert: IX, 33-44
199. Hatto H. Schmitt, Überlegungen zur Sympolitie: IX, 35-44
200. Monique Bile, La πατρõιõκος des Lois de Gortyne: Etude linguistique: IX, 45-51
201. Sima Avramović, Response to Monique Bile: IX, 53-60, 1 fig.
202. Michael Gagarin, The Economic Status of Women in the Gortyn Code: Retroactivity and Change: IX, 61-71
203. Alberto Maffi, Risposta a Michael Gagarin: IX, 73-78
204. Kenneth J. Burchfiel, The Myth of 'Prelaw' in Early Greece: IX, 79-104
205. Diederich Behrend, Diskussionsbeitrag zum Referat Kenneth J. Burchfiel: IX, 105-107
206. Robert W. Wallace, The Athenian Laws against Slander: IX, 109-124
207. Stephen C. Todd, Status and Contract in Fourth-Century Athens: I, 125-140
208. Edward E. Cohen, Status and Contract in Fourth-Century Athens: A Reply to Stephen C. Todd: IX, 141-152
209. Douglas M. MacDowell, The Case of the Rude Soldier (Lysias 9): IX, 153-164
210. Martin Dreher, Diskussionsbeitrag zum Referat Douglas M. MacDowell: IX, 165-168
211. Edward M. Harris, 'In the Act' or 'Red-Handed'? Apagoge to the Eleven and *furtum manifestum*: IX,169-184
212. Julie Vélissaropoulos-Karakostas, Altgriechische πίστις und Vertrauenshaftung: IX, 185-190
213. Éva Jakab, Bemerkungen zur Vertrauenshaftung im altgriechischen Recht: IX, 191-197
214. Joseph Mélèze-Modrzejewski, Στέρησις θήκης. A propos du délit religieux dans l'Égypte grecque et romaine: IX, 201-214
215. Adam Łukaszewicz, Artémisia – l'Antigone de Memphis? (A propos de la στέρησις θήκης): IX, 215-218
216. Naphtali Lewis, 'Εμπολεύευιν as a Punishable Offense: IX, 219-224
217. Hans-Albert Rupprecht, Die Vererblichkeit von Grund und Boden im ptolemäischen Ägypten: IX, 225-238
218. Arnold Kränzlein, Diskussionsbeitrag zum Referat Hans-Albert Rupprecht: IX, 239-240
219. Mario Amelotti – Livia Migliardi Zingale, Dalle tabelle bronzee di Locri alle tavolette cerate di Pozzuoli: IX, 241-249
220. Dimitri C. Gofas, Encore une fois sur la Tabula Pompeiana 13 (Essai d'une interprétation nouvelle): IX, 251-266
221. Gerhard Thür, Die Aestimationsabrede im Seefrachtvertrag. Diskussionsbeitrag zum Referat Dimitri C. Gofas: IX, 267-271

X. Symposion 1995 (Corfou, 1-5 septembre 1995)

222. Fritz Gschnitzer, Zur Terminologie von 'Gesetz' und 'Recht' im frühen Griechisch: X, 3-10
223. Henri et Micheline van Effenterre, Du nouveau sur le 'Code' de Gortyne: X, 11-15
224. Alberto Maffi, Processo di libertà e rivendicazione in proprietà dello schiavo a Gortina e ad Atene: X, 17-25
225. Jean-Marie Bertrand, De l'usage de l'épigraphie dans la cité des Magnètes platoniciens: X, 27-47
226. Remo Martini, Sul contratto d'opera nell'Atene classica: X, 49-55
227. Edward E. Cohen, The *Astoi* of Attika: Nationality and Citizenship at Athens: X, 57-95
228. Eva Cantarella, Filiazione legittima e cittadinanza: X, 97-111
229. Stephen C. Todd, Status and Gender in Athenian Public Records: X, 113-124
230. Michael Gagarin, Oaths and Oath-Challenges in Greek Law: X, 125-134
231. Evanghélos Karabélias, L'arbitrage privé dans l'Athènes classique: X, 135-149
232. Robert W. Wallace, On not Legislating Sexual Conduct in Fourth-Century Athens: X, 151-166
233. Eberhard Ruschenbusch, Drei Beiträge zum Strafrecht Athens (I. Solon F 26: Vergewaltigung? II. Echinos. III. δίκη κατά τινος und πρός τινα): X, 167-171
234. Gerhard Thür, Der Rechtsgewährungsvertrag aus Stymphalos (IPArk 17; IG V2, 357): X, 173-178
235. Stavros Perentidis, *Apaulia – Epaulia – Anakalyptèria*: définition et fonction des rites et des dons nuptiaux: X, 179-204 et 8 fig.
236. Arnold Kränzlein, Überlegungen zu den Freilassungsinschriften aus Bouthrotos: X, 205-210
237. Felice Costabile, Constitutions de *poleis* italiotes et siceliotes: X, 211-219
238. Francisco Javier Fernández Nieto, Los reglamentos militares griegos y la justicia castrense en época helenística: X, 221-244
239. Joseph Mélèze-Modrzejewski, 'Paroles néfastes' et 'vers obscènes'. À propos de l'injure verbale en droit grec et hellénistique [résumé]: X, 247-248
240. Bernard Legras, La prostitution féminine dans l'Égypte ptolémaïque: X, 249-264
241. Joachim Hengstl, Petita in Petitionen gräko-ägyptischer Papyri: X, 265-289
242. Hans-Albert Rupprecht, Zwangsvollstreckung und dingliche Sicherung in den Papyri der ptolemäischen und römischen Zeit: X, 291-302
243. Livia Migliardi Zingale, Dal testamento ellenistico al testamento romano nella prassi documentale egiziana: cesura o continuità?: X, 303-312
244. Éva Jakab, Gaius kommentiert die Papyri? Vertragsklauseln im Weinkauf: X, 313-324
245. Andrea Jördens, Erlasse und Edikte. Ein neuer Erlass des Präfekten M. Sempronius Liberalis und die Frage der statthalterlichen Rechtssetzungskompetenz: X, 325-352
246. Angelos Chaniotis, 'Tempeljustiz' im kaiserlichen Kleinasien. Rechtliche Aspekte der Sühneinschriften Lydiens und Phrygiens: X, 353-384
247. Julie Vélissaropoulos-Karakostas, Épilogue [Symposion 1995]: X, 385-387

XI. Symposion 1997 (Altafiumara, 8-14 septembre 1997)

248. Mario Amelotti, Arnaldo Biscardi †: XI, IX
249. Eva Cantarella, Modelli giurisdizionali omerici: il giudice unico, la giustizia dei vecchi: XI, 3-19
250. Henri et Micheline van Effenterre, Le vocabulaire de l'appartenance dans la loi de Gortyne: XI, 21-31
251. Remo Martini, Su due norme transitorie del codice di Gortina: XI, 33-39
252. Michael Gagarin, The Gortyn Code and Greek Legal Procedure: XI, 41-52
253. Pietro Cobetto Ghiggia, Una testimonianza sull'*apokeryxis* nell'*Alcesti* di Euripide: XI, 53-60
254. Athina Dimopoulou-Piliouni, La Constitution des Athéniens du Pseudo-Xénophon: une approche comparative: XI, 61-74
255. Edward M. Harris, How to Kill in Attic Greek. The Semantics of the Verb (ἀπο)κτείνειν and their Implications for Athenian Homicide Law: XI, 75-87
256. Robert W. Wallace, *Diamarturia* in Late Fourth-Century Athens: Notes on a 'Cheese Pot' (SEG XXXVI 296): XI, 89-101, 2 pl.
257. Julie Vélissaropoulos-Karakostas, Remarques sur la clause κυρία ἡ συγγραφή: XI, 103-115
258. Maria Youni, The Different Categories of Unpunished Killing and the Term ἄτιμος in Ancient Greek Law: XI, 117-137
259. Gerhard Thür, Recht im hellenistischen Athen (Ephebie, Kassel/Austin, Adespota 1152. Basanos): XI, 141-164, 2 pl.
260. Léopold Migeotte, Quelques aspects légaux et juridiques de l'affermage des taxes en Grèce ancienne: XI, 165-174
261. Franco Ghinatti, Di nuovo sulle tabelle dell'Olympeion locrese: XI, 175-207
262. Alberto Maffi, La *lex sacra* di Selinunte e la purificazione dell'omicida: XI, 209-214
263. Francisco Javier Fernández Nieto, Zum Problem der öffentlichen Überwachung der Privatkorrespondenz in der griechischen Welt: XI, 215-224
264. Mario Amelotti, Leggi greche in diritto romano: XI, 225-234
265. Martin Dreher, Die Asylstätte des Romulus – eine griechische Institution im frühen Rom?: XI, 235-252
266. Andrea Jördens, Papyri und private Archive. Ein Diskussionsbeitrag zur papyrologischen Terminologie: XI, 253-268
267. Bernard Legras, L'homosexualité masculine à travers les papyrus grecs d'Égypte: droit et morale: XI, 269-284
268. Livia Migliardi, Ancora sui *prostagmata basileon* nella provincia romana d'Egitto: XI, 285-294
269. Éva Jakab, 'Wo gärt der verkaufte Wein?' Zur Deutung der Weinlieferungskäufe in den graeco-ägyptischen Papyri: XI, 295-318
270. Adam Łukaszewicz, A propos des jardins sacrés en Égypte romaine: XI, 319-321

XII. Symposion 1999 (Pazo de Mariñán, La Coruña, 6-9 septembre 1999)

271. Bibliographie: Joseph Mélèze Modrzejewski: XII: XIII-XXX
272. Julie Vélissaropoulos (Athènes), Homère et Anaximandre de Milet. Aux origines de la justice grecque: XII, 3-19, 1 fig.

273. Henri van Effenterre, Un mort parle toujours: XII, 21-26
274. Micheline van Effenterre, Les servitudes en droit grec archaïque: XII, 27-35
275. Alberto Maffi, La legittimità a stare in giudizio del kosmos gortinio (IC IV 72 I 51-55 e IC IV 41 IV 6-16): XII, 37-56
276. Gerhard Thür, Sachverfolgung und Diebstahl in den griechischen Poleis (Dem. 32, Lys. 23, IC IV 72 I, IPArk 32 u. 17): XII, 57-96
277. Michele Faraguna, Vendite di immobili e registrazione pubblica nelle città greche: XII, 97-122
278. Adele C. Scafuro, IG II^2 204: Boundary Setting and Legal Process in Classical Athens: XII, 123-143
279. Lorenzo Gagliardi, Dove giudicavano gli efeti ?: XII, 145-165
280. Robert W. Wallace, *Phainein* in Athenian laws and legal procedures: XII, 167-181
281. Michael Gagarin, Who were the *kakourgoi*? Career Criminals in Athenian Law: XII, 183-191
282. Lene Rubinstein, *Synêgoroi*: their Place in our Reconstruction of the Athenian Legal Process: XII, 193-207
283. Martin Dreher, Der Prozess gegen Xenophon: XII, 209-227
284. Klaus Hallof, Zur Gerichtsbarkeit in attischen Kleruchien des 4. Jh.: XII, 229-234
285. Stephen C. Todd, Lysias on Abortion: 235-256
286. Inés Calero Secall, Los órdenes sucesorios en derecho griego. Un testimonio etolio (IG IX 1^2 2): XII, 257-271
287. Remo Martini, Testamento e adozione ad Atene (e Roma): XII, 273-295
288. Léopold Migeotte, Taxation directe en Grèce ancienne: XII, 297-313
289. Kaja Harter-Uibopuu, Der Hellenenbund des Antigonos I Monophthalmos und des Demetrios Poliorketes 302/1 v.Chr.: XII, 315-337
290. Víctor Alonso Troncoso, L'institution de l'hégémonie: entre la coutume et le droit écrit: XII, 339-354
291. Francisco Javier Fernández Nieto, E1 derecho privado sobre el botin de guerra en el ámbito dorio (s. V-II a.C.): XII, 355-386
292. Sophie Adam, Environnement et droit dans l'Antiquité grecque: XII, 371-411
293. Jean-Marie Bertrand, De la fiction en droit grec. Quelques réflexions: XII, 387-411
294. Pietro Cobetto Ghiggia, Fonti tarde εὐθυδικία: XII, 413-430
295. Adam Łukaszewicz, Quelques observations sur les chrématistes de Syène (P. Eleph. DAIK. 1): XII, 433-442
296. Bernard Legras, La sanction du plagiat littéraire en droit grec et hellénistique: XII, 443-461
297. Andréas Helmis, Entre les vivants et les morts. La fondation à la mémoire d'Aleximachos fils de Critolaos (IG XII.7, 515; IIe siècle av. J.-C.): XII, 463-480
298. Hans-Albert Rupprecht, Die Streitigkeiten zwischen Satabous und Nestnephis: XII, 481-492
299. Éva Jakab, Bankurkunden und Buchführung. (TPSulp. 60 und die graeco-ägyptischen Papyri): XII, 493-530
300. Bernhard Palme, Pflichten und Risken des Bürgen in byzantinischen Gestellungsbürgschaften: XII, 531-555

XIII. Symposion 2001 (Evanston, Illinois 5-8 septembre 2001)

301. Raymond Westbrook, Penelope's Dowry and Odysseus' Kingship: XIII, 3-24

302. Eva Cantarella, Response to Raymond Westbrook: XIII, 24-32
303. David Cohen, Women in Public: Gender, Citizenship, and Legal Status in Classical Athens: XIII, 33-46
304. Lin Foxhall, Response to David Cohen: XIII, 47-50
305. Adele C. Scafuro, Parent Abusers, Military Shirkers, and Accused Killers: The Authenticity of Dem. 24.105B: XIII, 51-70
306. David C. Mirhady, Response to Adele C. Scafuro: XIII, 71-78
307. Douglas MacDowell, The Athenian Procedure of Dokimasia of Orators: XIII, 79-80
308. Lorenzo Gagliardi, The Athenian Procedure of Dokimasia of Orators. A response to Douglas M. MacDowell: XIII, 89-90
309. Lin Rubinstein, Dangerous Liaisons? Litigants and Witnesses in the Athenian Courts: XIII, 99-120
310. Gerhard Thür, Response to Lin Rubinstein: XII, 121-124
311. Edward M. Harris, Feuding or the Rule of Law? The Nature of Litigation in Classical Athens. An Essay in Legal Sociology: XIII, 125-142
312. Matthew R. Christ, Response to Edward M. Harris: XIII, 143-146
313. Robert W. Wallace, 'Listening to' the Archai in Democratic Athens: XIII, 147-158
314. Edward E. Cohen, Unintended Consequences? The Economic Effect of Athenian Tax Laws: XIII, 159-174
315. Sima Avramović, The Rhetra of Epitadeus and Testaments in Spartan Law: XIII, 175-186
316. Stephen C. Todd, Epitadeus and Juridice. Response to Sima Avramović: XIII, 187-196
317. Éva Jakab, Sale with Earnest Money in the Papyri: XIII, 199-218
318. Hans-Albert Rupprecht, Antwort auf Éva Jakab: XIII, 219-222
319. Bernard Legras, Droit et culture dans le Sarapieion de Memphis: les rêves d'Apollonios fils de Glaukias: XIII, 223-236
320. Bernhard Palme, Antwort auf Bernard Legras: XIII, 237-246
321. Joseph Mélèze Modrzejewski, Chronotomie grecque dans l'Égypte hellénistique et romaine: XIII, 247-262
322. Martin Dreher, Rom und die griechischen Asyle zur Zeit des Tiberius: XIII, 263-282
323. Alberto Maffi, Riposta a Martin Dreher: XIII, 283-303
324. Léopold Migeotte, Les pouvoirs des agoranomes dans les cités grecques: XIII, 287-301
325. Claude Mossé, Remarques sur le texte de Léopold Migeotte: XIII, 302
326. Julie Vélissaropoulos-Karakostas, Justice and Games: The Brabeus: XIII, 303-316
327. Michael Gagarin, Response to Julie Vélissaropoulos-Karakostas: XIII, 317-320
328. Michele Faraguna, La figura dell'*aisymnêtês* tra realtà storica e teoria politica: XIII, 321-338
329. Jean-Marie Bertrand, Réponse à Michele Faraguna: XIII, 339-346

XIV. Symposion 2003 (Rauischholzhausen, 30 septembre-3 octobre 2003)

330. Joseph Mélèze Modrzejewski, Eröffnung: XIV, 3-7
331. Michael Gagarin, Inscribing Laws in Greece and the Near East: XIV, 9-20
332. Raymond Westbrook, A Response to Michael Gagarin: XIV, 21-25
333. Adele C. Scafuro, Magistrates with Hegemony in the Courts of Athens: XIV, 27-52
334. Lin Foxhall, A Response to Adele Scafuro: XIV, 53-56

335. Robert W. Wallace, Withdrawing *graphai* in Ancient Athens. A Case Study in 'Sycophancy' and Legal Idiosyncrasies: XIV, 57-66
336. Edward Harris, A Response to Robert Wallace: XIV, 67-72
337. Edward E. Cohen, Consensual Contracts at Athens: XIV, 73-84
338. Éva Jakab, Antwort auf Edward Cohen: XIV, 85-91
339. Stephen C. Todd, Some Notes on the Regulation of Sexuality in Athenian Law: XIV, 93-111
340. Lorenzo Gagliardi, Risposta a Stephen Todd: XIV, 113-120
341. Douglas M. MacDowell, Mining Cases in Athenian Law, : XIV, 121-131
342. Mario Talamanca, Intervento sulla relazione di MacDowell: XIV, 133-139
343. Michele Faraguna, La città di Atene e l'amministrazione delle miniere del Laurion: XIV, 141-160
344. Gerhard Thür, Antwort auf Michele Faraguna: XIV, 161-165
345. Marietta Horster, Die Olivenbäume der Athena und die Todesstrafe: XIV, 167-185
346. Hartmut Leppin, Antwort auf Marietta Horster: XIV, 187-190
347. Jean-Marie Bertrand, À propos de la *Rhétorique* d'Aristote (I, 1373b1-1374b23), analyse du processus judiciaire: XIV, 191-202
348. Andréas Helmis, Réponse à Jean-Marie Bertrand: XIV, 203-206
349. Francisco Javier Fernández Nieto, Titularidad y cesión de los derechos de la pesca marítima en la antigua Grecia: XIV, 207-232
350. Léopold Migeotte, La gestion des biens sacrés dans les cités grecques: XIV, 233-246
351. Martin Dreher, Antwort auf Léopold Migeotte: XIV, 247-254
352. Rudolf Haensch, Das öffentliche Siegel der griechischen Staaten – zwischen Kontrollmittel und Staatssymbol: XIV, 255-279
353. Evangélos Karabélias, Réponse à Rudolf Haensch: XIV, 281-283
354. Julie Vélissaropoulos-Karakostas, Une inscription inédite de Corfou: XIV, 285-292
355. Kaja Harter-Uibopuu, Antwort auf Julie Vélissaropoulos-Karakostas: XIV, 293-298
356. Alberto Maffi, Studi sulla giurisdizione nei regni ellenistici: XIV, 301-314
357. Dieter Nörr, Antwort auf Alberto Maffi (Das Erbgesetz von Dura-Europos – P. Dura 12 – und das sog. *oikos*-Prinzip): XIV, 315-322
358. Barbara Anagnostou-Canas, Effets juridiques de la filiation dans l'Egypte grecque et romaine: XIV, 323-339
359. Jakub Urbanik, A Response to Barbara Anagnostou Canas: XIV, 341-346
360. Uri Yiftach-Firanko, Regionalism and Legal Documents: The Case of Oxyrhynchos: XIV, 347-365
361. Andrea Jördens, Antwort auf Uri Yiftach-Firanko: XIV, 367-374
362. Bernhard Palme, Spätrömische Militärgerichtsbarkeit in den Papyri: XIV, 375-408
363. A.J. Boudewijn Sirks, Antwort auf Bernhard Palme: XIV, 409-414
364. Fritz Mitthof, Neue Evidenz zur Verbreitung juristischer Fachliteratur im spätantiken Ägypten: XIV, 415-422
365. Mario Amelotti – Livia Migliardi Zingale, Risposta a Fritz Mitthof: XIV, 423-424
366. Livia Migliardi Zingale – Mario Amelotti, Omologia e quietanza? A proposito di alcune vendite di età postgiustinianea: XIV, 425-434
367. Eva Cantarella, L'insegnamento del diritto greco a trent'anni dal primo Symposion: diffusione, approcci e prospettive di sviluppo: XIV, 435-442

XV. Symposion 2005 (Salerno, 14-18 septembre 2005)

368. Michael Gagarin, From Oral Law to Written Laws: Draco's Law and its Homeric Roots: XV, 3-17
369. Eva Cantarella, Response to Michael Gagarin: XV, 19-22
370. Laura Pepe, A proposito di una legge siceliota sull'omicidio: XV, 23-53
371. Felice Costabile, Risposta a Laura Pepe: XV, 55-56
372. Martin Dreher, Das Bürgerrecht im griechischen Sizilien zwischen Recht und Politik: XV, 57-78
373. Antonio Banfi, Risposta a Martin Dreher: XV, 79-87
374. Karen Rørby Kristensen, Inheritance, Property, and Management: Gortynian Family Law Revisited: XV, 89-100
375. Alberto Maffi, Risposta a Karen Rørby Kristensen: XV, 101-104
376. Éva Jakab, SEG XLVIII 96: Steuergesetz oder Frachtvertrag?: XV, 105-121
377. Michele Faraguna, Risposta a Éva Jakab: XV, 123-130
378. Gerhard Thür, Das Prinzip der Fairness im attischen Prozess: XV, 131-150
379. Mario Talamanca, Risposta a Gerhard Thür: XV, 151-158
380. Edward Harris, Who Enforced the Law in Classical Athens?: XV, 159-176
381. Sophie Adam, Réponse à Edward Harris: XV, 177-182
382. Robert W. Wallace, Law's Enemies in Ancient Athens: XV, 183-196
383. Alberto Maffi, Risposta a Robert W. Wallace: XV, 197-199
384. Edward E. Cohen, Laws Affecting Prostitution at Athens: XV, 201-224
385. Adriaan Lanni, Athenian Approaches to Legal Predictability in Contract Cases: XV, 225-235
386. Jean-Marie Bertrand, À propos de la *Rhétorique* d'Aristote (I, 1373b1-1374b23), analyse du processus judiciaire: XV, 237-251
387. Stephen C. Todd, A Response to Jean-Marie Bertrand: XV, 253-258
388. Andréas Helmis, La privation de sépulture dans l'antiquité grecque: XV, 259-268
389. Lene Rubinstein, "*ARAI*" in Greek Laws in the Classical and Hellenistic Periods: Deterrence or Concession to Tradition?: XV, 269-286
390. Adele C. Scafuro, A Response to Lene Rubinstein: XV, 287-290
391. Bernard Legras, Les testaments grecs dans le droit hellénistique: la question des héritières et des testatrices: XV, 293-306
392. Barbara Anagnostou-Canas, La réparation du préjudice dans les papyrus grecs d'Égypte: XV, 307-326
393. Andrea Jördens, Anwort auf Barbara Anagnostou-Canas: XV, 327-334
394. Kaja Harter-Uibopuu, Zum Gerichtswesen im kaiserzeitlichen Sparta: XV, 335-348
395. Mario Amelotti, Risposta a Kaja Harter-Uibopuu: XV, 349-350
396. Federico Morelli, *Grammatêphoroi* e vie della giustizia nell'Egitto tardo antico: XV, 351-371
397. Livia Migliardi Zingale, Risposta a Federico Morelli: XV, 373-376
398. Jakub Urbanik, Compromesso o processo? Alternativa risoluzione dei conflitti e tutela dei diritti nella prassi della tarda antichità: XV, 377-399
399. Bernhard Palme, Antwort auf Jakub Urbanik: XV, 401-410
400. Joseph Mélèze Modrzejewski, De Rheda à Salerno – quinze Symposia: XV, 413-437

INDICE DELLE FONTI

a cura di Nunzia Donadio, Milano

1.1. Autori greci e latini

1.2. Lessicografi

2. Fonti giuridiche romane

3. Iscrizioni

4. Papiri, *Tabulae*

5. Fonti legislative di età moderna e contemporanea

6. Altre fonti